ORACLE8™ DATA WAREHOUSING

GARY DODGE
TIM GORMAN

WILEY COMPUTER PUBLISHING

JOHN WILEY & SONS, INC.

New York • Chichester • Weinheim • Brisbane • Singapore • Toronto

Publisher: Robert Ipsen

Editor: Robert M. Elliott

Managing Editor: Brian Snapp

Text Design & Composition: SunCliff Graphic Productions

Designations used by companies to distinguish their products are often claimed as trademarks. In all instances where John Wiley & Sons, Inc. is aware of a claim, the product names appear in initial capital or ALL CAPITAL LETTERS. Readers, however, should contact the appropriate companies for more complete information regarding trademarks and registration.

ORACLE is a registered trademark of Oracle Corporation, Redwood City, California, U.S.A. Oracle7 and Oracle8 are trademarks of Oracle Corporation, Redwood City, California, U.S.A.

This work is a publication of John Wiley & Sons, Inc. and is not sponsored by or affiliated with Oracle Corporation.

This text is printed on acid-free paper. ∞

This publication is designed to provide accurate and authoritative information in regard to the subject matter covered. It is sold with the understanding that the publisher is not engaged in rendering legal, accounting, or other professional services. If legal advice or other expert assistance is required, the services of a competent professional person should be sought.

Library of Congress Cataloging-in-Publication Data
Dodge, Gary, 1951–
    Oracle data warehousing / Gary Dodge, Tim Gorman.
      p. cm.
    "Wiley Computer Publishing."
    Includes index.
    ISBN 0-471-19952-4 (pbk. : alk. paper)
    1. Data warehousing. 2. Oracle (Computer file). I. Gorman, Tim,
1962–   . II. Title.
QA76.9.D37D63 1998
005.75'85—dc21   97-29335
                                          CIP

Printed in the United States of America
10 9 8 7 6 5 4 3 2 1

DEDICATION

To my father who made learning important,
to Luann who makes living worthwhile,
and to Brigid and Ryan who make both fun.

GD

To Jarmila, my best friend who is also my wife,
To Peter and Marika, my kids and heart and soul,
And to Gary, my friend and mentor.

TG

CONTENTS

Chapter 3   Oracle Software Architecture and Features   65

Chapter 4   Designing the Oracle Data Warehouse   113

Chapter 5   Building the Oracle Data Warehouse   157

Chapter 6   Populating the Oracle Data Warehouse   211

Chapter 7   **Post-Load Processing in the Data Warehouse**   **283**

Chapter 8   **Administering and Monitoring the Oracle Data Warehouse**   **313**

Chapter 9   Data Warehouse Performance Tuning   383

Chapter 10   Parallel Operations in the Oracle Data Warehouse   441

Chapter 11   Warehousing with Oracle Parallel Server   493

Chapter 12   Distributing the Oracle Data Warehouse   553

Chapter 13   OLAP Processing in the Oracle Data Warehouse   587

ACKNOWLEDGMENTS

A number of people provided assistance in the development of this book. Our thanks go to Bill Pass for his timely help with the hardware architectures of Chapter 2. Our gratitude is owed to Kim Wilson for his contributions to material on building the data warehouse in Chapter 6. Karl Johnson's guidance and insight into the workings of Oracle Express for Chapter 13 are appreciated. We are also grateful to Ulla-Carin Johnson, who helped in the production of many of the drawings. Armand Perry read the manuscript with a non-technical eye and helped identify several opportunities to clarify technical material.

Finally, we must express our heartfelt thanks Valerie Borthwick and Doug McArthur, our regional management within Oracle Consulting Services, for their encouragement and support in both initiating and completing this project.

INTRODUCTION

Forget the former things;

   do not dwell on the past.

See, I am doing a new thing!

   Now it springs up; do you not perceive it?

I am making a way in the desert

   and streams in the wasteland.

Isaiah 43:18-19

This book arose, as all should, from a need. Many books, articles, and seminars that address data warehousing have been available in the last several years. These sources all seem to describe what a data warehouse is and why an organization should build one. They describe the process of organizing a data warehouse implementation team. They describe the general design concerns of a warehouse and the process of identifying, extracting, and cleansing data from source systems.

What seemed to be missing was a nuts-and-bolts "how to" manual for the technical team chartered with actually creating the data warehouse. Of course there are many products that can be used to design, build, and manage a data warehouse and no general audience book could attempt to deal with the specifics of each.

Oracle7™ and the newly released Oracle8™ are among the most popular and effective tools available for managing the large amounts of data required in a data warehouse. As consultants for Oracle® Corporation we have worked with clients to develop data warehouses over many years, using Oracle version 6, Oracle7, and now Oracle8. Along the way we've acquired or developed a lot of very practical knowledge of how the Oracle RDBMS product can be used to address the problems faced in data warehousing. These problems come in many colors and flavors; some are related to performance of queries and of large data loads and related activities. Other common problems are related to the administration of very large databases. Still other difficulties arrive in the form of just selecting from the many technology options provided in each new release of Oracle.

It is our intent in writing this book to share as much of this practical knowledge as we can. Each revision has gotten longer as we continue to identify other topics, tips, and "gotchas." The time has come to stop adding and start sharing. There is certainly a lot more that could have been included! It is our sincere hope that the subject matter that eventually made it into this volume will be the most practical and useful subset of the universe of Oracle knowledge.

Audience

This book is directed to two groups of readers. First, we anticipate that experienced data warehouse developers who have worked with a different RDBMS product and are about to use Oracle for the first time will find this book very useful. While it will not replace the shelf full of manuals (or their digital equivalent) shipped with each copy of Oracle, we know firsthand how daunting the prospect of absorbing Oracle documentation can be. This was true when we started over ten years ago (with Oracle version 5) and the number of features and the corresponding documentation has mushroomed in the interim. This book can serve as the technical roadmap to the specific Oracle7 or Oracle8 features that are relevant to building, tuning, and administering an Oracle data warehouse. Once the function and usage of a particular feature or option are understood, the reader can locate the more detailed information in the relevant Oracle reference manuals. We have provided many "pointers" to official documentation throughout this book.

The second intended audience is the individual who has been working with Oracle, perhaps for years, as a developer or DBA but who is new to data warehousing. It is not intended that this book be the only reference for learning about data warehousing—the many books mentioned above do a much more thorough job of covering the concepts—but it will provide a guide to thinking about how to use Oracle technology in a different way. Experienced users of Oracle7 may find special value in the description of how to use new Oracle8 features, such as partitioning and the updated star query optimization. Knowing that data warehouses will continue to be built using both Oracle7 and Oracle8 for several years, we have attempted to cover features of both products in each section of this book where there are differences. Of course, there is a lot more experience with Oracle7 to draw upon and future releases of Oracle8 will continue to add new features and improvements to current ones.

Organization

This book has been developed in thirteen chapters. Chapter 1, "Warehousing" is a quick overview or review of the basic concepts of data warehousing. We address current developments in the data warehousing world such as data marts and OLAP.

Chapter 2, "Hardware Architectures for Oracle Data Warehousing" describes various hardware platforms which can be used to support the Oracle data warehouse. Common architectures such as symmetric multi-processor (SMP) computers are described along with more exotic configurations such as clusters and massively parallel processor (MPP) hardware. Hardware and software technology, such as RAID, for handling data file storage are covered as well. This chapter may be safely skimmed by readers who are not responsible for selecting hardware for the warehouse. You may find it sufficient to just review the description of the particular hardware architecture that your organization has already chosen.

Chapter 3, "Oracle Software Architecture and Features" is an overview of the architecture of Oracle7 and Oracle8 and a description of various standard and optional features that may be used to enhance the workings of a large data warehouse. Experienced Oracle7 DBAs may wish to just review this chapter for an introduction to the many Oracle8 enhancements.

Chapter 4, "Designing the Oracle Data Warehouse" discusses design considerations, including the need for warehouse metadata and how to deliver it to users. This chapter also introduces a case study situation of a warehouse, which will be used throughout subsequent chapters to demonstrate specific features or techniques.

Actually constructing the data warehouse using Oracle7 and Oracle8 database technology is addressed in Chapter 5, "Building the Oracle Data Warehouse" Several very useful techniques using SQL*Plus, the Oracle interactive SQL environment, are demonstrated. Then we cover the specifics of creating Oracle databases and database objects.

The Chapter 6, "Populating the Oracle Data Warehouse" describes techniques for loading data into the Oracle data warehouse.

Chapter 7, "Post-Load Processing in the Data Warehouse" builds upon this foundation by providing information on the processes used for summarizing and aggregating data within the warehouse.

Chapter 8, "Administering and Monitoring the Oracle Data Warehouse" and Chapter 9, "Data Warehouse Performance Tuning" address administration and performance tuning requirements and techniques using a varienty of tools available to the developer and database administrator.

Chapter 10, "Parallel Operations in the Oracle Data Warehouse" describes the "divide and conquer" capabilities of Oracle7 and Oracle8 for performing parallel operations in order to accomplish massive tasks more quickly. These features are virtually indispensable in developing and maintaining large Oracle data warehouses.

Chapter 11, "Warehousing with Oracle Parallel Server" deals with an optional feature, Oracle Parallel Server, which enables simultaneous access to a single Oracle database from multiple computers in either a clustered or MPP configuration.

Chapter 12, "Distributing the Oracle Data Warehouse" presents various reasons for choosing a distributed architecture and describes specific features and techniques for implementing it.

Finally, Chapter 13, "OLAP Processing in the Oracle Data Warehouse" provides an overview of the Oracle Express product set, which provides online analytical processing (OLAP) capabilities for the data warehouse. Express can operate independently as a multidimensional database or provide "reach through" access to a relational warehouse built with Oracle7 or Oracle8 RDBMS.

In essence, this book is not a work of reference. The standard Oracle Server documentation set should provide that. Given the pace at which Oracle is adding new features, attempting to duplicate the Oracle7 and Oracle8 Server reference manuals would be a Quixotic effort. Rather, consider this book to be a series of recommendations, already proven in the field, and readily adaptable to different warehousing situations.

Additionally, whenever possible, we have identified techniques for verifying the internal workings of Oracle features, particularly the various parallel operations. Use these techniques to verify that Oracle is, or is not, doing what you expect in the way you expect it. Use the knowledge imparted in these chapters to verify whether the approach you are considering is reasonable or not. There is almost never a single "right answer" to questions regarding data warehouse design and usage, but we will try to provide you with the information needed to steer you away from the wrong answers.

An Invitation

Do not dwell on the past. There is much that may initially seem counter-intuitive to OLTP developers and administrators about Oracle's new features to support data warehousing. Read on and learn. Then, go forth and *do the new thing!*

We welcome your feedback. If you have comments, suggestions, or questions please feel free to E-mail us at "artful-dodger@worldnet.att.net" and "tgorman@ us.oracle.com". Please don't consider this offer as an alternative to Oracle Worldwide Support and please don't expect fast turnaround; we cannot respond to E-mails marked URGENT. Also, be sure to allow for additional delays during the winter months . . . after all, there are certain priorities during ski season in Colorado!

Enjoy!

CHAPTER 1 WAREHOUSING

So, you've been given the assignment of building a data warehouse. Congratulations! The CIO read an article in *Computerworld* that said a data warehouse is a fundamental component of a modern information technology (IT) department. The CEO has also read articles in *Business Week* and *Forbes* that imply a data warehouse is *the* vehicle for competitive advantage as we approach the twenty-first century. Everybody seems to agree that we need a data warehouse because everyone else seems to be building them.

Without any scientific studies to back it up, our observation is that most data warehouse projects begun in the past five years have failed to achieve the lofty rewards promised for them. This doesn't mean that most have been complete failures resulting in project cancellations (although that has certainly happened in many cases), but many so-called data warehouses have produced very modest returns on their implementation investments.

Some organizations' data warehouse failures have been due to technical implementation issues. But most failures (or modest successes) have missed the mark on more basic levels. Failing to understand the underlying concepts, philosophy, objectives, and success factors of data warehousing presents far greater risks than technical issues such as the choice of hardware or relational database management system (RDBMS). Within the correct conceptual and managerial context one can successfully deliver a useful warehouse using virtually any vendor's hardware or software offerings.

The material in this chapter is intended as a review and summary of information that should already be familiar to the reader of this book. If these topics are new, then we strongly recommend that you also study the less technical and more conceptual books and articles on data warehousing written by Bill Inmon and others.

Before tackling the specifics of implementing a data warehouse using Oracle7™ or Oracle8™, we'll spend one chapter covering many of the nontechnical concepts and critical success factors of data warehousing.

For More Background Information

Many books, articles, courses, and seminars have been developed to teach the concepts of data warehousing. This book is primarily devoted to the specific issue of implementing a data warehouse using the Oracle® RDBMS. This first chapter will briefly summarize data warehousing concepts, but it is certainly not intended to be the reader's first or only exposure to this topic.

To offer an analogy, you might consider this book to be like the shop manual for your new sports car. It is designed for a specific, technical audience, but it presupposes all the knowledge contained within the car's owner manual as well as a fundamental understanding of engine, suspension, electrical, braking, and other automotive systems. Many drivers (data warehouse users) will need only the owner's manual and not the shop manual. The technicians who need the shop manual will find that it doesn't attempt to cover all the conceptual basics that would be included in the owner's manual and a driver's education course.

What Is a Data Warehouse?

As the latest apparent panacea for all the ills confronting the IT provider, one might think that data warehousing would be the final hurdle. Needless to say, however, data warehousing joins all the other failed panaceas: structured programming, relational databases, CASE tools, 4GLs, client-server and object-oriented development. To be sure, each of these technologies has provided great improvements and is not, in and of itself, a failure. The failure has been in our expectation that we've finally reached the last hill of our journey and, if we can just climb it, we'll soon gaze upon the Promised Land.

As one example, during the 1980s hundreds of organizations bought CASE tools with the expectation that they'd receive tenfold increases in productivity. But when the dust settled and the organization's first CASE project was not completed any sooner than a non-CASE project, the company put the CASE tool on the shelf and went back to doing things the way it always had. What failed in almost every case (pardon the pun) was not the tool or the technology. What failed was the organization—it did not adopt and internalize the philosophical change of perspective required by a new way of doing things. CASE development is primarily a change in thinking; the tools are just supporting aids to help mechanize the new way of thinking. Without transforming the organization to the new discipline of CASE development, the tools just got in the way.

A similar explanation lies behind every one of the other "panacea" technologies just mentioned. They were demonstrably successful in those organizations that had realistic expectations, introduced the new philosophy and technology in a controlled manner, and ensured that all the participants adopted the philosophy first and then used the tool to support it. For the other organizations, those

Introducing CASE Tools

In several client consulting engagements over the years as part of Oracle Consulting Services we have been asked to bring in Oracle's CASE tools to help rescue a behind-schedule project. In some of those engagements, our answer has been a firm "no" backed up with an explanation of this phenomenon: On their first project, new tools inevitably consume far much more time than they save.

that did not change their way of thinking and developing systems, the new tools were frequently seen as failures.

To be successful with data warehousing, it is thus essential to view it first as a new philosophy, a new way of thinking. Only then should the various technologies be introduced. If you have purchased a new Sun UNIX server, Prism Solutions's ETT tool, and the Oracle8 RDBMS and expect to simply put them together to build a data warehouse, you are virtually doomed to disappointment. Data warehousing is not fundamentally about technology.

The following sections discuss some other misconceptions about what a data warehouse is that should be addressed.

A Data Warehouse Is Not a Project

Projects have defined starts and schedules; projects have defined results and specified constraints. Projects have budgets and assigned resources. Most importantly, projects have definite ends. (Of course, we've all been on projects that never seemed to end, but this is how it is *supposed* to work!)

A successful data warehouse does not have an end. The data warehouse is implemented in a series of miniprojects, each of which should have all the project characteristics just described. There are two risks associated with the misconception that a data warehouse is a project.

The first risk is that when the project ends everybody assumes the warehouse is done. Most of the benefits of the data warehouse will not be realized in the first delivery. Both users and developers of the first warehouse release will learn at least as much about what additional warehousing needs were not addressed as they will about the business entities represented within the warehouse. The sponsor, the implementation team, and the first set of warehouse users should all have the attitude that they're going to deliver something during the first project, but it will not be perfect. It will be a foundation for the next, improved version that will, in turn, form the foundation of the next, further improved version. This process should continue for as long as the organization has a data warehouse, although the changes and enhancements should be expected to become less radical over time.

The second risk of confusing a data warehouse with a project is that the project team is dangerously tempted to try to do everything and meet every need right out of the starting gate. There is absolutely no problem with deciding to severely limit the initial scope of the warehouse. Successfully providing integrated data about a small handful of business subject areas in a few months is far healthier than spending years attempting to get it all right in one giant release. It is, truthfully, impossible to do the latter. You cannot anticipate all the uses to which the warehouse may be put. It cannot be done. It has never been done. You will not be the first to have tried and failed.

Plan, therefore, to initially disappoint some or most prospective users. The very fact that they begin using the data that you have provided and then start asking for additional, related data is your first sign of success! What they learn from the first release will lead them to new questions that will lead you to new data structures and the like.

Data Warehousing Is a Process

A data warehouse is not a project. It is implemented in a series of projects. Through successive iterations we gradually build our data warehouse. In the first release, we might implement only three or four entities that are closely tied to each other and are of interest to one specific department or group of users. Each successive release adds some additional information based upon what was learned from using the prior release. The additional information may be about existing subject areas, perhaps adding additional columns or some new summaries. We may also choose to add entirely new subject areas.

In an ideal implementation, our first release is made available to a particular user group within six months or less. As they begin to use the data warehouse two things happen. First, they find useful information that leads them to ask new questions. Some of these questions cannot be answered by the limited scope of data provided in the first release, which then leads to enhancements that are rolled out in future releases. Second, however, is another byproduct of our early success with our initial release: the word spreads from our initial targeted group of users to other potential users within other departments. The initial success with the finance department produces interest and access requests from marketing and production and sales and so on.

As this word-of-mouth reputation spreads throughout the organization, the data warehouse team is presented with new opportunities and new risks. The opportunities, of course, are related to supplying the additional data subject areas that are of interest to all those other departments now clamoring at the door. The risks, too, are in letting the first-round success trap us into trying to satisfy every newly identified opportunity in our second release. It is critical that we maintain the same discipline that allowed the first release to be successful. The warehouse team should prioritize specific subject areas and user groups for inclusion in each release. Each version of the warehouse should incrementally add new data to allow for three- to six-month intervals between releases.

Each release should follow closely enough on the heels of the prior release so that we maintain momentum and build a string of small success stories rather than attempt to do too much at once. Just as in baseball, grand slam home runs make the headlines, but they don't happen often. Nine out of ten long fly balls are caught for an out rather than clearing the fence. To continue the analogy, the teams that win games consistently are those that can regularly get runners on base and then systematically advance them into scoring position and then bring them home. Baseball games are generally won by a series of singles and doubles (and sacrifices) rather than home runs. Data warehousing is the same. By the time a three-year grand slam warehouse project is completed (if it ever is) the interest of the sponsor and users will have waned, and funding will have been diverted to some timelier project.

Begin thinking early of the warehouse as an ongoing process rather than a single project or event.

A Data Warehouse Is Not a Product

Many vendors are reacting to the current data warehousing fervor by offering a "data warehouse in a box" or a "data mart." Vendors, consultants, and authors offer predefined enterprise data models for manufacturing, retail, or other industries. All of these prepackaged solutions are attempts to appeal to the desire for an easy solution to a tough problem. Building a data warehouse requires making very tough decisions about the data model, the naming of attributes, the agreement on definitions (and other metadata) of each attribute, the source of each data element, the transformations that will be applied to the source data . . . the list goes on and on.

TIP

Metadata is special data that describes the other data in the data warehouse. Metadata is discussed in Chapter 4, "Designing the Oracle Data Warehouse."

A vendor who promises to give us a ready-made solution is like the snake oil salesman roaming the countryside with a one-dollar bottle of elixir that promises to cure whatever ails you. Gee, a dollar isn't much; it's certainly less than the surgery that my doctor told me I needed—why not? Perhaps a more contemporary analogy would be the late-night television infomercials offering some device that can promise "rock-hard abdominal muscles" or the "thighs of a supermodel" with *"absolutely no exercise in only ten minutes a day while you watch your favorite TV show!"* Of course, in reality these magic solutions to difficult problems don't work, and they end up gathering dust under the bed or in a closet.

In most cases, the data warehouse will store its data within the control of a RDBMS, but this is not a requirement. The data warehouse is not the database. Some historical or foreign data for the warehouse may be realistically stored on tapes, microfiche, or even paper. It may not even be in the possession of the organization that built the data warehouse. The data warehouse is a means of discovery. Sometimes the discovery is conveniently fast because the data needed for a particular question are nicely organized within the online files of a single relational database. It is just as valuable, although not as convenient, for the database to be able to answer the first of three questions, for example, and perhaps only provide direction for the user to find the answers to the final questions.

As an example, consider a data warehouse that supports the marketing functions of a multinational corporation. The warehouse could be realistically expected to contain a lot of information about the corporation's past sales results and the success of several marketing campaigns in various geographic territories. The warehouse might also have industry statistics obtained from trade organizations or the U.S. Department of Commerce. Some information on the corporation's competitors would certainly be valuable. It might, however, be impractical to physically store images of each of the competitors' various advertisements. Would you want 150 copies of the actual ad or information about the 150 placements and perhaps a pointer to a single copy of the ad layout? It might be useful to be able to find every article ever written that mentions our products or those of our competitors. If our company has a traditional library in which trade publications and other reference materials are held, it is a reasonable accommodation for the warehouse to store only references to the physical magazines. If potentially useful journal articles (or, for instance, Ph.D. theses) are already stored electronically by their copyright owners and made available over the Internet, it isn't critical that a copy be maintained within the warehouse's database. It would be very handy, however, if our warehouse were able to store the means for locating the information later.

As much as we might like to digitize and store a copy of everything anyone might ever want within our warehouse, realistically, there are costs associated with storage. Those costs have to be traded off against (1) the probability of access, (2) the likely value of that access, and (3) the probability that the currently available copy will remain available until we might want to reference it. Storing the table of contents for each issue of our industry publications and journals and providing a text search against them may be nearly as useful as trying to electronically store every word ever published in them. It will certainly be a lot cheaper and probably more prudent legally.

As one final example, it is very common for the most detailed operational data used to build the data warehouse to be made available for inquiry for a period of time, frequently several months or even a year, as part of the warehouse. At some point, however, the sheer volume of detailed data produced by any large organization forces it to do something other than continue storing the data online for immediate access. One alternative is to purge the data without keeping a copy. Purging is appropriate for some data, but most data warehouse developers tend to have a defensive "pack-rat" mentality about such things. "What if somebody finds a need for that data in a form other than the historical summaries we've built?" Anything is possible, so in many cases the developers will archive the data rather than purge it. By archiving, they move a copy of the data to some low-cost medium, such as magnetic tape or CD-ROM, before removing it from the online database. If, by chance, someone in the distant future needs to access the data, they'll retrieve it and make it temporarily available again.

Objects and Data Warehousing

Much effort is underway within the RDBMS vendor community to better integrate the storage of complex data other than the traditional numeric and character data currently stored in the data warehouse. Oracle8, for example, has greatly enhanced its capability for storing images, sounds, video clips, and even more complex objects. What is still missing is an appropriately engineered set of end-user query tools that are able to manipulate and retrieve these complex data types. These will come, however, and we predict they will be available within the life cycle of Oracle8. Unfortunately, the data warehouses being built and used today cannot exploit these capabilities yet.

Archived data may not be in the database, but it can still be considered part of the data warehouse. Access archival data is obviously slower, but the cost of storage is substantially less. Remember that the speed with which data can be accessed is only one of several factors to be considered when designing the data warehouse. Other factors include the cost of storage, the cost of retrieval, the probability of retrieval, and the value of the data when retrieved. We can't keep everything. And what we can keep can't necessarily be retrieved immediately forever.

Likewise, prepackaged "data mart" products sound like they are an easy way to bypass all the tough issues surrounding the design and integration of a data warehouse. However, the primary value of the data warehouse comes directly from the integration of data. A standalone data mart in each department or regional office may independently meet some organizational information needs, but it will not begin to resolve problems that result from creating proprietary "islands of information."

Data Warehousing Is a New Way of Thinking about Data

Programmers and users of traditional transaction processing systems have unconsciously adopted a very short-term perspective on data. What is the current value of QTY_ON_HAND in the INVMSTR file for PROD_ID = 'BD112786'? How many employees are enrolled today in the 401(k) plan? Why didn't order number 19374730 from our biggest customer ship today as promised? How much money needs to be transferred tonight to cover the accounts payable check run?

All these questions are important to the operation of the business. They cannot be ignored or avoided. As new transactions are processed within our operational systems, the specific values associated with each of these questions constantly changes. New orders as well as new inventory receipts will constantly change the quantity on hand of many products. Newly hired employees and those leaving the company will change the retirement plan enrollments daily. Today's critical order will be forgotten tomorrow as we focus on the next critical order. Treasury management will have to assess balances and requirements again tomorrow and every day.

When (and only when) all of those operational questions are handled by stable, predictable data processing systems is it possible for an organization to start asking questions from a different perspective. The operational manager is like an airline pilot who has a specific destination to reach and a specific route to fly. He or she certainly has decisions to make (in conjunction with air traffic control) about finding the most economical and comfortable altitude or about detouring around a large thunderstorm, but they are all decisions regarding this flight, on this one day. Someone other than the pilot, however, needs to take a different perspective and consider such questions as whether that particular route is profitable or if the departure and scheduled arrival times are optimal for passenger loading, gate operations, equipment and crew utilization, and so on. Such questions don't affect the pilot flying today's flight. They do, however, involve information about many flights, routes, and even competitors' schedules.

Similarly, the effective user of a data warehouse has to be able to pull away from the details of today's operations and take a broader view of the business. The data warehouse can facilitate questions asked from the new perspective, but it cannot generate the new perspective. "Build it and they will come" is not a healthy way to approach data warehousing. In fact, they may or may not come; and if they do, they may not be ready to think in the way that a data warehouse can enhance.

One of our health care clients recently began building its first data warehouse. The sponsoring group of initial users was the actuarial department. I initially thought that actuaries would probably be interested in big-picture trends and would be perfect consumers of the summarized, long-term data normally found in a data warehouse. Wrong! In reality, the actuaries insisted on having access to the lowest level of detailed data; nothing would budge them from this position. What we eventually learned was that there was an immense backlog demand for detailed, operational reporting within this department. The actuaries required specific case data on morbidity and mortality for last month, and the currently available operational reports did not meet their needs. They needed consolidation of current data across geographic boundaries, and the current systems were only capable of reporting independently for each state in which the provider did business. They were not attempting (at that moment) to identify which procedures or doctors provided a long-term reduction in follow-up medical costs. They were just trying to find out how many patients, in total, died from cancer last month. They needed an operational data store to meet some current operational system deficiencies.

A Data Warehouse Is Not a Reporting Subsystem

We frequently see consulting clients who claim to be implementing a data warehouse. Upon closer inspection, however, we find that their driving business requirements are to be able to do faster or more flexible reporting on their operational data. There is nothing wrong with recognizing this business need.

Maslow's Hierarchy of Needs

For any reader who may have somehow escaped attending virtually any management or organizational motivation seminar or college course in the past thirty years, Maslow theorized in 1943 that every person has a hierarchy of needs. Basic physiological needs such as food and water must be met before the individual will be motivated by needs of safety. Only when physiological and safety needs are met can the person begin to seek love and interpersonal interaction. At that point, the individual begins to seek esteem and position within a social organization. Finally, upon the foundation of satisfied physiological, safety, love, and esteem needs, the individual can begin to "self-actualize" and become concerned about self-fulfilling activities.

Frequently, organizations do have unfulfilled operational reporting needs. Organizations have a hierarchy of information needs that is similar to A. H. Maslow's famous hierarchy of individual needs.

Organizational Information Needs

Just as a person requires the satisfaction of basic physical needs for food, shelter, and the like, an organization must first be able to manufacture its product or deliver its service. If it can't, then more sophisticated information needs are irrelevant. A small startup business, such as a "single-shingle" consultant, may well survive based only on the owner's ability to remember the who, what, where, and when of his promised deliveries. The first information needs can be met simply by keeping a logbook and handwritten invoices. If the consultant is at all successful, a more complete information system will eventually be needed to meet tax reporting requirements (which obviously correspond to Maslow's safety needs!)

As the business grows and additional consultants are added there will be additional information needs. The different people in the organization will require information to support assignment schedules, payment of commissions, and the like. Like Maslow's love and esteem need categories, the organization's information needs at this point are functionally ones of communication, cooperation, and coordination. The organization will need to have a new awareness of cash flow and the days outstanding of accounts receivable. Eventually, the mature organization will have developed various information systems to handle these operational requirements.

Only when the organization has met these operational requirements will it be ready, like Maslow's self-actualizing individual, to address data warehousing needs. If the operational reporting needs of an organization have not been met, what might be called a data warehouse will end up becoming what Inmon has termed an *operational data store*. There is absolutely nothing wrong with building an operational data store that will hold a copy of operational data in order to support various otherwise unmet reporting requirements. This is a common phenomenon in a large mainframe shop whose assembler and COBOL programs date back to the 1960s and 1970s and whose file structures don't lend themselves to easy ad hoc reporting. The need to see additional operational reports from these ancient systems cannot be met through the labor-intensive process of writing more COBOL programs.

Without a good understanding of data warehousing (and a perspective on where the organization is in this informational needs hierarchy) it is very tempting to start copying data to a relational database environment and letting the users build their own reports—and then just calling it a data warehouse. The operational data store meets the level of need being felt by the organization. These reporting needs must be met *before* the organization will be capable of doing data warehousing.

Data warehousing is *not* equivalent to ad hoc queries and reporting. There may well be ad hoc processing of operational data. The risk of confusing the two is that an organization that claims to have developed a data warehouse when it's really built an operational data store doesn't recognize that there is still an opportunity before it. Its managers begin to wonder why they are not receiving the wonderful competitive benefits that *Computerworld* and *Business Week* told them to expect.

As a final comment on the topic of operational data stores, it should be noted that extracting operational data to populate the operational data store is a very helpful step to have completed when one does start to build a true data warehouse. It is often much simpler to obtain operational data for the warehouse from a relational operational data store. If someone has already done some of the hard work of identifying and extracting data from the various legacy system files then the remaining work of integrating and time-dimensioning the data during warehouse design may be simplified.

Operational Data

The transaction processing systems used to run the business generally have a very current focus: What is the current stock level for product number 7582 at warehouse 3? How many hours did Luann work last week for which she needs to be paid? Which orders are currently waiting to be fulfilled because of stock outages? How many blue casings are we supposed to produce before retooling the injection-molding machine? These are all important questions that must be capable of being answered. If the operational systems don't somehow provide screens or reports to handle these and similar questions then an operational data store may be the appropriate next step.

The warehouse will, by contrast, allow us to ask a different set of questions: During which months do we sell the most of product number 7582? Are we spending more money on temporary, hourly workers this year than last? Which of our vendors' late deliveries to us have caused us to delay production and shipment of the greatest dollar volume of orders to our customers? What is the average number of days between identical machine setups to produce the same part? These are new questions that deal less with running today's business and allow us to begin to manage the business at a higher level of understanding. This ability to view historical data and to analyze current data within a historical context is the key benefit of a data warehouse.

Just keep in mind that users who can't take or fill orders or cut a paycheck are probably not yet ready to start analyzing business performance on these levels. Satisfy the more basic needs before embarking on a data warehouse.

A Data Warehouse Is Not a Place

It may be obvious to some, but a data warehouse is not a specific location to which information consumers come to get data. Data warehousing has grown out of a tradition of decision support processing that, a dozen years or so ago, included just such an actual physical place. Today's data warehouse is not the same as a 1980s-vintage information center, which typically provided a special room equipped with terminals, PCs (remember, this was before every desk came equipped with a computer), printers, plotters, and trained support staff.

A data warehouse need not be housed in a single place. And even those warehouses whose databases are implemented on a single server are still not likely to be in a place ever physically visited by a user. Information is distributed to users at their normal place of work—their desk—in response to their requests. This model fits the image of a warehouse as a distribution center: Orders for specific warehouse contents are located, picked, packaged, and shipped to the original requester.

The difference, of course, is that data within the warehouse are not depleted in the same way as a physical warehouse. Multiple users may request the same data, or the user may "browse" through the warehouse requesting various things

Extending the Metaphor

The term *data warehouse* presents a useful metaphor for characterizing the mass storage and distribution of information. Various authors (and vendors) have attempted to extend the metaphor . . . sometimes even usefully. We have seen the advent of the term *data mart,* which has been used variously to describe a small standalone data warehouse or a distributed secondary level of storage and distribution in conjunction with a data warehouse. We've also acquired the terms *data mining* and *data publishing* as other industrial metaphors. Recently, vendors have announced new products that they have dubbed the "data mall" and the "data factory." Eventually, we will probably all be subjected to "data service stations," "data condos," "data retirement homes," and "data amusement parks" as vendors and consultants climb over each other to find new (and annoying) variations on the industrial building metaphor.

until he or she finds something interesting. Data, though, does have to be re-plenished in the data warehouse—not, however, because of depletion, but for the sake of renewal. To have ongoing value the data of the data warehouse has to be both current and historic. We constantly add new data to the warehouse that can be compared to and combined with the historical record of data. It is within this context that the warehouse provides value in a way that the organization's operational systems cannot.

Data Warehousing Is a Supplement to Traditional Data Processing

Traditional transactional systems are oriented toward holding a data value until that value is changed, at which point the systems are chartered with holding that new value until it is changed again. Each of those transactions, however, sees many interesting data relationships as it executes but does not traditionally record them. For example, we record the fact that our particular order was for twenty lawn mowers and we incidentally record the fact that on that same day we needed to replenish our inventory of lawn mowers. All sorts of other poten-tially interesting connections between these two "independent" transactions, however, are lost within our traditional systems.

These operational systems don't record coincidental circumstances that might occur at the time of a transaction. One transaction might note that John Smith ordered a set of four tires; a separate transaction orders a new supply of tires to be delivered to the shop. No record, however, is likely to be kept that it was specifically John Smith's order that caused our local inventory to drop below the reorder level. That may or may not be something of interest to an analyst. It might, however, be more interesting to know that right before Mr. Smith's order, we processed an order from a rental car fleet for four hundred of the same tires. The actual reorder was "caused" by a small order, but we may want to investi-gate the impact of large orders. How often do these large orders occur? What is their impact on stock outages and reorders? How many small orders are affected when we receive a large order like this? What is the cost of maintaining suffi-ciently high inventory levels to handle these occasional large orders versus the additional cost of shipping large orders from a centralized warehouse while maintaining smaller inventory at each of our regional warehouses?

Neither do our operational systems track weather events around the country. Why should they? But an analyst might be very interested to know which prod-ucts show an increase or decrease in sales when a geographic region experi-ences an early frost.

What products show a change in purchasing trends when a market has a pro-fessional sports team in the playoffs? Again, our operational systems are not ex-pected to record such information.

The systems that we build or buy to help us run our daily business are de-signed and tuned for efficient operation. They don't keep track of what data val-ues might have been last month or last year. They aren't supposed to. But there is great value in observing the trends in how values have changed over time and in being able to see what other data have also changed—and possibly discovering connections. This is where a data warehouse can supplement the operational systems. By keeping regular snapshots of the operational data, the warehouse accumulates years of data that we can analyze. By incorporating data from external sources (like the weather data or the sports playoffs), the warehouse can become the place where we discover things about our data that were never visible in the day-to-day operational files and databases.

Inmon's Four Characteristics of a Data Warehouse

Bill Inmon, who is widely credited with founding the data warehousing movement, has written and lectured extensively on data warehousing and the ways to design and build a data warehouse. His books and articles on these topics should be read by anyone embarking on a warehouse implementation effort. He has repeatedly and consistently defined a data warehouse in terms of four defining characteristics. According to him, a data warehouse is a "subject oriented, integrated, nonvolatile, and time variant collection of data in support of management's decisions" (from Inmon's *Building the Data Warehouse*, 2nd Ed., Wiley, 1996). It is, of course, possible to quibble with minor details or provide an exceptional case in which this definition doesn't precisely apply. As a general statement, however, this is the widely accepted definition of data warehousing. Let's examine each of the four points in greater depth.

Subject Oriented

We have traditionally built systems with an applications or functional focus. When we build or buy the operational systems for a cable TV provider we deal with the billing function, the program-scheduling function, the maintenance physical plant, and installation of equipment. We build other systems to handle order entry for monthly services and pay-per-view events. We will need to be able to schedule installation and repair visits. Frequently, each of these systems may be purchased from a different vendor or internally built or replaced at different times. Each application is supported by its own set of databases or files. We would commonly interface between these applications through extract files that pull a copy of information from, for instance, order entries to populate needed data in our installation, service, and billing systems. Our cable company would also use this order data to identify specific set-top devices and their authorized services and features for the network control and transmission systems.

Each of these systems (except for program scheduling) has some awareness of the CUSTOMER entity. The billing function and the network control function, as an example, have totally different views of what a customer is. Billing cares about a name and address and what service packages have been ordered by the customer. The network control function is aware of, say, two set-top devices with cryptic network addresses and that these devices are connected to a specific headend controller. The process of enabling a particular set-top device to receive this evening's heavyweight championship fight does not require any knowledge of the customer's name or mailing address or whether the customer disconnected the Disney Channel last week. Conversely, billing doesn't care what encryption algorithm will be used by the headend controller to transmit the fight.

In the data warehouse, however, we want to look across these multiple applications to distill the essential gestalt of CUSTOMER. Some of the data about a customer is likely to be found in the operational billing system. Other customer data may be extracted from the service calls database, which needs to be included with customer data taken from our pay-per-view system. Likewise, we might also need to retrieve data from billing, customer service, repair, and physical plant maintenance systems to capture and present all the necessary information about a service outage.

Within the OUTAGE subject area in the warehouse we will want to see the cause of each incident, the number of customers affected, the duration of the outage, the cost of repair, the refund costs committed to customers who complained, and the like.

In the warehouse, the subject orientation around CUSTOMER or OUTAGE is primary. Everything we store will be brought together around one of these subjects. If we stumble across some interesting bit of data from an operational system that does not apply to one of the subject areas of our data warehouse we will set it aside until some future release in which its subject is implemented.

Data warehouse design is data-driven design. There have been several pushes for data-driven design of application systems, but the reality of application projects is that we first define the functional scope of the project and then design the data needed for the included functions. Within the data warehouse there are no functional barriers, and we, as designers, are free to be more pure in our data focus. We identify the subject areas, we construct our design, and then we go seek the data from its various operational sources. In some cases, the data we would like to include about one of our subjects cannot be obtained because of limitations imposed by the operational source systems or by the availability of external data. We mark that particular part of our subject area as unavailable and continue on. When possible, we'll request modifications to the existing legacy systems to better capture or retain the data we're interested in or we'll investigate other sources.

What we don't do in constructing our data warehouse is to build it "bottom up" by finding what data can be obtained and then loading it into an unstructured shell.

Integrated

Very closely related to the topic of subject orientation is that of integration. Once we have a cohesive, data-driven design we have the foundation for an integrated data warehouse. As we pull together the disparate data to form each subject effort we must make a conscious effort to effectively integrate it. As designers of the data warehouse we can and must take the time to force consistency and discipline onto data that, in the operational sources, are anything but consistent and integrated.

We find that each system frequently uses a different name for a piece of data and that each system has stored the item with different encoding or different units of measure.

- What the payroll system calls SEX_CD and stores as either M or F corresponds to the benefits systems GENDER field that contains either 1 or 0.
- The benefits department registers 401(k) contributions by percentage of income, but payroll tracks contributions in dollars and cents while treasury reports fund balances as percentages of total contribution.
- One system has lots of fields suffixed with _IND (for indicator) that contain T and F values. Another system was built using _FLAG names for fields that store 1 or 0, while a third has no standard naming but seems to have lots of fields containing either Y or N.
- Purchasing orders liquid lubricants by volume measured in barrels or by weight measured in tons. Our warehouse system tracks inventory of all fluids in gallons. Our installation and service departments dispense oil by the liter.

As we bring all this discovered data into the data warehouse, we are responsible for modifying the names, standardizing the encoding, and imposing consistency in our units of measure. Of course, each of the departments is used to naming, encoding, measuring, and even thinking in the way that its supporting systems have been written. As designers we have to resolve such conflicts in some manner, such as the following:

- by what seems logical to us
- by the common usage of the first sponsoring department
- by the common usage of the department with the biggest budget
- by flipping a coin
- by inviting all departments to a "last-man standing" wrestling match

Seriously, there is no clear-cut way of deciding such issues. As we'll discuss later, one of the critical success factors in developing a successful data warehouse is to form a project team with active representation from each department likely to use the warehouse. Even if the initial release of the warehouse is going to include only the subject areas of interest to the finance department, other departments will someday use some of that data as well, especially after we include some additional subjects and data in releases two and three. Certain subject areas such as CUSTOMER and PRODUCT tend to cross many organizational boundaries. It is essential to resolve questions about the naming and storage of this data through discussion and compromise with all the groups that will eventually want to access the warehouse.

When old departmental conflicts prevent cooperation and compromise, it becomes necessary for the core warehouse development team to make decisions. Sponsoring executives need to be told before the start of the effort that their departments' representatives must be oriented toward the corporate benefit rather than parochial, departmental tradition. They (sponsors and design participants) need to understand that *any* standard is far better than the chaos created by decades of unintegrated applications.

When all else fails, it is possible (though not advisable!) to incorporate aliases into the warehouse design and to store and present specific data in more than one way. We can carry a field measured in inches and another in centimeters, or we can write conversion functions into the database and incorporate them into views that will allow each warring faction to see the data in their customary way. Rarely is this the right approach, for it misses one of the side benefits of a data warehouse—fostering improved communication across functional and organizational boundaries to discuss business subjects.

Nonvolatile

Data once entered into the data warehouse is almost never changed. Data records an event or state as it existed at some point in time. If some other event occurs that changes that state, it should be included in the warehouse as a separate, distinct event with a later time stamp. The data should reside as it was loaded for as long as the data is retained. Thus, there are only a few operations performed on warehouse data: It is loaded, it is accessed (for building summaries or by user queries), or it is eventually purged or archived. Data in the warehouse is not generally updated.

Any pressure to violate this simplified processing model should be viewed with extreme suspicion. If someone is asking to have adjusting entries or returns applied against the original transaction's data, either they are confused about the nature of the data warehouse or they are really attempting to extend their operational systems into an operational data store. If they need additional operational reporting, this is a need that should be met outside of (and prior to) the data warehouse.

One exception that may legitimately be made to this rule is when the integration of data from multiple sources is delayed because of the different availability of the source data. Remember that we did a pure, data-driven design of our warehouse. Data to satisfy the design is commonly pulled from multiple sources, not all of which are made available at the same time. As one example, if the design for our CUSTOMER entity includes data fields for SIC code, annual sales, and the like that do not originate within our internal systems, we may legitimately decide to load our internal data and later include the missing data when it becomes available. When we obtain the external data (from their quarterly 10Q filings, for instance) we can add it to the warehouse record of the customer.

Another exception is sometimes made to allow for data summaries of the "year-to-date" type. If your design is made simpler by this denormalization and you consciously choose to include this current data focus to an entity, you risk having operational questions ("What are the current year-to-date sales to Acme Corporation?") directed to your warehouse. This may lead to improper interpretations of answers since we may only update that field monthly while the user may think they are truly getting *current* values. Also, it adds complexity (and potentially locking issues) to our data warehouse if we begin doing single row updates. If you anticipate many questions of this type, you may wish to make life simpler for the user by supplying "to-date" summaries, but be very careful not to mix them with more appropriate nonvolatile summaries.

It might be preferable to create a view that meets the users' convenience needs without requiring frequent updating of data. The following example is built upon detailed data in the ORDERS table, but a better performing view could be built on top of a MONTHLY_ORDERS table if such a summary were already available:

```
CREATE VIEW YEAR_TO_DATE_SALES
    AS
SELECT CUSTOMER_ID, CUSTOMER_NAME, SUM(SALES)
  FROM ORDERS
  WHERE SALES_DATE BETWEEN ROUND(SYSDATE, 'YEAR') AND SYSDATE
  GROUP BY CUSTOMER_ID, CUSTOMER_NAME;
```

Time Variant

Most data stored for operational use has an implied time dimension: now. Each new transaction modifies the current state of data, such as an inventory level, to form a new current state. Even data that are created by the transaction (such as a new order) are typically modified to show changes in current state, such as the order status changing from "taken" to "credit checked" to "picked" to "shipped." Order data that isn't modified tend to have a rather short life span within the order processing system. Operational data is generally kept only until its innate workflow cycle is completed. This might mean until the order is shipped or until the end of the next billing cycle or perhaps, somewhat arbitrarily, for six months.

For performance reasons the designers of operational systems try to keep databases and files as small as possible. Most details about last year's orders are of relatively little use in running today's business.

Contrasted with this operational focus on currency of data and minimizing storage space and access speeds, the data warehouse has very a different perspective on time. First, data in the warehouse is expected to be retained for much longer periods, commonly five or ten years. One of the most frequent types of analysis performed in the warehouse involves identifying trends and correlations over time.

Data, whether in the originating application system or the data warehouse, can be classified as being related to an event or a state. Events are the triggers that initiate a transaction. Event data includes the order that was taken at a particular time and shipped on a particular day. Events are easily positioned in time, although not all of a company's operational systems do so explicitly.

State data is changed by a transaction. Examples of state data include inventory levels, customer credit limits, and cash flow. State data can be sampled at any time and can generally change at any time. State data does not have a pre-defined time element, but only an implicit one—the current time when it is sampled. We can take a nightly snapshot of our inventory levels or make a monthly calculation of cash on hand. Alternatively, we can sample the current value of state data on an irregular schedule, perhaps tied to some event.

Finding a correspondence between events and state data is one of the most difficult aspects of decision support processing. Problems arise because of this dichotomy between event and state data. First, the order of events has profound effects on the changes in state. Several events may commonly occur between captures of state data, and it is frequently difficult to rebuild the successive state changes that occurred between the samples. Second, events are not necessarily discrete, and there is potentially more than one way to determine the time of an event.

A common part of taking an order is to check the state of inventory and the customer's credit limit. Another part is adjusting both the inventory level and the credit limit. If the customer makes several purchases, returns some items, and makes a payment all on the same day, it is possible for one of the purchase requests to be refused because of a credit limit violation, but the nightly report of customers who are over their credit limits may not include the customer. Why? Several events have occurred between our snapshots of state. Depending upon when the payment and return transactions are processed in relation to the attempts to purchase, this customer may or may not have had a purchase refused. Similarly, a bank that does its nightly posting of checks and other debits before it posts deposits would likely have some very irate customers who were bouncing checks even though they had deposited adequate funds to cover those checks.

Another example, familiar to most businesspeople who travel a lot, is the credit card postings for airline travel. Charges seem to be posted by the airlines to your credit card immediately. Return an unused ticket to the airline or travel agency, however, and it will probably not get credited to your account for at least one extra billing cycle. The reason, of course, is that the airline is playing cash flow games using your money. But when the monthly billing statement is produced (state data) your account will not reconcile to your personal calculation of your outstanding balance. The statement is accurately reflecting the posted activity (events) that have completed, but your own balance is also accurately reflecting the events that have been initiated. This is because you've measured the start of an event (returning the ticket), and the credit card company has recorded the completion of the event (posting the credit). In between these two parts of the same event a variable amount of time may occur.

Resolving these issues and correlating event data and state data is one of the great opportunities and great challenges for the data warehouse designer. Virtually all data that enters into the data warehouse must be given a time dimension. This means that events are time-stamped, and samplings of state data are also given a time stamp. Ideally, we would like to have these perfectly correlated, but this is rarely possible. Commonly, we have an available transaction time-stamp for events, but it may vary widely in its precision. Orders are recorded with date and time, perhaps provided by a database trigger that reads the system clock. Shipping events are recorded only by the day processed. Once a package is addressed, weighed, and placed in the outbound bin, it is considered shipped even though the shipping carrier may not come to the dock for several hours.

Similarly, it would be possible to record the current state data as part of every transaction, but the additional workload and storage requirements would be prohibitive for most operational systems. So we compromise by taking snapshots at regular intervals. In some cases, this might be hourly, in others it might be nightly, and in still others it might only be monthly. To illustrate this point, it would be possible as part of order taking to record the standard price of each item along with the negotiated or volume discounted price. Our order processing system may have been designed, for storage economy, to ignore standard pricing whenever a negotiated price for this customer is available. Order processing is streamlined by this design, but our decision support users may later legitimately wish to analyze discounting and its correlation with order volume. If we can't convince the maintenance team for order entry to add some additional logic and data fields (and we probably can't) we may have to do the additional work as part of building the data warehouse. We may choose to record (and time-stamp) the events of all changes to standard and negotiated prices. Alternatively, we may choose to snapshot the pricing data nightly. Either way, we have a means of adding standard price and discount percentage to each order when we add it to the warehouse. The first approach may be harder to accomplish but provides greater accuracy. The second approach is programmatically simpler but loses precision if multiple pricing changes happened during one day or if some orders were processed before and others after the price change.

Choosing an appropriate sampling frequency is a compromise between costs and accuracy. Even though the detailed data initially loaded into the data warehouse is time-stamped with different levels of precision we are not hopelessly out of synch. In most cases, the detailed data loaded into the warehouse will be used primarily for building various summaries. Summaries, like all other data in the warehouse, should have a time dimension as part of their key structure. Sales are summarized by region and month. Hiring is summarized by department by month. In summarizing along the time dimension, we typically compress the data by giving up precision. We may summarize activity by day, week, month, quarter, and/or year. If we have captured our state data to at least the first level of summarization of our events then most of the warehouse processing can correlate the two with adequate precision.

All data in the data warehouse should be identifiable by its position in time in addition to its other identifying attributes.

What Is a Data Mart?

Some people use the term *data mart* to mean a small data warehouse. They create several data marts to meet the needs of several departments and everyone is happy. Well, maybe. The risk of using data marts in this way is that it may easily

Refreshing the Data Warehouse

One side note on the impact of time on the warehouse: In addition to forcing a time dimension on all data as it is entered or built through aggregation, there is an issue of timing our warehouse processing. Data should be entered into the warehouse on a regular schedule. Summarizations, too, should be processed according to a regular schedule. For the past twenty-five years, the emphasis of data processing has been to move as much processing as possible from batch mode to online mode. (Newcomers to the industry who don't have an IBM mainframe background don't even use the term batch.) We have been brainwashed into thinking that everything must happen immediately and that delays in processing data are inherently bad. For several reasons this thinking must be reversed when working with the data warehouse.

First, performance of batch operations on large amounts of data is almost always more efficient than single-record processing. Loading ten million rows to an Oracle database via direct path SQL*Loader is orders of magnitude faster than loading the rows individually. Likewise, building a summary table in Oracle using the parallel, unrecoverable CREATE TABLE AS SELECT command is many times faster than processing each detail row in a SQL cursor and applying changes to an existing summary. Performance requirements for a warehouse are generally relaxed over those of an OLTP system, but throughput concerns are often more stringent.

Second is the (somewhat underhanded) value of introducing an intentional delay in making data available in the data warehouse. Even if your data volumes are such that you can load daily transactional data overnight, it is almost always preferable to load data only weekly or even monthly. "How can that be?" the OLTP-trained masses cry. The answer is that if yesterday's data is made available today, there is an immediate temptation to start using that data for operational purposes. To keep warehouse users focused on the bigger picture of analysis and discovery we should not encourage them to get mired in details.

Finally, by making data available in batches rather than piecemeal, we can keep the warehouse better synchronized. We avoid the problem of users asking the same question at different times and getting different answers because we were loading relevant data between the two submissions of the query. Users should receive either the complete answer to a query or no answer. Data, ideally, should be an all-or-nothing resource.

sidestep the tough issues of integration that must be addressed in a data warehouse. By avoiding these issues we can certainly get several independent data marts operational more quickly. Each department works in isolation and thinks it is receiving valuable information from its private decision support system (DSS) environment. What naturally follows is that the independent data marts foster the same "islands of information" typified by the old application systems, which are functionally delineated. Using this independent data mart model we still find the marketing department and the manufacturing department getting two very different answers to what appears to be the same question.

To be useful, the concept of a data mart needs to be an extension of the data warehouse. Data is integrated as it enters the data warehouse. Data marts, then, derive their data from the central source, the data warehouse. Each department (or whatever organizational unit gets its own data mart) determines which of the data warehouse contents are of primary interest. These subject areas are then replicated onto the smaller, local data mart so that users can get to the data they are interested in with less interference.

Of course, if we were truly just replicating the identical data we would probably be able to save a lot of money by just increasing the query processing capacity of the data warehouse and retaining just one copy of the data. In fact, the distribution of data from data warehouse to data marts provides an opportunity to build new summaries to fit a particular department's needs. A common approach to data marts is to load detailed data into the data warehouse and perform the first level of summarizations (what Inmon refers to as "lightly summarized data"). The data marts, by contrast, keep only higher levels of summarization, which are derived from the warehouse's lightly summarized data. No detail data is copied to the data mart, and the central data warehouse does not attempt to keep every possible summary. This approach keeps the size of each local data mart relatively small. It also allows the complete data mart to be quickly refreshed. Since the data mart can be reconstructed quickly, backup and recovery concerns are virtually eliminated.

In this hierarchical model, whenever users of the data mart need to drill down from their local level of summarization their queries are routed to the primary data warehouse. This can be done automatically and transparently through the distributed capabilities of Oracle, although it may be preferable to make users aware of the change of venue. As they ask more detailed questions they should understand that the warehouse, with its larger volume of data to process and potentially greater number of users contending for system resources, will generally provide slower response times.

A good analogy for effective data mart design is that of a public library system. The central, downtown library attempts to obtain a large number of books, periodicals, and other more obscure publications. The local branch library maintains a much smaller inventory of materials. For average users, their local branch provides nearly all their needs. Children doing school papers and adults looking for an interesting mystery novel find what they need most of the time. But in the occasional situation in which the local resources are not sufficient, the local branch can obtain any of the main library's resources on an overnight basis. The electronic card catalog available in each branch shows the total set of resources, their location, and their availability status. The user of the data mart should have the same capability to view the entire catalog of available data and decide whether the immediately available local summary data will meet his or her needs or whether to wait for delivery of a more detailed set of data from the central data warehouse.

More complete discussion of data mart implementation is provided in Chapter 12, "Distributing the Oracle Data Warehouse."

What Is OLAP?

OLAP, online analytical processing, is complementary to data warehousing. There are two variations of OLAP.

MOLAP (multidimensional OLAP) provides analysis capability on data stored within a specialized multidimensional database system (MDBS). This specialized MDBS can be on an individual analyst's personal computer or it may be considered a departmental data mart. MOLAP databases are optimized for rapid analysis across different dimensions of generally numeric data. MDBSs are not designed to support the same operations as transaction processing databases (relational, network, or hierarchical), such as transaction management and high concurrency of access. Generally, the structure of the multidimensional "cube" is fairly rigid. Modifying the structure and reloading the cube is often a very time-consuming task.

ROLAP (relational OLAP) applies analysis tools to data stored within a relational database. ROLAP processing may be applied to the data warehouse or to a data mart. Relational databases are best known for their flexibility. Until recently they were weak in their ability to perform the same kind of multidimensional analysis that the MDBS is specifically optimized for. The introduction of hybrid relational systems with enhanced abilities to manipulate star schemas, such as the Red Brick product, brought much of the OLAP capability to the relational world. Oracle7, release 7.3, introduced star schema processing to the Oracle RDBMS product. This star schema processing has been greatly enhanced in Oracle8.

These improvements still do not enable ROLAP to meet the "slice and dice" analysis speeds offered by a dedicated MDBS. But coupled with the traditional flexibility of the relational database and ROLAP's ability to gracefully incorporate more complex data types and structures, ROLAP is an attractive option.

Both forms of OLAP processing, using Oracle's Express line of products, are covered in Chapter 13, "OLAP Processing in the Oracle Data Warehouse."

What Is Data Mining?

Data mining software is a recently invented class of tools that apply artificial intelligence (AI) techniques to the analysis of data. The promise of data mining tools is that, given access to the raw data, the tool can dig through the data looking for patterns and discovering relationships that the user might never have suspected. These tools are still maturing and can be expected to improve over the next several years. Whether they will eventually deliver on their promise or, like the AI products and techniques so widely touted a decade ago, end up living only in academic laboratories is still to be determined.

OLAP tools and most query tools used with data warehouses require the user to identify specific queries for investigating data that is expected to be of interest. The user must formulate his or her own hypothesis and then investigate the data to see if the hypothesized data relationships exist. Data mining tools can work against the data stored in operational systems or in a data warehouse. Because of the processing-intensive nature of data mining, it is likely that these tools, if they are ever widely adopted, will be commonly used in a data warehouse or operational data store environment.

Critical Success Factors in Data Warehousing

Certain characteristics are common to data warehouses that have been implemented successfully. Success is defined by user acceptance and usage. It is common to justify the development of a data warehouse by forecasting a return on investment that assumes a dollar value for business decisions made more accurately or quickly because of information gleaned from the warehouse. In a small percentage of cases, the warehouse team has solicited the users' valuation of the warehouse after deployment as well. In some publicized cases, users have been able to point to specific decisions made using warehouse data that have earned their companies millions of dollars in new business opportunities or saved costs.

Such cases are no doubt real, but they are isolated. Most data warehouses provide their value through hundreds of small, incremental decisions whose individual value is difficult to quantify. Even if users cannot point to a million-dollar cost savings, a data warehouse is successful if its users are finding it subjectively valuable and if they are continuing to ask for enhancements and extensions.

Some of the common factors seen in data warehouses that are successful and growing include the following:

- **An identified, involved user community.** Successful data warehouses are not built in a vacuum. The only reason to keep data in a warehouse is for the users who will request it. The library analogy applies here as well. A successful library listens to the needs of its users and adds books, periodicals, and technology that will enhance its patrons' usage. Trying to determine their needs without involving them can at best be only partially successful.
- **Executive sponsorship.** An organization makes a large commitment when it decides to begin data warehousing. This commitment involves potentially large sums of money for funding hardware, software, and human resources. The opportunity cost of what those people might otherwise be doing should not have to be constantly reviewed. Only with an executive sponsor who can champion the effort through its gestational period can the warehouse team keep its focus and move toward success.
- **A project team.** Warehouse teams don't have to be large. The most successful ones aren't. They do, however, need a variety of skills and knowledge, both technical and business-related. It is easy to fall into the trap of

thinking that the primary team players will have technical backgrounds. In reality, the representatives of the business units that will be the warehouse users will have the greatest impact on the eventual warehouse results. The IT analysts and DBAs are best considered as the facilitators who bring the others' business knowledge together into a design.

- **Quick, small, incremental successes.** As stated at the beginning of the chapter it is not advisable to attempt to build the corporate data warehouse in a single, massive project. Given a very high-level outline of the subject areas that will eventually be represented in the warehouse, the first implementation effort should only attempt to satisfy a small manageable portion. By completing that portion quickly, the team can demonstrate benefits, cement management support, and begin learning how to improve the design for future releases.

- **An architectured environment.** Simply throwing transactional data into a relational database and calling it a data warehouse is a recipe for failure. Unless the warehouse implementation team commits to making the difficult design decisions required to integrate the data into a subject-oriented plan, users will not find relevance in the warehouse. (Very likely they won't be able to find *anything* in the warehouse!) Of all possible characteristics, irrelevance is the one that will doom the warehouse fastest.

Summary

Data warehousing is not a project but an ongoing process. A data warehouse is not a product or set of products but a new way of thinking about the data of an organization. A data warehouse is also not the same as an operational data store. If an organization has unmet reporting needs about the current operational data these needs should be addressed separately and before building a data warehouse. Finally, a data warehouse is not a specific place. It does not replace current application systems but is a supplemental outgrowth of traditional data processing.

As noted earlier, according to Bill Inmon a data warehouse is a "subject oriented, integrated, nonvolatile, and time variant collection of data in support of management's decisions." This means that a lot of work goes into the data-driven design of a data warehouse in order to allow users to visualize data across application and organizational boundaries and across time. Gary Larson's *Far Side* comic strip once displayed a big pile of horses and cowboys heaped in the street in front of the sheriff's office. The sheriff is seen saying to his deputy, "and so you just threw everything together? Mathews, a posse is something you have to organize!" So, too, is the data warehouse.

HARDWARE ARCHITECTURES FOR ORACLE DATA WAREHOUSING

CHAPTER 2

An Oracle data warehouse may be implemented on a wide variety of systems with a number of options for data storage, fault tolerance, backup, and recovery. Each of these systems can be categorized in terms of broader hardware architectures (i.e., SMP, MPP, clusters, etc.). This chapter describes each of these architectures and discusses their suitability to the Oracle data warehousing environment. The ability of each architecture to support the Oracle Parallel Query and Oracle Parallel Server options is discussed. Oracle Parallel Query is discussed because it is considered essential for most Oracle data warehouses. Oracle Parallel Server *may* be required if the workload exceeds the capacity of a single node.

Data storage hardware and software continue to evolve side by side with the core computer systems architectures. In the later sections of this chapter, data storage technologies are discussed as they relate to the data warehouse.

The Audience for This Chapter

This chapter describes and compares the different hardware environments in which the Oracle7 and Oracle8 RDBMS can operate. The non-technical reader who is not involved with making hardware selection decisions may safely choose to skim this material quickly. The information on clustered and MPP architectures, however, is important background for the understanding of Chapter 11, "Warehousing with Oracle Parallel Server."

Throughout this chapter the terms node and system are used to identify components of a hardware architecture. A node is the smallest hardware component of an architecture that is capable of independently running its own operating system and database instance. A system is composed of one or more nodes that together provide the hardware infrastructure for implementing the Oracle data warehouse.

Computer Architectures

A key factor in determining the likely success of a data warehouse is, in part, the organization's ability to select the architecture that best meets most of the requirements. It will probably be cost-prohibitive or technically unfeasible to meet all of an organization's requirements. Some compromises will inevitably have to be made. In this chapter we identify why it is important to develop a set of requirements in conjunction with the end users of the system, what these requirements should contain, and how to evaluate an architecture based on these requirements. We will then discuss the computer architectures currently available and describe their strengths and weaknesses.

Requirements Definition

When evaluating an architecture it's necessary to assess how well the architecture satisfies your organization's requirements. These requirements need to be developed with the cooperation of the end users of the data warehouse and should take into account their expectations. They should be documented on paper so that all parties are in agreement about what the data warehouse should provide. These requirements form the basis for evaluating the various architectures and for selecting the one that best fits an organization's needs.

The requirements that impact the warehouse architecture are distinctly different from the requirements that define the contents of the data warehouse. Architectural requirements define in a quantitative manner the reliability, availability, performance, and scalability of the data warehouse. There are also other consid-

Ongoing Architectural Assessment and Improvement

Regardless of the architecture selected, there will always be software and hardware failures. There is a natural tendency for the operations staff to blame the hardware or software vendor for these failures. Although this may be warranted in some cases, it does not address the needs of the users. To address these needs, an assessment and improvement process should be adopted to investigate the causes for each failure. This should lead the organization to identify new procedures or architectural changes to prevent the failure from reoccurring in the future or to mitigate the impact of such a failure.

erations (e.g., manageability and cost) that should be taken into account once these basic requirements are satisfied but that are not part of the architectural requirements.

The requirements document can also be used (with some additions) as the basis for a service-level agreement. This agreement serves as the contract between the users and the operations staff. It establishes an ongoing method for measuring the effectiveness of the chosen architecture as well as the performance of the operations staff. The service-level agreement serves to pinpoint weaknesses in the architecture or deficiencies of the operations staff and point the direction for improvement.

Evaluation Criteria

There need to be objective criteria in place by which alternative architectures may be evaluated. The following five classifications will be described in the sections that follow and then used to evaluate the available architectures:

- reliability
- availability
- performance
- scalability
- manageability

Reliability

Users view reliability as the frequency of unexpected system outages. The systems staff may alternatively view reliability as the amount of time between failures. Vendors typically express this as the Mean Time Between Failures (MTBF). Based on their testing, they will estimate the MTBF for each individual component in a system. Considered in total, the reliability of these components will determine the total reliability of the system.

Another aspect of reliability is the impact of a specific outage. It is important to remember that a single query on a data warehouse may require several days to complete. An outage in the middle of such a query would typically require that the query be restarted from the beginning. (There is one exception to this—when running Oracle7's Oracle Parallel Server option. If there is a single node failure in a multinode system, no portion of the query is running on the failed node, and the disks of the failed node are available through another node, then the query will continue running. Oracle8 extends this concept through a new application failover capability that will allow queries to failover and reconnect to another node even if the node that a query started on should fail.)

The KISS principle (Keep It Simple, Stupid) generally applies to reliability concerns. Complexity is the enemy of reliability. The more independent components there are in a system, the more likely the system is to fail. Reliability is tightly coupled with the next criterion—availability. Insufficient or inadequate components can lead to poor availability. For example, if redundant disks are not available, then a single disk failure (a reliability issue) could result in a lengthy outage (an availability issue) while the database is restored to a consistent state.

When evaluating an architecture's reliability characteristics consider the following:

- maturity of the product(s)
- simplicity of design
- system load
- usage in similar environments
- MTBF

Unless a new, unproved component, product, or configuration provides considerable cost savings or is backed by significant support resources, it is not advisable to select it as the basis for any critical project including a data warehouse. On the other hand, if a product is so mature as to be approaching obsolescence, then it may not be a good idea to depend on it either. As products approach their intended life expectancy, they are not supported as well as the newer products. Also, in our industry new products typically provide superior cost-performance to previous generations. Be wary of products that depart from a vendor's existing product line. This does not necessarily mean that you should avoid the product that has a higher clock rate or faster system bus but is basically the same as a previous version. These, too, can have risks associated with them, but it is a lower level of risk than that typically associated with a completely new architectural approach.

Examine each proposed architectural design for its simplicity. After eliminating all the redundant components in the design, how many nodes are there and how are they connected? As the number of nodes goes up, the potential for hardware and software problems also increases. This is due to the necessarily complex hardware and software needed to coordinate the activities of all these nodes to make them function as a single system. In general, if you can meet your performance and scalability requirements with fewer nodes, that will probably be a more reliable path than a design with many more nodes.

Operating a system at or near capacity can expose hardware and software problems that would not be exposed at lower workload levels. Architectures that will allow your data warehouse application to operate at a fraction of capacity while still delivering the required performance are preferable to those that would require running it at maximum capacity.

The suitability of an architecture for the data warehouse role can be determined, in part, by talking with reference accounts that have implemented data warehouses on the proposed architecture. The vendor should be able to provide such accounts. If they can't then the architecture is probably too new or may be inappropriate for the data warehouse role. When discussing the architecture with the reference account representative(s) be sure to inquire about the size of the total system and workload. It should be similar in size to the system you are expecting to build. A four-node cluster may be very reliable but a sixteen-node cluster of the same hardware components may prove far less reliable. A related issue, scalability, will be discussed later.

The final step in considering a system's reliability is to examine and compare the MTBF numbers of the components for the various architectures. By multiplying the MTBF by the number of components of each type you should arrive at an expected failure frequency. By example, if a disk drive component is rated as 150,000 hours MTBF but you intend to deploy two hundred of these disks, you should expect a failure about every 750 hours (once a month!). This can be used to guide your decisions about where redundancy is needed to meet your availability requirements. If you choose not to build in redundancy for certain components or if it is not feasible to do so then the calculated system reliability number must not exceed the MTBF requirements of the users.

Availability

Availability is the amount of time the system is available to the end users. The system may be unavailable due to either planned or unplanned events. The service-level agreement should define the expected hours of operation. Reliability is one factor that affects system availability, but it is not the only one. Each failure may make the system unavailable for users to do their work. A related factor is the amount of time it takes to return the system to a usable state after a failure. This is typically expressed as the Mean Time To Repair (MTTR). A final factor relates to the amount of time needed to perform planned maintenance tasks that require that the system (or database) be taken away from the users.

Another characteristic that impacts availability is degraded performance and brownouts. If performance degrades to the point that the performance criteria for user queries cannot be satisfied, then the system is not available at the required performance level. Also, Oracle Parallel Server on Oracle7 and Oracle8 may experience temporary brownouts when a node fails. When this happens all queries are temporarily suspended. Assuming that no portion of the queries was running on the failed node, they will resume where they left off after the automatic recovery of the failed node.

It is important to set realistic availability requirements. Beware of simplistic availability models that state something like "The data warehouse must be available 98 percent of the time." This approach is unrealistic because it doesn't allow for differences between planned and unplanned downtime. There may very well be requirements for loading, indexing, summarizing, and possibly backing up data that will exceed the allowed 2 percent downtime. If users expect they'll have query access 98 percent of the time, they are likely to be disappointed. An additional reason that this simplistic availability requirement statement is unworkable is that mere percentages don't reflect the duration and impact of an incident of unavailability. A system could make the 98 percent availability target either by being down for one fifteen-hour period a month or by being down 1.2 seconds of every minute! The former situation will allow completion of a lot more work during the month than the latter.

The cost of achieving higher availability levels is not linear. A user or manager who requires that a warehouse be unavailable no more than once a month for no more than one hour needs to be shown the cost of such a solution. If he or she is willing to accept a more relaxed availability requirement of, say, one

The "A data warehouse is not an operational system" Syndrome

There is a tendency to design data warehouse environments that do not provide adequate availability. The rationale for this may be explained as "a data warehouse is not an operational system." While this may be true, the number of people who come to work every day and expect to ask questions of the warehouse may not see it quite that way. This situation can be avoided by working with the user community to develop realistic availability requirements and then investing in technology capable of meeting those requirements. Designing within both budget tolerance and availability requirements is essential to the success of a data warehouse.

event per week of up to two hours then the cost may be only half that of the more stringent solution. Frequently the "desire" is greater than the "requirement." The tradeoffs between the business requirements, the availability requirements, and the ultimate cost of providing the solution need to be carefully considered.

When evaluating an architecture's availability characteristics consider the following:

- redundancy
- auto failover capabilities
- failover speed
- recovery speed

The availability of a system can be increased by providing redundant hardware and software components that can continue to provide service when the primary component fails. Just as we added up the probability of failure of independent components, we can multiply the reliability factors of redundant components. As a very simplified example, if the probability of failure of a particular disk device can be estimated as 1/100,000 then a database stored on two of these disks should have a failure probability of 1/50,000 since the loss of either disk would make the database unavailable. However, if the data is stored redundantly on both disks, then the probability of both disks failing simultaneously is only one in 10,000,000,000 hours (1/100,000 * 1/100,000).

Consider providing redundancy for those hardware components with the lowest MTBF in order to reduce downtime. Selecting components with reduced MTBFs over more reliable components is not a wise investment unless the savings are used to provide redundancy. Always begin consideration of redundancy with the component that has the highest failure rate (e.g., disks). It is not always necessary to provide a one-for-one mirror for each of these components. Some logical volume management (LVM) software and high availability (HA) software technologies provide the ability to implement redundancy with fewer hardware components. These technologies will be discussed later in this chapter.

In addition to hardware failures the warehouse's ability to survive operating system and database failures should be considered. Assuming there is sufficient hardware, the use of HA software or Oracle Parallel Server can provide a means for reducing downtime. Using HA software without Oracle Parallel Server requires that the database instance that failed be restarted on a surviving node after the failure occurs. With Oracle Parallel Server, a database instance is already running on the other nodes, and another instance simply has to perform recovery on behalf of the failed instance. This approach provides slightly higher availability.

In conjunction with redundancy, an automatic method of detecting failures and initiating failover or recovery operations is needed to reduce downtime. Some hardware vendors build in the ability to detect hardware failures (power supplies, disks, CPUs, memory, system buses) and automatically reconfigure the system around the failed component. These automatic facilities are preferable to manual intervention. However, they may require that a node be rebooted in order to reconfigure around the failed components. When this occurs the system will be temporarily unavailable. HA and/or Oracle Parallel Server software can be employed to detect software failure and initiate failover operations automatically. These software technologies may also be used in conjunction with automatic hardware failure detection and recovery to reduce or even eliminate the temporary loss of service caused by the reconfiguration reboot.

The method and performance of the automatic failover facility will impact system availability. Each of the potential hardware and software failures that can occur should be evaluated for the potential loss of service they may cause for each proposed architecture. When evaluating architectures preference should be given to those that accommodate these failures with a minimal loss of service. Be sure to include any database recovery time for HA or Oracle Parallel Server enhanced solutions.

In the event of a failure that requires the initiation of database recovery, the performance of the recovery mechanism should be considered in reducing downtime. Each recovery scenario (database file[s], tablespace, entire database, import) should be tested and benchmarked to determine the best approach for each type of recovery that may be required. These procedures should be scripted to reduce confusion and ensure timely recovery when they are needed.

In some cases it may be faster to rebuild or refresh some or all of the database rather than perform recovery on it. Most newer tape technologies can sustain higher I/O rates than most disks. However, most recovery/backup software will support only one stream of data between a single disk file and tape device. (Oracle8's recovery manager, working in conjunction with tape management software and hardware, can support a multiplexed backup of multiple files to maximize the streaming capacity of the tape device.) In virtually all cases, however, utilizing multiple tape devices to backup or recover a large number of disk files in parallel can significantly decrease both backup and recovery times. This is an opportunity for using component redundancy that is commonly (and improperly) overlooked in the interest of economy.

Performance

OLTP environments typically have a large number of concurrent users who execute a small number of simple, predefined transactions that operate against small amounts of data in the database. In contrast, data warehouse environments typically have fewer users executing complex ad hoc queries that require vast amounts of data and processing resources. In addition to the online user queries the data warehouse will need to be periodically refreshed. As a result, the typical measure of performance for OLTP environments (i.e., response time) cannot be applied to data warehouse environments. For data warehouses, a method for measuring performance that covers both the online users as well as the refresh requirements must be defined.

Performance metrics for online data warehouse users should define the workload in terms of how many concurrent users can query the database and still provide reasonable response time. To define what reasonable response time is, it's necessary to establish a series of benchmark queries that can be run under various load conditions. The emphasis should not be on the absolute response time of any single query but on the throughput of total user workload.

Another method for establishing performance requirements for the batch refresh jobs is also needed. One method is to define the total amount of time available to complete the various load, summarization, and indexing jobs. Since the load may vary for weekly, monthly, quarterly, or yearly refreshes it will be necessary to define the time window for each of these jobs. Of course, it will also be necessary to define the conditions under which these jobs will run:

- Will backups be running?
- Which jobs can/should be run simultaneously?
- What degree of parallelism will be used for these jobs?
- How many users, if any, will be permitted access during these refresh periods?

Additionally, the amount of time to perform many of these tasks (especially indexing and backups) can be expected to increase over time as data volumes in the warehouse grow. Allowance for this increased processing load must be made during the initial design of the system.

There are numerous technical areas of an architecture that must be examined when evaluating its performance. The TPC-D benchmark provides one data point for comparing architectures under a hypothetical data warehouse load. This particular benchmark provides a more complex query mix than previous TPC benchmarks. However, it is a hypothetical load and is not necessarily indicative of how any specific warehouse will perform. Also, hardware and DBMS vendors tend to try every possible trick in the book to achieve performance that may not be realistic in a real-world environment. By way of example, the benchmark results may depend upon specific data partitioning that would be administratively burdensome in a real warehouse. A good approach for evaluating how an architecture will perform with an Oracle7 or Oracle8 data warehouse is to analyze

Oracle Parallel Server and Oracle Parallel Query Will Not Increase Performance on a System with Limited Resources

Oracle Parallel Server and Oracle Parallel Query provide the ability to parallelize certain operations (see Chapter 10 for a list) in the Oracle7/Oracle8 data warehouse. However, they cannot shorten the run-time of an existing job if the supporting system is already limited on resources. You will be disappointed if you expect Oracle Parallel Query to significantly shorten the run-time of a job on a system that has only 10 percent CPU idle time or that is already I/O bound. In this situation, using Oracle Parallel Query in conjunction with adding CPUs or striping the datafiles may dramatically increase performance.

how quickly certain database operations can be performed. From an architectural standpoint, the chief factors that influence this are as follows:

1. **Disk Transfers.** How long does it take to transfer data between the SGA and disk (msecs [milliseconds])? The primary concern here is sequential read access times. Write times also become a factor during refresh operations and any intensive recoverable data manipulation language (DML) operations. Placement of data files and the number of concurrent database operations can lead to disk contention (also called "hot spots"). Another factor is over how many spindles the load is spread. In general, the more disk spindles, the better the performance. Differing RAID levels also impact I/O performance (this will be discussed in more detail later). System bus throughput may become an issue (especially on nodes that have multiple CPUs). Oracle Parallel Server presents some additional demands for disk transfers. It requires that all database files be accessible from every node. Some of the platforms on which Oracle runs provide this accessibility through software instead of through shared direct access to the disks. These platforms impose an additional overhead in terms of software and the intranode communications required for all disk operations that cannot be satisfied locally. Also, each node increases the contention on the disks.

2. **Lock Conversions (Oracle Parallel Server only).** How long does it take to convert a lock with the Oracle Parallel Server option (μsecs [microseconds] to msecs [milliseconds])? This is a factor involving the latency of the communications path between the requesting node and the node containing the lock directory, the node mastering the lock, and the node (if any) that has the lock in exclusive mode. Additionally, if a node has the lock in exclusive mode, you must consider the amount of time to flush any dirty buffers covered by the lock as well as the rollback and redo associated with the transaction that requested the lock to disk. Lock conversion is only an issue during insert, update, and delete processing during warehouse refreshes, not during periods of exclusive query activity.

3. **SGA Access.** What is the latency for access to the SGA (nsecs to μsecs)? Each CPU on a node will require quick access to the shared Oracle SGA. Since CPU caches are less efficient in deferring memory requests for the large SGA (especially in multi-CPU environments), latency (not to be confused with throughput) is critical. Also, as the number of CPUs on a single node increases, competition for access to the SGA can cause contention on the system bus. Therefore, system bus throughput also has an impact on SGA access.

4. **Execution Speed.** How many CPUs are there and how fast are they (MHz/SPECint)? More CPUs provide the ability to increase the number of users doing work concurrently as well as the ability to increase the degree of parallelism with Oracle Parallel Query. The former is really a scalability attribute, while the latter decreases execution time for some database operations. More CPUs also permit the Oracle background process to run concurrently with user requests. Of course, the faster the CPU, the faster nonblocking operations can be performed. However, if there are too many CPUs contending for access to common resources (memory, disks, communications channels), then more or faster CPUs will not substantially improve performance.

Scalability

Scalability is the ability of an architecture to meet current demands as well as to grow easily to meet greater needs in the future. To determine if the architecture will meet these demands it will be necessary to look into the crystal ball and project data and processing growth over some period of time. In addition to the amount of data that will be stored, the number of new applications and users that are projected to start using the data warehouse during that same period need to be defined. The users' expectations in terms of performance in light of this additional load should also be defined.

Note that we can address the scalability of an architecture in which specific components or nodes may not necessarily scale. Adopting a distributed data warehouse architecture or one based upon clustering may allow the warehouse to scale even though individual computers are not modified.

There are two primary means for scaling up a data warehouse to support additional users and/or applications with Oracle7 or Oracle8:

- increasing the number of CPUs within existing nodes
- increasing nodes/instances within a system

Most vendors boast about how well their hardware architecture scales. However, when running a database the ability to scale a hardware architecture is highly dependent on system bus and/or high-speed interconnect bandwidth. When scaling up a system by adding CPUs or replacing existing CPUs with faster ones the common system bus is typically the limiting factor. Likewise, when scaling up by adding additional nodes/instances the high-speed interconnect is typically the limiting factor. Attempting to scale beyond a point at which these buses or interconnects become saturated results in diminishing returns or even degradation.

Oracle Parallel Server adds another layer of software to coordinate activities between nodes/instances. Although adding Oracle Parallel Server can help you achieve higher availability goals or scale beyond the capabilities of a single node, it does not scale as efficiently as a pure hardware scale up. So when you consider the expected growth of the system over the new few years, determine if it is possible to achieve this growth within the confines of a single node/instance. If it is, then consider Oracle Parallel Server for high availability only.

On the other hand, if you see that additional nodes will be required, then installing multiple reduced capability nodes initially will alleviate some of the migration difficulties later on. Starting with two clustered nodes, each containing two processors, and later upgrading each node to four processors will generally be easier than starting with a single four-CPU node and then later adding a second node and migrating to Oracle Parallel Server. Oracle Parallel Server requires certain database design considerations and prohibits the use of file systems for multiple-instance access.

Whichever approach you take, you need to ensure that it will accommodate the increasing disk storage demands of the growing data warehouse. Also, as the number of users and jobs increases, so does the demand for memory. A growth path that will not unnecessarily limit the ability to accommodate these increased demands is essential.

Manageability

Although the users of the warehouse are not concerned with the manageability of the system, they are directly impacted by a lack of manageability in terms of system availability. The operations staff should be keenly concerned with how manageable the system will be, especially since they are on the hook for living up to service-level requirements. This is another area where the KISS principle applies. A more complex architecture means more to monitor and manage. Even the use of sophisticated monitoring and management tools may not be sufficient to overcome the complexity of the architecture. You may have to enlarge your operations staff.

Several aspects of a system need to be proactively monitored and managed. Effective tools that work together and provide the ability to manage by exception are key to the success of a complex data warehouse environment. There are a lot of tools that provide too much information but not necessarily the right information to the people who must manage the system. It is essential to properly select and configure monitoring and administration tools. Also consider the required experience and training level of the staff that will be using these tools. If the operations staff is not adequately trained you cannot expect them to use the tools effectively. A partial list of areas that require monitoring and managing follows:

- **Hardware.** You need tools that provide online and offline diagnostics and alerts that inform the operations staff when a component (disk, memory, CPU, I/O controller, node) has failed or is experiencing recoverable errors that may foreshadow a failure in the near future.
- **Operating System.** Operations staff must have the ability to monitor operating system metrics including disk I/O rates, memory utilization, CPU utilization, file system utilization, paging/swapping, active jobs, and rogue jobs. Also, job scheduling and/or tape management packages may be required.
- **Network.** Tools to monitor the network for hardware failures, link failures, excessive errors or collisions, and utilization are necessary in today's client-server environments.
- **Database.** Tools are required that provide the ability to backup and recover the database; perform administrative activities; and monitor space usage, latch contention, locks, parallel operations, and user sessions.

The primary architectural issue that impacts manageability is the complexity of the architecture at initial implementation and as it scales up. The more components there are in the architecture, the harder it will be to manage. This complexity may be manageable with more sophisticated tools, but expect to add personnel to the operations staff as the system becomes more complex.

Uniprocessor Systems

The uniprocessor architecture is the simplest computer configuration on which you can implement an Oracle database. The ability to run Oracle, however, does not mean that a data warehouse application, other than a small data mart, is feasible on this architecture. The following description of a uniprocessor system provides a comprehensive background for the other architectures available today and introduces the simplest of architectures in order to set the stage for the more complex architectures presented later.

A uniprocessor system is characterized by a single node containing a single CPU, which is directly attached to all the other components in the systems via a common bus. This node must do all the processing for the entire system. This includes the operating system, database queries, and any applications that may be resident. Figure 2.1 depicts the major components of the uniprocessor system architecture.

Reliability

Uniprocessor architectures are very mature and simple. They have been around since the dawn of the computer age and because of the single processor design do not require sophisticated bus interface logic to implement cache coherence.

Figure 2.1 Components of the uniprocessor architecture.

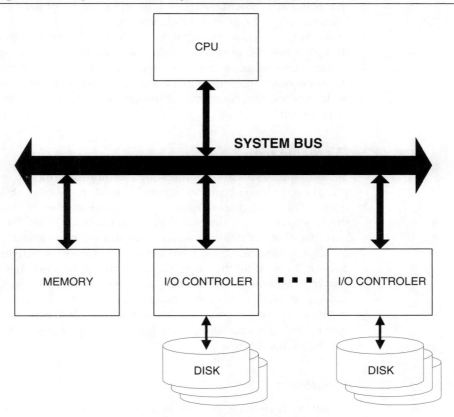

Likewise, the bandwidth of these buses may be kept low in comparison to other architectures. This further simplifies the design. Architecturally, this is the most reliable design. One potential area of investigation is the MTBF of the components used. A quick review of the components used should be done to ensure that they are of high quality and have MTBF numbers similar to those of components of other architectures being considered.

From a software perspective the probability of failure is also low. The software does not have to be as sophisticated as that required for multiple-CPU architectures, and timing issues present less of a challenge. On the other hand, there is no hardware or software redundancy so any outages are likely to result in a complete loss of service.

Availability

The simplicity of the uniprocessor's architecture provides for excellent reliability, which benefits availability. A few vendors provide the ability to implement redundancy for disks. However, redundancy at the CPU, memory, and system bus level is typically not available for this architecture. As a result, hardware failures that result in a system outage will be significantly longer than for designs that do implement more robust redundancy features.

Software redundancy capabilities are not inherent with this architecture, although it may be possible to add this capability (see the section on high availability later in this chapter) to compensate for a lack of hardware redundancy. At some point, the addition of software and hardware to improve availability adds expense and complexity corresponding to other architectures, such as MPP or clustered.

Performance

Since uniprocessor architectures are not normally meant for large database applications they will typically support a small number of disk devices. More care must be taken in placing data on the limited number of disks to avoid hot spots that could adversely impact disk access times. Oracle Parallel Server is not a consideration for uniprocessor architectures (unless it is a uniprocessor node in an MPP architecture, discussed later), therefore lock conversion times are not a concern. With only the single CPU and the limited number of disk devices, system bus contention and throughput as well as memory access times are not typically a problem with uniprocessor architectures.

Since the single processor must perform all the work on the system, user queries will contend with Oracle background processes and other operating system functions for time on the CPU.

Scalability

Scalability is severely limited on a uniprocessor architecture. There are practical as well as physical limits on the amount of disk storage and memory that can be added to these systems. The only CPU upgrade path is to replace the single CPU with a faster one. As the clock rate of the CPU increases it may be necessary to replace the system bus and/or memory on these systems. If your data warehouse is expected to grow then this is probably not the path for you.

If you are considering the uniprocessor architecture to support multiple, distributed data marts as extracts from a central data warehouse then the uniprocessor architecture may well serve the lighter needs of a departmental data mart.

Manageability

With only one copy of the operating system, applications, and database instance, the uniprocessor architecture is by far the easiest architecture to manage. Because of its simplicity this architecture does not require a lot of monitoring and management tools. You can probably get by with simple scripts developed in house. However, most of the tools that make more complex architectures manageable are also available on the uniprocessor architecture.

Figure 2.2 Components of the SMP architecture.

Symmetric Multiprocessing (SMP) Systems

As shown in Figure 2.2, on the surface the symmetric multiprocessing system (SMP) appears identical to the uniprocessor architecture but with the addition of multiple CPUs. However, each of the major components attached to the system bus requires complex logic to arbitrate between the multiple CPUs and to ensure cache coherence between them.

Reliability

SMP architectures have been around for a number of years and have established themselves as fairly reliable systems. They are quite a bit more complex than uniprocessor architectures and are always pushing technology to improve performance. Each new generation of SMP uses newer technology and tricks (e.g., shortening system buses) to overcome the limitations of physics to achieve the next level of performance and scalability. As this occurs the systems become more delicate and sensitive to timing issues that can cause failures. These may be manifested as hardware failures or as operating system or even database

CPU Caches and Cache Coherence

Each CPU (regardless of architecture) has a small amount of memory to cache instructions and data, which are referenced frequently (this is similar in function to the Oracle SGA). This memory is called cache and is significantly (orders of magnitude) faster to access than main memory. A CPU that can fetch instructions and data found in the cache will operate much more efficiently. Fetching from the cache instead of main memory is called a cache hit. When the fetch cannot be satisfied by the cache, it is called a cache miss. Most cache implementations are also used to defer store operations (i.e., data is immediately stored in cache and written back to main memory in the background). This prevents the CPU from pausing when storing to main memory. For these reasons, bigger caches tend to benefit CPU performance.

Another issue that is of particular concern in multi-CPU environments is cache coherence. Cache coherence is the mechanism employed to synchronize identical memory locations when cached by multiple CPUs. Hardware vendors use a variety of techniques to ensure that any single memory location contains only a single value regardless of where it is currently cached. Most approaches involve watching or "snooping" the system bus for memory requests. When an address is seen that corresponds to an address that's in the local cache, the local copy may be sent in response to the request (instead of the copy in main memory), or the local copy may be invalidated when a remote copy is modified.

Caches are more effective at caching instruction execution streams and local data. The CPU cache is less effective in caching the large amounts of data stored in the Oracle SGA. This is due to the limited size of the cache and the higher probability of repeatedly accessing the same instructions and local data memory. Since database execution is tightly coupled to how quickly structures in the SGA can be accessed, the resulting cache misses will dramatically influence performance. Therfore, it is critical to performance that the system bus provide short latencies and high throughput.

Oracle utilizes a latching mechanism to ensure protected access to memory structures stored in the SGA. These latches are usually implemented by a test-and-set operation on a shared memory address. If the latch is not immediately available Oracle will spin a number of times on the test-and-set operation. If the latch is still not available, then the Oracle process may sleep for a period of time before attempting to gain access to the latch again. As multiple Oracle processes on multiple CPUs attempt to obtain these latches a great deal of system bus traffic is generated to maintain cache coherence. CPU execution will pause momentarily when obtaining the latch from another CPU's cache or from main memory. This is another justification for high system bus throughput and low latencies.

bugs. Hardware failures can be overcome by increasing the redundancy and automatic failover capabilities of the systems. Software bugs, on the other hand, can only be overcome by subsequent software releases or patches. For this reason, it may not be prudent to be the vendor's guinea pig for these new systems until they have proven themselves.

As the size of these systems increases, simple multiplication of the MTBF will lead to higher failure rates. Small variances in the MTBF of specific components between systems can have a dramatic effect when multiplied by the number of components needed to reach the proposed configuration. These numbers are an excellent indication of the long-term stability of the system.

As with uniprocessor architectures, the SMP architecture also depends on a single operating system and database instance. Failures of any one of these components will likely result in a compete outage.

Availability

Availability in SMP architectures varies greatly and is dependent on the amount of hardware redundancy built into the system and the method of reconfiguring around these failures. Consider all single points of failure and the system's ability to reconfigure and continue running in the event of a component failure. Single points of failure should be carefully considered as they can lead to lengthy outages while you wait for a replacement part to be shipped and replaced. Most SMP vendors support a method of reconfiguring around a failed disk (assuming redundant disks are available). Some capability for redundancy at this level should be considered mandatory for large data warehouse applications. Also consider whether the disk storage technology supports hot swapping for increased availability. Fewer vendors support the ability to reconfigure around CPU, memory, system bus, or power supply failures. Those that do may require an outage for the system to automatically reconfigure, or even worse, may require a manual reconfiguration in order to return the system to a degraded mode of operation. All these factors must be taken into consideration when evaluating vendors' alternative solutions.

Software impacts on availability will be primarily affected by the maturity of the software release and the load placed on it. Since there is only one operating system and database instance running, the system will be unavailable in the event of a failure. The amount of time needed to restart the system can dramatically affect availability. Restart times vary between architectures and vendors. SMP architectures will generally have faster restart times than an MPP or cluster architecture. However, since the MPP and cluster architectures may have built-in failover capabilities, the probability of restarting the entire system is lower than with SMP systems.

Performance

Implementing cache coherence in SMP architectures places an enormous load on the common system bus. As the number of CPUs increases, so does contention on the system bus. Compounding this is the number of cache misses that occur when accessing the Oracle SGA or when obtaining a latch. As a result, it may not be feasible to effectively utilize all the CPUs that may be theoretically configured for a given SMP architecture. When evaluating SMP architectures, the following prioritized factors should be compared for maximum configured systems.

- System bus latency
- System bus throughput
- CPU cache size
- CPU speed
- Number of CPUs

Even with the common system bus contention issues, SMP architectures provide excellent performance within their scalability range when compared to other architectures. The two best performers according to the current TPC-D benchmarks are SMP-based architectures. Of course, as vendors upgrade their products and perform additional benchmarks, TPC-D results will change frequently. In fact, the previous leader of the TPC-D benchmark was an MPP architecture.

Since the SMP architecture uses hardware to apply multiple CPUs to a problem, it is more efficient than architectures that use software (i.e., MPP and cluster) to apply multiple CPUs to the same problem. As such, SMP architectures require less hardware to provide equal levels of performance. Another way of saying this is that the SMP architecture is more efficient since it needs to spend less of its available CPU time coordinating the activities of multiple nodes.

Scalability

Implementing cache coherence in SMP architectures places an enormous load on the common system bus and limits how many CPUs can effectively be added to the system. In the previous section, we discussed how to evaluate SMP architectures for maximum performance. These same evaluation criteria can also be used to determine the scalability of an SMP architecture. In addition to the practical limit on how many CPUs may be effectively utilized in an SMP node, a physical limitation also exists. For this reason, SMP architectures have limited scalability when compared to MPP and cluster architectures. Scalability improvements are frequently seen even between releases of the vendor's operating system on identical hardware. As CPU contention issues are identified they are researched and fixed as bugs.

If a single SMP node can satisfy the growth requirements of your organization then that is an acceptable option. However, if the growth requirements are beyond the capabilities of a single SMP node then the MPP or cluster architectures should be examined.

Manageability

The SMP architecture is inherently as simple as the uniprocessor architecture to manage since it has only one operating system and database instance to monitor and control. However, SMP architectures can support a lot more users and storage than the uniprocessor architecture can. As a result, more sophisticated tools for monitoring system performance are required. Also, with the increased storage capacity, more sophisticated tools may be needed for managing database backup and recovery. Note that this additional administration overhead is due to the larger configuration capacity, not to limitations in the SMP architecture itself.

Nonuniform Memory Access (NUMA) Systems

Nonuniform Memory Access (NUMA) architectures are similar to cluster architectures. However, they run a single operating system and database instance and provide a single memory address space, like SMP architectures. The NUMA architecture connects one or more CPUs to local memory and local I/O devices via a local shared bus to form a local processor group. This local processor group is, in turn, connected to other processor group(s) via a high-speed interconnect. Each local processor group provides a portion of the total memory space that is available to the node. Operations that can be satisfied within the memory of the local processor group do not generate traffic on the high-speed interconnect. Accesses to local memory are faster than accesses to the memory in remote processor groups, thus the term *nonuniform memory access*. Figure 2.3 depicts the components of the NUMA architecture.

Reliability

The NUMA architecture is the newest of the architectures described here and therefore is not as mature as the others. Also, there are only a few vendors offering systems based on the NUMA architecture. Because of this there are only a few organizations that have actually implemented data warehouses based on these systems. As more organizations adopt this architecture for their data warehouse applications more information will be available on its reliability.

From a hardware perspective, the NUMA architectures are based on the same technology as the other architectures. The difference is in the manner in which the components are assembled and connected. So from a hardware perspective, reliability is expected to be similar to that of SMP solutions (assuming similar MTBF numbers). From a database and applications software perspective, there are no changes required in order to run on this architecture. There may, however, be some performance benefits to modifying database and applications software to run on it.

The operating system, obviously, must be modified to support this new architecture, just as uniprocessor operating systems had to be modified to support SMP configurations. These changes may introduce unanticipated bugs as the vendors port their SMP-based operating systems to the NUMA systems. However, these problems should be resolved as these systems become more prevalent in the marketplace.

The complexity of the NUMA architecture is similar to that of the SMP architecture and should have similar reliability once it becomes mature.

Figure 2.3 Components of the NUMA architecture.

Availability

Availability of the NUMA architecture is influenced by the exact same factors as those of the SMP architecture and should be comparable for similar levels of redundancy. These systems may initially experience decreased availability owing to some of the reliability concerns addressed in the previous section. However, once the reliability stabilizes, availability should be very similar to that of SMP architectures.

Performance

My limited, early experience with NUMA systems has shown them to have excellent performance characteristics. Certainly, if the high-speed interconnect of the NUMA architecture can deliver performance similar to that of the SMP system buses, then it should provide better performance. However, the NUMA vendors are not currently implementing high-speed interconnects that operate at the same throughput and latencies as the high-end SMP configurations. Therefore, it is essential to reduce the number of accesses that must cross the high-speed interconnect. The caches in NUMA architectures should be as effective as SMP architectures at reducing requests for instructions and local data over the high-speed interconnect. However, the same issues that were of concern with the SMP architecture are also of concern in the NUMA architecture. Oracle SGA accesses and Oracle latch accesses will frequently have to be resolved over the interconnect.

The Oracle SGA is a large, shared memory area that all Oracle foreground and background processes must access. Assuming no special changes are made to the Oracle server code, the location of the SGA is up to the operating system. Likewise, the contents of the SGA are not partitioned to localize accesses by processor group. As such, the probability that an Oracle process running in a local process group will be able to find a portion of the SGA it requires locally will be a factor of the percentage of the SGA that is local. It is probable that the total number of accesses to the SGA that result in traffic on the high-speed interconnect will be lower than accesses over the system bus in SMP architectures. It is not clear that the reduced number of remote accesses will be sufficient to overcome the higher latency paid for these accesses when compared to high-end SMP architectures. Of course, if in some future release Oracle were able to partition the shared pool and buffer cache (which are structures in the SGA) evenly across all the local processor groups' memories and provide local processor group affinity, then the number of remote accesses might be dramatically reduced. This presumes that the NUMA system's operating system can provide process group affinity for individual processes.

The same issues that resulted in remote SGA accesses also impact latch requests by the Oracle foreground and background processes. Without any changes to the Oracle server code the result may be a lot of remote accesses that result in slower CPU execution because the CPU has to wait on a consistent copy of the latch to be retrieved from a remote processor group's memory. This is another situation in which it is not clear that NUMA architectures will necessarily outperform a similarly configured SMP system. It is also a situation in which Oracle could someday optimize access by partitioning these latches along with the SGA to reduce remote requests and to speed execution.

Based on these issues, it is not clear that NUMA will always deliver higher performance than comparably configured SMP systems without making significant changes to the Oracle server. In situations in which an SMP architecture is overloaded and is experiencing a lot of contention on the system bus, a NUMA architecture should provide better performance. However, if an SMP architecture is not experiencing system bus contention then the SMP architecture should be able to perform better because it has lower bus latencies than the NUMA architecture.

When evaluating NUMA architectures the following prioritized factors should be compared for maximum configured systems.

- High-speed interconnect latency
- High-speed interconnect throughput
- Local processor group bus latency
- Local processor bus throughput
- CPU cache size
- CPU speed
- Number of CPUs per processor group
- Number of processor groups

Scalability

During the discussion of cache coherence for SMP architectures it was explained how cache coherence and system bus throughput/latency impact CPU performance and scalability. The NUMA architecture is a direct response to these issues. The concept is this: If the majority of accesses can be satisfied within a local processor group, less contention will be generated on the high-speed interconnect. This should allow a single-node NUMA-based system to scale better than single SMP nodes.

Although performance is impacted by the increased latency for the Oracle SGA and latches with NUMA architectures, scalability is not impacted. This is because the high-speed interconnect has high throughput and very little contention. This, combined with the fact that more processors can be added to the NUMA architecture than to the SMP architecture, should provide for better scalability within a single-node system.

As with SMP architectures, if more scalability is required than can be addressed within a single node, then clustered or MPP options must be considered.

Manageability

The manageability of NUMA architectures should eventually be identical to that of SMP architectures. Enhancements will be required to various monitoring and administration tools to provide visibility to the additional structures and connections within the NUMA configuration.

Clustered Systems

Clustered architectures combine multiple nodes of the uniprocessor, SMP, or NUMA architectures to increase availability, scalability, and/or performance. The nodes may be connected by a system interconnect that is based on either a standard network or a specialized high-speed interface. This interconnect is used to support the lock management communications required by the Oracle Parallel Server option or the heartbeats required for non-Oracle Parallel Server high availability (HA) software. Cluster systems also share a common pool of disks that can be directly accessed from all systems in the cluster. When using Oracle Parallel Server, disk accesses from Oracle are coordinated by using a lock management protocol. If HA software is used in lieu of Oracle Parallel Server, then only one node at a time has exclusive access to the shared disks. This is enforced by the HA software. The advantage of Oracle Parallel Server is that in addition to providing higher availability, higher performance and scalability may be achieved. Figure 2.4 depicts the components of the cluster architecture.

Reliability

Clusters have been around for quite a while, and Oracle has a long history of running on these architectures. This architecture was introduced by Digital Equipment Corporation over a decade ago with VAX clusters, and Oracle version 5 provided a multi-instance mode that was the predecessor to Oracle Parallel Server. Thus, the basic cluster architecture is a mature and proven technology, although vendors of UNIX systems have begun providing clustered solutions only much more recently. Reliability of the cluster architecture will actually be lower than the constituent nodes that comprise it. This is due to the multiplication effect on the MTBF for the additional hardware. The addition of Oracle Parallel Server or HA software can also result in more frequent outages. This is due to the criticality of timing to the HA software and the complexity of the Oracle Parallel Server software. If availability (not scalability) is the goal when using Oracle Parallel Server, then using only one system to support online users at any point in time may reduce the potential for outages.

Availability

One of the primary objectives of cluster architectures is to increase system availability by eliminating the node as a single point of failure. When a node fails another node is available to take up the load of the failed node. Depending on which approach is taken (Oracle Parallel Server or HA), the amount of time the system is unavailable will vary. When using Oracle Parallel Server, the database is already up and running on the other node(s). When a node failure occurs a surviving node recognizes the failure and initiates recovery for the failed instance. During this recovery all user requests at all surviving nodes temporarily pause. The amount of time it takes for this recovery to take place depends on the amount of time that has passed since the last checkpoint and the number of PCM locks. Processing of these requests resumes once recovery is complete. With Oracle7, users that had queries running on the failed node will need to re-

Figure 2.4 Components of the cluster architecture.

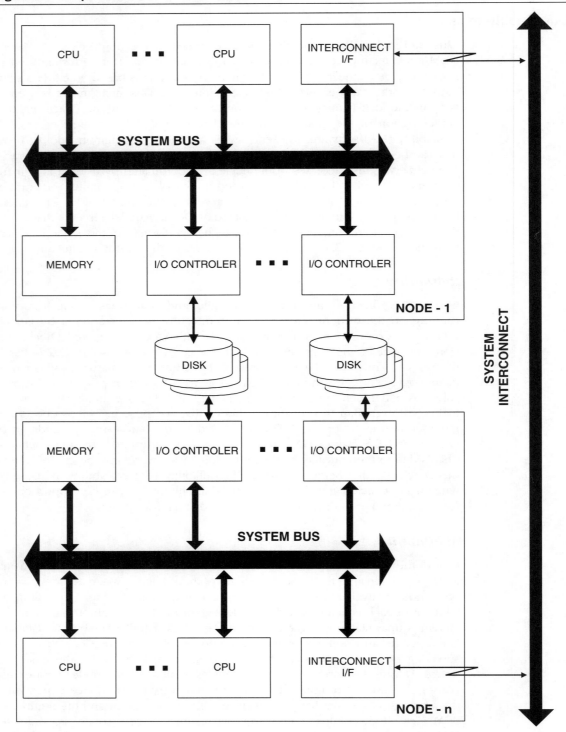

connect/resubmit their jobs. Oracle8 can be configured so that the reconnection and resubmission of queries is invisible to the end user. Data modification (INSERT, UPDATE, DELETE) activities, however, must be resubmitted. If there are a large number of PCM locks then the recovery time can cause the temporary pause in service to be longer than the time required to shut down and restart the database. (However, shutting down and restarting would result in the termination of all currently executing queries, requiring them all to be resubmitted.)

The HA approach continuously polls all the nodes in the cluster for a node failure. Upon detecting that a node has failed, the HA software starts up the Oracle instance of the failed node on another node and optionally takes over its network address so that users do not realize the instance has moved. The amount of time required to return the instance to an operational state is dependent on the amount of time it takes to obtain access to the shared disk and to start up the replacement for the failed database instance. The database instance startup time may be quite lengthy if it has been a long time since the last checkpoint of the failed instance. The HA approach may be faster than Oracle Parallel Server in restoring access to an instance, but it does not provide the performance and scalability advantages of Oracle Parallel Server.

Performance

For the cluster to provide better performance than SMP or NUMA architectures, Oracle Parallel Server (and usually Oracle Parallel Query) must be used to implement a parallel database.

Given an equal number of CPUs in a single node versus the same number of CPUs spread across multiple nodes, the single-node approach provides better performance (up to the point at which contention issues limit scalability). This is due to the overhead of the lock manager software that is used to coordinate access to the shared disks from multiple nodes. However, if more CPUs are needed than can be configured in a single node, the cluster architecture is an excellent second choice for data warehousing.

Clusters are more efficient than MPP architectures since they require fewer nodes to implement a parallel database using Oracle Parallel Server for a comparable level of performance. This is due to smaller operating system overhead as well as the method for implementing shared disks. MPP architectures also depend upon software and high-speed interconnects to provide access to all disks at all nodes. This is in comparison to the very simplified coordination effort required for direct shared disk access within a cluster.

Scalability

When combined with Oracle Parallel Server, clusters provide the ability to scale a data warehouse up from single-node NUMA or SMP machines to multiple-node systems composed of these same systems. The ability to scale in this manner is limited by the number of nodes a disk subsystem can concurrently connect to and the bandwidth of the system interconnect. In practice, the disk subsystem is the primary concern. Most hardware vendors support only a small number of concurrent connections to their disk subsystems. Because of this physical limitation, cluster-based architectures cannot scale to the extent that MPP architectures can.

Oracle Parallel Server presents severe database and application design requirements for OLTP systems in which users must simultaneously perform INSERT, UPDATE, and DELETE activity. There is very little impact, however, on simultaneous query performance, so nearly linear scalability within the warehouse environment is achievable—two nodes can provide almost double the workload of a single node.

Manageability

Managing a cluster is more difficult than managing a single-node SMP or NUMA architecture, but it is not as difficult to manage as an MPP architecture, which typically has many more nodes. More sophisticated tools are required to monitor the parallel database when using the Oracle Parallel Server option in conjunction with the cluster architecture. The multiple operating system copies and Oracle instances required for a multinode cluster require coordination. Care must be taken to ensure that configuration changes on one node are propagated to the other nodes.

Massively Parallel Processing (MPP) Systems

The MPP architecture provides for maximum scalability of an Oracle parallel database using Oracle Parallel Server and Oracle Parallel Query. This architecture overcomes the physical limitations of the cluster architecture disk subsystems to connect multiple nodes by utilizing a high-speed interconnect and software to make it appear that disks that are actually local to a single node are available at all nodes in the system. The Oracle Parallel Server option requires direct access to all disks in the database from all nodes in the system, and this approach satisfies that requirement. An MPP node is an autonomous system with its own CPU(s), I/O devices, memory, and operating system. Each node also runs an instance of an Oracle parallel database. The high-speed interconnect ties all of the nodes together. Figure 2.5 depicts the components of the MPP architecture.

Although Oracle software runs on several varieties of MPP hardware, the majority of MPP data warehouses today are implemented on the IBM RS/6000 SP (commonly still referred to as the "SP2," even though IBM dropped that designation quite a while ago).

Reliability

The reliability of the MPP architecture is worse than all the other architectures. The MPP architecture requires many more components than the other architectures to provide a comparable level of performance. The autonomous nature of

Figure 2.5 Components of the MPP architecture.

each node contributes to lower reliability from both a hardware and software perspective. Each node has an operating system and a database instance that can potentially fail. The software used to implement the virtual shared disk and Oracle Parallel Server capability is complex and more prone to failure as the number of nodes increases. There is also limited redundancy.

Availability

The MPP architecture is identical to the cluster architecture in terms of the handling of node failures with Oracle Parallel Server. Although this is not depicted in Figure 2.5, it is possible to "twin tail" disks between multiple nodes so that in the event of a single node failure, another node can provide access to the rest of the system for that node's disks. It is also possible to provide redundant disks so that a single disk failure will not make database files unavailable. Because of the large number of nodes in a typical MPP system, it can absorb many more node failures than a cluster architecture typically can.

Startup times for today's MPP systems are longer than for clusters. This is due to the large number of separate redo threads (each node has its own redo thread) that must be recovered at database startup. Because of the way in which Oracle keeps track of transactions, it is not possible to perform instance recovery on all nodes in parallel. Only one node will perform the instance recovery on behalf of all the nodes on the system at startup. Also, at system boot all the nodes in the cluster must go through their own boot process and restart the virtual shared disk software before starting the Oracle database. The amount of time required to start large systems can exceed an hour.

Performance

The MPP architecture is the least efficient of all of the multi-CPU architectures. This is due to the overhead imposed on each node to run its own operating system and database instances as well as the overhead necessary to implement the virtual shared disk subsystem and lock manager for coordinating access.

The nodes of the MPP system are connected by a high-speed interconnect. Depending on the implementation of this interconnect and the number of nodes in the system, contention can become a problem. The vast majority of traffic over this interconnect is disk data being transferred in support of the virtual shared disk subsystem. This represents a massive amount of data. As the data warehouse grows so grows the amount of data that must be transferred over the interconnect. In contrast to the buses in SMP and NUMA architectures, the main concern here is throughput rather than latency.

Some efforts have been made with Oracle Parallel Server to reduce the amount of disk data being transferred over the high-speed interconnect. In later versions of Oracle7 disk affinity was implemented for parallel operations. Disk affinity gives preference to nodes on which data physically resides in order to perform operations on that data. As a result, the disk data does not need to be transferred across the interconnect. In Oracle7 there are only a few operations that can be parallelized. With Oracle8 a larger number of operations are parallelized, resulting in reduced internode traffic. Subsequent releases of Oracle8 can be expected to continue this trend toward reducing the amount of data that must be moved across the interconnect. Much of the need for data transfers over the interconnect is determined by the physical design of the database and its partitioning of data.

Scalability

MPP architectures have the fewest physical restrictions on the number of nodes that can be interconnected. As a result, they can scale to many more processors and nodes than can all the other architectures. The interconnect is the primary hardware limitation on how far this architecture can be scaled. As more nodes and their disks are added to the system they place higher demands on the high-speed interconnect. The resulting contention effectively limits how far this architecture can be scaled.

Another consideration is the design of Oracle Parallel Server itself. For certain operations, there are a few global enqueues that must be obtained in exclusive mode across all instances in a parallel database. Waiting on these enqueues can cause jobs to serialize. They are highly dependent on the operations performed by users and, as such, can be subject to contention as the system scales. When this occurs, adding more nodes to the system may provide no additional capacity or may even reduce total system throughput. Again, partitioning the database and the application tasks plays a critical role in avoiding this situation.

Manageability

Managing current MPP systems is very difficult. With a large number of nodes, each running its own operating system and database instance, it is difficult to keep configuration changes in synch across all the nodes. Software upgrades must be coordinated across all nodes. Monitoring the system is also complicated by the large number of nodes. When attempting to track down a problem it is not unusual to jump from node to node looking for the cause. Although there are some good tools for managing this environment, they fall short. It is often necessary to develop custom scripts to monitor and manage these systems. Even with all these tools it takes a large staff to operate a large MPP system.

Backup and recovery also require a carefully considered plan and a sophisticated backup/recovery tool. Not only do you need to back up all the database files, but you must be able to restore the operating system and configuration for every node in the MPP system.

Summary: Computer Architectures

The Oracle Parallel Server and Oracle Parallel Query options give you the ability to parallelize operations across multiple CPUs and nodes. Table 2.1 summarizes the computer architectures discussed in this chapter and the combinations of

Table 2.1 Oracle Option Recommendations by Architecture

Hardware Architecture Options	Oracle Parallel Query	Oracle Parallel Server
Uniprocessor	Not Necessary	Not Necessary
SMP	Preferable	Not Necessary
NUMA	Preferable	Not Necessary
Cluster	Preferable	Preferable
MPP	Required	Required

Oracle parallel options that are required, preferable, or unnecessary. Using Oracle Parallel Server and Oracle Parallel Query where they are not necessary or appropriate may result in poorer performance. In the situations in which Oracle Parallel Server and Oracle Parallel Query are preferable, you can improve performance by using them.

All the architectures discussed earlier in this chapter are capable of supporting a data warehouse. Table 2.2 summarizes the architectures and how they rate in each of the evaluation criteria. Of course, only a really small data warehouse or data mart with very few users can use the uniprocessor architecture. The SMP and NUMA architectures are similar and are simpler to manage than the cluster and MPP architectures. These should be considered first before moving on to the more complex cluster and MPP architectures. Should higher availability or performance be required than can be achieved with standalone SMP or NUMA architectures, the cluster architecture is the next step. Finally, should the performance requirements exceed the capabilities of a cluster, then the MPP architecture provides the ultimate in scalability, although at the cost of manageability and reliability.

Data Storage Architectures

As computing architectures have evolved to meet the computing requirements of the data warehouse, so have data storage technologies. The primary motiva-

Table 2.2 Architecture Evaluation Ratings

Criteria/Architecture	Reliability	Availability	Performance	Scalability	Manageability
Uniprocessor	Excellent	Poor	Poor	Poor	Excellent
SMP	Good	Okay	Excellent	Okay	Good
NUMA	Good[1]	Okay	Good[2]	Okay[3]	Good
Cluster	Okay	Excellent	Good	Good	Okay
MPP	Poor	Good	Okay	Excellent	Poor

Notes: 1. There is insufficent infomation available on NUMA to accurately evaluate reliability. The relative score is based on the SMP architecture with which it is most closely associated.
2. This evaluation would be upgraded to excellent if the SGA could be partitioned.
3. This evaluation would be upgraded to good if the SGA could be partitioned.

Oracle File I/O Requirements

For data integrity, Oracle requires that for each disk write the data be flushed all the way to persistent storage. If data were to be written to a file system cache and not flushed to disk and then a system crash occurred, the database would be left in a corrupted state. When the system was rebooted and the database instance restarted it might not detect that a block was not flushed. In other situations media recovery might be required in order to restart the instance. Any data storage technology that does not provide the ability to perform synchronous writes is not appropriate for storing Oracle data.

tions for this evolution are the higher processing speeds of these new computer technologies and the rapid growth in the amount of information being stored in data warehouses. This evolution has come through advancements in both software and hardware technology. This section focuses on these advances and their applicability to the data warehouse.

Software

Software advances have occurred in the areas of file systems and redundant storage technologies. New file systems have been developed that decrease the amount of time needed to recover from system outages, increase performance, and reduce the waste of valuable disk space. Methods of storing data on multiple disks have been developed that provide higher data availability through varying degrees of redundancy.

Raw Files

The most direct and efficient method for accessing database files is through raw files. Raw files provide the ability to bypass the file system and access data without the overhead associated with accesses through the file system. File systems are layered on top of raw files and introduce CPU and memory overhead, which results in reduced I/O performance. On the other hand, raw files are more rigid in their configuration and typically require a system administrator as well as a DBA to move or resize a database file. For this reason they are less flexible than file system files. Without special logical volume management software, only a

ORACLE PARALLEL SERVER REQUIRES RAW FILES

At present, Oracle Parallel Server in UNIX requires that all database files (including control, redo, rollback, temp, and data files) be stored as raw files. This is due to the buffering of file system data and lack of a cache coherence policy for these buffer caches between multiple systems. Work is continuing to create file systems that can be shared between systems, but these are not yet available.

small number of raw files may be defined on a single disk, and a raw file cannot span multiple disks.

Because of the difficulty of managing raw files they are not recommended for development environments or production environments where it is anticipated that data files will need to be resized or moved often. Raw files and file system files may be mixed within a single Oracle database, although this is rarely recommended.

Logical Volume Managers (LVM)

Logical Volume Management (LVM) software provides the ability to combine multiple disk partitions or entire disks so they appear as a single raw file (called a logical volume). Several methods for combining these disks to provide increased performance and/or redundancy exist; I will discuss them in more detail in the following section on Redundant Arrays of Inexpensive Disks or RAID. Once a raw logical volume has been defined using the LVM, a file system may be on the raw file, thus providing the same performance and redundancy benefits for all files (including database files) stored in the file system.

The LVM software typically provides GUI and command line tools for configuring and monitoring logical volumes. Since most LVMs provide a finer granularity of control over the placement of raw files than raw files by themselves, they may reduce some of the management burden of raw files alone.

Because of the usefulness of LVM software for both raw files and file systems, it should be considered mandatory for any large data warehouse environment.

Redundant Arrays of Inexpensive Disks (RAID)

Redundant Arrays of Inexpensive Disks (RAID) is an engineering approach to organizing multiple disks that provides varying degrees of performance and redundancy. Multiple disks are used together to provide reliability or performance characteristics that could not be economically provided by a single disk. RAID may be implemented solely in software via an LVM or it may be implemented through intelligent array hardware combined with LVM software. The currently defined levels for RAID are as follows:

- **RAID 0.** Provides for nonredundant disk striping. Each disk is subdivided into smaller units called stripes. Stripes from multiple disks are concatenated together to provide a larger striped logical volume that then appears to be a single raw file. Performance and concurrency are increased by spreading I/O requests across multiple devices.
- **RAID 1.** Provides for mirroring of data between multiple disks. Each disk has a mirror copy on another disk, providing 100 percent redundancy.
- **RAID 0+1.** Combines RAID levels 0 and 1 to provide striped/mirrored logical volumes. When combined in this manner RAID 0+1 provides increased performance and redundancy.
- **RAID 3.** Provides for storage of parity data on a single disk. Multiple disks are grouped together into a single logical volume with one disk dedicated to storage of parity. If any single disk fails the data can still be recon-

structed from the remaining disks by using an XOR (exclusive or) operation, resulting in increased availability.

- **RAID 5.** Combines RAID levels 0 and 3 to provide striped parity across multiple disks. Parity is distributed across a number of disks at the stripe level, thus providing the availability attributes of RAID 3 with increased performance benefits similar to RAID 0.

Each of the RAID levels provides varying degrees of redundancy and performance for different types of I/O operations. Table 2.3 summarizes the various RAID levels and ranks them based on performance and redundancy for normal operations. Some RAID levels (5 and 3) experience dramatic reductions in performance when a single disk fails since all disks must be accessed for I/O that is directed to the failed drive. These rankings are for software-only RAID implementations and do not take into account array hardware, which may accelerate the performance of certain RAID levels. Hardware RAID implementation will be discussed in a subsequent section.

Some vendors are coining their own RAID levels and terms for describing what is essentially one of the previously defined RAID levels combined with intelligent array hardware for overcoming some of the performance limitations associated with certain RAID levels. We will discus hardware-embedded RAID solutions later in this chapter.

One of the key factors that affect the performance of striped RAID levels (0, 0+1, and 5) is the stripe width (or stripe size). Stripe width is the amount of data that is stored across all disks in a logical volume before wrapping around to the first disk in the logical volume. When a single write request is larger than the stripe width, then the single logical I/O results in more than one physical write to one of the disks. This causes the I/O request to enqueue on itself, resulting in diminished performance.

A stripe segment (or stripe unit) is the amount of data written to one disk before starting to write to the next disk. The stripe width is equal to the size of the stripe unit multiplied by the number of disks in the striping group. Raw files are mapped in a round-robin fashion across the set of disks, which provides for an even distribution of data (and usually I/Os) in the logical volume.

Stripe size has a direct impact on how well certain access methods (sequential or random) perform under certain load conditions (high or low concur-

Table 2.3 RAID Level Rankings (higher numbers are better)

RAID Level	Redundancy	Sequential Read	Sequential Write	Random Read	Random Write
0	1	3	3	1	3
1	3	3	2	1	2
0+1	3	3	2	1	2
3	2	1	1	3	1
5	2	2	1	2	2

Table 2.4 RAID Stripe Size Recommendations

Data File Type	Access Method	Concurrency	Recommended Minimum Stripe Size
Control Files	Sequential	Low	2 * DB_BLOCK_SIZE
System Tablespace	Random	High	2 * DB_BLOCK_SIZE
Redo Logs	Sequential	Low	DB_BLOCK_SIZE
Rollback Segments	Sequential	Low	2 * DB_BLOCK_SIZE
Temp Segments (Sort Space)	Sequential	High	2 * DB_FILE_MULTI_BLOCK_READ_COUNT * DB_BLOCK_SIZE
Indexes	Random	Varies	2 * DB_BLOCK_SIZE
Tables	Mixed	Varies	2 * DB_FILE_MULTI_BLOCK_READ_COUNT * DB_BLOCK_SIZE

rency). Low concurrency means a small number of nearly simultaneous I/O requests while a large number of I/O requests indicates high concurrency. Table 2.4 summarizes the various types of data files that make up an Oracle data warehouse, their access patterns, and the recommended *minimum* stripe sizes.

In general, the objectives of striping are to spread the I/O load evenly across multiple disks while avoiding any single I/O request from enqueing on itself. Rather than attempt to individually tune each type of file, selecting a uniform stripe size of one or two megabytes can provide the best balance of performance and simplicity.

File Systems

Another method of storing database files is in a file system. A file system is an extra layer of software that allows the storage of multiple files per raw file. File systems are built on top of raw files. Therefore, my previous discussion of LVM and RAID also applies to file systems (i.e., file systems may be mirrored, striped, etc.). The biggest advantage of file systems is their flexibility. Files can be created, moved, resized, and deleted at will without the need to coordinate with a system administrator every time you wish to make a change. On the other hand, this extra layer of software does add extra CPU overhead for every I/O request. Depending upon the file system implementation, this overhead can range from very small for some of the new specialized file systems to as much as 10 to 15 percent for older file systems such as the UNIX file system. Also, if the file system utilizes a buffer cache (and most do) then you will need additional memory for storing database blocks twice (once in the file system cache and once in the SGA). In this section we will examine three different file systems and their associated overhead and performance characteristics.

UNIX FILE SYSTEMS (UFS)

The UNIX file system (UFS) is the oldest of the file systems we will consider. It has been around since the genesis of UNIX but has evolved over time, with each vendor making its own improvements and customizations. In many cases the vendors have coined new names for their particular implementation of UFS.

UFS was designed to provide efficient access and storage of relatively small files. Large files, on the other hand, are not as efficiently stored. Each file in a UFS is accessed via its inode, which contains information on where each block of the file is stored. As files become large, multiple inodes are required to keep track of all the blocks. These inodes are structured in a hierarchical fashion like a B*Tree index in a database. The more inodes there are, the more I/Os are required to locate and access a single data block. The overhead of database files in UFS can be as high as 15 percent in terms of access times as well as additional CPU load. More and/or faster CPUs are required to accommodate database files in UFS compared to raw files.

As files are created in a UFS, the blocks are allocated from a free pool. This pool is not defragmented when blocks are returned to it. This can lead to individual files being scattered all across the disks underlying the file system. This can result in poor performance when doing sequential I/O operations, as is often required with data warehouses.

Untuned UFS file systems also waste a lot of space when database files are stored in them. Since they are typically meant to contain large numbers of small files, the default storage parameters are not optimized for storing a few large database files. If you intend to store database files in a UFS be sure to tune the file system to hold back less space and to allocate fewer inodes. It is also advisable to store only database files or program files in a given UFS. Mixing file types within a single file system is not recommended.

A UFS employs caches for more frequently accessed data blocks (similar to the database block buffers of the SGA) and inodes for files that are open. Blocks that are part of the database end up being double cached (once in the file system cache and once in the SGA block buffer). When using UFS for database files, plan on configuring additional memory for this purpose.

ARE RAW FILES ALWAYS FASTER THAN FILE SYSTEMS?

Because of the default way in which Oracle avoids SGA buffering of blocks retrieved as part of a full table scan, UFS buffering can occasionally improve performance when a table is scanned repeatedly.

JOURNAL FILE SYSTEMS (JFS)

A Journal File System (JFS) is any file system that provides the ability to record file system metadata in a log similar to the redo log in Oracle. Only metadata is written to the JFS; file data is written directly to the file system. The advantages of a JFS are that it reduces the probability of file system corruption and decreases file system recovery time. The JFS log is used to recover metadata changes that had not yet been applied prior to doing the file system integrity check. As a result, the check typically completes almost instantaneously when the system is being rebooted. One disadvantage of a JFS when used in conjunction with an Oracle database is that there will be a minimum of two synchronous writes for each database write operation: one for the data block that must be synchronously written through the file system to the underlying disks and one for the metadata (for any write operation, the last modification time stamp in the file's inode must be updated), which is stored in the JFS log.

Placing the log for a JFS is critical to the performance of a JFS file system. The log itself is written sequentially in a circular fashion and is typically relatively small. It should be placed either on disks separate from the JFS it is protecting or striped across a small portion of all the disks in the file system to reduce contention with regular file data transfers. The JFS logs should also be mirrored to provide an extra level of protection against file system corruption.

If you are planning to use file systems to store your database files, a JFS is highly recommended to protect that data against potential loss and to increase availability. Even if you do not plan on using the file system for database files it is a good idea to protect the remaining system components and the archive log files with a JFS.

Some implementations of JFS use a log for both metadata and file data changes. This significantly increases the amount of data being logged. Since Oracle does synchronous writes, data logging is not needed. For this reason this implementation of JFS is not recommended for storage of Oracle database files.

Extent-Based File Systems (XFS)

Extent-based File Systems (XFS) is a relatively new file system design that does not utilize an inode structure to map data blocks to files. Instead of mapping individual data blocks, XFS groups contiguous blocks into extents. Multiple extents (if required) can be grouped together to access the entire data file. This approach is far more suitable for storing large files such as those required by a database. It is not suitable for very dynamic environments containing small files. The allocation/deallocation of these files will result in fragmentation and reduce the effectiveness of XFS in handling large files. When used for database files only, however, XFS has far less overhead for finding data blocks. Also, data files are more likely to be stored contiguously. Some implementations of XFS provide tools to defragment a file system (in some cases while it is online) or to implement a strict contiguous storage policy.

Although XFS implementations typically provide a caching capability similar to UFS, this feature can often be turned off or bypassed, resulting in performance similar to that of raw file accesses. Bypassing the cache also results in less memory wastage due to the double-buffering effect seen in UFS implementations.

XFS, like UFS, is implemented as a software layer on top of raw files. As such, XFS can be used with the RAID technologies previously discussed to increase its performance and/or redundancy characteristics.

XFS provides an effective compromise between the performance of raw file access and the flexibility of UFS, while overcoming each technology's shortfalls. Assuming that Oracle Parallel Server is not required, XFS should be considered before raw files due to its UFS-like manageability characteristics. In the future there are likely to be XFS implementations that support Oracle Parallel Server. Until that time, however, warehouses that require Oracle Parallel Server must continue to use raw files.

Hardware

There have been several advances in hardware storage technology to keep abreast of the increasing performance, availability, and growth demands originating from data warehouse applications. These advances have manifested themselves as intelligent controllers that can handle a large number of disks, commonly referred to as disk arrays. In this section we will consider three types of arrays, which offer varying degrees of intelligence.

Caching Arrays

Caching arrays are used to increase the performance of all read/write operations by utilizing a persistent cache embedded in the array controller. The size of these caches varies and has a direct impact on performance. Although this technology increases the performance of the RAID levels described earlier, it does not directly implement any of them. Software running on the host operating system is completely unaware of the caching going on in the controller and must continue to implement any required RAID support.

Write operations are the main beneficiaries of this technology. Whenever Oracle requests a write operation, the block being written must be persistently stored before control is returned to Oracle. The disk block in question is transferred to the array's persistent cache for storage, and control is immediately returned. The array then has a process that ensures that the dirty block gets written to disk in background. The write-to-cache operation completes in a fraction of the time required to write directly to disk. The cache must be persistent so that in the event of a power outage, the data is not lost. Once power is restored, the background process resumes writing the dirty blocks to disk. The cache should be sufficiently large so that the background write process in the controller can stay ahead of demand. Should the write process consistently fall behind, performance will revert to writing directly to disk.

Data blocks that are cached in the array because of a recent read or write operation may be used to satisfy read requests. However, the SGA and file system cache (if you are using file systems) will satisfy most read requests that might be cached in the array. Those read requests that eventually make their way to the array are more likely to request data that is not cached, resulting in a physical disk read operation. As such, the benefit of caching arrays for read operations in a data warehouse environment is limited.

Embedded RAID Arrays

The embedded RAID array, in addition to providing the caching array functionality discussed earlier, also implements some or all of the RAID levels in hardware. This effectively off-loads the host operating system from performing the multiple I/O operations required by software implementations of the various RAID levels. Each I/O request results in a single request from the operating system to the intelligent controller. The controller satisfies the request and returns control to the operating system.

In general, embedded RAID arrays will react in a manner similar to caching arrays. Overall performance will be better and system load will be reduced compared to caching arrays. However, write operations will continue to benefit more than read operations for the same reasons described for caching arrays. Embedded RAID arrays typically provide larger caches than caching arrays, resulting in better cache hit rates and higher performance. Some RAID arrays allow replacement of a failed disk without interrupting access to the array. This feature is commonly referred to as "hot swappable" disks. Arrays that support hot swapping of disks will hide the performance degradation for resynchronization better than software implementations.

Several embedded RAID array solutions on the market provide a variety of other capabilities. Some provide read ahead capabilities that attempt to guess which data blocks may be requested next. Others provide hot swap capabilities to increase availability. They may also support connections from multiple hosts (required for Oracle Parallel Server cluster solutions).

One drawback to the embedded RAID array is that it becomes a single point of failure that can bring your entire system down. This risk can be mitigated with arrays that provide for multiple host connections from the same host coupled with automatic sensing and failover circuitry. Some arrays may even provide redundant power supplies and intelligent controllers to further increase availability.

Remote Replication Arrays

Remote replication arrays provide the ability to replicate data over great distances. This capability provides the ultimate in availability, redundancy, and disaster recovery. Should any disaster cause a system or array to become temporarily or permanently unavailable, the remote site can be activated using an up-to-date copy of the data from the failed site. The replication capability is an option that is added to either the caching or embedded RAID arrays.

The remote site is a read-only site (from an application perspective) until it is activated. As writes occur at the online site they are synchronously transferred to the remote site to keep it up to date. In order for the remote site to be viable from an Oracle perspective, updates must occur synchronously. They cannot be propagated via a write-behind approach. Depending on the amount of write activity to the array, one or more parallel communications paths may be needed to keep up with the demand without impeding the online database performance. In addition to the throughput needed to keep up with this demand, communications delay must be considered when replicating over long distances.

Oracle software provides some similar capabilities through replication and the standby database feature (introduced in Oracle7, release 7.3). This level of protection and investment, however, is rarely considered necessary for data warehousing.

Summary

Five computer architectures (uniprocessor, SMP, NUMA, clusters, and MPP) have been introduced and evaluated in relation to several criteria of reliability, availability, performance, scalability, and manageability. The uniprocessor architecture is recommended only for small-scale data marts. Most Oracle data warehouses today are implemented with SMP configurations. The newer NUMA architecture extends many of the benefits of SMP. When a single SMP or NUMA computer cannot provide the performance of scalability that is required, Oracle Parallel Server in conjunction with clustered SMP or NUMA nodes may be the answer. For extremely high-end warehousing needs an MPP solution may be required, albeit at a cost of both dollars and administrative time.

Complementing the evolution of computer architectures has been a corresponding evolution in data storage technology. Raw disk files and various file systems implementations were described. Logical volume managers, various levels of RAID, and three types of storage array hardware were presented.

There is clearly no one single computer or storage architecture that is ideal for every data warehouse. Each architecture offers specific advantages and disadvantages when compared to the others. From the descriptions and evaluations provided in this chapter you should be able to begin evaluating alternative configurations from various vendors.

ORACLE SOFTWARE ARCHITECTURE AND FEATURES

CHAPTER 3

The Oracle data warehouse is created, accessed, and managed through the facilities of the Oracle Server. The majority of these facilities are provided through the core Oracle Server product while others are only available through separately licensed options.

We'll begin our examination of Oracle's architecture from the outside and identify and describe the components that can be observed from the operating system level—what we'll call the external architecture. Then we'll move inside of the Oracle database to see the components and substructures that Oracle uses to perform its various functions—what we'll term the internal architecture.

Oracle Server: External Architecture

This chapter introduces the architecture that underlies the Oracle Server. Experienced Oracle DBAs may feel comfortable skimming over this introductory mate-

Oracle Server Features and Options

The packaging of features by Oracle Corporation into its base Server product and its various options (e.g., the Oracle Parallel Server) has changed over time for both technical and marketing reasons. Some of the features described thoughout this book are available only as extra cost options to the Oracle7 or Oracle8 Server. The user is responsible for compliance with current licensing restrictions.

rial. More detailed information on this topic is available in the Oracle7 and Oracle8 *Server Concepts* manuals published by Oracle Corporation.

The external architecture includes those things that can be seen or monitored from the operating system. It includes various disk files, several processes (or threads, depending on the operating system's design), and the allocation of memory by those processes. Figure 3.1 illustrates the primary components of Oracle's external architecture.

We will discuss each of the components in more depth later in this chapter. Before getting into the specifics of the Oracle architecture, it is important to clarify some terminology that is specific to the Oracle environment.

Oracle Database versus Oracle Instance

New Oracle users and administrators who are familiar with other DBMS products commonly get confused about Oracle's use of the terms *database* and *instance*. In Oracle's terminology, a database is a set of physical files that exist on permanent storage, usually disk. The database continues to exist even if the computer system is shut down. The additional software processes and shared memory structures that are needed to access and use the database are referred to, in Oracle terms, as an instance.

In normal operations one database is associated with one instance; typically, they even have the same name. It is no wonder then that, in casual conversation, even an experienced Oracle administrator, consultant, or support representative may use the terms interchangeably—which, of course, helps feed the confusion. There are times, however, when it is important to understand the distinction between these terms.

An Oracle database can exist even without an instance. The instance may have been shut down, for instance, to perform an offline ("cold") backup of the database. If an instance does not have the database open, no information within the database can be accessed, read, or manipulated. Only operating system functions (such as the cold backup) on entire files can be performed on the database.

Less intuitively, however, it is possible to have an Oracle instance without an Oracle database. Specifically, when creating a new database the administrator will start up an instance and then issue the CREATE DATABASE command. Even with an existing database, the process of starting up Oracle and making the database available to users has three distinct steps. Not until the third step is the database actually involved.

Instance Startup and Database Opening

In the first step, the *startup* phase, only the instance is started. That is, several processes are started by the operating system, each of which runs the Oracle RDBMS software. An allocation of shared memory is made that is accessed by each of these Oracle processes. To perform this first step, Oracle reads a file containing initialization parameters that define how to configure the instance.

Figure 3.1 High-level external architecture.

These parameters provide such important information as the name of the database, how much memory should be allocated, and which optional Oracle processes should be started.

In the second step, called the *mount* phase, the Oracle software opens a special file associated with the database, called the *control file*. The control file contains information about all other files that make up this database. Because of the critical nature of the control file it is important that you keep multiple copies of it. Oracle will automatically maintain these copies. The names of each copy of the control file are provided to the instance through the CONTROLFILES parameter in the initialization parameter file opened in step one.

Finally, in the third step (the open phase) each of the files that make up the database is opened. At this point, the instance and the database are associated with each other until the administrator shuts the instance down. Oracle can now retrieve specific data from the database files for a user. Any changes made to the data will be recorded in the redo log files and the database files.

Multi-instance Oracle

One other situation makes it critical to understand the distinction between an Oracle instance and an Oracle database. In clustered architectures and massively parallel processor (MPP) configurations (introduced in Chapter 2), multiple computers, each having its own memory and processes, can all access a set of database files on disk. In these hardware configurations, a special Oracle option, the Oracle Parallel Server Option, must be used to control simultaneous access to the database from the separate computers. Using Parallel Server, an Oracle instance is started on each of the computers in *multi-instance mode*. In this mode, each instance agrees to cooperate with each of the other instances to protect the integrity of the data in the database. Only one instance, for example, will be allowed to actively work with a specific block (or, more typically, a set of contiguous blocks) at a time. Figure 3.2 illustrates Oracle's ability to start two instances on two nodes of a clustered configuration, which then share access to a single Oracle database. Each instance has its own set of redo log files, but they share access to the database files.

In Chapter 11 we discuss the issues involved in designing, loading, and administering a data warehouse using Oracle Parallel Server in clustered and MPP environments.

File Architecture

Since by definition a database is the organized storage of data—and generally large amounts of it—it is appropriate to begin our examination of Oracle architecture by considering the data files that provide the storage. In addition to the files that actually hold the data, Oracle uses other files to provide integrity controls to ensure that the data is not lost or corrupted. These various Oracle files are shown in Figure 3.3. The database data is stored in database files. Changes made to blocks in the database files are logged in redo log files, which are later permanently copied to archive log files. Control files keep track of the status of all the database and log files. Initialization parameter files are read during instance startup to properly configure the instance.

Database Files

An Oracle database is created using the SQL command CREATE DATABASE. (The Oracle Installer can issue this command automatically, if requested, when the Oracle Server software is installed.) Several files are created in this process that will comprise the actual physical database stored on disk. Whenever the computer system hosting the database is powered down and all memory is erased, these physical files will remain until the next system startup. When you need the database again, issue the Oracle STARTUP command (from SQL*DBA,

Figure 3.2 Multi-instance Oracle.

Oracle Server Manager, or Oracle Enterprise Manager programs, depending upon which version of the Oracle Server is being used), and the files will be open to make the database available.

Figure 3.3 Oracle File Architecture.

tablespace

When you create a database you must create at least one database file for the SYSTEM tablespace (which we will discuss further in the section on Oracle internal architecture). This tablespace contains the essential components that must be part of every Oracle database, namely, the data dictionary. Your data warehouse will, of course, require you to create other database objects, such as tables and indexes, to store the information that your users want to see. Oracle uses the data dictionary to store its information about those other objects you will create.

Each database file stores some special control information in its file header. This information is not generally seen or used by the database administrator or end user. It is used by the Oracle RDBMS software to ensure the integrity of the database and prevent a file from being substituted or overlaid in error. As an example, consider a fairly common situation in which a disk failure causes one (or more) of the database files to become unavailable. The database administrator then restores an old copy of the database from a tape backup and attempts to restart the Oracle instance and open the database. When Oracle compares the control file information to the data stored in the header of the restored data files, it immediately recognizes that the restored files are out of date and some changes may have been lost. The instance forces the administrator to complete the recovery before allowing any users to connect.

Redo Log Files

An additional set of files is automatically created as part of the Oracle database. At least two redo logs must be part of every Oracle database. Redo logs are Oracle's journal of the changes being made to database data. In case of the failure

Figure 3.4 Online redo log file processing and archiving.

of a disk or other hardware, Oracle can use the redo logs' record of changes to perform recovery so the changes are not lost. There must be at least two redo log files because Oracle must switch between the two files repeatedly as changes are logged. The operation of redo logs is illustrated in Figure 3.4.

At time T1, we see all changes being written to log-1 until it is filled. At T1, log-1 is currently holding the 333rd log file created by this instance. When log-1 is filled (at time T2) Oracle begins writing changes out to log-2. At time T3, the second log (sequence #334) has completely filled and Oracle again performs a log switch to start writing change records into the log-1 file again—this time as log sequence #335.

Each log switch also initiates a checkpoint. During checkpoint processing Oracle writes out every database block within the buffer pool of the System Global Area (or SGA, discussed later in this chapter) that has been modified but not yet written out to disk. Remember that Oracle does not write the actual data blocks to disk as changes are made. If the instance should fail due to a hardware, operating system, or Oracle software problem, the unwritten changes stored within the SGA's memory structures would be lost—except for the record maintained within the redo log. Therefore, Oracle cannot overwrite the information in log-1 until all the modified data blocks are safely stored out on disk. When the checkpoint is completed we are assured that the change information that was written out to log-1 is no longer needed in case of an instance failure, and Oracle can begin reusing the log-1 file when log-2 is full, as shown at time T3.

A problem can arise in a database in which many changes are occurring. What happens if log-2 fills up before the checkpoint can be finished? Well, a bad thing happens: All insert, update, and delete activity in the database comes to a complete halt until the checkpoint finishes. Oracle will not allow the possibility of changes getting lost by being prematurely overwritten or not being recorded in a log file. The solution to this problem is for the administrator to increase the number of log files.

Another risk to the integrity of the database is presented by the possible loss of an online log file due to a disk failure. For this reason, Oracle provides a simple facility for keeping multiple copies of the redo logs. The copies are called members of a log file group. So, instead of log-1 and log-2 we have two log file groups, each with two members. The first, log group 1, has members log-1a and log-1b. The second, log group 2, has members log-2a and log-2b. I strongly recommend that you multiplex all logs of any production Oracle database in this way. Redo logs are generally small (usually between thirty and three hundred megabytes), so keeping a second copy is likely to require at most two extra disks. With most data warehouses today requiring hundreds of gigabytes of data storage, making the additional copy of all redo logs adds only 1 or 2 percent to the overall disk expense for the warehouse. For simplicity, Figure 3.4 does not show the two log files being duplexed, but in practice these critical files should always be multiplexed (either by the Oracle facility or by storing the files on mirrored disks).

Since the change information written to the online redo logs is kept until the actual data blocks are safely written to disk, Oracle is able to recover from the various types of hardware and software failures that would cause the volatile memory that contains the SGA to be destroyed. All committed changes are either stored on disk in the database files or are available in the online redo logs so they can be "replayed" during instance recovery to ensure than no committed changes are lost.

Yet another risk may threaten the database—loss of a database file from disk failure. When a database file is lost, the change information since the last backup of the file must be available in order for the database to be recovered. If redo log files are being reused, say, every hour or so, how do we possibly recover from a file backup made one or more days before the disk loss?

Oracle conveniently provides for this situation through an optional process called redo log archiving. When enabled, the database is said to be operated in *archivelog mode*. When in archivelog mode, the instance will make a copy of the online redo log whenever it fills and before it can be overwritten. At time T2

Instance Recovery

During instance recovery the database is returned to a consistent state. That is, all completed (committed) transactions will be fully restored. Incomplete (uncommitted) transactions will be fully undone (rolled back). Since these transactions never had the chance to complete before the instance failure, Oracle will not allow the partially completed changes to be visible after recovery. Every transaction is either fully completed or fully erased.

in Figure 3.4 the archiver process (ARCH) begins copying the contents of log-1 to a new archive log file. This copy is assigned a file name that corresponds to the log sequence in which it was created. In this example, it inherits the number 333. Later, at time T3, when log-2 is filled and Oracle switches back to writing changes to log-1, ARCH again goes to work copying the contents of the filled log file to an archived log file. Just like checkpoint processing, the archiving must be completed before Oracle will be able to reuse an online log file.

If recovery from a media failure is necessary, Oracle will automatically prompt the DBA to provide the necessary archived logs (in the proper order) to replay all the changes since the backup copy of the lost datafile was created. We cover this topic in much more depth in the discussion of backup and recovery in Chapter 8.

Even though archivelog mode is not the default mode of operation for the database, nearly every production Oracle database should be run in archivelog mode to protect the database from media failures. The few exceptions to this rule are also discussed in Chapter 8.

Control Files

Creating a database also creates at least one control file. The control file is where Oracle keeps a record of every other file (database and redo log) that is part of the database. Although only one control file is required for the database, because of its critical nature and small size it is highly recommended that several control files be defined on different physical disks. Oracle will then maintain each of them as identical copies so that no single disk failure will make the database unusable. Oracle uses the control file(s) during database startup processing to find every other file that must be opened and also to verify that each of those files is indeed the correct file and has not been dropped or substituted while the database was shutdown.

Information identical to that stored in the header of each database file and redo log is also kept in the control file. Oracle will maintain this information automatically without any direct intervention by the administrator or user. This information includes such things as the file name and the last time Oracle checkpointed the file (when all changes made in memory were flushed out to the physical file). Also, whenever the administrator issues a command that adds a file to the database (e.g., CREATE TABLESPACE, ALTER TABLESPACE . . . ADD DATAFILE, ALTER DATABASE . . . ADD LOGFILE), drops a file, or renames a file Oracle updates the control files as well as the header of the affected file.

If during the open phase of startup Oracle finds that there is any difference in the file header information and the information maintained in the control file, it will interrupt the startup process and direct the DBA to correct the problem. This check is one of the primary integrity features of the Oracle RDBMS, which prevents accidental corruption of the database.

Initialization Parameter Files

There are literally hundreds of parameters that can affect the way Oracle behaves. Most, luckily, have default values that work well without an administrator having to set them. A few (e.g., DBNAME and DB_BLOCK_SIZE) control how the database is initially built and cannot be changed once the database is created. Some parameters (such as DB_BLOCK_BUFFERS, SHARED_POOL_SIZE) control how the allocation of shared memory will be made. Others (NLS_LANGUAGE, MTS_SERVERS, for instance) control various optional features of the Oracle RDBMS. Still others are used to configure security options, and others provide "knobs" for performance tuning. Some initialization parameters that are particularly relevant to data warehousing are shown in the list below.

Descriptions of each of these parameters is provided in the *Oracle7* and *Oracle8 Server Reference* manuals. The warehouse DBA should become familiar with the listed parameters. (An asterisk indicates the parameters that are new to Oracle8.) Two of these parameters (PARTITION_VIEW_ENABLED and STAR_TRANSFORMATION_ENABLED) control important data warehouse features but default to False. These two parameters, in particular, will need to be explicitly set to True to enable these features.

Initialization Parameters for Data Warehouses

BITMAP_MERGE_AREA_SIZE *	PARALLEL_MAX_SERVERS
BUFFER_POOL_KEEP *	PARALLEL_MIN_PERCENT
BUFFER_POOL_RECYCLE *	PARALLEL_MIN_SERVERS
CREATE_BITMAP_AREA_SIZE *	PARTITION_VIEW_ENABLED
DB_BLOCK_BUFFERS	SORT_AREA_RETAINED_SIZE
DB_BLOCK_SIZE	SORT_AREA_SIZE
DB_FILE_DIRECT_IO_COUNT *	SORT_DIRECT_WRITES
DB_FILE_MULTIBLOCK_READ_COUNT	SORT_WRITE_BUFFER_SIZE
HASH_AREA_SIZE	SORT_WRITE_BUFFERS
HASH_JOIN_ENABLED	STAR_TRANSFORMATION_ENABLED *
HASH_MULTIBLOCK_IO_COUNT	

Each database has its own initialization parameter file and may sometimes have several alternative files. One file might be used to configure the instance for normal daily operations, and another might be used to configure the instance differently for special weekly database load and summarization processes. When more than one parameter file is available, the administrator (or the startup scripts he or she has written) will have to specify the name of the parameter file to be used during startup whenever it is not the default name or if it is stored in a directory other than Oracle's default location.

Undocumented Initialization Parameters

Some undocumented initialization parameters whose names are prefixed with an underscore and some documented ones should not be modified except under the direction of Oracle Worldwide Support.

Although this file is properly known as the *instance initialization parameter file*, many Oracle administrators find that to be more than a simple mouthful and continue to refer to it by the shorthand term *init.ora* (init dot ora). This more manageable name comes from the common format of the names assigned by Oracle to these files: *init_instname.ora* (where *instname* is the name of the instance to be controlled by this particular file).

Memory Architecture

Oracle uses a combination of shared and private memory structures. The System Global Area is a shared memory structure that is allocated during instance startup. It provides a means of communication and coordination for the many processes, both system and user, that need to access data within the database. Additionally, each process may need some memory usage that is irrelevant to any other process and is allocated privately by the individual process.

System Global Area (SGA)

The primary memory structure, which is accessible to all Oracle processes, is called the System Global Area, or, more commonly, the SGA. Figure 3.5 shows the primary structures within the Oracle SGA. It is common for the SGA to be the largest single consumer of memory on a computer dedicated to running an Oracle database application. The SGA may often be several hundred megabytes or even a gigabyte in size. How this shared memory structure is created and attached by processes varies by operating system. In UNIX, the most common platform for Oracle data warehouses, the SGA is created during instance startup as a shared memory segment.

Database Buffer Cache

The SGA holds three very important structures. The largest, typically, is the database buffer cache. The buffer pool for a data warehouse will commonly be defined as having several hundred or even a few thousand database buffers. A

Figure 3.5 SGA structures.

single buffer pool is used for all the database blocks needed by all users. Each buffer is capable of holding one database block of data. This database block (or *Oracle block*) size applies to every block in the entire database and is defined by the value of the DB_BLOCK_SIZE parameter when the database is created. It cannot be modified without completely recreating the database.

In normal operations, the data needed by a user can only be manipulated after it is retrieved from the database files and stored in one of the buffers in this pool. In Figure 3.1, note that the server processes assigned to users' requests are able to retrieve data blocks from disk into the database buffer. When changes are made to a block in the buffer pool, the block must be written back out to disk by the database writer (DBWR) process. These changes are not written as part of the transaction that made the change, but asynchronously. At the longest, this write will be performed as part of the next checkpoint.

The various buffers in the pool are managed using a least recently used (LRU) algorithm. An LRU list keeps track of how recently each block in the pool has been used. Each time a block is read or modified it is moved to the tail of

Setting DB_BLOCK_SIZE

DB_BLOCK_SIZE is normally between 2,048 (2 KB) and 16,384 (16 KB) bytes, but allowable values vary by operating system and Oracle version. It is the amount of data Oracle will either read or write at a time. Generally, for data warehousing applications the larger block sizes should be chosen over the small (usually 2 KB) default. Ideally, for best performance the Oracle block size should be the same as the operating system's block size. This will have to be coordinated with the system administrator, who is otherwise likely to choose a smaller block size than this ideal.

the LRU list—that is the "most recently used" end. If a block is brought into the buffer pool and then not used again, it gradually moves toward the "least recently used" end of the LRU list. Buffers at this end of the list become candidates to be "stolen" for use as another user's blocks that need to be read in from disk. Each server process that performs the reads will use the LRU list to determine the buffers in which to store newly read blocks.

There is an exception to this LRU process that is used for handling full table scans. Since a single table may consume far more space than the total number of database buffers in the SGA, a full scan using the normal LRU mechanism would completely flush all other blocks from the buffer cache. This would hurt performance for other queries that would otherwise find blocks in memory but now must reread them from disk. To prevent this effect from occurring, when a server process is performing a full table scan by default it places the buffers it uses at the least recently used end of the LRU list. These buffers, then, tend to get immediately reused even by the same query. The downside of this special behavior is that, for a smaller table that various queries are likely to want repeatedly, the table must be repeatedly read from disk by each subsequent query! To balance these conflicting needs, Oracle allows the DBA to modify table scan behavior to record retrieved blocks of certain tables on the most recently used end of LRU list, just like blocks that are accessed randomly. Blocks of a table created with the CACHE keyword will be retained in the buffer cache after a table scan so they may be accessed by another query. The DBA must be careful in assigning the CACHE behavior to tables in the data warehouse. Use it for relatively small reference tables, but avoid using it for very large tables that do not fit entirely within a portion of the buffer cache or are not likely to be repeatedly queried.

MULTIPLE SUB-POOLS IN ORACLE8

Oracle8 provides the administrator with another technique to more carefully control the handling of blocks of particular tables. The large database buffer cache may be divided into sub-pools with independent LRU handling. Up to three sub-pools may be defined using the BUFFER_POOL_*name* initialization parameter. Objects may then be assigned to the sub-pool using the new BUFFER_POOL clause on the CREATE TABLE, ALTER TABLE, CREATE INDEX and ALTER INDEX commands.

The first sub-pool, the KEEP cache, may be defined to hold blocks from small reference tables (such as dimension tables) and high performance indexes which might otherwise be flushed by the overwhelming numbers of blocks from large (e.g., fact) tables and indexes.

The second, the RECYCLE cache, may be specified to store blocks of large tables that are accessed randomly but have a low probability of reusing any specific block before it ages from the buffer pool. Whatever remains of the total buffer pool after defining either or both of these special sub-pools is assigned the DEFAULT cache. The DEFAULT cache behaves identically to the Oracle7 single buffer pool and will contain blocks of all objects not specifically assigned to the KEEP or RECYCLE caches.

Some experimentation is required to determine the optimal size and contents of each sub-pool in order to actually improve on Oracle's default LRU handling. More information on the use of multiple buffer pools is provided in the *Oracle8 Server Tuning Reference* manual.

Conventional Oracle wisdom holds that a larger buffer cache is almost always better for performance than a smaller cache. This is not always true for OLTP applications, and it is often not true for data warehouses. If at least some tables aren't defined with the CACHE attribute, relatively few buffers may be used if lots of full table scans are performed. This may be the case in data warehouses based primarily upon summary tables. (This isn't the case, however, with warehouses built around star schemas, which will frequently use indexes to identify and retrieve random blocks from tables.) To use the memory allocated to a large database buffer cache effectively, ensure that you strike a balance between random block requests, scans of small cached tables, and scans of large tables without the CACHE attribute.

SHARED POOL

The second structure in the SGA is the *shared pool,* which is a common area of memory used for two different functions. The shared pool contains the *dictionary cache* and the *library cache.*

When a user issues a SQL statement (or invokes a block of code written in PL/SQL, Oracle's procedural programming language) that statement or block of code is loaded into the library cache. The statement (or program) is parsed to validate syntax and ensure that all the referenced objects (such as database tables or other stored procedures) exist and are accessible with this user's current security privileges. To do this parsing and security checking, Oracle must reference the data dictionary, which is the part of the database where Oracle keeps track of everything about the structure of the database. Definitions of all the users, tables, indexes, and the like are maintained in the data dictionary tables, which are stored in the system tablespace. To avoid the disk I/O expense of repeatedly having to go out to the database files associated with the SYSTEM tablespace to look up this information, Oracle keeps a copy in the dictionary cache.

Sizing the Database Buffer Cache

To determine whether the buffers currently being allocated are being used effectively, set the parameter DB_BLOCK_LRU_STATISTICS to true and query the X$KCBCBH table. This table has one row for each allocated buffer and will provide a count of how many times each relative position on the LRU chain was used for a subsequent access. The results are generally more easily interpreted if the large number of rows is grouped together into about 10 to 20 buckets. A query to do this grouping along with more detail about how to interpret the results can be found in the *Server Tuning* manuals for Oracle7 (Chapter 8 for releases 7.2 and 7.3 and Chapter 13 for release 7.3.3) or Oracle8 (Chapter 14). These manuals also describe how to use DB_BLOCK_ LRU_ EXTENDED_STATISTICS and the X$KCBRBH virtual table to determine the potential benefit of increasing the value of DB_BLOCK_BUFFERS.

When the statement has been parsed and security checks are completed, the Oracle query optimizer develops an execution plan that will determine how best to retrieve the information requested by that SQL statement. (Oracle security mechanisms and query optimizer are discussed later in this chapter.) All the information about referenced objects and execution plans is then stored in the library cache along with the original text of the SQL statement.

Prior to the release of Oracle7, this statement parse information was stored in private memory by each user's server process instead of by a shared memory structure. Making the information shareable provides major savings in memory and parse effort in OLTP systems. Typically, dozens or hundreds of users of a large OLTP system are running one application and issuing identical SQL statements. Instead of forcing each user's process to individually absorb the overhead of parsing and determining an optimal execution plan and storing this information privately, in Oracle7 and Oracle8 only the first process to issue a particular SQL statement will incur these costs. All other users' server processes will be able to take advantage of most of this effort. (Each user must still be individually evaluated for necessary security privileges associated with the statement.)

Of course, data warehousing and OLTP systems operate in many fundamentally different ways. One of the key differences is in the amount of shared SQL processing typically performed. In the OLTP situation, it is common for many users to issue the same SQL statements as they navigate through application screens or submit application reports for processing. Data warehouse users, on the other hand, tend to issue different SQL statements.

There are several reasons why data warehouse users are less likely to be issuing identical SQL statements. First, the data warehouse has fewer simultaneous users (although each one may be causing the database to do much more work!). Secondly, each user is more likely to be investigating different data relationships. One analyst may be looking at the last quarter's average cost of sales for a new product line across each sales region. Another may be examining the correlation between manufacturing rejection rates at various factories and the suppliers of various raw materials. Yet another might be trying to determine the relative effectiveness of a recent change in the marketing organization structure in the international divisions.

For these reasons, Oracle's shared SQL feature of the library cache does not provide the same memory and processing savings for the data warehouse that it does for a database used for OLTP applications. The dictionary cache, however, provides potentially greater advantage to the data warehouse since more SQL statements are being parsed and, therefore, more references to data dictionary information must be made. Even though the many decision-support queries submitted to the data warehouse are likely to be different, they will generally be referencing the same set of tables and will need the same data dictionary information about tables, columns, indexes, and so on.

Oracle maintains space within the shared pool dynamically using an LRU algorithm. Each time a SQL statement or dictionary element is referenced, it is, in effect, time-stamped. As additional parsing is performed, the new SQL statement or retrieved data dictionary information will reuse space within the shared pool by flushing out the information that has the oldest time stamp. Oracle maintains statistics about how frequently items in the shared pool are flushed and then have to be reloaded. These allow the administrator to determine when additional space should be allocated by changing the value of the SHARED_POOL _SIZE initialization parameter and restarting the instance.

REDO LOG BUFFER CACHE

Every time a user changes the value of data in the database, Oracle must record the specifics of the change into the current redo log. Each of these changes typically requires recording only a few bytes—an identification of the data block affected, the transaction making the change, and the specific bytes modified. Because of these small record sizes, it would be very inefficient to write these changes out as they occur. Also, since several transactions (at least in an OLTP database) are likely to be occurring simultaneously, controlling and coordinating a large number of writes would be a bottleneck to performance and a nightmare for administration.

To avoid these two problems, Oracle buffers the change information and then the Log Writer (LGWR) process issues a write request after several changes, by multiple users, are accumulated. The write is triggered by any transaction issuing a COMMIT statement or whenever this buffer pool reaches one-third full. The administrator controls the size of the redo log buffer cache using the LOG _BUFFER initialization parameter.

Program Global Area (PGA)

Each user's session will require some allocation of private memory to maintain information that is of no value to other processes connected to the database. Generally, this memory is allocated within the Program Global Area (PGA) by the server process that is working on that user's behalf. This memory is used for functions like keeping track of how far a specific query has progressed in its retrieval of data or storing values for variables that may be declared within the session. Additional memory may also be allocated by the user's server process for performing sort operations.

The introduction of the shared SQL feature in the Oracle7 release greatly reduced the amount of private storage needed by each user's server process.

Process Architecture

Several processes make up the Oracle instance. Four of these processes perform key background functions and are required. These four are shown in bold boxes in Figure 3.6. Several other background processes are optional and will be initiated during instance startup based on initialization parameters. Finally, a third set of processes are created to do server work on behalf of users who connect to the instance. One of these server processes is started for each user and is dedicated to performing work for that user until he or she disconnects from the database. These dedicated server processes are represented in Figure 3.6 with dashed boxes.

Figure 3.6 Oracle process architecture.

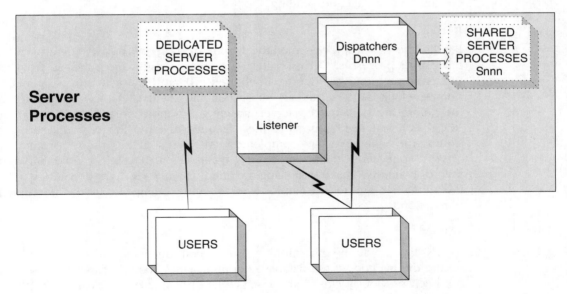

Required Processes

There are four required processes: DBWR, LGWR, PMON, and SMON.

DBWR

The database writer process (DBWR) is responsible for writing modified data blocks from the database buffers of the SGA out to the database files.

In Oracle version 6 DBWR was the only process that ever wrote to the database files. As new features have been added in Oracle7, two special exceptions to this rule have been made. When loading large volumes of data using SQL*Loader in direct path mode, the dedicated server process doing the load is allowed to directly write to an empty part of a database file. This feature is discussed in depth in Chapter 6. The second exception is the SORT_DIRECT_WRITES feature, added in release 7.3, which speeds sorting operations by allowing the dedicated server process to bypass the database buffers in the SGA when writing intermediate sort results to temporary storage. This capability is discussed as part of Sort Operations later in this chapter.

LGWR

LGWR, the redo log writer process, has responsibility for doing all writes to the online redo log files. Each time any user or program ends a transaction by issuing a COMMIT command, LGWR is awakened to write the accumulated contents of the redo log buffers out to the current redo log. Log writer is also signaled to begin writing log information out to disk whenever the redo log buffers reach one-third full. This can occur when large batch jobs do large amounts of work with only infrequent COMMITs. Such batch jobs may be used in a data warehouse environment to load data into the database or to do summarization processing on that data after loading.

PMON

PMON, the Oracle process monitor, has the responsibility of cleaning up after failed user processes. Occasionally, a user process gets disconnected from its Oracle server processes due to an aborted program or a lost network connection. Any locks held by the user transaction and any data changes made prior to the failure are held by the server, awaiting a transaction-ending COMMIT or ROLLBACK statement. But since the user process is no longer connected, the transaction will never be completed. PMON recognizes these "orphaned" servers, connects to them temporarily, and issues a ROLLBACK command and then disconnects. This restores any modified data to its state prior to the start of the transaction and releases all locks and memory being held by the interrupted transaction.

SMON

SMON, the Oracle instance monitor, has several functions. Its primary job is to ensure the integrity of the database during instance startup. If the database had not been previously closed and instance had not shut down cleanly then there may have been change records placed in the redo logs whose actual data buffers were never written down to the database files. During the startup process, SMON checks the logs and the headers of the database files and then performs the necessary recovery to ensure that any previously committed transactions are restored. Additionally, SMON has several other responsibilities, including cleanup of leftover temporary segments that are no longer needed and the coalescing of adjacent free extents.

Optional Processes

In addition to the four required processes just discussed (DBWR, LGWR, PMON, and SMON), there are several other processes that may be initiated as part of the startup of the Oracle instance. These optional processes are started depending on which options of the Oracle Server are in use and what the values of various initialization parameters are.

ARCH

The archiver process, ARCH, is only present when the database is operating in archivelog mode. It is started automatically if the DBA has issued the ARCHIVE LOG START command. This is the normal method for invoking archiver, but the DBA may manually initiate the archiving of each redo log with other variations of the ARCHIVE LOG command. Only in very rare circumstances should a database be operated in *noarchivelog mode*.

RECO

The recoverer process, RECO, is only used with the Distributed Option. RECO's function is to recover distributed transactions that might fail during the very brief span between phases of a two-phased commit process. The first phase of committing a distributed transaction ensures that every participating site is prepared to complete the commit. If all sites are prepared, then the second phase makes the transaction's changes permanent on all sites. Should one of the instances or the network fail between the prepare phase and the commit phase, the transaction at that site is left in the prepared state. After restarting the failed instance or recovering the connecting network, RECO resolves each pending transaction found in the prepared state by contacting its partner database to determine the final disposition (either committed or rolled back) of the transaction. It then commits or rolls back the local portion of the transaction to match the action taken at the transaction coordinator site.

CKPT

The checkpoint process, CKPT, can be initiated by the DBA through the CHECK-POINT_PROCESS initialization parameter. When active, CKPT takes over some of the coordination duties normally performed by LGWR during a checkpoint.

WMON

The wakeup monitor and probably the most obscure of the background processes, WMON, is seen on only a few operating system ports of Oracle. It aids in the wakeup signaling of the other Oracle background processes, which are designed to operate intermittently.

SNPn

The snapshot processes, SNPn, are used by Oracle replication facilities to copy data changes from one database to another. These processes also perform other scheduled jobs that have been submitted to the Oracle Job Queue maintained with the DBMS_JOB package.

LCKn

The Oracle Parallel Server lock processes, LCKn, coordinate the actions of multiple Oracle instances that have opened a single database using the Oracle Parallel Server option (n is an integer, from 0 to 9, used to uniquely identify each lock process that is part of an instance). The Oracle Parallel Server option is discussed briefly later in this chapter and then more completely in Chapter 11.

Dnnn

Multithreaded server dispatchers, Dnnn, are part of the Multi-Threaded Server (MTS) feature of the Oracle Server (nnn is a three-digit integer that uniquely names each dispatcher associated with the instance.) This feature is discussed more fully under "Server Processes" in the next section. A user connected to an Oracle instance via MTS does not get a dedicated server to process his or her requests. Instead, the user commands are passed to a dispatch process to which the user remains connected. The dispatcher then passes the request to one of a pool of shared servers. The temporarily assigned server performs the requested work and then passes its response back to the same dispatcher, which then relays them back to the user. Each dispatcher handles requests of several users.

Snnn

Shared servers, Snnn, are also a component of the MTS architecture. The next section on "Server Processes" will discuss these processes in more depth.

Server Processes

The standard configuration for Oracle uses a *two-task* architecture. Each user session (or batch program) has a second task (or process) that starts automatically to perform its database work. On UNIX, the most popular operating system for large data warehouses, it is dangerous to let a user session or program connect directly to the SGA. Since the SGA is a shared resource, any program that connects to it could possibly corrupt data in the SGA that is needed by other users. To prevent this, the user session or program passes its requests (in SQL or

Single Task

In some operating systems, such as Digital Equipment Corporation's OpenVMS, this high level of isolation can be provided within a single process. In this environment, Oracle can be run in single-task mode, and no additional server process is required. It is possible to link programs as single-task in the UNIX environment, but this exposes the shared SGA to corruption by program code, which might inadvertently address into the Oracle server code. Therefore, with the single exception of Oracle-provided utilities such as IMP, this approach is never recommended.

PL/SQL) to its dedicated server process, which is running Oracle-provided code. The server process, connected to the SGA, performs the requested database operations and passes results back to the user process. This effectively insulates the critical SGA structures from any possible program bugs in user code.

An alternative server architecture provided by Oracle is called the Multi-Threaded Server (MTS). When users connect to the database through MTS they do not receive a dedicated server. Instead, user requests are processed by a shared pool of server processes. MTS is useful for situations where a large number of users need to be connected simultaneously, but each has relatively infrequent interaction with the database. This commonly occurs with OLTP systems that might support hundreds of connected users doing data entry into online screens. The user might take a few seconds to enter data into a screen field and then a very quick validation query might be programmed to occur. Only when several fields have been entered is the data submitted to the database for insertion. The database might be actively in use for only a small percentage of the total time the user is connected. MTS is designed to allow the server to be working for many other users in the interim.

MTS is rarely used with data warehouses, however, for at least three reasons. First, data warehouses usually have far fewer simultaneously connected users than the number needed for MTS to become useful. The additional process overhead of dedicated servers for fifty or even a hundred users is negligible on the large computer systems typically used for data warehousing. MTS is even less useful for the dozens of users who typically might be interacting with a data mart on a smaller UNIX or NT server. Second, the server usage pattern of data warehouse users is not uniform as in the OLTP example given earlier. Typically, the warehouse analyst will spend many minutes composing a query that may then take many seconds, minutes, or sometimes hours to complete. This pattern doesn't fit well with the MTS load-balancing paradigm. Third, passing large amounts of data back from the shared server to the user takes longer than doing so from a dedicated server. Warehouse users frequently issue queries that retrieve large result sets. The extra work performed in returning the data might nullify whatever process relief MTS provided.

Oracle Server: Internal Architecture

There are many structures internal to the Oracle database that do not correspond directly to the physical database file structure. The organization of these structures cannot be seen except from within the database. These structures include tablespaces, segments, and extents and are shown in Figure 3.7. Each database typically has several tablespaces. Each tablespace holds one or more segments. Each segment is comprised of at least one extent. Each extent is a contiguous set of database blocks.

Several types of segments exist, including tables and indexes as well as more specialized segments used for system functions. The data dictionary is a special set of tables, clusters, indexes, and views that provide the means for observing the rest of the internal structure of the database.

Figure 3.7 Oracle internal database architecture.

Tablespaces

Since the introduction of Oracle version 6, the *tablespace* has been the fundamental unit of Oracle database object storage, backup and recovery, and other administrative functions. Whenever an object that requires storage is created, it must be created within a currently available tablespace. Whenever the database administrator performs on online ("hot") backup, it is done for an entire tablespace at a time. If a database file is lost because of a disk problem, the entire tablespace becomes unavailable until the problem is resolved.

A tablespace is the link between the physical files observable at the operating system level and all the logical database objects (such as tables and indexes) that are only visible from within the Oracle environment. Each tablespace consists of one or more operating system files that, in total, define the size of the tablespace. A tablespace is created using the CREATE TABLESPACE command. When the tablespace is created (or enlarged through the ALTER TABLESPACE . . . ADD DATAFILE command) the space from the database file on disk is immediately allocated to that tablespace and cannot be used for any other purpose.

The following example shows the SQL statement for creating a tablespace called USER_DATA in an NT environment, which uses a single 100-megabyte file. Oracle takes over the 100 megabytes, which are then considered freespace in the USER_DATA tablespace. By querying the dictionary view DBA_FREE_SPACE, as shown in the following example, we see that this space is now available. When an object is created in the tablespace, the amount of freespace is reduced by the object's size.

```
SQL> CREATE TABLESPACE USER_DATA
  2    DATAFILE 'H:\ORADATA\DWP1\USER_DATA_01.DBF' SIZE 100M
  3    DEFAULT STORAGE
  4       (INITIAL      1M
  5        NEXT         1M
  6        PCTINCREASE 0)
  7  /

Tablespace created.
```

```
SQL> SELECT SUM(BYTES)
  2     FROM DBA_FREE_SPACE
  3     WHERE TABLESPACE_NAME = 'USER_DATA'
  4   /

SUM(BYTES)
----------
 104855552

1 row selected.

SQL> CREATE TABLE TEST_TABLE
  2     (CUST_ID       NUMBER(6,0),
  3      CUST_NAME     VARCHAR2(30),
  4      REP_ID        NUMBER(5,0))
  5      TABLESPACE    USER_DATA
  6      STORAGE
  7         (INITIAL     1M
  8          NEXT        1M
  9          PCTINCREASE 0)
 10   /

Table created.

SQL> SELECT SUM(BYTES)
  2     FROM DBA_FREE_SPACE
  3     WHERE TABLESPACE_NAME = 'USER_DATA'
  4   /

SUM(BYTES)
----------
 103800832
```

Every Oracle database must have at least one tablespace, named SYSTEM. Occasionally, inexperienced Oracle administrators will not create additional tablespaces and will place all the application tables and indexes within the SYSTEM tablespace. For a small database that resides entirely on one or two disks this may not present any problems. Typically, however, the large database will occupy multiple disk drives, and the administrator must take explicit control of where database objects get stored. This is done by creating multiple tablespaces and then creating specific objects in appropriate tablespaces. Objects are assigned to tablespaces either to group certain objects together or, more commonly, to separate specific objects and keep tablespaces to a manageable size.

Why Doesn't the Initial Freespace Equal 100 MB?

The actual initial freespace, 103,800,832bytes, is 2,048 bytes (the size of one Oracle block on this example database), smaller than the actual 100 megabytes allocated in USER_DATA_01.DBF. This block contains the file header and cannot be used to store user-created database objects.

Optimal Flexible Architecture (OFA)

Several years ago, Cary Millsap of Oracle Consulting Services' System Performance Group published a white paper on an Optimal Flexible Architecture (OFA) for Oracle version 6 databases. He has updated the paper several times over the years to account for Oracle7 changes and adapt to the issues raised by the ever larger databases being maintained in Oracle. The concepts of OFA have been included in the Oracle product documentation. Beginning with Oracle7 release 7.3, they have also been incorporated into the Oracle Installer product so that the "default" database optionally created as part of installing the Oracle RDBMS will follow the guidelines of OFA.

OFA deals with many database configuration issues beside tablespaces, but effective decisions about tablespaces and their assigned objects is one of its key principles. The goal of the OFA recommendations for tablespace assignment is to be able to characterize each tablespace with respect to segment growth patterns (and fragmentation), administrative requirements, and I/O loads. Segments with short life spans (such as temporary segments that are dynamically created and destroyed) should never be placed in the same tablespaces as permanent objects. Objects (tables, partitions or indexes) that are to have data added or modified should not be located in tablespaces with static, read-only tables. Tables that are frequently scanned should not be placed in the same tablespace with objects that are normally accessed in a random manner. Objects expected to have high I/O demands should be separated from those that will not be accessed frequently. The entire Oracle7 OFA paper and other excellent white papers from the System Performance Group are available for public download from www.europa.com/~orapub. I highly recommend that this paper be reviewed before you install Oracle7 or Oracle8 and create the warehouse database.

Segments

Each database object that requires space for its storage will be created in a specific tablespace. Tables and indexes are the most common database objects of this type, although the DBA will have to make arrangements for rollback segments and temporary segments. Oracle's term for these created objects is *segments*. Using the same example as in the discussion on tablespaces, we can query the data dictionary to find out information about segments stored within our USER_DATA tablespace.

```
SQL> SELECT SEGMENT_NAME, OWNER, SEGMENT_TYPE, BYTES
  2    FROM DBA_SEGMENTS
  3    WHERE TABLESPACE_NAME = 'USER_DATA'
  4  /

SEGMENT_NAME OWNER     SEGMENT_TYPE           BYTES
------------ --------  ----------------  ------------
TEST_TABLE   GDODGE    TABLE               1,054,720
```

Why Isn't the Segment Exactly 1 MB?

The segment is 1,054,720 bytes in size, slightly larger than the one megabyte we specified when we created it. To avoid small fragments of freespace, Oracle may round up the requested size of an object by as much as five blocks.

We see that the table we created in the earlier example is the only segment in USER_DATA.

In addition to the basic tables, clusters, indexes, and specialty segments (rollback and temporary) found in Oracle7, Oracle8 adds some new variations. An Oracle8 partitioned table consists of multiple segments—each partition of the table is stored as a separate segment. Also, a new hybrid structure, the index-organized table, is introduced that combines the data storage of a table with the hierarchical organization of an index.

Tables

Tables are the type of segment most easily recognized by users of the data warehouse. They are where the warehouse data is actually stored. When the analyst wishes to see information about customers, he or she will issue a SQL SELECT statement against the CUSTOMERS table. To see information about which products have standard prices at least 50 percent higher than their cost, he or she would probably need to query the PRODUCTS table.

When the DBA creates a table, both the logical structure (column definitions) and physical structure (tablespace name, storage parameters) are defined. Setting these properly before loading data makes the future life of the DBA much easier; it is generally an unpleasant situation when the DBA finds that a 20-gigabyte table has to be reorganized because a storage parameter was incorrectly defined! Oracle7 and Oracle8 do not yet provide automatic utilities for reorganizing or rebuilding a table, so this task, if required, may mean hours of effort during which the data in the table may have to be made unavailable to users. (A new utility for reorganizing indexes, ALTER INDEX . . . REBUILD, was introduced with release 7.3.) The best solution to the table reorganization problem is to avoid having to do reorganizations. In Chapter 5, we discuss effective space management techniques that can eliminate the need for table reorganization.

A new specialized type of table, introduced in Oracle8, is the partitioned table. Data warehouse tables frequently hold millions of rows and may require many gigabytes to store. Managing segments of this size can be a particular burden on the warehouse DBA. An Oracle8 table may be created with multiple partitions. Each partition is defined to contain a particular subset of the total table's rows. Values in any column (or columns) can be used to do the partitioning, but in most cases data warehouse tables are partitioned by some date field. This allows a partition to be loaded as one month (or other period) and then have its tablespace converted to read-only status. When a partition's data is sufficiently old, the entire partition can be archived or purged easily. Each partition is also defined independently with respect to its tablespace location and storage parameters. Each partition can be independently administered, which makes the total management task more manageable. Partitioning is discussed in more depth in Chapter 5.

Indexes

Users of the data warehouse generally are not concerned about the names or location of index segments. Unless they are including optimizer hints in their queries, they never need to specify anything about indexes. The DBA, however, is responsible for determining which tables should have indexes on specific columns to help queries execute faster. An index allows Oracle to rapidly find specific rows in a table when a query includes conditions that limit the requested rows. As an example, the following query wishes to retrieve only those customers whose address is in the primary zip code assigned to downtown Denver:

```
SELECT CUST_ID, CUST_NAME
  FROM CUSTOMERS
 WHERE ZIPCODE = 80202;
```

If we have a million customers, but only 1,500 are in downtown Denver, then an index on the column called ZIPCODE would allow this query to execute very quickly. Without the index, Oracle would have to examine each of the million rows in the CUSTOMER table and test the value of ZIPCODE to see if it equals 80202. The relative performance gain from using the index is determined by several factors, including the size of the table, the percentage of the total number of rows that needs to be found, and how the rows are distributed in the table. Deciding where indexes will be useful is one of the primary responsibilities of the DBA and is examined in the next chapter. In general, however, data warehouses tend to have more indexes per table than most OLTP systems because of the wide variety of selection criteria used in data warehouse queries.

B*TREE INDEXES

Oracle provides two types of indexes. The first is based on a balanced B*Tree structure that is processed hierarchically to find the values of interest. Figure 3.8 shows a small B*Tree index. If a query wants to find information about product number 21694, Oracle will have to first read the top block of the hierarchy (called the "root" block) to determine which of the second-level blocks to read next. Reading the appropriate block from the second-level block determines which third-level block to read. In this small example, the third level is the last (known as the leaf nodes) and will contain the ROWIDs (addresses) of the actual data block that contains the data we want to see. Oracle will then retrieve the specific data block and present us with our answer. This allowed us to find

Figure 3.8 B*Tree index.

the data for product number 21694 with a total of four logical block reads—three in the index and one in the table. This access path would be particularly efficient compared to reading the hundreds of data blocks that might comprise the entire PRODUCTS table.

Two varieties of B*Tree indexes are available in Oracle. A unique index allows at most one data row to contain any particular value. This is how Oracle enforces *unique* or *primary key* constraints. These constraints are useful for preventing the corruption of an OLTP database, which would occur if someone were able to enter two employees with the same employee number or two customers with the same customer identifier value. The DBA would typically define the PRODUCT_ID column of the PRODUCTS table with the primary key constraint to ensure that no duplicate customer IDs would ever be allowed in the table. The example shown in Figure 3.8 appears (from the limited data shown) to be a unique index.

The other type of B*Tree index, nonunique, is the type created by the CREATE INDEX command. In a nonunique B*Tree index, multiple pointers to data rows are allowed for any particular value. This type of index would be appropriate for indexing the CUST_ID column of the ORDERS table where it is reasonable (and desired!) that a given customer would place multiple orders. Retrieving all of a customer's orders quickly could be facilitated by creating this nonunique index. Generally, nonunique indexes will speed query processing whenever a small percentage of the total rows needs to be retrieved. Building a B*Tree index on a very nonselective column (such as the SEX_CODE of the EMPLOYEES table) is generally of little value, since it is likely that finding all the women or all the men would involve reading every data block anyway. Simply reading the blocks sequentially (doing a full table scan) would be more efficient than using the index.

Oracle8 introduced a new variation on the B*Tree index structure. An Oracle8 reverse key index uses the same B*Tree structure, but reverses the order of the data bytes when building the index. This helps randomize where an entry to the index needs to be made. This can be particularly helpful when indexing a column whose new values are constantly increasing while the oldest values are being regularly purged. A normal B*Tree index will have new values always added at the right side of the index structure but will never reuse the space being emptied by the deletes occurring on the left side of the structure. In the reverse key index, inserted rows and deleted rows can be equally dispersed across the entire width of the index structure. However, the ability to do index range scans is sacrificed in reverse key indexes because contiguous data values will not be stored adjacently in the index.

Oracle8 allows indexes, just like tables, to be partitioned into multiple segments. This is generally done to make each segment smaller and more manageable.

Bitmap Indexes

The second type of index structure provided by Oracle is a bitmap index. This type of index was introduced to the Oracle7 product with release 7.3. Bitmap indexes are particularly useful in situations where traditional B*Tree indexes are useless—when we have a large number of rows but only a small number of distinct values. Figure 3.9 shows a logical layout of the organization of bitmap indexes. For each distinct value in the indexed column, a bitmap contains one bit corresponding to each row in the indexed table. When we examine all the bitmaps associated with the values bitmap index we find that each row will be represented in only a single bitmap with a 1 and in all others by a 0.

Physically, the bitmap index is identical in hierarchical structure to a B*Tree index except in the layout of the leaf nodes. Where a B*Tree index stores the ROWID pointer to each data row with a particular data value, the bitmap index contains a bitmap that includes one bit corresponding to each row in a contigu-

Figure 3.9 Bitmap index.

EMPLOYEE TABLE

EMPID	EMPL NAME	SEX	STATUS	DEPT	JOB_TITLE
1234	Foley	Male	Full	Marketing	Clerk
1397	Pass	Male	Part	Manufacturing	Assembler
8372	Simpson	Male	Full	Shipping	Manager
3875	Tai	Male	Part	Marketing	Clerk
9736	Birk	Female	Full	Sales	Sales Rep
6430	Stack	Male	Full	Shipping	Clerk
8757	Livingston	Male	Part	Marketing	Brand Mgr
8876	Fosnight	Male	Full	Shipping	Clerk
3732	Parker	Male	Full	Manufacturing	Assembler
3309	Melgaard	Male	Full	Sales	Manager
9393	Johnson	Male	Part	Manufacturing	Assembler
3984	McConahay	Female	Part	Manufacturing	Assembler
3857	Shouldice	Female	Full	Sales	Sales Rep
8439	Bush	Female	Part	Marketing	Brand Mgr
9496	Wikstrom	Femail	Full	Manufacturing	Manager
7495	Windle	Male	Part	Sales	Clerk

BITMAP INDEX ON "DEPT" column of EMPLOYEE TABLE

EMPLID	"Manuf"	"Mrktng"	"Sales"	"Shipng"
1234	0	1	0	0
1397	1	0	0	0
8372	0	0	0	1
3875	0	1	0	0
9736	0	0	1	0
6430	0	0	0	1
8757	0	1	0	0
8876	0	0	0	1
3732	1	0	0	0
3309	0	0	1	0
9393	1	0	0	0
3984	1	0	0	0
3857	0	0	1	0
8439	0	1	0	0
9496	1	0	0	0
7495	0	0	1	0

BITMAP INDEX ON "SEX" column of EMPLOYEE TABLE

EMPID	"Male"	"Female"
1234	1	0
1397	1	0
8372	1	0
3875	1	0
9736	0	1
6430	1	0
8757	1	0
8876	1	0
3732	1	0
3309	1	0
9393	1	0
3984	0	1
3857	0	1
8439	0	1
9496	1	1
7495	1	0

BITMAP INDEX ON "STATUS" column of EMPLOYEE TABLE

EMPID	"Full"	"Part"
1234	1	0
1397	0	1
8372	1	0
3875	0	1
9736	1	0
6430	1	0
8757	0	1
8876	1	0
3732	1	0
3309	1	0
9393	0	1
3984	0	1
3857	1	0
8439	0	1
9496	1	0
7495	0	1

BITMAP INDEX ON "JOB TITLE" column of EMPLOYEE TABLE

EMPLID	"Assembler"	"Brand Mgr"	"Clerk"	"Manager"	"Sales Rep"
1234	0	0	1	0	0
1397	1	0	0	0	0
8372	0	0	0	1	0
3875	0	0	1	0	0
9736	0	0	0	0	1
6430	0	0	1	0	0
8757	0	1	0	0	0
8876	0	0	1	0	0
3732	1	0	0	0	0
3309	0	0	0	1	0
9393	1	0	0	0	0
3984	1	0	0	0	0
3857	0	0	0	0	1
8439	0	1	0	0	0
9496	0	0	0	1	0
7495	0	0	1	0	0

ous range of data rows in the table. (Multiple ranges of contiguous blocks, such as from multiple table extents, will each be represented by a separate bitmap entry in the index.) Each row will be represented with a 1 if that row has this particular value or by a 0 if it doesn't. Oracle performs compression on the bitmap strings so that a long series of zeros (as may frequently be expected) can be stored in less space than the actual string would require.

The SEX column of the EMPLOYEES table in Figure 3.9 is a perfect example of a candidate for bitmap indexing. There are only two values across our entire list of employees, so only two bitmap strings need to be created. If we also build bitmap indexes on other columns within the same table (such as STATUS, which includes only two values, DEPT and JOB_TITLE, each having only a small set of allowable values), then Oracle can very efficiently combine the informa-

Figure 3.10 Using multiple bitmap indexes to satisfy a query.

"How many part-time, male clerks are employed in the marketing department?"

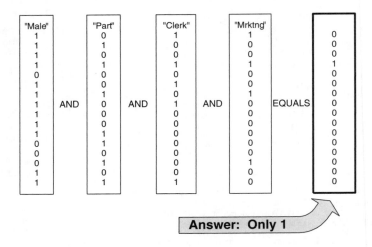

Answer: Only 1

tion in these four bitmap indexes to answer questions such as "How many part-time, male clerks are employed in the marketing department?" Bitmap indexes provide an excellent component, therefore, in the complete data warehouse solution. Figure 3.10 demonstrates Oracle's use of these four bitmap indexes to quickly answer this question. Queries of this type, which look for the highly selective intersection of several criteria that are individually very nonselective, are commonly used in decision-support queries.

Doing this type of "AND" (as well as the similar "OR") processing between the equal-length bitmaps is extremely fast. Performing the next step, if the query requires it, of looking up the actual data rows is done using a normal ROWID lookup into the table. As we'll see in Chapters 4 and 5, we'll exploit this feature of bitmap indexes to quickly access rows in the central fact table in an Oracle8 star query. (Oracle7 performs star queries but requires a concatenated B*Tree index and cannot use the more effective and efficient bitmap indexes for this purpose.)

Index-Organized Tables

Oracle8 introduces a new type of segment called an index-organized table. This structure is a hybrid between a table and a B*Tree index. An index-organized table is a table and is created by including the ORGANIZATION INDEX clause on a CREATE TABLE statement. It contains all the data columns defined for the table. However, the data in the table is stored inside a B*Tree index structure. By using the hierarchical search facility inherent in the hierarchical index structure and then storing all the data in that structure, Oracle can optimize retrieval of table data by primary key values. This is in contrast to a normal B*Tree index that would store the key data and also a ROWID pointer, which Oracle would use to look up the rest of the data in the separate table segment.

The index-organized table does not include a ROWID as part of the data. This saves a little bit of storage (six bytes in Oracle7, either six or ten bytes in Oracle8). The primary key data is also just stored once in the index-organized table instead of twice (once in the index and again in the table), which saves some more storage space. The total space savings can be significant if the primary key data makes up a large percentage of the total data row length.

The retrieval speed and storage space advantages of index-organized tables can be significant. However, there are also disadvantages to index-organized tables that make them generally of more use in transaction processing applications than in data warehousing. The index-organized table is highly optimized to benefit lookups of data based on primary key (either by equality lookup or by range scan) but other secondary forms of access are eliminated. Specifically, since no ROWID is assigned to each data row it is not possible to build additional indexes on an index-organized table. Another restriction, at least in the initial release of Oracle8, is that index-organized tables cannot be partitioned or replicated.

Clusters

Oracle provides a means, called a *cluster*, for physically organizing data from one or more tables based on the values of a particular column or set of columns. The *cluster key* is the data shared by the various rows that are to be stored together. Typically, the cluster key is the primary key of one table and the associated foreign key column(s) from other tables. The cluster key will be used to determine where each newly inserted row gets placed.

This physical organization may on first examination seem like a violation of a basic axiom of relational database—that row order is not important. However, clusters should be simply considered a physical access optimization similar to indexing. SQL access to each table remains unchanged, and the users/programmers do not need to modify their code because of clustering. As an example, Figure 3.11 shows all the sales order data for a particular customer as physically stored in the same block.

ORDER_ID was defined as the cluster key, and a cluster index was built on this key. Data from both the ORDERS and ORDER_LINES tables is then sorted so that everything about order number 1234 can be found in a single data block. This can provide exceptional performance in some OLTP systems that commonly need to retrieve all this information or perform joins on ORDER_HEADERS rows and their associated ORDER_LINES entries. The DBA needs to determine how much total storage will be needed for all the data about an order. This SIZE parameter (part of the CREATE CLUSTER command) will determine how many ORDER rows (and associated ORDER_LINE data) will be stored in each block.

Figure 3.11 A block of an index cluster in which related data from two tables are physically stored together.

2 Logical Tables

```
CREATE TABLE ORDERS
  (ORDER_ID              NUMBER(12,0),
   CUST_ID               NUMBER(8,0),
   ORDER_DT              DATE,
   SALES_REP_ID          NUMBER(5,0),
   TOT_ORD_COST          NUMBER(7,2),
   CONSTRAINT ORDERS_PK
        PRIMARY KEY (ORDER_ID),
   CONSTRAINT ORDERS_CUST_FK
        FOREIGN KEY (CUST_ID)
           REFERENCES CUSTOMERS;
```

```
CREATE TABLE ORDER_LINES
  (ORDER_ID              NUMBER(12,0),
   ORD_LINE_NUM          NUMBER(2,0),
   PRODUCT_ID            VARCHAR2(9),
   QUANTITY              NUMBER(3,0),
   UNIT_PRICE            NUMBER(7,2),
   CONSTRAINT ORDER_LINES_PK
        PRIMARY KEY (ORDER_ID, ORD_LINE_NUM),
   CONSTRAINT ORDER_LINES_ORDERS_FK
        FOREIGN KEY (ORDER_ID)
           REFERENCES ORDERS,
   CONSTRAINT ORDER_LINES_PRODUCT_FK
        FOREIGN KEY (PRODUCT_ID)
           REFERENCES CUSTOMERS;
```

Sample Table Data

ORDERS TABLE DATA

ORDER_ID	CUST_ID	ORDER_DT	SALES_REP_ID	TOT_ORD_COST
1234	10239487	4-DEC-97	4526	130.34
1452	12987674	5-DEC-97	3397	49.97

ORDER_LINES TABLE DATA

ORDER_ID	ORD_LINE_NUM	PRODUCT_ID	QUANTITY	UNIT_PRICE
1234	1	8383202	2	23.75
1234	2	8633993	1	17.99
1452	1	5645J33	1	24.99
1234	3	5447302X	5	12.97
1452	2	7339309	2	12.49

Stored in 1 Physical Block

Block Header Data

```
1234  10239487  4-DEC-97  4526  130.34
1 8383202   2  23.75
2 8633993   1  17.99
3 5447302X  5  12.97

1452  12987674  5-DEC-97  3397  49.97
1 5645J33   1  24.99
2 7339309   2  12.49
```

There is some benefit from reduced storage requirements as well, since the cluster key data needs to be stored only once instead of in each row. For very long key values this savings can be significant.

A second type of cluster, called a hash cluster, was introduced with Oracle7. In this type of structure, rows are organized by applying a hash algorithm to the value of the cluster key and then calculating the relative block address within the total set of blocks allocated to the cluster. No index is required to determine where to insert (or later retrieve) all the rows that have a particular cluster key value. This makes lookups based on the value of the cluster key very fast, but only equality searches can be performed. This is because rows with "adjacent" key values may be hashed into data blocks anywhere in the cluster, so no range scans (where we wish to find all matches for a range of values rather than for one specific value) can be performed unless an index is also created on the same column(s) as the hash cluster key.

Both types of clusters are useful in very specific situations in which one type of data access needs to be optimized. Other forms of access are, unfortunately, compromised in either type of cluster. Full table scans, in particular, suffer in both cases. The nature of data warehouse processing is so varied that it is generally impossible to predict that one particular type of access to a table should be optimized to the detriment of all other forms of access. Full table scans (especially when the Parallel Query Option is available) are common within the data warehouse environment. Clusters, however, typically spread data out over more data blocks so that a full table scan has to read more blocks to find all the rows. This is particularly true with hash clusters, which must be initially created with enough blocks to store the projected maximum number of rows. The first row inserted into a hash cluster table is equally likely to be inserted into the last physical block or the first. This means that every full table scan of a hash cluster may have to read a large number of empty blocks.

For this reason, clusters are rarely, if ever, used in the design of a data warehouse. In very specific cases, a DBA who is familiar with clusters and the many trade-offs involved with them might find a way to incorporate one into a warehouse design. Dave Ensor, formerly of Oracle's consultancy in the United Kingdom, provided the best advice on the use of clusters: "Used properly, a cluster might provide a 10 percent performance boost for one out of a hundred situations; in the other ninety-nine cases, however, the improper use of clustering might easily cause a severalfold performance degradation!" His comments were primarily directed to OLTP configurations. The data warehousing scenario, where flexibility and overall throughput are generally of greater importance than the performance of any single query, is even less encouraging.

Rollback Segments

Rollback segments are Oracle's structure for keeping track of *undo* information—the "before" image of data prior to a transaction's modifications. Should the transaction end with a ROLLBACK statement or have to be undone because of a transaction failure, the information stored in the rollback segment is sufficient to restore all the data to its condition before the transaction started. Should a transaction end with a COMMIT statement then the undo information is no longer required and that portion of the rollback segment is marked as available for use by another transaction.

Rollback segment information is also used by Oracle to provide *read consistency* across multiple transactions. Read consistency is needed when a transaction wishes to look at a block that has been modified but not yet committed by a second transaction. Rather than allow the transaction to see the uncommitted changes (which are not yet completely finished and, possibly, may be rolled back and never made permanent), Oracle uses undo information from the rollback segments to rebuild, in memory, a temporary copy of the data block as it would look if the second transaction were not occurring. Thus, each transaction or query sees the database as if no other transaction were active in the database. Because of this feature the Oracle user does not need to do anything special to ensure that he or she is not reading "dirty" data. In other popular DBMSs the user commonly has to specify an isolation level such as "repeatable read" and acquire locks on each data block as it is read.

In the pure, theoretical data warehousing model where access is always read-only, read consistency is not a critical feature. However, no data warehouse is ever completely read-only. Data in the warehouse has to be periodically loaded and resummarized. Ideally, no users should be executing queries against tables that are being loaded or modified. Even if read consistency isn't required during normal warehouse operations, it also incurs absolutely minimal additional cost, —except when block image has to be reconstructed because a query and a modifying transaction are simultaneously active in the block.

Temporary Segments

As one might guess from the name, temporary segments are database objects that are only used during the operation of a single SQL statement and are then released so their space can be reused for another purpose. The most common use of temporary segments in the data warehouse is supporting large sort operations. (Sort operations will be discussed more completely later in this chapter.)

Each user is allowed a specific amount of memory in which to perform sorts. In the data warehouse environment, a SELECT statement may frequently retrieve large amounts of data. If the query includes an ORDER BY or GROUP BY clause that causes the data to be sorted, it may be impossible to fit all the data into the allocated memory. In this case, Oracle will sort whatever portion of the data will fit into memory and then write the intermediate sort results out to temporary storage in the database.

In Oracle7 Server releases prior to 7.3, each time a disk sort was needed by a SELECT statement it was dynamically allocated. After the query was completed, the temporary segment was recovered by SMON. In a system, such as a data warehouse, where large sorts are frequently required, the overhead of dynamically allocating temporary space could be significant. Additionally, because SMON has several functions and does not run continuously, there is sometimes a delay and additional overhead when recovering the temporary segments released by completed queries.

Release 7.3, however, introduced a new tool for the DBA to alleviate this unnecessary overhead in dynamically allocating and deallocating temporary segments. Now when the DBA creates a tablespace to be used for storing temporary segments, he or she may create it with the TEMPORARY keyword. Oracle will then be able to avoid the extra space management overhead of dynamically creating temporary segments for each query by preallocating temporary extents in the tablespace. When a SELECT statement (or other SQL statement) requires sort space, these temporary extents can be quickly "checked out" for temporary use. Oracle prevents the creation of any permanent segments in a tablespace created with (or altered to) TEMPORARY status.

Extents

Each segment, of any type, is made up of one or more extents. The *extent* is the unit of space allocation by which a segment is initially created and later grows. When the DBA creates a table, index, or other segment, he or she is able to specify several parameters in the STORAGE clause that affect the size of the segment's extents. The following CREATE TABLE command illustrates these parameters:

```
CREATE TABLE SALES_REPS
       (EMPL_ID            NUMBER(7,0) PRIMARY KEY,
        EMPL_NAME          VARCHAR2(30),
        SALES_REGION       VARCHAR2(12),
        QUOTA              NUMBER(9,0))
  TABLESPACE DIM_DATA
  STORAGE
       (INITIAL            10M
        NEXT               20M
        PCTINCREASE        100
        MINEXTENTS         1
        MAXEXTENTS         20);
```

In this simple example, one extent of ten megabytes will be created initially. As rows are added and that extent is filled, a second extent of twenty megabytes will be added. When the second extent is filled a third extent of forty megabytes will be added to the segment. This third extent will be forty megabytes because the PCTINCREASE parameter was set to 100 percent. Each additional extent will be twice the size of the previous extent. Incidentally, the value of PCTINCREASE shown in this example is rarely used. The default value for this parameter is 50 percent, which leads to odd-sized extents and various space management difficulties for the administrator. Typically, the DBA sets PCTINCREASE to 0 (zero) so each additional extent will be the same size.

In some cases, the DBA wishes to initially allocate more than one extent rather than wait for growth to trigger the creation of additional extents. Each extent is a contiguous set of database blocks and, therefore, must be contained within a single database file. If a table of nineteen gigabytes needs to be created and the operating system only allows filesizes up to two gigabytes, then a minimum of ten files will be required. Therefore, a minimum of ten extents will have to be created. The DBA can do this at table creation time by specifying MINEXTENTS equal to 10.

TIP

The DBA can also take explicit control of the size and placement of extents through the ALTER TABLE . . . ALLOCATE EXTENT command, which will be discussed in Chapter 11.

Database Blocks

We introduced Oracle database blocks earlier in this chapter. Each time Oracle reads from or writes to the database files it moves data in units of database blocks; the data buffers within the SGA are each sized to fit one database block.

The database block size may be set as a multiple of the underlying block size used by the operating system. (Ideally, the Oracle block should correspond directly to one underlying operating system block.) The default database block size used by Oracle in most operating systems is 2,048 (2K) bytes. To override this default value, the DBA must specify a value for the DB_BLOCK_SIZE initialization parameter when creating the database. In almost every case, the large data warehouse benefits from using a larger block size of 8K or even 16K. The maximum value allowed for the DB_BLOCK_SIZE parameter is dependent both on the Oracle release and the operating system you are using.

The Oracle Data Dictionary

The SYSTEM tablespace is the home of the data dictionary where Oracle will store its information about all the other data to be put into the database. Every Oracle database must have a SYSTEM tablespace. The structure of the data dictionary consists of tables and indexes (just like our data warehouse will have), but the dictionary is owned by the Oracle system (a schema, or user, named SYS). The user and even the database administrator have very little reason to directly query the actual tables that make up the data dictionary. Such direct access can be very confusing because many of the table and column names are rather cryptic and because most useful queries require data from more than one table. To avoid these problems, a large number of data dictionary views have been created that make the dictionary much friendlier. There are data dictionary views to tell us about tables, indexes, tablespaces, and many other things involving the contents and structure of the database. Most of these views are named with a prefix like USER_, ALL_, or DBA_ to identify their intended use.

As an example, three dictionary views describe the tables defined in the database. The first view, USER_TABLES, shows information only about the tables owned by the user querying the view. If we issue the query SELECT TABLE_NAME FROM USER_TABLES we will see the names of the tables in our schema. If you issue the same query you will, most likely, get a different list of table names reflecting the contents of your schema. The second view, ALL_TABLES, shows us information about the tables we own as well as all other tables whose owners have given us the ability to access them. Even if we don't own any tables ourselves (a common configuration for a data warehouse in which all the data is contained within one or more special schemas that are not associated with actual users), when we issue SELECT OWNER, TABLE_NAME FROM ALL_TABLES, we will get a listing of all the tables we have permission to access. The final view, DBA_TABLES, is only accessible to those with special database administrator privileges. This view shows all the tables in the entire database.

In addition to these views of database tables, the Oracle data dictionary contains information on all other database objects. A complete listing of all the data dictionary views is contained in the Oracle7 and Oracle8 *Server Reference* manuals. The actual structure of the data dictionary views varies somewhat in each release of the Oracle Server and also depends upon which server options have been installed. The basic dictionary views have remained fundamentally the same since the introduction of Oracle version 6 nearly a decade ago.

Metadata

Metadata is data about the structure of the "real" data stored in the data warehouse. The Oracle data dictionary contains much of the metadata needed to navigate through the data warehouse. Unfortunately, the data dictionary can be somewhat cryptic to users who don't work with it on a regular basis like DBAs. Additionally, there is some metadata that is important to the data warehouse but is not tracked automatically by the data dictionary, such as identification of the source location and transformation algorithms used to populate the warehouse. Chapter 4 will present suggestions for structuring metadata in a way that can be used more conveniently by warehouse users.

Qualifying Object Names

Table names must be unique within a *schema*, but two schemas may each own a table of the same name. (These are, however, completely separate tables and must be differentiated by specifying OWNER as well as TABLE_NAME.) The following is a query of the dictionary view ALL_TABLES that reports multiple tables named CUSTOMERS:

```
SELECT OWNER, TABLE_NAME
  FROM ALL_TABLES
 WHERE TABLE_NAME = 'CUSTOMERS';

OWNER                           TABLE_NAME
------------------------------- ------------------------------
CANADA_SALES                    CUSTOMERS
EAST_SALES                      CUSTOMERS
WEST_SALES                      CUSTOMERS

3 rows selected.
```

This situation is similar to the church youth group of Gary Dodge's son, Ryan. His best friend there is also named Ryan. If the group leader needs to get the attention of one of them, calling "Ryan" is not sufficient. He needs to call either "Ryan Dodge" or "Ryan Flanders" to uniquely identify which Ryan he wants. Even though they share the same name, they are certainly not the same boy! In Oracle terms, we refer to this unambiguous naming as "qualifying the object name." It is done by specifying the owner, then a period separator, and then the table name. So the customer table, owned by the schema WEST_SALES would be uniquely identified as WEST_SALES.CUSTOMERS (generally, this would be spoken as "westsales dot customers").

Taking a quick look at the number of rows in each of the CUSTOMERS tables shows that they are, indeed, different objects. Note that the table names had to be qualified in these two queries so Oracle could determine which specific object we wanted to see.

```
SELECT COUNT(*)
  FROM WEST_SALES.CUSTOMERS;

COUNT(*)
---------
   234984

SELECT COUNT(*)
  FROM EAST_SALES.CUSTOMERS;

COUNT(*)
---------
   763916

SELECT COUNT(*)
  FROM CANADA_SALES.CUSTOMERS;

COUNT(*)
---------
      926
```

The Distributed Data Dictionary

If desired, the Oracle data warehouse can be distributed across multiple databases on multiple servers. This topic will be discussed in much more depth in Chapter 12. From the perspective of the data dictionary, however, it is important to recognize that each of these databases in a distributed warehouse is autonomous. Each physical database will have its own data dictionary, independently tracking its database objects, users, and privileges.

If a user connected to database A wishes to access the CUSTOMERS table that is stored on database B (and assuming the user has been granted access to the table by the administrator of B) then a further level of qualification is necessary. It is possible (though potentially confusing) for a CUSTOMERS table to be owned by a schema of the same name on both databases A and B. To identify the remote CUSTOMERS, the user would have to further qualify the table name with its location as well as its owner. Here we query the remote data dictionary to find other CUSTOMERS tables on a database known as INTERNATIONAL:

```
SELECT OWNER, TABLE_NAME
  FROM ALL_TABLES@INTERNATIONAL
 WHERE TABLE_NAME = 'CUSTOMERS';
```

The location qualifier INTERNATIONAL in this query is a database link. These database links are created by the database administrator using the CREATE PUB-

LIC DATABASE LINK command. It is possible for individual users to create their own private database links, but most administrators will see the advantages of creating and maintaining public database links to all the other databases that their users may need to access.

LOCATION TRANSPARENCY THROUGH SYNONYMS AND VIEWS

In many cases the users of the distributed data warehouse don't want to know about the physical distribution of schemas and tables. Why should the user have to remember that CANADA_SALES data is kept in the same database as the East and West regions of the United States, but EUROPE and ASIA SALES information is kept in a separate INTERNATIONAL database? To remove this complexity (and to give the administrator the freedom to move objects to accommodate hardware capacity, processing schedules, or other considerations) Oracle allows the qualification or even the actual table names to be hidden through the use of *synonyms*.

A synonym is an *alias* or nickname for an object. It can be created by the administrator to give a simple, consistent name to objects that hides the physical implementation decisions from the users. The decision to create multiple CUS-TOMERS tables in separate schemas and then to deploy them onto multiple servers may have been necessary for administrative reasons. Unless these administrative reasons correspond to functional or organizational structures that all the users understand, however, it may be best to disguise the physical complexity by providing a simple logical structure to the users. The following series of commands will develop a simple, consistent structure:

```
CREATE PUBLIC SYNONYM EAST_US_CUSTOMERS
    FOR EAST_SALES.CUSTOMERS;
CREATE PUBLIC SYNONYM WEST_US_CUSTOMERS
    FOR WEST_SALES.CUSTOMERS;
CREATE PUBLIC SYNONYM CANADA_CUSTOMERS
    FOR CANADA_SALES.CUSTOMERS;
CREATE PUBLIC SYNONYM EUROPE_CUSTOMERS
    FOR EUROPE_SALES.CUSTOMERS@INTERNATIONAL;
CREATE PUBLIC SYNONYM ASIA_CUSTOMERS
    FOR ASIA_SALES.CUSTOMERS@INTERNATIONAL;
```

Now we have created five synonyms that are consistent and easy to remember. There is no longer a need to know which regions are represented in the "domestic" database and which are stored in the INTERNATIONAL database.

If desired, we can even remove the fact that there are five separate sales organizations by creating a view that combines information from all five customer tables into a single CUSTOMERS view:

```
CREATE VIEW CUSTOMERS AS
    SELECT 'EAST_US' REGION, *
      FROM EAST_SALES.CUSTOMERS
  UNION ALL
    SELECT 'WEST_US' REGION, *
```

```
        FROM WEST_SALES.CUSTOMERS
UNION ALL
  SELECT 'CANADA' REGION, *
    FROM CANADA_SALES.CUSTOMERS
UNION ALL
  SELECT 'EUROPE' REGION, *
    FROM EUROPE_SALES.CUSTOMERS@INTERNATIONAL
UNION ALL
  SELECT 'ASIA' REGION, *
    FROM ASIA_SALES.CUSTOMERS@INTERNATIONAL;
```

This approach presents a simple perspective on our global customers list. A user can find information about any customer by querying the CUSTOMERS view. There are, of course, many other issues besides user simplicity that must be considered. The view just described, for example, which combines data from multiple databases, may introduce unnecessary performance problems. This is because each query for customers in say, Cleveland, will be resolved by searching the CITY column in five tables spread across both databases even though a more informed query could have been directly executed against just the EAST_SALES.CUSTOMERS table.

This trade-off between simplicity and performance is a common enigma that the data warehouse designer and administrator must somehow solve. One step toward reaching a solution is possibly to identify multiple audiences among the user community. There are commonly some warehouse users who will use the warehouse infrequently and will not take the necessary training to become sophisticated in their access. For these users, the administrator should probably only provide simplified access to summary data that, due to its smaller volume, will not present opportunities for truly painful performance problems. The tables containing more voluminous detailed data may only be made available for drill-down by warehouse "power users" who receive additional training on query tuning and warehouse navigation.

We will discuss design alternatives and metadata for warehouse users in the next chapter. Performance issues related to the use of views and distributed queries are treated in Chapter 9.

Security Features

Oracle has very strong security capabilities that provide the necessary granularity for the most demanding separation of responsibilities. These security features are used extensively in OLTP systems, but, all too often, minimal consideration of security is given in the data warehouse. Even though there may be less stringent security demands in the warehouse, it is generally not appropriate to simply say that all users may have SELECT privilege on all tables. The designers of the data warehouse should be familiar with Oracle security facilities and make an analysis of the data needs of various user groups. Oracle7 makes the management of security relatively easy. Oracle8 security has been enhanced to provide better control over users' passwords.

As a universal rule, no Oracle user can perform any action in the database until a specific privilege to perform that action is granted to that user. The default set of privileges, therefore, is the null set—no privileges at all.

Schemas and Users

Before Oracle7, Oracle users were each assigned a username and a password for connecting to the database. Depending upon the system privileges granted by the DBA, some users could create tables or other objects and others could not. Oracle7 introduced a new term, *schema*, which can be considered equivalent to the older concept of *user*. The newer term more precisely includes the concept of ownership of database objects. Even though the two terms are synonymous, within the data warehouse it may be useful to consider them distinctly.

A schema may be considered a special form of user account that is used to hold a set of tables and indexes to store warehouse data. In doing warehouse design it is helpful to create a separate schema to hold all the database objects related to a subject area. Normally this will mean that a warehouse will have a handful of schemas used for storing data. Generally, no user will ever actually connect to the database using one of these accounts—they are reserved for special administrator functions.

LIMITS ON THE DBA's PRIVILEGES

There is actually only one activity that must be done from within the table-owning schema: Initially granting access to the tables of a schema cannot be done from the administrator's schema. All other actions, including creating or dropping schema objects, loading data, truncating tables, and building indexes can be done by the administrator without first connecting to the owning schema.

The warehouse will have another, larger group of users who will need to access the data stored in the table-owning schemas but will not ever need to create objects of their own.

System Privileges

There are a large number (approaching one hundred) different privileges that may be granted to users, which give them the ability to perform some type of action. These system privileges include basic capabilities such as CREATE SESSION (which allows the user to make a database connection) and more exotic ones such as ALTER RESOURCE COST or BACKUP ANY TABLE, which would be expected to be granted only to administrators.

Normally, an entire group of users will need a consistent set of system privileges. Three or four groups would be typically identified for a data warehouse: ADMINISTRATORS, SCHEMA_OWNERS, USERS, and POWER_USERS might be four candidate groups that would each need a different set of system privileges. Rather than repeatedly grant the necessary set of privileges to each member of a group, the set of privileges can be granted to a role (discussed later), and then a single grant of the role to each new user will provide them with the full set of privileges.

Object Privileges

Just as system privileges allow their recipients to do some type of action, object privileges provide recipients with the ability to perform a particular action on a specific object. Thus, the schema owner DW_OWNER may grant SELECT privilege on the PRODUCTS table to the user account JSMITH. This then allows JSMITH to read the data stored within the DW_OWNER.PRODUCTS table.

Roles

Just as with system privileges, object privileges are more easily managed through roles. *Roles* are named collections of privileges. The administrator creates a new role and then grants privileges to the role. The administrator can then subsequently grant that role to a group of users.

A large number of tables and views may be defined in the warehouse. There may also be a large number of users who are to access those tables and views. If 500 warehouse users are going to be given access to 200 tables, individual grants of these privileges would require 10,000 grant statements. However, if access to the 200 tables had been granted to a DW_USER role and then that role were granted to the 500 users, then a total of only 700 grants would be required—a 93 percent savings in administrative workload. (This example assumes that all users require access to all tables—a more granular approach is generally recommended, however.)

A role should be created that includes access to the tables within each subject area. Users in the finance department might then be granted the roles corresponding to the three or four subject areas of interest to their analysis. Users within manufacturing will likely require access to a different set of subject areas, as would the users from the marketing department. Of course, there is not usually a simple, distinct mapping of users to subject areas. There will be overlaps. Some users in one department will be granted multiple roles, and roles associated with a given subject area will need to be granted to more than one group of users. The user groups don't generally align neatly along organizational boundaries, although this is a good place to start. The reality of cross-group responsibilities is facilitated by creating two levels of roles, as shown in Figure 3.12. Here, the typical users from each department are granted access to a subset of the data warehouse subject areas. The chief financial officer is, however, granted access to the roles created for both marketing and finance users.

The other advantage of using two levels of roles, as shown in Figure 3.12, is that we can very easily make a portion of the data warehouse inaccessible during maintenance by revoking a small number of the grants between the two levels of roles. After the maintenance window is over and the data has been checked and validated, the access may quickly be restored by remaking the in-

Figure 3.12 Usage of roles.

terrole grants. This is much simpler to manage than trying to handle the large number of individual grants based upon the total user base or the total number of warehouse objects.

Oracle Optimizer

An RDBMS optimizer is given the task of deciding between multiple access paths to satisfy the data needs of a particular SQL statement. Oracle provides several alternative methods for performing joins. There may well be several potential indexes that might be used, and Oracle always has the option of scanning a complete table.

Both Oracle7 and Oracle8 actually provide two optimizers. The rule-based optimizer remains basically unchanged from Oracle version 6. Without specific action on the part of the administrator, both Oracle7 and Oracle8 will default to using the rule-based optimizer. For applications that were written and tuned specifically for the rule-based optimizer in version 6 or early releases of Oracle7, this default choice may still be appropriate. The rule-based optimizer chooses between alternative access plans by following a predefined list of rules and selects the access path that uses the highest-level rule. Thus, the rule-based optimizer will always choose to use an available index on a small table even though it might be more efficient to scan the entire table.

The second optimizer available with Oracle7 or Oracle8 is cost-based. The initial releases of Oracle7 had several difficulties that made the cost-based optimizer a problem in many cases. However, enhancements made in release 7.3 and 8.0 make the cost-based optimizer a far better choice, especially for the unplanned queries typical of the data warehouse. Several access options of particular interest to data warehouse queries have been added in these releases. These new access path options are not available to the older rule-based optimizer.

Before the cost-based optimizer will be used to resolve a query plan, statistics must be gathered on the data in the tables and indexes of the data warehouse. These statistics are gathered using the ANALYZE TABLE command. Two options on this command allow the administrator to gather very accurate statistics based upon reading every row of the table (ANALYZE TABLE . . . COMPUTE STATISTICS) or potentially less accurate statistics (ANALYZE TABLE . . . ESTIMATE STATISTICS) based upon reading only a sample of the rows in the table. When a table is analyzed, statistics are also gathered for each index on the table. If needed, an index may be analyzed directly with the ANALYZE INDEX command.

One of the improvements made in successive releases of the cost-based optimizer has been in the sampling process. Each new release has allowed accurate estimates to be made based upon smaller sample sizes. By release 7.3 (and Oracle8) it is possible to obtain sufficiently accurate statistics based upon sample sizes of 4 or 5 percent of the total rows. The ideal sample size is a balance between the shorter execution time of a small sample and the increased accuracy of a large sample. The optimal sample size will vary by table, however. If the data in the table is very consistent and evenly distributed, a very small sample will do nicely. If the data is very irregular in its distribution then a large sample will be needed to get a good estimate. To find the correct sample size for a given table the administrator should first issue the ALTER TABLE . . . COMPUTE STATISTICS command and save the resultant values from DBA_TABLES, DBA_INDEXES. Then the table should be analyzed several more times using various sample sizes. Each set of values should also be saved before the next ANALYZE. Comparing the resultant values will allow the administrator to determine the smallest sample size that yielded the same (or very nearly the same) statistics as the initial COMPUTE STATISTICS. Once determined, this same sample size will probably be appropriate for future statistics gathering on that table.

COLUMN HISTOGRAMS

Column-level statistics can be gathered in the form of a height-balanced histogram when the data in one particular column deviates substantially from a uniform distribution. Histograms allow the optimizer to make a better decision about how many rows are likely to be retrieved on a particular range of values specified in a WHERE clause condition. Building a histogram on a column is done with ANALYZE TABLE . . . ESTIMATE STATISTICS FOR COLUMNS. These statistics are viewed in DBA_TAB_COLUMNS and DBA_HISTOGRAMS.

A table (and its indexes) should be reanalyzed whenever changes made to the data are likely to have altered the distribution of data enough to make the old statistics inaccurate and potentially cause the optimizer to make an improper choice. If one hundred thousand rows are added to a table of ten million rows, it is likely that the statistics will not change materially. If those one hundred thousand rows are added to a table with only two hundred thousand rows it is almost guaranteed that the table needs to be reanalyzed. Even the first example with a small percentage of newly added rows may require the regathering of column-level statistics if the added data rows cause a skewing that might affect a particular column's histogram.

Most warehouse administrators tend to include statistics gathering as a regular step in their periodic data loading/summarization cycles. After each load, indexes are built (as needed) and estimated statistics are obtained. When Oracle8 partitioned tables (or partitioned indexes) are used then only the newest partition (assuming partitioning is done by date) where rows have been added will need to be analyzed. New syntax for analyzing a single partition has been added to Oracle8 to handle this chore.

I/O Operations

Oracle performs I/O in different ways on different file types and for different types of access. Modified data blocks and index blocks are always written to the database files by DBWR in single Oracle blocks. Reading index blocks and individually requested blocks from disk is done in units of single Oracle blocks. If the underlying operating system blocks are smaller than the Oracle block size, then the I/O request may turn into multiple underlying I/O requests.

One major exception to this rule of requesting single Oracle blocks is during performance of a full table scan. During a full table scan, the Oracle server process will request a number of sequential blocks in each I/O request as defined by the initialization parameter, DB_FILE_MULTIBLOCK_READ_COUNT, which defines the number of Oracle blocks to be requested in each request. To determine the total I/O request size this value must be multiplied by the value of DB_BLOCK_SIZE. By example, a database with 8KB Oracle blocks and with DB_FILE_MULTIBLOCK_READ_COUNT set to 4 would request transfers of 32KB of data in each successive read during each table scan.

Another exception to the standard I/O request size of one Oracle block is while performing direct read or direct write operations. These occur, for instance, during direct path SQL*Loader jobs or when SORT_DIRECT_WRITES is enabled in the initialization parameter file. These direct read and write operations are performed using the value of DB_FILE_DIRECT_IO_COUNT. Just like the previous example, this parameter is the number of Oracle blocks to be transferred in each request.

Sort Operations

Oracle typically has to do sorts when a user issues a query that includes an ORDER BY or GROUP BY clause. Some joins (those using the SORT_MERGE or HASH join method) also require a sort operation. Index builds also require sorting data. When possible, Oracle will perform these sorts entirely in memory. This is determined by the value of the initialization parameter SORT_AREA_SIZE, which controls the amount of memory that can be allocated by the server process to perform a sort. If the entire sort can be completed within this memory allocation then no disk sort activity will be needed.

If the amount of data to be sorted exceeds this value then Oracle will sort as much data as it can within memory and then write it to disk in a temporary segment. Each subsequent set of data will be read, sorted, and written to the temporary segment until all the data is processed. Each of the sets of data written to the temporary segment is then merged to finish the sort process.

Where the temporary segment is created for a particular user is determined by the TEMPORARY TABLESPACE attribute, which was set using the CREATE USER or ALTER USER commands. Each database should have one (or possibly more) tablespaces set aside for just this purpose. Each user should then be altered to direct their sort activity to this location. If the user is not altered to set this attribute then sorts will be directed to the SYSTEM tablespace, the absolutely worst possible location!

Beginning in release 7.3, the tablespace that is created for this purpose can be dedicated to this single function using the ALTER TABLESPACE . . . TEMPORARY command. This command prevents any other segments from being created in this tablespace and will preallocate the entire tablespace into temporary extents for use by queries. This reduces the overhead associated with allocating temporary space for a sort. The administrator should set the TEMPORARY attribute for each temporary tablespace.

Backup and Recovery Features

Oracle provides several options for backing up data so it can be recovered after a disk failure. Backups of data can be either logical or physical. Logical backups can be performed on a table using the export utility, EXP. This approach allows the data in a single table (or Oracle8 partition) to be restored to the point in time that the export was performed. In most cases, data warehouses are too large to use EXP as the primary backup method.

Physical backups involve copying the datafiles to a safe location and later restoring them when the actual datafile is lost due to media failure. Two types of physical backup are available in Oracle7. A cold backup is the simpler approach, requiring the database instance to be shut down and a copy made of every datafile and redo log file. Recovery from a failure requires every file from the most recent backup to be restored from its backup location, usually on tape. Cold backups are time consuming and take away time from user availability. Cold backups may be sufficient for the data warehouse as long as the time required for performing the backups fits within the scheduled window for unavailability.

The second physical backup option is to use hot backups. Hot backups require that the database be operated in archivelog mode in which the ARCH process will make permanent copies of each log file before it is reused. Hot backups do not require the database to be shut down, which may be critical for a data warehouse with high availability requirements, perhaps because of a global user base. Hot backups can be performed on individual tablespaces. When a database file is lost, only the lost file needs to be restored, and then tablespace recovery will allow the logged changes to be replayed in order to bring the datafile back up to the point of failure.

Many of the backup and recovery features of Oracle7 can be automated by using the Enterprise Backup Utility, which coordinates backup activity with tape management software. Oracle8 introduces some additional backup capabilities above and beyond those of Oracle7. The new Oracle8 Recovery Manager enhances the functions of Enterprise Manager and adds a new capability for doing incremental backups of only the blocks in a datafile that have changed since the last backup.

Oracle Server Options

This book describes the use of several features of Oracle7 and Oracle8 that are not part of the base Oracle server. Some of these features, such as bitmap indexes or partitioning, are bundled with upgraded levels of the Oracle server (such as the Oracle8 Server Enterprise Edition but not the base Oracle8 server). Others are provided as part of special options that must be separately licensed. Features are bundled into these optional product packages for a variety of technical and marketing reasons.

Over the history of Oracle version 6, Oracle7, and Oracle8 there have been several of these features that were initially introduced as part of an extra-cost option but later incorporated into the base server product. The reader should verify, before installing or using a feature, that it has been properly licensed.

Some of the server options that have been offered as supplements to various Oracle releases include the following:

- **Transaction Processing Option** (version 6): Provided the ability to execute anonymous PL/SQL blocks within the RDBMS and enabled row-level locking.

- **Procedural Option** (Oracle7): Allowed the creation of stored procedures, functions, packages, and database triggers.
- **Parallel Query Option** (Oracle7): Allowed multiple processes to share the work of performing large queries, loads, and index builds.
- **Parallel Server Option** (Oracle7 and Oracle8): Allows multiple Oracle instances to simultaneously access a shared database from the various nodes of a clustered or MPP system.
- **Distributed Option** (Oracle7): Enabled the two-phased commit protocol necessary to support distributed transactions.
- **Advanced Replication Option** (Oracle7): Provided for updateable snapshots and multiple-master replication.
- **Objects Option** (Oracle8): Allows the use of Oracle8's new object types, tables, and views.
- **Partitioning Option** (Oracle8): Enables the ability to partition tables and indexes and to use parallel DML operations on those partitioned objects.
- **ConText Option** (Oracle7) and **ConText Cartridge** (Oracle8): Provide special indexing features for manipulating large-text objects.

Several other data cartridges are offered with Oracle8 to manage particular types of data, such as video, images, time-series data, and so on. It is likely that more changes and additions to the offered options and cartridges will continue throughout the life of Oracle8. In would therefore be inappropriate (and impossible!) to attempt to present an accurate and complete list in this book.

Summary

This chapter provides an overview of the architectural components of files, memory structures, and processes that make up the Oracle7 and Oracle8 server products. An Oracle *database* consists of data files, redo log files, and control files. Initialization parameter files are used to control the characteristics of the Oracle *instance*. The Oracle instance is made up of a series of processes that all access a shared memory structure known as the *System Global Area (SGA)*.

Within the database, objects such as tables and indexes are stored as segments that are created within tablespaces. Tablespaces are made up of one or more operating system data files. Special segments are used internally by the database for storing rollback (or undo) information and temporary sort data. A special set of tables and indexes make up the Oracle data dictionary, which keeps track of all the other structures within the database.

DESIGNING THE ORACLE DATA WAREHOUSE

CHAPTER 4

The success of a data warehouse project is dependent upon many factors, such as the need for an executive sponsor and an effective project team organization. In the final accounting, however, the measure of success of the warehouse itself will be based on how useful it is to its users. Is useful information available? How easily can users find that information? How easily and accurately can users interpret the data they retrieve? Is performance of the warehouse acceptable to users? Can administrative tasks, such as data loads, purges, and backups and recovery be performed within the available processing windows so that users will have access when they need it?

All these questions reflect the quality of the warehouse design. Inaccurate, disjointed, or unintelligible data cannot be used to make effective business decisions. Questions that take too long to answer will, in short order, cease to be asked. A warehouse that can't be accessed can't be used. The tasks of loading and summarizing data, performing necessary administration, and providing adequate performance are all impacted—for better or worse—by the quality of the underlying design.

Before discussing specific techniques of database design for the Oracle data warehouse, we will address the issue of providing information about the contents of our data warehouse through metadata.

Metadata

Metadata is data about data. It is a description of what data is stored in the data warehouse, including where it is stored, how it is stored, where it originated, or how it was derived. As the designers of our corporate data warehouse, we will make many design decisions that will impact our users. All the decisions and compromises we make while designing the data warehouse will potentially impact how the users locate, utilize, and interpret the data we work so hard to make available.

Our warehouse users, for instance, will need to know that within our data warehouse:

- The data in the SALES table is summarized on a daily basis by CUSTOMER_ID (the detail of multiple SALES invoices for a given customer on a given day is not retained).
- The data in the SALES table is only retained for the past thirteen complete fiscal months, then purged.
- Warehouse users can obtain weekly, monthly, quarterly, and annual summarizations of that SALES data for the past four years by querying the PERIOD_SALES table.
- The CUSTOMER_NAME and CUSTOMER_ADDRESS columns in the SALES table were obtained by referencing the corporate accounts receivable system rather than the various regional sales support systems.
- Daily SALES data from all international regions has been converted from local currency to U.S. dollars based upon the currency conversion factor in effect on the last day of the fiscal month.
- The column of the SALES table named SALES_DATE corresponds to the BOOKING_DATE field in the order entry system for all transactions that required credit checks and corresponds to the DATE_OF_SALE field for all others.
- Split transactions that involve sales across multiple regions reflect the actual percentage split of the transaction and do not include the 20 percent "cooperation incentive" bonus introduced in 1995 in the Sales accounting system.

These and thousands of other decisions that seem perfectly reasonable to the warehouse designers may be anything but intuitive to the regional compensation analyst in Chicago who can't understand why her warehouse reports don't balance with the monthly sales commission reports she works with daily.

Besides informing our warehouse users, metadata serves as a record of decisions and activities that are valuable to the analysts and administrators of the warehouse over time. Remember that a data warehouse is not a single project; it is not an event; and it is definitely not a product. It must be an ongoing process. By the very nature of decision-support processing—a discovery process—it is impossible to know in advance what uses may be found for the data stored within the warehouse. As users become familiar with the available data they will think of new questions to ask. It will not be possible to answer many of those questions based on the current warehouse design. New data, whether from existing or new transaction processing systems—or perhaps purchased from external sources—will need to be identified and integrated into the warehouse structure. Maintaining a data warehouse is a much more active role than maintaining operational systems. As support personnel inevitably change during the never-ending "design" phase, the newcomers will need to refer to metadata about the data sources (and rejected alternative sources), transformation algorithms, and other details of the current structure.

Recording Warehouse Processing as Metadata

Even "processing logs" need to be kept that record details of when extracts were performed, when and how much data was loaded (whether refreshed or appended), when summaries and indexes were rebuilt, and so on. Traditionally, system logs of this type are generated as text files by the batch processes that perform the work. These text files are generally unavailable to all but the system administrators—and are rarely examined even by them! Much useful information, however, can be gleaned from the statistics, volumes, and timings that can be obtained from these batch jobs.

Imagine a simple table added to your data warehouse in which each routine batch job does a single insert when it starts and a single update when it ends. (Note that the overhead incurred by this extra recording is negligible within the total amount of work done by any of these processes.) In a simple case, the data to be recorded might include the following:

- the name of the process (and perhaps its version/release number)
- input file name, size, and the like (if applicable)
- the date and time of job start and end
- the job completion status
- the number of rows processed (inserted, updated, purged, etc.)
- the number of rows rejected or errored (if applicable)

Another newly defined process can be added at the end of the regular maintenance window to snapshot additional statistics about the data warehouse itself. These statistics are gathered automatically by Oracle whenever a table or index is analyzed. (See Chapters 5 and 9 for more information about using the ANALYZE command to gather statistics for use by the Oracle query optimizer.) The optimizer statistics are available in the data dictionary using simple, low-overhead queries. They need to be captured, however, into another table before they are overwritten by the next cycle of loading and analyzing. In this way you

Viewing the Statistics Gathered by ANALYZE

The primary tables containing these useful statistics are DBA_TABLES and DBA_INDEXES. A more complete monitoring might also find interesting statistics from DBA_TAB_COLUMNS, DBA_IND_COLUMNS, DBA_HISTOGRAMS (Oracle7), DBA_TAB_HISTOGRAMS (Oracle8), DBA_TAB_COL_STATISTICS (Oracle8), and DBA_FREE_SPACE. If auditing is used to track warehouse usage, it may be helpful to regularly snapshot information from DBA_AUDIT_OBJECT, DBA_AUDIT_SESSION, or DBA_AUDIT_TRAIL. For Oracle8 partitioned objects, additional useful statistics can be obtained from DBA_TAB_PARTITIONS and DBA_IND_PARTITIONS.

will retain a history of these statistics that can be examined to observe changes over time.

Having this information in the database allows the administrator to ask a variety of interesting new questions about trends (Why is the weekly load cycle seeming to take longer than it used to? Which specific processes are taking more time than they used to? When did this start? Did it occur suddenly or gradually? Is it related to changes in the volume of data being processed or the total being stored?) Specific observations of B*Tree indexes growing out of proportion to their tables can identify the need for rebuilding them to accommodate a load/purge cycle that leaves older branches of the index sparsely populated even while newer branches are being created.

If one job should fail to complete, there may be a logical discrepancy in the implied relationships between data in different tables. Consider the case of a summary table that fails to be re-created after loading additional data into a corresponding detail table. Attempts to drill down from the summary to detail may return bizarre, confusing results.

Even warehouse users can find useful information within this "processing log" type of metadata. Just knowing that a particular load or summarization

Controlling User Access During Warehouse Refresh Processing

Ideally, the administrator of the warehouse should prevent access to the warehouse, or a specific subject area, if data in one table is not properly synchronized with data in other related tables because one process out of several failed to complete. As we'll see later in this chapter, the normal OLTP system practice of using declarative foreign key constraints to ensure data integrity is not widely used in the data warehouse. Also, because of the large volumes of data typically processed in a load cycle, updates to more than one table in the warehouse are not coordinated through the normal transaction processing capabilities of Oracle. Each table is typically loaded or summarized independent of others. Either automatically or manually, the administrator should ensure that inconsistent data should not be viewed by users. Access to warehouse data should be controlled using Oracle's role-based security feature. Roles make it very easy for the administrator (or subject area owner) to add new users to the warehouse and give them access to appropriate data. As a side benefit, this same facility makes it very easy to temporarily restrict access to one portion of the warehouse. Each subject area should be controlled by a different pair of roles. To prevent users from accessing a particular subject area during the time that data is being maintained (loaded, indexed, summarized, purged, etc.), the administrator need only issue a single REVOKE statement; after completion of all related maintenance within that subject area, only a single GRANT statement will reopen the warehouse for access. Should any portion of the maintenance cycle fail to complete, the GRANT statement should not be issued until the problem is investigated and process did not complete successfully can help an analyst avoid (or explain!) a query that might return erroneous results. Also, the stored trend information about number of rows processed (or rejected) may be of more interest to the business analyst than the administrator. Why were last week's store receipts from the central region 23 percent less than the week before? The answer might be a business issue (spring flooding in the Midwest?) or it might be because a processing problem in the Chicago office's computer prevented delivery of one of five extract files. If the analyst can see only that the dollar volume was down for the region, he or she may have a hard time understanding the cause; if, on the other hand, he or she can also investigate the record volume and processing log then the investigation may take a totally different direction.

The Data Design Process

Typically, departments use different operational systems to support their part of the business and therefore use different names to describe identical data and, sometimes, the same name for very different data. The warehouse design team, however, must attempt to derive single, unambiguous data names, formats, cal-

resolved.This process can be performed manually. In this situation, the administrator or subject area owner will manually review the results of the most recent maintenance cycle. After verifying that all processing completed properly, the GRANT statement is executed manually. The advantage to this approach is that the verification process can be more intelligently performed; the administrator or subject area owner can examine the data for reasonableness by issuing a variety of queries rather than just verifying the completion of jobs. The disadvantage, of course, is that someone must assume this responsibility after each maintenance cycle, whether that is monthly, weekly, or daily. As a daily responsibility, this may present problems. Vacations, illness, weather, and the like may all prevent the timely granting of access to other users. The manual approach does not require that all of the run statistics be kept in the database, although doing so is likely to facilitate the process. Optionally, this process can be performed automatically. To do so, run results must be made available in the database as recommended. A simple program or stored procedure needs to be written that will examine whichever results and statistics are determined to be important to reasonably assure the integrity of the just completed data maintenace cycle. If each of these checks is successful, then the program or procedure will issue the appropriate GRANT statement (and add its own execution record to the processing log). Should any problems be detected, Oracle provides stored procedures capable of sending an e-mail message (or, with some additional programming, a page) to the appropriate administrators and subject area owners. Once written, this program or procedure needs to be added to the processing schedule after all the jobs whose execution it will verify.

culations, and meanings. Ideally, representatives of the various departments are consulted during the design of warehouse entities they are likely to use. Not infrequently, these discussions of what data is to be included, where it is to be obtained, and what it is to be called become spirited or even confrontational, with each representative honestly believing that his or her way is the only right way. The warehouse designer must combine excellent communication, negotiation, mediation, and peacemaking skills to facilitate progress and avoid project "paralysis by analysis."

Inevitably, however, compromises have to be made that conflict with the common usage of one or more groups. Even if the representative from marketing finally agrees that manufacturing's definition of the term PRODUCT is acceptable, there are likely to be dozens of other marketing employees who will someday access the data warehouse. If they interpret PRODUCT in their department's customary way, they are likely to make erroneous conclusions or ask nonsensical questions.

The data warehouse design and delivery team must have a means for telling the users of the data warehouse all about the data they are being given. This is a similar, but significantly more difficult, task to communicating database design information throughout the programming staff of a traditional IT project. It is similar because the handful of programmers all need to share a common understanding of what data they're working with and how it is stored. It is more difficult, however, for several reasons:

- Data warehouse users are not professional programmers and may not be used to dealing with such issues.
- Data warehouse users are typically not all from the project team (or even department) and therefore are not as likely to share a common understanding of how the data is used.
- The number of users of a successful data warehouse is likely to be very large, making personal Q&A sessions much more burdensome.
- Many data warehouse users are only occasional users. Unlike members of a programming project team who work with a database every day, some warehouse users may access the data warehouse only once or twice a month. The nature of decision support activity means that, frequently, they will need to investigate data and data relationships they've not previously explored.
- Data warehouse users are, in many cases, located in different buildings, cities, or even countries from the warehouse designers. The users of the data warehouse are likely to have no more than one training session at which they will have a chance to discuss such issues with a member of the design team. Future users may receive their training only casually from another local user in their own department.
- Data warehouses are evolutionary in their design. New data is defined and added to the data warehouse regularly. Users must be able to identify, access, use, and interpret the data added in each new release as easily as the original data on which they were trained.

Because of these factors, and many others like them, the data warehouse team must find a way to communicate unambiguously to a large, possibly casually trained audience with minimal personal contact. The training warehouse users needs to follow the model of the old proverb, "Give a man a fish and you feed him for a day, teach him to fish and you feed him for a lifetime." Rather than try to teach a new user every detail about the contents of the data warehouse, the goal should be to provide a means to let them find those details in the metadata.

What Metadata Does Oracle Provide?

At a bare minimum, users will need to be able determine the name and structure of each table that contains information important to them. As we'll see shortly, this information is available via the Oracle data dictionary. Figure 4.1 shows a slightly simplified diagram of the level of metadata about the logical structure of the warehouse that is maintained by the Oracle data dictionary. Un-

Figure 4.1 Metadata maintained by the Oracle data dictionary.

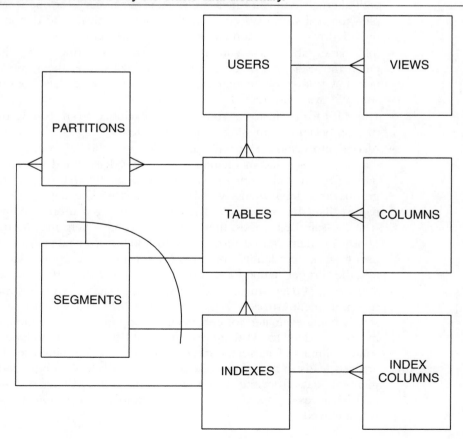

fortunately, this level of metadata may not be sufficient to allow the warehouse users to make informed decisions about which warehouse data they need, how to form a query to retrieve it, or how to interpret their results.

Additional metadata that may be helpful to the users of our warehouse can include the following:

- Information about the source of warehouse data. This might name the operational system, file, and field from which the data was extracted, or it might identify where external data was acquired. Rarely will this be a simple 1:1 mapping of a warehouse table back to a single file or table in the legacy systems world.
- Information about how the data is transformed, filtered, and preprocessed during the extraction and loading of detailed data.
- A schedule and history of load, summarization, purge and other administrative jobs including record counts and other control information.
- Definition of units of measure. As data is loaded into the warehouse, it is transformed into standardized units of measure. This allows the direct comparison of different data. Some users, however, will be more familiar with alternative units of measure (meters versus feet, for one simple example—the real world is frequently far more complex), and they need to be provided with conversion factors to help interpret results.
- Information about how summarizations were performed. This should also guide the user in how to perform drill-downs from the summary to the next lower level of summarization or to the detailed data from which the summary was constructed.
- The rules for exclusion if some data is excluded from loading or summarization because of missing or invalid values.
- Aliases information. Since all data loaded into the data warehouse is integrated (as discussed in Chapter 1) we have determined a single standard name for each element of warehouse data. Invariably, different work groups and departments will be familiar with the data under different names than the one standard name chosen. Until users become familiar with the standard names, they will need to have help making the translations. This help can be provided with additional metadata that allows the user to look up a familiar business (or specific legacy system) term and be told the "proper" name for that data within the data warehouse.
- Versioning of data structures and definitions. Data warehouse structures are not permanently frozen. Almost by definition, data warehouses are constantly being evaluated for enhancement opportunities. Additional data elements are added to existing tables, new tables are added and, occasionally, some columns of current warehouse tables may be eliminated. New DSS analysis leads to new types of questions, which lead to new data requirements. If data from the warehouse is archived and later restored, it will also be necessary to restore the metadata that was current when the data was archived.

- Job execution status. As we discussed earlier in this chapter, the failure of one or more load or summarization jobs may invalidate the results of some queries. If the monthly regional summaries of SALES_REVENUES completed successfully but the corresponding summaries of COSTS_OF_SALES did not, then queries that seek to determine profitability by region are not going to deliver meaningful answers. In some such cases, the failure will be obvious and the queries will simply fail. In other cases, the queries may be complete but with erroneous results.

Delivering Metadata

There are several alternative means for allowing users to view metadata about the contents of the warehouse. They are discussed in the following sections.

Printed Metadata Reports

Early data warehouses typically provided metadata to their users via printed reports—often generated directly from the Oracle data dictionary. Each new user was provided with a book of simple metadata, often limited to the same type of physical database design information that DBAs would provide to a programming team for an operational system. This book typically included a layout for each table, which showed column names, data types, and length. This simple approach to providing users with information about the contents of the data warehouse has several drawbacks:

- As discussed earlier, the need for additional metadata was recognized over time as the warehouse support staff found themselves having to repeatedly explain where some data element originated and how it was processed en route to the warehouse. Warehouse users have a greater need to correctly interpret the data they work with than do programmers, and they therefore need more than just physical layouts. The additional information about the warehouse data can, of course, be added to these reports using a word processor, but other problems remain.
- A printed report is of use to the user only when he or she takes the time to look something up in it. It is inherently passive. Modern query tools, however, are able to take advantage of metadata when it is stored in the database. As the user of one of these tools browses through the data warehouse and develops a query, the tool can become an intelligent helper by automatically displaying descriptive aliases on reports, by graphically displaying probable join criteria, or by referencing statistical information from the database to roughly predict query performance.
- Another major deficiency of printed metadata reports is that they become rapidly outdated as the warehouse evolves. New subject areas are added, each with multiple tables and relationships. Existing subject areas are frequently enhanced with new summary tables as analysts identify expensive

queries that repeatedly summarize detailed data. Finally, new columns may be added to existing tables as users request additional data. Printed reports, therefore, have to be regenerated and redistributed frequently. Users who don't receive or file their updates are unable to take advantage of new warehouse features.

The Oracle Data Dictionary

The Oracle data dictionary lies at the core of each Oracle database. Oracle uses it to keep track of all database objects, freespace, users, and security. An incredible amount of detail is maintained in the data dictionary that is quite helpful to the DBA, who frequently has the need, time, and experience to delve into the gory internal workings of the database and its objects.

Many query tools also take advantage of the Oracle data dictionary to assist the user in navigating through the data warehouse. These tools can often present a graphical view of the database, including relationships and join criteria. (This capability may require defining foreign keys, which are often a problem in a data warehouse; see the discussion of database constraints later in this chapter.)

There are, however, two characteristics of the data dictionary that limit its usefulness to general data warehouse users: incompleteness and excessive detail.

NOT COMPLETE

First, the information that is maintained in the data dictionary is very heavily oriented toward physical database structures. Warehouse users certainly have some need for physical descriptions of the tables they access. They need to know the names of tables and of columns within those tables. They need to know what type of data is stored in each of those columns. They need to know about the primary keys that define how the data in a table is organized. More experienced users will be interested in knowing which indexes are available to speed the execution of a contemplated query. Unfortunately, the data dictionary does not hold other information needed by the warehouse user. The data dictionary does not, for instance, keep track of which operational system a particular data element is populated from or what calculations were performed on it. The data dictionary does not remind the user that a specific column name has several alternative names.

Further, the data dictionary only provides a current view of the database structure—it does not maintain any history. Given the evolutionary nature of the data warehouse, it is important to be able to understand the changes in structure that have occurred. This is particularly true when archival data is maintained in an older format than current data.

TOO DETAILED

Second, the level of physical detail that is needed by the DBA is not easily navigated by a less technically trained user. The warehouse user is not likely to recognize that the name of the "table" in his or her SELECT statement might actually be known in the data dictionary as a table, a view, or even a synonym to another schema's table or view. Even experienced Oracle developers sometimes get confused about the actual location of data they're accessing when they create a private synonym, table, or view that supercedes an intended public synonym reference to another object. All this complexity is confusing to the business analyst trying to use the data warehouse to obtain answers to business questions. Ideally, the average warehouse user should be able to see metadata for all his or her available objects in one standardized set of metadata objects.

Extending the Oracle Data Dictionary

The simplest means of extending the Oracle data dictionary is to use comments. The standard data dictionary has a built-in capability for storing additional textual information about each table and each column defined in the database. It is surprising how few Oracle database administrators are aware of this capability or use it at all.

USING COMMENTS

Comments are appended to the definition of the table or column using the COMMENT command. As an example, to add source system information for the CUSTOMERS table in the schema named DW, the administrator might issue the following SQL command:

```
COMMENT ON TABLE dw.customers
    IS 'Source is CUSTMSTR file within the ORDPROC system.';
```

Views can be commented just the same as tables. Use the COMMENT ON TABLE command just as if the view were a table. Here is a comment added to the definition of the LOCAL_CUSTOMERS view:

```
COMMENT ON TABLE dw.local_customers
    IS 'Local customers are those with HQ located in Colorado.';
```

To further note that the CUSTOMER_NAME column of this table has been edited before loading it into the warehouse, an additional column-level COMMENT command could be issued:

```
COMMENT ON COLUMN sales.customers.customer_name
    IS 'Name edited to all capital letters during load.';
```

Once the information has been added to the data dictionary with COMMENT commands for each table and column, it can be viewed by inquiring on the dictionary views ALL_TAB_COMMENTS and ALL_COL_COMMENTS using the OWNER (schema name), TABLE_NAME, and COLUMN_NAME columns as keys. This is fairly easy to do if printed reports are to be generated. To provide this data to warehouse users without forcing them to do two queries or to repeatedly join the data, the administrator may create two new views (perhaps just called TABLES and COLUMNS) which predefine the joins to effectively add the

COMMENTS column to the other information. Here is an example that builds the TABLES view:

```
CREATE OR REPLACE VIEW dw.tables As
   SELECT T.TABLE_NAME, TC.TABLE_TYPE, TC.COMMENTS
     FROM ALL_TABLES T, ALL_TAB_COMMENTS TC
    WHERE T.OWNER = TC.OWNER
      AND T.TABLE_NAME = TC.TABLE_NAME
      AND T.OWNER = 'DW'
   UNION ALL
   SELECT VIEW_NAME, TC.TABLE_TYPE, TC.COMMENTS
     FROM ALL_VIEWS V, ALL_TAB_COMMENTS TC
    WHERE V.OWNER = TC.OWNER
      AND V.VIEW_NAME = TC.TABLE_NAME
      AND V.OWNER = 'DW';
```

During training, the users can be instructed to use these views to obtain their metadata:

```
SELECT * FROM dw.tables;

TABLE_NAME                        TABLE_TYPE
----------------------------      -----------
COMMENTS
--------------------------------------------------------------------
CUSTOMERS                         TABLE
Source is CUSTMSTR file within the ORDPROC system.
LOCAL_CUSTOMERS                   VIEW
Local customers are those with HQ located in Colorado.
TABLES                            VIEW
3 rows selected.
```

There are, however, a few limitations on using the COMMENTS feature to extend the Oracle data dictionary:

- The textual data is unformatted by Oracle. It is treated only as a character string, so any structure to the information must be carefully defined and enforced by those who enter the COMMENTS.
- The comments for any one table or column can not exceed two thousand characters in Oracle7 or four thousand in Oracle8. This may not provide enough room to maintain all the additional metadata needed by an organization.
- At any given time, there can be only one comment for each table, view, or column known to the data dictionary. There is no historical record of dictionary structure or of our extended comments.
- Comments can only be added to tables, views, and columns. Other structures, such as sequences or clusters, cannot be commented. Individual Oracle8 partitions cannot be separately commented.

- Most query tools are not likely to automatically perform the joins to ALL_TAB_COMMENTS and ALL_COL_COMMENTS in order to display comments since the comments feature is so rarely used.
- The information stored in comments cannot be easily edited. It is replaced each time another COMMENT command is issued on the table or column. To make changes to existing comments the administrator would need to retrieve the current information to a text file, edit the text file, and then reissue the COMMENT.

EXTRACTING DATA DICTIONARY INFORMATION TO A FILE

Extract data from the data dictionary to a text file using the SPOOL command in SQL*Plus followed by a SELECT statement for the specific data you want written to the file. To generate the extracted data in the form of the necessary SQL statements to re-create the data, use SQL to generate SQL. This technique is presented in Chapter 5.

If the limitations of using comments to extend the Oracle data dictionary impair the designer's ability to document and present metadata, it may be time to consider another alternative.

CREATING ADDITIONAL TABLES

The entire Oracle data dictionary is composed of standard Oracle tables, indexes, clusters, views, and sequences. Application developers routinely create other tables, indexes, and the like to store data needed by their applications. The warehouse developer can just as easily build an application to handle warehouse metadata.To employ this option, the warehouse developer will need to have a solid understanding of the Oracle data dictionary because everything built in the metadata application will need to be coordinated with it. An Oracle DBA assigned to the project should provide this necessary knowledge. However, an additional skill in building online screens to maintain the metadata will be needed. Normally, a warehouse project does not have an assigned programmer familiar with Oracle*Forms, Visual Basic, or other screen development tools. If your project elects to provide metadata using custom tables, be sure to include this resource early in the project plan.

There is no one right set of tables and views that will satisfy the metadata needs of a warehouse. The design will be driven partly by the sophistication of the users, partly by the choice of query tool (or tools), and partly by the design of the warehouse itself. Some warehouse builders will not choose to implement a versioning strategy. Some may want to document archived data; others may not. Oracle Discoverer creates over forty tables to maintain its metadata and support its queries.

Whichever approach is chosen to supplement the Oracle data dictionary, it will be necessary to provide a means of maintaining metadata in the repository.

MAINTAINING THE EXTENDED DATA DICTIONARY

If comments are used to extend the metadata stored about tables and columns in the dictionary, then the additional metadata stored within those comments must be maintained by reissuing the COMMENT command. Each new COMMENT command will overwrite the previous comment on the object. The easiest way to maintain the data will be in an external file using a text editor. The data dictionary will be used primarily to present the data to the user, via SQL queries, but the real maintenance will be done outside of the database and then applied via a COMMENT command.

If, on the other hand, extended metadata is provided via additional tables, then maintenance can be performed using the shop's chosen application development tools. Oracle's Developer/2000 tools, Microsoft's Visual Basic, or other 4GLs designed for quickly developing SQL applications will fit the bill.

The biggest difficulty with this approach of keeping extended metadata in separate tables will be encountered when you try to keep the tables synchronized with the Oracle data dictionary. Since actual SQL statements issued by the user will interact with the tables, views, and columns as known to the data dictionary, it is essential that the helpful metadata provided to the users be consistent with the data dictionary. If we add a column to a table (via the ALTER TABLE SQL statement) the data dictionary will be immediately updated to reflect its existence. We must simultaneously add the same information to our extended metadata tables. Unless the administrator is very careful, there is a strong possibility that errors will be made while performing dual maintenance.

There are three approaches to ensuring that updates to the basic data dictionary and our extended dictionary are coordinated:

1. The first approach is after-the-fact verification. Simple SQL scripts can be run to validate that the contents of your extended metadata tables are synchronized with Oracle's data dictionary record of the actual physical structure of the warehouse.

2. The second approach is to generate skeleton updates to the extended tables from the data dictionary. Using the SQL to generate SQL technique (presented in Chapter 5), a script can read the data dictionary to initially populate the extended metadata repository. Screen-based programs would then be used to allow the warehouse designer to fill in the blanks with the additional logical metadata needed by the user and future maintainers of the warehouse.

3. The final approach is to make all the changes directly to the extended metadata tables and then generate the corresponding SQL DDL to update the Oracle data dictionary. This approach, which also uses SQL to generate SQL, has the advantage of providing the best support for historical versioning of metadata.

Building and maintaining your own metadata repository as part of the data warehouse design process is a challenging and time-consuming task. Unless the data warehouse project faces severe budget limitations (as during a proof-of-concept phase) it is preferable to acquire a predefined repository that can accomplish the same goals with much less effort.

Predefined Metadata Repositories

Even though the Oracle RDBMS's built-in data dictionary does not include all the information needed to support a data warehouse, other components of the complete data warehouse solution may provide the necessary capabilities.

ETT TOOLS

Most data warehouse projects will require the use of specialized tools for extracting, transforming, and transporting data from various legacy systems into the warehouse. Frequently data warehouse projects are initiated on a shoestring budget and the organization decides to save money by not acquiring an ETT tool. These products are, admittedly, rather expensive with price tags commonly well into six figures. However, the opportunity cost of using in-house programmers and the actual cost of engaging contractors and/or consultants to manually write and maintain the necessary extract programs, transformation logic, and file transfer scripts (and, of course, metadata) will eventually exceed the software licensing costs for a well-designed ETT tool.

One of the benefits provided by these tools is a metadata documentation layer. Each tool will vary in the emphasis it provides to user metadata as well as how and where it will store the metadata. The tool needs to store metadata for its own use. It needs to remember where to find the needed source data and how to transform it. This is also information of interest to the users. To be completely functional as a metadata repository, however, it should also be capable of storing the additional information needed by warehouse users. As discussed earlier, this should include items such as aliases, definition of standardized units of measure, conversion factors, methods of summarization, and so on. One of the many criteria for selecting an ETT tool should be the completeness of the metadata it is capable of storing as well as how easily it can be maintained by the warehouse designer or administrator and accessed by users.

The ETT tool developers have several alternative locations in which to store their metadata. Be sure that the one you select is capable of storing its repository in the data warehouse so that users can access it using their standard query tools. An external repository on a dedicated ETT workstation may be most convenient for the ETT tool, but it will not meet the additional metadata needs of the warehouse users.

A Standardized Metadata Repository

An effort is currently underway within Oracle Corporation to define and provide a standardized metadata repository for data warehousing that would be used by all of Oracle's decision support tools. When completed, this effort will result in much simpler and more useful data warehouses.

QUERY TOOLS

As an alternative to maintaining warehouse metadata manually or on the "front end" in an ETT tool, many of the current generation of end-user query tools provide a metadata layer as well. If your data warehouse project will be selecting a single, standardized query tool then this is a perfect opportunity to provide a robust navigation and interpretation tool at the same time. Using the "administrator" mode of the query tool, the analyst can document everything the user might want to know about the structure, contents, and meaning of the warehouse. The tool can then help guide the user easily through the navigation of the warehouse and automatically perform joins, drill-downs, and star and snowflake consolidations.

Of course, the end-user query tool's metadata will not directly support the needs of the extraction, transformation, and transportation functions. One potential risk in piecing together an entire data warehouse solution is that the warehouse administrator will need to maintain multiple metadata repositories with some overlapping needs. If this is the case, keeping the multiple repositories in synch with each other (and the real data!) will become an additional point of concern.

CASE TOOLS

A third alternative for acquiring a metadata repository is the set of tools used by designers of application systems to document their table and process models. Some Computer Aided Systems Engineering (CASE) tools are very good at defining and using multiple levels of metadata. Others are little more than diagrammers for drawing pretty pictures. There are, however, a few limitations of the current crop of CASE tools that may limit their applicability to providing metadata for a data warehouse.

The Promise of CASE Tools

CASE tools were widely touted in the late 1980s as the salvation of information technology. (Relational databases, GUI development tools, object-oriented development, and the web have all taken their turn in this limelight.) Like any product, some CASE tools were (and are) better than others. Many organizations purchased and then discarded even the best CASE tools because their first in-house usage did not generate the 50 percent (or more) project time savings touted by the CASE vendors. In virtually all of those situations the problem was not in the tool but in the organization. Systems engineering, supported by CASE, is fundamentally a change in organizational discipline. Organizations without the necessary discipline (or the endemic desire to adopt it) were doomed to fail. A carpenter who fails to measure carefully will not become more successful because he replaces his handsaw with the best circular saw; he will just be able to make a mess more quickly.

- Most CASE tools have not been designed to handle the special design considerations of a data warehouse. OLTP systems focus on the current value for any data element, while data warehouses provide a historical view of changes in values. Entity relationship diagramming (ERD) techniques are useful for designing a traditional detail-and-summary style of warehouse. Newer techniques are required for dimensional analysis of a star schema warehouse.
- Some CASE tools support versioning of applications but generally with a revolutionary mind-set. That is, version 2 is being built to replace version 1. In a data warehouse, it is frequently necessary to maintain data in version 1 format for years, even after new data has been added in the format of versions 2, 3, and 4.
- Relational OLTP systems have a strong emphasis on foreign keys based on value equality between two tables. These relationships are generally clouded in the data warehouse where time becomes part of most tables' key structures. The warehouse relationship of summary-to-detail is not the same as OLTP's parent-to-child.
- Star and snowflake schemas are unique to the data warehouse. CASE tools designed for OLTP systems design will not support this diagramming technique or generate the appropriate supporting DDL.
- Most OLTP systems do not require active interaction with extended metadata at run-time. CASE tools are generally oriented toward generating DDL or application code offline. Most users of the data warehouse will not be using code generated by a programmer but will be interacting directly with the database and metadata repository to discover new information.

As data warehouses have become a main thrust of the entire IT field in the 1990s, some of these capabilities are being included into CASE tools. If your organization is currently using a particular CASE tool successfully, you should evaluate its capabilities for supporting the specific design requirements of a data warehouse. Perhaps you need to get an upgrade from the vendor to obtain necessary features. Beyond its usefulness as a design tool, you should also evaluate its capabilities for presenting an active metadata interface to users and their investigative tools.

Eventually these separate classes of tools (RDBMS, ETT, query, and CASE) may become better integrated into the entire data warehouse process. When that occurs, we will no longer have to maintain multiple repositories of our metadata.

Logical Schema Design Process

The process of designing the data warehouse database is a variation of that used in designing traditional OLTP systems' databases. Figure 4.2 demonstrates the typical "waterfall" approach used in the design of OLTP systems. Countless systems design methodologies have been developed that follow this general approach.

Figure 4.2 Traditional OLTP "waterfall" methodology.

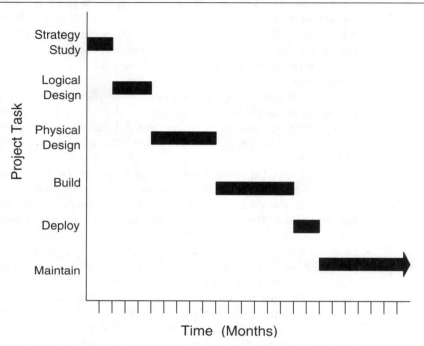

The warehouse design process shares some characteristics with the OLTP "waterfall" methodology. We have the same general steps to complete, but we visit the steps in a very different pattern. Figure 4.3 demonstrates our very short phases. For each phase, we iterate through the entire set of steps.

For the data warehouse, we typically still perform a strategy study that presents a case for management to justify building a data warehouse and defines the objectives, costs, rough implementation schedule, and resources needed. We will develop a logical design that documents the data requirements and relationships. Since the data warehouse is developed in incremental stages, we will typically start logical design by doing a very high-level subject area design that will be used to plan several phases of implementation. This corresponds to the preliminary design of the OLTP design methodology.

We can then do the detailed data modeling for Phase 1. The logical design does not take into account the specific implementation issues (such as clustering, partitioning, or indexing) of a particular database management system. When we have a complete logical model for a particular phase we translate it into a physical design that is very specific to the chosen DBMS. At this point we introduce specific features and capabilities of the DBMS that make our warehouse more manageable and provide optimal performance. We also take into account any DBMS limitations that might influence us to avoid specific design/implementation options.

Figure 4.3 Data warehouse iterative methodology.

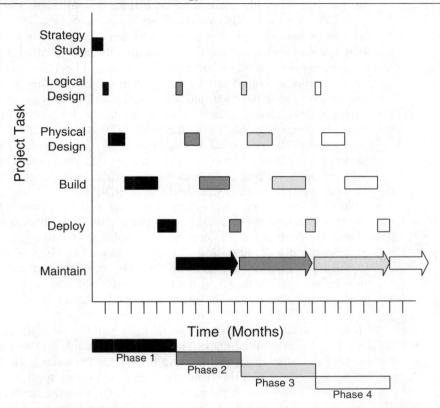

After completing the physical design for Phase 1, we will begin the actual development (build) and deployment tasks. As soon as Phase 1 has been released to the users, we will immediately return to review and possibly revise the high-level subject area design and then start on the detailed logical design phase for Phase 2. That will lead to the physical design and deployment for Phase 2 and so on.

Natural Keys versus Artificial Keys

The debate over whether to use naturally occurring keys or generate artificial keys when designing tables has raged for years within the ranks of experienced DBAs and database designers. There are valid arguments to be made for each approach.

Natural keys are the identifiers of entities in the real world. People and companies have names. Automobiles have license plates. Buildings have addresses. Unfortunately, these real-world keys are not as pure and precise as our systems and databases require. Natural keys fail in three common ways:

- **Uniqueness:** People and companies find that they do not have unique names when they are considered on a large enough scale. Just look at the repetition of names in phone books for a couple of large cities. Even automobile owners change license plates to create a unique persona. In databases, sometimes an artificial key has already been created and has been in use long enough that it functions like a natural key. Taxpayer IDs (social security numbers) and automobile VIN numbers fill this same role. But even these, as we have learned, are not always perfectly unique.

- **Complexity:** Timecard entries are naturally keyed by the company (or possibly division within the company!), by the identification (whatever it might be) of the employee whose time is being reported, by the date on which the employee worked, and by the specific project and task that was worked on. Very long and cumbersome natural keys like these are difficult to work with, both for people and for the RDBMS.

- **Absence:** Some things and events in the real world just do not have identifiers. A household watching a particular television show and changing channels during a specific commercial might be of interest to a marketing analyst, but it would be difficult to find a key much short of the total data available. Telephone calls fall into the same category. Operational systems that have been designed to track, measure, bill, and report such events have been forced to generate artificial keys for them.

With all these failings, perhaps artificial keys are the one right answer. Some designers would take this position. There are many Oracle OLTP systems in production that use sequence-generated artificial keys for every table. Within the processing logic hidden in the database foreign keys and application programs this works very efficiently. If properly designed, the resulting systems don't put a big burden on users to have to remember or reenter these key values. This potential user burden (and source of error) is the major argument against using artificial keys.

The same questions arise when designing the data warehouse database. Frequently, however, the issue becomes moot within much of the data warehouse. Unique identifiers on each row are particularly important in an operational system when we need to get to a specific row unambiguously and efficiently. As we load data into the data warehouse from the operational system, we want to avoid accidentally inducing duplicates by running a load job more than once. Other than that precaution, we typically won't have much need to quickly grab specific rows. Data validation and the enforcement of integrity rules are the responsibility of the operational source systems. Our responsibility is primarily to not introduce any additional errors during our processing; only secondarily do we have a responsibility to identify problems in the source system so we can pass that information back to the application support teams for investigation and correction.

Our two most common accesses to the data will be scripts to generate summary tables or user queries based upon a variety of user-specified conditions. In the first case, we generally will be summarizing data in such a way that its unique identifiers get lost in the summary. When we examine timecard data summarized to the monthly level, the artificial key that identified each row in the TIMECARD or TIMECARD_ENTRIES tables disappears—it is not part of our GROUP BY or calculated summarization columns.

In the second case, user-specified conditions are most easily specified in terms of the real-world keys where they exist. The second most useful conditions turn out to be those based on artificial keys introduced by the operational systems that have become "almost natural" through repeated use. Retrieving all the consultants and their total hours worked on a particular project during the third quarter of 1997 could be done by the project name or through a drill-down from the client name. If the user issuing the query were the departmental administrator who works every day with all the current project numbers, it might be simpler to enter that artificial key instead. The point is that in the data warehouse we have to provide for both accesses depending on our users' needs.

An additional difficulty arises when assigning artificial keys in the data warehouse. Since the data is not processed as a transaction, we commonly load new data into multiple tables independently. It can be very difficult to assign an artificial key to a new row in a dimension table and then later be able to assign the same value during loading of rows into the fact table. Doing so will prevent direct path loading of the data. Direct path SQL*Loader, described in Chapter 6, is the fastest means of loading large amounts of data.

So, in the context of the data warehouse, artificial versus natural keys is not much of a debate. We need not introduce new artificial keys just because a pure relational system's table must be "dependent upon the key, the whole key, and nothing but the key (so help me, Codd)." Where artificial keys are part of the source data, we may carry them forward into our detail data of the warehouse whenever there is user value in having them available. As always, a strong demand for being able to report on specific detail data should raise a red flag about the users' expected use of the warehouse—they may well be planning to perform some form of operational reporting that has not been satisfied within the source application.

Two Approaches to Warehouse Schema Design

To make our warehouse useful to our users we will go beyond loading raw data and letting them figure it out. We will load the raw data, probably preprocessing it to resolve name and formatting inconsistencies. We will then perform various aggregations to produce summary data in a form useful for our users. Through interviews and prototyping we discover that the finance department wants to view information about consulting projects from a monthly revenue perspective. Marketing, however, wants to ask questions about the amount of business being performed in various industries. Our recruiting and internal training groups are interested in spotting trends in the hours being worked in various job functions being performed so they can keep ahead of a growing demand for certain skills. Each of these groups anticipates issuing multiple queries that will need to see data summarized in different ways.

Detail and Summary Schema

We have already talked in some depth about detailed and summary data. Within traditional data warehouse design (does "traditional" mean anything in a field as new as data warehousing?), we provide data in a somewhat predigested form for our users. The raw source data (from various sources) contains all of the information that can potentially be derived from the warehouse. Without any processing constraints imposed by our hardware and RDBMS software we could just add a time stamp, load the voluminous raw data, and call it a warehouse.

There are, however, constraints that prohibit this approach. We don't want to incur the processing costs entailed in having multiple users repeat very large queries to get related information. We also don't want to force our users to traverse a confusing network of relational tables and foreign keys to build eight table joins with multiple-level correlated subqueries!

Detailed Data

Because of the large volume of detailed data produced by any modern corporation organizations must seek ways to limit their need to store and repeatedly process it. In some data warehouses detailed transaction data is never loaded. Light summarization is done during the extract process to minimize the cost and time transferring and loading the extract files. If you can accurately determine the lowest level of summarization that will be needed then this approach has merit. It also helps avoid the operational reporting trap that can accompany detailed data into the warehouse.

In other situations the decision is made to load detailed data. Early in the design of Phase 1 of the data warehouse a "requirement" is frequently stated that data will be retained for some extensive period of time, such as five years. One should at least question the need to view specific detailed transactional data from that far back. An alternative approach is to retain the detailed data for, say, twelve months and various summarizations for the five (or more) years.

A decision will eventually have to be made about retention, archival, or purging of old detailed data. Fortunately, this is not one of the pressing decisions during the initial setup and design of the first phase of the data warehouse. A tentative plan to purge thirteen-month-old detailed data each month can be reconsidered anytime during the first year of the warehouse's operation. You may later determine that archival may be a better strategy or that an eighteen-month retention period is more appropriate. Until you actually perform the first purge you have the freedom to reevaluate.

Summary and Aggregate Data

In most cases users will find the summarized data much easier to navigate. In building a summarization we can incorporate data from other related tables to avoid having to do joins from the summary. Of course, relational purists have to make some adjustments to their thinking—in the warehouse such denormalizations are proper.

The only difficulty arises from changes in the nonkey data. Is it possible for an organizational unit's name to change? For most companies, the answer is, "of course." How will that be addressed in the warehouse? What approach will accommodate the name change in February when doing a summarization on a quarterly or annual basis? You face a Hobson's choice dilemma:

- Include one name or the other in the summary row and only allow selection based on that name.
- Include neither name but allow a query-time lookup (still of one name or the other).
- Report separate results for queries based upon the two different organizational names (but merged data if a similar query were issued based on ORG_ID).

None of these three alternatives is perfect. Each will cause some confusion and the potential for erroneous results (or rather, erroneous interpretations of the results!). Generally, warehouse designers go with the third alternative. When nonkey data changes, we create a new row in whatever table (or, more likely, tables) includes that data and set appropriate values for effective and expiration date-time columns in both rows.

In our example of changing organization names, we might see the following entries in our summary data:

```
ORG_ID ORG_NAME        AREA  DIV MONTH QTR  YEAR INDUSTRY  HOURS  EXPENSES
123    Colo-Wyo-Utah   West  US  JAN   1    1997 Telecom   1,469  37,124
123    Colo-Wyo-Utah   West  US  FEB   1    1997 Telecom     897  19,459
123    Rocky Mountain  West  US  FEB   1    1997 Telecom     664  14,882
123    Rocky Mountain  West  US  MAR   1    1997 Telecom   1,629  42,668
```

Users who issue queries based on the new organizational name will only receive results starting with February 1997, and those results might be misinterpreted to suggest, for instance, that month-to-month growth between February and March (or Q1 1997 versus Q1 1998) was greater than it actually was. Users who queried based on the ORG_ID value would see a more complete picture of the telecom-related business performed within a given geographic territory. Actually, as this example illustrates, there is no single answer to this issue other than to keep data only in its most detailed form and process through it explicitly for each query. Since we cannot realistically do that with today's hardware and software this approach is the least offensive alternative. (We should not hold out hope for advances in hardware and software to resolve this issue in the future either. Even as quickly as these technologies evolve, our ability to create data seems to grow even faster.)

There are two other difficulties that arise when providing data through multiple summarizations. The first is anticipating what summarizations are necessary. Frequently users won't know what questions they will eventually need to ask until after they've worked with the warehouse for a while. This is the normal evolutionary development pattern of a data warehouse. There is not a problem adding additional summary tables in later phases while also expanding the variety of subject areas and data sources. This approach does, however, require that a sufficiently low level of detail be available upon which to base new summary tables. In the absence of a "final" warehouse design (which should never be expected) deciding to initially load and retain sufficiently detailed data is a reasonable insurance policy. After several design and delivery iterations the warehouse team will have a much better grasp of what data is likely to be needed in the future.

Introduction to a DW Case Study

The primary business at our fictitious "Consultants 'R Us" case study company is providing a variety of consulting services to many clients in a number of different industries. We employ thousands of consultants who provide these services. They have different skills and different levels of experience. Each consultant is assigned to a specific organization, but they often work on projects managed by a different organization. Each organization focuses on a geographic territory or a specific industry. Because of our excellent staff and high-quality engagements we frequently obtain repeat business and consult on many different projects for the same customer.

Our business tracks consulting assignments using a time and expense system that was developed in house about five years ago. Every project, client, consultant, and organization exists in the TEAM (Time Expense And Management) system. Each consultant is required to enter his or her time into the system every week and must assign every working hour to some project. We have created some nonclient projects associated with internal assignments, training, vacations, and the like so a time record will frequently have hours assigned to more than one project. Further, we have established function codes that are used to indicate the specific activities on any project. Although our transactions occur at least on a weekly basis, we will need to aggregate and report data for a given consultant, project, organization, and function on a monthly basis. Our extract and load procedures run monthly.

Our management wants to better understand the fundamental nature of our consulting business and wishes to conduct a range of analyses. Some of the expected analyses are as follows:

- comparative analysis of budget and actual revenues among organizations over time
- revenue associated with different types of consulting services
- revenue and profitability associated with our work in different industries or geographies
- profitability of specific projects, organizations, etc.
- utilization rates of consultants in various organizations

We have been asked to develop a data warehouse to support these types of analysis.

Figure 4.4 OLTP source system database design.

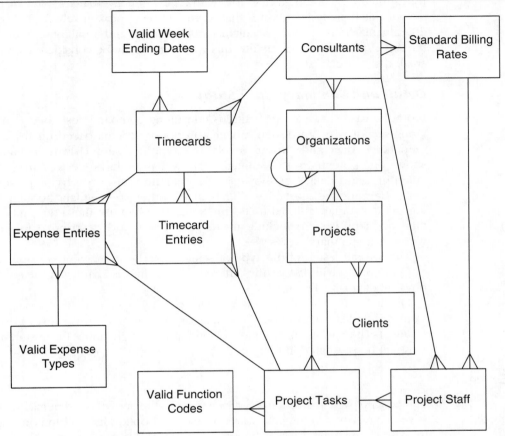

Figure 4.4 shows the logical model for the "Consultants 'R Us" TEAM operational system. The programming team that maintains TEAM system will be extracting data for our warehouse into flat files that will be transmitted to us after the close of each monthly billing cycle.

Organizations are grouped into regions, regions are grouped into areas, and areas are rolled up into divisions. This is a classic hierarchy, and for the TEAM application our company's development team designed the hierarchy with an ORGANIZATIONS entity and a recursive relationship that would allow us to combine each element in the hierarchy with its parent organization. This type of design would provide flexibility for changing the hierarchy, and Oracle's CONNECT BY function would allow us to rebuild the hierarchy structure. Such a design is not appropriate for a data warehouse, however. The performance overhead we would incur by having to process a CONNECT BY in order to calculate summaries at different levels of the hierarchy would simply be too great. For the warehouse, we will collapse the organization structure to a single level with a time component so we can later accommodate changes in the organization structure by adding a new row with a new effective date.

Our initial analysis indicates that there will be approximately 25,000 projects, 200 organizations, 10,000 consultants, 50 functions, and 5 million transactions in the ACTIVITY table. Incidentally, this would generally be considered a relatively small data warehouse.

Detail and Summary Case Study

From the case study of our fictitious consulting company described in the previous section we can design a data warehouse schema based on the concept of detailed data and various levels and types of summarization. Figure 4.5 shows one potential set of summary tables that might be derived from the detailed timecard data. Not shown in the diagram, but necessary to perform the denormalization discussed earlier, will be other source data about projects, consultants, organizational units, and so on. We will use these during our summarization process to include meaningful real-world descriptive information within our summary tables.

The logical design of this type of schema can be implemented using Oracle7 or Oracle8. We will discuss the differences later in this chapter in the section on physical database design.

Oracle7 and Oracle8 provide efficient parallel operations for populating the summary tables from the detailed data (or from another lower level of summarization). The specific techniques for building or maintaining these summary tables will be presented in Chapter 7.

Star Schemas

The concept of a star schema (or its variation, the snowflake schema) was a relatively late arrival in the data warehouse design option list. Bill Inmon's writings from 1992 and 1993 don't make reference to this design alternative. The primary reference work on this topic is Ralph Kimball's *The Data Warehouse Toolkit* (1996, Wiley-QED). This book is highly recommended for a more in-depth explanation of star schema concepts and application than is possible here.

The relational star schema is derived from multidimensional database design. The central fact table is related to several dimension tables. In relational terms, the fact table has a foreign key relationship to each dimension table. That is to say that each row inserted into the fact table will have values in the foreign key columns that correspond to primary key data in the various dimensions.

Other than these foreign key columns, the fact table consists of one or more columns that describe the volume, frequency, dollar value, or other numeric measure that can be summed, averaged, or aggregated in a query. Fact tables, by their very nature, are highly normalized—they consist of a concatenated key (which is the intersection of the various dimension keys) and one or more mea-

FOREIGN KEY RELATIONSHIPS

Even though these *relationships* between a fact table and its dimension tables are foreign keys, Oracle does not require them to be defined using foreign key *constraints*.

Figure 4.5 Relational "detail and summary" schema.

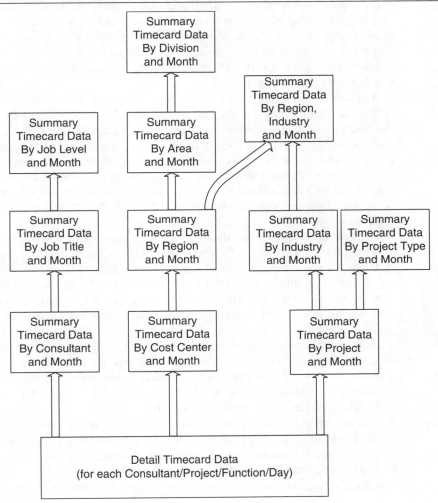

sures or attributes that are related directly to that key. Textual attributes are of little value in fact tables since they cannot be arithmetically combined when a query seeks to retrieve many rows, but are rather displayed in a few summarized output rows. Virtually all attributes in a fact table turn out to be measurements that can be meaningfully summed. In most cases the text attribute is more properly assigned to one of the dimensions.

True to traditional relational design, any descriptive attributes about the dimension will be stored in the dimension tables rather than the fact table. Numeric values that wouldn't make sense being summed (such as a consultant's hourly billable rate) would be dimensional attributes, not facts. These dimensional attributes can be used to help select data to be reported or included in the query output.

Dimension tables may be normalized around the specific dimension key. In many cases, however, where the dimension is naturally hierarchical, the hierarchy may be collapsed so that all but the lowest level of the hierarchy becomes nonkey attributes of the dimension. Figure 4.6 shows an example of taking a natural hierarchy from our company as it might be implemented in our OLTP systems. (In Figure 4.4, the OLTP schema ERD showed this as a recursive relationship on ORGANIZATIONS.)

Any additional attributes of the higher levels of the hierarchy (such as DIVISION_NAME, REGION_NAME, and AREA_NAME) will also be made attributes of the resulting collapsed dimension. This is a denormalization but continues to reflect the reality in that each value of ORG_ID is associated with a single value of DIV_CD. Instead of being reflected via the one-to-many relationships of the hierarchy this is reflected in a single value of the attribute for each individual key. Within the OLTP world such a denormalization would potentially require additional maintenance since a change of DIVISION_NAME would require updates to multiple rows.

Collapsing the hierarchy results in a single dimension within our star schema in which the user may specify any level of the hierarchy in his or her query. By specifying a value for any one of the attributes derived from the higher levels of the hierarchy, multiple rows of the ORGANIZATIONS dimension will be used to restrict the associated rows in the fact table to which the dimension is joined. As long as the number of rows in the resulting collapsed dimension is relatively small, this is an acceptable design.

One of the dimensions of virtually every star will be related to time. This dimension may be collapsed so that each daily record includes the week, month, quarter, and year associated with that day. Alternatively, the designer may choose (as we did in our case study) to maintain the week as the lowest level of granularity, or detail, in the fact table. This is identical to the decision made in designing the detail tables of the summary-based warehouse. After selecting a particular level of granularity, the designer is preventing warehouse users from ever obtaining information at a lower level of detail. The balance must be made between the possible uses of the data and the capability for storing even greater volume. Fortunately, new features for partitioning of large fact tables, combined

Dimensional Data Changes over Time

Note that changes to the name or other attribute of any level of the collapsed hierarchy still present a problem for reflecting history in the data warehouse. This problem is unchanged by collapsing the hierarchy. It can only be avoided by adding a time element (or version number) to the key of each dimension just as in the detail-and-summary schema discussed earlier in this chapter. This is an unfortunate aspect of the real world that complicates the purity of both forms of design.

Figure 4.6 Collapsing a hierarchical dimension.

**Hierarchy of
Organizational
Units**   (asterisk indicates a key)

**Collapsing the
Dimension
Hierarchy**

with improvements in the star query algorithm, allow Oracle8 to conveniently manage much larger volumes than were feasible before.

Dimension tables tend to be relatively small compared to the fact tables. Dimensions may include a few dozen or a few thousand rows. Fact tables frequently hold millions of rows. The voluminous fact tables would be very difficult to process frequently, even with index lookups. The objective of the star schema is to be able to efficiently select a subset of the total fact table by restricting the number of fact rows through limiting conditions specified about the dimensions. Consider an artificially simplified case in which a ten-million row fact table has six defined dimensions. Each dimension has one hundred rows. A query that selects a single row from each of only three dimensions would, assuming a normal data distribution, only retrieve ten rows out of the ten million (.01*.01*.01*10,000,000). This fact lookup (assuming appropriate indexes) can be performed very efficiently!

Oracle7 release 7.3 requires that a concatenated index on the foreign key columns in the fact table be used to perform the joins to the dimensions. The difficulty with this approach is that, to be useful, the index must include as its leading edge the columns used in the lookup. An index on columns A, B, C, D, E, and F could be used by a query that provides values (or join conditions) to A and B or A, B, and C, for instance. It could be used for a query that specifies A, B, and D, but would only use the restrictions obtained from A and B (not D). The index would not be used at all for a query that specified B, D, and E since the leading edge (A, B . . .) is not available. This situation results in the frequent need to create multiple indexes over various combinations of the foreign key tables in order to satisfy a wide variety of queries using different dimensions. These concatenated indexes on several columns of a multimillion-row table take a lot of effort and time to build and maintain. Keeping multiple indexes compounds the problem and requires a lot of storage space.

Oracle8 provides a great improvement on this optimization scheme. Rather than require use of a concatenated B*Tree index on the foreign key columns being used to join to the dimension tables, Oracle8's star transformation optimization will work with a separate bitmap index on each foreign key column. This is a perfect combination. The relationship of small dimensions to large fact tables naturally creates low cardinality (i.e., few valued) indexes (ideal for bitmaps). The specification of multiple dimensional criteria allows the use of the very efficient bitmap merge operation to precisely determine the correct rows from the fact table.

Star schemas in Oracle8 are much more efficient, in both space consumption and processing load, than in Oracle7 release 7.3. Further, the large fact table may, in Oracle8, be partitioned on a frequently specified dimension. In many cases, an Oracle8 star schema query can be executed in comparable time to a corresponding query against a predefined summary table. The star schema design, however, is much more flexible and saves a lot of space and advance processing effort. Eventually, using Oracle8, it is likely that more data warehouses will be designed around star schemas than traditional summary tables.

More exotic variations of the star schema, known as snowflake schemas, extend this model further. The snowflake "branches" correspond to different predefined levels of summarization in a traditional detail-and-summary warehouse schema. Kimball describes such designs extensively in his book. The implementation techniques demonstrated in this book for the simpler star design are directly extended to form a snowflake.

Star Case Study

The same information included in the detail-and-summary schema of Figure 4.5 can be modeled in a star schema as in Figure 4.7. Instead of predetermining which summary levels and GROUP BY columns are appropriate, the star schema allows the user to select the dimensions that interest them and display whatever aggregate values are important.

Generally, we will create our dimension tables so that for the lowest level of dimension detail we will store all the hierarchy information in the same row.

Figure 4.7 Star schema.

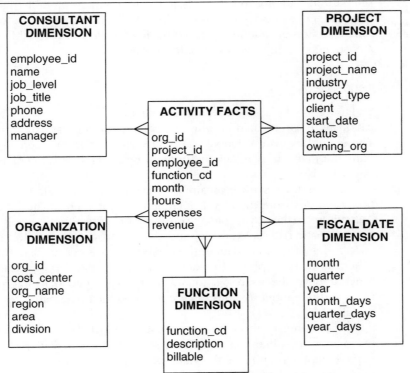

This makes maintenance of the dimension hierarchies more difficult, but presumably the hierarchical organizations change infrequently. We will deal with these slowly changing dimensions by maintaining multiple rows for the low-level detail information with an effective date column so that we can identify the correct hierarchy at any point in time if we have to maintain history. In our example, when a cost center is moved to a new region, we will create a new row in the dimension table with the new region and area data with a new effective date. This strategy allows us to look at the data from various points of view. We can look at our activity data by either the current organization projected back in time or the old organization projected forward in time or apportion the activity data to the correct organization according to a point in time.

We design the FISCAL_DATE table using similar reasoning. In this case, we flatten out what is essentially a time hierarchy. Time is a dimension of interest to users in almost every data warehouse. Given Oracle's capabilities for dealing with dates it is possible to manage a time dimension without actually having to implement a separate table. Our experience suggests that it is easier over the long run to implement a time table and treat it just like any other dimension. This is particularly true if a business uses accounting periods that are different from normal calendar time periods, for example, thirteen-week quarters with three months of four, four, and five weeks, respectively. In these situations, Oracle's standard date functions such as ADD_MONTH will not understand the non-standard accounting functions. Using a time dimension table makes such "artificial" calendar processing more simple. Users may still choose to use date functions in their queries to avoid having to join the date table when appropriate, such as when selecting data for a specific week.

External and Reference Data

So far we have discussed warehouse data as if it all originated within the application systems operated by our organization. To a great extent that may be true. There are, however, valuable sources of data that are not generated by our company but that can be integrated into our data warehouse to enhance the value of our own data.

One can, for instance, obtain an amazing range of data on industrial production and sales from the U.S. Department of Commerce. The U.S. Department of Agriculture makes available information on agricultural supply and consumption. Climatic data is available, and so on and on. One of the most commonly used forms of external data in the United States is census data, which provides a wealth of demographic information that can overlay an organization's sales territories to give the analyst a totally new insight into data interpretation. Postal code and telephone country/area code reference data can also be obtained externally.

The designer of the data warehouse should be constantly aware of the opportunities for obtaining data from sources outside of the company that will complement and enhance the value of internal data. In many cases, open-ended questions asked of the warehouse users will uncover the potential value of some form of external data. Then the research begins for where to obtain it, how much it will cost, how frequently it will have to be refreshed, and how to integrate it with other contents of the warehouse.

Physical Design

Physical database design is the process of translating the plan for either the detail and summary schema or the star schema into actual database structures. During this process the designer will accommodate the specific idiosyncrasies of the chosen database management system to meet the requirements of availability, performance, flexibility, and manageability.

Tablespace Design

An Oracle7 or Oracle8 database is organized into several tablespaces. Each tablespace receives an amount of disk space through one or more operating system file. Each object (e.g., table or index) that requires storage space is assigned to a tablespace and receives its necessary space allotment from the available space of the tablespace.

The primary design objective of tablespaces is to separate objects that have different requirements or "lifestyles." Tables should be separated from their indexes. Small tables should be separated from large tables. Two tables that are frequently joined should generally be in different tablespaces. Tables that are frequently scanned should be separated from those that are usually accessed randomly. Tables and indexes that are static—once loaded, data is not added or modified—should not be placed in the same tablespace with tables that receive regular maintenance. Extremely large tables or indexes are candidates to be split—partitioned—into smaller pieces that can then be placed into separate tablespaces.

Oracle's special types of segments (rollback and temporary) need to be placed in dedicated tablespaces of their own. The Oracle data dictionary, which resides in the SYSTEM tablespace, should not be impacted by putting any other data into SYSTEM.

OPTIMAL FLEXIBLE ARCHITECTURE

More detailed guidelines explaining why and how to separate segments into tablespaces are provided in the Optimal Flexible Architecture (OFA) whitepaper by Cary Millsap of Oracle Consulting Services' System Performance Group. This and other valuable whitepapers can be downloaded from www.europa.com/~orapub on the World Wide Web.

The only hard limit on the number of tablespaces is imposed by the number of files that can be included in a single database. In Oracle7 this is 1,022 files per database. Oracle8 effectively eliminates this restriction by increasing the number of files on most operating systems to 1,022 per tablespace and 65,533 per database.

The files associated with each tablespace should be striped across multiple disk drives whenever possible. This striping may be performed using the hardware or logical volume manager software techniques discussed in Chapter 2, or it may be done manually by creating multiple datafiles and then placing each onto a separate disk. The former approach will require less maintenance effort and will usually result in a better distribution of I/O. If raw files are used (for parallel server installations, for instance) then some small set of standard file sizes should be utilized across the entire database. If all raw files are sized at either 100 MB or 500 MB (as an example), it will be easier to redistribute I/O between busy and idle disks by exchanging files. Choosing a large variety of raw file sizes makes this sort of swap difficult or impossible.

Predicting Space Requirements

Chapter 5 discusses methods for predicting the size of individual tables and indexes. Unfortunately, this task is very difficult to do precisely before actually creating the tables and loading a sample of data. Once some data is loaded, the DBA should run ANALYZE to compute statistics that will provide a good estimate of the average length of a row and how many rows can be stored in each individual data block. Index storage is even harder to predict. To extrapolate an index's final size from sample data the sample must be well distributed across the full range of data values. If data from only one department is loaded, then an index on ORG_ID will not be representative of the storage requirements for all departments.

Planning for Growth

Data warehouse tables have very different growth patterns. Some detail tables (or fact tables) grow by a predictable number of rows each week or month. Some reference or dimension tables rarely change at all. In some cases, it is impossible to predict the volume of each periodic load because of the nature of the business application that feeds the data warehouse.

In every case, it is critical for the warehouse administrator to ensure that there is sufficient space available to accommodate the data to be loaded. Since load jobs tend to be scheduled in the wee hours of a weekend morning, it is essential that the processes are able to complete without manual intervention in order to add an additional datafile to a tablespace. Beginning with release 7.3, Oracle7 and Oracle8 have provided a way for a datafile to grow when its tablespace does not have enough freespace for the allocation of an object extent. It is implemented using the AUTOEXTEND clause as part of the file specification in the CREATE TABLESPACE and ALTER TABLESPACE . . . ADD DATAFILE commands. Allowing datafiles to automatically grow provides some insurance against the midnight failure of a load or index job. There is a downside, however, in controlling the use of disk space. When multiple datafiles are manually striped across several disks, the DBA will typically want to provide more space by manually adding an additional file on a different disk. If large file systems have been striped using either hardware or LVM software, then allowing files to automatically grow may be an appropriate strategy. (This feature has no value for use with UNIX raw files.)

Planning for Archival or Purging of Data

In addition to planning for the regular growth of the warehouse during periodic loads, the design team needs to consider the opportunity to remove older data when its value has passed. This seems like heresy to many first-time data warehouse designers. Most warehousing neophytes tend to think in a "first in, never out" manner. Keeping detail data forever may be appropriate for some subject areas in some data warehouses. Then again, it may be inappropriate in other situations. You should remain open to the opportunities for removing aged detail data from the warehouse. Keeping detail data from only the most recent twelve (or whatever appropriate number of) months will go a long way toward solving the warehouse growth problems. Specific techniques for performing archival and purging of data are presented in Chapter 6.

Partitioning Data

Extremely large tables should be considered as candidates for partitioning. Dividing a large object into smaller pieces can make each piece more manageable.

The data should not be split randomly. The objective should be to find one or more columns whose values will frequently be used to specify queries. This will allow the query optimizer to eliminate several partitions and look for data in just a small part of the total table. Ideally, these partitions should be roughly the same size.

Because of the normal time-related aspect of data warehouses, partitioning is typically done based on the transaction date of the source data. Each month (or quarter or year) of detailed data is assigned to a separate partition, which, in turn, is placed into its own tablespace.

Oracle7 and Oracle8 have very different approaches to partitioning. Oracle7 starts with separate tables and applies a UNION ALL view over them to make them appear to be a single object. This prevents a single index from being created to reference data in all the tables—each table must have separately created indexes. Keeping separate tables in Oracle7 requires more additional administrative work than does an Oracle8 partitioned table. In Oracle8, a single table can be created that has multiple partitions. A global index may be created on the entire table, and several maintenance options are provided for managing the partitions. A very large index can also be partitioned in Oracle8. Chapter 5 provides more information on this topic and gives examples of SQL syntax to create partitioned objects in both Oracle7 and Oracle8.

Indexing

In trying to find the data of interest to a particular query, Oracle always has the option of reading all the data in the table. For small tables, this is often the preferred access method. In many other cases, an index is needed to allow Oracle to more rapidly find a single row or a small subset of the total table. Indexes are created after the creation of a table and may be built based upon one or more columns of the table.

Which columns need to be indexed is determined by knowing the data and anticipating the types of queries that will be issued by users. The WHERE CLAUSE (and, in some rare cases, the ORDER BY clause) will determine which indexes can be used by the query.

The Oracle query optimizer's job is to determine which access path through the data will provide the fastest (or least-effort) solution. The newer cost-based optimizer should always be used in data warehouses managed by Oracle7, release 7.3, or Oracle8. Only the cost-based optimizer can take advantage of new access paths such as the star query optimization feature. To allow the cost-based optimizer to make informed choices between alternative solutions, current statistics on each table and index need to be gathered using the ANALYZE command (which is covered in Chapter 5).

By monitoring use of the data warehouse and the queries submitted by users, it will be possible to identify the need for additional indexes that might not have been anticipated when the warehouse was initially delivered. Unnecessary indexes, while wasteful of space, will generally not impair performance under the cost-based optimizer since it will choose to ignore an index that would cause additional work for the query. The older, rule-based optimizer, however, would go ahead and use an index even though doing so might be very inefficient.

B*Tree Indexes

B*Tree indexes are hierarchical structures that allow a rapid search (usually in no more than three or four logical I/Os) in order to obtain the address (ROWID) of a specific row in the data table that has a particular value. The structure of B*Tree indexes is covered in Chapter 3 and shown in Figure 3.8.

In a unique index only one row is pointed to by each index value. A nonunique index may have pointers to several different rows from each distinct value. As the number of rows addressed per key value increases, the efficiency of using the index falls. A B*Tree index on a two-value column, such as SEX_CODE, would generally point to rows in every block of the table. Simply scanning the entire table would be more efficient than bouncing back and forth between the index and the table.

COLUMN-LEVEL STATISTICS

When the data distribution is heavily skewed, a B*Tree index may have greater value to some queries than to others. An index on SEX_CODE might be very efficient for finding all the female patients in a Veterans Administration hospital assuming that they make up only a few percent of the total. On the other hand, using that same index to find all male patients would be very inefficent. For the cost-based optimizer to know the distribution of data within a column it is necessary to gather column-level statistics. This can be done by specifying the FOR COLUMNS option of the ANALYZE command.

Consider adding B*Tree indexes on a column of a large table when you anticipate queries that will need to return a small (less than 5 percent) subset of the total table based on WHERE clause restrictions on that column. (Nested loop joins will also be able to do this type of restriction based on looking up rows that match values found in another table.) Where multiple columns will be frequently used together to restrict rows returned by a query, then create one index on that set of columns. Select the most frequently specified column to be first in the index.

Bitmap Indexes

Bitmap indexes were also introduced in Chapter 3. Their logical structure and use are shown in Figure 3.9. Bitmap indexes are appropriate in situations where only a few distinct values occur within a column (or series of columns). This is called a low-cardinality column. Bitmap indexes are very efficient in their physical storage. A query can be very efficiently executed when the conditions of a WHERE clause allow multiple bitmap indexes to be used to restrict the rows of the table. The various nonselective bitmaps can be combined to provide a very narrowly restricted list of rows. An example of using multiple bitmaps was provided earlier in this chapter in the description of Oracle8 star query execution.

Consider using bitmap indexes on a table when there are likely to be several columns used in combination for many queries and each individual column has only a few distinct values and would be, on its own, very nonselective.

Other Structures

Oracle8 provides for several other types of structures that are less relevant to data warehousing. These include index-organized tables, reverse order indexes, index clusters, and hash clusters. Chapter 5 provides a description and syntax to create each of these objects.

Database Constraints and Triggers

Starting with Oracle release 6.0, the Oracle database designer has had the ability to declare data constraints as part of the definition of a table. Effective with Oracle7, the Oracle kernel enforces these rules to prevent data from being entered (or modified) that would violate the constraints. The types of constraints available to the Oracle7 or Oracle8 database developer include the following:

- **Check:** The check constraint allows the designer of a table to establish rules about the specific values that are allowed to be stored in a particular column. The rules allow comparison to constant values ("QTY_SOLD must always be greater than zero") or to the value of another column within the same row of the table ("SALES_DISCOUNT cannot be greater than LIST_PRICE"). Comparisons can be encoded using normal SQL comparison operators (such as =, >, <, IN, BETWEEN), and multiple conditions may be specified through the use of the SQL logical operators (NOT, AND, OR).
- **Not Null:** This one constraint has been enforced in releases of Oracle prior to Oracle7. It requires that some value be provided for the specified column in each row of the table. No row is allowed to contain a null (or absent) value. It is enforced by Oracle7 and Oracle8 as a special variety of a check constraint.
- **Unique:** The unique constraint on a column (or combination of up to sixteen columns in Oracle7 or thirty-two columns in Oracle8) of a table prevents two rows in the table from having the same value (or set of values) at the same time. Uniqueness is actually enforced by the automatic creation of a unique index that, before Oracle7, was the way this rule would have been enforced—the DBA would have manually created a unique index.
- **Primary Key:** Declaring a primary key for a table forces the values of data inserted (or updated) in the primary key column(s) to be both unique and not null. There can be at most one primary key defined for a table. The primary key on a table is used to define the identifier that can be used to uniquely distinguish between every row in the table.

- **Foreign Key:** This constraint is the only one that provides for evaluating data in one table based on values currently stored in another table. Rules such as "the PRODUCT_ID specified in an ORDER_LINE row must be a valid PRODUCT_ID in the PRODUCTS table" are implemented using foreign key constraints.

These five types of declarative constraints can represent most simple business rules as part of a table definition. More complex business rules can also be implemented by the database designer by writing database triggers. In Oracle7 and Oracle8, database triggers are developed in PL/SQL, Oracle's procedural language for database triggers, stored procedures and functions, and for the application logic within Oracle's application development tools such as Designer/2000.

Database Constraints in OLTP Systems

Designers of OLTP databases should always use Oracle's declarative constraints and triggers to ensure the integrity of the database. These constraints allow the database to do the important work of verifying that data being added or modified to a table follows some basic rules. When data in the database is corrupted, it frequently falls on the database administrator to develop a strategy for restoring data integrity. Even if the application programmers are to do some quick custom coding to restore order, while the database is under repair it is the DBA who frequently feels the heat from users and management. Self-preservation is reason enough for the DBA to insist on encoding basic data integrity rules into the OLTP database. There are, luckily, other more objective advantages to using database enforcement of rules.

It is preferable to have the database do this integrity checking in operational systems rather than depend upon the application code to enforce rules about the data. It isn't that the application programmers are irresponsible or untrustworthy; but frequently there are multiple application programs chartered with making changes to any one database table. Often these application programs are written by different programmers, frequently in different programming languages. Even when, twenty or so years ago, development teams made a concerted effort to write exhaustive analysis and design documents before starting to code, we frequently had problems with different interpretations of business requirements finding their way into the code of different transactions. For better or worse, today's 4GL client-server development environment is less disciplined and controlled than the old mainframe teams. Rules coded into the database only have to be written once as part of a table's definition and will apply to every transaction that affects that table. We get consistent enforcement of our rules.

Additionally, these constraints (and triggers) generally have performance advantages over equivalent rules embedded in application code. Performance is enhanced for many constraints by being implemented at a lower level of the Oracle kernel than SQL. These constraints therefore don't require the overhead of being parsed and executed as would application code. Even for more complex rules that are implemented using database triggers, there is efficiency in only having a single block of code to maintain in the shared pool as well as the significant savings in network traffic over a client-server dialog requiring multiple calls to the database.

Database Constraints in the Data Warehouse

In many ways, however, the data warehouse and the OLTP database have different objectives and approaches. Rarely is it appropriate to enforce the same level of constraints in the warehouse as in an operational system's database. This is true for several reasons.

PERFORMANCE

Performance considerations for the data warehouse are very different than those in the OLTP system. Transaction processing generally focuses on the performance of a single update. It is balanced against the integrity of the data touched in that single update. The overhead of a constraint or even a trigger acting on that one row is a small incremental cost when compared to the possibility of having inaccurate data entered into the database because of a data entry error or program logic bug.

Performance in the data warehouse must still be evaluated against data integrity, but the equation is different. Data integrity can be reasonably ensured because of the more limited source of data—existing application systems as opposed to multiple online screens and various batch postings. Also, because the data is initially entered into the data warehouse through large batch file loads as opposed to single row inserts it is easier to examine the data integrity of the entire file as one batch step prior to loading.

The other side of the equation, performance, is also affected indirectly by the batch nature of data loads. Typically, the warehouse builder will want to take advantage of some of the very specialized tools provided by Oracle for dealing with bulk data loads. Chapter 6 will cover the use of the direct path option of the SQL*Loader utility. Direct path SQL*Loader gains its speed by formatting and writing complete data blocks directly to disk, thus bypassing the overhead of buffer management and SQL-level processing in the Oracle kernel. Part of the overhead that is avoided is the handling of constraints and triggers.

Most constraints are automatically disabled on a table when it is loaded using the direct path. They can be reenabled after the load is completed, but this requires the complete examination of all data rows in the table. If the load added one million rows to a thirty-million row table, reenabling constraints will have to do a lot of extra work—thirty times as much! Unique and primary key constraints are enforced using indexes and are automatically reenabled (unless a parallel direct path load was performed) by building a new temporary index on the data that has been added and then merging it with the original index to form a new, bigger index. While this approach is usually faster than building the new index completely from scratch, it does require enough extra space in the tablespace to temporarily hold two copies of the index during the process. Triggers are also disabled during direct path loads. Data entered while the triggers are disabled will not be processed by the trigger logic, even when they are reenabled.

In short, one must choose between the potential integrity advantages of constraints or triggers and the substantial performance advantages of direct path SQL*Loader, particularly if it is run in parallel direct path mode.

RELATIONSHIPS

One of the most useful types of database constraint for ensuring integrity of data in a transaction processing database is the *foreign key constraint*. With a typical operational system database, relational tables are related to each other in a variety of ways. A common value for CUST_ID provides the linkage whereby a particular order is associated with a particular customer. The combination of CUST_ID and ORD_NUM link each of the appropriate order lines to that order and to that customer. Similarly, the sales order is linked to a particular salesperson record by embedding a value from the SALES_REPS table's primary key as a foreign key in the ORDERS table. Determining who the actual sales representative is, his or her department and manager, and so on can be done in the operational system by joining ORDERS to SALES_REP based on the equality of SALES_REP_ID in the ORDERS and SALES_REPS tables.

Occasionally, similar equality relationships exist in the data warehouse. Commonly, however, a different style of relationship is required for the data warehouse that is not based on a simple equality relationship. This is generally caused by the warehouse's different perspective on time. The operational system only has to track the current or latest state of the data. If a value is changed in the operational system, it is changed "in place" and supercedes the previous value.

In the data warehouse, by contrast, we need to track each of the various iterations of the data. As we examine historical data about sales on particular days or weeks or months, we may require related information as it existed at various points in the past. If the supplier for one of our products changed on October 1, we will later have warehouse queries wanting to know the cost of components that went into our product in September. We will also have to determine a different cost when we consider products manufactured in October. Depending on our accounting rules for inventory handling (FIFO, LIFO, etc.), we may discover interesting and valuable information in the warehouse besides the cost of sales shown in the accounting reports. We may also want to examine reliability differences in the product as it is delivered by the different suppliers.

But note the interesting change in the nature of the relationship. Instead of a straightforward equality of PRODUCT_ID in our operational ORDER_LINES table and PRODUCTS table, we have a warehouse PRODUCTS table with multiple entries for the same product, but each entry has effective dates included into the key structure. For a specific batch of our product we'll have to compare the DATE_OF_MANUFACTURE to the date ranges within our PRODUCTS table along with the equality comparison on PRODUCT_ID. This type of range comparison is just as valid a relationship as an equality test, but it cannot be implemented using a relational foreign key constraint.

Another kind of relationship is introduced into the data warehouse that does not have a counterpart in the operational world. The relationship of summary to detail data is not the same as a foreign key although it may often appear similar in that it is fundamentally one to many. As we build summary tables we may choose to partition or restrict data in different ways. The detail data (the "many" side of the relationship) may include specific CALL_DETAIL data for every call placed or received by one of our cellular customers. We might, however, create a summary table that includes a monthly summarization of only toll calls or roaming calls. The summary row in this table (the "one" side of the relationship) relates to multiple rows in the detail table. But not every row in the detail table has a corresponding row in this summary table. This would violate a relational foreign key relationship that requires each "child" to have a corresponding "parent."

As another example, we may choose to form several different summary rollups on our detail data. In one we might summarize domestic sales by region (excluding international sales) and in yet another aggregation we might just maintain a count of sales over $1 million by region, excluding smaller sales. The data in each of these aggregations is related to the detailed data from which it was developed, but not in the same sense as required by a foreign key relationship.

CHANGING BUSINESS RULES

Transaction processing systems are oriented around current rules and current snapshots of data. When a business rule or database structure change is needed, the current data in the OLTP system is restructured and processing continues. A data warehouse, however, generally keeps months or years of data. The data from two years ago was oriented around a set of business rules and structures that may no longer be current.

In some cases, it may be possible to restructure historical data to fit the new rules and structures. Even when possible, this is rarely a wise thing to do unless it can be done through an alternative rollup structure while preserving the historical integrity of the data as recorded.

In a much larger number of cases, there is no means of translating the historical data to cleanly fit the new business rule. Consider the changing sales territories in a fast-growing software company. Two years ago there may have been only twelve sales offices. The company's application systems may have included a check constraint to ensure that no other value could be entered. Last year, growth to twenty offices required an easy change in the operational systems' constraints. Now there are twenty-eight offices, and the rule has been changed accordingly. Which rule would you consider appropriate to add to the warehouse? The latest set of offices would have to be included to constrain current data. Data from two years ago would not be properly constrained, however, to the twelve offices current at that time. So what is the purpose of the constraint?

The proper approach to handling constraints would be to depend upon (and verify) the correctness of the operational systems so that extracted data is correct at the time it is added to the warehouse. Any additional information about sales offices should be kept in a separate table that includes a description of when each office was opened (and possibly closed).

But how would you change historical sales data if you decided to do so? If sales office territories are purely geographic, then it might be possible to determine which current office would have made the sale if it had been open. For some trend examinations, this might be useful information, but then we would lose access to other useful information, such as average annual sales per office over time. If the sales territories changed on more than just this one dimension, perhaps by the vertical industry and the size of the customer, it may not even be possible to determine a proper mapping. No record may have been saved of the customer size at the time of the sale two years ago. The customer may no longer exist or may be much smaller or larger today.

In general, it is not a good idea to try to restructure historical data in the warehouse. It is a difficult task to version your data structures and metadata, but it is a manageable one. Trying to constantly keep historical data in conformance with current organizational structures and business rules is an impossible quest.

Proper Uses of Constraints in the Data Warehouse

All this is not to imply that there is no place for database constraints in the data warehousing environment. Constraints have value and are sometimes required, but the warehouse designer also needs to understand their costs before employing them.

PARTITION VIEWS

Partition elimination using partition views in Oracle7 release 7.3 requires check constraints on each underlying table so that Oracle can be sure that data rows will be found in only the appropriate partition. Creation of partition views is described in the Chapter 5. (The equivalent declaration of partition boundaries in an Oracle8 partitioned table is done as part of the PARTITION clause syntax instead of check constraints.)

Database constraints serve two distinct purposes in an Oracle database. Oracle allows the administrator to either enable or disable any constraint. When enabled, a constraint will enforce a specific rule about the integrity of data in that table any time the data is inserted, updated, or deleted. When disabled, no en-

Disabled Foreign Keys

In Oracle version 6, constraints could be declared, but they were not enforced by the RDBMS. Few database designers took the time to declare them for just their documentation value. However, even back in the late 1980s users of data warehouses and some query tools discovered this trick of disabled foreign key constraints driving anticipated joins.

forcement is performed. The other purpose of a constraint is for documentation. The constraints are stored in and can be viewed from the data dictionary. This documentation may be of some value in meeting our metadata needs. It may also be of some value in supporting various query tools. Several query tools on the market do not install their own metadata layer, but they do attempt to use the Oracle data dictionary to support user query formation. When these tools determine that a foreign key relationship exists between two tables, they can anticipate the join criteria for any query that references both tables. In many cases, the tool is smart enough to see the relationship but (luckily) not smart enough to examine whether the relationship is enforced. Even if you don't want the overhead of enabling and enforcing constraints, sometimes it may be useful to "trick" a query tool into making life easier for your users.

NOT NULL CONSTRAINTS

Not null constraints are one exception to the general rule of constraints being disabled during direct path loads. Not null constraints are inexpensive to process, and they are automatically enforced during all loads. If the warehouse designer determines that a particular column should always have data and that there is some documentation or integrity advantage in having the database perform this check, then he or she should feel free (that is, unconstrained) in using the Not Null constraint.

PRIMARY KEY AND UNIQUE CONSTRAINTS

Primary key and unique constraints provide three functions for the data warehouse. One is to document the structure of the database and provide an identifier for locating individual rows within a table. The second is to benefit query performance through the underlying index. The final function is to help ensure data integrity; commonly, that might mean preventing a bulk data load from being executed a second time. The designer of the warehouse database should not necessarily follow the relational rule that every table must have a primary key. If there is a valid performance reason for needing the key to be indexed then, by all means, create the primary key constraint. However, there are cases in the data warehouse environment when tables may be created without a primary key.

The detailed data initially loaded into a warehouse may well not have a naturally occurring key. In an operational system, the Oracle designer faced with this situation would immediately define an artificial key and create a sequence generator to provide unique values. If, as is often the case, this lowest-level transactional detail data is being loaded into a warehouse strictly to allow the creation of various aggregations and summaries, then there may be no reason for a user to want to locate a specific row of detail. The designer should evaluate the potential documentation advantages. Perhaps they can be met by declaring, but not enabling, the constraint.

Further, there may be other cases when no anticipated query is going to take advantage of an index on the ORDER_ID column, which is the key generated for our ORDERS table back in its source operational system. Users may be expected to drill down to the detailed data to see particulars about a set of orders rolled up into some summary, but this drill-down would be based on the columns used in generating that summary. Normally, users of the data warehouse should not be trying to inquire into the details of order number 1873549. (If they are, there is a good chance that the warehouse is being misused to fill some deficiency in the operational systems.) If no query performance gain is expected from the underlying index, there may be no good reason to expend the effort to maintain the index.

Summary

One of the requirements for making a data warehouse useful is the need for metadata—data about the other data in the warehouse. There are various levels of metadata possible and various ways of maintaining and presenting metadata to our users.

One primary design decision is determining the appropriate level(s) of data granularity and the length of data retention. There are two primary models for designing an Oracle data warehouse—a traditional design based on precreation of summary tables and the newer alternative of star schemas. Either style of schema can be implemented using Oracle7 and Oracle8 features such as indexing and partitioning. Database constraints and triggers, commonly used in OLTP database design, have limited use in the data warehouse.

BUILDING THE ORACLE DATA WAREHOUSE

This chapter will examine the physical creation of a data warehouse in both Oracle7 and Oracle8. Careful planning when developing the database schema will help you ensure acceptable performance and avoid maintenance problems. This chapter will refer to a number of SQL commands and will provide some examples of the use of those commands. The chapter is not intended to be a tutorial on Oracle database administration and will not provide exhaustive descriptions of SQL command syntax. The Oracle reference manuals and other books are available for more complete syntax. Instead, we will focus on introducing commands and usage that are of particular relevance to implementing a data warehouse using the Oracle database.

We will introduce several development techniques that may seem obvious to experienced Oracle developers. In our experience, however, these may be unknown to developers new to the Oracle environment and are all too often ignored by experienced developers (yes, sometimes even painfully by ourselves).

Finally, we will actually demonstrate how to implement the data warehouse by creating the database, its tablespaces, and various types of tables, indexes, and views. We will show how to provide statistics about the tables and indexes to the Oracle cost-based optimizer. We will conclude with a discussion of the need for testing the data warehouse with a representatively large sample of data.

Using SQL*Plus to Create the Data Warehouse

In many cases the initial data warehouse project may not justify the purchase of CASE or ETT tools. Oracle's SQL*Plus provides a wonderful environment for both the developer and the DBA. We can just log into SQL*Plus, type in an SQL or PL/SQL command, execute it, edit it again, and reexecute until we get it right. Great—a developer's dream!

We should, however, resist the temptation to develop our warehouse in this haphazard fashion. No one would ever admit that this is how he or she works, but far too many of us slip into using just this approach when building a data warehouse. The warehouse tends to be evolutionary; it is easy to tweak and adjust, and at the margin there is never a clear need to create a formal script just to execute a fairly simple SQL command. There is one certainty to this approach, however: We will regret it eventually. We should always use scripts whenever we execute any SQL command. We will never do anything once, no matter what we may think at the time. We will execute the same command or something very similar in the future, we will be rewarded for the few extra minutes it may take to create a script file when we first execute a command. Moreover, to paraphrase the famous bumper sticker, "Bad Stuff Happens"—no matter how careful and how certain we are or how easy something is, we will occasionally make mistakes. Sometimes the mistakes manifest themselves in subtle ways and are not observed until much later during data loads or even user access. It makes life much easier (and promotes career longevity!) to maintain a record of exactly what actions were taken before the appearance of the error(s). It's easy to maintain a history of our activities using Oracle.

Keeping Logs of Your Actions

The SQL*Plus SPOOL command can be used to create log files for all our activities. Ensuring that we spool the output of our script will enable us to easily track any errors that may occur while we are creating the database schema.

```
SPOOL KEEP_LOG.LST
<list of SQL and SQL*Plus commands>
SPOOL OFF
```

In this simple example of a SQL*Plus script, everything from the SPOOL command through the SPOOL OFF command will be logged to the file named KEEP_LOG.LST. A long list of commands may scroll quickly by on our screen or may even require hours to run overnight. In either case, it will be easier to review the log after the completion of the script. We will also use SPOOL later in this section to help us save generated SQL output into a new SQL script file.

SQL*Plus Formatting Commands

The SQL*Plus environment provides a number of special commands that can be used to control how SQL*Plus displays output. We refer the reader to the Oracle7 or Oracle8 *SQL*Plus User's Guide and Reference* for a complete description of the SQL*Plus commands. SQL*Plus commands are completely different from SQL commands. SQL*Plus commands are only recognized in the SQL*Plus environment, and they are unique to Oracle. SQL commands are used in many different Oracle tools, and they are frequently standard across various vendors' RDBMS environments (most vendors use ANSI standard SQL with their own extensions). It is possible to create very sophisticated reports with totals and subtotals, word wrapping, titles, footers, and other complex formats using only SQL*Plus. Most developers will choose a more graphical reporting tool than SQL*Plus to create sophisticated reports.

Since our primary interest in this chapter is on creating the data warehouse and not creating reports, we will focus on the several commands that are indispensable to a data warehouse developer or manager. There are a number of variables that control SQL*Plus processing that can be manipulated using the SQL*Plus SET command. The general syntax of the SET command is SET *variable_name value*. We will simply include the necessary SET commands in our SQL*Plus script file to create the desired execution environment for our script.

For example, we may sometimes want SQL*Plus to print a page break after 62 lines when we are sending output to a laser printer. We may want to set page breaks to occur after every 22 lines when we are displaying to a monitor, and we don't want the output to scroll past too fast. We will use two SQL*Plus commands to create an environment where the page will display on one terminal screen and then prompt us to scroll to the next page of output. SET PAGESIZE 22 (typically abbreviated as SET PAGES) will produce a 22-line output page. Next we need to make sure the display just doesn't scroll right past the page break all the way to the end. We accomplish this with the SET PAUSE command. SET PAUSE ON will cause SQL*Plus to display a full page of data (which we just defined to be 22 lines) and then stop until the user presses a key on the keyboard. We would like to present a prompt (so the user knows to press a key and doesn't think the command is just executing slowly). We can use SET PAUSE message to pause and print the reminder message. When we use SET PAUSE More, SQL*Plus will print a page of output, print the message, "More" on the display, and pause until it receives a keystroke. Our script file will look like this:

```
SET PAGES 24
SET PAUSE ON
SET PAUSE More
SELECT TABLE_NAME FROM DICT;
SET PAGES 62
SET PAUSE OFF
```

We set our page size back to the value used for printing and turn off the pause function after we execute our SQL command.

There are a large number of SET commands available. Some of the more useful ones include the following:

- **ECHO (ON/OFF):** Controls whether the command file will display each command as it executes it. The default value is OFF.
- **FEEDBACK (OFF/ON/n):** Controls whether SQL*Plus will display the number of rows returned from a query at the bottom of the query result set. Setting FEEDBACK OFF suppresses the display. It is possible to provide a value so that FEEDBACK is provided only if there are more rows than the value specified. Setting FEEDBACK 10 will result in FEEDBACK only if there are more than ten rows returned. The default value is 6.

- **HEADING (OFF/ON):** Controls whether SQL*Plus will display the column heading at the top of each output page. SET HEADING OFF suppresses column headings.
- **LINESIZE (n):** Controls the width of the display before the line wraps. The default value is 80.
- **NEWPAGE (n):** Controls the number of blank lines printed at the top of each new page. Setting NEWPAGE 0 will result in a page feed before the start of each new output page.
- **PAGESIZE (n):** As demonstrated earlier, SET PAGESIZE controls the number of lines per output page. SET PAGES 0 will result in no page breaks at all. It also suppresses column headings.
- **TERMOUT (OFF/ON):** Controls whether the output displays to the terminal. Frequently, we will set TERMOUT OFF if we are executing batch scripts and are spooling output to a file. Even if we are executing scripts in an interactive session, it may be useful to set TERMOUT OFF to speed execution. Remember to spool the output to a file and be careful not to use the SET PROMPT command when setting TERMOUT OFF (SQL*Plus will wait for a keystroke, but the user will not be able to see the prompt).

Using SPOOL to Unload Table Data

We frequently need to create a "flat" file from a table, and using SQL*Plus commands allows us to do this easily. This is useful for dumping data from a source system to be loaded into the data warehouse or for archiving data from the warehouse into a file that could be easily loaded back into the warehouse using SQL*Loader. To unload a portion of our ACTIVITY table to a flat file we could use the following command file:

```
SET FEEDBACK OFF TERMOUT OFF PAGES 0 HEAD OFF
SPOOL FLAT_FILE.LST
SELECT ORGANIZATION_ID, REVENUE
  FROM ACTIVITY
 WHERE MONTH = '1997MAR'
/
spool off
```

Note that we can place several options to a single SET COMMAND on one line.

We will present a more complete example of using SQL*Plus to extract data from an Oracle source system and build a corresponding SQL*Loader control file in Chapter 6.

Passing Values to a Script at Run-time

Since one of our goals is to consistently use scripts for managing our data warehouse, we should strive to make them as generic as possible by using the SQL*Plus capabilities for passing variable values to a script. If we preface a variable name in the SQL*Plus command with a single ampersand (&), SQL*Plus will prompt for the substitution value by printing the variable name and waiting for input. SQL*Plus will prompt each time it encounters &*variable_name*. Suppose we want to run a simple script to check for the total number of records loaded into the data warehouse and the total revenue value for a given month. These values will be checked against totals calculated from our source systems to ensure we have accurately extracted and loaded the data. We can create a simple script using a substitution variable for the month we want to check.

```
SPOOL  CHECK_LOAD.DAT
SELECT COUNT(*), SUM(REVENUE)
  FROM ACTIVITY
 WHERE MONTH = '&MONTH';
SPOOL OFF
```

To avoid having to enter the same value repeatedly in a SQL*Plus script that references the &*variable* several times, we can use the &&*variable_name* construct. The double-ampersand variable will prompt for a value only the first time the particular variable is encountered and will automatically substitute thereafter. In the following example, we choose to use two SELECT statements that will both require specification of the MONTH variable. Because the first is referenced by &&MONTH, the value will be saved and we won't be asked for a value when the second SQL statement is executed.

```
SPOOL  CHECK_LOAD.DAT
SELECT SUM(REVENUE)
  FROM ACTIVITY
 WHERE MONTH = '&&MONTH';
SELECT COUNT(*)
  FROM ACTIVITY
 WHERE MONTH = '&MONTH'
SPOOL OFF
```

Frequently, we will want a more descriptive prompt than simply the name of the variable. We can use the SQL*Plus ACCEPT command to provide a more descriptive prompt. The ACCEPT command specifies the name of the variable and then specifies the keyword PROMPT followed by a string that defines what should be displayed on the user's screen when input is expected.

```
SPOOL CHECK_LOAD.DAT
ACCEPT  CHECK_MONTH  PROMPT 'Enter the month (YYYYMON): '
SELECT SUM(REVENUE)
  FROM ACTIVITY
 WHERE MONTH = '&&MONTH';
SELECT COUNT(*)
  FROM ACTIVITY
 WHERE MONTH = '&&MONTH';
UNDEFINE MONTH
SPOOL OFF
```

We issued the SQL*Plus UNDEFINE command at the end of this script, which clears the saved value from this variable. This is particularly useful if we are using the *&&variable* construct to maintain persistence of the variable across several references as the script runs but we would also like to be prompted again for the variable value each time the script is reexecuted. (*&&variables* are automatically UNDEFINEd when exiting SQL*Plus.)

Writing Scripts for Execution in Batch

Some scripts are best run as batch procedures because they may take a long time to run or should be executed during nonbusiness hours. It is easy to set up an environment to execute batch SQL*Plus procedures using parameters. This requires a slight modification to our SQL*Plus scripts. Since we are going to pass parameters from the command line, we will need to ensure that our scripts use substitution variables that are numbers (e.g., "&&1," "&&2," etc.). The number refers to the relative position of the parameter value on the command line. We will remove the ACCEPT command from script file because we are not going to prompt for a value interactively but will pass the parameter value from the command line when we invoke SQL*Plus.

When we enter SQL*Plus we must provide our Oracle userid and password, shown here as UID/PWD. We can also pass the name of a SQL*Plus command file using the @ symbol followed by the name of the command file to execute. We place our substitution values after the command file name, with each value separated by a space. To run our example script, we would issue the following command:

```
sqlplus UID/PWD  @CHECK_LOAD 1997MAR
```

Specifying Passwords on the UNIX Command Line

Entering the userid and password on the command line poses some security risks in the UNIX environment. Any user who issues a UNIX ps command will be able to see the full command line of executing processes. A more secure approach to providing connection information to scripts is to use Oracle's operating system authentication feature (frequently referred to as "OPS$" accounts for the default prefix given to the Oracle account name). Security checking by Oracle is simplified for Oracle accounts defined in this way. The user is automatically allowed to connect to the Oracle account that corresponds to his or her operating system account, which, presumably, has already been verified.

Since our script is going to run in the background, we will need to tell the script to exit SQL*Plus after completing our processing. The actual script that we modified now looks like this:

```
SPOOL CHECK_LOAD.DAT
SELECT SUM(REVENUE)
  FROM ACTIVITY
 WHERE MONTH = '&&1';
```

```
SELECT COUNT(*)
  FROM ACTIVITY
 WHERE MONTH = '&&1';
SPOOL OFF
EXIT
```

Now that we know how to execute a SQL*Plus script and pass parameters directly from the command line, we want to extend our ability to allow us to submit a job that will run in batch. Unfortunately, the exact syntax for that depends upon the operating system on which Oracle is run. Since many data warehouse projects are implemented on a UNIX operating system, we will describe how to create a simple batch procedure for UNIX. UNIX provides the nohup command that enables you to start a UNIX process that will continue to run even if the connection between your terminal and the UNIX server is broken. By combining the nohup command with the & command to execute a UNIX process in the background it is possible to create a very simple, yet flexible, method for submitting batch procedures on UNIX. We can execute our CHECK_LOAD.SQL script in batch mode using the following UNIX syntax:

```
nohup sqlplus UID/PWD @CHECK_LOAD 1997MAY > outfile &
```

The > in the UNIX syntax redirects the output to the specified file name ("outfile") and the & command instructs UNIX to run this command in the background. We can make this even easier by creating a generic UNIX shell script that will invoke "sqlplus" and pass our UID/PWD, SQL*Plus script file, and necessary parameters using the UNIX command processor. We create a simple UNIX shell script called GO_SQL as follows:

```
sqlplus "$1"  @"$2" "$3"
exit
```

The "$1," "$2," and so on are UNIX parameters that receive arguments from the UNIX command line and, where appropriate, substitute the values and pass them into the Oracle script. In our example, $1 represents the Oracle UID/PWD, $2 is the file system name of our SQL*Plus command file, and $3 is the SQL*Plus parameter that passes the date to our SQL*Plus script. Using the UNIX nohup

UNIX nohup Command

The UNIX nohup command gets its name from "no hangup." When UNIX was initially developed users frequently connected from a dial-up TTY device. When running long operations there was no guarantee that the online session could be maintained until the script completed. Thus, nohup was invented to allow the process to continue even if the user's connection was broken.

command described earlier we now have a flexible method for executing any SQL*Plus command file in batch mode as follows:

```
nohup GO_SQL UID/PWD CHECK_LOAD 1997MAY > output &
```

In the process of managing a data warehouse you will accumulate many different scripts. It is very convenient to store the names and functions of the scripts in the database. Simply create a table that includes a column for file name, a column for description, and a longer column for any appropriate documentation.

Oracle7 allows data in a VARCHAR2 column to be up to two thousand bytes in length. Oracle8 extends this limit to four thousand bytes. It would be possible to store larger amounts of documentation using either the Oracle8 CLOB data type (storing up to four gigabytes) or the LONG data type (in Oracle7, which can store up to two gigabytes). Before using the LONG data type, be sure that its many restrictions will not present a problem. LONGs cannot be replicated or used in the SELECT list of a CREATE TABLE AS SELECT statement. They cannot be used in a WHERE clause or in SQL character functions (such as SUBSTR), which makes LONGs difficult to search. In general, Oracle8 databases should be created using the CLOB data type rather than LONG.

```
CREATE TABLE SCRIPTS
      (SCRIPT_NAME        VARCHAR2(30),
       SCRIPT_TYPE        VARCHAR2(8),
          CONSTRAINT SCRIPT_TYPE_CK
CHECK (SCRIPT_TYPE IN ('SQL','SHELL')),
       SCRIPT_DESCRIPTION  VARCHAR2(200),
       AUTHOR             VARCHAR(30),
       LAST_MODIFIED      DATE,
       DOCUMENTATION      VARCHAR2(2000),
          CONSTRAINT SCRIPTS_PK
PRIMARY KEY (SCRIPT_NAME, SCRIPT_TYPE) )
   TABLESPACE USER_DATA
   STORAGE (INITIAL 1M NEXT 1M PCTINCREASE 0);
```

You can use the techniques just described to create a script that prompts for the necessary information and inserts it into the database. This makes it much easier to find a script that performs a particular function that you may have written months ago.

One additional advantage that naturally occurs when consistently using scripts to execute commands for managing the data warehouse is that we are far more likely to provide some documentation as part of the script. Don't plan on going back and documenting what each script does after the warehouse is up and running. Because a warehouse is an evolutionary creation, there is rarely a point at which we will feel we can "spare" the time to create the documentation. We just keep adding more and more routines (just a few at a time, so it doesn't seem that bad) until we have an unmanageable mess. Document the scripts as you create them. You will be glad you did!

Using SQL to Generate SQL

One additional technique that we need to explore in detail is a method for using SQL itself to create other SQL statements. This technique is very powerful, and we will use it frequently in managing our data warehouse. Let's suppose that we just happened to create some test tables in our data warehouse and, since we knew they were just test tables, didn't bother to create a script to execute the CREATE TABLE command. Those tables turned out to be so useful that we really want to move them into our production environment. We want to reverse-engineer our CREATE TABLE scripts from information in the data dictionary. (This is a good exercise even though this action would be easy using the Oracle EXP/IMP utilities or if we were using an automated design tool). This is a perfect opportunity to explore how to use SQL to generate other SQL statements.

Generating Text Output

First, it's obvious that if we were to issue the following SQL statement and spool it to a file, we would end up with a command file that could be used to create a very simple table.

```
SELECT 'CREATE TABLE TEST '||
'(TEST_COLUMN VARCHAR2(10), '||
'TEST_COLUMN2 NUMBER(5,2));'
FROM DUAL;
```

This SQL statement gives the following output:

```
CREATE TABLE TEST (TEST_COLUMN VARCHAR2(10), TEST_COLUMN2 NUMBER(5,2));
```

This works because we are simply selecting a constant string. We simply need to extend this to select information from the data dictionary. The data dictionary table DBA_TAB_COLUMNS contains the column names and data types for every column in every database table. We can issue a SQL SELECT statement to produce a list of the columns, data types, and data length for every column in our PROJECT_REV table:

```
SELECT COLUMN_NAME, DATA_TYPE, DATA_PRECISION, DATA_SCALE,DATA_LENGTH
  FROM USER_TAB_COLUMNS
 WHERE TABLE_NAME = 'PROJECT_REV'
   AND OWNER = 'DW';
```

COLUMN_NAME	DATA_TYPE	DATA_PRECISION	DATA_SCALE	DATA_LENGTH
PROJECT_ID	NUMBER	13	0	22
COST_CENTER	VARCHAR2			30
LEDGER_DATE	DATE			7
TOTAL_REVENUE	NUMBER	15	2	22

Generating Output from Multiple Queries

There are still a couple of problems we have to solve. First, our output has several sections that have different numbers of lines. The first section will be a single line of output that contains the CREATE TABLE *tablename* (phrase. This repeats only once for the table we are working with. Then we will need a second section with several lines of output corresponding to each of our column names and data types. This portion of the output will repeat as many times as we have columns in the table. Finally, we will need to end our output with a third section that will again occur only once for each table.

We can solve this problem—multiple parts of our desired output requiring different SELECT statements—using the UNION operator. UNION allows us to combine the results from several SELECT statements into a single result set. We can UNION any SQL statements together as long as the number and data types of columns in each SELECT statement are identical:

```
SPOOL CR_TAB_PROJECT_REV.SQL
SET PAGESIZE 0 FEEDBACK OFF
SELECT 'CREATE TABLE PROJECT_REV ('
  FROM DUAL
UNION
SELECT column_name||' '||data_type||'('||data_length||'), '
  FROM USER_TAB_COLUMNS
 WHERE TABLE_NAME = 'PROJECT_REV'
UNION
SELECT ')TABLESPACE PROJECT_TS;'
  FROM DUAL;
SPOOL OFF
```

Executing this SQL statement produces the following output:

```
COST_CENTER VARCHAR2(30),
CREATE TABLE PROJECT_REV (
LEDGER_DATE DATE(7),
PROJECT_ID NUMBER(22),
TOTAL_REVENUE NUMBER(22),
)TABLESPACE PROJECT_TS;
```

Sorting the Output

This is getting close, but we need to change the order so that the output of the first SELECT statement sorts at the top and output from the second SELECT sorts next (and in the proper column order), followed by the output of the third SELECT. We can control this by introducing a dummy column that is used for nothing more than controlling the sorting order. We use the SQL*Plus NOPRINT command to suppress output of the sorting column.

We still have another problem in substituting the correct values for each column's size specification. We can use the DATA_LENGTH column for our VARCHAR2 columns, but we need to specify a precision and scale for our NUMBER columns. For DATE columns, we don't need to specify a length at all. We can address the problem of providing precision and scale for NUMBER columns, length for VARCHAR2 columns, and no size arguments for DATE columns by using several different SELECT statements combined with the UNION operator. (There is a more elegant method for accomplishing the same thing that uses the DECODE function. We will discuss various uses of DECODE later in this chapter).

```
COL DUMMY NOPRINT
SELECT 1 DUMMY, 'CREATE TABLE PROJECT_REV ('
  FROM DUAL
UNION
SELECT 2, COLUMN_NAME||' '||
        DATA_TYPE||'('||DATA_LENGTH||'),'
  FROM USER_TAB_COLUMNS
 WHERE TABLE_NAME = 'PROJECT_REV'
   AND DATA_TYPE = 'VARCHAR2'
UNION
SELECT 3, COLUMN_NAME||' '||
        DATA_TYPE||'('||DATA_LENGTH||'),'
  FROM USER_TAB_COLUMNS
 WHERE TABLE_NAME = 'PROJECT_REV'
   AND DATA_TYPE = 'NUMBER'
   AND DATA_PRECISION IS NULL
UNION
SELECT 4, COLUMN_NAME||' '||
        DATA_TYPE||'('||DATA_PRECISION||','||DATA_SCALE||'),'
  FROM USER_TAB_COLUMNS
 WHERE TABLE_NAME = 'PROJECT_REV'
   AND DATA_TYPE = 'NUMBER'
   AND DATA_PRECISION IS NOT NULL
UNION
SELECT 5, COLUMN_NAME||' '||DATA_TYPE||','
  FROM USER_TAB_COLUMNS
 WHERE TABLE_NAME = 'PROJECT_REV'
   AND DATA_TYPE = 'DATE'
UNION
SELECT 6, ')TABLESPACE PROJECT_TS;'
  FROM DUAL;
 ORDER BY 1;
```

(handwritten annotations: } Varchar2 } num (no precision) } num (w/precision) } Date)*

This yields the following:

```
CREATE TABLE PROJECT_REV (
COST_CENTER VARCHAR2(30),
PROJECT_ID NUMBER(10,0),
TOTAL_REVENUE NUMBER(13,2),
LEDGER_DATE DATE,
)TABLESPACE PROJECT_TS;
```

Our sorting still isn't quite correct. So far, we've used a brute force method of handling each different data type appropriately, but we need to sort the columns based on their order in the original table. Fortunately, the USER_TAB_COLUMNS table includes a column, COLUMN_ID, that defines this order. We will add another sort column to do this sorting within our second section. Since the number and type of data columns in each SELECT of a UNION query must match, we'll also have to add another dummy column within our first section. We'll use the first DUMMY column strictly to control in which section an output line will appear. The new DUMMY2 column will control the order within the section. This leads us to our next iteration:

```
COL DUMMY1 NOPRINT
COL DUMMY2 NOPRINT
SELECT 1 DUMMY1, 1 DUMMY2, 'CREATE TABLE PROJECT_REV ('
  FROM DUAL
UNION
SELECT 2, COLUMN_ID, COLUMN_NAME||' '||
       DATA_TYPE||'('||DATA_LENGTH||'),'
  FROM USER_TAB_COLUMNS
 WHERE TABLE_NAME = 'PROJECT_REV'
   AND DATA_TYPE = 'VARCHAR2'
UNION
SELECT 2, COLUMN_ID, COLUMN_NAME||' '||
       DATA_TYPE||'('||DATA_LENGTH||'),'
  FROM USER_TAB_COLUMNS
 WHERE TABLE_NAME = 'PROJECT_REV'
   AND DATA_TYPE = 'NUMBER'
   AND DATA_PRECISION IS NULL
UNION
SELECT 2, COLUMN_ID, COLUMN_NAME||' '||
       DATA_TYPE||'('||DATA_PRECISION||','||DATA_SCALE||'),'
  FROM USER_TAB_COLUMNS
 WHERE TABLE_NAME = 'PROJECT_REV'
   AND DATA_TYPE = 'NUMBER'
   AND DATA_PRECISION IS NOT NULL
UNION
SELECT 2, COLUMN_ID, COLUMN_NAME||' '||DATA_TYPE||','
  FROM USER_TAB_COLUMNS
 WHERE TABLE_NAME = 'PROJECT_REV'
   AND DATA_TYPE = 'DATE'
UNION
SELECT 3, 1, ') TABLESPACE PROJECT_TS;'
 ORDER BY 1, 2;
```

This yields the following:

```
CREATE TABLE PROJECT_REV (
PROJECT_ID NUMBER(10,0),
COST_CENTER VARCHAR2(30),
LEDGER_DATE DATE,
TOTAL_REVENUE NUMBER(13,2),
) TABLESPACE PROJECT_TS;
```

Final Formatting

To make our script more generic, we'll remove the hard-coded table name from each of the SELECT statements' WHERE clauses and use a substitution variable.

We still have the problem of the extra comma on what should be the final line of our column definitions. Solving this problem will involve a quick usage of the DECODE function, which will be more fully described later in the chapter. On the surface it appears that our problem involves deciding which is the final line of output and then suppressing the comma. This approach is a bit complex because we don't know, in advance, how many columns any given table will contain. We can use a subquery to determine the maximum value of COLUMN_ID and print a comma for all lines that don't match this maximum value.

Another (simpler) solution is possible if we restate the problem. The goal is to separate each column's definition from other columns with a comma. Rather than thinking of putting a comma after every line but the last, we can choose to put a comma before every line except the first. It is very easy to find the first column (COLUMN_ID = 1) for every table. Putting the comma at the start of the next line will make our output will look a little odd, but it will function identically.

The DECODE function serves as a test. It takes, in this simple case, four parameters. Whenever the first two parameters are equal, the DECODE will return the value of the third parameter. If the first two are not equal, then the value of the fourth parameter will be returned. We will test the value of COLUMN_ID to see if it is equal to 1. If so, we will print a space, but if not we will print a comma. Here, then, is our final script to regenerate the basic CREATE TABLE statement for any table in our schema:

```
ACCEPT table_name PROMPT 'Generate CREATE TABLE for which table? '
COL DUMMY1 NOPRINT
COL DUMMY2 NOPRINT
SELECT 1 DUMMY1, 1 DUMMY2, 'CREATE TABLE &table_name ('
  FROM DUAL
UNION
SELECT 2, COLUMN_ID, DECODE(COLUMN_ID, 1, ' ', ',')||COLUMN_NAME||' '||
       DATA_TYPE||'('||DATA_LENGTH||'),'
  FROM USER_TAB_COLUMNS
 WHERE TABLE_NAME = '&table_name'
   AND DATA_TYPE = 'VARCHAR2'
UNION
SELECT 2, COLUMN_ID, DECODE(COLUMN_ID, 1, ' ', ',')||COLUMN_NAME||' '||
       DATA_TYPE||'('||DATA_LENGTH||'),'
  FROM USER_TAB_COLUMNS
 WHERE TABLE_NAME = '&table_name'
   AND DATA_TYPE = 'NUMBER'
   AND DATA_PRECISION IS NULL
UNION
SELECT 2, COLUMN_ID, DECODE(COLUMN_ID, 1, ' ', ',')||COLUMN_NAME||' '||
       DATA_TYPE||'('||DATA_PRECISION||','||DATA_SCALE||'),'
```

```
      FROM USER_TAB_COLUMNS
 WHERE TABLE_NAME = '&table_name'
   AND DATA_TYPE = 'NUMBER'
   AND DATA_PRECISION IS NOT NULL
UNION
SELECT 2, COLUMN_ID, DECODE(COLUMN_ID, 1, ' ', ',')||COLUMN_NAME||' '||
       DATA_TYPE||','
  FROM USER_TAB_COLUMNS
 WHERE TABLE_NAME = '&table_name'
   AND DATA_TYPE = 'DATE'
UNION
SELECT 3, 1, ') TABLESPACE PROJECT_TS;'  FROM DUAL
 ORDER BY 1, 2;
UNDEFINE table_name
```

Our final formatted result is as follows:

```
CREATE TABLE TEST (
 PROJECT_ID NUMBER(10,0)
,COST_CENTER VARCHAR2(30)
,LEDGER_DATE DATE
,TOTAL_REVENUE NUMBER(13,2)
) TABLESPACE PROJECT_TS;
```

This same technique can be used for any number of repetitive tasks the DBA may have to perform. As another example, if the DBA needs to drop and re-create a table it will be necessary to reissue GRANT statements to all the schemas or roles that have access to the original table. We can use SQL to generate all the GRANT statements before dropping the table:

```
SET PAGES 0 FEEDBACK OFF ECHO OFF HEAD OFF
ACCEPT table_name PROMPT 'ENTER TABLE NAME FOR GRANTS: '
SPOOL GRANT_&table_name.SQL
SELECT 'GRANT '||PRIVILEGE||' ON '||TABLE_NAME||' TO '||GRANTEE||'; '
  FROM USER_TAB_PRIVS
 WHERE TABLE_NAME = UPPER('&table_name');
SPOOL OFF
UNDEFINE table_name
```

Using SQL to generate other SQL statements is a very useful technique for the data warehouse developer and DBA. With practice, you'll see more and more opportunities to use it. This is one of the most flexible tricks to put into your toolkit. We will use this technique again later in this chapter and the next.

Creating an Oracle Database for the Data Warehouse

During the installation of Oracle a default database can be created for you. In most cases, however, the warehouse administrator will need to create a new database after completion of the install. There are a number of parameters that can be manipulated that will have a direct effect on performance. These parameters should be tuned so they provide the best performance for your specific applications that use the database. The defaults supplied by Oracle are very unlikely to be appropriate for a large data warehouse. Many of the parameters can be changed by shutting down the database instance, changing the desired parameters, and then restarting the instance. Some can even be changed "on the fly," but there are some critical parameters that can be set only at the time of database creation. We will have to use the CREATE DATABASE command to get our data warehouse started.

Unpleasant as it may be, we will have to do some analysis and planning before we create our database. We need to have a rough estimate of the size of our tables and indexes. We will need to understand the plan for using Parallel Query Option (PQO) to ensure that data is adequately spread across the available disk drives. We will need an estimate of the number of expected concurrent connections to the database.

Estimating the Size of the Database

It is useful to have an estimate of the size of objects in the data warehouse so we can ensure that our hardware architecture is adequate to support it. Estimating the size of the tables and indexes will allow us to allocate sufficient space to those objects when we create them. Although Oracle can dynamically allocate additional space (extents) to a table or index as it is required, this may result in fragmentation that could lead to administrative complexity and sometimes performance degradation. This is particularly true during data loading if Oracle has to frequently manage space. Contrary to much Oracle folk wisdom, fragmentation of a table is rarely a performance problem. Nevertheless, the safest approach is to allocate a sufficient amount of contiguous space to a table or index in only a few, properly sized extents.

Appendix A of the Oracle7 and Oracle8 *Server Administrator's Guides* presents several algorithms that can be used to estimate the storage requirements for a table and an index. These algorithms are perhaps too precise and too complex to obtain a ballpark estimate for our needs. (Moreover, there's a Catch-22: these formulas refer to some system data values that can be seen only by examining the data dictionary, which therefore requires the database be loaded and available; we want to do some rough estimates before creating our database.) Our basic position is that the best way to estimate space requirements is to use an empirical approach. Once a database is up and running, create the tables, load a subset of data into it, and execute a SQL query that shows how much storage space is being used for the known number of rows. These sizes can then be extrapolated (within a margin of error of one Oracle block) to project the final table size.

We can use the following methods (derived from Oracle's recommended algorithms) to give us the rough estimates that will be useful for some up-front planning before we have any database available.

First, we need to determine how much space we will have in our Oracle data blocks for our data. The critical factor is the size of our Oracle data block. The database block size has a substantial effect on database performance (particularly in index lookups) and storage efficiency. For now, let's assume a data block size of 4 KB. Oracle requires a small portion of each data block for some internal information, referred to as the block header. For our ballpark estimate, we can assume the block header requires 200 bytes. Second, we need to know how much space will be reserved for future updates of data and how much will be available for our initial inserts. This parameter is referred to as PCTFREE (percent free). PCTFREE also has an effect on data warehouse performance and storage efficiency. For now, let's assume PCTFREE is the default value of 10 (not an optimal value for a data warehouse, as we will see). So the amount of space in a data block available for our data is equal to DATA BLOCK SIZE - BLOCK HEADER - (PCTFREE/100 * DATA BLOCK SIZE). In our example, 4096 - 200 - 410 = 3486 bytes.

Now we need to determine how much space an average row in our table will require. We have to estimate the average column length for each column in our table. Most Oracle data types are stored in a variable length format so the average will be determined by the actual data loaded, not the length specified in the CREATE TABLE command. VARCHAR2 character data will require the actual length of the data entered. Dates will require 7 bytes to store. Numbers will require 1 byte more than one half the number of digits to be stored, rounded up. Estimating these variable lengths is, at best, difficult. To get a more precise estimate load a sample of the data and then query the AVG(VSIZE(column_name)) for each column.

We have to add one byte for column overhead if the length of the column is under 255 bytes and 3 bytes if the column length is over 255 bytes. We will add 4 bytes for row overhead. The length of a row is the sum of the column lengths and column overhead plus the row overhead. This calculation is not precise because Oracle stores different types of data differently, but it provides a generally conservative estimate.

You must repeat this estimation for each table in our database. Using a spreadsheet to calculate and track these estimates and then to sum them by assigned tablespace will prove very helpful. We see that, as expected with a star design, the vast majority of our space requirements are devoted to supporting the central fact table. The dimension tables require relatively little space. We need to ensure that our hardware environment is adequate for supporting this size of database.

Planning cannot stop at this point. It is also necessary to estimate the amount of space required for indexes and summary tables. A data warehouse will oftentimes have more space allocated to indexing and summaries than to the actual data. Again, there are some relatively complex algorithms presented in Appendix A of the Oracle8 *Server Administrator's Guide* (and in the Reference section of the same manual for Oracle7) that can help you estimate the space requirements for indexes. Estimating the amount of space needed for summary tables is done using the same approach as our detailed data tables, except that we'll need to estimate the number of rows to be stored in each summary based on knowledge of the GROUP BY clause used for building the summary.

We also need to have space for our temporary tablespace segments, our rollback segments, and the system tablespace. A very rough rule of thumb is to plan for three to four times as much required storage for the actual detailed data to support the indexing, summarization, and other requirements. One final note on space calculations. Our experience suggests that (1) people will underestimate the space requirements of a data warehouse and (2) it is far more difficult to manage a large data warehouse that has tight disk space constraints. We also have found that management does not like to deal with repeated requests for additional disk space (it makes us look like we don't really know what we're doing) and, unfortunately, management is unusually suspicious about requests for very large amounts of disk storage for a data warehouse project. Nevertheless, request sufficient disk storage for your planned growth for the first two years; unless your warehouse is quite unusual you will doubtless use it all in the first year. Be generous, you will have enough to worry about without concerning yourself over disk availability.

Number of Concurrent Logons to the Database

We need a rough estimate of the number of concurrent logons to the data warehouse so we can decide if we need to use Oracle7's Multi-Threaded Server (MTS), which effectively reduces the number of direct connections to the database. An overview of MTS was provided in Chapter 3. Each user connects to a dispatcher who handles individual requests by handing them off to one of a pool of shared servers, which perform the actual work for the user. If we expect fewer than fifty concurrent connections to the database we will not use MTS. If we expect hundreds of concurrent logons, we may want to consider MTS. The multithreaded server architecture was designed to support a large number of users doing relatively small transactions. It is very rare for a data warehouse to use the multithreaded server architecture. Many of the requests submitted to the warehouse typically take minutes or even hours to complete, which would tie up shared servers, defeating the design purpose of MTS.

Although the MTS architecture is still supported in Oracle8, it has been enhanced and supplemented by several new communication facilities. Net8's connection pooling feature allows for a larger number of "logical" connections to the database than the maximum number of physical connections. Idle connections are disabled (without being disconnected) to allow other connections to become active. In effect, this can allow a physical connection to be reused for a user with immediate needs while a current user either studies the results of his or her last query or waits for a current query to complete.

A new administrative tool, the Net8 Connection Manager, provides enhanced configuration and management of the Oracle network. A detailed discussion of Net8 and the Connection Manager are beyond the scope of this book but are documented in the *Net8 Administrator's Guide*.

Creating Tablespaces

Oracle stores tables and indexes in *tablespaces*. A tablespace consists of one or more data files. Before we can create any tables, we must have a tablespace for the table. Each user/schema may have a default tablespace defined in which objects will be created if a specific tablespace is not named. It is best to always explicitly name the tablespace in CREATE TABLE and CREATE INDEX statements rather than allow for default placement. Even if all the tables and indexes for a schema are to go into the same tablespace (not recommended) explicitly declaring the tablespace provides additional documentation value.

There are several considerations to be kept in mind as we prepare our data warehouse by creating tablespaces. We should, at a minimum, place index data and table data in separate tablespaces. Since tablespaces consist of one or more datafiles, it is possible to distribute the datafiles for a tablespace across several disk drives. This is particularly useful when we have not taken advantage of either hardware or software striping.

Each tablespace may be defined with a DEFAULT STORAGE clause that will become the default for all objects created in that tablespace, unless it is overridden in the CREATE TABLE statement. The following command will create the tablespace for our dimension tables.

```
CREATE TABLESPACE DIMENSION
    DATAFILE '/u002/oradata/dwp1/dim_data_01.dbs' SIZE 500M
    DEFAULT STORAGE (INITIAL 5M NEXT 5M PCTINCREASE 0)
    MINIMUM EXTENT 5M;
```

This creates a tablespace with a single datafile that is 500 MB in size. The DEFAULT STORAGE clause specifies that whenever a table or index is created in this tablespace it will, by default, initially be given 5 MB of storage. Whenever additional storage is required for a table or index, it will be assigned another 5 MB increment. PCTINCREASE is set to the recommended value of 0, which means that subsequent extents will also be allocated additional storage in 5 MB extents. If PCTINCREASE is nonzero, then each additional extent would grow by the percentage specified in PCTINCREASE. (PCTINCREASE defaults to 50, which eventually leads to very odd-sized extents that make it difficult to manage space within the tablespace.) The final parameter, MINIMUM EXTENT, is new syntax for Oracle8 and forces all objects' extents in this tablespace to be a multiple of 5 MB. If a user creates a table with a value for INITIAL of 13 MB, then Oracle8 will round the value up to 15 MB. This will further aid the administrator in maintaining regular extent sizes that can be easily reused if an object is dropped.

It is also possible to specify AUTOEXTEND in the CREATE TABLESPACE command. AUTOEXTEND can tell Oracle that if we exhaust the 500 MB allocated in our datafile, it should increase the datafile size by a predetermined amount. Oracle will continue to automatically increase the size of datafile until it reaches MAXSIZE. The use of AUTOEXTEND in the UNIX environment requires the use of filesystem files instead of raw files. AUTOEXTEND can help us avoid loading errors that may occur during our batch load window, but it does introduce the possibility of losing some control over your disk and datafiles. It should be used very cautiously, and we must institute monitoring procedures to maintain control over our datafiles. Most administrators of very large Oracle databases find that they want to take more explicit control over their disk utilization and add more datafiles to a tablespace when necessary.

Read-Only Tablespaces

It is possible to declare a tablespace to be a *read-only* tablespace. Obviously, once a tablespace has been declared read-only, you may no longer perform any DML operations on the tables and indexes in that tablespace. The primary advantage of a read-only tablespace is that you do not have to back it up once a first backup is made. For very large databases, the backup processes become very difficult and reducing the amount of backup volume is very beneficial. A read-only tablespace may be used to reduce the cost of data warehouse storage because it can be stored on less expensive media than a disk drive such as a CD-ROM or WORM device. For very large data warehouses, storing some read-only data on CD-ROM can result in sizable cost savings. Of course, there may be a substantial performance decrement if these devices do not support rapid access. Using read-only tablespaces as part of an archival strategy for older data that is infrequently accessed but needs to remain available can be an effective strategy. The procedure for creating a read-only tablespace is as follows:

1. Load all the tables (or build all the indexes) in the tablespace. You must identify tables that, once loaded, will not need any updates or future inserts. In our example, if we were storing each month's data from the ACTIVITY table into its own monthly ACTIVITY table (Oracle7) or partition (Oracle8), we would store a month's data in our read-only tablespace.

2. Execute a query on each table in the tablespace, which will induce a full table (or partition) scan. Oracle does not always complete the cleanout of lock information in the headers of newly loaded or modified blocks when the modifying transaction is committed. The next time the block is touched by another transaction or query, delayed block cleanout is performed. Performing a full table scan on each table will ensure that each block has been touched. (When block cleanout is performed can be controlled in release 7.3 and Oracle8 by the DELAYED_LOGGING_BLOCK_CLEANOUTS initialization parameter.)

3. Ensure that there are no active transactions anywhere in the database. This can most easily be accomplished by shutting down the database instance and starting it in RESTRICTED MODE. The key is to ensure that no transactions are active in any of the blocks in the tablespace, but Oracle does not provide any simple means of verifying the absence of transactions at a tablespace level.

4. Ensure that the only objects in the tablespace are tables, partitions and indexes. Rollback segments and temporary segments need to be written (or dropped), which requires that they be in a read-write tablespace.

5. Issue the command ALTER TABLESPACE *tablespace_name* READ ONLY;.

Temporary Tablespaces

Another special type of tablespace useful in a data warehouse is the TEMPO-RARY tablespace. When Oracle performs sorts, it attempts to sort in memory and then writes to disk when the sort is too large. If a TEMPORARY tablespace is provided, Oracle will use that as the disk area for sorting. This can result in substantial performance gains because Oracle is able to handle space allocation and deallocation more efficiently in a TEMPORARY tablespace. We can create a TEMPORARY tablespace by either issuing an ALTER TABLESPACE *tablespace _name* TEMPORARY command or using the TEMPORARY keyword in our original CREATE TABLESPACE command.

Spreading Data across Disk Drives

Now that we have some idea of our storage requirements we can ensure that we have a sufficient number of disk drives available to support our warehouse. Unfortunately, it is not quite that simple. We need to have a plan for how we will deploy our disks. There are some standard architectures that we should use when installing an Oracle database to ensure maximum performance. It is commonly understood that rollback segments, data segments, and index segments and temporary segments should be located in separate tablespaces so they can be placed on separate disk drives. If we plan on using Oracle's Parallel Query Option extensively for our data warehouse, we need to develop a plan to spread our data across disk drives.

The Oracle Parallel Query facility provides the capability to break a query (with Oracle8 this capability is extended to some DML operations on partitioned tables as well) into smaller tasks and then utilize multiple processes to complete the tasks. If there are multiple CPUs available, then these separate processes will execute in parallel, and the results from each component process will be merged into the final result set. The benefits of Oracle Parallel Query can be substantial; it is particularly effective in the data warehouse environment where large index builds and full table scans are common. If we can distribute the data for a table across several disk drives, we will reduce the probability that the parallel processes will contend for I/O resources. As a rough rule of thumb, we would like to ensure that large tables are distributed across as many disk drives as the Parallel Query processes we plan on using (as we will see in Chapter 10, there are several methods for telling Oracle how many parallel processes to use when processing a particular table). Ideally, we would also like to distribute the data across disk controllers in addition to just disk drives.

One of the implications of the need to distribute even an individual table across many disk drives is that we are far better off with a large number of smaller disk drives than fewer, larger drives. Most sites use some RAID strategy, implemented either in hardware or software, to manage striping across disk drives. RAID 0 (striping), RAID 0+1 (striping with mirroring), and RAID 5 (striping with distributed parity) are the most frequently utilized RAID configurations for the Oracle environment. These RAID levels were discussed in depth in Chapter 2.

If we do not have the capability for striping our data through RAID hardware or software, we can accomplish much the same thing by creating tablespaces that have multiple datafiles, with each file located on a different drive. Then we create a table with multiple extents, with each extent having a size that allows it to fit precisely into one of the data files. If more than one table is to be created in the manually striped tablespace, then the DBA will need to force each extent of each table into a separate datafile. This can be done by manually allocating extents before loading data, with the following command:

```
ALTER TABLE table_name ALLOCATE EXTENT DATAFILE 'file specification';
```

The result of this command will be a table that has extents located on different disk drives, and when data is loaded it will naturally end up distributed across disk drives. This "poor man's approach" to striping creates much more administrative work and is less effective than RAID striping at the individual file (or filesystem) level.

Creating the Schema

Before we dive into the syntax necessary to create tables for our data warehouse schema, we need to take a side tour into how Oracle processes requests for data from a table.

Full Table Scans

Until several years ago there was a mantra among Oracle database tuners: "Index Good, Full Table Scan Bad." This may still be generally good advice for tuning OLTP applications. It definitely does not apply to data warehouses. Oracle has spent much time developing efficient algorithms to optimize the performance of full table scans. The introduction of Oracle Parallel Query and its ability to use multiple query servers greatly improves the efficiency of full table scans. Full table scans are frequently the most efficient way to process large tables. The cost-based optimizer will frequently choose a full table scan for a wide range of different queries, especially when it has Parallel Query available. For these reasons, the data warehouse designer should spend at least as much attention implementing strategies to maximize the efficiency of full table scans as he or she used to spend trying to devise strategies to avoid them.

One obvious and effective strategy for improving the efficiency of a full table scan is to minimize the size of the table that must be processed. More specifically, we should reduce the number of data blocks that are read during a scan. There are several ways of doing this. First, minimize the amount of wasted space in each block by setting PCTFREE to 0 on tables that will not have rows updated (most tables in the warehouse). Second, minimize the number of empty blocks that must be read during the scan. This only becomes an issue when data rows have been deleted from a table. For warehouse tables that are regularly emptied and then reloaded, use the TRUNCATE command rather than DELETE. TRUNCATE is much more efficient and resets the table's high-water mark, unlike DELETE. A third approach to limiting the number of blocks to be scanned is to use Oracle8 partitioned tables or partition views in Oracle7, release 7.3. When a query's WHERE clause restricts the needed rows to a single partition (or view's underlying Oracle7 table) then the optimizer will eliminate the scanning of any other partitions.

The strategy we use to lay out our tables on the disk drives may also have a direct effect on the performance of full table scans. The goal is to ensure that we maximize the operating system's capability to process I/O requests simultaneously. This is particularly important if we are planning to use Oracle Parallel Query. To process I/O simultaneously, we typically need to have the I/O requests directed toward different disks or different disk controllers. This means we want our large fact table to be spread across several disk drives (typically, a fact table is large enough that it must be spread across different drives). We need to plan which drives we want to use for large fact tables. An important consideration of our physical design should be to maximize the capability to make simultaneous reads of the disks.

Be Wary of Denormalizing Star Tables

Another possible approach to improving the efficiency of a full table scan is less useful. In our standard star design, we tend to focus on the *fact table*. An intuitively appealing solution to designing the database is to denormalize the fact table and store much of the detail that is found in the dimension tables directly with the fact table, thereby avoiding the need to perform a join. There are several potential problems with this approach, however. First, the fact table frequently holds millions of rows, so adding extra information to the fact table will quickly result in a substantial increase in the size of the fact table. There is usually a rich amount of information contained in the dimension table, which means that it would be difficult to store all the useful analytic information in the dimension tables with the fact table—so we end up joining the fact table anyway. By moving all the dimension data into the fact table we eliminate the advantage of doing a star join: The objective of a star query is to quickly reduce the number of rows in the fact table that have to be examined. If all the dimension data were stored in the fact table then we would have to examine it all (or else create a large number of additional indexes on this very large table).

Denormalizing the fact table also makes it far more difficult to deal with changes in dimension information. In our project accounting data warehouse, we will have to deal with reorganizations that change the hierarchical organization structure, consultants' job levels change, function code classifications change, and so on. Managing changing dimensions is a classic challenge in data warehouse projects. If we have denormalized our fact table so that information subject to change is stored in the fact table, we have increased the challenge by

If we must stripe our ACTIVITY_TS tablespace manually, we can create it with the following command:

```
CREATE TABLESPACE ACTIVITY_TS
    DATAFILE 'datafile_on_disk1' SIZE 513M,
    DATAFILE 'datafile_on_disk2' SIZE 536879004,
    DATAFILE 'datafile_on_disk3' SIZE 536879004,
    DATAFILE 'datafile_on_disk4' SIZE 536879004
  DEFAULT STORAGE (INITIAL 512M NEXT 512M PCTINCREASE 0)
  MINIMUM EXTENT 512M
  NOLOGGING;
```

This provides just over four gigabytes of storage space for the ACTIVITY_TS tablespace, spread across four disk devices. Making each file slightly larger than the size of the object extents provides room for the file header block. Each file requires additional space equal to one database block (8 KB in this example). The MINIMUM EXTENT and NOLOGGING parameters are new with Oracle8. MINIMUM EXTENT forces all extents for segments created in this tablespace to be multiples of 512 MB. No odd-sized extents will be allowed. NOLOGGING is

an order of magnitude. Both performance and maintenance considerations suggest that we proceed very cautiously in deciding to denormalize our fact table (later in this chapter we will examine in more detail a technique that may in some circumstances let us do some denormalization while minimizing its effects on full table scans).

There are a few other issues to consider when designing the fact table. Eliminate long columns from your fact tables. The presence of a long column can require several data blocks just to store a single row. Reduce the number of columns in the fact table. There may be columns that are simply not required in a large percentage of queries. They may be important and we have to include them in the database, but we don't necessarily have to keep them in the same fact table as the commonly used information. We can use vertical partitioning to create several different fact tables. One fact table will store the more central information that is commonly referenced, and the other fact table will store the rarely used information. Both tables have the same keys and can be joined together to rebuild the logical fact table. This technique can provide substantial performance gains. Ideally, this method should only be used when there are sets of columns that are never accessed together, so we can safely break the table into subtables and not have to worry about the performance implications of joining several multimillion row tables. It is possible, however, to include some columns in both tables so related data will be found in a single fact table. Before deciding to vertically partition the fact table, it is critical to consider all the trade-offs between wasting storage on storing data twice and optimizing certain queries while slowing the performance of a separate set of analyses.

a segment (table, partition, or index) attribute that will be inherited by all the objects created in this tablespace unless specifically overridden when an object is created. It directs Oracle to perform minimal redo logging when creating an object or performing direct path loads. This speeds these operations but also means we will not be able to recover the object from a media failure after one of these operations. It is critical to immediately back up the tablespace after creating or loading data!

The strategies for maximizing full table scan performance are best applied to the large fact table(s) in a star schema design or the detailed data if we've elected to use a more traditional summary design. In most data warehouse implementations, the relative size difference between the fact table and the dimension table is so large that few meaningful benefits occur from attempting to minimize the size of dimension tables.

We will next examine how we can use this tablespace to create tables that are optimally designed for the typical queries in a data warehouse environment.

Creating Tables

We have created a tablespace, ACTIVITY_TS, that is manually striped across four disk drives. We want to create our large fact table, ACTIVITY, in this tablespace so we can take advantage of Oracle Parallel Query when doing full table scans. We also want to ensure that we have as few data blocks as possible. Since our fact table is never updated, we don't have to reserve space for updates to avoid chaining. We will use all the available space in each data block.

```
CREATE TABLE ACTIVITY
   (MONTH              VARCHAR2(7),
    ORG_ID             NUMBER,
    FUNCTION_CODE      VARCHAR2(2),
    PROJECT_ID         NUMBER,
    REVENUE            NUMBER,
    HOURS              NUMBER,
    EXPENSES           NUMBER)
TABLESPACE ACTIVITY_TS
STORAGE (INITIAL 512M  NEXT 512M MINEXTENTS 4 PCTINCREASE 0)
NOLOGGING
PCTFREE 0;
```

This command results in the ACTIVITY table receiving four extents at the time of table creation. The PCTINCREASE 0 clause tells Oracle that every data extent allocated to the ACTIVITY table should be 512 MB. The NOLOGGING attribute informs Oracle8 to minimize the amount of redo information which is logged for this table. Finally, we use PCTFREE 0 to make the best possible use of all the space available and minimize the number of data blocks required.

Several other optional clauses that can be used in CREATE TABLE may have limited use in a data warehouse project. Oracle reserves 23 bytes in a data block for each transaction that is simultaneously updating that data block. The parameters INITRANS and MAXTRANS control the number of transactions that can simultaneously modify a data block. These parameters can be quite important for OLTP but are less important for data warehouses. Generally, we will not have concurrent processes updating data blocks in our warehouse tables. Simultaneous inserts are directed to use different blocks through the FREELISTS parameter. INITRANS defaults to 1, which is usually appropriate for the warehouse. MAXTRANS should be allowed to default—the specific value varies by operating system but is always much higher than we'll ever need.

Oracle manages space allocation for a table by using a list that contains the addresses for blocks that are available for insertion in a structure called a *freelist*. If there are simultaneous processes attempting to insert into the same table, there can be contention in accessing the freelist. Oracle permits you to create a table with more than one freelist. Set FREELISTS to the number of simultaneous processes that will be loading data into the same table with INSERT statements. Direct path SQL*Loader does not require you to set FREELISTS since it avoids the use of SQL INSERTs and writes directly to new, empty blocks.

There are several places where we can tell Oracle how many parallel query processes to use when performing a query against a particular table. We can provide a hint as part of the query that directs the optimizer to use multiple processes (or not to use multiple processes); we can specify the number of query processes to be used when querying or indexing a specific table by including the PARALLEL clause in the CREATE TABLE command; finally, a default value may be defined for the entire instance through initialization parameters. The benefits of parallelizing queries will be limited by the I/O capacity of the disks used to store the large table. Ensure that large tables that you expect to scan with Oracle Parallel Query are spread over several disks.

We will enhance our CREATE TABLE command to include these additional clauses. Because we have four available processors on our data warehouse machine, we will create the ACTIVITY table to use four parallel query processes and to provide support for four simultaneous insert processes:

```
CREATE TABLE ACTIVITY
    (MONTH              VARCHAR2(7),
     ORG_ID             NUMBER,
     FUNCTION_CODE      VARCHAR2(2),
     PROJECT_ID         NUMBER,
     REVENUE            NUMBER,
     HOURS              NUMBER,
     EXPENSES           NUMBER)
   TABLESPACE ACTIVITY_TS
   STORAGE (INITIAL 499M  NEXT 499M MINEXTENTS 4 PCTINCREASE 0 FREELISTS 4)
   NOLOGGING
   PCTFREE 0
   PARALLEL (DEGREE 8);
```

Two other changes would be appropriate if our warehouse is being created on a clustered or MPP system using Oracle Parallel Server. The PARALLEL clause may be enhanced with the specification of the number of instances the parallel query processes should be spread across:

```
PARALLEL (DEGREE 8 INSTANCES 2)
```

Also, our means of dealing with INSERT contention by defining additional freelists may not be sufficient in the Oracle Parallel Server environment. An additional parameter, FREELIST GROUPS, should be set to the number of instances that may be simultaneously trying to insert data to the table. Usually, our warehouse tables are inserted through a single instance, but this parameter provides this way to spread heavy INSERT activity if necessary.

Partitioned Tables

Although we frequently focus on the challenges a large data warehouse poses to query operations, the greatest difficulties are commonly associated with loading, indexing, and general management of the data warehouse. If we have a limited "load window," it is imperative that we be able to complete data loading, transformations, summarization, and indexing as quickly as possible. There are usually things that can be done to improve query performance (i.e., creating summary and aggregation tables), but if the data cannot be made available in a timely fashion the warehouse will fail.

The primary challenge with data warehouses arises from the presence of the very large fact tables. A fact table may contain millions of rows and be many gigabytes in size. Several classes of problems must be addressed when we are confronted with the presence of a multimillion row table. Simply being able to load the actual data into the table in an acceptable period of time can be problematic. Even if we can get the data loaded, the problems associated with creating or maintaining even a single simple index on a table this size are daunting. It is typically necessary to maintain several indexes including concatenated indexes for a very large table, which makes the problems even more challenging.

Once we have the data loaded and the indexes created for the table, our challenges continue. Eventually we will want to remove old data from the table, and so we must have a purge or archive scheme that will enable us to delete rows from the fact table and possibly store them in some fashion outside of our main fact table. Finally, it is necessary have to have a recovery strategy that can restore or rebuild every table in a reasonable period of time.

Breaking up a very large table into smaller pieces that can be managed independently is the key to successfully meeting the challenges presented by multimillion row tables. Breaking up a single table into component parts is referred to as partitioning. Oracle7, release 7.3, supports partitions using partition views, and Oracle8 supports true table partitioning. Oracle8 provides a very simple method to migrate from Partition Views to a true partitioned table.

There are two conceptual ways to partition a table—*vertical partitioning* and *horizontal partitioning*. Vertical partitioning is useful when the very large table has many columns, and certain sets of columns are almost always referenced together. It is possible to create several separate tables that break the columns into their common sets and maintain a common key across tables. This approach reduces the overall size of a single table but does not reduce the number of rows in a table. Consequently, vertical partitioning does nothing to help solve the indexing problems associated with a very large table. In fact, vertical partitioning exacerbates our problems because now we have several multimillion row tables for which we must maintain indexes. Vertical partitioning rarely finds a use in a data warehouse architecture.

The other method of partitioning a table is to use horizontal partitioning. In a horizontal partitioning scheme, subsets of rows are stored together in separate segments. With Oracle7 partitioned views, each subset goes into its own table. This effectively reduces both the overall space requirements and the number of rows to be managed in each table.

The Oracle7 or Oracle8 optimizer must be able to determine which partitions to search (and which to ignore) in order to speed our queries. It is possible to choose any haphazard method to select the subsets of rows to place into each partition. However, to fully benefit from partitioned views or Oracle8 partitioned tables, you must use a selection criteria that can be implemented as a table constraint. That is, all the rows in a given table need to share some common data value (or range of values) in one or more of their columns. We refer to this as the *partition key*.

It is important to select the partition key carefully. It must not be updated (which would require a delete from one table and an insert into another partition), which should not be a problem for a data warehouse. The partition key should produce partitions that are of manageable and roughly equal size. Ideally, the partition key should work so that each data load will only load into one relatively small partition. If each periodic refresh needs to load and index every partition we still may have a problem completing the loading process for all twenty-five partitions in an acceptable amount of time.

Usually a date (some kind of transaction date) will meet the requirements for a good partition key. In our example, we would select MONTH as the partition key for our ACTIVITY table. Once we have loaded and indexed a month's worth of data into a partition, we will never have to load or index that data again. The tablespace containing the data can be made read-only and further backups avoided. Partitioning by date also addresses the issues of archival. When certain data no longer needs to be kept online, that table or partition can be backed up and then dropped. Since archiving is frequently based on the passage of time, date-based partition keys make the archiving and recovery scheme very easy to implement. There is no requirement, however, for partitioning by

Partition views in Oracle8

Even though Oracle8 supports the partition view facility for upward compatibility for databases migrated from release 7.3, the true partitioning available in Oracle8 is vastly superior in performance and administrative ease. This new capability is a key reason to move the data warehouse to Oracle8 technology.

date. An organization might well choose to partition by a regional or departmental code if the majority of queries will be constrained by that column, but this will limit the ability to take advantage of read-only tablespaces.

CREATING A PARTITIONED VIEW

Partition views were introduced in Oracle7, release 7.3, and remain available for backward-compatibility reasons in Oracle8, release 8.0. However, the README document included with release 8.0.4 of Oracle8 states that this feature will be desupported in a future release. This is due to the fact that partitioned tables in Oracle8 provide the main partition pruning and management advantages of Oracle7 partition views, but have fewer restrictions and provide many additional benefits.

There is no reason to use partitioned views in Oracle8.

The Oracle optimizer uses the partitioned view to eliminate specific partitions that it can determine are unnecessary to a specific query. For the optimizer to use a partitioned view for partition elimination, the tables must be created with a check constraint that will ensure that each table will only hold its partition key values. An index must then be created on the partition key columns. This is necessary so that the Oracle optimizer will able to efficiently process these tables. Finally, the DBA must set the PARTITION_VIEW_ENABLED initialization parameter to TRUE. There is a more detailed discussion of how partitioned views are processed in Chapter 9. Additionally, the types of parallelism available with partitioned views are described in detail in Chapter 10.

CREATING AN ORACLE8 PARTITIONED TABLE

The same considerations that led to the selection of the partition key for use with Oracle7 partition views also apply to the creation of an Oracle8 partitioned table. Rather than have to create and manage individual tables and then use a view to make them appear to be a single object, Oracle8 allows a single table to be stored in multiple partitions. The syntax to create our ACTIVITY table as a partitioned table with one partition for each month of 1997 would be as follows:

```
CREATE TABLE ACTIVITY
  (MONTH              NUMBER(6),
   ORG_ID             NUMBER,
   FUNCTION_CODE      VARCHAR2(2),
   PROJECT_ID         NUMBER,
   REVENUE            NUMBER,
   HOURS              NUMBER,
   EXPENSES           NUMBER)
  STORAGE (INITIAL 50M NEXT 10M PCTINCREASE 0)
  PCTFREE 0
  NOLOGGING
  PARALLEL (DEGREE 8)
  PARTITION BY RANGE (MONTH)
          (PARTITION ACT_97JAN VALUES LESS THAN ('199702')
                  TABLESPACE ACT_97JAN,
```

```
PARTITION ACT_97FEB VALUES LESS THAN ('199703')
        TABLESPACE ACT_97FEB,
PARTITION ACT_97MAR VALUES LESS THAN ('199704')
        TABLESPACE ACT_97MAR,
PARTITION ACT_97APR VALUES LESS THAN ('199705')
        TABLESPACE ACT_97APR,
PARTITION ACT_97MAY VALUES LESS THAN ('199706')
        TABLESPACE ACT_97MAY,
PARTITION ACT)97JUN VALUES LESS THAN ('199707')
        TABLESPACE ACT_97JUN,
PARTITION ACT_97JUL VALUES LESS THAN ('199708')
        TABLESPACE ACT_97JUL,
PARTITION ACT_97AUG VALUES LESS THAN ('199709')
        TABLESPACE ACT_97AUG,
PARTITION ACT_97SEP VALUES LESS THAN ('199710')
        TABLESPACE ACT_97SEP,
PARTITION ACT_97OCT VALUES LESS THAN ('199711')
        TABLESPACE ACT_97OCT,
PARTITION ACT_97NOV VALUES LESS THAN ('199712')
        TABLESPACE ACT_97NOV,
PARTITION ACT_97DEC VALUES LESS THAN ('199801')
        TABLESPACE ACT_97DEC);
```

There are a couple of things to note in this example. First, in order to tell Oracle8 which rows will be stored in each partition, we use the VALUES LESS THAN clause. The order in which partitions are created is important. Partitions with lower values for the partition key must be declared before those for higher values. Therefore, we must define the JAN97 partition before FEB97. Also, to make the sorting work based on the MONTH column it was necessary to change the way we planned to store the actual data. Earlier, our table design included MONTH as a seven-character VARCHAR2 column. If we were to partition based on that data, Oracle would be sorting by the alphabetic value of the month abbreviation (APR, AUG, DEC, FEB, etc.), which would be very confusing! Changing the data to be stored as a six-digit number with year followed by month will work much better. Of course, if the original definition of MONTH as character data were important for users' access, an additional column could have been added to the table (e.g., MONTH_NUM) and used for the partition key.

The next thing to note about the partitioned table is that we defined STORAGE, PCTFREE, NOLOGGING, and PARALLEL attributes at the table level. In this style, each partition will inherit those characteristics from the table. It is also possible to specify any of these parameters as part of the definition of an individual partition, in which case it will override the table-level value. This can be used, for instance, to adjust monthly storage requirements when the natural business cycle causes a large number of ORDERS to be taken in November and December and a much smaller number in January. Partitions do not have to be the same size or have the same degree of default parallelism.

If the data volume on the ACTIVITY table were smaller, we could very easily choose to partition by quarter instead of month. The change in syntax to accomplish this partitioning scheme would be as follows:

```
PARTITION BY RANGE (MONTH)
        (PARTITION ACT_97Q1 VALUES LESS THAN ('199704')
                TABLESPACE ACT_97Q1,
        PARTITION ACT_97Q2 VALUES LESS THAN ('199707')
                TABLESPACE ACT_97Q2,
        PARTITION ACT_97Q3 VALUES LESS THAN ('199710')
                TABLESPACE ACT_97Q3,
        PARTITION ACT_97Q4 VALUES LESS THAN ('199801')
                TABLESPACE ACT_97Q4)
```

To make things easier to understand and track, this example names each partition and tablespace identically, but this is not a requirement. Partitions do not have to be placed in separate tablespaces, and the names for partitions must only follow the standard Oracle naming of any object and must be unique within the schema. Using meaningful names will make the administrator's life easier in the long run.

Finally, we need to understand what happens if any data rows are inserted to this partitioned table with MONTH values prior to January 1997 or after December 1997. The first partition (JAN97) is defined as having all rows with MONTH less than 199702. So, a row with a MONTH value in 1996 would be placed into the JAN97 partition. This is probably not desired behavior, so a CHECK constraint can be placed on the table to prevent any values less than 199701 from being inserted. A row with a value greater than 199712 would be rejected during the INSERT process by this table. This is commonly the proper behavior for date-ranged partitions. Optional syntax is available, however, to deal with other situations. Rather than supply a value in the VALUES LESS THAN clause of the final partition, it is valid to use the keyword MAXVALUE. This would allow the final partition to take on any values greater than or equal to the range defined in the next-to-last partition. Using MAXVALUE would, therefore, allow any 1998 activity to be placed into the DEC97 partition.

MAINTAINING AN ORACLE8 PARTITIONED TABLE

The partitioned table created in the last example only provided for the storage of 1997 activity data. Of course, there will be a need to add additional data after each month of 1998 and beyond. Adding an additional partition to store the new data is very easy—much easier than re-creating views and synonyms as required with a partitioned view. There are two options for adding a new partition's set of data to the partitioned table. The first, and most obvious, way is to simply add an additional partition, such as

```
ALTER TABLE ACTIVITY
  ADD PARTITION ACT_98JAN VALUES LESS THAN('199802')
     TABLESPACE ACT_98JAN;
```

Once again it is possible, if necessary, to override the STORAGE or other parameters defined at the table level. Also, the tablespace must have been created before the partition can be created. Once the partition has been added, data can be loaded and validated and indexes created (or re-created).

A second alternative, which has many benefits, allows for taking a standalone table with data already loaded and adding it to the partitioned table. This approach allows the data to be loaded and completely validated (including enabling constraints that might be too expensive to enable on the very large partitioned table) before making it visible to the users. This is absolutely the best way to provide the verification and publishing function on newly added data as described in the next chapter. While working with the standalone table, the administrator can take as much time as necessary to validate the data and resolve any problems. When each table's new data has been checked and "blessed" as correct, a single script can be run to include the new partitions in each partitioned table. Adding partitions in this manner is a six-step process:

1. Create the new standalone table in the appropriate tablespace using the same column definitions as the partitioned table. Use appropriate STORAGE, PARALLEL, and other clauses. Using a subquery to obtain the table definition will save some typing and potential errors. (Generating it from a CASE tool would certainly work as well.)

   ```
   CREATE TABLE ACTIVITY_LOAD
           TABLESPACE ACT_98JAN
           STORAGE (INITIAL 50M NEXT 10M PCTINCREASE 0)
       AS SELECT * FROM ACTIVITY
           WHERE 1=2;
   ```

2. Load the new data to the standalone table.
3. Modify the table to create and enable whatever constraints are needed to verify data accuracy. Execute whatever PL/SQL procedures or SQL statements to further ensure the data is correct.
4. Add a new partition to the partitioned table. This partition will never be actually used. It is only a placeholder that will be swapped for the loaded standalone table and then dropped. Therefore, it can be made very small and placed in any convenient tablespace (such as USER_DATA).

   ```
   ALTER TABLE ACTIVITY
           ADD PARTITION ACT_98JAN VALUES LESS THAN('199802')
           TABLESPACE USER_DATA;
   ```

5. Exchange the standalone table with the placeholder partition. This is the only step that requires syntax not already familiar to the DBA. If any indexes were created on the standalone table that correspond to local indexes desired on the final partition, then INCLUDING INDEXES will convert them in the same operation. WITHOUT VALIDATION should be used if the data validation process on the standalone table has ensured that only rows with the proper range of the partitioning key are included. The default action is to verify each row's data during the exchange.

```
ALTER TABLE ACTIVITY
        EXCHANGE PARTITION ACT_98JAN WITH TABLE ACTIVITY_LOAD
            INCLUDING INDEXES
            WITHOUT VALIDATION;
```

6. Drop the new empty table that was originally the placeholder partition.

```
DROP TABLE ACTIVITY_LOAD;
```

Other forms of administering partitions are available. Partitions can be moved, renamed, split, merged, and truncated. The Oracle8 *SQL Language Reference* manual describes each of these actions. Individual partitions may also be exported. This is described in the Oracle8 *Utilities Reference* manual.

Purging from an Oracle8 Partitioned Table

When older data eventually needs to be removed from the partitioned table, the administrator may drop the partition using the following:

```
ALTER TABLE ACTIVITY
    DROP PARTITION ACT_97JAN;
```

You must use the export utility or other means of backing up the data before dropping the partition if archival is required.

As an alternative strategy for archiving data from a partitioned table, the old partition may be exchanged with a placeholder table (the reverse of the process by which a new partition is added). This makes the oldest partition into a stand-alone table still residing in its original tablespace. The tablespace can then be made READ-ONLY, copied to CD-ROM, and taken offline. This allows the data to remain part of the database but not kept on expensive disk storage. If the data is ever needed again, the tablespace may be brought back online. Oracle8's expanded limits on the number of files in a database makes this form of archival a viable possibility.

Database Constraints in a Data Warehouse

One of the greatest challenges in implementing a data warehouse is to ensure that only "clean" data is present in the warehouse. All data must be "fit for use." By "fit for use" we mean that only valid ranges are present, that all integrity constraints are met, and so on. Every warehouse development team finds that a substantial amount of time is spent defining just exactly what "fit for use" or "clean" data means and then implementing procedures to ensure that the data meet these requirements. Nothing can kill a data warehouse project as fast as having the end users decide they cannot trust the data in the warehouse. Inevitably, each end user ends up performing his or her own acceptance tests. They will identify some set of reports they can produce out of the operational systems and devise some query in the data warehouse that they believe should yield identical results. They will test it out. It is important that the data warehouse be able to pass this "sniff" test. It is possible that the warehouse will fail this test because the data in the warehouse is better, or more "fit for use" than the data in the operational systems. It is not at all unusual for a data warehouse to reveal flaws in business practices or operational systems. The critical thing is that the data warehouse not be incorrect. It is hard to recover credibility, hence the need for very close attention to issues of data quality.

Oracle offers a method for using the database itself to perform various validation checks (referred to as constraints) on the data when it is loaded into the database. One common constraint is referential integrity. The database itself can ensure that all foreign key columns refer to a valid primary key. In our example, we could use referential integrity constraints to ensure that every ORG_ID in the ACTIVITY table corresponds to a valid ORG_ID in the ORGANIZATION table. To create a referential integrity constraint on our ACTIVITY table to ensure no invalid ORG_ID is inserted into the database would require the following SQL commands:

```
ALTER TABLE ORGANIZATION ADD PRIMARY KEY (ORG_ID);
ALTER TABLE ACTIVITY
  ADD CONSTRAINT ORG_FK
      REFERENCES ORGANIZATION(ORG_ID)
      EXCEPTIONS INTO BAD_ORGS;
```

Before creating a foreign key constraint it is necessary to ensure that the corresponding column(s) in the parent (or referenced) table have been defined as a PRIMARY KEY (or UNIQUE) constraint. This is done by the first statement just given. The EXCEPTIONS INTO clause specifies a table in which Oracle will store the ROWID, EXCEPTION_NAME, and TABLE_NAME of any rows that fail to meet the ORG_FK data integrity constraint. This makes it easier to identify any offending data and make the necessary corrections.

In addition to referential constraints, Oracle provides CHECK constraints that enable the database to check for valid data values or perform other validation processes on the data as it is inserted into the database. To also ensure that all HOURS values are between the range of 0 and 80 (we have a firm policy that no one can work more than eighty hours in a week and, despite some managers' suspicions, we also find it impossible to work a negative number of hours) we can create a CHECK constraint on the ACTIVITY table:

```
ALTER TABLE ACTIVITY

  ADD CONSTRAINT CHECK_HOURS
      CHECK (HOURS BETWEEN 0 and 80)
```

A check constraint is able to use any columns' values from the data row as well as literals (constants) to perform its validation. Using Oracle's data integrity capabilities provides an easy method for ensuring consistent data and also provides a centralized location for metadata rules.

Many data query tools use the referential integrity rules present in the data dictionary to control their operations. These sophisticated data query tools are able to generate SQL statements that join tables automatically when required, based on referential integrity definitions. Such tools greatly ease the load on developers by reducing the need to create views or train users in joining tables. These tools can also provide a substantial performance benefit over pre-defined views because they only generate table joins when necessary, based on which columns a user wants to include in the query.

The relative merits and drawbacks of using database constraints were discussed in Chapter 4. If the amount of data to be loaded is small and the additional overhead for loading is acceptable, by all means employ constraints to help ensure valid data. On the other hand, if a large number of rows must be processed with a relatively short time window available, constraints may be too expensive. In these, data validation should be performed during the extract process or cleansing should be performed before the database loading process. As a third alternative, data can be direct path loaded into a relatively small, temporary table with constraints and be validated before moving it into the larger table on which constraints may not be appropriate.

In order to have the constraints present in the data dictionary (for both meta-data reference and to provide information to our query tools), it is possible to create the desired constraints and then disable them. A disabled constraint still exists in the data dictionary, but Oracle does not attempt to enforce it during data loads. To disable a constraint on the ACTIVITY table we can issue one of the following commands:

```
ALTER TABLE ACTIVITY DISABLE CONSTRAINT ORG_FK;
```

Whenever a constraint is disabled and then reenabled, Oracle will revalidate every row in the table. Keep this in mind before disabling a constraint on a large table. This may, in some cases, be used to advantage. In some situations it may be a valid compromise to load data that has been validated during the extract process (and presumed to be fit for use) every day, with the constraints disabled, and validate the data every weekend, when more time is available, by enabling the appropriate constraints.

Index-Organized Tables

As described in Chapter 3, Oracle8 provides a new segment type, the index-organized table. This segment uses the hierarchical structure of a B*Tree index but stores the complete data row in the index structure. This allows data to be accessed quickly based on the columns used to build the index structure. However, data rows in an index-organized table have no associated ROWID. This means that no additional indexes may be created to allow alternative access paths. This makes the index-organized table of relatively little value in the data warehouse. A large table would typically be expected to need multiple access paths, and a small table would not gain much benefit from avoiding the extra storage and I/O for normal B*Tree lookup.

The only likely use for an index-organized table in the warehouse is to provide a code-translation table that might consist of only a short CODE_VALUE and longer CODE_DESCRIPTION. Providing no user would ever want to query on CODE_DESCRIPTION (a dangerous assumption!), this table could be easily joined to another table when the description is needed. Most warehouse designers will choose to denormalize to include the CODE_DESCRIPTION in the base tables unless the space savings were extreme. (An alternative, using a hash cluster to store the code-translation table, would meet the same lookup requirement with even less I/O overhead.)

To create an index-organized table, a few additions are needed to the normal CREATE TABLE syntax:

```
CREATE TABLE CODE_VALUES
   (CODE_VALUE            NUMBER(3),
    CODE_DESCRIPTION      VARCHAR2(500),
    CONSTRAINT CODE_VALUES_PK PRIMARY KEY (CODE_VALUE))
   ORGANIZATION INDEX
   TABLESPACE LOOKUP_DATA
   PCTTHRESHOLD 10;
```

Index-organized tables are very sensitive to the length of the data rows being stored. PCTTHRESHOLD defines how much of each block should be reserved for each data row. Rows that do not fit within this amount of storage are, by default, rejected during INSERT processing. Optional syntax (not shown) allows an overflow area to be specified for data columns that don't fit in the primary storage block.

Using Indexes in the Data Warehouse

Indexes have two purposes in an Oracle database. They are used to enforce uniqueness of data values within one or more columns of a table, such as a primary key. They are also used to reduce the number of rows in a table that need to be examined to satisfy a query. The older, rule-based optimizer puts a high value on being able to use an index. It will blindly use an index even though it might be much more efficient to do a full table scan. The newer, cost-based optimizer is much more intelligent—assuming it has accurate statistics available—in determining when using an index is appropriate.

B*Tree Indexes

The original, and most common, form of index in Oracle is a B*Tree index. The structure and use of B*Tree indexes was covered in Chapter 3. B*Tree indexes may be created on a single column of a table or a series of up to thirty-two columns in Oracle8 (sixteen columns in Oracle7). B*Tree indexes may be optionally created as UNIQUE (no duplicate values allowed). A unique index is automatically created when a PRIMARY KEY or UNIQUE constraint is enabled on a table. Star queries in Oracle7, release 7.3, require a concatenated B*Tree index on the columns of the central fact table, which correspond to the primary keys of each dimension table.

CREATING A B*TREE INDEX

Creating and dropping indexes is quite straightforward. The CREATE INDEX has many of the same clauses found in the CREATE TABLE command. We can specify a tablespace to hold the index, the amount of free space to be reserved in the index blocks for future growth (PCTFREE), the maximum degree of parallelism to use when creating the index, or the way we want to allocate additional space to the index segment as it grows (using the standard STORAGE clause with INITIAL, NEXT, and PCTINCREASE parameters).

One very handy additional clause available when creating an index is UNRECOVERABLE (Oracle7) or NOLOGGING (Oracle8). Creating an index with one of these attributes tells Oracle not to log the creation of the index. This avoids a lot of overhead and speeds the index build but means that if media failure occurs before a backup is made, the index will not be present after we recover the tablespace. This is typically a reasonable risk for the data warehouse where index build times are often critical and where backups are generally made immediately after each load cycle.

We can also specify a degree of parallelism to use when building the INDEX. Using a parallel index build combined with the UNRECOVERABLE option will greatly enhance index creation. With our example, we will use the following command:

```
CREATE INDEX ACT_PRI on ACTIVITY (PROJECT_NUMBER, MONTH)
    UNRECOVERABLE
    TABLESPACE ACT_IDX
    STORAGE (INITIAL 5M NEXT 5M PCTINCREASE 0)
    PARALLEL (DEGREE 8);
```

There are a couple of issues to note when creating an index. Using the parallel option during the create of an index gives each parallel process a full extent allocation for space, determined by the supplied STORAGE clause parameters. In the example just given, the index segment will be allocated a minimum of 20 MB in four 5-MB extents. Take this into account when defining the storage parameters: divide the calculated space requirement by the number of parallel processes to derive the correct storage parameter values.

Index segments should always be separated from the tables they point to. Do this by placing the index segments and data segments in separate tablespaces. If necessary, index extents can be manually striped across multiple drives using the same procedures described earlier for table extents.

Finally, because B*Tree indexes guarantee equal search path length regardless of the path through the tree, the index must be occasionally rebalanced when new data is inserted. Rebalancing a large B*Tree can take some time. When loading a large number of rows the index will be rebalanced frequently, resulting in poor load performance. In many cases, when loading a large number of rows it may be faster to drop the index, load the table, then re-create the index using the UNRECOVERABLE/NOLOGGING and PARALLEL options.

NOSORT OPTION

On a newly loaded table it is sometimes possible to save much of the time required to create one index on the table by using the NOSORT option. This option allows Oracle to avoid sorting the data by simply reading the table and directly building the index structure. To use this feature, however, the data must have been presorted and then loaded in the sorted order. This prevents the use of parallel direct path SQL*Loader to initially load the data into the table since parallel loads would not preserve the presorted order.

ORACLE8 REVERSE ORDER INDEXES

It is possible in Oracle8 to build a B*Tree index in which the byte order of the indexed data is reversed. This avoids a common problem with B*Tree indexes that are defined on a column whose values constantly increase—new values are always added to the "right" edge of the indexed range. This commonly occurs in date columns with artificial primary keys that receive their values from Oracle sequence generators. The problem occurs when older data is also being regularly deleted from the "left" edge of the indexed range. Under these conditions, the index structure constantly grows to accommodate higher values while still maintaining the original (now empty) structure for the lower values.

By reversing the order in which the bytes of the indexed value are stored, new entries (and deleted old data) tend to randomize more evenly over the entire reverse order index structure. These indexes cannot, however, be used to perform index range scans in which the user's query uses the BETWEEN, > (greater than) or < (less than) operators.

To build a reverse order index, merely add the keyword REVERSE anywhere after the list of columns to be indexed. Bitmap indexes cannot be built in reverse order.

IDENTIFYING REVERSE ORDER INDEXES IN THE DATA DICTIONARY

Unfortunately, in the initial releases of Oracle8 (prior to 8.0.4) the dictionary views which describe indexes (e.g., DBA_INDEXES) do not include an attribute to identify a reverse order index. You must inquire directly on dictionary base tables to see this information. The following query will display all reverse order indexes in the database:

```
select o.obj#, u.name owner, o.name index_name
  from sys.ind$ i, sys.user$ u, sys.obj$ o
where i.obj# = o.obj#
  and o.owner# = u.user#
  and bitand(i.property,4) <> 0;
```

Only consider using a reverse order index in the warehouse when (1) values in the indexed columns constantly increase while old data is regularly purged,

(2) the index is too large to occasionally reorganize by rebuilding, and (3) it is known that users will only be issuing queries based on equality comparisons to the indexed columns. In short, there are few opportunities in data warehousing in which to effectively use a reverse order index.

Bitmap Indexes

Bitmap indexes were also introduced in Chapter 3. Bitmap indexes are used when there are a small number of distinct values in a particular column. They are much more compact than an equivalent B*Tree index in that only a single bit is required to represent a row as opposed to a full ROWID pointer.

Bitmap indexes can also be used just like B*Tree indexes to retrieve actual row data for computing summary information or retrieving individual row data. If a query actually has to retrieve row information and refers to only one bitmap-indexed column in the WHERE clause, it will usually be more efficient to perform a full table scan than to look up a large number of rows pointed to by the bitmap index. But if several bitmap-indexed columns are referenced in the query's WHERE clause then combining the restrictions made by the indexes can be very efficient. The bitmaps are combined using simple bit arithmetic corresponding to the AND and OR conditions of the WHERE clause. The number of rows that meet all the specified conditions is likely to be a very small subset of the table that can be efficiently retrieved.

BITMAP INDEXES IN ORACLE8

In addition to the uses for bitmap indexes described earlier, Oracle8 employs bitmap indexes to implement its star transformation algorithm. You may create a bitmap index on each foreign key column in the fact table to take advantage of this new Oracle8 way to perform star joins. In our example, bitmap indexes would be created on the PROJECT_ID, CONSULTANT_ID, ORG_ID, FUNC-TION_ID, and MONTH columns in the ACTIVITY table. When we issue a query that joins the ACTIVITY table with the dimension tables, Oracle will first use provided WHERE clause criteria to limit the rows from each dimension table. The primary key values of these remaining dimension table rows are then compared to the bitmap indexes to identify the fact table rows needed using the efficient bit merge operations to resolve these sets into a single result set of qualifying rows. The final step in executing the star join is to join that result set back to each dimension table, using the most appropriate join technique (e.g., hash join, sort merge, nested loop). The Oracle8 star transformation algorithm is extremely efficient, and we should ensure that it is enabled by creating the necessary bitmap indexes.

CREATING A BITMAP INDEX

The only change to the CREATE INDEX command described for creating a B*Tree index is to add the keyword BITMAP. To create a bitmap index on our PROJECT table for the SERVICE_LINE column we use the following command:

```
CREATE BITMAP INDEX PROJ_SL_I on PROJECT(SERVICE_LINE)
   UNRECOVERABLE
   TABLESPACE PROJ_IDX
   STORAGE (INITIAL 2M NEXT 2M PCTINCREASE 0)
   PARALLEL (DEGREE 8);
```

The storage requirements for the bitmap index will be less than those needed for an equivalent B*Tree index. The actual amount of savings will depend on the actual data distribution of the column(s) being indexed. Bitmap indexes on columns of lower cardinality will save more space than those with many values. Also, the storage efficiency increases with the number of rows being indexed. Creating bitmap indexes is also much faster than creating B*Tree indexes. The maintenance of a bitmap index, however, may be slower than equivalent changes in a B*Tree index because Oracle has to uncompress and recompress the bitmaps as data rows are modified. In some cases, it may be much faster to drop a bitmap index before performing table maintenance and then rebuild the index.

Each case may be different. The number of distinct values represented in the index and the type of operation being performed on the table will determine the relative efficiency of maintaining or rebuilding the index. Maintaining a bitmap index after a bulk addition rows to a table (such as via direct path SQL*Loader) may actually be faster than a B*Tree index. Since each row in the table is assigned one bit in each bitmap, the values from the newly added rows are sorted and then appended to the bitmaps without requiring the values in the existing bitmaps to be modified. It may turn out that leaving bitmap indexes in place during your weekly data loads of a particular table is faster but that dropping and rebuilding them is faster for your monthly purges. As in all situations, the designer's rule of thumb must be to first understand the available alternatives and then to test them under realistic conditions.

Oracle8 Partitioned Indexes

Just as large tables may be broken up into multiple segments, Oracle8 allows indexes to be partitioned. Both B*Tree and bitmap indexes may be partitioned. A partitioned index may be built on either a nonpartitioned or a partitioned table. In the latter case, the index may be partitioned on the same partition key as the table or on some other column or columns. An index that is partitioned identically with its partitioned table is called a *local* index. Oracle will automatically maintain any local indexes if the base table is repartitioned. Local indexes are identified using the LOCAL keyword in the CREATE INDEX command.

PREFIXED LOCAL INDEXES

Local partitioned indexes may be either *prefixed* or *non-prefixed*. Prefixed local indexes are partitioned by the same column(s) that form the leading (first defined) edge of the index. An index on our partitioned ACTIVITY table that is partitioned on MONTH is local. If the index is built on the MONTH column (or

MONTH followed by one or more other columns) is prefixed local. Since any query using this index must have specified a value (or range) for MONTH, the Oracle8 optimizer can determine the subset of index partitions that must be examined. This partition elimination feature makes prefixed local indexes the most efficient type of index for query performance.

NONPREFIXED LOCAL INDEXES

Of course, some of our queries need to specify conditions that do not include our partitioning key. We will probably need to index several of these columns as well. Another local (i.e., partitioned by MONTH) index, defined on the ORG_ID column, would be considered nonprefixed. Since each monthly index partition is likely to have timecard records from every organization, a lookup based on ORG_ID will not be able to eliminate any index partitions. This means that a range scan against a local non-prefixed partitioned index will require a search (or "probe") in each index partition. This may have performance impacts, of course, on queries using the index, especially if there are many partitions which must be probed. These searches in multiple index partitions can, luckily, be performed in parallel.

Nonprefixed local indexes cannot be created as unique. A unique index must either be global or include the partitioning key so that Oracle8 may verify that duplicate values do not occur across partitions.

GLOBAL INDEXES

A partitioned index that is partitioned differently than its base table is known as a *global* index. Each partition of a global index may have entries which point to any of the table partitions. There are several restrictions on the use of global indexes in Oracle8.

- Only prefixed global partitioned indexes are supported. This means that a global index must be partitioned by the leading edge column(s) of the index.
- Global indexes on partitioned tables must be B*Tree indexes. Global bitmap indexes are not supported.
- Partitioned bitmap indexes may not be created on non-partitioned tables.

Global indexes require additional maintenance when built on partitioned tables so they should be avoided whenever possible. A local nonprefixed index will generally provide acceptable performance with less administrative overhead. Unless the number of partitions is very large, the searches of multiple local partitions can be performed in parallel which will mitigate the adverse effects. (Incidentally, all nonpartitioned indexes are considered global.)

BUILDING PARTITIONED INDEXES

The following SQL statement will create a local partitioned bitmap index on AC-TIVITY to allow for quick lookup using both MONTH and ORG_ID columns. Because it is declared to be a LOCAL index, it is unnecessary (and actually forbidden) to specify the PARTITION BY RANGE or VALUES LESS THAN clauses. These index partitioning values are taken by Oracle8 from the table partitioning values.

```
CREATE BITMAP INDEX ACT_MONTH_ORD_IDX ON ACTIVITY (MONTH, ORG_ID)
  STORAGE (INITIAL 5M NEXT 5M PCTINCREASE 0)
  PCTFREE 0
  NOLOGGING
  PARALLEL (DEGREE 8)
  LOCAL
          (PARTITION ACT_97JAN_ORG_IDX
                  TABLESPACE ACT_97JAN_ORG_IDX,
           PARTITION ACT_97FEB_ORG_IDX
                  TABLESPACE ACT_97FEB_ORG_IDX,
           PARTITION ACT_97MAR_ORG_IDX
                  TABLESPACE ACT_97MAR_ORG_IDX,
           PARTITION ACT_97APR_ORG_IDX
                  TABLESPACE ACT_97APR_ORG_IDX,
           PARTITION ACT_97MAY_ORG_IDX
                  TABLESPACE ACT_97MAY_ORG_IDX,
           PARTITION ACT_97JUN_ORG_IDX
                  TABLESPACE ACT_97JUN_ORG_IDX,
           PARTITION ACT_97JUL_ORG_IDX
                  TABLESPACE ACT_97JUL_ORG_IDX,
           PARTITION ACT_97AUG_ORG_IDX
                  TABLESPACE ACT_97AUG_ORG_IDX,
           PARTITION ACT_97SEP_ORG_IDX
                  TABLESPACE ACT_97SEP_ORG_IDX,
           PARTITION ACT_97OCT_ORG_IDX
                  TABLESPACE ACT_97OCT_ORG_IDX,
           PARTITION ACT_97NOV_ORG_IDX
                  TABLESPACE ACT_97NOV_ORG_IDX,
           PARTITION ACT_97DEC_ORG_IDX
                  TABLESPACE ACT_97DEC_ORG_IDX);
```

Obviously, each organization may have activity data in multiple partitions of the ACTIVITY table that was partitioned by month. To create a global index with five partitions (to allow lookup in any table partition) by just the ORG_ID, use the following:

```
CREATE INDEX ACT_ORD_IDX ON ACTIVITY (ORG_ID)
  STORAGE (INITIAL 5M NEXT 1M PCTINCREASE 0)
  PCTFREE 0
  NOLOGGING
  PARALLEL (DEGREE 8)
  GLOBAL PARTITION BY RANGE (ORG_ID)
          (PARTITION ACT_ORG1_IDX VALUES LESS THAN ('200')
                  TABLESPACE ACT_ORG1_IDX,
```

```
PARTITION ACT_ORG2_IDX VALUES LESS THAN ('400')
        TABLESPACE ACT_ORG2_IDX,
PARTITION ACT_ORG3_IDX VALUES LESS THAN ('600')
        TABLESPACE ACT_ORG3_IDX,
PARTITION ACT_ORG4_IDX VALUES LESS THAN ('800')
        TABLESPACE ACT_ORG4_IDX,
PARTITION ACT_ORG5_IDX VALUES LESS THAN MAXVALUE
        TABLESPACE ACT_ORG5_IDX);
```

Note that this syntax to create a global partitioned index applies only to B*Tree indexes. Bitmap indexes must be local or else nonpartitioned.

Local partitioned indexes are administratively simpler than global indexes because of the automatic handling provided by Oracle8 when repartitioning the table. A local index is generally smaller than a global index and only needs to be maintained when data in the corresponding table partition is modified. Other local index partitions, for instance, are unaffected when we load data into the most recent table partition.

Because we frequently need to index columns that don't include the table's partition key and want to avoid the performance penalty of probing many local index partitions, it will sometimes be necessary to create global indexes. Additional processing by Oracle8 is needed to deal with global indexes because they are affected whenever data in any table partition is added, modified, or deleted. The administrator must also perform additional work to deal with global indexes. Anytime a partition of the partitioned table is added, dropped, split, moved, truncated, and so on, all global indexes are marked as unusable and must be recreated by the DBA. This activity needs to be planned and pre-scripted to accommodate the required global index maintenance whenever table repartitioning is performed.

Global index partitions may be repartitioned (using ALTER INDEX SPLIT PARTITION and ALTER INDEX DROP PARTITION commands) in a manner similar to partitioned tables, as described earlier in this chapter. Local indexes are automatically maintained when their base table is repartitioned. Individual partitions, local or global, may be rebuilt independently when necessary.

TABLESPACE FOR INDEX PARTITIONS

It is critical that the DBA specify a tablespace whenever a partition is added to an index partition. Without an explicit tablespace declaration Oracle8 places the new partition into the same tablespace as the base table.

Oracle Database Clusters

Oracle provides several methods for allowing rows that share common data values to be stored together in the same data blocks. The result of storing rows together is that they can be retrieved more quickly when they are used together such as in a join.

Index Clusters

Index clusters were also described in Chapter 3. There are some OLTP situations in which clustering a hierarchy of tables can provide optimized access for join processing. Rarely can the warehouse designer as the developer of an OLTP database predict join requirements precisely.

There is one use for index clusters in a data warehouse. That is to cluster a single table. A table with many rows that have a common data value in a column (or series of columns) may be a candidate for a single table cluster. The advantage of a single table cluster is to reduce the number of data blocks required to store the table. This is possible because the cluster key is stored only one time, and all the rows for that cluster key simply reference that cluster key. If the cluster key columns are large, the space savings of a single table cluster can be substantial. Additionally, any queries that need to retrieve these common-valued rows as a set will require less physical I/O to locate them.

A possible alternative to the star design might be denormalized by including information that is normally stored in the dimension tables in the actual fact table, essentially prejoining the fact table and several of the dimension tables. By using data from several dimension tables, we are able to create a cluster that would be impossible with a multitable cluster. For example, we could store our organization hierarchy information in the fact table by including the cost center, region, area, and division names in the fact table. We could also store some of the information from the PROJECT table, such as service line, industry, and project type in the fact table. This would eliminate the need to join the ACTIVITY, ORGANIZATION, and PROJECT tables for a large percentage of our queries. Without a cluster, we would avoid doing this because of the huge price we would pay in extra storage requirements. If we had one million rows in the ACTIVITY table and we attempted this kind of denormalization to a normal table (adding approximately 300 bytes of denormalized columns from dimension tables), we would require approximately 50,000 data blocks (assuming an 8-KB block size). By creating a single table cluster using these denormalized columns as the cluster key, we will require approximately 10,000 data blocks.

This alternative has drawbacks (as alternatives usually do in database design) in that we will have to create additional bitmap indexes on a million-row table in order to efficiently answer all the possible queries that might be posed using criteria from dimension data. Additionally, we must be able to predict the total amount of space needed to store the entire set of rows that share any given cluster key value. Unless this space requirement is fairly uniform, storage efficiency in the cluster will be lost. In most cases, the possible performance and storage gains are not sufficient to warrant making this denormalizaton.

However, as an example, the following SQL commands would be used to create a prejoined ACTIVITY table as an indexed cluster:

```
CREATE CLUSTER PREJOIN_ACTIVITY
   (CCNUM          VARCHAR2(4),
    MONTH          VARCHAR2(7),
```

```
              SERVICE_LINE    VARCHAR(40),
              INDUSTRY        VARCHAR2(40),
              REGION_NAME     VARCHAR2(40),
              AREA_NAME       VARCHAR2(40))
           TABLESPACE ACT_CLUSTER
           STORAGE (INITIAL 100M NEXT 100M PCTINCREASE 0)
           PARALLEL (DEGREE 8);

       CREATE INDEX PREJOIN_IND1 ON CLUSTER PREJOIN_ACTIVITY;

       CREATE TABLE ACTIVITY
          (MONTH         VARCHAR2(7),
           CCNUM         VARCHAR2(4),
           INDUSTRY      VARCHAR2(40),
           SERVICE_LINE  VARCHAR2(40),
           REGION_NAME   VARCHAR2(40),
           AREA_NAME     VARCHAR2(40),
           CONSULTANT_ID NUMBER,
           FUNCTION_CODE VARCHAR2(2),
           HOURS         NUMBER(11,2),
           EXPENSES      NUMBER(11,2),
           REVENUE       NUMBER(11,2))
          CLUSTER PREJOIN_ACTIVITY
              (CCNUM, MONTH, SERVICE_LINE, INDUSTRY, REGION_NAME, AREA_NAME)
          PARALLEL (DEGREE 8);
```

The order in which the statements are executed is important. The cluster must be created first, then the cluster index, then the table. The storage parameter in the CREATE CLUSTER works as the default storage parameters for tables created in the cluster, and the PARALLEL parameter sets up the number of parallel processes that can operate on the cluster and tables in the cluster. (There are a number of other parameters that relate to creating a cluster; these are described in detail in the Oracle7 and Oracle8 Server SQL reference manuals.) We can create regular B*Tree indexes on any column in the clustered table. Applications are not aware of whether a table exists in an indexed cluster, so we can move tables into and out of a cluster with no effect on any application SQL code.

Even though Oracle7, release 7.3, is optimized to perform star joins, there may occasionally be a substantial improvement in query performance using the single table cluster. On our example data warehouse, we observe performance improvements ranging from 0 to 300 percent depending on the nature of the query. The best performance with a single table cluster will result when the leading (i.e., first defined) columns in the cluster key are referenced in the WHERE clause. Just as with a regular B*Tree concatenated index, when the leading edge of the cluster key is referenced in the WHERE clause, the cluster index may be used for the query. Careful analysis of user access patterns and selectivity is required when choosing the order of columns cluster key. The prime considerations in choosing a cluster key are that (1) it can be used in as many queries as possible and (2) it is selective enough that chaining will be minimized. If (as is usually the case) the queries cannot be predicted, then multiple indexes might have to be created. Ideally, data columns in the cluster key should not be updated.

Using a single table cluster may slow performance on INSERT operations because Oracle must locate the appropriate data block for the specific cluster key for each row rather than just select an available block from the table's freelist. A single table cluster may not be effective for tables with millions of rows for which we cannot create a cluster key that is sufficiently selective to avoid chaining. Although we would not generally recommend the use of single table indexed clusters for data warehouses, the technique can be effective in certain situations and is worth exploring. The improvements made to star query optimization in Oracle8 make this technique less appealing.

Hash Clusters

Oracle offers an additional type of clustering, *hash clusters*. Hash clusters differ from indexed clusters primarily by the way Oracle determines where the data block is located. A hash cluster creates a hash key based on either an internal algorithm or an algorithm supplied by the developer as part of the table data. The hashing algorithm processes the cluster key columns and computes the hash key. The hash key points Oracle directly to the data block containing that set of cluster key columns. Hash clusters operate faster than indexed clusters for lookups based on specific key values because there is no need to traverse a B*Tree index to locate the address of the cluster columns. This can result in a substantial improvement in performance for a specific subset of queries. Unlike an indexed cluster, a hash cluster stores the cluster key values for each row in the cluster. Consequently, we cannot use the single table clustering technique discussed in the previous section as a way to prejoin our tables. Index range scans and full table scans generally suffer when the table is placed in a hash cluster. Adding data to a hash cluster also presents difficulties—the entire table's space must be allocated at initial creation and cannot later allocate additional extents. Hash clusters are also very sensitive to chaining. For these reasons, there is rarely an opportunity to take advantage of hash clusters in a data warehouse.

The syntax to create a hash cluster is very similar to that shown earlier to create an index cluster. An additional clause, HASHKEYS (and optionally HASH IS), must be provided to tell Oracle how to organize the data within the allocated data blocks.

Analyzing Schema Objects

Once tables and indexes have been created, we need to ensure that the cost-based optimizer has sufficient information to make an intelligent choice among various alternative query execution strategies. Oracle uses the ANALYZE table command to gather information about the number of rows, the distribution of index values, and the like. To analyze a table we issue the following command:

```
ANALYZE TABLE ACTIVITY COMPUTE STATISTICS;
```

When we analyze a table we analyze both the table and the indexes on that table. In order to analyze a table, Oracle must perform a full table scan and sort the table data. This requires a substantial amount of CPU and memory resources. For very large tables (multimillions of rows) analyzing the table is quite an expensive operation. It is possible to analyze a table and only sample a subset of rows. The command is as follows:

```
ANALYZE TABLE ACTIVITY
  ESTIMATE STATISTICS SAMPLE 10 PERCENT;
```

It is possible to sample any percentage of the rows in a table or to specify a number of rows to sample. Each release of Oracle7 has shown improvements in the sampling algorithm that allow good statistics to be gathered with smaller sample sizes. By release 7.3 it appears that sampling about 5 to 10 percent of the rows yields acceptable results in most cases. Large detail or fact tables should be analyzed whenever about 10 percent of the data in the table changes. A smaller load, however, that significantly alters the distribution of data in one or more columns may justify obtaining a new set of statistics. Most warehouse administrators try to schedule an ANALYZE step after each periodic load whenever possible. The dimension tables and individual partitions of partitioned tables are usually sufficiently small that the ANALYZE command is relatively inexpensive and can be executed after each load.

To gather statistics on a single partition of an Oracle8 partitioned table, the modified syntax is as follows:

```
ANALYZE TABLE ACTIVITY PARTITION ACT_98JAN
    ESTIMATE STATISTICS SAMPLE 10 PERCENT;
```

An optional clause can be added to the ANALYZE TABLE command in order to build a histogram of the data values in various columns:

```
FOR ALL INDEXED COLUMNS SIZE 20
```

This example shows one of several variations of the optional syntax for gathering column-level statistics. Statistics for each indexed column will be stored in twenty histogram "buckets." It is also possible to name specific columns or to request statistics for all columns in the table. (This final option provides no real value to the optimizer since retrieval based on data from nonindexed columns will require a full table scan.)

The syntax to gather (COMPUTE, in this example) statistics on an individual index is as follows:

```
ANALYZE INDEX ACT_PK
   COMPUTE STATISTICS;
```

The cost-based optimizer will not work correctly if the tables and indexes have not been analyzed. Users will receive no error messages, but the optimizer will simply make assumptions (that are probably not valid) about the data and proceed. This generally results in suboptimal query performance. There is a PL/SQL package that can be used to analyze all the objects in a schema. DBMS_UTILITY.ANALYZE_SCHEMA takes two arguments, the name of a schema and the analysis method (COMPUTE or ESTIMATE). However, this package does not allow you to specify the percentage of rows on which to base the estimate.

Using Views in the Data Warehouse

A view is a virtual table that gives a data warehouse developer the ability to control exactly how the underlying data structures in the database appear to the user. Views can be used to hide complicated underlying physical database designs from the user. Even though one of the strengths of a star design is that the relationships between the tables are simple and intuitive, we would still like to avoid having to teach our users about joining tables. This becomes even more important if we can avoid having to introduce the concepts of outer-joins and antijoins (an antijoin is when a query is used to select rows that belong to one table that do *not* have a corresponding row in another table) to the users. Using views enables the user to "prejoin" tables, ensuring that the join is correctly defined and efficient. Some simple but useful views that we will use in our project accounting data warehouse might include PROJECT_REVENUES and ORGANIZATION_REVENUES to present summary information. Another candidate view might be BAD_CONSULTANT_IDS which is an antijoin used to identify any CONSULTANT_IDS that are in the ACTIVITY table but are not in the ORGANIZATION table.

```
CREATE OR REPLACE VIEW PROJECT_REVENUES AS
   SELECT PROJECTS.PROJECT_ID, PROJECT_NAME, SUM(REVENUE)
    FROM PROJECTS, ACTIVITY
    WHERE PROJECT.ID = ACTIVITY.PROJECT_ID
    GROUP BY PROJECTS.PROJECT_ID;

CREATE OR REPLACE VIEW ORGANIZATION_REVENUES AS
   SELECT ORGANIZATIONS.ORG_ID, ORGANIZATION_NAME, SUM(REVENUE)
    FROM ORGANIZATIONS, ACTIVITY
    WHERE ORGANIZATIONS.ORG_ID = ACTIVITY.ORG_ID
    GROUP BY ORGANIZATIONS.ORG_ID;

CREATE OR REPLACE VIEW BAD_CONSULTANT_ID AS
   SELECT CONSULTANT_ID
    FROM ACTIVITY
```

```
WHERE CONSULTANT_ID NOT IN (SELECT CONSULTANT_ID
                              FROM CONSULTANT);
```

This last view could be rewritten using the MINUS operator or as an outer-join. In any event, it is an antijoin view. The Oracle optimizer will frequently re-cast antijoin SELECT statements into a form that can be processed in the most efficient manner.

Using Views and DECODE for Complex Analyses

Users frequently want to display information that is stored in separate rows in our database as columnar data. This capability allows them to produce cross-tab or matrix reports. Consider an example from the project accounting data warehouse. Each of the external projects has been assigned to a specific service line. Warehouse users would like to analyze the total revenue associated with each service line for each organizational unit. We will create a view that presents the data as a matrix between ORG_ID and SERVICE_LINE.

In order to create columns out of rows, we will need to use the DECODE function. DECODE works much like an IF statement. The basic DECODE function takes four arguments: two data values, expressions, or columns and two possible output values. If the two data parameters are equal then the DECODE returns the first output value. If the two values are not equal, it will return the second answer. The syntax is as follows:

```
DECODE(first_test_value, second_test_value, result_if_equal, other_result)

CREATE OR REPLACE VIEW SERVICE_REVENUE AS
    SELECT CCNUM, MONTH,
           SUM(DECODE(SERVICE_LINE,'INTERNET',REVENUE,0))     INTERNET,
           SUM(DECODE(SERVICE_LINE,'APPLICATIONS',REVENUE,0)) APPLICATIONS,
           SUM(DECODE(SERVICE_LINE,'DATABASE',REVENUE,0))     DATABASE,
           SUM(DECODE(SERVICE_LINE,'BPR',REVENUE,0))          BPR,
           SUM(DECODE(SERVICE_LINE,'EDUCATION',REVENUE,0))    EDUCATION,
           SUM(DECODE(SERVICE_LINE,'OTHER',REVENUE,0))        OTHER
      FROM ACTIVITY A, PROJECT P
     WHERE A.PROJECT_ID = P.PROJECT_ID
     GROUP BY CCNUM, MONTH;
```

Each column will be the sum of the value of REVENUE for each row in which SERVICE_LINE equals the constant provided in the second parameter. All other rows will contribute 0 to the sum. Executing the query

```
SELECT *
  FROM SERVICE_REVENUE
 WHERE CCNUM IN ('477', '488')
   AND MONTH IN ('1997NOV', '1997DEC');
```

results in the following matrix report:

CCNUM	MONTH	INTERNET	FINANCIALS	DB	BPR	ED	OTHER
477	1997NOV	55,120	47,620	25,050	11,270	12,450	53,200
477	1997DEC	43,830	52,500	22,110	12,335	12,500	52,400
488	1997NOV	37,442	41,207	13,400	9,500	7,000	27,000
488	1997DEC	34,300	40,270	12,530	10,110	8,430	25,600

A common criticism of a RDBMS being used in data warehousing is that it is difficult, if not impossible, to perform time-based analyses. Even relatively simple time-based analyses like comparing last year's data with the current year can be challenging with a relational database. This is functionality that multidimensional databases such as Oracle Express (covered in Chapter 13) typically manage better than relational databases. However, this technique of creating views with the DECODE function will allow us to easily manage time-based analyses. To create a view for the project accounting data warehouse that will allow analysis of each month's revenue by organization use the following:

```
CREATE OR REPLACE VIEW MONTHLY_REVENUE AS
   SELECT CCNUM,
          SUM(DECODE(MONTH,'1997JAN',REVENUE,0)  JAN1997,
          SUM(DECODE(MONTH,'1997FEB',REVENUE,0)  FEB1997,
          SUM(DECODE(MONTH,'1997MAR',REVENUE,0)  MAR1997,
          SUM(DECODE(MONTH,'1997APR',REVENUE,0)  APR1997,
          SUM(DECODE(MONTH,'1997MAY',REVENUE,0)  MAY1997,
          SUM(DECODE(MONTH,'1997JUN',REVENUE,0)  JUN1997,
          SUM(DECODE(MONTH,'1997JUL',REVENUE,0)  JUL1997,
          SUM(DECODE(MONTH,'1997AUG',REVENUE,0)  AUG1997,
          SUM(DECODE(MONTH,'1997SEP',REVENUE,0)  SEP1997,
          SUM(DECODE(MONTH,'1997OCT',REVENUE,0)  OCT1997,
          SUM(DECODE(MONTH,'1997NOV',REVENUE,0)  NOV1997,
          SUM(DECODE(MONTH,'1997DEC',REVENUE,0)  DEC1997
     FROM ACTIVITY
    GROUP BY CCNUM;
```

Obviously, this could be extended to include as many years' worth of data as desired. Once the view is created the user simply can refer to any desired months in the select list of their query and combine months to show quarterly results, compare differences between time periods, and the like. Grouping months into quarters could be done with a query such as the following:

```
SELECT CCNUM,
       NVL(JAN1997,0)+NVL(FEB1997,0)+NVL(MAR1997,0) Q1,
       NVL(APR1997,0)+NVL(MAY1997,0)+NVL(JUN1997,0) Q2,
       NVL(JUL1997,0)+NVL(AUG1997,0)+NVL(SEP1997,0) Q3,
       NVL(OCT1997,0)+NVL(NOV1997,0)+NVL(DEC1997,0) Q4
  FROM MONTHLY_REVENUE
 GROUP BY CCNUM;
```

We can use this technique along with SQL to generate SQL and information in the database to create these views dynamically. That way, after we load new data we can run the script to create a new view based on the new data in the database. The view will always be up to date. To maintain the MONTHLY_REVENUE to always have a running twenty-four-month history in the view we can use the following SQL statement to create the necessary SQL script for us:

```
COL DUMMY NOPRINT
COL DUMMY2 NOPRINT
SET FEEDBACK OFF PAGES 0 HEAD OFF
SPOOL CREATE_MONTHLY_REVENUE.SQL
SELECT 1 DUMMY, SYSDATE,
       'CREATE OR REPLACE VIEW MONTHLY_REVENUE AS SELECT CCNUM '
  FROM DUAL
UNION
SELECT 2, TO_DATE(MONTH,'YYYYMON'),
       'SUM(DECODE(MONTH,'''||MONTH||''''||',REVENUE,0)'||'  '||
       SUBSTR(MONTH,5)||SUBSTR(MONTH,1,4)
  FROM FISCAL_DATE
 WHERE MONTHS_BETWEEN(SYSDATE,TO_DATE(MONTHS,'YYYYMON') < 25
UNION
SELECT 3, SYSDATE, 'GROUP BY CCNUM'
  FROM DUAL
ORDER BY 1, 2;
SPOOL OFF
```

We want to ensure that the columns are created in ascending order, so that the first column is the oldest month, the second column is the second oldest, and so on. We include a second "dummy" column in the query that will be used to sort the rows returned by the second SELECT statement. Since each query in a UNION must have the same number of columns and each column must have the same datatype, we must include a dummy value (SYSDATE) in the first and third SELECT statements. These dummy columns are not used other than as placeholders. In the middle query we return the date value; when we sort by the second column, this results in the rows being sorted in the desired order. The subsequent CREATE VIEW statement will have the columns created in the proper order.

USE DECODE INSTEAD OF PROCEDURAL IF-THEN-ELSE

The DECODE statement provides powerful capabilities that will be used frequently in a data warehouse project. A common use for DECODE is to test and transform data values during load processing. Because DECODE is a SQL function and is used in SELECT statements, we can take advantage of parallel processing for our test and transformations. This is contrasted to the common alternative of using a series of IF tests in a PL/SQL procedure. While the PL/SQL procedure is more intuitive to a programmer, PL/SQL does not take advantage of parallel processing capabilities. Using DECODE can provide substantial performance benefits over using PL/SQL and processing each row one at a time.

There is one caution to keep in mind when using views to hide the complexity of joins from end users. Typically, we create a view that has all the useful columns from each table that we join. The end user is presented with a list of available columns that all appear from the same table. One column seems as good as another column in the view. If the end user should happen to select a set of columns that are all in a single base table the query will still have to suffer the performance overhead of performing the joins. The use of views from ad hoc query tools means that every query will have to join all the tables.

A better approach would be to use a query tool that allows the administrator to provide the end user with a single list of available columns but have the tool maintain its own metadata so that each query only accesses those tables absolutely necessary to resolve the query. Oracle Discoverer 3.0 has this capability.

Summary Views or Summary Tables?

In our project accounting data warehouse, we have created some views that are used to present summary information. An alternative approach would be to create actual summary tables for the same purpose. Summary tables will provide more rapid response to queries. Does this mean that summary tables are always to be preferred over views? Not necessarily. Summary tables can be expensive to create and to store. It is not unusual for a substantial portion of the periodic loading time to be spent creating summary tables.

Because summary tables collapse the detail data across one or more dimensions, many summary tables are typically required. A "traditional" data warehouse can consume more disk space for storing summaries than is devoted to the detail data. As the number of summary tables grows, the task of the DBA becomes more complex. The user also can be overwhelmed by a large number of summary tables and his or her inability to figure out which table he or she should access to answer a particular question (this latter concern applies equally to the presence of a large number of views).

Some sophisticated query tools help us deal with the proliferation of summary tables and views. Oracle Discoverer 3.0 allows the administrator to specify the relationship between a summary table and the detail tables on which the summary is based. Discoverer 3.0 then determines which table will provide the correct answer to a query and the fastest response time to the query. It directs its generated query to the summary table when possible or to the detail table when necessary. The user does not have to be aware of the presence of summary and detail tables.

If we decide to implement summary tables we can use Oracle's parallel CREATE TABLE table_name AS SELECT (pCTAS) command to quickly calculate the summary data:

```
CREATE TABLE ORG_REVENUE_SUMMARY
    UNRECOVERABLE
    PARALLEL (DEGREE 8)
    STORAGE (INITIAL 5M  NEXT 5M PCTINCREASE 0)
    PCTFREE 0
```

```
AS SELECT CCNUM, MONTH, SUM(REVENUE)  MONTHLY_REV
   FROM ACTIVITY A, ORGANIZATIONS O
   WHERE A.ORG_ID = O.ORG_ID
   GROUP BY CCNUM, MONTH;
```

This command will typically execute very quickly if sufficient hardware resources are available. Creating summary tables using pCTAS is covered in depth in Chapter 7.

The primary reason for creating summary tables is to improve query performance. We expect that, as more data warehouses are implemented using Oracle8, the role of summary tables will be reduced because adequate performance will be available with star joins against the detail (fact) table.

Testing the Data Warehouse

Like all large projects, a data warehouse needs extensive testing. Typically, insufficient time is set aside for testing (or the planned time is consumed with resolving data extract problems!) All data extraction, data cleansing, transportation, and load, summarization, and aggregation processes must be tested. Additionally, expected data access methods need to be verified.

These types of tests can be referred to broadly as data quality testing. Does our data warehouse provide data of sufficiently high quality to be useful? Although the data quality testing should start early, it is not possible to complete it until all the various components are finished and the equivalent of integration testing can begin. The amount of time required for this wide range of testing will be considerable. The data warehouse implementation plans must provide enough time for testing and making changes based on the results of the testing.

In addition to the data quality testing that must be conducted, you should also conduct architecture feasibility tests using sufficiently large volumes of data. There is a bit of a Catch-22 in volume testing. Since the testing is of fundamental architecture features, like the physical database design, hardware and network design, and so on, this testing must occur sufficiently early in the project to allow time to make changes. Waiting until the week before the warehouse opens to test the architecture's ability to support the planned data volumes may leave the project in serious trouble! It is very difficult to make fundamental architectural changes late in the project. The Catch-22 is that there generally isn't enough data early in the project that can be used for volume testing. Without data extraction and loading procedures completed, how can we have a sufficient amount of data to perform any useful tests?

The primary concern in generating test data is to maintain the necessary referential integrity between the fact table and the dimension tables. Because the dimension tables tend to be relatively small, it is feasible to use simple manual methods to populate them with meaningful data. The fact table will need to have thousands or millions of rows, and each row will need to properly reference each of the dimension tables. Unfortunately, you can't just populate the fact table with random data and be able to adequately test your warehouse. It is possible, though, to generate a "quick and dirty" set of test data for your data warehouse using PL/SQL. Create referential key constraints for the fact table and the dimension tables. If you supply the name of a fact table, it is possible to determine from the data dictionary all the referenced dimension tables and the name of their primary key columns. The following SQL statement demonstrates this for a fact table named ACTIVITY:

```
SELECT COLUMN_NAME, UCC.TABLE_NAME
  FROM USER_CONS_COLUMNS UCC, USER_CONSTRAINTS UC
 WHERE UCC.CONSTRAINT_NAME = UC.R_CONSTRAINT_NAME
   AND UC.TABLE_NAME = 'ACTIVITY'
```

The output of this SQL statement will be the name of each table and the associated primary key column in the table for every table that is referenced by the fact table. This information can be used to generate SQL statements that insert records into the fact table that will maintain the necessary referential integrity. Use the SQL-to-generate-SQL (or in this case PL/SQL) methods discussed at the start of this chapter to create a PL/SQL routine that will load the fact table. The first step in the PL/SQL routine will be to create CURSOR FOR LOOPS that reference each dimension table and column. There will be one CURSOR FOR LOOP for each dimension table. Loop through each table, selecting the primary key values into a PL/SQL table. (A PL/SQL table works much like a single-dimension array.) At this point you will have several PL/SQL tables, one for each dimension table. You are now ready to create an insert statement for the fact table. The insert statement can reference some random data for the data fields and reference one of the values in each PL/SQL table for the foreign key values. The PL/SQL table values are referenced as variables in the INSERT statement. Control the number of rows inserted by using nested loop logic, with the inner loop processing each row in the PL/SQL table and the outer loop processing N times (where N is a parameter passed to the procedure).

Regardless of the method used to load the data warehouse with test data, the effort to load and test the data warehouse with large volumes of data early in the project will be richly rewarded. It is impossible to overemphasize the need to validate the warehouse design with large volumes of data. Don't limit testing to query response times, but test the time it takes to perform the incremental loads, indexing, archival, and planned backup/recovery processes. It is very likely that procedures that work well with smaller data volumes simply will not be acceptable with large volumes. The only way to ensure that volume-related problems are identified and addressed is by thorough testing. To be useful, this testing must begin even earlier in the development life cycle than in a custom application development project.

Summary

This chapter introduced several features of the SQL*Plus environment that can be exploited by the administrator of an Oracle data warehouse to make life simpler. These included spooling and formatting of output, the use of substitution variables, and the use of SQL to generate SQL.

We then described the process for creating an Oracle database, tablespaces within the database, and then various database objects in these tablespaces. The primary object types that make up the warehouse are tables (including partitioned tables) and indexes (both B*Tree and bitmap).

The use of ANALYZE to gather statistics for the cost-based optimizer was covered along with the use of views to simplify the way data appears to the warehouse users. The chapter concluded with an exhortation to plan for (and execute!) early testing of the warehouse using realistic volumes of data.

POPULATING THE ORACLE DATA WAREHOUSE

CHAPTER 6

Of all the work done before the data warehouse is ready to open, the average warehouse development team will spend less than 20 percent of its time designing the warehouse, configuring hardware, installing software products, and the like. Easily 80 percent of the work involved in setting up a data warehouse is devoted to locating, extracting, filtering, scrubbing, and finally loading data. Of these tasks, loading is by far the easiest. Resolving the various (and nefarious!) problems that arise when we bring together data from multiple source systems is invariably more difficult than we anticipated.

We haven't devoted a lot of space in this book to planning an overall data warehouse project, but we will provide one guideline here. Take whatever amount of time you believe will be necessary for data extracts, data scrubbing, and data loading; then double that total amount and add it into the schedule for resolving data problems. And then make sure there is some additional slack in the schedule to allow for the data that still isn't quite right!

It is always hard for the first-time warehouse analyst to accept, in advance, the fact that the majority of the operational systems (with which we are successfully running our businesses) are not internally consistent—that somehow they continue to function even with dirty data! After the first warehouse load experience, however, a healthy dose of skepticism is inevitably introduced. Among many other valid reasons for starting on a small scale, this is sufficient justification for basing Phase I of the warehouse on only a very small number of subject areas and source systems.

The complexity of the integration process grows rapidly as the number of subject areas and source systems are increased. For a very simplified example, Figure 6.1 demonstrates that the probability of a data conflict is proportional to the number of system integration points to be resolved. If we are integrating data from two sources, there is only one integration point to be resolved. With a triangle of three sources, there are three "edges" to be integrated. As we move

Figure 6.1 Complexity effect of multiple data sources.

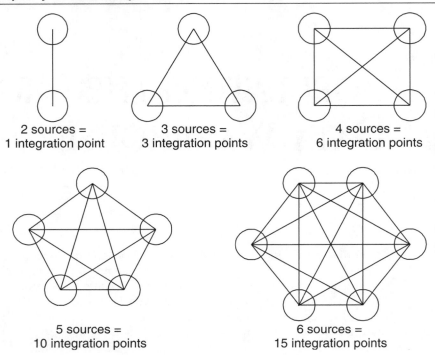

2 sources =
1 integration point

3 sources =
3 integration points

4 sources =
6 integration points

5 sources =
10 integration points

6 sources =
15 integration points

to four sources, we have to deal with six potential conflicts. Five sources yields ten opportunities for integration problems, while with six sources we have to resolve discrepancies arising from fifteen different integration points.

It is easy to see how the complexity of integrating data from many sources rapidly becomes unmanageable. By starting the data warehouse with, say, three subject areas or sources, we can gain experience while dealing with a relatively small number of data integration points. A second phase can then add three more data sources to the existing warehouse with only an additional six areas of potential conflict (since the existing integrated warehouse now acts as a single source). This phased approach actually presents less total work (3 + 6 = 9 integrations) than attempting to do a "big bang" implementation (15 integrations!) and is more manageable.

Dealing with Dirty Data

Integrating data from multiple sources is difficult under the best of circumstances. Unfortunately, we have never seen the best of circumstances! One should expect differences between the names, formats, and encoding of data being extracted from multiple sources. An organization's many operational systems should naturally be expected to have been designed by different teams at different times and probably built using different file or database management systems. The old payroll system tracks employees by social security number in VSAM files while the newly purchased project accounting system tracks consulting employees by name. Sometimes project accounting's employee name doesn't exactly match the name carried in the payroll system. Payroll also keeps track of all employees, some of whom aren't in project accounting because they don't work on billable projects. To make things worse, the project accounting system tracks some independent contractors who aren't even company employees.

On top of these expected differences that have to be resolved, it is virtually guaranteed that we will find other surprises in the data we extract. Our newly designed data warehouse has a carefully architectured environment in which we document and incorporate specific data rules. We find that many of our existing operational systems were built without rigorous enforcement of various business rules. In other cases, we find that the application code has been enforcing some rules that aren't documented—we "discover" these rules as we try to make sense of the extracted data.

It may seem surprising, but it is not uncommon, to encounter dirty data: duplicate records, missing "parents" from what should be parent/child relationships, denormalized data that can't be renormalized. Imagine a system developed in COBOL and VSAM files in which the record layout is designed to hold everything necessary about an employee's weekly timesheet. (This design allowed the original COBOL programmer to avoid complex multiple input logic.) The record contains repeating groups to track the multiple projects, hours, and days on which an employee might work during the week. The record also carries the information about the employee, their pay grade and organization code. Such a structure makes the payroll processing fairly simple. What happens, however, if the organization code or other employee information changes from one week to the next? The next week's payroll record simply carries the new values, and payroll churns along happily. What happens, however, if the pay grade changes on the first day of a month that falls on a Wednesday? Well, the original programmers found an easy solution, they just create two timesheet records for that employee for that week, one with sixteen hours and the other with twenty-four hours at the higher rate of pay. Payroll processing still works fine, but when we extract for the data warehouse we expect to load data into a normalized structure with primary keys. We have to resolve the two records into one parent row with multiple child rows for each day and project code.

We also expect that every project code we encounter in a payroll record will already be part of our PROJECTS dimension table. Since the payroll system is only concerned with how many hours the employee worked and how much money to pay per hour, it never cared about specific project codes. During our warehouse integration effort we have to reconcile discrepancies.

Dealing with Missing Data

One special case of dealing with dirty data is the situation in which not all data needed for an extract has been entered as of the time of the extract. In our case study of data taken from a company's project accounting system, we expect each employee to file a timecard each week. But what if they are late? The vacationing consultant who didn't enter his or her time report before leaving for two weeks in Hawaii will not be represented in our extract. On returning, he or she will probably be chastised and will enter the missing weeks' data, and the operational systems will be able to pay the employee and issue client invoices. But what about the data warehouse?

Similar situations can occur in lots of operational systems besides project accounting. There is no straightforward technical solution to this problem. We have several possible ways of dealing with it:

- Ignore the missing data. In some cases, the amount of missing data may be insignificant in relation to the whole. When combined with the next option, this solution works well in many cases.
- Wait to do our extracts until we can be sure that all (or virtually all) of the necessary data is entered. Of course, this approach will require more or less waiting depending on the source system. This approach is, generally, the best answer. Those critics who argue that they absolutely need the data warehouse to be updated within twenty-four hours of a transaction are probably trying to do some form of operational reporting instead of pure data warehouse analysis.
- Mark rows/records as they are extracted so that unextracted data can be identified at the time of the next extract. One disadvantage to this approach is that it requires more work to do an UPDATE in addition to a SELECT during extract processing. Another major disadvantage is that any summaries performed on a time basis (as most warehouse rollups are) will have to be reexecuted after the missing data is later obtained. This approach, unlike the first two, requires updates to warehouse data. Updating warehouses should be avoided so that users do not receive different answers to the same question asked at different times.
- Extract data based on time of data entry as opposed to the business period to which it applies. This is tempting when the source system time-stamps records, but it is generally not a very satisfactory solution. It shares the disadvantage of requiring that summaries be reexecuted to include late-arriving data. Additionally, it may cause a corollary problem by getting small amounts of data from the next period. Doing a summarization based on less than a statistically significant sample of the data may lead to erroneous decisions based on incomplete data. We will further address the concept of "publishing" data later in this chapter.

Our next decisions are how and where to do the required data resolution and reconciliation. We have three general choices: we can use a tool that automates the extraction, transformation, integration, and transfer of the data from sources to warehouse; we can perform the complex transformation and reformatting as part of custom-written extraction programs and scripts; or we can extract the necessary data in "raw" form and then perform the necessary transformations and integration on the warehouse side during (or after) the load process.

Updating Warehouse Data

Although not absolutely forbidden, updating data in the warehouse after it has been "published" to users leads to problems when the same query issued on different days yields different results. This has the same negative effect as creating multiple departmental "data marts" with different data sources—it causes confusion and doubts about the accuracy of all warehouse information. We should avoid making changes to data in the warehouse.

Reconciling with ETT Tools

We've already discussed the use of data extraction, transformation, and transfer tools in the context of defining and building the data warehouse. In addition to these functions, your ETT tool will also aid in the loading of data into the warehouse.

Figure 6.2 demonstrates the option of performing data scrubbing and integration using an ETT tool to define the extract processing, to perform necessary data reengineering, and then to control the load process.

The primary advantage of using an ETT tool is that it can provide a single "control panel" to handle several steps in the data warehouse design, develop-

Figure 6.2 Data reconciliation using an ETT Tool.

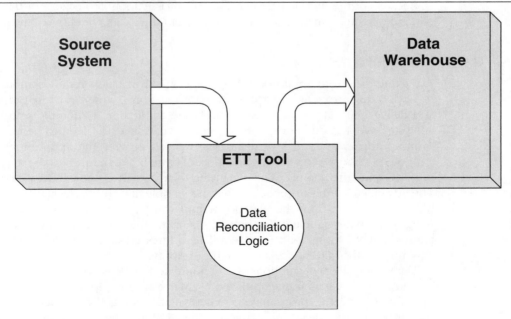

ment, and implementation. The ETT tool can serve as the repository of all warehouse design metadata. It can generate the needed extract programs to process the source data. It can control the transfer of extract data files from their source system to the computer hosting the warehouse. Finally, the ETT tool can control the loading of data into the Oracle warehouse.

The primary disadvantage of ETT tools is their cost. It is not uncommon to spend as much or more on the ETT tool as on the Oracle RDBMS that will host the data warehouse. The tool may be worth the price if it is used to its full advantage. There is a risk of an organization acquiring such a tool but not investing enough commitment into training and the subsequent learning curve. Management that funds the purchase must also understand the total costs and insist that the tool be used rigorously.

There are several criteria that should be considered when selecting an ETT tool. The warehouse team should evaluate the user interface of the repository. Will the analysts and programmers assigned to the warehouse use the ETT tool for all their work, or will they be tempted to hand-modify the generated code? How fully does the tool understand the Oracle database's features? What about newer features such as table and index partitioning, bitmap indexes, parallel operations, direct path SQL*Loader, and star schemas? How easily can the analyst define the structure of both the source systems and the warehouse? Especially important is the ease with which the tool modifies the design. If you change the structure of a table in the warehouse, can the tool generate the necessary DDL to make the change? If the change cannot be performed without rebuilding the table (e.g., in dropping a column), does the tool generate all the necessary code to perform the operation? Does it do so with PARALLEL CREATE TABLE AS SELECT (pCTAS) or by unloading and reloading?

Because of the high initial licensing cost of ETT tools or because of the discipline they require, many shops choose to build their data warehouse "manually."

Reconciling during Extract

Extracting data from application files in specific formats just requires another set of application programs. We develop specifications, write and test programs, and deliver the output to the data warehouse for loading. When the warehouse analysts have a good conception of exactly what data will need to be extracted from an application's files or databases, we can provide the applications team with the necessary program specifications. Figure 6.3 demonstrates the approach of performing the complex data cleansing logic as part of the extract process. The advantage of this approach is that the complexities of the legacy application files are removed from the warehouse and will be addressed by the programming team, which already knows and maintains the application. The disadvantage is that the complexities must still be addressed, and the application team may not see the warehouse as its highest priority.

Many Oracle data warehouses are populated, at least partly, with data extracted from IBM mainframe applications. Many of those applications are written in COBOL, and the programmers who will be doing the extraction are frequently going to write those extracts using COBOL. The assigned programmers

Figure 6.3 Data reconciliation during extract processing.

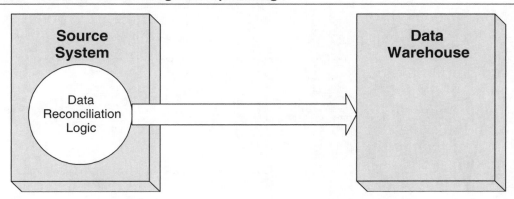

will typically already have the file definitions for the input application files or database. They will have to write the necessary procedure division code. In most cases, it will take some complex logic to properly reconcile, extract, and format normalized data out of the chaos of legacy systems whose quirks have frequently taken decades to develop!

The data that is extracted from the source system will need to be loaded into the data warehouse, usually with the SQL*Loader utility. We'll discuss SQL*Loader in more depth later in this chapter. SQL*Loader has the capability to load logical records from multiple physical input records. If possible, this feature should be avoided since it adds complexity to the loader setup and slows the load process. Try to get the extract programmers to provide the data in simple physical records that map neatly to the tables into which the data must be loaded.

You can help the application programmers provide all the necessary data in a convenient format by specifying the layout of the extract files. The following SQL*Plus script will generate an appropriate COBOL DATA DIVISION layout in a format that will be very easy to process using SQL*Loader. Each extract file will correspond to a single table to be loaded.

```
set heading off
set feedback off
set pagesize 0
set echo off
set linesize 80
set verify off
accept ownerid Prompt 'Enter schema of table for copybook generation: '
accept tablename Prompt 'Enter tablename for copybook generation: '
define outfile = ''
column out_file_name new_value outfile
select  decode(comments,'',table_name,substr(comments,1,8)) out_file_name
  from dba_tab_comments
 where owner      = upper('&ownerid')
   and table_name = upper('&tablename')
```

```
/
column var1 noprint
column var2 noprint
spool &outfile..cpy
select 1 var1, 1 var2,
       '      *********************************************************'
    from dual
union
select 1, 2, '          *  COBOL DECLARATIONS FOR ORACLE TABLE: '||
                 upper('&tablename')
  from dual
union
select 1, 3,
       '      *********************************************************'
  from dual
union
select 1 , 4 , '        01  DCL'||replace(upper('&tablename'),'_','-')||'.'
  from dual
union
select 2, column_id,
       '             05 '||
       rpad(substr(comments,4,4)||'-'||replace(column_name,'_','-'), 32)||
       decode(data_type,'VARCHAR2'    ,'PIC X('||data_length||').',
                        'VARCHAR'     ,'PIC X('||data_length||').',
                        'CHAR'        ,'PIC X('||data_length||').',
                        'DATE'        ,'PIC X(5).',
                        'NUMBER'      ,'PIC '||
                                        lpad('9', nvl(data_precision,38)
                                            -nvl(data_scale,0)+1, '-')||
                                        decode(data_scale,0,'','','','.'||
                                            rpad('9',data_scale,'9')) ||
                                          '.',
                        'UNDEFINED')
  from dba_tab_columns dtc,
       dba_tab_comments dtcm
 where dtc.owner = upper('&ownerid')
   and dtc.table_name = upper('&tablename')
   and dtc.owner = dtcm.owner
   and dtc.table_name = dtcm.table_name
 order by 1, 2
/
spool off
undef ownerid
undef tablename
undef outfile
```

A few notes about this script are in order. To generate a meaningful and legal name for this copybook member, the script will use the first eight characters of the table's comments, if available. Otherwise, the file will be named the same as the table. These names may then have to be edited before transferring the file to the mainframe programmers.

The script handles the Oracle data types most commonly used in data warehouses, but it does not know how to specify a COBOL PICTURE clause corresponding to other Oracle data types. For LONG, RAW, LONG RAW, CLOB, BLOB, or any object data types, the output will print the string UNDEFINED? instead. Because Oracle allows for numbers of up to thirty-eight digits of precision, the COBOL PICTURE clause may also not be legal for very large precision numbers (or columns defined as NUMBER without specification of precision). If you expect to use this technique to aid in the extract process, be sure to use only these basic data types in the tables of your warehouse that will be populated from COBOL programs. Otherwise, you will have to determine how you wish to map other data types back to the COBOL file layouts and modify the script accordingly.

If your extract programmers will be working with a language other than COBOL, similar scripting can be used to generate the appropriate file descriptions for FORTRAN, C, or any other language. Later in this chapter we'll use a similar technique to generate an SQL*Loader control file and an SQL*Plus file for unloading data from an Oracle table.

Once you've developed the extract specifications and provided a file layout, you can then write the rather simple SQL*Loader control files to process the files in the Oracle warehouse. Then you can just wait for the files to appear.

Reconciling during Load

Most data warehousing project teams are given responsibility for the data warehouse but not for the extract process. The current application owners are generally very protective of their files and databases. They are hesitant when they aren't downright obstructive!) to allow "outsiders" direct access to these precious resources. Instead, the applications team typically volunteers to do the extract processing for the warehouse. The warehouse team typically accepts the offer as an easy way to offload some work while the application team thinks they're volunteering for a one-time effort that will get the warehouse pests off their back.

Partnering with the Applications Team

An "us versus them" division between the owners of the application and the owners of the data warehouse develops all too easily and much too frequently. An ideal warehouse project team involves a partnership between the application and the warehouse. As we discussed in Chapter 1, a data warhouse should be considered as an extension of the operational systems. In forming a warehouse team, whenever possible, get the owners of the applications that will feed the warehouse involved. Otherwise, the warehouse team is likely to be viewed as just an extra, unnecessary burden. Let the applications teams share in some of the glory of delivering additional benefits to the users who are the real owners of the data. Their active assistance and cooperation will be well worth the investment!

Although it's unfortunate, it is also common to find that there are major unexpected project delays introduced each time we ask the applications team to create or modify an extract file. Because of the iterative, heuristic nature of data warehouse development, the warehouse team frequently needs to ask for additional files or fields that it hadn't requested earlier. As each extract request is received (and then prioritized) by the applications team, the warehouse team ends up waiting for days or weeks to get the new extract. Meanwhile, progress on the warehouse is stalled.

One way to avoid these frequent requests for extract changes is shown in Figure 6.4. In this model, we take a generic extract (or complete file copies) from the application systems. We then pick and choose which specific data fields to use and how to manipulate them during the load process. If we later determine that some additional source data is needed, we just change the load process to include the new data. The extract process is unaffected, and the applications team isn't interrupted. The trade-off for this simplicity may be much larger extract files to transfer and process.

The warehouse team can now absorb all the responsibility and work of getting the data right. Of course, they must also take on the additional responsibility of accommodating any changes in file structures introduced by application changes. So the need for close communication between applications and warehouse teams is not eliminated, but rather shifted. In most cases, this approach will work as long as the warehouse team has a full-time commitment from an experienced programmer transferred or on rotation from the applications team. The data complexities and exceptions embedded within the applications files will still have to be unraveled!

An additional benefit of performing our data scrubbing and integration on the warehouse side is that we have access to the data from multiple source systems. This is, of course, the crux of the integration problem. Most of the integration work will have to be performed here even if the choice is made to do complex extract processing at each application source.

SQL combined with PL/SQL provides an easy means of manipulating raw data once it has been loaded into the warehouse. In some cases, however, it may not be terribly efficient. When the raw data can be processed using SQL's set processing features, joins, and Oracle's parallel capabilities, the work can usually be done very efficiently. If the processing must be performed in a row-at-a-time manner using PL/SQL cursors, then special care must be taken to design the postprocessing tasks. One of the final sections of this chapter will explore this topic of postprocessing data after initial bulk loading.

Loading Data

For those shops that invest in an ETT tool, it will usually become the primary means of extracting data from their source systems, moving it to the data warehouse, transforming it to the warehouse's standard format and encoding schemes, and then loading it into the data warehouse. However, for the majority of shops that are just starting their first data warehouse project, a less automated approach is frequently adopted. In this section we will examine Oracle's

Figure 6.4 Data reconciliation during load processing.

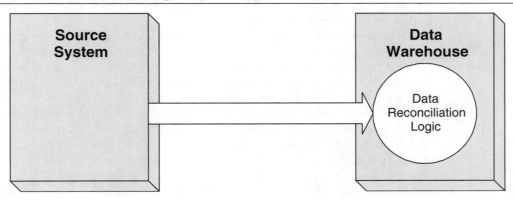

SQL*Loader utility in depth. SQL*Loader is the most common means of adding large volumes of data to the Oracle data warehouse. We'll then explore some other means for getting smaller amounts of data into your Oracle data warehouse including Oracle's gateway technologies and some special facilities for loading data that is already maintained in an Oracle database.

We'll close the chapter with a discussion of several topics closely related to loading data. We'll explore the need to further process bulk-loaded data to integrate it with existing data. We'll discuss the issues related to index maintenance whenever large amounts of data are being added to a table. Then we'll tackle the topic of verifying and publishing data. Finally, we'll look at how to get data back out of the data warehouse—either to purge or to archive detailed data once its useful lifetime has passed.

Using SQL*Loader

Oracle provides a general purpose utility, SQL*Loader, for loading large amounts of data into an Oracle database. SQL*Loader is a very easy product to use, but it has dozens of options that can present a formidable puzzle to the first-time user. The best approach is not to attempt to memorize all the specifics of the utility— few users will ever use even half of the optional syntax—but to learn the basic concepts and functions and then tackle one data loading task at a time. With a basic idea of what the product can do, it is fairly easy to use the examples provided in the Oracle7 or Oracle8 *Server Utilities* manuals to solve a specific problem.

In this section, we'll discuss SQL*Loader's capabilities, its major options, and its few limitations. We will provide several examples of using SQL*Loader in a data warehousing environment. We will not attempt to explore every option and keyword.

*SQL*Loader Concepts*

Whenever you find yourself with a file of data that needs to be entered into the Oracle data warehouse, your first thought should generally be to use SQL*Loader.

With only a few exceptions (which we'll discuss at the end of this section), SQL*Loader is the proper tool for processing any file of data that needs to be loaded into the Oracle data warehouse.

SQL*Loader takes an input file of raw data and loads the data into one or more Oracle tables. A control file is used to tell SQL*Loader the format of the input data file and to map these fields to the proper Oracle columns. The control file also allows the user to define WHEN clause criteria that instruct SQL*Loader to bypass the loading of certain input records.

In addition to the data loaded into the database, SQL*Loader can create up to three output files. The log file records a summary of the activity performed by each invocation of SQL*Loader. The BAD file is written whenever records are rejected by SQL*Loader because of errors in the input file or by the Oracle database because of errors that prevent the data from being inserted. This may include violations of the database's data type definitions or constraints defined on the table being loaded. The DISCARD file is created only when requested via the control file. It then receives a copy of each record that SQL*Loader did not attempt to load because of WHEN conditions specified in the control file.

SQL*Loader has two modes of operation—conventional path and direct path—which we will discuss more fully later in this chapter. In its conventional path, SQL*Loader issues SQL INSERT statements for loading the data. These INSERT statements can use the efficient array insert facility of Oracle. However, there is still significant overhead associated with performing SQL processing—Oracle processes each row through the SGA's buffer cache and performs all the constraint checking and index maintenance that would be performed on any INSERT. As we'll see, the faster direct path avoids most of this overhead but imposes some other limitations.

Invoking SQL*Loader

SQL*Loader is intended to be used as a noninteractive "batch" program, so it normally cannot be called from graphical user interface (GUI) front-end presentations. The Personal Oracle7 products, intended for single-user operating systems such as MS-DOS and Windows 95, provide an icon for SQL*Loader and a simple graphical front end, but Oracle7 Workgroup Server, Oracle8 Server (i.e., which corresponds to the Oracle7 Workgroup Server), and Oracle8 Enterprise Edition do not. For the most part, these products are expected to be invoked through the operating system command-line prompt, thus ensuring that SQL*Loader can be readily used in the native batch scripting language.

Once you are at the operating system command-line prompt, finding out how to invoke SQL*Loader is easy. Simply entering

```
$ sqlldr
```

at the UNIX shell command-line prompt or

```
C:\> sqlldr80
```

for Oracle8 SQL*Loader or

```
C:\> sqlldr73
```

for Oracle7.3 SQL*Loader at the Windows NT command prompt will cause basic help text to display, as follows:

```
SQL*Loader: Release 8.0.2.0.2 - Beta on Sun Sep 28 9:45:30 1997
Copyright (c) Oracle Corporation 1979, 1994, 1996.  All rights reserved.


Usage: SQLLOAD keyword=value [,keyword=value,...]

Valid Keywords:
    userid -- ORACLE username/password
   control -- Control file name
       log -- Log file name
       bad -- Bad file name
      data -- Data file name
   discard -- Discard file name
discardmax -- Number of discards to allow         (Default all)
      skip -- Number of logical records to skip   (Default 0)
      load -- Number of logical records to load   (Default all)
    errors -- Number of errors to allow           (Default 50)
      rows -- Number of rows in conventional path bind array or between
              direct path data saves
                 (Default: Conventional path 64, Direct path all)
  bindsize -- Size of conventional path bind array in bytes  (Default 65536)
    silent -- Suppress messages during run (header,feedback,errors,discards,
              partitions)
    direct -- use direct path                      (Default FALSE)
   parfile -- parameter file: name of file that contains parameter specs
  parallel -- do parallel load                     (Default FALSE)
      file -- File to allocate extents from
skip_unusable_indexes -- disallow/allow unusable indexes or index partitions
              (Default FALSE)
skip_index_maintenance -- do not maintain indexes, mark affected indexes as
              unusable  (Default FALSE)
commit_discontinued -- commit loaded rows when load is discontinued
              (Default FALSE)


PLEASE NOTE: Command-line parameters may be specified either by
position or by keywords.  An example of the former case is 'sqlload
scott/tiger foo'; an example of the latter is 'sqlload control=foo
userid=scott/tiger'.  One may specify parameters by position before
but not after parameters specified by keywords.  For example,
'sqlload scott/tiger control=foo logfile=log' is allowed, but
'sqlload scott/tiger control=foo log' is not, even though the
position of the parameter 'log' is correct.
```

The last paragraph of this display, starting with PLEASE NOTE, is helpful. In addition, it should be noted that all but the first two parameters, USERID and CONTROL, have default values and are therefore optional. The parameter PARFILE has no default, but if it is not specified it is simply not used.

And, of course, the entire topic of SQL*Loader is explained in very fine detail in the Oracle7 or Oracle8 *server utilities* guides, which is part of the standard Oracle documentation set for their respective versions. Starting with basic concepts, SQL*Loader is explained with numerous examples across five or six chapters.

SQL*Loader's parameters can be specified on the operating system command-line prompt, as follows:

```
$ sqlldr userid=scott/tiger control=test.ctl
```

Or they can be stored inside a SQL*Loader parameter file, which is specified at the command-line prompt:

```
$ sqlldr parfile=test.par
```

The parameters inside the parameter file are listed one per line:

```
userid=scott/tiger
control=C:\TEMP\TEST.CTL
log=D:\APP\ORACLE\ADMIN\LOAD\LOG\TEST.LOG
data=C:\TEMP\TEST.DAT
```

. . . and so on. Of course, it is possible to mix the use of parameters specified on the command line as well as inside the parameter file, as follows:

```
$ sqlldr userid=scott/tiger data=test.dat parfile=test.par
```

The salient question, however, must be "Why would you specify parameters one way or the other?" For the most part, it is a matter of style, but there are some situations in which one method is clearly superior to the other. One method involves password security, which is compromised in UNIX systems when a password is specified at the command-line prompt. In this case, the invocation:$ sqlldr userid=scott/tiger control=test.ctl data=test.dat can be picked up in its entirety by any other user on the system, thereby rendering the password of the Oracle account SCOTT public to the world. By embedding the userid parameter and its values in a parameter file and then setting the permissions for reading that file appropriately, the Oracle account password can be safeguarded. Many people tend to ignore basic security like this, but security risks are not defined simply as malicious teenagers with Internet access and too much time on their hands. Rather, security risks include all situations in which an unauthorized individual can see, change, or remove data, even accidentally. Allowing an account password to be plucked off the UNIX command line is a very preventable example of this.

Whether they are specified directly on the operating system command line or embedded in a parameter file, the parameters may be briefly explained as follows:

Parameter Name	Description	Default Value	Comments
userid	Oracle account username, password, and optional SQL*Net connect string.		required parameter
control	Name of the SQL*Loader control file.		required parameter
parfile	Name of the SQL*Loader parameter file.		not used if not specified
data	Name of the input file containing data to be loaded into Oracle. Can be specified in the INFILE clause in the SQL*Loader control file. Specification here overrides specification in the control file.	If not specified in the control file, then the name of the control file is stripped of it's file extension and replaced with a file extension of ".dat".	
log	Name of the output file to hold a log of all activities performed by SQL*Loader.	If not specified in the control file, then the name of the control file is stripped of its file extension and replaced with a file extension of ".dat".	
bad	Name of the output file to hold all the input data records that were rejected because they violated either the SQL*Loader control file specification or some kind of database constraint.	If not specified in the control file, then the name of the control file is stripped of its file extension and replaced with a file extension of ".dat".	
discard	Name of the output file to hold all the input data records that were discarded because they did not satisfy the WHEN clause in the SQL*Loader control file.	If not specified in the control file, then the name of the control file is stripped of it's file extension and replaced with a file extension of ".dat".	
discardmax	Number of discarded records to allow in the discard file.	All	
skip	Number of logical records from the input data file to skip over.	0	
load	Number of logical records from the input data file to load.	All	
errors	Number of logical records to allow to fail due to violations of either the SQL*Loader control file specification or a database constraint, before forcing the SQL*Loader to quit.	50	
direct	Use "direct path" load mechanism, which bypasses Oracle's normal INSERT mechanism (a.k.a. "conventional path") in favor of performance but with possible reduced flexibility and functionality.	FALSE	

(continues)

Parameter Name	Description	Default Value	Comments
rows	Number of logical records in bind array, to be included in a single INSERT operation. A COMMIT is performed after each array INSERT.	64	conventional path only
rows	Number of rows between direct path data saves. Setting this to a finite integer value allows periodic saves, which can decrease the impact of failure during loading, at the cost of some performance overhead and restart complexity in the event of failure.	ALL	direct path only
silent	Suppress messages during run (header, feedback, errors, discards, partitions). Header is the banner produced by SQL*Loader that shows versions. Feedback is the output shown after each commit or data save (see the ROWS parameter). Errors is the logging of all error messages in the log file (see the ERRORS, LOG, and BAD parameters). Discards is the logging of messages in the log file each time a record is discarded (see the DISCARD and DISCARDMAX parameters). Partitions is the logging of summary statistics for each partition to the log file. All covers all of the above keywords.	none (all forms of feedback are produced unless suppressed)	partitions is for Oracle8 only
bindsize	Size of the bind array in bytes. If the ROWS parameter multiplied by the width (in bytes) of each logical record exceeds BINDSIZE, then the ROWS parameter will be reduced to fit.	65536	conventional path only
parallel	Setting to TRUE allows multiple direct path loads on the same table to be performed in parallel; normally only one direct path load can be performed on a table at a time. PLEASE NOTE that this parameter is not necessary when using conventional path, since Oracle allows multiple concurrent INSERT statements as part of its base functionality.	FALSE	direct path only
file	Internal Oracle datafile in which to allocate extents. The datafile must belong to the tablespace in which the table being loaded resides. The datafile must be specified by its full name, as shown in the FILE_NAME column in the view DBA_DATA_FILES.	Oracle chooses where to allocate extents in the tablespace by default	direct path only

Parameter Name	Description	Default Value	Comments
skip_unusable _indexes	If TRUE, allows SQL*Loader to load into tables that indexes in UNUSABLE state prior to the start of the load, without causing the SQL*Loader session to fail.	FALSE	direct path for Oracle8 only
skip_index _maintenance	If TRUE, does not maintain indexes during the load, leaving them in UNUSABLE state when the load completes successfully.	FALSE	direct path for Oracle8 only
commit _discontinued	Save (commit) rows already loaded if the SQL*Loader session fails for having exceeded the number of errors allowed by the ERRORS parameter.	FALSE	for Oracle8 only

Altogether, SQL*Loader has two input files: the input data file and the SQL*Loader control file. The input data file contains the data to be loaded and can be a regular operating system file, a tape device, or a UNIX named pipe. The latter two choices are useful in the event the input data file is simply too large to reside in an operating system file; many operating system have a limit of two gigabytes on file size. Also, being able to use either a tape drive or a named pipe saves time during loads, removing the need to "stage" the input data file onto disk before loading it into Oracle.

The control file contains a description of what the input data file looks like, using SQL*Loader's own data definition language. This language is very similar to Oracle's internal data definition language, used for creating tables and specifying columns. The important thing to remember is that these are two separate data definition languages, despite their similarities. One very common mistake when using SQL*Loader is to specify a data type for a field in the SQL*Loader control file using a data type from the Oracle RDBMS, and vice versa.

The Oracle RDBMS has very few predefined data types: CHAR, VARCHAR2, NUMBER, RAW, and DATE. In Oracle7, there are LONGs and LONG RAWs, but in Oracle8 these are supplemented by character CLOBs and binary BLOBs. Additional predefined data types that are valid in the RDBMS, such as INTEGER, are just variations on these basic data types.

SQL*Loader, however, has to be able to recognize far greater numbers of data types, so it's set of defined data types is larger and richer. Rather than provide you with a list of these data types here, it is very much worth your while to consult the chapters on SQL*Loader in the Oracle7 or Oracle8 *Server Utilities* guides, both for the references on data types as well as the many different control file scenarios.

One important thing to remember that will help clear up confusion: Names of objects in the SQL*Loader control file refer to tables and columns in the database, while everything else in the control file refers to items in the input data file. The control file provides a mapping between the input data file and the database tables into which data is being loaded, nothing more. It provides a guide for SQL*Loader, enabling it to read appropriate data items from the input data file, interpret them correctly in order to translate them from the external format to Oracle's internal format, and then insert them into the correct table and column.

The basic format of a SQL*Loader control file is simple:

```
LOAD DATA
INTO TABLE table-name
(
    column-name          external-datatype,
    column-name          external-datatype,
    ...
)
```

Of course, there is a world of options excluded from this basic description. In fact, there are optional keywords and phrases to enable a multitude of functionality that can be inserted just about everywhere in this oversimplified example. But the important point is that even this basic example shows all the basic components for loading data into a database. The input data file has been specified either as a SQL*Loader command-line parameter or here in the control using the INFILE clause (not shown in the example). At least one database table to be loaded from the input data file has been identified with the INTO TABLE clause. In that table, one or more database columns have been identified, which have been mapped to input data file *fields*. Since SQL*Loader can access the Oracle data dictionary, it already knows what the internal Oracle data type of each database column is. The control file syntax that specifies the external data type provides most of the information needed to perform a translation, if one is necessary. If the input data file is in a character set or language different from that of the database, this too can be specified as an option.

Two important points that are missing from this brief example are record format and field format. SQL*Loader supports three basic record formats: stream, fixed-length, and variable-length. The default record format is stream, which is also the default text file format for UNIX systems. The stream record format implies a "stream" of characters separated by a record-separator, which is usually a line-feed character on UNIX systems. Thus, SQL*Loader is designed to load free-format text files from UNIX systems by default. However, be aware that the stream record format is best used only with text data. If you are loading any nontext (i.e., binary) information such as binary integers or packed-decimal data, it is not good to use this record format. This is due to the fact that the character chosen as a record-separator can easily appear in the binary data field and thus cause SQL*Loader to confuse the binary information for the end of the current record of data.

For large-scale data loads from mainframe systems, the most common record format is fixed, where each record comprises a fixed number of bytes. This is in fact the most efficient record format to use for loading with SQL*Loader because the SQL*Loader process is freed from the chore of reading ahead for the next record-separator character. SQL*Loader can simply allocate a buffer large enough to hold one or more records and then read the data straight into that buffer for additional processing. If you are trying to optimize performance in SQL*Loader, use a fixed-length record format.

The last record format, variable-length, is the least often used. Variable-length record format implies that each record is preceded by a record-length field. The format of the record-length field can vary from operating system to operating system, consisting of anything from a two- or four-byte binary integer to a five-digit character text field. Consult the Oracle7 or Oracle8 *Server Utilities* reference manuals for more detail.

Once the record format has been specified, you should now be aware of the field format. Luckily, for each record format there is a particular field format that is commonly used. For stream record formats, it is common for fields to be delimited by a field-separator character, much as records are delimited by record-separator characters. Common field-separator characters include the comma (i.e., ",") or pipe characters (i.e., "|"). Another common alternative is for fields to be enclosed by single quote (i.e., "'") or double-quote (i.e., """) characters and optionally separated by commas. SQL*Loader has syntax to cover all these possibilities and more.

With a fixed-length record format, it would be quite odd to use anything other than fixed-length field formats. The most common way to specify fixed-field formats is to use the POSITION(p, n) syntax, where p is the byte offset within the record where the field starts, and n is the length of the field. Of course, delimited or variable-length fields are possible in fixed-length records, but this is not common.

With variable-length records, either variable-length fields or fixed-length fields are common. Generally, the reason the record is variable-length has to do with one or two fields that are variable length, usually located toward the end of the record.

At any rate, these are only the simplest of situations that can be handled by SQL*Loader. Once again, please be sure to at least browse the relevant chapters in the Oracle *Server Utilities* guides to decide whether SQL*Loader can effectively solve the issue of loading data into your data warehouse database.

One important note: SQL*Loader for Oracle8 does not handle very well the loading of data into object-oriented constructs such as nested tables or user-defined columns. These limitations should exist until Oracle 8.1 or perhaps later 8.0 releases. If you are loading into tables using object-oriented features, you may want to use SQL*Loader to load into non-OO temporary tables, then finish the load using PL/SQL or it may be necessary to write custom OCI programs (using a third-generation programming language such as C) to perform the load.

Conventional Path SQL*Loader

As mentioned earlier, the two methods used by SQL*Loader for inserting data into the Oracle database are *conventional path* and *direct path*.

Conventional path means that SQL*Loader uses normal SQL "INSERT" statements. Based on the information provided in the control file, the SQL*Loader program uses OCI to construct INSERT statements dynamically. This mechanism

Figure 6.5 SQL*Loader conventional path.

has been in place since SQL*Loader was known as ODL (Oracle Data Loader), before version 6 of Oracle. Figure 6.5 illustrates the operation of SQL*Loader's conventional path.

The use of conventional path is the default in SQL*Loader. Because it uses SQL statements, conventional path provides the most flexibility and functionality. With SQL INSERT statements, indexes are maintained automatically, database triggers are fired appropriately, database constraints are enforced at the time of insert, and normal COMMIT/ROLLBACK mechanisms are used.

Direct Path SQL*Loader

Starting with Oracle7, the *direct path* mechanism was introduced. This option, enabled by setting the parameter DIRECT to TRUE (from its default of FALSE), permits better performance by bypassing the entire SQL layer in Oracle. Instead of dynamically constructing and issuing SQL INSERT statements, the direct path mechanism formats database blocks entirely in the SQL*Loader process' private memory space, and then writes these preformatted database blocks directly down to the datafiles within the Oracle tablespaces. Normal SQL INSERT statements merely access database blocks cached in the buffer cache in the System

Figure 6.6 SQL*Loader direct path.

Global Area (SGA), and the writes of the blocks are performed by the database writer (DBWR) process. Figure 6.6 shows the ability of SQL*Loader direct path to bypass the Oracle kernel's SQL layer and write directly to the database files.

Obviously, it is much faster for SQL*Loader to perform all this work itself rather than possibly contend with other Oracle processes for access to the SGA while waiting for the DBWR process to wake up and do its job. The problem is, how does this "antisocial" behavior on the part of the direct path mechanism fit in with the highly social structure of normal SQL operations in Oracle?

Fast Loader in Oracle for MVS, Version 6

Actually, the predecessor to SQL*Loader direct path was introduced with Oracle for MVS during the version 6 product life cycle. Designed to provide competitive parity with the loading capabilities of IBM's DB2 database, the feature was originally dubbed "fast loader." The technology to perform direct disk writes was made part of the general SQL*Loader product on all ports, effective with the release of Oracle7.

The answer is that direct path operations do not take place in the currently utilized space of a table or index. With direct path, space above the table's high-water mark is used. This is space that has already been allocated for use by the table but into which data has not yet been inserted by the normal SQL layer. Thus, space above the high-water mark is unused and can therefore be restricted for use by one process alone.

When the direct path load is finished, the high-water mark of the table is moved so the data loaded in direct path is now below the high-water mark and now accessible by all users.

RESTRICTIONS ON DIRECT PATH LOADS

Triggers are disabled for all rows added via direct path. Integrity constraints are not validated until after completion of the load. SQL functions are unavailable to the load. Tables in clusters may not be loaded in direct path mode. No other transactions (INSERT, UPDATE or DELETE) may be active in the table during the load.

If direct path loading to a single partition of an Oracle8 partitioned table, no global indexes on the table may exist and no referential integrity or check constraints may be enabled on the table. Also, all triggers on the table must be disabled.

As you can tell from the description, the direct path mechanism does place restrictions on concurrent access of the table. No other transactions may obtain locks to do DBL operations. Constraints and database triggers will be disabled. Thus, only SELECT operations can proceed against the table while the load is running but even SELECT statements may cause problems when the direct path load finishes and needs to rebuild the table's indexes. While direct path loads are occurring, a table is pretty much unavailable.

PARALLEL LOADING

Another point that may not be obvious from the description just given is that only one direct path load can occur on a table at a time because of its exclusive locking. After all, each table has only one high-water mark, and one direct path load process is potentially using all the space currently above that high-water mark.

Starting with Oracle7, release 7.1, the PARALLEL parameter was added to SQL*Loader. This pertains only to direct path, since conventional path SQL*Loader has always had the ability to perform "parallel loads" on the same table, just like any program or utility that uses SQL INSERT statements. This ability is shown in Figure 6.7, where multiple direct path SQL*Loader sessions are simultaneously writing to the database files.

If parallel direct path SQL*Loader is going to be used for a table, then all SQL*Loader processes need to set the PARALLEL parameter to TRUE. Thus, instead of simply using currently allocated space above the high-water mark, parallel direct path processes actually allocate new, separate TEMPORARY segments in the same tablespace, and load data into the TEMPORARY segments.

Figure 6.7 SQL*Loader parallel direct path.

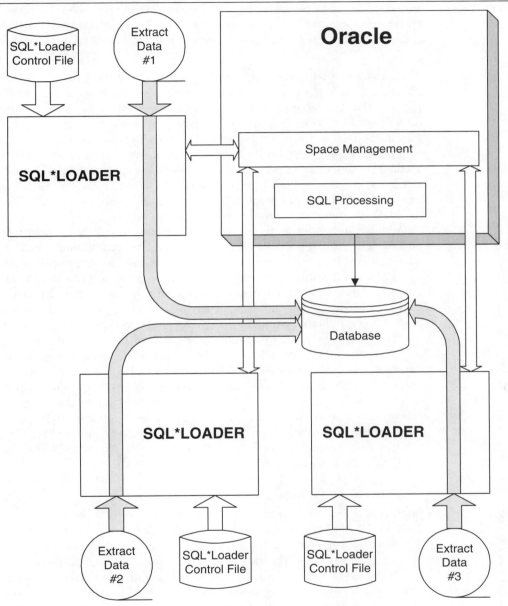

Therefore, the space above the existing high-water mark is not touched, and multiple such processes can work concurrently. When each parallel direct path process finishes its loading, it merges the TEMPORARY segment into the table being loaded.

An index-organized table cannot be loaded in parallel direct path mode. Only the APPEND option for adding rows is valid; you may not specify REPLACE, TRUNCATE, or INSERT options. No indexes, either global or local, are automatically maintained by the load processes.

To minimize I/O contention, each parallel direct path load process should, ideally, be loading into a part of the table that is located on a separate disk. This requires that the table be striped across as many disks as there are concurrent direct path load jobs. This striping can be performed by creating multiple data files in the tablespace and then manually allocating extents in each file. Alternatively, the striping may be done "below the covers" at the hardware or logical volume management (LVM) software levels. If manual striping of the tablespace has been done (as would be appropriate in Oracle Parallel Server environments—see Chapter 11) then each parallel load control file should also specify the FILE parameter to determine where its data will be loaded.

Parallel direct path loads are ideal for loading data into a single partition of an Oracle8 partitioned table. This is facilitated by partitioning along the same keys that will be used to separate load jobs. Usually loads are performed based upon time—each month or each week a new set of data needs to be loaded. This presents a strong recommendation for partitioning by time as well.

If partitioning is done by some other value, such as by ORGANIZATION, then performing a full table parallel load (each parallel job can load to more than one partition) requires that all partitions be located in the same tablespace in order to specify the FILE keyword. Generally, however, we want to separate partitions into their own tablespaces. This complication can be avoided by partitioning the input data into separate load files that correspond with the table partitions. In this way, each partition can be loaded independently from the others, and you can use the FILE keyword to control exactly where the data will be placed.

For more information on the benefits and usage of parallel direct path SQL*Loader, see the appropriate section in Chapter 10, "Parallel Operations in the Oracle Data Warehouse."

UNRECOVERABLE OPTION

Another nice feature important to data warehousing debuted in Oracle7, release 7.1—the UNRECOVERABLE option of SQL*Loader.

It was noticed quite early on that data warehouse data was not like data in operational databases. The data in data warehouses originates somewhere else and is copied to the data warehouse. Frequently, this happens in huge volumes. Oracle's redo logging mechanism faithfully copied all this data to the redo log files. In turn, this meant that the log writer (LGWR) process became very busy, as the huge volumes of data being loaded meant that sometimes LGWR was hard-pressed to keep up. As you are aware, a database COMMIT does not complete until the LGWR process(es) has finished writing redo information safely to the redo log files, so frequently a data warehouse would become bottlenecked on the redo logging subsystem.

Unrecoverable Option in OLTP Databases

The unrecoverable option of SQL*Loader was actually included in the initial release of Oracle7. For some reason, however, it was not documented until release 7.1. Use of this option became critical at one client site in which several hundred gigabytes of data needed to be loaded into an early Oracle7 OLTP database as part of the conversion from a legacy mainframe system. Without the unrecoverable option we found that our load processing filled 300 MB log files in about an hour. Unfortunately, the archiving process was taking about eighty minutes to copy each log. This quickly became a bottleneck to the loads. Starting multiple archiver processes helped, but the final solution was to get special permission to utilize the undocumented unrecoverable parameter, which completely eliminated the bottleneck and allowed the large loads to procede unencumbered.

This might not have been so terrible if the information being stored in the redo logs was important, but as we just mentioned, the data being loaded into a data warehouse is generally a *copy* of operational data that originated elsewhere. Therefore, saving this information in the redo logs is unnecessary. If something were to happen to the Oracle database, the data warehouse could be rebuilt relatively easily and reloaded; restoring from backups and recovering from the redo logs may not be the most expeditious way of recovering.

As a result, the UNRECOVERABLE option was first added to SQL*Loader circa 1994, and over the following years it was added to other features of Oracle, such as CREATE INDEX, CREATE TABLE AS SELECT, and parallel DML in Oracle8. With Oracle8, the name of the feature has largely been changed to NOLOGGING and can now be applied as an attribute of a table, but the mechanism and concept is the same.

When the UNRECOVERABLE option is used, it does not mean that the table in question can never be recovered in the event of media failure (i.e., disk drive failure). Rather, it means that data loaded during the SQL*Loader session was not logged to the redo logs and therefore cannot be recovered from there. This option is available only with the direct path mechanism in Oracle7 and is superseded by the NOLOGGING table option in Oracle8.

The standard recommendation from Oracle Corporation is to perform a backup of the appropriate tablespace immediately after completing an UNRECOVERABLE load. This is to ensure that a restore operation is possible even if recovery from redo logs is not. The important point is that there is nothing wrong with the data loaded using UNRECOVERABLE, but that the normal methods of recovering data in the event of media failure have been disabled.

If a database restore and recovery of a tablespace with tables previously loaded UNRECOVERABLE is performed, the tables in question will have to be truncated and fully reloaded.

Initial versus Periodic Loads

A very common mistake committed by many project teams is to forget the difference between an *initial load* and the *periodic loads* that will occur during the lifetime of the data warehouse.

Take for example the idea that SQL*Loader will be used to periodically (i.e., every day) load data from the operational source system into the data warehouse. Due to availability requirements, this load should not cause any interruptions in service.

The choices here are quite clear. SQL*Loader conventional path should be used for this type of load, since conventional path uses "normal" SQL INSERT statements. Thus, if there are any triggers on the tables being loaded, they will fire. If there are any constraints on the table or its columns, they will be obeyed. Indexes on the table will be maintained automatically and not be invalidated. The volume of data to be loaded is not excessive, so the periodic loads should be completed in an acceptable time. All in all, this is the kind of situation for which conventional path SQL*Loader is ideally suited.

But something has been overlooked. When the data warehouse is initially loaded, the volume of information to be loaded is orders of magnitude greater. While this load is occurring, there are no availability requirements, since there are no users on the system until the loads are completed. In this situation, the use of conventional path SQL*Loader would be a mistake, as the amount of overhead incurred by using INSERT statements, maintaining indexes, firing triggers, and checking constraints would result in what would probably be a prohibitively slow rate of loading. Obviously, the best idea here is to change the SQL*Loader parameter values from DIRECT=FALSE to DIRECT=TRUE, and possibly set PARALLEL=TRUE as well, and make use of the "direct path" insert mechanisms in SQL*Loader.

Now, using the exact same SQL*Loader control files and scripting routines developed for the periodic loads, the rate of loading should be sufficient to meet the higher volume demands of an initial load. In this way, by flipping a few switches, SQL*Loader can cover the needs both of high-volume initial loads as well as lower-volume, high-availability periodic loads.

What about the reverse situation? Should the high-performance "direct path" be used for periodic loads, so they are completed faster? Probably not. Remember that the direct path mechanism does not fire database triggers, does not maintain constraints during the load, and does not maintain indexes during the load. As a result, the use of direct path SQL*Loader in situations requiring table availability is not recommended.

Additionally, since direct path SQL*Loader always writes its blocks above the table's current high-water mark, it can never reuse space that might have been available below the high-water mark. Managing the space consumption of a table being periodically loaded in this way becomes more complex, especially when regular data archival or purges are being performed.

This is yet another valid illustration of a basic trade-off inherent throughout computing: speed versus flexibility. When you opt for speed, you typically give up something in terms of flexibility. When you opt for flexibility, you typically give up something in terms of speed.

Using Custom Load Programs

It is possible to write custom programs to handle the reconciliation and loading of data. There are only a few cases when this choice would be chosen instead of using SQL*Loader:

- When data must be loaded into clusters, you cannot use the direct path mode of SQL*Loader. This is rarely an issue in data warehousing as clusters are not widely used or recommended.
- When data being loaded must be processed using data already in the database or in some other source. SQL*Loader does not have the ability to do procedural logic involving looking at data outside of the individual input record being processed. An example would be to include decoded data into a row being inserted by looking up the value for the code supplied in the raw data. A similar decoding capability could be implemented using conventional path SQL*Loader and database triggers, but this approach is likely to have performance problems if large amounts of data must be processed. Another alternative used in many situations is to quickly load the raw data using direct path SQL*Loader into a temporary table and then postprocess the data using custom-coded PL/SQL stored procedures. The postprocessing step would perform whatever lookups and reformatting were needed and then insert the data into the proper permanent table or partition.
- When using Oracle8's new object data types. Eventually, we should expect SQL*Loader to handle these data types, but they are not supported in the initial production release (8.0.3). Note that in the initial Oracle8 release, object data types are incompatible with several of the large database features, such as partitioning and parallel query, which are commonly required for data warehousing.

In short, there are relatively few cases when data warehousing teams have to write custom programs for loading their data. Whenever possible, attempt to take advantage of the bulk-loading speed provided by SQL*Loader's direct path mode. As a second choice, exploit the many parallel capabilities of Oracle, such as parallel CREATE TABLE . . . AS SELECT (and parallel INSERT and UPDATE in Oracle8). Only as a last resort, choose to write custom load programs.

Using Oracle's Gateway Products

Oracle provides a series of Open Gateway products that allow Oracle to access data maintained by a foreign database management system or file system. Some of these gateways allow for read-only access to the foreign data; others allow for read-write access and even the coordination of distributed transactions. Oracle

Figure 6.8 Oracle Open Gateway.

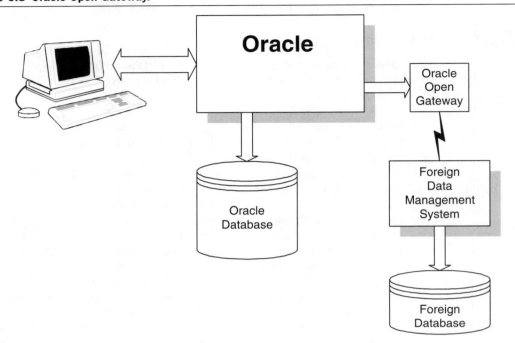

also provides procedural gateway products that allow an Oracle PL/SQL call to invoke procedural logic on the remote site. Depending on the specific data source you wish to reach, you may find that an Oracle Transparent Gateway product exists that can make your remote data appear to the Oracle data warehouse just as if it were another Oracle database. For less common data sources, you may be able to "roll your own" using Oracle's Procedural Gateway Developer's Kit (PGDK). Figure 6.8 shows the relationship between the Oracle Open Gateway and the source system and the Oracle data warehouse.

Most Oracle data warehouses are fed through the extract and load model we have discussed throughout this chapter. Occasionally, there may be a need to directly access data from a non-Oracle database. When relatively small amounts of data need to be retrieved from a remote site, issuing a simple SQL SELECT statement may be much simpler than performing extract, transfer, and load processes. Selecting data from a foreign source using a gateway should not be considered a replacement for extracting and loading when large amounts of data need to be transferred.

The other potential use for Oracle's Open Gateway products is to develop a distributed data warehouse in which one or more sites are implemented using a DBMS other than Oracle. Distributed data warehouses will be discussed in Chapter 12.

One final consideration about using gateways or operational Oracle databases requires mention. The ease with which remote queries can be executed may tempt warehouse designers to provide "real-time" access to operational data. Just because it is possible to provide such access doesn't mean it is wise. Be wary of allowing the data warehouse to become an operational data store in which users attempt to perform operational processing and reporting. Executing queries against the remote data should, in general, be limited to the administrators of the warehouse who will use the facility to load portions of the warehouse. The only exceptions should be to enable access to a different level of a distributed warehouse when it may be appropriate for users to issue queries directly or for administrators to perform modifications to data on the remote site.

Extracting Data from Oracle Sources

There are several alternative means for moving data from one Oracle database to another. This section will discuss the following:

- the export/import of entire tables
- using triggers to identify changed rows
- an unload/reload utility
- CREATE TABLE . . . AS SELECT
- the SQL*Plus COPY command

Each of these five alternatives has relative merits and drawbacks that make them useful in different situations. In some cases, the best solution may be a combination of these techniques. For instance, if a subset of the rows in a large table needs to be identified and copied you might choose to use triggers to time-stamp changed rows, use CREATE TABLE . . . AS SELECT in parallel to extract the selected rows to a local temporary table, then export that table for transport and import into the warehouse.

Using Export/Import Utilities

Oracle has provided special-purpose export (EXP) and import (IMP) utilities. Originally, these utilities were used for backup and recovery purposes. More recently, with much the larger databases and enhanced backup capabilities introduced in Oracle version 6, EXP/IMP has been used more for table reorganizations for moving data from machine to machine. One of the advantages of EXP/IMP is that it allows data to be exported from an Oracle database on one operating system and then imported to an Oracle database on a completely different operating system. It will, for instance, allow for migration of data between a mainframe EBCDIC database and an ASCII database on a UNIX or Windows NT machine. Figure 6.9 illustrates the use of the EXP and IMP utilities to move data from one Oracle database to another.

REFERENCE

EXP and IMP are documented in the *Server Utilities* manual for Oracle7 and Oracle8.

Figure 6.9 EXP and IMP utilities.

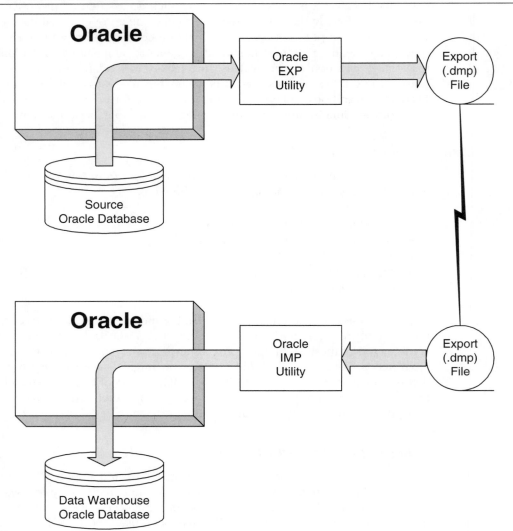

EXP writes out a single file that contains the data definitions and data for all the data being exported. This file is commonly referred to as a "dump" file and is written with a default file extension of ".dmp." The dump file's format is not documented, is designed to be readable only by the IMP utility, and should not be processed by any user-written programs. The Oracle8 IMP utility is able to read an export file created by the Oracle7 version of EXP. This may be used to assist in copying a portion of an Oracle7 database while migrating to Oracle8, although the Oracle8 migration utility will generally be used if an entire database is to be converted.

Linking as Single-task

EXP and IMP utilities and other programs are generally linked in "two-task" configuration for execution on UNIX platforms. This means that EXP or IMP run as a separate process and communicate with the Oracle kernel processes through an interprocess communication facility. This configuration is safer in that a client application is separated from the Oracle SGA and cannot accidentally corrupt these critical shared memory structures. This configuration does exact an additional cost for the extra communication. It is possible to link client programs "single-task," in which case they will include the Oracle kernel code and will be able to directly access the SGA. This configuration is not recommended for any user-developed programs but is frequently done with Oracle utilities such as EXP and IMP. IMP especially benefits from the speed-up associated with linking single-task. Instructions for linking utilities single-task are included within the operating-specific Oracle documentation.

EXP can back up data from a single table, a named series of tables, all of the objects in a schema, or all of the database objects in the entire database. In Oracle8, it is also possible to export single partitions of a partitioned table. IMP allows for the importing of specific objects (table, partition) out of a dump file created from an entire schema or database.

EXP was enhanced in release 7.3 to include a direct read mode. This greatly speeds the process of exporting data. IMP, however, still relies on doing SQL inserts to reload the data.

Since the individual table (or individual partition in Oracle8) is the lowest granularity of data access supported by EXP/IMP, it is uncommon to use these tools in data warehousing. Full table copies between the operational database and the data warehouse are uncommon. Usually we need to reformat, rename, and filter data before it enters the data warehouse. Also, in most cases, we only wish to extract and load data that has been entered or modified during the period since the last refresh. EXP/IMP will transfer an entire table's contents.

Because of processing constraints on the operational Oracle database, it may not be feasible to perform complex selection and extraction processing on that database. We have seen one situation in which the administrator of a small OLTP database was only willing to provide a copy of an export dump file. In such a case, the warehouse administrator may have to use IMP to load a copy of the relevant tables into a temporary (nonpublic) area of the data warehouse and then perform necessary selection and reformatting processing in the warehouse.

It is possible to export from an Oracle7 database and then import into an Oracle8 warehouse. Moving data in the opposite direction is a bit tougher. This may not be much of an issue, since most shops are more likely to use Oracle8 to build (or migrate) their data warehouse before operational systems. To import

Specifying SQL*Net or Net8 Service Names

How SQL*Net (Net8 with Oracle8) service names are specified varies by operating system and telecommunications protocol. In general, the name is provided by the user either through an operating system environment variable or as part of the command-line invocation of a specific program or tool. The provided name is translated into the necessary network routing and connection information through an entry in a local TNSNAMES.ORA file or through a lookup on a centralized Oracle Names Server. Additionally, Net8 provides new alternatives for using other naming services provided through network operating system facilities. To verify how to connect to a remote database, check your operating system-specific Oracle documentation or with the local administrator who has configured your Oracle network.

data into an Oracle7 database, it needs to be exported from an Oracle8 database using the Oracle7 version of EXP. If you have both Oracle7 and Oracle8 on the same server this will only require pointing to the Oracle8 database by specifying its SID when invoking the Oracle7 EXP utility.

EXPORTING FROM ORACLE8 FOR IMPORT TO ORACLE7

If you are upgrading from Oracle7 to Oracle8, you may wish to retain a copy of the Oracle7 EXP executable before removing the original ORACLE_HOME directory tree. This will facilitate exporting data from the Oracle8 database should you ever need to IMP into Oracle7 on another server. Note that Oracle7 IMP will not be able to export new Oracle8 database objects such as partitioned tables or those with object data types.

If, however, you are running Oracle7 and Oracle8 on different servers, particularly with different operating systems, you will have an additional problem. Since the EXP executable from one operating system cannot be moved and executed on a different platform, it will be necessary to run EXP over the network. This is done by specifying the appropriate SQL*Net service name for the remote Oracle8 database when invoking EXP. Be advised, however, that performance of EXP over the network will be significantly slower than EXP run locally and linked single-task.

INVOKING EXP

EXP can be run interactively by just invoking EXP from the command line. It will then prompt the user for values of the most commonly used parameters. Run in this manner, you will not have the ability to change some of the less commonly used parameters, but for most types of export this is the easiest way to get started.

For example:

```
$ exp

Export: Release 7.3.3.0.0 - Production on Mon Sep 29 06:02:00 1997
Copyright (c) Oracle Corporation 1979, 1994, 1996.  All rights reserved.

Username: joebob
Password:                        <-- note that the password is not displayed

Connected to: Oracle7 Server Release 7.3.3.0.0 - Production Release
With the distributed, replication, parallel query and Spatial Data options
PL/SQL Release 2.3.3.0.0 - Production

Enter array fetch buffer size: 4096 >    <-- default taken

Export file: expdat.dmp >     <-- full path-name of file to be exported

(1)E(ntire database), (2)U(sers), or (3)T(ables): (2)U >   <-- default taken

Export grants (yes/no): yes >         <-- default taken

Export table data (yes/no): yes >        <-- default taken

Compress extents (yes/no): yes > no     <-- see COMMENTS below

Export done in US7ASCII character set

About to export specified users ...
User to be exported: (RETURN to quit) > joebob

About to export JOEBOB's objects ...
. exporting snapshots
. exporting snapshot logs
. exporting job queues
. exporting refresh groups and children
. exporting database links
. exporting sequence numbers
. exporting cluster definitions
. about to export JOEBOB's tables via Conventional Path ...
. . exporting table              GUN_COLLECTION      1,584 rows exported
. . exporting table              FAVORITE_BEERS        966 rows exported
. . exporting table              PICKUP_TRUCKS          23 rows exported
. . exporting table              SAT_NIGHT_DATES         0 rows exported
. exporting synonyms
. exporting views
. exporting stored procedures
User to be exported: (RETURN to quit) >  <-- press RETURN to quit

. exporting referential integrity constraints
. exporting triggers
. exporting posttables actions
Export terminated successfully without warnings.
```

If you don't want to run EXP interactively this way, you can specify all these options from the operating system command line and possibly run EXP as a "batch" job. A complete reference on using the EXP utility is in the Oracle7 and Oracle8 server utilities guide. To get online help on the command-line parameters available, enter the following:

```
$ exp help=y
```

from the UNIX shell command-line prompt, or

```
C:\> exp80 help=y
```

for Oracle8 EXP or

```
C:\> exp73 help=y
```

for Oracle7.3 EXP from the Windows command prompt. In return, you'll see something like the following display:

```
Export: Release 8.0.2.0.2 - Production on Mon Sep 29 05:53:08 1997
Copyright (c) Oracle Corporation 1979, 1996.  All rights reserved
You can let Export prompt you for parameters by entering the EXP
command followed by your username/password:

    Example: EXP SCOTT/TIGER
```

Or, you can control how Export runs by entering the EXP command followed by various arguments. To specify parameters, you use keywords:

```
    Format:  EXP KEYWORD=value or KEYWORD=(value1,value2,...,valueN)
    Example: EXP SCOTT/TIGER GRANTS=Y TABLES=(EMP,DEPT,MGR)
```

Keyword	Description (Default)	Keyword	Description (Default)
USERID	username/password	FULL	export entire file (N)
BUFFER	size of data buffer	OWNER	list of owner usernames
FILE	output file (EXPDAT.DMP)	TABLES	list of table names
COMPRESS	import into one extent (Y)	RECORDLENGTH	length of IO record
GRANTS	export grants (Y)	INCTYPE	incremental export type
INDEXES	export indexes (Y)	RECORD	track incr. export (Y)
ROWS	export data rows (Y)	PARFILE	parameter filename
CONSTRAINTS	export constraints (Y)	CONSISTENT	cross-table consistency
LOG	log file of screen output	STATISTICS	analyze objects(ESTIMATE)
DIRECT	direct path (N)		
POINT_IN_TIME_RECOVER	tablespace point-in-time recovery (N)		
RECOVERY_TABLESPACES	List of tablespace names		

The available parameters are as follows:

Parameter Name	Description	Default Value	Comments
userid	ORACLE account username and password.		required
buffer	Size of the data buffer (in bytes) internal to the EXP process.	4096	
file	Name of the file to be written.	expdat.dmp	
compress	When exporting CREATE statements, should STORAGE parameters be recalculated to compress all allocated extents into the INITIAL extent?	Y	Choosing "N" for this option preserves the STORAGE parameters assigned to the segment at CREATE. Many DBAs prefer not to compress; see Chapter 8 on administering and monitoring.
grants	When exporting tables, should all GRANTS for those tables be exported as well?	Y	It is wise to accept the default, as GRANT statements typically do not take much room.
indexes	When exporting tables, should CREATE INDEX statements be exported as well?	Y	It is wise to accept the default, as CREATE INDEX statements do not take much room.
rows	When exporting tables, should the data in the tables be exported along with the table definitions?	Y	Sometimes you just want to export the table structure, instead of the table data.
constraints	When exporting tables, should table constraints (such as PRIMARY KEY and FOREIGN KEY) be exported as well?	Y	It is wise to accept the default, as ALTER TABLE statements do not take much room.
log	Log output from the EXP session to the specified file.		
direct	Use "direct path" EXP?	N	
full	Export the entire database?	N	Only available to privileged accounts (i.e., with EXP_FULL_DATABASE role).
owner	Export the indicated ORACLE accounts.		Unless this is the same account as specified in userid, this requires special privileges.
tables	Export the indicated tables and/or partitions.		Unless these tables are owned by the account specified by userid, this requires special privileges and each table must be specified as OWNER.TABLE. If exporting specific partitions of an Oracle8 partitioned table, use TABLE:PARTITION.
recordlength	Length of I/O buffers used during writing.		

(*continues*)

Parameter Name	Description	Default Value	Comments
inctype	When FULL=Y, INCTYPE= COMPLETE exports everything, INCTYPE=CUMULATIVE exports everything changed since the last COMPLETE or CUMULATIVE export, and INCTYPE = INCREMENTAL exports everything changed since the last COMPLETE, CUMULATIVE, or INCREMENTAL export.	complete	Requires EXP_FULL_DATABASE role.
record	Track the incremental export.	Y	To use "N" would imply that the subsequent incremental exports would be unaware of this EXP session.
parfile	Retrieve EXP command-line parameters from the indicated file.		Can be used to safeguard the password for the userid by setting file permissions for the parameter file appropriately.
consistent	All tables exported will be read-consistent to the exact same point in time.	N	Setting this parameter to "Y" causes EXP to issue the SET TRANSACTION READ ONLY command.
statistics	Should an ANALYZE to generate cost statistics be run during import of the exported data? Values are COMPUTE, ESTIMATE, or NONE.	estimate	In environments where the Oracle cost-based optimizer is in use, it would be wise to accept the default or specify COMPUTE for smaller tables.
point_in_time _recover	Is the import from this export going to be used during an Oracle8 "Tablespace Point-In-Time-Recovery"?	N	Available only with Oracle8.
recovery _tablespaces	Specifies the tablespaces to be exported for an Oracle8 "Tablespace Point-In-Time-Recovery" operation.		Available only with Oracle8.

Using all these command-line options, the EXP session performed interactively previously could be performed in batch using the following

```
$ exp userid=joebob/jimmyray compress=n owner=joebob
```

because all the other parameter value defaults were used. As mentioned previously, for SQL*Loader it may be dangerous for security reasons to leave the password for the Oracle account JOEBOB on the UNIX command line like this, since anybody running the UNIX utility *ps* could view it. Instead, using a parameter file as a standard method of operation would help here, as follows:

```
$ exp parfile=exp_profile.par owner=joebob
```

The contents of the parameter file *exp_profile.par* would look like this:

```
userid=joebob/jimmyray
compress=n
```

Then, read permissions can be set on this file so that only appropriate people can read it or edit it.

DIRECT PATH EXP

Like SQL*Loader, EXP has both a *conventional path* and a *direct path* mechanism. The conventional path mechanism is implemented using normal SQL SELECT statements, generated dynamically using the Oracle Call Interface (OCI).

The much faster direct path mechanism bypasses SQL and reads directly from the datafiles in the Oracle tablespace. Because SQL statements are not generated to do this, the Shared SQL Area in the Shared Pool in the System Global Area (SGA) is not used. Also, the data queried for the export bypasses the shared buffer cache in the SGA. All in all, this can significantly reduce contention in a very busy system, making the direct path export much faster just by itself and, by reducing contention in the SGA, allowing the database instance overall to perform much faster.

Although using DIRECT=Y on EXP is essentially a transparent performance boost, not affecting the exported data in any way, there are (of course!) a few restrictions on direct path export. One is that direct path export is unable to translate from one character set to another.

Be sure to read the section on other dependencies for using direct path export in the Oracle7 or Oracle8 *Server Utilities* guides.

INVOKING IMP

Just like EXP, the IMP utility can be run either interactively or entirely from the operating system command line. Once again, the relevant documentation in the standard Oracle documentation set is the Oracle7 or Oracle8 *Server Utilities* guide.

Running IMP interactively from the operating system command line would look something like:

```
Import: Release 7.3.3.0.0 - Production on Mon Sep 29 07:55:58 1997
Copyright (c) Oracle Corporation 1979, 1996.  All rights reserved.

Username: joebob
Password:

Connected to: Oracle7 Server Release 7.3.3.0.0 - Production Release
With the distributed, replication, parallel query and Spatial Data options
PL/SQL Release 2.3.3.0.0 - Production

Import file: expdat.dmp >                              <-- default taken
```

```
Enter insert buffer size (minimum is 4096) 30720>        <-- default taken

Export file created by EXPORT:V07.03.03 via conventional path

List contents of import file only (yes/no): no >

Ignore create error due to object existence (yes/no): no >

Import grants (yes/no): yes >

Import table data (yes/no): yes >

Import entire export file (yes/no): no >
Username: joebob

Enter table names. Null list means all tables for user
Enter table name or . if done:                         <-- default taken

. importing JOEBOB's objects into JOEBOB
. . importing table              GUN_COLLECTION      1,584 rows imported
. . importing table              FAVORITE_BEERS        966 rows imported
. . importing table               PICKUP_TRUCKS         23 rows imported
. . importing table             SAT_NIGHT_DATES          0 rows imported
Import terminated successfully without warnings.
```

Just like the EXP utility, online help for the command-line parameters can be obtained by running

```
$ imp help=y
```

from the UNIX shell command-line prompt, or

```
C:\> imp80 help=y
```

for Oracle8 IMP or

```
C:\> imp73 help=y
```

for Oracle7.3 IMP from the Windows command prompt. In return, you'll see something like the following display:

```
Import: Release 8.0.2.0.2 - Production on Mon Sep 29 08:04:35 1997
Copyright (c) Oracle Corporation 1979, 1994, 1996.  All rights reserved.


You can let Import prompt you for parameters by entering the IMP
command followed by your username/password:

    Example: IMP SCOTT/TIGER
```

Or, you can control how Import runs by entering the IMP command followed by various arguments. To specify parameters, you use keywords:

```
Format:  IMP KEYWORD=value or KEYWORD=(value1,value2,...,valueN)
Example: IMP SCOTT/TIGER IGNORE=Y TABLES=(EMP,DEPT) FULL=N

Keyword  Description (Default)          Keyword       Description (Default)
--------------------------------------------------------------------------
USERID   username/password             FULL          import entire file (N)
BUFFER   size of data buffer           FROMUSER      list of owner usernames
FILE     output file (EXPDAT.DMP)      TOUSER        list of usernames
SHOW     just list file contents (N)   TABLES        list of table names
IGNORE   ignore create errors (N)      RECORDLENGTH  length of IO record
GRANTS   import grants (Y)             INCTYPE       incremental import type
INDEXES  import indexes (Y)            COMMIT        commit array insert (N)
ROWS     import data rows (Y)          PARFILE       parameter filename
LOG      log file of screen output
DESTROY  overwrite tablespace data file (N)
INDEXFILE write table/index info to specified file
CHARSET  character set of export file (NLS_LANG)
POINT_IN_TIME_RECOVER  Tablespace Point-in-time Recovery (N)
SKIP_UNUSABLE_INDEXES  skip maintenance of unusable indexes (N)
ANALYZE  execute ANALYZE statements in dump file (N)

Import terminated successfully without warnings.
```

The parameters for IMP are explained as follows:

Parameter Name	Description	Default Value	Comments
userid	ORACLE account username and password.		required
buffer	Size of the data buffer (in bytes) internal to the IMP process.	30720	
file	Name of the file to be read from.	expdat.dmp	
show	Just list the contents of the export file without writing anything to the database.	N	
ignore	Ignore any errors caused by the prior existence of objects when IMP tries to CREATE them?	Y	Set to "N" only if you are certain that the tables, indexes, sequences, and related PL/SQL objects do not already exist.
grants	Should the GRANT statements exported and saved in the export file be imported?	Y	

(continues)

Parameter Name	Description	Default Value	Comments
indexes	Create indexes upon import?	Y	Sometimes you just want to import the table structure and its data, without incurring the overhead of index maintenance.
rows	Import table data after tables are created?	Y	Sometimes you just want to import the table structure, instead of the table data.
full	Import the entire database from the FULL database export?	N	Only available to privileged accounts (i.e., with IMP_FULL_DATABASE role).
fromuser	List of ORACLE account names to which objects in the export file are going to be imported.		
touser	List of ORACLE account names to be imported into.		
tables	Import the indicated tables and/or partitions.		Unless these tables are owned by the account specified by userid, this requires special privileges and each table must be specified as OWNER.TABLE. If importing specific partitions of an Oracle8 partitioned table, use TABLE:PARTITION.
recordlength	Length of I/O buffers used during reading.		
inctype	When FULL=Y, INCTYPE= COMPLETE imports everything, INCTYPE=CUMULATIVE imports everything changed since the last COMPLETE or CUMULATIVE import, and INCTYPE = INCREMENTAL imports everything changed since the last COMPLETE, CUMULATIVE, or INCREMENTAL import.	complete	Requires IMP_FULL_DATABASE role.
commit	Commit after each array INSERT?	N	COMMIT=N will perform a commit only after the entire import is completed.
parfile	Retrieve EXP command-line parameters from the indicated file.		Can be used to safeguard the password for the userid by setting file permissions for the parameter file appropriately.
log	Log output from the IMP session to the specified file.		
destroy	Recreate the datafile in the tablespace?	N	Only with FULL database import.

Parameter Name	Description	Default Value	Comments
indexfile	Write DDL commands, such as CREATE TABLE and CREATE IN-DEX, to the specified file?		Ideal if you want to edit any DDL for the exported objects prior to importing.
charset	Specifies the National Language Support (NLS) character set used during the export of the export data file. IMP will automatically translate from that character set to the one used by the database.		
point_in_time _recover	Is this IMP session being used to import data as part of an Oracle8 "Tablespace Point-In-Time-Recovery"?	N	Available only with Oracle8.
skip_unusable _indexes	Should indexes previously marked UNUSABLE be automatically maintained by this IMP session?	N	Available only with Oracle8.
analyze	Should an ANALYZE to generate cost statistics be run during import of the exported data, provided that the EXP parameter STATISTICS was set to either COMPUTE or ESTIMATE during the export?	N	In environments where the Oracle cost-based optimizer is in use, it would be wise to set ANALYZE=Y.

From this list, it can be seen that the previous interactive IMP session can be run using the following command-line parameters:

```
$ imp userid=joebob/jimmyray fromuser=joebob
```

This is because all the other parameter value defaults were used. As mentioned previously, for SQL*Loader and for the EXP utility it may be dangerous for security reasons to leave the password for the Oracle account JOEBOB on the UNIX command line like this, since anybody running the UNIX utility *ps* can view it. Instead, using a parameter file as a standard method of operation would help here, as follows:

```
$ imp parfile=imp_profile.par fromuser=joebob
```

The contents of the parameter file *imp_profile.par* would look like this:

```
userid=joebob/jimmyray
```

Then, read permissions can be set on this file so that only appropriate people can read it or edit it.

One important point should be made about importing and IMP. Database objects are imported in the exact same order as they were exported. In the case of the EXP and IMP of the Oracle account JOEBOB, the tables GUN_COLLECTION, BEERS, PICKUP_TRUCKS, and SAT_NIGHT_DATES were all imported in the same order as they were exported. This is fine if there are no referential integrity constraints between these tables, but just suppose that the table GUN_COLLECTION had a FOREIGN KEY to the table PICKUP_TRUCKS, implying that each pickup truck can have zero, one, or more guns stored in it. If this is the case, a straight import like those illustrated would fail.

Instead, it may be necessary to structure the running of IMP to accommodate these relationships. For example, it would work better if all tables that do not have any FOREIGN KEYS are imported first:

```
$ imp parfile=imp_profile.par fromuser=joebob \
                tables=beers,pickup_trucks,sat_night_dates
```

Then, once that first import is complete, a *second pass* from the same export file can be run as follows:

```
$ imp parfile=imp_profile.par fromuser=joebob tables=gun_collection
```

Obviously, this kind of thing can grow quite complicated. You may find it useful to use the Oracle data dictionary view DBA_DEPENDENCIES to help find each layer of tables in a referential integrity hierarchy, if this has not been otherwise documented already.

Using Database Triggers in Operational Systems

EXP copies all data from a table (or Oracle8 partition). In most cases, our real need is to copy only the data that has been entered or changed since the last copy. This requires some means of identifying the modified rows. This is an issue for all source systems, not just Oracle-based ones. In some cases, this identification will require keeping a copy of the database or files at each extract cycle and comparing data between the current copy and the previous one. For sequential files this "file rubbing" works well. For large databases, however, this may be expensive in terms of disk space and processing time. If only a small percentage of the rows have been touched, it is inefficient to have to examine every row and compare it to the previous database copy.

Another means of capturing data from an Oracle operational system is to use database triggers to either flag data rows that have changed or to copy the changed data into a temporary table for later movement to the warehouse. An Oracle database trigger is procedural logic, coded using Oracle's PL/SQL language, which is attached to a particular table. The trigger defines additional processing that should be performed each time a row in the table is acted upon by SQL data manipulation language (DML) commands such as INSERT, UPDATE, or DELETE.

TRIGGERS AND TIME-STAMP COLUMNS

Some Oracle applications have already been written to use a trigger to flag each row with a time when it was last modified. If this is the case, it may be possible to build your extraction based upon these time stamps. The extract SELECT statement for each table in the operational system would include a WHERE clause condition similar to the following:

```
SELECT *
  FROM EMPLOYEES
 WHERE DEPARTMENT= 'CONSULTING'
   AND LAST_CHANGED >= '1-NOV-97'
   AND LAST_CHANGED < '1-DEC-97';
```

TIP

By default, all Oracle DATE columns include both a date and time portion. Unless the trigger maintaining the LAST_CHANGED column were specifically coded to store only the date, the time of day would be stored in the LAST_CHANGED data as a fractional portion of a day. Coding the conditions as shown will get all transactions time-stamped starting just after midnight on the morning of November 1 and up through midnight on the evening of November 30.

This example would let us retrieve the current information about any consultants who were hired, promoted, reassigned, and the like during the month of November. This data can then be added to the warehouse. (Of course, in this example it might be more appropriate to select data based on a transaction effective date, which is stored as part of the CONSULTANTS' data as opposed to the transaction's processing date. This is one of several design issues that must be evaluated by the warehouse analyst in determining extract strategies.)

Other Oracle applications (or other tables within the same application) may not already have time-stamp columns that are being maintained. It may be necessary to add such triggers in order to assist the regular extract process in finding the appropriate data. This will likely be a touchy point of negotiation between the warehouse team and the application maintenance teams. Such a change will require adding a column to the tables of interest that will affect storage requirements, and it will involve creating a simple trigger to those tables. The logic for each table's trigger can be identical and similar to the following:

```
CREATE OR REPLACE TRIGGER TIMESTAMP_TABLE_X
BEFORE INSERT OR UPDATE OR DELETE
ON TABLE_X
FOR EACH ROW
BEGIN
    if inserting or updating then
        :new.last_update := SYSDATE;
    else if deleting then
        INSERT INTO TABLE_X_HISTORY (<column-list>,…, LAST_UPDATE)
```

```
                    VALUES (<column-list-values>, …, SYSDATE);
        end if;
END;
```

TIP

Making such changes to a production OLTP application is not likely to be enthusiastically embraced by the team responsible for ensuring the performance of that application. This is another reason for a close cooperative involvement between the warehouse team and the application maintenance teams! Generally, the only way to invoke that cooperation is to have an executive sponsor from the user organization responsible for both the online application and the decision-support function. He or she can help reinforce the shared commitment to successfully implementing the warehouse as a supplement to the traditional application functions.

The extra processing load required by such a trigger is minor for each row (except when deleting!), but it may be significant when considered in terms of the total load of many rows being inserted or updated by the application. The processing load may be further increased if it is determined that an index is required on the column in order to efficiently locate the rows. Such an index will have to be updated every time a row in the table is inserted, updated, or deleted.

There is an additional issue with respect to using triggers to update a time-stamp column within application tables. This technique works well for identifying rows that are inserted or updated, but it fails to capture information about delete rows since the DELETE command also deletes our time-stamp column! Whether deleted rows need to be recorded in the data warehouse or not is a

Locating a Small Subset of Rows in a Table

An Oracle B*Tree index only stores non-null values. Before the introduction of the Parallel Query Option in release 7.1, we frequently used this feature to our advantage when we needed an index to locate a small subset of rows from a larger table. Rather than keep a LAST_CHANGED value in every row, we can reset the column value to null in every row once it has been extracted. Then the only rows that will be included in the index at the time of the next extract will be those that have been touched during the period between extracts. The index remains smaller and is more easily rebuilt.

As another approach, because of the speed-up provided by parallel query, it may be possible to avoid using the index entirely. Testing will determine whether the performance of the parallel full table scan will be acceptable. If so, then there will be no need to reset values to null. Each extract will read the entire table in parallel to find the rows changed during our period of interest.

very specific design issue. For example, our warehouse might need to receive information about each order when it is taken, modified, shipped, and so on. There may be no value, however, in recording the fact that a completed order was purged from the operational system at some later point. The purge is not a business transaction of interest to us; it is an administrative transaction used to keep the online operational database to a manageable size.

In other cases, however, the delete may be part of a business transaction that is needed in the warehouse. If so, we'll need to use a different recording technique.

TRIGGERS AND CHANGE LOG TABLES

Rather than having our database trigger to update a time-stamp column within the modified row, we can have the trigger insert a row into another table that we will create just for this purpose. That table becomes a log of changes made to our application's base table. This is the basic approach used by the Oracle snapshot and symmetric replication facilities. A simple example of a change log table might be designed as follows:

```
CREATE TABLE CONSULTANTS_CHANGES
    (EMPLOYEE_ID        NUMBER(7),
    LAST_CHANGED       DATE,
    CHANGE_TYPE        CHAR(1)
        CONSTRAINT CONS_CHANGE_TYPE_CK CHECK CHANGE_TYPE IN ('I','U','D'),
    CONSTRAINT CONS_CHANGE_PK PRIMARY KEY (EMPLOYEE_ID, LAST_CHANGED);
```

An example trigger to populate this change log might look like this:

```
CREATE OR REPLACE TRIGGER LOG_CONSULTANT_CHANGES
    BEFORE INSERT OR UPDATE OR DELETE
  ON CONSULTANT
  FOR EACH ROW
DECLARE
    v_change_type   VARCHAR2(1);
BEGIN
    --
    IF INSERTING THEN
        v_change_type := 'I';
    ELSIF UPDATING THEN
        v_change_type := 'U';
    ELSE
        v_change_type := 'D';
    END IF;
    --
    INSERT
      INTO consultant_changes (employee_id, last_changed, change_type)
    VALUES (:old.employee_id, SYSDATE, v_change_type);
    --
END;
```

Several alternatives to this approach may be considered. In the example just given we used the primary key of the base table (EMPLOYEE_ID) to track which row was modified. Some DBAs or programmers may suggest we use the ROWID of the base table row as the identifier of the source row. This is tempting because finding a specific row during the extract process will be faster using the ROWID than an index lookup based on the primary key. This minor performance benefit should be avoided, however, for several reasons:

- Although ROWIDs do not change as long as a row exists in the database, they do get modified if the DBA does a table export/import to reorganize the table. Should this happen, the originally recorded ROWID will be useless.
- Using ROWIDs raises the same problem with DELETEs that we saw using time-stamp columns—the ROWID will no longer point to a row after the row is deleted. (It may well even point to a new row that may have been inserted into the same block after the delete was completed!)
- In the data warehouse, we will store data based upon real-world primary key values, not upon the Oracle physical storage convenience of ROWID. We should make our connections to the source data based upon the same real-world key.
- The ROWID format changes between Oracle7 and Oracle8. Building your extract process on an Oracle7 ROWID will present additional difficulties for the applications team when they someday need to migrate the source database to Oracle8.

Another option in using a change log table is to copy additional source data into the change log in order to avoid having to look it up at extract time. This approach has the disadvantage of requiring additional storage in the change log table. It has, however, several advantages to recommend it:

- If a row changes more than once during the period between extracts, we will be able to capture each of those successive changes in the warehouse. In our example, it may well be important for us to know that a particular consultant was promoted on the fourth of the month and then transferred to a new organization on the twenty-seventh of the month. For time reports entered for days between the fourth and the twenty-seventh, we would want to properly summarize his or her activity into the proper organization and job title. Recording only a primary key "pointer" to the row would only provide us with the final image when we try to capture the change made on the fourth.
- Having all the necessary warehouse data stored in the change log makes our extract process more efficient since we don't have to individually look up the original source rows. We can obtain all our data through a simple table scan of a relatively small table. In either case. we will have to make a second scan of the table to purge the rows that have been extracted.
- Data from deleted rows can be retained. In some uncommon situations, the warehouse may need the data after the DELETE even though it might

not have been captured when inserted. This might occur when the operational inventory system's transaction removes a stock record rather than setting the quantity on hand to zero when inventory is depleted.

- Once we've found a way to identify which rows need to be extracted, we'll need to copy them to our data warehouse. We can do that in a variety of ways. We'll examine three methods, all of which allow the specification of a qualified query to retrieve specific rows from the source database and transfer them to the data warehouse for loading.

Unload and Reload

The import utility is notoriously slow in loading large volumes of data. IMP, at least through release 8.0, cannot be automatically parallelized and uses standard INSERT SQL processing. As we discussed earlier, the direct path mode of SQL*Loader processes large volumes of data much more efficiently by bypassing most of the work involved in SQL processing. In some cases, you may wish to move a large amount of data from one Oracle database to an Oracle data warehouse and may find that IMP is too slow for the volumes involved. Import also processes entire tables rather than a selected subset of rows.

We can use another variation on the SQL-to-generate-SQL technique to generate a SQL*Plus script that will extract data from an Oracle database, using parallel query processing when appropriate, and then generate a SQL*Loader control file to load the extracted data into the warehouse. Figure 6.10 illustrates this using a script to generate and execute the unload and reload tasks.

The generated unload script will probably run slower than EXPORT (especially direct path EXPORT) even when run with parallel query. The direct path SQL*Loader portion will, however, run in a fraction of the time required to IMPORT the same amount of data. Performance is related to the length of the records written to the intermediate file. A table with many columns defined with very long VARCHAR or VARCHAR2 specifications but that actually contain relatively little data will involve writing out lots of spaces in this fixed format file.

Similar wasted bytes (and decreased performance) arise from NUMBER columns specified without precision and scale. In an ideal Oracle world, tables would not be defined with unspecified NUMBER columns, but there are certainly Oracle systems around that do not constrain the size of numbers. Oracle will store up to thirty-eight digits of precision in such columns. To avoid writing out all such columns' data using thirty-eight bytes, the script prompts the user for different default lengths to use for unspecified precision and scale. When responding to these prompts, the user needs to know the data well enough to avoid artificially trimming the precision of actual data being extracted in any column.

EXECUTING THE UNLOAD/RELOAD SCRIPT

When you execute this script, it will prompt for the name of the schema that contains the table and the name of the table (or view). In order to deal with any

Figure 6.10 Using the unload/reload generation script.

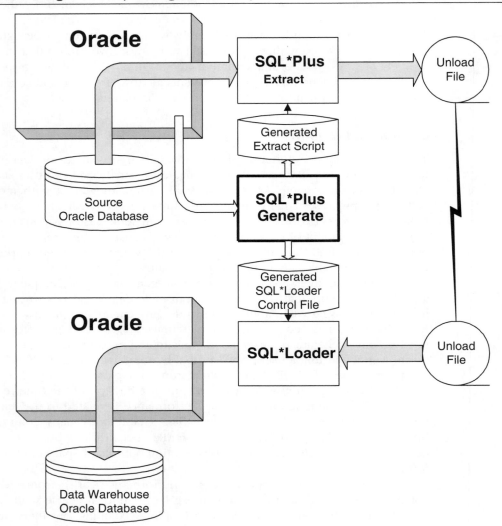

NUMBER columns that might have been defined without precision or scale, the script will prompt you for a default value to use for precision and scale of these fields in the unload file.

The generated SQL*Loader script (named unload2.sql) assumes that fields of blanks should be loaded as NULLS—if the table has columns for which SPACES are valid values, then it will be necessary to edit the generated unload2.sql script to concatenate double quotation marks before and after the affected column(s) as well as change the length (linesize in unload2.sql and the individual field's length in the generated .ctl file) by two bytes.

If a numeric column is encountered that has no defined precision or scale, then this script will use default values (prompted for). This poses three risks: (1) you may overspecify the precision and thereby waste space in the unload file; (2) you may underspecify the precision and thereby get overflow indicators in the unloaded data that may not be caught prior to loading; (3) you may underspecify the scale and introduce truncation that will not be found by either the unload or load processes. For this reason, it is strongly recommended that numeric table columns be defined in the source database with appropriate precision and scale values.

ADVANTAGES OF THE UNLOAD/RELOAD SCRIPT

This unload/reload utility has some other advantages besides speed. The unload can easily select a subset of the original table (for statistical sampling or retrieving rows for a particular department or range of business dates), whereas EXP/IMP deals with entire tables. Additionally, if desired, the unload script can be easily enhanced with an ORDER BY clause to sort the output in order to speed index builds and/or increase buffer cache hits on the reloaded data based on loading frequently used rows contiguously.

Finally, the generated unload script might have a GROUP BY appended to the SELECT statement that would facilitate initial loading of summary tables. In the project accounting case study used in this book, each week actual timecards are entered with data keyed down to the day, but we load data into the data warehouse based on a calendar month. At some point (during the extract, during the load or in a summarization step after the initial load), this data will have to be summarized. The following script could be used to perform that level of summarization while unloading the data from the Oracle-based project accounting system.

One big advantage of using this utility is that it can also unload data from a view, which is not possible using EXP. By unloading data as defined in a view, this facility may be used to do subsets—selection (specific rows), projection (specific columns), joins, GROUP BY summaries, or to apply functions (either Oracle built-in or user-defined) during the selection without having to edit this script or its generated output scripts, other than possibly changing the name of the table in the SQL*Loader control file.

Finally, by manually editing the generated unload2.sql and SQL*Loader control files, it is possible to remove columns or modify them with SQL or PL/SQL functions during the extract. In general, however, you should avoid manually editing the files by using the capability of unloading from a view.

LIMITATIONS OF THE UNLOAD/RELOAD SCRIPT

This script is not a complete replacement for the Oracle EXP and IMP utilities. In addition to being slower on the unload step than EXP, it has other limitations. This script only moves data from one table or view at a time. EXP/IMP can export database objects other than tables (such as indexes, synonyms, views, users, and roles). Use this tool only to help move data from an Oracle source system to the data warehouse.

It doesn't handle LONG, RAW, LONG RAW, ROWID, MLSLABEL, or any of the new Oracle8 object data types. These data types are not widely used in data warehousing but may be part of the source system from which you unload data. If the data you need to move includes "exotic" data types, EXP/IMP, or the SQL*Plus, the COPY command may provide a better solution.

This unload/reload script will not automatically make translations when the unload file is moved between Oracle databases running on machines with different data encoding schemes, such as ASCII and EBCDIC. Only a relatively small number of shops run Oracle in MVS or VM shops, so moving to or from EBCDIC is not a large concern. Other translations may be necessary for organizations with operations in multiple countries where various machine-encoding schemes are commonly used. Since all data is written in external formats, one should expect that file transfer utilities that do such conversions should work. SQL*Loader allows for specification of the data encoding used in the input file so, as an alternative, one could edit the SQL*Loader control file to specify the alternative encoding scheme.

THE UNLOAD/RELOAD SCRIPT

```
set tab off heading off heading off feedback off echo off verify off
set space 1 pagesize 0 linesize 120
ACCEPT owner            PROMPT 'What schema owns the table to be unloaded? '
ACCEPT table_name       PROMPT 'What table is to be unloaded? '
ACCEPT default_precision PROMPT -
    'How many TOTAL digits for numbers without defined precision? '
ACCEPT default_scale PROMPT -
    'How many DECIMAL digits for numbers without defined scale? '
---------------------------------------------------
-- Generate the unload script
---------------------------------------------------
SPOOL unload_fixed2.sql
Select 'SET HEADING OFF FEEDBACK OFF ECHO OFF VERIFY OFF SPACE 0 '
         || 'PAGESIZE 0 TERMOUT OFF'
  FROM dual
/

-- Calculate the sum of all output field lengths and set the output record size
SELECT 'SET LINESIZE '
       || (SUM(DECODE(data_type,
                      'CHAR',data_length,
                      'VARCHAR',data_length,
                      'VARCHAR2',data_length,
                      'DATE',14,
                      'NUMBER',DECODE(data_precision,
                                '',&default_precision+2,
                                GREATEST(data_precision-data_scale,1)
                                +DECODE(data_scale,0,0,1)+data_scale)+1,
                      'FLOAT',&default_precision+2,
                      data_length)))
```

```
  FROM dba_tab_columns
 WHERE owner=UPPER('&&owner')
   AND table_name=UPPER('&&table_name')
/
--  Generate a SQL*Plus COLUMN command to control formatting of each output
field
SELECT 'COLUMN ' || rpad('"'||column_name||'"',32)
       || ' FORMAT '
       || RPAD(DECODE(data_type,
                    'CHAR','A'||data_length,
                    'VARCHAR2','A'||data_length,
                    'VARCHAR','A'||data_length,
                    'DATE','A14',
                    'NUMBER',DECODE(data_precision,'',
                                      RPAD('0',&default_precision-
&default_scale,'9')
                                          ||'.'||RPAD('9',&default_scale,'9'),
                                      RPAD('0',GREATEST(data_precision-
data_scale,1),'9')
                                          || DECODE(data_scale,0,'','.')
                                          ||
DECODE(data_scale,0,'',RPAD('9',data_scale,'9'))),
                    'FLOAT',RPAD('0',&default_precision-&default_scale,'9')
                                  ||'.'||RPAD('9',&default_scale,'9'),
                    'ERROR'),40)
       || ' HEADING ''X'''
  FROM dba_tab_columns
 WHERE owner=UPPER('&&owner')
   AND table_name=UPPER('&&table_name')
 ORDER BY column_id
/

--  Generate the actual SELECT statement to unload table data
SELECT 'SPOOL /tmp/&&owner..&&table_name..DAT'
  FROM dual
/
COLUMN var1 NOPRINT
COLUMN var2 NOPRINT
SELECT 'a' var1, 0 var2, 'SELECT '
  FROM dual
UNION
SELECT 'b', column_id, DECODE(column_id, 1, '     ', ' , ', ')
                      || DECODE(data_type,'DATE',
                              'TO_CHAR('||'"'||column_name||'"'
                                      ||','''YYYYMMDDHH24MISS'') '
                                      ||'"'||column_name||'"',
                              '"'||column_name||'"')
  FROM dba_tab_columns
 WHERE owner=UPPER('&&owner')
   AND table_name=upper('&&table_name')
UNION
```

```
SELECT 'c', 0, 'FROM &&owner..&&table_name'
  FROM dual
UNION
SELECT 'd', 0, ';'
  FROM dual
 ORDER BY 1,2
/
SELECT 'SPOOL OFF'
  FROM dual
/
SELECT 'SET TERMOUT ON'
  FROM dual
/
SPOOL OFF
------------------------------------------------------------------------------
--  Generate the SQL*Loader control file
------------------------------------------------------------------------------
SET LINES 120 PAGES 0
SPOOL &&owner..&&table_name..CTL
SELECT 'a' var1, 0 var2, 'OPTIONS(DIRECT=TRUE)'
  FROM dual
UNION
SELECT 'b', 0, 'LOAD DATA'
  FROM dual
UNION
SELECT 'c', 0, 'INFILE  ''/tmp/&&owner..&&table_name..DAT'''
  FROM dual
UNION
SELECT 'd', 0, 'BADFILE  &&owner..&&table_name..BAD'
  FROM dual
UNION
SELECT 'e', 0, 'DISCARDFILE  &&owner..&&table_name..DSC'
  FROM dual
UNION
SELECT 'f', 0, 'DISCARDMAX 999'
  FROM dual
UNION
SELECT 'm', 0, 'INTO TABLE &&owner..&&table_name'
  FROM dual
UNION
SELECT 'n', column_id,
            RPAD(DECODE(column_id,1,'(',',')||'"'||column_name||'"',31)
                || DECODE(data_type,
                        'CHAR','CHAR('||data_length||')',
                        'VARCHAR','CHAR('||data_length||')',
                        'VARCHAR2','CHAR('||data_length||')',
                        'DATE','DATE(14) "YYYYMMDDHH24MISS"',
                        'NUMBER','DECIMAL EXTERNAL('||
                                DECODE(data_precision,
                        '',&default_precision+2,
                        GREATEST(data_precision-data_scale,1)
```

```
                                   +DECODE(data_scale,0,0,1)+data_scale+1)||')',
                         'FLOAT','DECIMAL EXTERNAL('||
                                 TO_CHAR(&default_precision+2)||')',
                         'ERROR--'||data_type)|| ' NULLIF ("' ||
                                 column_name||'" = BLANKS)'
      FROM dba_tab_columns
   WHERE owner = upper('&&owner')
     AND table_name = UPPER('&&table_name')
UNION
SELECT 'z', 0, ')'
   FROM dual
  ORDER by 1, 2
/
SPOOL OFF
-----------------------------------------------------------------------
-- Cleanup
-----------------------------------------------------------------------
CLEAR COLUMN
CLEAR BREAK
CLEAR COMPUTE
UNDEF owner
UNDEF table_name
UNDEF default_precision
UNDEF default_scale
```

Incidentally, this same script can be used for reorganizing a table that, due to improper PCTFREE and PCTUSED parameters coupled with unexpected patterns of UPDATE, INSERT and DELETE processing, has become internally fragmented with many blocks with unnecessary and unusable free space.

Copying Data with CREATE TABLE . . . AS SELECT

It is possible to use the SQL CREATE TABLE command with a subquery to retrieve data from an existing table (or join of multiple tables). For small amounts of data, this feature can be used directly across a database link to retrieve data from a remote database and use it to create a table in the data warehouse. The following is an example:

```
CREATE TABLE NOV_ACTIVITY

      (consultant_id,
       project_id,
       function_code,
       revenue,
       hours,
       expenses)
   TABLESPACE temp_loads
      STORAGE (INITIAL 50M NEXT 50M PCTINCREASE 0)
AS
SELECT t.employee_id, t.project_code, t.function_code,
```

```
              sum(t.labor_hrs * p.rate) sum(t.labor_hrs), sum(t.expense)
   FROM TIMECARD@TEAM T, PROJECT_ASSIGNMENTS@TEAM P
  WHERE t.project_code = p.project_code
        t.employee_id = p.employee_id
    AND t.timecard_dt BETWEEN p.start_date AND p.end_date
    AND t.timecard_dt >= '1-NOV-97'
    AND t.timecard_dt <  '1-DEC-97'
  GROUP BY t.employee_id, t.project_code, t.function_code;
```

This will create a local table (called NOV_ACTIVITY) in our data warehouse that will be populated with the lightly summarized timecard records from the source system (identified by the database link named TEAM) for days worked during November 1997. (The specifics of the query and how it found the needed data in the TEAM database are not important. The key is that the subquery executes entirely in that remote database and performs the necessary join to find the data needed for the data warehouse.)

In many cases, however, the extracted data volume will be too large to pass over a SQL*Net connection efficiently. CREATE TABLE . . . AS SELECT can still be used, however, to extract the data from the source system and create a temporary table. Once the subset of data is extracted, the resulting temporary table can be exported (or unloaded) for transport to the warehouse for importing or loading. In this situation, the CREATE TABLE would be executed entirely on the source system.

PARALLEL CTAS (PCTAS)

When sufficient CPU and I/O resources are available, the CREATE TABLE . . . AS SELECT can be performed much more quickly using the parallel query capabilities of Oracle7 or Oracle8. Use of the UNRECOVERABLE option on this command is especially useful for this type of task. There is no reason to endure the additional overhead of redo logging each of the INSERTs into our new temporary table. We expect to immediately back up (via the export) the data in this table as soon as it is created. Should the CREATE TABLE command fail to complete we can simply reexecute it when the system is available. In no event would we expect to recover an incomplete CREATE TABLE, so UNRECOVERABLE costs us nothing.

Much more information on the specifics of Parallel CREATE TABLE . . . AS SELECT (pCTAS) is provided in Chapter 10. This command is frequently the fastest means of extracting a compact subset of Oracle data from a very large table to make the selected data available for transport to the data warehouse.

*Using the SQL*Plus Copy Command*

SQL*Plus includes a command called COPY that provides a means of copying data from one database to another or from one table to another within the same database. Note that COPY is not a SQL command and cannot be used from within an Enterprise Manager WorkSheet or other SQL interface. In most cases, it is preferable to use CREATE TABLE . . . AS SELECT or INSERT . . . SELECT SQL syntax. There are several reasons for this preference. SQL language commands should be used whenever possible over the proprietary syntax of any tool. Additionally, Oracle8 allows for parallelizing both of the alternative SQL commands (Oracle7 can parallelize the CREATE TABLE . . . AS SELECT) but COPY cannot.

There is one particular situation in which the SQL*Plus COPY command is valuable. Oracle has provided a LONG data type as a way of storing character data that would not fit within the allowable storage of the character data types (CHAR, NCHAR, VARCHAR2, NCHAR2, and VARCHAR), which have been variously limited to 255, 2,000, or 4,000 bytes, depending on the Oracle release. LONG (as well as LONG RAW, which is used for noncharacter data) have been allowed to store from 64 KB (through version 6) to two gigabytes in Oracle7 and Oracle8. LONG data is further limited to only 32 KB when referenced in PL/SQL.

Along with the greater storage capacity, the Oracle LONG data type has always had several limitations, which are documented in the Oracle7 and Oracle8 *SQL Reference* manuals. Among these limitations is a prohibition against including a LONG column in the SELECT list of CREATE TABLE . . . AS SELECT or the subquery of INSERT . . . SELECT. Incidentally, the Oracle replication facility also shares this inability to directly move LONG data between databases.

In general, we've traditionally recommended avoiding the use of LONGs when designing Oracle systems except when absolutely required. Oracle8's new CLOB and BLOB data types have been created to provide the capability to store long data without the severe limitations imposed by the LONG data type. Unfortunately, there are many systems around that have included LONG columns, often unnecessarily. We recently worked with a client who needed to copy data from a purchased application to a reporting database. The vendor of this particular application included LONG columns in several tables to store "memo" data. No row in this client's database ever stored more data than could have been accommodated by the Oracle7 VARCHAR2 data type, but the chosen design severely constrained our ability to replicate data for the client.

If your source data includes data stored in LONG columns that you need to move to the data warehouse, your solutions are generally limited. The EXP/IMP utilities will work with LONG data, providing you wish to copy entire tables. PL/SQL procedures can work with LONGs providing none of the data exceeds PL/SQL's 32-KB size limitation on character variables. Of course, writing custom programs (e.g., in Pro*C) is another option that offers the most flexibility but also requires the most effort. The SQL*Plus COPY command is a simple means of copying data, including LONGs, between databases with the flexibility to specify particular columns and conditions for row selection.

DEFINING THE MAXIMUM LENGTH OF LONG DATA IN SQL*PLUS

Define the maximum size of LONG data for COPY to transmit through the SQL*Plus SET LONG command. The value of this variable defaults to only 80 bytes. Any LONG data that exceeds the set value will be truncated by SQL*Plus!

The basic syntax of COPY has four basic parts:

```
COPY FROM source_db_connection
     TO destination_db_connection
     ACTION destination_table_specification
     USING query
```

You must specify either the FROM or TO database connection. If you omit one or the other then SQL*Plus will default that connection to the currently connected database. For example, if you are connected to the warehouse database and need to copy data from the PROD instance, you would specify the FROM connection to point at PROD and let the TO connection default to the warehouse. *source_db_connection* and *destination_db_connection* are of the form *userid/password@database_spec*. You must provide a valid Oracle userid and password in the database specified by *database_spec*. *database_spec* must be a valid SQL*Net (or Net8) connection, which can be resolved by SQL*Net's Transparent Network Substrate (TNS) facility. In general, this means it will be specified either in Oracle Names or your local TNSNAMES.ORA file.

The ACTION must be one of four keywords: CREATE, APPEND, REPLACE, or INSERT. The chosen keyword determines how SQL*Plus treats the destination table into which data is to be copied.

- CREATE will create a new table in the database schema specified in the TO clause (or defaulted to current database connection). If a table of the specified name already exists in the destination database schema then COPY . . . CREATE will return an error.
- APPEND acts just like CREATE except that, if the table already exists, COPY will then insert rows into the existing table rather than return an error.
- REPLACE will drop an existing table of the name specified, if it exists. Then it will create a new table of the *destination_db_specification* using data retrieved via the *query*.
- INSERT will copy the rows into an existing table in the destination database schema. The column list specified in the *query* must match the columns of the destination table. An error is returned if the table does not already exist.

destination_table_specification is of the form *table_name* (column name list). The *destination_table_specification* must provide a valid *table_name* for the destination database schema. Although not documented, you may specify an existing view name in *destination_table_specification* if doing an INSERT or APPEND. The column name list is optional syntax and allows for changing the names of columns retrieved by query when creating a new table through CREATE, REPLACE, or APPEND. The columns must match the order of columns specified in query and will be created with corresponding data types. If rows will be added to an existing table then the data types of the columns in the destination table must match those specified in query. SQL*Plus will allow minor data type translations, for instance, between CHAR and VARCHAR2 columns, but it will not allow you to change a LONG data type in the source to a VARCHAR2 in the destination. It will allow you to copy data into a column with a smaller maximum size provided the actual data is short enough to fit. Thus, you can copy from a column defined as VARCHAR2(20) into a column defined as VARCHAR2(10) as long as no row contains data longer than ten characters. Copying data from a CHAR column, incidentally, into a VARCHAR or VARCHAR2 column requires the destination to be at least as long as the original CHAR column.

The USING clause specifies a query that will retrieve data from the *source_db_connection*. This is in the form of a standard SQL SELECT statement embedded in the SQL*Plus command. If you wish to add rows to an existing table using INSERT or REPLACE, then the column names of the destination table must match those in the query. You may use column aliases in query to force the names to match.

The COPY command is not, however, an efficient way of moving very large volumes of data. It does not take advantage of any parallel capabilities (other than the possibility of performing a full table scan in the query). The total volume of rows will be transmitted from the source database to the destination database in a serial manner over SQL*Net, although it can bundle multiple rows together for transmission. The number of rows handled in each "batch" is controlled by the SQL*Plus SET ARRAYSIZE command.

Consider using COPY only when you must move a modest amount of data, particularly when it contains a column defined as LONG.

Postprocessing of Loaded Data

In some cases, it is possible to complete all reformatting and cleanup of data during the extract and load processes. In such cases, the data can be directly loaded into the actual warehouse tables that will be accessed by users. When completely reformatted and scrubbed, data can be extracted (or preprocessed) via an ETT tool or customized extract programs; then loading will be extremely easy and fast.

In other cases, some additional processing will be needed on the warehouse side. If the volume of data to be loaded is not too large, database triggers on the warehouse tables can complete data validation and reformatting on data being entered via SQL*Loader's conventional path.

In many cases, however, the data being extracted will require some level of additional processing. Frequently, the volume of data to be loaded requires the use SQL*Loader's direct path, which precludes trigger processing during the load. In such cases, it is common to load the data initially into a temporary table and then use PL/SQL to further massage the data and insert it into the final warehouse table.

Index Builds and Rebuilds

One of the frequently executed steps after loading data is to create the necessary indexes on that data. Whenever loading data to an empty table (or partition), it will be faster to build the indexes after the data is loaded than to incur the overhead of maintaining the indexes with each row inserted.

ENSURING UNIQUENESS

When an index is needed to provide uniqueness (indexes created to support a PRIMARY KEY or UNIQUE constraint), it may be appropriate to incur this overhead to ensure that no duplicate rows are encountered. If you have confidence that the data has been properly cleansed before loading, even these indexes can be built after the load. Do this by disabling the constraint (with the ALTER TABLE command), then loading the data and enabling the constraint. If duplicates are discovered during the rebuild of the index, an error will be returned and the index build terminated. You can use the EXCEPTIONS INTO syntax on the CREATE INDEX and ALTER TABLE commands to obtain a listing of duplicate values.

The direct path mode of SQL*Loader generally avoids this overhead by deferring the index maintenance until after completing the load. Before making the new data part of the table (raising the table's high-water mark) it builds a mini-index on just the newly added data. It then merges this mini-index with the existing table index to create a new index that covers all the table's data. This means that at the completion of the load each index on the table will require roughly double its normal storage allotment. Ensure that index tablespaces have sufficient space to accommodate the original, the mini-index temporary segment, and the final merged index.

There is one exception to this process of performing an index merge. By specifying the SINGLEROW option on the direct path load you can cause SQL*Loader to maintain indexes on a row-by-row basis. This will, of course, slow the load process, especially if there are several indexes to be maintained. This option should be used when there is a shortage of space in the tablespace and the number of rows to be loaded is relatively small compared to the current size of the table. In this case, the choice is made to slow the load in order to save space or the time needed to perform a complete rebuild of the index.

If any problem occurs during the index merge (such as running out of space or an instance failure) Oracle8 will leave the index in the index unusable state (in Oracle7 this was called the direct load state). No SQL statements will be able to use or maintain an index left in this state. Therefore, one of the necessary steps in postload processing will be to examine all indexes and verify that they are usable. Any which are not usable must be dropped and re-created.

IDENTIFYING UNUSABLE INDEXES

To determine whether an index has been left in the index unusable or direct load state, look at the STATUS column within DBA_INDEXES table.

Another restriction when using SQL*Loader direct path is that when loading data into a partition of an Oracle8 no global indexes on the table may be in place. Drop all global indexes before loading and rebuild them after completing the load.

Finally, parallel direct path SQL*Loader always leaves indexes in an unusable state. All indexes (both global and local in the case of an Oracle8 partition) on the segment being loaded will need to be dropped and re-created after each parallel direct path load.

Creating indexes on very large tables (including global indexes on Oracle8 partitioned tables) can be a very time-consuming effort. An index build consists of three steps:

1. scanning the table (or partition) to determine the values of the indexed columns

2. sorting the values (unless the NOSORT option is specified)

3. building and loading the hierarchical B*Tree or bitmap structure

The first two of these steps are the most resource intensive, but luckily they lend themselves nicely to parallel operations. In almost every case, indexes for the data warehouse should be built with the PARALLEL and NOLOGGING (UNRECOVERABLE in Oracle7) options. Details for parallel index builds are presented in Chapter 10.

"Publishing" Data

It is important that users see a consistent view of data within the warehouse. It is not appropriate for a user to see some data that updated as of April and other data within the subject area that was current as of May. Running the same query a day later, when the May update had been completed, would give different results. A similar inconsistency could occur when new detail is loaded but the summarizations based on that detail have not been updated. Users attempting to drill down from one layer to another will receive conflicting results.

To avoid these situations, the warehouse administrator should prevent access to the data from the time that periodic loads start until the entire process is verified as complete. When the entire load, index, and summarize process can be completed in the available batch window then "closing" the warehouse may be appropriate. This can be done on a subject area basis through the use of the ROLE features of Oracle security. As described in Chapter 3, each group of users should be assigned a role. The SELECT privilege on each subject area's data should be granted to a different role. To make access temporarily unavailable, the second role is revoked from the first. To make the subject area's data available to the group of users after the data is completely updated, only a single GRANT statement is executed.

The revoke, load, and grant approach works well when users are able to wait while the load and associated processes complete. This approach breaks down, however, when the load process takes a very long time or when users have a very high availability requirement, perhaps due to global access. An additional problem arises in warehouses in which some queries might take many hours or even days to complete. In these situations it is important to find a way to perform the most time-consuming parts of the periodic maintenance while still allowing the users to access the existing warehouse data in a consistent manner.

There are three techniques, all of which have been introduced already, to perform this sleight of hand:

- The first is to divide the data warehouse into multiple subject areas and update each of the areas under a different schedule. This might mean delaying part of the weekly warehouse maintenance to Monday, Tuesday, and Wednesday evenings even though the source data is all made available over the weekend.
- The second technique is to work with temporary tables. If extensive processing of the new data is necessary, perhaps through trigger processing or other procedural code, then load the data into tables that users can't access. Complete as much massaging of the data as possible, including generating summarizations into additional temporary tables. Then close the warehouse (or individual subject area) while adding the processed data and new summary rows into their permanent tables.
- The third useful technique for limiting the time that the warehouse needs to be closed is partitioning. Working with a separate table and then adding it to an existing Oracle7 partitioned view or an Oracle8 partitioned table is an ideal way to minimize the time required to make data available in a coordinated, controlled manner.

Figure 6.11 illustrates this third means of adding data to a very large Oracle8 partitioned table. The data is initially loaded into a standalone table. Data validation, reformatting, and other processing can be completed while users continue to access the partitioned table. Indexes on the standalone table can be created. When the entire process is complete and verified (which might even take several days) the administrator swaps the standalone table with an empty partition of the permanent table. Each index is also swapped and becomes a local index on the partition. As long as no global indexes need to be rebuilt, the entire process can be completed with only a few minutes of downtime. This allows several partitioned tables to be maintained in what seems, to the user community, a very short window. In fact, most of the difficult work was done while they were able to access the warehouse but in an area they can't see.

For related tables that are not large enough to warrant partitioning, such as many summaries or dimension tables, the effort required to INSERT new rows from their temporary "staging areas" is usually manageable. Oracle can easily copy hundreds of thousands of rows from one table to another within a few minutes. To further shorten the required time, it is possible to unload the data in the temporary table and then add it to the permanent table using direct path SQL*Loader. Keep in mind the cautions mentioned earlier for performing periodic loads with direct path, but this approach does provide a means for buying

Figure 6.11 Publishing data in the Oracle8 warehouse.

processing time at the cost of some additional space management and index maintenance concerns. (The other issues regarding triggers and constraints should not be a problem since the data is preprocessed before being added to the table. No triggers or constraints would be used on the permanent table.)

Purging and Archiving Warehouse Data

It is impossible to keep all detailed data in the data warehouse forever. The cost of storing and administering the data goes up as the data volume grows. The cost of accessing data also goes up as the total volume increases. Luckily, the value of individual transaction data diminishes over time. This relationship—increasing cost and decreasing value—leads us eventually to start removing data from the data warehouse. Typically, we will want to retain the rows for old data in our summary tables as queries that span multiple years will only need summarized data for comparison. The details that fed those summaries are far less important as they age.

The warehouse team must evaluate the potential future value of the old detailed data. When we recognize that old data is no longer being used for online queries, we must consider whether there may be other uses. Sometimes we may anticipate a need to someday build a new summary that will require the old details. In some cases, it will be determined that there is no chance of ever needing to access the data again. In the former case, we will want to archive the data—copy it to a low-cost storage location outside the online data warehouse—so it may be made available again at some future time or through a different means. In the latter case, we may feel safe in purging the data—removing it from the warehouse without retaining a copy. When in doubt, it is much safer to retain the data in archival form. The cost of a few tape volumes each month is negligible compared to the cost of data that is needed but unavailable.

Figure 6.12 illustrates the conceptual process for archiving and purging data from the data warehouse. Multiple techniques exist for actually performing the archival and purge tasks.

Techniques for Archiving Data

Making the archival copy before removing data from the data warehouse can be accomplished using the same techniques described earlier for moving data from an operational system's Oracle database to the data warehouse.

The EXP utility works well if the data to be archived is stored in a separate partition of an Oracle8 partitioned table or is segregated into a table that is then included with other similar tables in an Oracle7 UNION ALL view. The data from the single table or partition can be exported simply and quickly. So far, Oracle has made a commitment to maintaining upward compatibility between earlier releases of EXP and newer versions of IMP. Of course, there may be some future change to that strategy, so if you choose to use EXP as your archival strategy be sure to verify the new version's capability for importing data from each prior version when you test and validate it.

Figure 6.12 Archiving warehouse data.

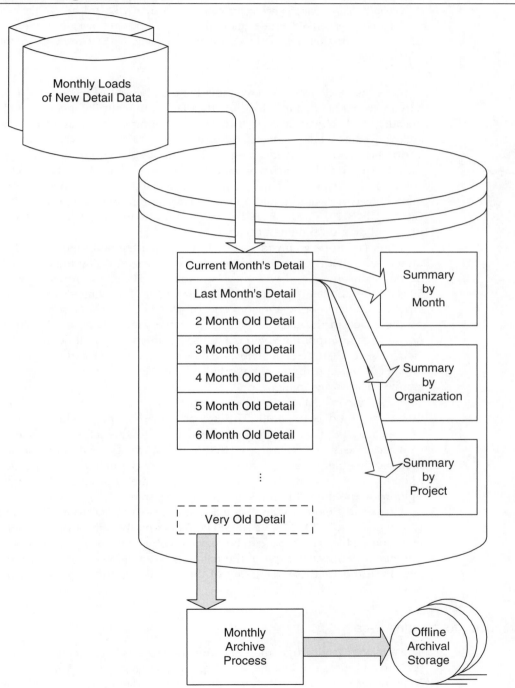

Downward Compatibility of EXP/IMP

Downward compatibility is not guaranteed. You may not be able to use the export feature of a new version of Oracle to move the data to a previous release. You can generally fall back to a previous release by exporting data using the EXP version from the earlier release.

If you use EXP you will have the additional benefit of having the data dictionary metadata needed to reload the data later automatically included. Other user metadata will, however, need to be copied along with the archival data. If the archived data needs to be reloaded in a year or two, it will be important to know the structure and meaning of the data as of the time it was exported. If metadata is stored in tables within the database, then those tables can be included in the export. If only the pertinent metadata for the specific table(s) being archived is desired then copy just that data into new temporary tables using CREATE TABLE . . . AS SELECT, include those temporary tables in the data export, and then drop the temporary tables.

If the data to be archived is stored in a nonpartitioned state with a larger volume of data that is not going to be removed then exporting the entire table may be time-consuming and wasteful. An export of 20 million rows (of which only 500,000 are about to be removed) will consume forty times as much space on tape, which may not be a major concern. However, a greater concern is likely to be the space in the database required in the future if those 500,000 rows are needed again; importing all 20 million to get them back will be a problem especially if several successive archival data sets are required and each requires that another 20 million rows be imported! Therefore, it is critical to ensure that the archival data size is minimized.

If a subset of data must be archived from a very large table, an alternative archival method is required. The unload/reload script provided earlier in this chapter may be used for this purpose. This technique allows that specific rows be selected as specified in the WHERE clause of the generated unload script. Remember that the primary performance benefit of the unload/reload is during the reload process. For archival purposes, reloads are anticipated to be infrequent; optimizing the unload process is far more important.

A better technique for archiving a small subset of data from a very large table is to use CREATE TABLE . . . AS SELECT to copy the subset of rows into a new temporary table. This table can be exported efficiently and then dropped.

Once a permanent copy of the data has been archived, you can remove the data from the database using any of the techniques for purging data described next.

Techniques for Purging Data

The ability to retain large amounts of detail data has been greatly enhanced with each major release of Oracle. Very large databases in Oracle version 5 were typically measured in a few hundred megabytes of data. Large version 6 databases might consist of several gigabytes. One early Oracle7 database that we helped develop in 1992 was considered very large at 300 gigabytes. Today, there are several Oracle7 databases that exceed a terabyte in size. Oracle8 has removed many of the explicit and implicit limitations of Oracle7. We will certainly see Oracle8 databases exceeding 100 terabytes within a few years.

Each Oracle7 database may consist of a maximum of 1,022 files. In Oracle8, each tablespace of the database is now subject to the 1,022 file limit. Of course, in addition to relaxing such limitations, Oracle8 has several new enhancements that make it possible to administer the much larger databases that are now physically possible. The most significant of these is the ability to partition tables and indexes. We've discussed the use of partitioned objects extensively throughout this book in relation to the performance benefits of loading, indexing, and querying individual partitions rather than entire very large tables.

Partitioning

Partitioning is also one of the key tools to help you move data back out of the Oracle8 warehouse when its value has faded. If the detailed data has been partitioned based on transaction dates, as is most common, then removing an old partition is as simple as adding a new one. A single partition may be dropped with the syntax

```
ALTER TABLE table_name DROP PARTITION partition_name;
```

As an alternative that might aid in archiving the data it is possible to switch the partition with an empty table, then drop the now empty partition and export the table. This is the same technique described earlier regarding publishing the newly loaded data. The syntax is as follows:

```
ALTER TABLE partitioned_table_name
  EXCHANGE PARTITION partition_name WITH TABLE unpartitioned_table_name;
```

Figure 6.13 illustrates the exchange of a partition.

Once the data has been moved to a standalone table, unavailable to the warehouse users, the administrator may archive the table at his or her leisure.

TRUNCATE

When the entire contents of a table (or cluster) are to be removed, the SQL TRUNCATE command is the fastest way to accomplish the task. TRUNCATE immediately resets the table's high-water mark to indicate an empty table. No undo or redo information is generated for the individual rows, which are, in effect, deleted so this command is permanent and cannot be rolled back! Truncate is most useful for emptying a temporary table that will be used repeatedly as part of a regular load or summarization process. Any indexes on the table are also truncated simultaneously. Figure 6.14 illustrates the effect of TRUNCATE on a table.

Figure 6.13 Exchange of a partition.

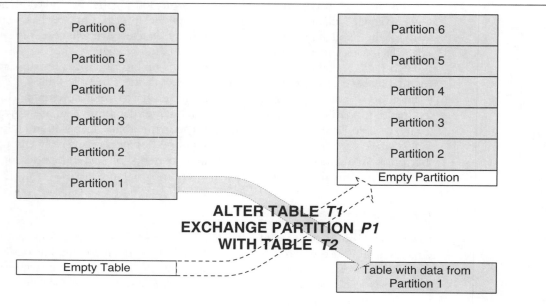

Figure 6.14 Truncating a table.

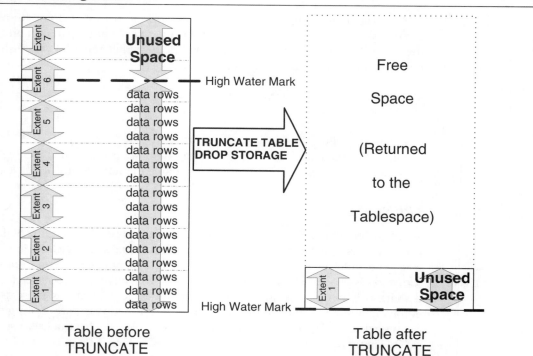

The syntax for truncating a table is simple, with only one significant option:

```
TRUNCATE TABLE table_name [REUSE STORAGE];
```

If you do use the REUSE STORAGE option, then the entire table's current storage will be retained. Without this optional syntax, the truncated table will release all additional extents allocated beyond the extents originally allocated.

It is not possible to truncate a single partition from an Oracle8 partitioned table. If you have this need, the EXCHANGE PARTITION facility will provide a suitable substitute.

SQL DELETE

If the data has not been partitioned (or has been partitioned by criteria other than those used for purging) the data to be purged will need to be removed from the table with an SQL DELETE command. Syntax for deleting rows from a table is straightforward:

```
DELETE
  FROM table_name
 WHERE conditions;
```

Undo information (in a rollback segment) and redo information (in the redo logs) will be generated for each row deleted. It will be necessary to properly size these structures to accommodate large purge jobs. The NOLOGGING attribute, discussed earlier for parallel INSERT to a partitioned table, does not apply to DELETE (or UPDATE) activities.

The SQL DELETE command is not parallelized in Oracle7. In Oracle8 it is parallelized only for partitioned tables and only to the limit of one parallel process per partition. To utilize parallel DELETE the partitioned table may have only local indexes and no enabled triggers.

DELETING FROM A SINGLE PARTITION

New Oracle8 syntax allows you to specify the name of a partition in a DELETE statement. This is useful when some, but not all, data from a single partition of a partitioned table needs to be deleted. This provides a shorthand method to avoid having to specify the additional WHERE clause conditions that would also limit the DELETE to data within that partition. The syntax is DELETE FROM table_name PARTITION (partition_name) WHERE conditions.

When rows are deleted from a table, the space they occupied in each data block is theoretically made available for additional rows to be inserted. If new rows are added by direct path SQL*Loader, however, the new rows cannot use space in data blocks that have been used before. Direct path only writes to new blocks above the table's high-water mark that it can initially format and fill. Also, depending on the value of the PCTUSED parameter defined for the table, the space in individual blocks might actually never be used for regular SQL inserts either. The default value of PCTUSED is 40 percent, meaning that new rows will be inserted into a block, provided that at least 40 percent of its available space is emptied by the DELETE statement. Generally, this value will work well to ensure that blocks are reused efficiently. Should PCTUSED be set to a higher value of, say 80 percent, then, the table could end up with a significant amount of wasted space within its allocated storage.

PCTFREE controls when new inserts should stop adding rows to a table. In OLTP systems where rows are expected to be UPDATED, it may be appropriate to reserve a significant portion of each block for future growth of existing data rows. Within a data warehouse it is rare that this type of activity would occur on detail tables, so generally the PCTFREE should be set to zero. The default value of 10 percent would lead to an automatic 10 percent wastage in each block of a table. For data warehouse tables in which no UPDATES will be performed, it is appropriate to set PCTFREE to 0 when creating the table.

PL/SQL

In some cases, a single DELETE statement might not be able to remove data rows in the manner desired. This may be because a very large number of rows must be deleted, which generates more undo information than can be accommodated by one of the available rollback segments. It may because the archive process needs to do more than just delete each row, for instance, to reformat and move a portion of the rows to an archival area while purging some other rows.

With any exotic requirements (and relatively low volumes!) it may be appropriate to write some procedural code to handle the archival and purge of a table. The procedural code should be written in PL/SQL and stored in the database as either a database "ON DELETE" trigger or as a stored procedure. If the extra procedural work affects a small number of rows out of the total number to be deleted, then, with an appropriate trigger in place, an SQL delete statement will cause the extra logic to be invoked for the appropriate rows. This approach will be most efficient when the identification of appropriate rows can be performed as part of the trigger's WHEN clause. The WHEN clause of a row-level trigger specifies the data conditions under which the rest of the trigger logic will be invoked. For each row that does not meet the WHEN conditions, the row is simply deleted with no additional action. WHEN clause conditions may not include a subquery or any user-defined PL/SQL functions.

If the objective is to avoid the undo associated with a massive DELETE then it may be more appropriate to write a "purge" procedure. Within the procedure you may open a cursor defined on the set of rows to be deleted. The procedure can then delete a specific number, say ten thousand, of rows from the cursor and then COMMIT WORK to release the rollback segment. The cursor can then be repeatedly reopened and another ten thousand rows deleted and committed until all the rows have been removed.

The primary disadvantage of using a PL/SQL trigger or procedure is the performance decrement when compared to a simple SQL delete, which, in turn, is far more expensive than a table TRUNCATE or drop of a partition.

Indexing Issues with Purging Data

Whenever you delete rows from a table, the corresponding entries in every index on the table must also be removed. This has an immediate performance impact on the DELETE. It may also have a negative effect on the organization of the index. A common problem with B*Tree indexes in Oracle7 occurs when new entries are consistently made at the "high" end of the indexed range and subsequently removed from the "low" end. Figure 6.15 illustrates this phenomenon. In this example, the CUSTOMER table has a large number of rows grouped within a tight range of sequenced values. The index has become disorganized and has split to a fourth level even though the left side is mostly empty. This

---

Figure 6.15 Normal B*Tree index after sequential inserts and purge.

suggests that there were once many rows before the current range that have since been deleted.

This situation commonly occurs in indexes built on date columns and numeric columns that get their value from a sequence generator. In these cases, new rows are always of a higher value than the previous entry, and deletes are usually done of the oldest data—and the lowest values in the index.

Over time the structure of the index can become lopsided—the blocks that were originally built to hold the early data are now empty, but new blocks continue to be built for new data. The index continues to grow even though the number of rows may remain relatively constant. The administrators of the warehouse database should anticipate this behavior in indexes that have this usage pattern. By running the ANALYZE command regularly, the DBA can monitor a few key statistics to determine when an index needs to be reorganized. The primary statistic to observe is the BLEVEL column in the DBA_INDEXES view. This indicates the number of levels in the index hierarchy that must be read to reach the leaf node that points to a specific data block. When the value of BLEVEL increases (especially when the value of NUM_ROWS has remained relatively unchanged) the index should be considered a candidate for rebuilding.

Even more specific statistics can be obtained for an index by performing an ANALYZE INDEX . . . VALIDATE STRUCTURE and then observing the values displayed in the INDEX_STATS dictionary view. Note that this view only shows the statistics for the last index validated. Make sure to capture the values before analyzing the next index! The PCT_USED column will tell you the percentage of space in the index that is currently being used. The DEL_LF_ROWS statistic will tell you how many values have been deleted from the index, while DEL_LF_ROWS_LEN will provide the number of bytes of those deleted entries. Monitoring these statistics for changes will indicate when a rebuild is required.

Oracle8 provides another facility for avoiding this problem—the reverse order index. When a B*Tree index is created with the REVERSE keyword, Oracle stores the bytes of each index value in reverse order. Figure 6.16 illustrates this concept. By storing the bytes in reverse order, the low-order bytes that change most frequently get stored in the leading edge. Thus, when successive rows are entered they will be distributed evenly over all the branches of the B*Tree. When older rows are deleted they, too, will be evenly distributed. Thus, regular insert and purge cycles will tend to balance each other and maintain a stable structure.

When the Oracle8 DBA identifies an index that will grow in one direction while being purged from the other (older) end, rebuilding the index with the REVERSE keyword may be in order. This will greatly reduce the future need for index rebuilds. The disadvantage of reverse order indexes is that they cannot be used to perform range scans. This means that, in most warehouses, the proper solution will be to rebuild indexes when they become lopsided after large purges. This is done with the ALTER INDEX REBUILD command. Be sure to specify an appropriate tablespace for the newly created index—otherwise it will attempt to build the index in the user's default tablespace!

Figure 6.16 Reverse order index after sequential inserts and purge.

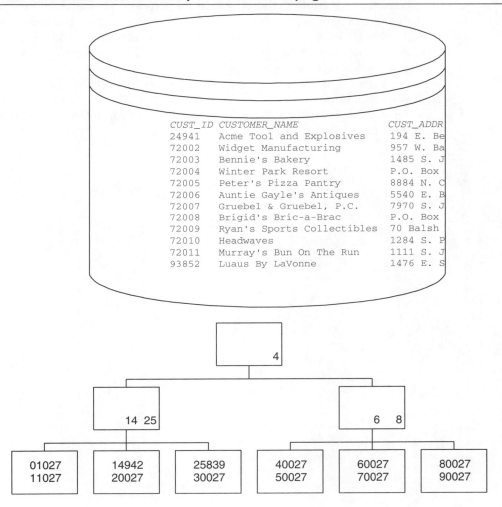

CUST_ID	CUSTOMER_NAME	CUST_ADDR
24941	Acme Tool and Explosives	194 E. Be
72002	Widget Manufacturing	957 W. Ba
72003	Bennie's Bakery	1485 S. J
72004	Winter Park Resort	P.O. Box
72005	Peter's Pizza Pantry	8884 N. C
72006	Auntie Gayle's Antiques	5540 E. B
72007	Gruebel & Gruebel, P.C.	7970 S. J
72008	Brigid's Bric-a-Brac	P.O. Box
72009	Ryan's Sports Collectibles	70 Balsh
72010	Headwaves	1284 S. P
72011	Murray's Bun On The Run	1111 S. J
93852	Luaus By LaVonne	1476 E. S

Summary

Once the data warehouse has been designed and built, it is necessary to load data and make the warehouse available to users. Typically, the warehouse will be loaded with data from multiple sources including various corporate transaction processing systems and purchased external data. Frequently, this data suffers from problems with quality or consistency, particularly when it has been combined with data from other sources. Reconciling data quality problems may be performed during the extract from the operational system, during the load into the warehouse, or sometime in between.

We examined several alternative methods for loading data into the warehouse, including SQL*Loader, custom-written load programs, and Oracle's gateway products. We discussed several special ways of moving data from one Oracle database to another. These include the Export and Import utilities, a utility for generating unload/reload scripts, the SQL*Plus COPY command, and the SQL CREATE TABLE . . . AS SELECT command. This final option is particularly effective when run in parallel with the UNRECOVERABLE option to make an extract table that can then be exported.

After data is loaded it must be verified, indexed, and "published" to make it available to users.

Finally, we presented the need and techniques for archiving and purging—that is, removing data from the warehouse when it is no longer needed.

POST-LOAD PROCESSING IN THE DATA WAREHOUSE

CHAPTER 7

Populating with detail data from the operational systems, which was described in the previous chapter, is by far the biggest ongoing task in the building and running of a data warehouse. Without this grist for the mill that is the data warehouse, nothing further can happen.

Many data warehouse initiatives run into serious problems early on because the task of populating the data warehouse was not given the emphasis it was due. Other aspects of building the data warehouse may occupy the attention of the project management, such as data model design and query/analysis tools. The ability to populate the data warehouse with data and then manipulate that data into the desired format is dismissed as an easy-to-solve technical problem. We hope the previous chapter shed light on that misconception.

But simply populating the warehouse with data may well be only the first half of the story. Often, the processes that populate the data warehouse cannot load the data into a format that is ready for use. This involves transforming the data from one (or more) operational data models into the data warehouse data model.

One reason could be that the utilities used to load the data are simply not capable of completing this transformation. The Oracle import utility (i.e., IMP) is a good example of this. IMP will import exactly what resides in the exported "dump" file. SQL*Loader, while it has some very powerful capabilities for transforming data, is also not capable of performing a radical transformation of the data.

Another reason may have to do with the complexity involved in performing the transformation. Radical transformation may best be done in several discrete simplified stages, rather than in one complex step.

Another consideration is performance. According to the old saying—and with all due respect to animal lovers everywhere—"there is more than one way to skin a cat, but some are faster than others." Each utility can do the required task, but some do the job faster. An example might be the use of Oracle snapshots or

SQL*Loader in conjunction with database triggers. Each of these mechanisms can do the required tasks. But both these particular methods do the job *transactionally* rather than in *bulk*. Neither of these methods is built primarily for speed but rather for transactional integrity and transparency of operation. If performance is a major consideration because of the amount of data to be transferred, then certain methods quite simply cannot be considered, even if they do the job correctly.

Last, having the detailed operational data complete with the original operational data model has the added advantage of potentially offloading some of the tactical reporting from the operational systems. By freeing the operational systems from this kind of reporting, you are freeing up both CPU and memory resources as well as disk space in the operational environment. If the operational environment has a purge capability, it can now be used after the data is extracted to the operational data store in the data warehouse.

Thus, the second half of the load phase is manipulating this data into a level of detail appropriate for analysis, strategic reporting, and data mining. Typically, this processing is treated as *postload* functionality in the final step of the load phase.

Once the original detail data has been loaded into the data warehouse database, there are three basic kinds of postload processing to be performed:

- summarization and aggregation
- filtering
- merging

The reasons for these operations are quite well documented in this book and in others. Decision-support systems such as data warehouses and data marts generally produce *strategic* reports, not *tactical* reports. Tactical reporting is operational in nature and generally shows operational levels of detail, possibly with summarizations. Strategic reports cover large volumes of data over wide ranges of time. It is not possible to show any level of detail in such reports without causing the report hard copy itself to outweigh your automobile. Also, the people who read strategic reports are simply not interested in details. They are looking at the "big picture."

As we mentioned in Chapters 1 and 4, there is no reason why a data warehouse should not hold detailed operational data. But if the true purpose of the system is to process and produce tactical reports, then we have an *operational data store*, not a data warehouse.

Summarization and Aggregation

It is easy to think of rollup summarization as a *saved intermediate step* (see Figure 7.1). There may be dozens or hundreds of queries that first perform a summarization or aggregation on the way to the final result. Creating tables with this summarized information essentially allows programmers to skip this initial step and start querying using the intermediate information.

Figure 7.1 Rollup summarization.

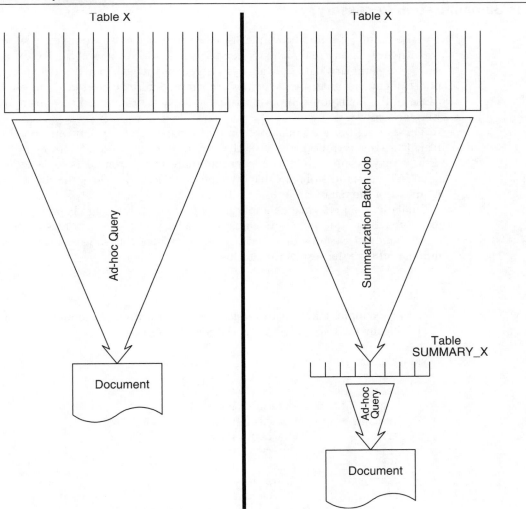

This can have an enormous positive impact on query performance. Although many database vendors (including Oracle) may tout their parallel capabilities as able to substitute for indexing, it is not always a wise strategy to depend on this capability. Although it is true that the parallel queries against huge tables can indeed rival the performance of a nonparallel scan against a smaller table for some queries, there is the matter of *scalability* to be considered. Parallelized full table scans against huge tables may indeed be able to rival nonparallel scans against smaller tables when the system is virtually empty, but it is unlikely that *one hundred* simultaneous parallel queries can match the performance of *one hundred* simpler nonparallel queries. Parallel queries on huge tables simply consume too many resources to scale effectively. Rollups eliminate that problem.

Is Summarization Necessary?

The use of any of these techniques is, in a very strict sense, completely superfluous. There isn't any real business need to summarize or aggregate, for example, since the summary data can always be reconstructed from the detail data. A purist might sniff that such activities are simply intermediate steps, imposed because of the limitations on performance and capacity imposed by existing hardware and software.

This is true, but the limitations on performance and capacity are nonetheless real. If a data warehouse is tasked with storing five to ten years of historical data, it may be unrealistic to expect the entire five to ten years to be stored in detail. The costs in storage capacity might significantly reduce the return on investment of the data warehouse, and we can't have that!

Similarly, the performance implications of constantly reaggregating detail data to answer basic questions are staggering. Why waste the resources to perform an operation thousands or millions of times when you can perform it once a month and save the results for later use?

For example, take our example schema for a project accounting application, specifically the two tables ACTIVITIES and PROJECTS.

```
CREATE TABLE PROJECTS
(       PROJECT_ID          NUMBER(10),
        PROJECT_NAME        VARCHAR2(40),
        SERVICE_LINE        VARCHAR2(40),
        INDUSTRY            VARCHAR2(40),
        TYPE                VARCHAR2(40),
        CLIENT              VARCHAR2(60),
        START_DATE          DATE,
        CLOSE_DATE          DATE,
        STATUS              VARCHAR2(5),
        CONSTRAINT PROJECTS_PK PRIMARY KEY (PROJECT_ID)
)
CREATE TABLE ACTIVITY
(       PROJECT_ID          NUMBER(10),
        ORG_ID              NUMBER(10),
        EMPLOYEE_ID         NUMBER(10),
        FUNCTION_ID         NUMBER(10),
        FISCAL_YR           NUMBER(4),
        FISCAL_MONTH        NUMBER(2),
        HOURS               NUMBER(11,2),
        EXPENSES            NUMBER(11,2),
        REVENUE             NUMBER(11,2)
)
```

Figure 7.2 Relationship between ACTIVITIES and PROJECTS.

In terms of an entity-relationship diagram, these two table belonged to the relationship illustrated in Figure 7.2.

A large number of decision-support queries are likely to be at the PROJECTS level as opposed to the ACTIVITIES level. Thus, instead of forcing each user to query ACTIVITIES like this:

```
SELECT SUM(HOURS) SUM_HOURS,
       SUM(EXPENSES) SUM_EXPENSES,
       SUM(REVENUE) SUM_REVENUE
  FROM ACTIVITIES
 WHERE PROJECT_ID = 9999999
 GROUP BY  PROJECT_ID;
```

the new columns SUM_HOURS, SUM_EXPENSES, SUM_REVENUE could be added to the PROJECTS table and modified whenever new data is added to the ACTIVITIES table.

Obviously, it pays to be aware of what kinds of queries are being issued. Usage tracking is one of the most important activities a data warehouse administrator performs, because if you understand what kinds of questions the users are asking, you can optimize the answers by presummarizing or preaggregating. Thus, it could be important to determine whether additional columns such as AVG_HOURS, AVG_EXPENSES, and AVG_REVENUE might be useful as well.

Usage Tracking from the Database

Different tools exist to aid in usage tracking. At a minimum, database administrators can periodically sample the SYS.V$SQLAREA data dictionary view for commonly used SQL statements.

```
SQL> SELECT sql_text, buffer_gets, disk_reads, executions
  2    FROM v$sqlarea
  3   WHERE buffer_gets > 10000
  4   ORDER BY buffer_gets desc;
```

This simple query will display the queries currently cached in the Oracle Shared Pool that cause the greatest number of logical reads (i.e., buffer_gets).

Although this is certainly not a foolproof method for determining which queries could be optimized by creating summarization or aggregation tables, it does screen out the queries that are of little or no consequence.

The advantages of this approach include the following:

- simplicity: cheap and easy
- covers all access points to the database, from any application

Disadvantages of this approach include the following:

- easy to miss some queries because of the transient nature of data in V$SQLAREA
- extra research is needed to link a query with the application or user issuing it
- administrators have to build their own usage analysis reports and build their own usage summary tables, and refresh routines

Usage Tracking from the Application

An alternative approach is to have the application, such as the Oracle Discoverer 3.0 tool, keep a record in its database repository of all queries issued against the database. It will analyze this repository to "suggest" opportunities for summarization based on the kinds of SQL statements that have been issued.

Discoverer will even generate the SQL necessary to create the summary table, utilize Oracle mechanisms to refresh the summary at a specified interval, and redirect its own behavior in subsequent queries to use the presummarized data.

The advantages of this approach include the following:

- simplicity: it's an integral feature of the product
- Discoverer manages creation of the new summary table and the refresh mechanism

The disadvantage of this approach is that it only covers access from Discoverer. This won't solve the problem for shops that use a variety of query and reporting tools.

Usage Tracking from Intercepts in the Network

Another approach is installing a layer of software at the network layer, in SQL*Net, that captures usage information. One such product is Pine Cone from Pine Cone Systems, Inc. of Englewood, Colorado. This product *intercepts* traffic entering Oracle through SQL*Net, extracts desired information from the SQL*Net packets, and passes the SQL*Net packets through to SQL*Net essentially unchanged. Traffic in both directions (both inbound to Oracle and outbound from Oracle) can be captured so that not only SQL statements and usage are tracked, but also the data returned (i.e., *content*) can be tracked.

The advantages of this approach include the following:

- It covers all access points to the database, from any application, that use SQL*Net connections.
- It is transparent to all applications; data gathered is imported back to Pine Cone Systems, Inc., where it is analyzed, and the results are returned in the form of recommendations.

Disadvantages of this approach include the following:

- Changes to SQL*Net affect the usability of this product; no matter what Oracle does to its networking, Pine Cone must remain transparent.
- Pine Cone essentially spawns a *mirror listener* to match SQL*Net listeners, and a *mirror server process* must be spawned to track every Oracle *server process* or *shadow process*. In situations where the number of Oracle server processes is high, this can strain the resources of the UNIX system.

Access to Appropriate Levels of Detail

The preceding examples show only one level of summarization, but there is no restriction on how many levels of summarization may be useful. Query performance is not always the only criteria; there may be security implications involved.

Continuing with the example schema started with ACTIVITIES and PROJECTS, it might be appropriate to summarize by quarter and year and by project, service line, and industry. For example, one of these summaries might be the following:

```
CREATE TABLE PROJECTS_QTR
       PARALLEL (DEGREE 12)
AS
SELECT P.PROJECT_ID,
       F.FISCAL_QTR,
       SUM(A.HOURS) SUM_HOURS,
       SUM(A.EXPENSES) SUM_EXPENSES,
       SUM(A.REVENUE) SUM_REVENUE
   FROM ACTIVITIES      A,
        PROJECTS        P,
        FISCAL_PERIODS  F
  WHERE P.PROJECT_ID = A.PROJECT_ID
    AND F.FISCAL_YEAR = A.FISCAL_YEAR
    AND F.FISCAL_MONTH = A.FISCAL_MONTH
  GROUP BY P.PROJECT_ID,
           F.FISCAL_QTR;
```

This view of the data might still be too "granular" for certain purposes, so a higher level of summarization might be as follows:

```
CREATE TABLE SERVICE_LINE_QTR
AS
SELECT P.SERVICE_LINE,
       PQ.FISCAL_QTR,
       SUM(PQ.HOURS) SUM_HOURS,
       SUM(PQ.EXPENSES) SUM_EXPENSES,
       SUM(PQ.REVENUE) SUM_REVENUE
  FROM PROJECTS_QTR PQ,
       PROJECTS P
 WHERE P.PROJECT_ID = PQ.PROJECT_ID
 GROUP BY P.SERVICE_LINE,
          PQ.FISCAL_QTR;
```

Please note that this second summarization used the results of the first one. Far fewer processing resources were used to obtain this result in two steps rather than one. Going a level further could yield the following:

```
CREATE TABLE INDUSTRY_QTR
AS
SELECT P.INDUSTRY,
       SLQ.FISCAL_QTR,
       SUM(SLQ.HOURS) SUM_HOURS,
       SUM(SLQ.EXPENSES) SUM_EXPENSES,
       SUM(SLQ.REVENUE) SUM_REVENUE
  FROM SERVICE_LINE_QTR SLQ,
       PROJECTS P
 WHERE P.SERVICE_LINE = SLQ.SERVICE_LINE
 GROUP BY P.INDUSTRY,
          SLQ.FISCAL_QTR;
```

Again, since the results of the previous summarization were used, far fewer resources were necessary to process this result.

The fact that the latter two summarization tables were easy to create is significant. Doesn't it indicate that we're going too far in summarizing? The answer: Only from a performance standpoint. What if we wanted to abstract the data to a high enough degree to protect the details? Suppose some of the users who were going to query this information were not supposed to have access to the finer granularity of information, to the PROJECTS_QTR or ACTIVITIES table? This might be true for an Internet-accessible Web site, where information in the company's annual report is made available to shareholders. For various reasons, we might provide shareholders with the ability to query by industry and drill down to service line, but not to the individual project or activity detail. Other users of the same data mart may have this additional privilege to drill down to the bottom-level details. A similar situation might occur with different groups even internally—we might not allow every user to query the detail tables unless they've received some training on SQL performance tuning. Access of this kind can be controlled by database views, roles, and object privileges.

Consider the security used for our example web-based access:

```
CREATE ROLE website_access;
GRANT SELECT ON dw.industry_qtr TO website_access;
GRANT SELECT ON dw.service_line_qtr TO website_access;

CREATE USER web IDENTIFIED BY web;
GRANT CREATE SESSION, ALTER SESSION TO web;
GRANT website_access TO web;
ALTER USER web DEFAULT ROLE website_access;
```

What we have is a user account named WEB with very few privileges. It can connect to Oracle, it can perform the ALTER SESSION command in Oracle, and it has permission (granted by the role WEBSITE_ACCESS) to query two tables in another Oracle account's schema. That's all it can do. Since this is information that is publicly available via the company's annual report, there is not much to worry about in terms of security.

However, company managers accessing this database via the company intranet may want a different, more detailed view of the data:

```
CREATE ROLE internal_access;
GRANT SELECT ON book.activities TO internal_access;
GRANT SELECT ON book.project_qtr TO internal_access;
GRANT website_access TO internal_access;

CREATE USER mgr IDENTIFIED BY i_cant_w8;
GRANT CREATE SESSION, ALTER SESSION TO mgr;
GRANT internal_access TO mgr;
ALTER USER mgr DEFAULT ROLE internal_access;
```

Now we have a role named INTERNAL_ACCESS that has all the permissions of the role WEBSITE_ACCESS, as well as access to the two finer-granularity tables in this schema. Of course, the management of the password is the weak point in this entire scheme, but that can be handled by assigning the role INTERNAL_ACCESS to individual Oracle accounts for each person requiring access and then using the Oracle8 password management utilities such as automatic expiration and password history restriction to ensure that passwords are kept somewhat secure.

Filtering

Data marts are generally differentiated from data warehouses by being focused on specific subject matter, such as financial, sales and marketing, or product service history. Creating each of these subject-matter specific subsets involves filtering information from the greater mass (see Figure 7.3).

For example, using our example of the ACTIVITIES table we have:

```
CREATE TABLE ACTIVITY
(    PROJECT_ID          NUMBER(10),
```

```
        ORG_ID              NUMBER(10),
        EMPLOYEE_ID         NUMBER(10),
        FUNCTION_ID         NUMBER(10),
        FISCAL_YR           NUMBER(4),
        FISCAL_MONTH        NUMBER(2),
        HOURS               NUMBER(11,2),
        EXPENSES            NUMBER(11,2),
        REVENUE             NUMBER(11,2)
    )
```

We may want to extract just revenue information for the business purpose of analyzing revenue separately.

We may also wish to extract information about projects based within a certain geography or employees with specific job titles.

Figure 7.3 Filtering specific subsets of information.

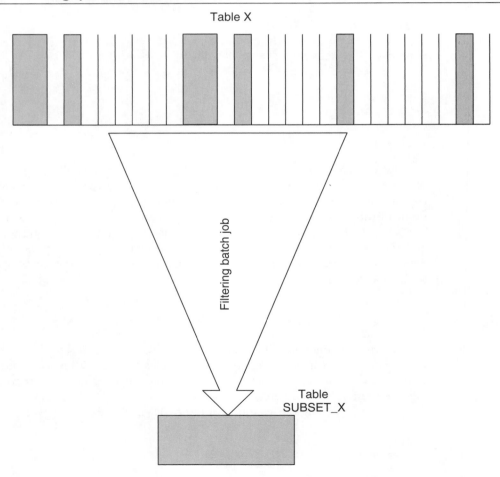

Filtering is a way of reducing a complex question into easily answered components. If we can create a set of information comprised of data that has already been filtered against several initial criteria, then the complexity involved in reaching the final answer can be reduced.

```
CREATE TABLE EAST_REVENUE
AS
SELECT org_id
       revenue
  FROM activities
 WHERE org_id IN
       (SELECT org_id FROM organizations WHERE region = 'EAST')
```

Since organizations in the West may not need to know about issues in the East, we now have a smaller set of data for each region to query.

Merging

Often, strategic data is created by merging data together. For example, merging customer service history with invoicing and customer billing information produces a more complete picture of the customer. Further merging of this customer information with demographic data or psychographic data can yield a completely unexpected portrait of the customer. This process is illustrated in Figure 7.4.

For instance, with the addition of demographic data you could realize that all customers with specific buying patterns live within a certain area, close to one another. This could lead to insights in focusing marketing efforts as well as shifting inventory to meet demand that could pay for the cost of the entire data warehouse with a single decision.

Parallel Create Table As Select (pCTAS)

The pCTAS command is one of the most useful commands in Oracle's arsenal for performing summarization, aggregation, filtering, and merging (see Figure 7.5). It is explained in much greater detail in Chapter 10 (on parallel operations), but for our purposes here its advantage is that it can quickly create an entire table based on the results of a parallel query. Although the actual table creation operation is not performed in parallel (it is not necessary), both the INSERT phase and the SELECT phase of the command are completely parallelized.

The query inside the pCTAS command can be an aggregation or summarization, making it ideal for re-creating summary tables after a complete refresh of the detail data.

The parallel CREATE TABLE . . . AS SELECT command can query from partitioned tables, but it cannot be used to create Oracle8 partitioned tables or their individual partitions, at least directly. However, using the ALTER TABLE . . . EX-

Figure 7.4 Merging information to create derived information.

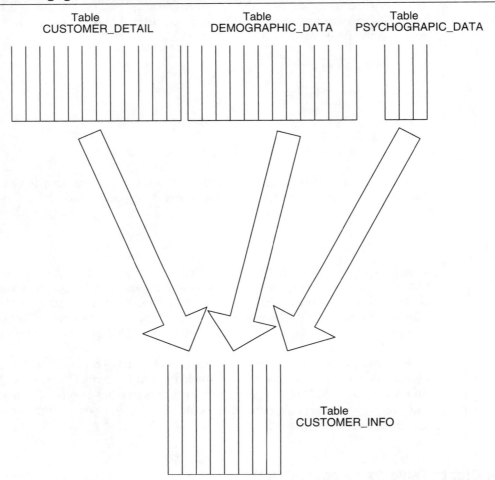

CHANGE PARTITION command, a table created by pCTAS can be merged into a partitioned table as a new partition.

The pCTAS command has been available since Oracle7, version 7.2.

Parallel DML

As we describe in Chapter 10, there is a variety of parallel Data Manipulation Language (DML) operations. All of these operations are available starting with Oracle8.

Parallel DELETE and UPDATE operations are available with partitioned tables only, while parallel INSERT statements can be performed both on partitioned and nonpartitioned tables.

Figure 7.5 Parallel CREATE TABLE . . . AS SELECT.

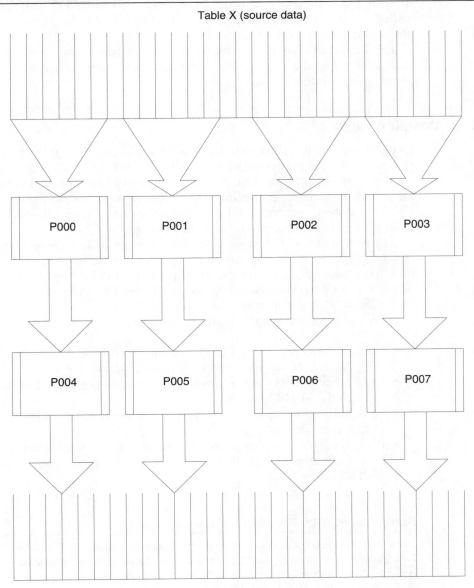

Table X (source data)

Table XX (target data)

Thus, in addition to all the benefits partitioned tables offer for managing large amounts of data, they also facilitate data manipulation in parallel, as the INSERT, UPDATE, or DELETE can be decomposed to run simultaneously on each of the table partitions.

Additionally, the mechanism used with the pCTAS operation can also be utilized by parallel INSERT. This operation becomes exactly like parallel CREATE TABLE . . . AS SELECT with the exception of the nonparallel operation of actually creating the table prior to INSERT.

This flexibility allows summary tables to be dropped and then re-created in their entirety, as the source detail data may have been either refreshed completely or appended.

PL/SQL for Complex Logic

Quite frequently, it is difficult to perform all the necessary logic in a single nonprocedural SQL statement such as a parallel CREATE TABLE . . . AS SELECT or a parallel INSERT, UPDATE, or DELETE. What is sometimes needed is procedural logic, with familiar programming constructs such as IF conditionals or looping. PL/SQL can be incorporated into parallel operations through the use of stored PL/SQL functions and packaged PL/SQL functions.

By creating stored functions in PL/SQL, it is possible to extend the Oracle SQL language, to effectively customize it. This is done by using these custombuilt functions in SQL statements, either in the SELECT clause of queries; in the SET clause of UPDATE statements; or in the WHERE clauses of queries, UPDATE, or DELETE statements.

There are some restrictions on this functionality:

- PL/SQL functions used in SQL statements (SELECT, VALUE, SET and WHERE clauses) cannot perform DML on database tables.
- Only IN arguments are allowed. The only output from the function is through the RETURN value.
- PL/SQL functions to be executed remotely or in parallel may not read or modify the values of package variables.
- PL/SQL functions which modify the values of package variables may only be called within the SELECT, VALUE and SET clauses, but not within the WHERE clause.

RESTRICTING PL/SQL FUNCTIONS TO ALLOWED ACTIONS

These restrictions are enforced on packaged functions using the PRAGMA operator in PL/SQL while the package or function is being compiled. The PRAGMA operator is a package compile-time construct very similar to PRAGMA in the Ada programming language. PL/SQL was closely modeled after the Ada programming language.

However, outside of these restrictions PL/SQL function developers are permitted to use PL/SQL package variables and PL/SQL tables, which provide a broad and powerful range of possibilities.

For example, suppose that a value to be inserted into a table created with pCTAS could be retrieved from one of several different tables, depending on the data value in a certain column. For example, if the value in column TYPE was "REVENUE," then a table named REVENUE would be queried for the value to be inserted. If the column TYPE contained the value "MARGIN," then a table named MARGIN would be queried. If TYPE = "COST," then the table named COST would supply the value to be inserted. Last, if the column TYPE had a NULL value, then the value would come from a table named OTHER multiplied by a value from the table named MISCELLANEOUS.

As you can imagine, this could become a very complex SQL statement. It would be possible to process using outer-joins:

```
CREATE TABLE big_mess
            PARALLEL (DEGREE 8)
AS
SELECT f.key_value,
       DECODE(f.type,
              'REVENUE', r.value,
              'MARGIN', m.value,
              'COST', c.value,
              NULL, o.value * x.value,
              NULL) VALUE
  FROM fact f,
       revenue r,
       margin m,
       cost c,
       other o,
       miscellaneous x
 WHERE r.key_value (+) = f.key_value
   AND m.key_value (+) = f.key_value
   AND c.key_value (+) = f.key_value
   AND o.key_value (+) = f.key_value
   AND x.key_value (+) = f.key_value;
```

Although both the pCTAS command and the parallel DML commands fully support and parallelize outer-join operations, you can see how this overly simplified, but not so far-fetched, scenario can quickly become a nightmare in non-procedural SQL programming.

Compare this with the following:

```
CREATE OR REPLACE PACKAGE example_package
AS
     PRAGMA RESTRICT_REFERENCES(example_function, WNDS, RNPS, WNPS);
     FUNCTION example_function
         (in_key_value     IN NUMBER,
          in_type          IN VARCHAR2)
         RETURN NUMBER;
END example_package;
/
CREATE OR REPLACE PACKAGE BODY example_package
AS
```

```
FUNCTION example_function
    (in_key_value    IN NUMBER,
     in_type         IN VARCHAR2)
    RETURN NUMBER
IS
    v_rtn_value      NUMBER;
BEGIN
    IF in_type = 'REVENUE' THEN
        SELECT value
          INTO v_rtn_value
          FROM revenue
         WHERE key_value = in_key_value;
    ELSIF in_type = 'MARGIN' THEN
        SELECT value
          INTO v_rtn_value
          FROM margin
         WHERE key_value = in_key_value;
    ELSIF in_type = 'COST' THEN
        SELECT value
          INTO v_rtn_value
          FROM cost
         WHERE key_value = in_key_value;
    ELSIF in_type IS NULL THEN
        SELECT o.value
          INTO v_rtn_value
          FROM other o,
               miscellaneous m
         WHERE o.key_value = in_key_value
           AND m.key_value = o.key_value;
    END IF;
    RETURN V_RTN_VALUE;
END;
END example_package;
/
```

Please note the PRAGMA statement used during the creation of the package header. The "purity levels" are as follows:

RNDS   Read No Database State (includes no SELECT statements)

WNDS   Write No Database State (performs no INSERT, UPDATE, or DELETE statements)

RNPS   Read No Package State (does not reference PL/SQL package variables)

WNPS   Write No Package State (does no updating of PL/SQL package variables)

As we mentioned earlier, in order for it to be used in a non-parallelized SQL statement's SELECT clause, the PL/SQL function must be able to pass the WNDS purity level as a requirement. It does not have to pass any of the other purity levels, although it does not hurt to do so. To allow the function to be used in a parallelized SQL statement, it must also pass the WNPS and RNPS purity levels.

Using the PL/SQL function inside an SQL statement then becomes as easy as this:

```
CREATE TABLE big_mess
        PARALLEL (DEGREE 8)
AS
SELECT key_value,
       example_package.example_function(key_value, type) value
  FROM fact;
```

This simple example doesn't begin to delve into the power of this technique. It allows very complex programming logic to be encapsulated inside easy-to-use program units and is also fully parallelizable.

Availability during Processing

Both the parallel CREATE TABLE . . . AS SELECT (pCTAS) command and the parallel INSERT commands using the APPEND option have negative impacts on table availability while they are running. One reason is that, on the one hand, one of these commands is a CREATE TABLE, and a table cannot be available before its creation is complete.

On the other hand, for parallel INSERT operations, using the APPEND clause causes the direct path mechanism to be used. Direct path, while swift, has many restrictions when compared to conventional SQL INSERT statements:

- Database triggers are automatically disabled
- Indexes are automatically disabled and rebuilt at the end of the operation
- Referential integrity constraints are automatically disabled

For all intents and purposes, a table is essentially unavailable while parallel INSERT with APPEND is operating against it, whether the table is partitioned or not.

This still leaves several options that employ conventional SQL operations such as INSERT, UPDATE, and DELETE. Parallel UPDATE and DELETE always use conventional SQL statements but only become parallel against Oracle8 partitioned tables. Parallel INSERT without the APPEND option uses conventional INSERT statements but, again, will run in parallel only against partitioned tables. In these usages, one parallel query process can be assigned to each partition.

More Complex PL/SQL Techniques

Depending on your tolerance for complexity, there are options for reaping the benefits of partitioning and parallel execution even without the parallel CREATE

TABLE . . . AS SELECT, parallel INSERT (APPEND or not), parallel UPDATE, and parallel DELETE commands.

These are situations that use either extremely complex logic that exceeds the restrictions on the previously mentioned operations or that must be performed in versions of Oracle before Oracle8 or against nonpartitioned tables. Other situations include extremely long-running operations that, for a variety of factors, may need to be "killed" and restarted exactly where they left off. Incidently, Oracle8 supports such restart functionality.

PL/SQL "Histogram" Processing

There is another option for performing conventional INSERT, UPDATE, and DELETE statements in parallel against nonpartitioned tables.

The general idea is to break the table up into manageable "buckets" for processing. If the total task can be divided into many smaller equal-sized tasks and all the smaller tasks can be run simultaneously, then we have manually parallelized the task at hand. What's useful about this is that this functionality was developed under Oracle7, version 7.1, and could have been developed under Oracle version 6, when PL/SQL was first introduced. As a matter of fact, there is no reason why this functionality has to be performed in PL/SQL; it can even be done using the Oracle Call Interfaces (OCI) or the Precompilers, using a third-generation programming language such as C or COBOL.

A prerequisite for this type of processing is an indexed column. The values in this indexed column can be numeric, text, or a date. The values in this indexed column don't have to be unique, but uniqueness makes the job of creating buckets somewhat easier.

The first step in processing is to count all the rows in the table, using a simple COUNT(*). For speed, this is best done in parallel. Once the total number of rows to process is known, it becomes simple to determine the number of rows per bucket: TOTAL-ROWS divided by NBR-OF-BUCKETS, rounded down in case the result is a fraction. The last bucket will have rows added to make up for the rounded-down fraction.

We now know how much work, how many rows, are to be in each bucket.

Once the NBR-ROWS-PER-BUCKET is known, we can now run a second query across the table. This query is designed to return the number of rows between two key values separated by a fixed range.

We can then loop through each of these fetched rows, filling bucket after bucket. We start off with the low range of the first row as the low-range value of our bucket, and when we've retrieved enough rows to fill the bucket, we use the high-range value of the last row as the high-range value for our bucket. Then, the next bucket starts with the value of the high-range value of the previous bucket *plus* one, and we continue. When we reach the beginning of the last bucket, we stop processing and simply apply a MAXVALUE for the data type as the high-range value for that last bucket.

And so we are left with the following distribution in a small example:

```
BUCKET_NBR LOW_VALUE   HIGH_VALUE NBR_ROWS
---------- ---------   ---------- --------
1          1           197        150
2          198         1002       150
3          1003        9836       150
4          9837        9998       150
5          9999        23512      150
20         1102387     9999999999 151
```

Despite the varying spreads between the LOW_VALUEs and the HIGH_VAL-
UEs, each of the 20 buckets has 150 rows.

Now, how can this be used?

Sample Code for "Histogram" Processing

First, create the stored procedure HISTPL, which will take the numeric column
indicated by the parameter *in_column* on the table or view indicated by the parameter *in_table* and execute the PL/SQL procedure indicated by the parameter
in_job_name the number of times indicated by the parameter *in_nbr_of_jobs*.
Each time *in_job_name* is executed, it will be passed two parameters of its own,
which will be a low and high value for a key range.

The code to create HISTPL looks like this:

```
CREATE OR REPLACE PROCEDURE histpl

    (in_job_name       IN VARCHAR2,
     in_table          IN VARCHAR2,
     in_column         IN VARCHAR2,
     in_nbr_of_jobs    IN NUMBER)
IS
    --
    c                     INTEGER;
    v_rtn_code            INTEGER;
    v_interval            INTEGER := 0;
    v_rowcount            INTEGER := 0;
    v_range_from          INTEGER;
    v_range_to            INTEGER;
    v_nbr_of_rows         INTEGER := 0;
    i                     BINARY_INTEGER := 0;
    j                     BINARY_INTEGER := 0;
    type int_array        IS TABLE OF INTEGER INDEX BY BINARY_INTEGER;
    v_from_array          INT_ARRAY;
    v_to_array            INT_ARRAY;
    v_rows                INTEGER;
    v_fetch_granularity   INTEGER;
    --
    v_errcontext          VARCHAR2(200);
    v_errmsg              VARCHAR2(200);
```

```
      --
BEGIN
   --
   /*
    * ...open cursor to execute first the COUNT(*) query and then the
    * "histogram"ing query...
    */
   v_errcontext := 'dbms_sql.open_cursor';
   c := dbms_sql.open_cursor;
   --
   /*
    * ...use dynamic PL/SQL (i.e. DBMS_SQL package) to count how many rows
    * there are in the table.  The SQL statement will look something like:
    *
    *     SELECT /*+ FULL(X) PARALLEL(X,4,1) * / COUNT(*)
    *        FROM table X;
    *
    * ...where "table" is the table name and "4" and "1" are the PQO
    * "degree" and "instances", respectively...
    */
   v_errcontext := 'dbms_sql.parse (count)';
   dbms_sql.parse(c, 'SELECT /*+ FULL(X) PARALLEL(X,4,1) */ ' ||
                     'COUNT(*) FROM ' || in_table || ' X', dbms_sql.v7);
   --
   v_errcontext := 'dbms_sql.define_column (count)';
   dbms_sql.define_column(c, 1, v_rowcount);
   --
   v_errcontext := 'dbms_sql.execute (count)';
   v_rtn_code := dbms_sql.execute(c);
   --
   v_errcontext := 'dbms_sql.fetch_rows (count)';
   IF dbms_sql.fetch_rows(c) <= 0 THEN
      RAISE no_data_found;
   END IF;
   --
   v_errcontext := 'dbms_sql.column_value, 1 (count)';
   dbms_sql.column_value(c, 1, v_rowcount);
   --
   /*
    * ...find out how many rows should be assigned to each job,
    * rounding the fractional part up to the next higher integer...
    */
   v_interval := trunc(v_rowcount / in_nbr_of_jobs) + 1;
   --
   /*
    * ...determine what the proper "block-size" should be used in
    * the following query, so that we pull back the proper number
    * of "buckets"...
    */
   v_fetch_granularity := trunc(v_interval / 10);
```

```
IF v_fetch_granularity < 2 THEN
    v_fetch_granularity := 2;
END IF;
/*
 * ...using the "histogram" query, assign "v_interval" rows
 * to each job (or just try to come close)...
 *
 * ...use dynamic PL/SQL (i.e. DBMS_SQL package) to build a SQL
 * statement with which to build the histogram itself.  The SQL statement
 * will look something like...
 *
 *     SELECT /*+ FULL(X) PARALLEL(X,4,1) * /
 *             granularity * TRUNC(column / granularity) + 1 RANGE_FROM,
 *             granularity * (TRUNC(column / granularity) + 1) RANGE_TO,
 *             COUNT(*) NBR_OF_ROWS
 *       FROM table X
 *       GROUP BY TRUNC(column / granularity)
 *       ORDER BY TRUNC(column / granularity);
 *
 * ...where upper-case text indicates fixed text in the statement, and
 * lower-case words indicate values to be plugged in...
 */
v_errcontext := 'dbms_sql.parse (histogram)';
dbms_sql.parse(c, 'SELECT /*+ FULL(X) PARALLEL(X,4,1) */ ' ||
                  v_fetch_granularity ||
                  ' * TRUNC(' || in_column || ' / ' ||
                  v_fetch_granularity || ') + 1, ' ||
                  v_fetch_granularity ||
                  ' * (TRUNC(' || in_column || ' / ' ||
                  v_fetch_granularity || ') + 1), ' ||
                  'COUNT(*) FROM ' || in_table || ' X GROUP BY ' ||
                  'TRUNC(' || in_column || ' / ' ||
                  v_fetch_granularity || ') ORDER BY ' ||
                  'TRUNC(' || in_column || ' / ' ||
                  v_fetch_granularity || ')', dbms_sql.v7);
--
v_errcontext := 'dbms_sql.define_columns (histogram)';
dbms_sql.define_column(c, 1, v_range_from);
dbms_sql.define_column(c, 2, v_range_to);
dbms_sql.define_column(c, 3, v_rows);
--
v_errcontext := 'dbms_sql.execute (histogram)';
v_rtn_code := dbms_sql.execute(c);
--
v_rowcount := 0;  -- ...reset to zero so we can use it again...
--
LOOP
    --
    v_errcontext := 'dbms_sql.fetch_rows (histogram)';
    IF dbms_sql.fetch_rows(c) = 0 THEN
```

```
        EXIT;
    END IF;
    --
    v_errcontext := 'dbms_sql.column_value (histogram)';
    dbms_sql.column_value(c, 1, v_range_from);
    dbms_sql.column_value(c, 2, v_range_to);
    dbms_sql.column_value(c, 3, v_rows);
    --
    /*
     * ...initialize the first element of "v_from_array" on the first
     * iteration into the loop...
     */
    v_rowcount := v_rowcount + 1;
    IF v_rowcount = 1 THEN
        v_from_array(i) := v_range_from;
    END IF;
    --
    /*
     * ...if we have enough rows for one job, then output a
     * job assignment (i.e. range and tally) and then reset...
     */
    IF v_nbr_of_rows + v_rows >= v_interval THEN
        --
        IF v_nbr_of_rows + v_rows > v_interval THEN
            --
            v_rows := (v_nbr_of_rows + v_rows) - v_interval;
            v_nbr_of_rows := v_interval;
            --
        END IF;
        --
        /*
         * ...reset running totals...
         */
        v_nbr_of_rows := 0;
        i := i + 1;
        v_from_array(i) := v_range_from;
        --
    END IF;
    --
    v_nbr_of_rows := v_nbr_of_rows + v_rows;
    v_to_array(i) := v_range_to;
    --
END LOOP;
--
/*
 * ...now, using the FROM and TO values saved in the arrays, go back and
 * execute the JOB for each range of values...
 */
FOR j IN 0..i LOOP
    --
```

```
        v_errcontext := 'dbms_sql.parse (jobexe)';
        dbms_sql.parse(c, 'BEGIN ' || in_job_name || '(' ||
                           to_char(v_from_array(j)) || ',' ||
                           to_char(v_to_array(j)) || '); END;', dbms_sql.v7);
        --
        v_errcontext := 'dbms_sql.execute (jobexe)';
        v_rtn_code := dbms_sql.execute(c);
        --
END LOOP;
--
v_errcontext := 'dbms_sql.close_cursor';
dbms_sql.close_cursor(c);
--
EXCEPTION
    --
    WHEN OTHERS THEN
        v_errmsg := sqlerrm;
        raise_application_error(-20001, v_errcontext || ': ' || v_errmsg);
    --
END histpl;
/
SHOW ERRORS
```

Now that HISTPL is created, it would be nice to be able to test it to make sure it works properly. The following stored procedure TEST_HISTPL is intended to do just that.

```
CREATE OR REPLACE PROCEDURE test_histpl(in_from IN NUMBER, in_to IN NUMBER)
IS
BEGIN
    --
    dbms_output.put_line('TEST_HISTPL: FROM=' || in_from || ', TO=' || in_to);
    --
END test_histpl;
/
SHOW ERRORS
```

As you can see, this rudimentary procedure simply accepts two numbers as parameters and displays them using the DBMS_OUTPUT package.

Now, to see what HISTPL can do, let's test it against one of the data dictionary views, DBA_OBJECTS:

```
SQL> SET SERVEROUTPUT ON SIZE 1000000
SQL> EXECUTE histpl('test_histpl', 'dba_objects', 'object_id', 10)
TEST_HISTPL: FROM=1, TO=250
TEST_HISTPL: FROM=251, TO=500
TEST_HISTPL: FROM=501, TO=750
TEST_HISTPL: FROM=751, TO=1000
TEST_HISTPL: FROM=1001, TO=1250
```

```
TEST_HISTPL: FROM=1251, TO=1500
TEST_HISTPL: FROM=1501, TO=1775
TEST_HISTPL: FROM=1776, TO=2025
TEST_HISTPL: FROM=2026, TO=2275
TEST_HISTPL: FROM=2276, TO=2650

PL/SQL procedure successfully completed.

SQL>
```

What HISTPL did was count all the rows in DBA_OBJECTS, and then divide that by ten (i.e., the requested number of jobs) to come up with the number of rows per *bucket* of work. Then, it queried the table and found what ranges of the column OBJECT_ID would produce ten equal-sized buckets of work. It then executed the TEST_HISTPL stored procedure, which simply displayed those ranges.

Now, imagine that you are in Oracle7 or Oracle8 and have a nonpartitioned table against which you must perform a massive, complex UPDATE or DELETE statement. You could try to just code that UPDATE or DELETE and run it, hoping that it finishes. Or you could code the statement (or statements) then encapsulate it inside a PL/SQL-stored procedure that takes two parameters. Those parameters would be low- and high-range values on an indexed numeric column on the table in question.

All that would be necessary would be to add an additional condition to the WHERE clause of the SQL statement(s) inside the new stored procedure, to restrict it by the given range values:

```
UPDATE <table-name>
   SET <stuff-to-be-updated>
 WHERE <original-WHERE-clause>
   AND <indexed-numeric-column-name> BETWEEN in_low_value AND in_high_value;
```

This is quite simple and a viable high-performance alternative to partitioned tables. (Partitioning still provides other administrative advantages, as described in Chapters 5 and 6.)

PL/SQL "To-do List" Processing

This next technique is geared toward situations where a large amount of processing is expected and it may be necessary to stop or kill the concurrently processing jobs before the job is completed. This implies that there must be the ability to restart processing from exactly where the job previously left off, rather than have to restart the job from the beginning.

The key to this technique is a separate specialized table known as a *to-do list*. A query is run against the table on which the work is to be performed, inserting one row for each individual *unit of work* into the to-do list table. The to-do list table contains columns to identify uniquely each atomic unit of work to be performed, along with columns to store possible error messages and possibly the exit status. For example:

```
CREATE TABLE TODO_LIST_TABLE
(
    KEY_COLUMN       VARCHAR2(200)    NOT NULL,
    STATUS           VARCHAR2(200)    NOT NULL
)
    INITRANS   10  /* to optimize concurrent db block updates */
    PCTFREE    20; /* to leave room for UPDATEs to STATUS column */
```

Now, how can this be used? The KEY_COLUMN column is intended to hold all the information necessary to uniquely identify a "unit of work." If you wish, it could be any number of columns. The STATUS column is intended to indicate what phase of processing a unit of work is ready for. At the start, it might hold a value like "READY." After successful completion, it might hold a value like "DONE." If an error occurred during processing, it might hold a value like "ER-ROR:" followed by some error message text to help diagnose the error.

Once the TODO_LIST_TABLE has been populated, one or more *work* programs can be started against it, to process all the rows in the table concurrently. A work program will query the TODO_LIST_TABLE, and for each row it finds it will process the corresponding unit of work that the row represents. Generally, the work program will be a *batch program*.

Most batch programs have the following general format:

```
connect to Oracle
perform some kind of initialization
loop on a SQL cursor
    do some unit of work
end loop
perform some kind of finalization
disconnect from Oracle
```

With a little bit of modification, just about any such batch program, whether it's written in a third-generation language such as C or COBOL or in PL/SQL, can be adapted to use the to-do list table and run in parallel. This is done in two steps.

First, take the SQL cursor mentioned in the preceding example and make it the INSERT statement that populates the to-do list table.

```
INSERT INTO TODO_LIST_TABLE (KEY_COLUMN, STATUS)
      SELECT key-value, 'READY'
        FROM <table-list>
       WHERE <search-conditions>;
```

Next, modify the algorithm of the batch program slightly to accommodate the use of a to-do list table:

```
connect to Oracle
perform some kind of initialization
loop on the rows in the to-do list table
    try to lock the current row in the to-do list table
    if it is already locked or STATUS is not 'READY', skip to the next row
    do some unit of work
end loop
perform some kind of finalization
disconnect from Oracle
```

Please note that only one line has been changed and two lines have been added to the interior of the processing loop. First, instead of driving the batch program from a query against the table to be manipulated, the batch program is now driving from a simple query of all rows in the to-do list table. Next, inside the loop, an attempt is made to place a *row lock* on the currently fetched row in the to-do list table. If this lock can't be made because somebody else has the row locked, or if the row can be locked but the STATUS column does not have a value of READY (indicating that it has already been processed), then skip this row and fetch the next row.

AVOIDING CONCURRENCY PROBLEMS IN THE TO-DO LIST

It is possible for parallel jobs to end up running serially if care is not taken in programming the lock function. A second job can queue up trying to obtain the same row lock already held by the first job. There are two ways to avoid this problem. Each job can quickly modify the row's STATUS column and then COMMIT the change before starting the actual job. Alternatively, the lock should be requested in NOWAIT mode (as demonstrated in the following example). This will return an error immediately rather than wait for the lock to be released.

With these minor changes, you can now start multiple, concurrent copies of this batch program, and they will cooperatively process the work in parallel. One advantage of this technique is that the query used to drive the batch program can readily be adapted to populate a to-do list table. This makes this technique ideal for converting existing batch programs. Next, this technique is fully restartable. If the jobs are ever terminated before completion, they are easily restarted exactly where they left off; unprocessed rows in the to-do list represent the work remaining. Also, error conditions that are logged can be examined for possible correction. Once the errors have been corrected somehow, the corresponding rows in the to-do list table can be set so that the column STATUS is given the value of READY, meaning ready to be processed. Then, just start one or more batch programs to process the contents of the to-do list.

Sample Code for "To-Do List" Processing

This code could be implemented in PL/SQL, Pro*C, PRO*COBOL, or any other programming language; PL/SQL has been chosen here because it is relatively easy to read, even for people who are not programmers.

An example of a work procedure follows. Please note that this stored procedure is doing several things:

- Each executing copy of this procedure can exist by itself or coexist with one or more concurrently executing copies of this procedure. In this fashion, a form of parallelism is being implemented. As mentioned earlier, much of this functionality can be retrofitted relatively easily into existing batch programs; the ability to *row-lock* (using the FOR UPDATE . . . NOWAIT clause) and to trap the failure to lock (using the ALREADY_LOCKED exception) is the key for implementing this.
- This procedure is restartable. If one or all the work procedures should fail for any reason (including database or system failure), subsequent job starts will pick up right where they left off. The fact that the main cursor always checks the value of the STATUS column together with the query by ROWID that performs the locking ensure that previously completed work will not be repeated.
- Its main cursor loop, against the TODO_LIST_TABLE, has been made "tolerant" of the Oracle SNAPSHOT_TOO_OLD (i.e., ORA-01555) error, which can occur with queries against extremely volatile tables. This can be a useful technique for any *restartable* process in Oracle programming.

```
CREATE OR REPLACE PROCEDURE work_on_todo_list
IS
--
    CURSOR get_todo_list
    is
    SELECT rowid
      FROM todo_list_table
     WHERE status = 'READY';
    --
    already_locked              EXCEPTION;
    PRAGMA EXCEPTION_INIT        (already_locked, -54);
    snapshot_too_old            EXCEPTION;
    PRAGMA EXCEPTION_INIT        (snapshot_too_old, -1555);
    v_key_column                todo_list_table.key_column%TYPE;
    v_status                    todo_list_table.status%TYPE;
    v_errcontext                VARCHAR2(200);
    v_errmsg                    VARCHAR2(200);
    skip_this_row               BOOLEAN;
    x                           get_todo_list%ROWTYPE;
    --
BEGIN
--
errcontext := 'open get_todo_list cursor';
OPEN get_todo_list;
--
LOOP
```

```
/*******************
 *
 * ...HANDLE POSSIBLE "SNAPSHOT TOO OLD" ERROR DURING FETCH...
 *
 *******************/
BEGIN
    v_errcontext := 'fetch get_todo_list cursor';
    FETCH get_todo_list INTO x;
    EXIT WHEN get_todo_list%NOTFOUND;
EXCEPTION
    WHEN snapshot_too_old THEN
        v_errcontext := 'close get_todo_list (ORA-01555)';
        CLOSE get_todo_list;
        --
        v_errcontext := 're-open get_todo_list (ORA-01555)';
        OPEN get_todo_list;
        --
        v_errcontext := 're-fetch get_todo_list (ORA-01555)';
        FETCH get_todo_list into x;
        EXIT WHEN get_todo_list%NOTFOUND;
END;
--

/*******************
 *
 * ATTEMPT TO LOCK ROW JUST RETRIEVED FROM "TO-DO LIST"...
 *
 *******************/
v_errcontext := 'lock row in todo_list_table';
BEGIN
    SELECT key_column
      INTO v_key_column
      FROM todo_list_table
     WHERE rowid = x.rowid
       AND status = 'READY'
       FOR UPDATE OF status NOWAIT;
    --
    /*

     * row successfully locked
     */
    skip_this_row := FALSE;
    --
EXCEPTION
    /*
* if ALREADY_LOCKED is encountered, then another process
* is currently processing the "unit of work" represented
* by this row
         *
* if NO_DATA_FOUND is encountered, then this means that
* another process has already finished processing the
```

```
* "unit of work" represented by this row
*/
        WHEN already_locked OR no_data_found THEN
            skip_this_row := TRUE;
    END;
    --
    /*******************
     *
     * PROCESS ONLY IF ROW NOT ALREADY LOCKED AND NOT ALREADY
     * PROCESSED...
     *
     ******************/
    IF skip_this_row = FALSE THEN
        --
        /*
* use the value retrieved into "v_key_column" to identify
* a "unit of work" in the tables actually being worked on
*
* set the variable "v_status" to either "DONE" or
* "ERROR: error-message-text" upon completion of the "unit of
* work"
*/
        <PERFORM "UNIT OF WORK" LOGIC ***HERE***>
        --
        /*******************
         *
         * mark "to-do list" row according to value in "v_status"
         *
         ******************/
        v_errcontext := 'update sample_todo_list';
        UPDATE sample_todo_list
           SET status = v_status
         WHERE rowid = x.rowid;
        --
    END IF; -- ...end of "skip_this_row" = FALSE logic...
    --
    /*
     * ...perform the COMMIT even if no processing was performed, to
     * release the row-lock...
     */
    v_errcontext := 'commit';
    commit;
    --
END LOOP;
--
errcontext := 'close get_todo_list';
close get_todo_list;
--
EXCEPTION
    WHEN OTHERS THEN
```

```
                    v_errmsg := sqlerrm;
                    raise_application_error(-20001, v_errcontext ||
                                                ': ' || v_errmsg);
END work_on_todo_list;
/
SHOW ERRORS
```

This style of programming is not new, by any means. Even if parallelization is not desired, the restartability is certainly a desirable feature.

Summary

Without exception, data requires a great deal of transformation during the journey from its source operational system to the destination data warehouse. Some of the transformation may occur during extraction from the source operational systems. Some transformation may occur during the actual transportation, or transfer, from the source system to the data warehouse. Some may occur during the load into the data warehouse. But, based on past experience, it is likely that the majority of data transformation will occur after the detailed operational data has been loaded into the data warehouse.

There are three major kinds of postload processing: summarization/aggregation, filtering, and merging. Some of the tools available to perform these tasks are as follows:

- parallel CREATE TABLE . . . AS SELECT
- parallel INSERT (with APPEND) on Oracle8 nonpartitioned tables
- parallel INSERT (with or without APPEND) on Oracle8 partitioned tables
- parallel UPDATE on Oracle8 partitioned tables
- parallel DELETE on Oracle8 partitioned tables
- custom-written PL/SQL for partitioning certain tasks by ranges of a key
- custom-written PL/SQL for parallelism and restart logic

Using these techniques should enable you to handle almost any eventuality in the Oracle data warehouse.

ADMINISTERING AND MONITORING THE ORACLE DATA WAREHOUSE

CHAPTER 8

Lights out.

That's how we want all our systems to run: off by themselves in a darkened machine room, humming away busily. Running themselves. Monitoring themselves. Calling for help only when absolutely necessary. Not demanding help from people unless something is about to go wrong.

Technical people like this idea because they hope it will allow them a utopian existence: working from home, playing golf, coaching Little League, surfing the Web, or reading Dilbert comics. Management likes the idea because it also conjures up pleasant images of trouble-free 24×7 operation, bonuses and kudos from the CEO, a guest column as management guru in *Business Week*, and perhaps a fellowship at the Harvard business school (but maybe not the Dilbert comics).

Well, maybe. . . . but there's no doubt that is the goal. Existing system running themselves, freeing the systems staff to enhance or create new systems. The path to this utopia starts with *responsibility.*

Occasionally, as Oracle consultants, we teach classes for customers through Oracle Education Centers. Recently, while teaching the class on database administration, the students were asked the standard question, "Who are you, and what do you hope to gain from this class?" The majority of folks in the class were either application developers or programmer/analysts who wanted to find out more about how the Oracle RDBMS works. Another large segment were information systems (IS) managers tasked with leading a development effort involving Oracle who wanted to know what their subordinates should be doing.

Only a small handful of people were actually database administrators (DBAs), about one-quarter of the class. After the first two or three days of the class, it was clear that there were two mind-sets in the class: conservative and "put the pedal to the metal." The former seemed more interested in nailing down the core concepts; the latter were most interested in probing the outermost reaches of the features of the RDBMS. Without formally polling the class, it seemed clear that the folks who were already administrators fell into the conservative category, and the application developers and programmer/analysts fell into the progressive category.

After a lively discussion that pitted the two mind sets against one another, the instructor commented, "You know, the most important thing about being a DBA is not so much what you know but being able to stare at anyone, including the company CEO, and growl, 'Not on my production database, you're not!' And mean it."

Most of the class laughed, thinking it was a recommendation that DBAs be obstructive and possessive. The conservative faction in the class nodded grimly. They understood that the instructor's comment did not imply that the identifying characteristics of a DBA are inflexibility, sociopathic tendencies, and a penchant for career-limiting moves. The issue is not *power* or *authority,* but *responsibility.* The DBA should always hold the goal of meeting the business and systems requirements of his or her database above all else and emphatically defend against the erosion of the database's abilities to meet those requirements. In practical terms, DBAs simply don't want to be paged at 2:00 A.M. with a downed system. In short, they are *responsible.*

For example, take the case of the DBA of a mission-critical order entry system who is in a meeting regarding a proposed new data warehouse that will extract from the order entry database. The team tasked with loading data into the data

Administration tools

There are several tools provided by Oracle Corporation for administering Oracle7 and Oracle8 databases. Among these are SQL*DBA, Server Manager, and the latest, Enterprise Manager. Various third parties provide additional products to aid the DBA in managing the Oracle environment. This chapter does not provide a tutorial on using any specific tool. The official documentation for each product can do a more complete job of that task. Repeating that material here would waste your time as well as ours.

We do, however, provide a philosophical discussion of the real-life role of a DBA and some very specific practical techniques to allow the DBA to do a better job of avoiding and, if necessary, solving problems that can occur in the very large Oracle database arena. All of the example code is provided in generic SQL and PL/SQL (with occasional minor SQL*Plus formatting commands) scripts that can be readily adapted to whichever administration tool you are using.

warehouse has just requested a read-only logon to the order entry system for the purpose of developing and testing extract programs. The CIO of the company has just unthinkingly said, "Sure, why not?" in the interests of keeping momentum on the data warehouse project, which is enthusiastically sponsored by the company's CEO and CFO.

But hold it—stop right there. In this example, the DBA knows that this particular order entry system has very strict performance requirements. If certain EDI transactions take longer than N number of seconds, the system sending the transaction cancels it and routes it elsewhere. Essentially, if response time is too slow, the company loses the transaction. If X number of transactions are lost in this manner within an hour, then the reservation company feeding the transactions decides that this company is having problems and disconnects. Reconnections won't happen until after the following midnight, meaning the company is effectively shut down until then.

Should a team of people unfamiliar with the order entry system be blindly consuming resources, even if they only have read-only privileges? Although it's true they can't harm the existing data, should they be allowed to even consume resources? Even if the upper-level management team makes a decision, the DBA may be in a position to educate everyone about the potential impact of the decision. Those who made the request and those who made the decision may not have realized the importance.

Obviously, the answer in this case is not to emphatically deny access. But because of the importance of maintaining the response time on transactions, a great deal of care should be taken to ensure not only that the data is safe but also that system resources are consumed modestly and in a controlled fashion, in a way that does not jeopardize the primary function of the system.

The issue is responsibility. It's not that other people are irresponsible; it's just that they may have many or conflicting priorities. The DBA has one priority: to keep the production database up and running and serving the business. It doesn't make sense to take responsibility for something without having a plan. That is where this chapter is intended to help—in developing a plan for administering an Oracle data warehouse. It also doesn't make sense to establish a plan that can't be adjusted to meet changing conditions. That is the other area in which this chapter will provide guidance—monitoring the system to prevent surprises.

Who Are We? Why Are We Here?

To paraphrase James Stockdale's famous statement in the 1992 vice presidential debates, we have to focus on basic issues. Because of Vice Admiral Stockdale's somewhat strained and nervous oratorical abilities and delivery, his opening statement, "Who am I? Why am I here?," came out sounding like the words of a confused (possibly senile) old man asking where he was, rather than an attempt to establish a logical base from which to proceed in a reasoned discussion.

Although it is seems like a good idea to establish basic principles and work forward from there, it is possible to be boring or condescending in the process. In many IS and DP shops, it is possible (even necessary, in the interests of time) to skip over basic principles and address the questions at hand. Unfortunately, a surprising number people walk into a data warehousing project believing that the objective is to do cool new things using neat new technology, to learn new techniques, and to gain marketable new skills. All that is possible and desirable, but only if it meets the objectives of the business.

It is not possible to make rational technical decisions without having a complete understanding of business requirements. Once the business requirements are understood, then system requirements can be defined.

Business Requirements

As countless texts and articles on data warehouses have made clear, the primary purpose of the data warehouse is to provide the most efficient reporting on tactical and strategic data. Because this book is a practical guide to implementation, we should assume, at this point, that all business requirements have been dealt with, especially with respect to designing the data warehouse in the first place. However, other business requirements that affect administration and monitoring mainly have to do with expectations. These requirements were described in Chapter 2 as some of the evaluation criteria for the selection of a hardware architecture. They include the following:

- reliability and availability expectations of the data warehouse
- overall performance expectations by end users or downstream data marts
- mean–time–to–repair expectations should an outage occur

These expectations may not have been set down explicitly and, as a result, different people may have different expectations. It is important to document these expectations so that everyone is clear on them, from the top of the organization chart to the bottom. Once these expectations are understood, then the technical team can start turning these expectations into system requirements.

System Requirements

These expectations, once quantified, can then be translated into system requirements. For example, let's assume that the development team for a proposed data warehouse has been told the following:

- The data warehouse only needs to be available five days a week (Monday through Friday) for eight hours a day.
- Response-time expectations are 30 seconds for formal reports and "canned queries" and no more than four hours for "ad hoc" queries.
- Should the system crash, missing a day of downtime would not cause the world to stop.

Sound familiar? Let's examine this further . . .

So-called 5×8 availability (i.e., eight hours per day, five days per week) implies that the system need only be up and running between 9:00 A.M. and 5:00 P.M. Suppose the company operates in several time zones, say, just in the continental United States (i.e., four time zones). This means that the system will need to be available from 6:00 A.M. Pacific Time (which is 9:00 A.M. Eastern Time) until 5:00 P.M. Pacific Time, which spans 11 hours. So the requirement should expand from 5×8 to 5×11. But wait . . .

The response-time expectations indicate at least four hours for ad hoc queries. Based on the habit of some end users of composing last-minute queries and firing them off at 5:00 P.M., this means that the system should probably remain available until 9:00 P.M. Pacific Time. If this is in fact the business user's expectation, then the hours of required availability just expanded from 5×11 to 5×15.

Okay, by asking a few questions, we've found that the uptime expectations are double what was originally stated. Let's keep going. . . .

Given the expected size of the data warehouse, how likely is it that reports and queries could run longer than four hours? Will data mining techniques be used on the system? Will online analytical processing (OLAP) tools be used, or will end users have unrestricted access to "ad hoc" queries using SQL? If they will have unrestricted ad hoc access, how proficient are they in tuning SQL statements on Oracle?

Depending on the answers to these, and other, questions, it is probably reasonable to at least double the expected duration of some reports and queries from four to eight hours (or more). Now, since the system has to stay up eight hours after 5:00 P.M., this means we now have a 5×19 system supporting four time zones.

Time zones. Aren't we expanding into Europe and Asia? If not, should we be? There goes the remaining downtime during the week: we're now at 5×24. Now let's look at those weekends. . . .

Anyway, it seems clear that no matter what anyone says, you should try to plan for the effects of globalization, which implies a 7×24 operation. But before you tell anyone you're going to try to run a 7×24 operation, let's look at the record. On planet Earth (and, to our knowledge, throughout the neighboring worlds), there is not a single computer system that truly runs 24 hours a day, seven days a week, and 52 weeks a year, year after year. There are some that come excruciatingly close, but they do shut down once a year for something like 45 minutes. While this seems close to 100 percent uptime, it is in fact 99.9914 percent uptime.

Systems like this (American Airline's SABRE computerized reservations system is an example) have been in existence for several decades. It has literally taken billions of dollars of investment in equipment, people, training, research, and experience to get to this level of availability. Is your company prepared for this level of investment? Is an investment of this magnitude appropriate for a decision-support system?

At the beginning stages of any project, it is probably prudent to consider more attainable goals. It makes a lot of sense for a data warehouse to have a significant chunk of time set aside for the load phase, backups, and other maintenance in the form of patches, upgrades, and card swap-outs. During these time periods, the end-user community should expect the data warehouse to be unavailable for their use. The administrators can then perform whatever mainte-nance actions are necessary during this time. If the administrators do not have anything to do, or if they complete their tasks early, then they can "give back" the time to the end-user community.

If this can be agreed upon, then the end-user community can be assured that the data warehouse will remain available during the time periods allocated to them, and the administrative staff can be assured they will have scheduled downtime available to them in order to perform necessary maintenance on the systems.

Given the initial requirements mentioned earlier (i.e., 5×8 availability, one day mean–time–to–repair), it is likely that this technical implementation team should stake out one or both days of every weekend as "owned" by them. Over time, this scheduled downtime could be renegotiated to become less and less frequent, until some point of equilibrium is reached.

Administration Roles

There are many distinct roles in administering an Oracle data warehouse. Quite often, all these roles will be performed by one or two people, but regardless of whether the IT department is one person or five hundred, it is important to un-derstand the roles that must be fulfilled.

Understanding these roles and keeping them separate, distinct, and private is not a matter of authority or power. It is a matter of responsibility. Should a prob-lem occur, it is best that the resolution of that problem be routed to the person most capable of handling it.

Database Administrator (DBA)

The database administrator (or DBA) is responsible for the Oracle database. The configuration, growth, and well-being of the database and its software is the re-sponsibility of this role. Most of the discussions in this chapter (indeed, in this entire book) center on this role.

System Administrator

The system administrator (or "SysAdmin", "SyAd", "SA" or whatever) is generally responsible for the computer machinery itself, along with system software. The computer, its subsystems, and most of its peripheral devices fall under this juris-diction. In a UNIX environment, the SysAdmin "owns" the password to the "root" superuser and should not share it with anybody else.

Security Administrator

The security administrator is responsible for setting up access to system re-sources (i.e., operating system logons, Oracle accounts, network logons, etc.) for developers, administrators, and end users. In some organizations, this role can occupy several full-time people; in others, it is a small part of the other administrative roles.

Network Administrator

The network administrator is generally responsible for network devices, peripherals, and client machines outside the data centers.

Application Administrator

Each application on the system should have one or more people responsible for configuring, maintaining, and troubleshooting it. All changes to the application should be approved by this role. All problems not due to the hardware, operating system, network, or database should be resolved by this role. The data warehouse is such an application.

Help Desk and Problem Resolution

This is perhaps the most important, yet most overlooked, role of all. The help desk is the single point of contact for the end-user community when something goes wrong. Help desk personnel need to be able to route the problem to the appropriate administrator after recording pertinent facts. An effective help desk allows you to control the amount of work that flows to the various administrators. An ineffective, poorly trained help desk can make a bad situation worse, and a well-trained help desk can ensure that the system runs smoothly.

The reasons go beyond the obvious. The obvious reason is that an effective help desk can understand and resolve problems faster, handling many of the problems without involving the rest of the IT organization.

The less obvious costs of an ineffective (or non-existent) help desk lie in the resolution of more complex problems. If no help desk exists, end users and developers alike tend to resolve their problems using their own personal network. Using a personal network of "gurus," "power users," and system administrators can be an effective way to resolve problems when the number of problems is few, but if there are a great many problems to be resolved, it has a disastrous effect.

As the most highly trained people spend time resolving problems that are not their normal tasks, they become unable to perform their own jobs during a normal workday. As a result, their own productivity suffers, and they become frustrated and disgruntled. Management, unable to record, track, or react to problems handled in this manner, only notices the decreased productivity and may take steps that do not address the real problem.

Data Warehouse Security Issues

Security administration is just one of the many facets of warehouse administration. In some IT shops security is assigned to a special individual or team. In others it is one of the responsibilities of the DBA. Even the shops that do a thorough job of effectively controlling access to their operational systems may be tempted to overlook security issues when planning and implementing the data warehouse. This is probably because of the mistaken perception that read-only access has less potential for abuse than other types of access. This is only partly true. True, a user of the warehouse cannot misuse the tool to enter fraudulent invoices into accounts payable. But the value (and risks) of an organization's computing resources are not limited to fraud and sabotage. Information is a key resource of the corporation—that is the justification for building the warehouse, isn't it? If a user prints out a customer list and takes it to a competitor, has the corporation been damaged? Probably. Would the fictitious "Consultants 'R' Us" company in our case study want the effective billing rates and project profitability numbers of its warehouse distributed to other consulting companies in their market? I doubt it. Would you like your competitor to have a copy of your standard pricing and volume discount policy? If not, then you probably don't want to make it available to every employee of the company. Whatever information is considered strategic to your organization's success is potentially just as valuable to someone else (and damaging to you if they get it).

Unfortunately, a common opinion of warehouse planners is that if everyone has access to everything they will be empowered to make better decisions. This attitude has fostered a very laissez-faire attitude toward security. Well, frankly, not everyone in the organization needs to make decisions about everything! Some thought needs to be given to who should be using the warehouse and what areas they should be allowed to investigate. A straightforward process needs to be created to allow for requesting, approving, and providing additional access when justified.

In designing the security plan for the data warehouse there are three objectives to balance. Security should be effective, unobtrusive, and simple.

Effective Security

Far too many warehouses have been built and delivered without consideration for the security of the information contents. It is simple, but inappropriate, to give every user access, SELECT ANY TABLE privilege, and unlimited resources. Each subject area in the warehouse should have one or more assigned owners who should specify guidelines for who may receive access (or even review and approve each specific user request for access). A particular subject area may need to be divided even more granularly in order to properly separate "public" information from potentially sensitive data.

One frequently ignored element of an effective security policy (for any system) involves education. Each user, as part of obtaining access to the warehouse, should be instructed on the value, confidential nature, and need for securing the information in the warehouse. They should be taught how (and why) to change their passwords regularly. They should also be made aware of the specific policies for accessing and distributing that information and the potential penalties for violating security policies. Finally, each user needs to understand the process for obtaining additional access where warranted.

Unobtrusive Security

Applying the security plan to the warehouse should not impair the user from doing legitimate operations. They should be generally unaware that certain operations are forbidden. Other than having to remember and occasionally change their passwords, user should be generally unaware of the existence of security measures. They should be trained in the process of requesting additional privileges, however, if they find legitimate reasons for access to objects in a part of the warehouse not currently available to them. The security administrator should be prepared to quickly obtain the necessary authorization from the "owner" of that new subject area.

Simple Security

Just as security should not be obtrusive on the users' legitimate pursuit of business decisions, it should also not become a burden on the DBA or security administrator. Oracle has provided excellent features for simplifying the administration of security once an effective and unobtrusive plan has been designed. Three of these features (roles, auditing, and password management) meet this need for administrative simplicity particularly well.

Roles

It is common for any particular user of the warehouse to need a wide variety of privileges—both system level and object level—to perform their analysis. As introduced in Chapter 3, there may be hundreds or thousands of privileges to be granted. The roles feature allows a common set of privileges to be grouped together as a role, assigned a name, and then distributed as a unit with a single GRANT or REVOKE statement. Two levels of roles are recommended for the data warehouse. One role is defined for each group of users who will need the same privileges. This is frequently done on the basis of department and of SQL sophistication. You may wish to limit new or untrained users to summary tables rather than allowing them to plow through large detail tables.

A second set of roles is then created, one per warehouse subject area (or portion of subject area if the owner has decided that access to some data needs additional restriction). Finally, the subject area roles are granted to the appropriate user group roles. This provides a simple network of grants between the two levels of roles (as depicted in Chapter 3, Figure 3.12). When a section of the warehouse needs to be made unavailable for maintenance, only the handful of grants between roles needs to be revoked and later restored. This is far simpler than having to revoke privileges on dozens of objects or hundreds of individual users.

Auditing

Later in this chapter we will recommend that session level auditing be used to track warehouse usage. There is very little overhead involved in recording when users connect and disconnect from the database. The advantage, from a security perspective, is an easy means to identify when unauthorized access is attempted. If auditing is not used for any other purpose, it should be enabled to record each unsuccessful attempt to access the Oracle7 warehouse database (Oracle8's new account locking feature, described in the next section, is an alternative solution). This is done by enabling auditing with the AUDIT_TRAIL initialization parameter and then specifying specific objects or actions to be tracked using the following AUDIT command:

```
AUDIT SESSION WHENEVER UNSUCCESSFUL;
```

This command will ensure that every unsuccessful attempt to log on to the database is recorded in the audit trail. You should expect to see an occasional entry when a user misspells a password. Your concern should be for situations where dozens or hundreds of entries appear which indicate someone is attempting to "crack" a password. The audit trail will tell you what username(s) were being attempted. You should contact that user (assuming a valid username was being entered) to find out whether they were having trouble or to have them change their password in case it was eventually guessed.

Gathering usage statistics would use the same AUDIT SESSION command, but without the WHENEVER UNSUCCESSFUL restriction. This usage along with relocation and maintenance of Oracle's internal audit trail table are described later in this chapter.

Password Management

This topic is mentioned last not because of limited value but because it is a new set of features in Oracle8. For instance, in earlier releases there was no automatic means of ensuring that users changed passwords regularly or that they selected a password of some minimum length or complexity. These new features are described in depth in Chapters 19 and 20 of the Oracle8 *Server Administrator's Guide* so they will be presented very generally here.

Password expiration: The administrator may define how long a password may remain valid before the user is required to change it.

Password history: Oracle can maintain a list of the previous passwords used by the user to prevent them from immediately resetting their current password.

Password complexity verification: The administrator may develop a PL/SQL script that will be executed whenever a user password is changed. This routine can ensure that passwords are of sufficient length, that they contain an appropriate mix of special characters, that they are not the same as the username or other common words (such as "welcome" or "oracle").

Account Locking: This feature can cut off access to a particular user account for a designated length of time whenever a specified number of unsuccessful logon attempts are made. This is a preemptive measure to prevent unauthorized access, in contrast to the auditing approach described earlier which only detects attempted breaches.

All four of these new features are implemented through entries in the user's resource profile. Profiles were introduced in Oracle7 for controlling the resource usage by groups of users. Using profiles is a two-step process. First, the administrator creates a profile with a specific list of resource limits or any of these new password management features. This is done with the CREATE PROFILE command or modified later with ALTER PROFILE. Then the profile is assigned to users using the ALTER USER command. Different profiles may (and should) be created to control different groups of users who have different responsibilities. Resource limits (especially on logical I/O per call) should be assigned based on a user's training, experience, and awareness of SQL performance issues.

Data Warehouse Configuration Issues

The following issues are covered in this section:

Optimal Flexible Architecture (OFA): a file directory structure for successful growth

Build/rebuild documentation: *semper paratus*

Identifying all inbound data and its sources: the importance of easily available metadata

Job scheduling: give yourself a fighting chance to prevent being overwhelmed

Identifying all outbound data and its destinations: know thy users

Capacity planning: space capacity planning and resource capacity planning

Development, test, and training environments: despite what you may have read or heard, data warehouses are serious business too

Backup and recovery: data warehouses *are* mission-critical

Enabling and optimizing auditing: it's not just for security any more; it helps track resource utilization, too

Optimal Flexible Architecture (OFA)

As of release 7.3 of the Oracle7 RDBMS, the OFA's directory structure will be enforced by the Oracle Installer. This means that users of Oracle products will either have to comply with OFA or fool the Installer into believing that there is compliance. It is probably a good idea to become OFA compliant, as long as you understand the reasoning behind it.

As briefly introduced in Chapter 4 in the context of tablespace design, OFA was developed primarily by Oracle Consulting Services' System Performance Group (SPG), led by Cary Millsap, in the early 1990s to help manage the increasingly large databases being developed using Oracle version 6. Although the documentation on OFA (available from www.europa.com/~orapub) describes the purpose of OFA in detail, the guidelines of OFA have three main objectives:

- separate software from database and configuration/log/trace files
- allow easy load balancing across disk devices as well as systems
- establish a cross-platform standard for directories and files for Oracle (and other) products

Understanding these goals is key to understanding why the OFA standards are what they are. To attempt to implement them without this understanding would be an exercise in jumping through hoops for no purpose.

In versions of Oracle prior to version 7.3, the Oracle Installer would attempt to perform the simplest possible install. This usually meant that, unless nondefault directory locations were specified, all the Oracle software files went into a single directory tree, usually known as ORACLE_HOME. The Oracle software; the database; and all configuration files, log files, and trace files would reside underneath this directory structure (see Figure 8.1).

As you may expect, this works well in very simple environments that remain small and simple. But as the environment grows managing this single directory tree becomes more and more complex (see Figure 8.2). In fact, since the maximum size of most UNIX file systems is 2 gigabytes, it's clear that the database it-

Figure 8.1 Everything in ORACLE_HOME.

Figure 8.2 Growing pains.

self will need to be relocated to another directory structure almost immediately. Archived redo logfiles also represent another growth risk, as they can accumulate rapidly in very busy database environments. Last, even log files (such as "alert.log") and trace files can exceed the available space quite rapidly.

So, it makes sense to plan for this kind of growth right from the beginning, so it can be planned properly. OFA guidelines therefore provide direction for creating similar directory structures under several similar *mount points*, where each mount point represents a separate file system or disk drive (see Figure 8.3). This scheme has the dual advantage of allowing the installation to exceed one file system and of balancing the I/O load across the multiple mount points.

One other fact of life that OFA enables is upgrades. Unless OFA (or some similar guidelines are utilized), a software upgrade may prove more exciting than it needs to. An upgrade should just replace the software without changing anything else. Ideally, it should also allow the DBA to schedule independent upgrades to multiple databases on the same server to allow for testing and controlled migration. If the software, database files, configuration files, log files, and trace files are all mixed up in the same directory structure, then it would be very difficult to accomplish an upgrade without affecting (even jeopardizing) everything else. However, since OFA separates the software from everything else, upgrades under an OFA-compliant installation are quite uneventful affairs.

Also, this standard can easily be adapted across platforms: UNIX, NT, VMS. In place of the UNIX mount points named in Figure 8.3, just replace those names with NT or VMS drive specifications. If a single group of DBAs has to manage

Figure 8.3 Optimal Flexible Architecture.

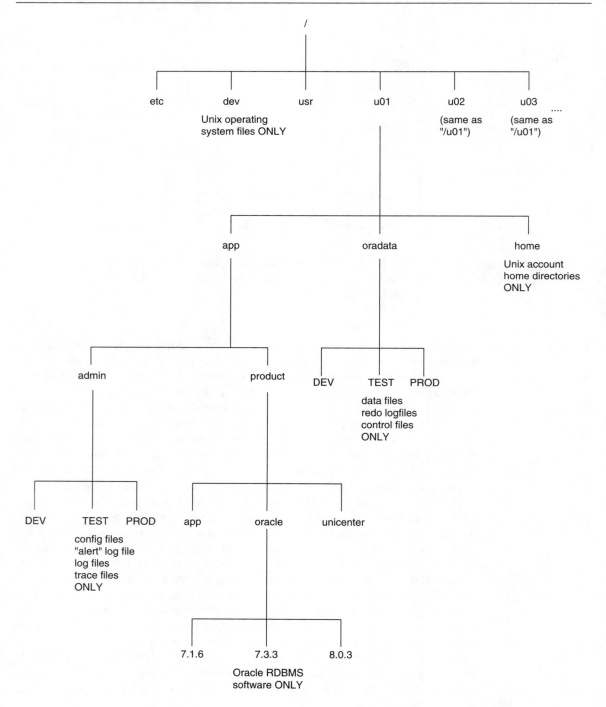

Oracle databases on many platforms or if Oracle Support is dialing into your system to work on a problem, using OFA makes everyone's job easier.

Build/Rebuild Documentation and Scripts

For a number of reasons, at any time it may be necessary to rebuild all or part of your database. Restores from backups can prevent this from being necessary, but in certain situations sometimes the best approach is to simply rebuild. Situations where this is true aren't necessarily due to mishaps or failures; you may be rebuilding the data warehouse environment on a different platform, either for migration or testing purposes or even to train new DBAs.

However, there are some situations where rebuild scripts and documentation may be useful as a recovery strategy instead of restoring from backups.

To illustrate this, let's consider some typical data warehousing environments. In many situations, a significant portion of the data is downloaded regularly as "complete refreshes" of the data. Sometimes, the frequency between refreshes is weekly or even daily. Does it make sense to back this data up regularly? Or, since this data is short lived on the system anyway, should the affected tablespaces simply be dropped, re-created, and reloaded in the event of media failure or corruption? This is known as the *restore-versus-rebuild* debate.

There are many things to consider when deciding which recovery strategy (i.e., restore from backups or rebuild and reload) to implement.

First, Oracle tablespaces such as SYSTEM and the tablespace(s) containing rollback segments should always be backed up with ARCHIVELOG mode enabled with the archived redo logfiles backed up as well. Losing SYSTEM (which contains the data dictionary) and the rollback segments can cause problems that may necessitate a complete database rebuild. Because of this, always implement the RESTORE FROM BACKUP strategy for these tablespaces.

If database auditing is enabled and you have relocated the SYS.AUD$ table to another tablespace outside of the SYSTEM tablespace, you may also want to use the RESTORE FROM BACKUP strategy here as well. While the loss of auditing data will not threaten structural integrity of the database, it should seem obvious that if auditing information is worth recording, it is worth restoring completely rather than losing it completely.

What about data that cannot be reloaded easily? Of course, it can be argued that even historical tables that contain aggregated data accumulated over many years could eventually be reloaded, but who would want to go through the effort? And who could decide whether the reloaded and reaggregated data is accurate? If a mistake is made, how would it be verified? As a rule of thumb, any data that cannot be reloaded in one step should not be considered for a REBUILD THEN RELOAD strategy but instead should be RESTORED FROM BACKUP.

Always consider the mean–time–to–repair. If you are not sure that you can quickly and reliably recall the data for reload, then don't consider REBUILD THEN RELOAD. What you may not be aware of is that data from legacy systems used to load a data warehouse one day may be overwritten with new data the next. Or sent to deep off-site storage. Or it may be misplaced.

If the tablespace contains an end-user layer for a development tool such as Oracle Developer/2000, Oracle Designer/2000, or Oracle Discoverer, don't assume that it will be acceptable to simply reinstall the tool. Developers using the tool may have many months of work stored in these tables and may not share a laissez-faire attitude toward this data.

Altogether, probably the only kind of data that is well suited for a REBUILD THEN RELOAD strategy is short-lived data that is frequently refreshed completely anyway. In this situation, which can sometimes consume several hundred gigabytes in a data warehouse, the idea of not performing backups has great appeal. If a media failure situation should occur, it can be quite easy to drop and re-create the affected tablespaces and then simply restart the normal load processes to reload them.

Tablespaces which have been made READ ONLY are ideal candidates for RESTORE FROM BACKUP. These files can be truly restored from backup and immediately made available. No roll forward recovery from archived redo logs is necessary provided they are backed up once after being altered to the READ ONLY state. Partitioning of large tables can frequently allow the majority of the table's data to be maintained in READ ONLY tablespaces.

Many DBAs and SysAdmins like the idea of REBUILD THEN RELOAD because they think it implies less work for them. But REBUILD THEN RELOAD really implies a custom-built recovery solution that must be as reliable and as easy to perform as RESTORE FROM BACKUP. Although a DBA will likely be performing the recovery, it might not necessarily be the DBA who is intimately familiar with the database in question.

Identifying All Inbound Data and Its Sources

The need for metadata is well documented in all references on data warehousing. More than other kinds of systems, data warehouses must make all metadata, both for the data warehouse itself as well as its sources, easily and readily available to everyone. End users, developers, and administrators alike need to understand what data is available, where it came from, and what transformations (if any) were performed in bringing it on board.

The administrators of a data warehouse must be able to accurately describe the source of all the data being loaded into the data warehouse. At one basic level, this documentation could simply be a listing of all the load jobs, their frequencies, how they are invoked, the primary contact for the load jobs on the data warehouse system, and the contact who maintains the extract programs on the source system. This could then be expanded using CASE tools to be comprised of complete metadata repositories of the source systems and the data warehouse.

Whatever the depth and degree of this documentation, it should be made accessible to all systems and end-user personnel using the data warehouse. Access mechanisms can include intranet web sites, documentation on network drives, CASE repositories, or hard copy in binders in libraries.

Metadata can be integrated into the tools that users will be utilizing for reporting and analysis. As an ad hoc query and report tool, Oracle's Discoverer

3.0 is an excellent choice for this reason. Most OLAP tools such as Oracle Express, Cognos Impromptu, and Business Objects come with extensive metadata facilities.

Metadata could also be a separate, nonintegrated part of the toolset; for example, an intranet web site. Providing metadata in this manner could allow end users to share a common repository instead of having to learn how to navigate through each tool's metadata facilities. Naturally, this option implies (at the least) purchasing another product or (at the most) extensive additional development effort to develop this web-based documentation. But with a diverse and dispersed end-user community utilizing many different tools (not to mention different versions of tools!), a web-based metadata repository may prove extremely cost-effective in the long term as a common repository.

Job Scheduling

It has been said that 80 percent of the work of a data warehouse is getting the doggone thing loaded, day after day, week after week, month after month. The queries and reporting, while they represent 100 percent of the work performed by end users, pale in comparison to the amount of human and computer effort involved in keeping the data warehouse up-to-date and functional.

It stands to reason that this work should be automated rather than depend on human intervention to initiate, track, and sequence job submissions. It is fairly common for data warehouse developers and administrators to perform job scheduling and submission manually, purportedly until the development phase transitions into production. Unfortunately, during the transition there never seems to be enough time to automate the process, and by that time extra software cannot be purchased anyway as the budget has been exhausted until the next budget cycle.

There is an old adage, which has been attributed both to Confucius and Murphy: "Things that are thought to be temporary are actually permanent, and things that are thought to be permanent are actually temporary." In this spirit, the bad habits and inefficiencies acquired during development and implementation cannot be corrected at a later date because the bad habits themselves leave no time to implement the correction.

Although some environments such as VMS, MVS, and AS/400 have very well-developed job scheduling facilities built in, it is unfortunate but true that most UNIX platforms have extremely primitive job scheduling facilities; namely, "at" and "cron." Without a significant amount of custom development, these utilities are not sufficient for production job scheduling.

Therefore, it is highly recommended that a full-featured job scheduling package be obtained for the data warehouse right from the beginning of the development phase. Job scheduling is not something that should be retrofitted in at a later date, nor would it be easy to convert manual processes over to automated job scheduling. When people develop manually initiated jobs, they generally implement them in a highly personalized fashion. This alone makes it very difficult and labor intensive to convert to the single format expected by an automated job scheduling system.

Automated job scheduling software should have at least the following features:

- time-based job submission
- event-based job submission
- job-dependency submission
- reporting on job schedules
- queue management (queue creation and removal, queue quiesce/pause, queue bandwidths, queue workshifts, job assignments to queues, job viewing, job resubmission to different queues, job prioritization/reprioritization within queues, job hold/release/termination)
- job history (log files, output files, records of elapsed time, queue, submitted by, scheduled at, began at, finished at, management reports, performance trend reports by queue, job, job type, user, time of day, etc.)

Additional desirable features include the following:

- cross-platform support
- integration with other job scheduling systems
- unified console management of distributed heterogeneous systems
- records of resources consumed

Job scheduling is not something that should be limited to administrators, however. End users should be encouraged to utilize the job scheduler for their repetitive jobs as well. Most data warehouse query tools, analysis tools, and OLAP tools do not have the ability to submit "batch jobs" or interface with job scheduling systems. They are generally designed to be executed interactively from a console or workstation.

Nonetheless, when evaluating such tools during the purchasing cycle, it would be wise to consider whether the query tool, analysis tool, or OLAP tool is capable of integrating with a job scheduling system, especially in the event of long-running queries. In this manner, the load on the system can be controlled to some extent, jobs that fail can be resubmitted automatically, and usage trends can be tracked more readily.

Identifying All Outbound Data and Its Destinations

Without prior planning, outbound data can be very difficult to document, and once documented it can be very difficult to keep up to date. Outbound data that is extracted from the data warehouse by means of batch jobs is not the problem. If a job scheduling package is used, batch jobs that extract data for reporting or transportation to other destinations such as data marts are quite easy to document and keep documented. With the job control features specified in the previous section, it is also very easy to restrict jobs running on the system and to terminate them if needed.

The real problem is potentially the ad hoc access to the data warehouse. More often than not, it is access via ad hoc tools (such as SQL*Plus) that causes performance degradation and security breaches in data warehouses. To guarantee the response time on specific load jobs, queries, and reports in a data warehouse, the administrators of the warehouse must be able to account for everything that is happening on the system. While Oracle DBAs can accomplish this after the fact using internal views such as V$SESSION and V$SQLAREA, it is far more effective to invest some planning into how ad hoc jobs will be submitted, tracked, and accounted rather than react to situations on an as-needed basis.

One way to document all outbound data is to restrict the tools being used, if possible. SQL*Plus allows rather unrestricted and completely ad hoc access to the database. This kind of access is very difficult to monitor and almost impossible to control.

Tools such as Oracle Discoverer 3.0 and Oracle Express provide additional levels of security, the ability to restrict what queries are running, and the ability to analyze those queries that do run (see Figure 8.4).

See Chapter 13 for a more detailed explanation of Oracle Express and its capabilities.

In short, both batched and ad hoc activity should be tracked to effectively regulate resource consumption in the warehouse. Toward this end, you should favor tools such as Discoverer 3.0, which have features to predict resource consumption and cache data on the client side and which store submitted SQL statements for later analysis and optimization. Simplistic tools such as SQL*Plus should be used only very rarely, using lockout features (such as the PRODUCT_USER_PROFILE table) provided by the vendor.

This is not to say that SQL*Plus does not have its place in a data warehouse environment; it simply lacks facilities to allow its usage to be moderated. It is a simple interface into the Oracle database, and as such it will allow careless end users to *code-and-fire* some truly resource-intensive SQL statements (affectionately referred to as "queries from hell" by DBAs). Make sure that only knowl-

Controlling SQL*Plus Activities

If ad hoc access using SQL*Plus is a problem in your data warehouse, then consider selectively disabling the functions that can be performed from SQL*Plus using the SYSTEM.PRODUCT_USER_PROFILE table in Oracle7 or the SYSTEM.SQLPLUS_USER_PROFILE table in Oracle8. The use of these two tables is documented in the SQL*Plus *User's Guide and Reference*. They won't prevent a user from connecting to the database with SQL*Plus, but they will prevent a user from executing the commands you specify (i.e., SELECT, INSERT, UPDATE, DELETE, HOST, SPOOL, EXECUTE, etc.) from SQL*Plus. Please note that this feature pertains to SQL*Plus only and does not have anything to do with object permissions, system permissions, and roles granted and revoked using the GRANT and REVOKE commands. This is an entirely different level of security particular only to access to the database through SQL*Plus.

Figure 8.4 Query tools and OLAP tools: End user layers.

edgeable developers and users are using SQL*Plus by using the PRODUCT
_USER_PROFILE table to limit SQL*Plus access to certain Oracle accounts.

Also, SQL*Plus is a worthy batch-processing tool for running reports and updates against the data warehouse. It is a good idea to have Oracle accounts for
batch processing separate from developer's normal logon accounts.

For example, take the example of a developer who has an Oracle account
named SALLY on a production data warehouse for the purpose of testing and
analysis. This account is set up to allow read-only access to most of the data
warehouse, and it has a *resource profile* that prevents intensive queries from
consuming too many resources (resource profiles were described in the Security
Issues section earlier in this chapter). In this account, Sally can develop, test,
and play around without consuming too many resources and without damaging
any data. If she is doing anything that temporarily requires more resources, the
DBAs can change her resource profile to something less restrictive, temporarily
or permanently.

However, the batch jobs that Sally develops are never executed under the account SALLY. Rather, the DBAs have set up another account named
SALLY_BATCH that is entirely under their control. Sally can develop the batch
processes, specify a schedule for their submission, and receive the results of the
jobs, but access to this account is limited to the warehouse administrators. The

reason for this is to give the people responsible for keeping the data warehouse up and running efficiently more control over how and when the data warehouse's resources are consumed.

Capacity Planning

There are two kinds of capacity in a computer system: space and resources. *Space* refers to storage; how much data can be stored in the data warehouse. *Resources* refers to the amount of work that can be performed on the data stored in the data warehouse.

Space Capacity Planning

There are many formulas that can be used to predictively calculate the amount of space that will need to be allocated in order to store a set of data in an Oracle database. Appendix A in the Oracle *Server Administrator's Guide* has formulas for predicting the sizes of tables, indexes, and clusters given the average sizes of each column in these objects.

But herein lies the rub: the formulas are based on *average sizes* and will therefore produce size estimates that will accumulate any errors made in estimating average column sizes. Thus, if you inaccurately estimate the average size of the data in a VARCHAR2(20) column as ten characters instead of eleven for a table that will hold one million rows, you are going to be off by 1 MB, just on the basis of that one column. In data warehousing, tables are frequently denormalized and contain dozens or hundreds of columns. Now the margin of error will be larger unless scrupulously accurate values are used.

Can scrupulously accurate sizing data be obtained? The answer, frequently, is no. The only way to obtain accurate sizing data is from existing data, and frequently the existing data itself or the ability to analyze it is not available. For example, imagine making the request to find the average size of all fields in all files to the administrators running a legacy order entry system. You can imagine that there are many good reasons, as well as a few equally real frivolous ones, why this task will never even be initiated, never mind completed. Therefore, database designers, in order to use these predictive formulas, must guess. Try to imagine the margin of error now. . . .

So, while these documented formulas are useful in helping one understand Oracle datablock formats and the factors involved in data storage, they are rarely useful in actual practice. As a matter of fact, there is a much faster, easier, and more accurate way to predict storage needs: data sampling and extrapolation.

The idea is this: obtain a few thousand data records. Create a table in Oracle and load the data. Observe how much space is consumed. Since you know how many records occupy this space, you can now calculate how many rows are in each database block. From this value (i.e., rows per block), you can now extrapolate how many database blocks would be necessary to hold N number of rows, where N is your estimated total table size. In addition to normal statistical sampling error, the maximum error introduced by this approach is an overestimate of nearly one Oracle block (assuming the worst case of only a single row being loaded into the final allocated block). Both forms of potential error are reduced by using larger sample sizes.

Of course, if you cannot obtain any of the data in the first place, this method is useless as well. In this event, where you can neither obtain data for extrapolation purposes nor obtain detailed and exhaustive information on size averages, you may as well just make simple guesses at space requirements. Simple guesses are faster than plugging guessed-at values into the sizing formulas, and either way the results are irrelevant to some extent.

But it is somewhat reasonable to expect that a data warehousing effort would be able to acquire some data to test with. Submitting a request to the harried administrators of a legacy order entry system for a certain number of records from each file might be treated more kindly than a request to analyze the data itself, which will likely entail extra effort on their part. Additionally, since some test data will be required at an early stage of the data warehouse project anyway, obtaining data samples for the purpose of sizing will kill two birds with one stone.

Next, create the sample table using reasonable parameters reflecting the expected behavior of the table. The Oracle *Server Administrator's Guide* has chapters entitled "Managing Tables" and "Managing Indexes" that describe the use of PCTFREE and PCTUSED and INITRANS and MAXTRANS. In a largely read-only environment like a data warehouse, it is doubtful that the values of INITRANS and MAXTRANS will need to be changed from their defaults, but it might be possible if the loads of the data warehouse incur contention for datablocks. Altogether, it is likely that the settings for PCTFREE and PCTUSED will require the most consideration for this exercise. It is completely valid to perform this extrapolation multiple times, each time using different values of PCTFREE, PCTUSED, INITRANS, and MAXTRANS, to observe their effect on storage. As described in Chapter 5, PCTFREE should generally be set to 0 for most warehouse tables. The value of PCTUSED will depend upon whether you will ever DELETE rows from the table.

When the data has been loaded, you can run the following query in Oracle7:

```
SELECT AVG(COUNT(SUBSTR(ROWID,10,4))) avg_rows_per_blk
  FROM <name-of-the-table>
 WHERE ROWNUM <= <total-#-rows-minus-some>
 GROUP BY SUBSTR(ROWID,1,8),
          SUBSTR(ROWID,15,4);
```

Or, for Oracle8:

```
SELECT AVG(COUNT(DBMS_ROWID.ROWID_ROW_NUMBER(ROWID))) avg_rows_per_blk
  FROM <name-of-the-table>
 WHERE ROWNUM <= <total-#-rows-minus-some>
 GROUP BY DBMS_ROWID.ROWID_OBJECT(ROWID),
          DBMS_ROWID.ROWID_RELATIVE_FNO(ROWID),
          DBMS_ROWID.ROWID_BLOCK_NUMBER(ROWID);
```

Knowing something about the meaning and contents of a ROWID is helpful. In Oracle7, a ROWID is stored internally as a *block-number*, a *row-number-within-block*, and a *file number*. In Oracle8, the ROWID has been expanded to include an *object-number* as well.

Of course, you need to substitute *<name-of-the-table>* for the name of the table itself, and you should substitute *<total-#-rows-minus-some>* with a value that is at least a couple of hundred or thousand rows less than the actual total number of rows in the table. The reason for this is to avoid counting partially filled database blocks, which would normally reside near the "end" of the table. These blocks may have been left partially filled when the load ended, and including them in this calculation may skew the average, however slightly.

Depending on the size of the database blocks, the settings of PCTFREE and INITRANS, and (of course) the characteristics of the data itself, you will get a value that can be used when extrapolating the eventual full size of the table. For example, if one of the queries just shown returned a value of 48.3, this means that—on average—each database block will hold 48.3 rows. Therefore, if you know that you'll need to store 100 million rows, then it will take just over 2 million (2,070,394 to be exact) database blocks to store this. If each database block is 8 KB, then this table should require 15.8 gigabytes.

Don't forget indexes. Again, it may be simplest to extrapolate; create the proposed indexes, see how big they are, and project their final size. If the sample version of the table contains 100,000 rows, and an index created against that consumes 1,000 blocks (according to the USED_BLOCKS column in the USER_INDEXES view following an ANALYZE INDEX), then it stands to reason that when the table is at its full size of 100 million rows the index will also be approximately 1,000 times larger as well (1 million blocks at 8 KB, which is about 7.6 gigabytes). (Index growth is not exactly linear, because of the hierarchical nature of B*Tree indexes, compression in the branch blocks and the capability of storing multiple ROWIDs for each key value.)

There is another issue regarding index space utilization that must be considered. When using parallel CREATE INDEX, each parallel slave temporarily allocates space according to the INITIAL and NEXT parameters specified in the STORAGE clause. During the course of the CREATE INDEX, the amount of space consumed will briefly equal about twice the eventual size of the final in-

Sizing Data after Parallel Direct Path Loads

If you used parallel SQL*Loader direct path to load this table, then there are likely to be as many partially filled blocks scattered throughout the table as the number of parallel jobs executed. In this case, don't bother using the WHERE ROWNUM clause, as it may only filter out one of several partially filled blocks. If you don't use SQL*Loader direct path parallel for this sizing exercise (and we recommend that you don't), then use the WHERE ROWNUM clause.

dex segment. This is due to a merge operation in which all the results of each parallel slave are merged into a single index structure. In essence, this is a kind of trade-off between *speed* and *space* during the CREATE INDEX operation: the nonparallel CREATE INDEX operation consumes less space during index creation, but it's slower; the parallel CREATE INDEX operation completes the index creation faster but uses lots of "scratch space" while doing so.

Since data warehouse environments are generally large enough to make the use of Parallel Query Option (PQO) features such as parallel CREATE INDEX (pCI), always remember that enough space should be left unused in a tablespace to accommodate the parallel creation of the largest index. This same allowance needs to be made in anticipation of reorganizing indexes using ALTER INDEX . . . REBUILD. For example, say you have sized four indexes at 8 gigabytes, 9 gigabytes, 10 gigabytes, and 12 gigabytes, and they are all going to reside in the same tablespace. Should you size the tablespace at 40 gigabytes (9 + 10 + 11 + 12 = 39)? Only if you intend to create these huge objects using regular old nonparallel CREATE INDEX. If you intend to make use of parallel CREATE INDEX, you should plan on leaving at least the equivalent of the largest index as unused space (see Figure 8.5); in this example, this implies that the tablespace should be sized at around 52 gigabytes! If disk space is at a premium, you could get away with sizing this tablespace with the equivalent of the smallest index as unused space, but that would imply that if you wished to re-create the largest (12 gigabyte) index, you would have to drop the two smallest indexes as well and re-create them after the large one had been re-created!

So far, we have discussed table and index space capacity planning, but there is more to an Oracle database than just the tables and indexes that comprise your data warehouse applications.

Oracle Database Space Requirements

Within the Oracle database, there are several types of special "internal use" tablespaces to consider (see Figure 8.6).

SYSTEM TABLESPACE

The *data dictionary* resides within the SYSTEM tablespace and is owned by the SYS account. The size of the data dictionary is generally quite fixed and usually starts at around 10 MB at initial configuration. The space required by the data dictionary after that initial configuration is affected by the number of schema objects in the database and the number of PL/SQL packages and triggers in the database. Generally, the typical data warehouse applications will not include a large number of tables and indexes or PL/SQL stored procedures. Numbers of tables and indexes in the low hundreds is considered small, as is a couple of dozen PL/SQL stored packages or procedures. By contrast, prepackaged software (such as Oracle Financials or Oracle Manufacturing) can sometimes consist of many thousands of tables, twice or four times that number of indexes, and hundreds or thousands of PL/SQL stored objects. For situations like these, it is not uncommon to see the data dictionary require up to 500 to 700 MB. Size your

Figure 8.5 Leaving room for parallel CREATE INDEX.

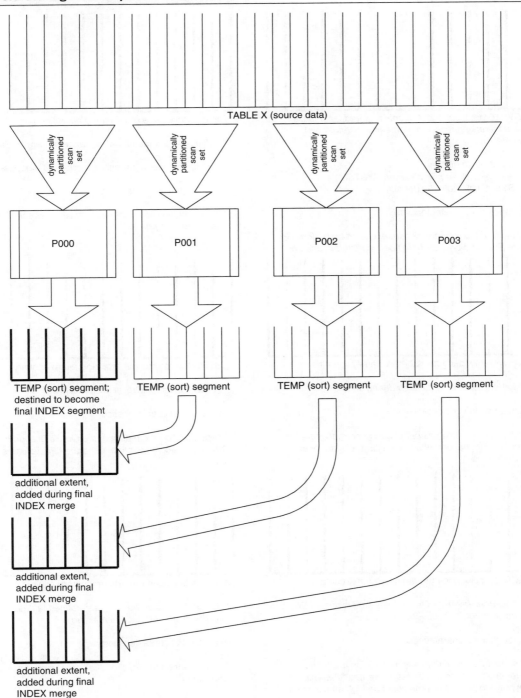

Figure 8.6 Oracle "internal use" tablespaces.

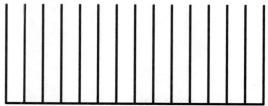

SYSTEM tablespace (the only required tablespace, and the only one whose name is unchangeable) contains:

* Oracle data dictionary
* one rollback segment named SYSTEM
* SYS.AUD$ table (by default)

Expected I/O characteristics:

* most of Oracle data dictionary should be buffered in the SGA; heavy I/O should be a cause for concern

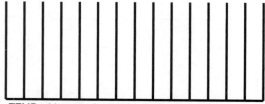

TEMP tablespace (an arbitrary name) contains:

* temporary segments used during sorting

Expected I/O characteristics:

* expect high volumes of I/O during normal operation, and during the load phase when indexes are being created

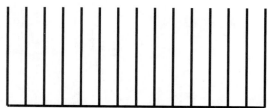

TOOLS tablespace (an arbitrary name) contains:

** **end-user layer** for Oracle tools (i.e Developer/2000, Designer/2000, Discoverer)*

Expected I/O characteristics:

* should be low, if the tools in question are tuned properly. If the tool in question creates "sharable hyper-cubes", I/O volume could be high on occasion

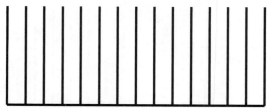

RBS_1 tablespace (an arbitrary name) contains:

* rollback segments for one instance of Parallel Server
or
* rollback segments for entire "exclusive" database

Expected I/O characteristics:

* expect high volumes of random, single-db-block I/O during the load phase

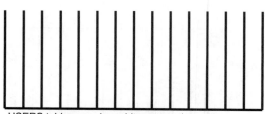

USERS tablespace (an arbitrary name) contains:

** **scratch area** for Oracle accounts*

Expected I/O characteristics:

** dependent on the nature of the Oracle accounts. **Developer** accounts might generate high volumes of I/O...*

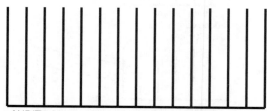

AUDIT tablespace (an arbitrary name) contains:

* SYS.AUD$ table and any user-defined tables and indexes used for database auditing

Expected I/O characteristics:

* dependent on the level of auditing, but anticipate high levels of I/O...

SYSTEM tablespace accordingly. If you think you may have a couple of hundred tables and indexes, then sizing SYSTEM at 30 to 100 MB is not unreasonable, regardless of the amount of space those tables and indexes will consume. The data dictionary does contain extent and free space information, which is affected by object size, but in general the sizing needs of the data dictionary are more dependent on the number of objects than the size of the objects (other than stored packages, procedures and functions, which are stored in SYSTEM). If you think that your database will eventually hold thousands of tables and thousands of indexes and will be heavily dependent on PL/SQL-stored packages and procedures, then sizing your SYSTEM tablespace from 500 to 1000 MB is not unreasonable.

ENLARGING THE SYSTEM TABLESPACE

If needed, additional space can be added to the SYSTEM tablespace using ALTER TABLE-SPACE SYSTEM ADD DATAFILE.

TOOLS TABLESPACE

Objects belonging to the SYSTEM schema (not to be confused with the SYSTEM tablespace) are not part of the data dictionary. Generally, the SYSTEM account owns the *end-user layers* for such tools as Oracle Developer/2000 and Advanced Replication option. The Oracle Installer program creates a tablespace named TOOLS as the default tablespace for the SYSTEM account, and the size of the TOOLS tablespace should take into consideration whether tools such as Developer/2000 and Advanced Replication will be installed and used, now or in the future.

ROLLBACK SEGMENT TABLESPACE

It is also a good idea to keep all rollback segments in one or more tablespaces named RBSnn (i.e., RBS01, RBS02). There are no specific rules as to whether one tablespace is better for rollback segments or several. Losing any tablespace (due to disk failure) that contains an online rollback segment may make the database unusable. Of course, disk mirroring should make such a possibility extremely remote, but even mirroring can be defeated by extremely bad luck.

The size and number of rollback segments has provided fodder for a great many books, white papers, and presentations, but I tend to follow these general guidelines for starters:

- Each rollback segment should have a minimum of 20 extents, perhaps 40 for very busy transactional systems. This means MINEXTENTS should be set between 20 and 40.
- The OPTIMAL setting for each rollback segment should be set to the size implied by MINEXTENTS.
- The size of extents in rollback segments should reflect the anticipated duration of the "average" transaction. If you are running an OLTP-type system

where there are hundreds or thousands of transactions concurrently active, but each is very small, then size rollback segment extents smaller (i.e., 64 to 128 KB). If the average transaction is larger, tending more toward batch and less toward online operations, you should size extents larger (i.e., 1 MB). Most data warehouse applications tend toward the latter.

- Extremely large transactions require more rollback space. If a large transaction cannot be split into smaller pieces or modified to run UNRECOVERABLE (Oracle7) or NOLOGGING (Oracle8), it may be necessary to create one or more very large rollback segments. The large transaction will need to specifically request the large rollback segment using the SET TRANSACTION USE ROLLBACK SEGMENT command.

Next is an example in rollback segment sizing:

Jane is building an Oracle database for a data warehouse that is expected to have about 200 gigabytes in data and 300 gigabytes in indexes at initial load. The nature of the application is that half that data will be reloaded completely (a complete refresh) every week (on Sunday); the other half will grow at a rate of 100 percent per year.

Outside the Sunday load phase, tablespaces will be "locked down" into READ ONLY mode to prevent any updates. The complete refreshes will utilize parallel SQL*Loader direct path, and the remaining loads will use SQL*Loader conventional path and PL/SQL and PRO*C programs to massage the data into its final form.

How Many Rollback Segments Are Needed?

We like to follow the Oracle guidelines of one rollback segment for every four concurrently *active* DML (data manipulation language, such as INSERT, UPDATE, or DELETE) transaction on the system, with a minimum of four and a maximum of 50 to 60. In an online application, it is not uncommon for 90 to 95 percent of all sessions to be *inactive*, leaving only 5 to 10 percent of all connected sessions *active* at any point in time. Thus, when there are 200 connected users, only 10 to 20 user sessions might actually be actively performing DML at any one time. This implies the need for 4 to 5 rollback segments. In a mostly batch-oriented application, it is likely that 90 percent of all sessions to be *active* running DML operations at any one time, with only 5 to10 percent *inactive* or read-only (i.e., non-DML). This is the exact reverse of online applications. So, if you have a batch-oriented system with 30 connected sessions, this might also imply that 25 or more of those sessions are active, which implies 6 to 8 rollback segments for starters. Again, most data warehouses tend toward the latter during their load phase. During their read-only phase, most data warehouses provide few issues involving rollback segments whatsoever, since read-only operations only involve read-consistency issues when there is simultaneous DML in the database.

The Sunday load phase is allowed to take a full twenty-four hours if absolutely necessary, but if hardware maintenance is scheduled or if software upgrades or patches are necessary, they will also have to be accomplished during Sunday. Therefore, it is in everybody's best interests to make the utmost use of the parallel capabilities of the hardware platform to finish the load phase in as short a time as possible.

Given this information, it is difficult to anticipate sizing needs for rollback segments. But let's assume that Jane knows she has 20 to 30 tables to load via complete refresh. Using SQL*Loader direct path means that rollback segments are not utilized at all. She has another 20 to 30 tables that will be loaded using SQL*Loader conventional path, PL/SQL, and PRO*C. Assuming that parallelism will allow her to run at least two separate processes (SQL*Loader, PL/SQL, or PRO*C) against each table, about 40 to 60 load processes requiring rollback segments will result. Using the basic formula of TRANSACTIONS / 4, this gives about 10 to 15 rollback segments. Since these are batch load transactions, Jane decides to size extents at 1 MB apiece for starters. Taking the conservative route of using MINEXTENTS 20, this means that Jane has 15 rollback segments, each requiring 20 MB at OPTIMAL, which means a minimum of 300 MB. Figuring also that each of these rollback segments can triple (or more) in size, Jane decides to double the minimum size figures and create an RBS01 tablespace of size 600 megabytes.

TEMPORARY SEGMENT TABLESPACE

Most Oracle databases also have a tablespace set aside strictly for use by TEMPORARY segments during sorting operations. These tablespaces, which beginning with Oracle7, release 7.3 should be marked as TEMPORARY, are usually named TEMP or TEMP_DATA, and all Oracle accounts should use this tablespace as the account's TEMPORARY TABLESPACE. The amount of temporary space a database will require for sorting is, again, dependent on the application. Many online (OLTP) systems don't do much sorting; they may generally do short, quick queries. They use queries that utilize indexes and retrieve only one or a few rows at a time. Although such systems also usually have reporting processes that may perform a great deal of sorting, overall they do not require much in the way of space in the TEMP tablespace.

On the other hand, data warehouse applications may require enormous amounts of sort space. Many data warehouses do not have large numbers of users logged in at any one time, but each user who is connected might very well be running enormous queries that are either sorting due to explicit ORDER BY or GROUP BY clauses, or they may be requiring temporary segments because they are using join methods that imply sorting or temporary space (i.e., SORT-MERGE joins). Additionally, the use of Parallel Query Option may increase these needs many times. If the typical large query in a data warehouse utilizes Parallel Query Option to a DEGREE of eight, this means that up to sixteen parallel query slave processes are working simultaneously on a query where previously only one process may have worked (eight for data retrieval and eight for sorting). This may mean that the demands for sorting space may have just increased eightfold (although hopefully for only one-eighth of the time as a nonparallel query). It is not uncommon for a data warehouse application that is going to make heavy use of Parallel Query Option to require a significant percentage of its space in the TEMP tablespace. Ratios of 10 to 25 percent of total database size may be valid. We recommend starting with 5 to 10 percent of total data size (i.e., 10 to 20 gigabytes in Jane's example, based on 200 gigabytes of data) at initial configuration. If during the development of the data warehouse that proves insufficient, feel free to dedicate more space to the TEMP tablespace, especially if Parallel Query Option is in use. If the ratio starts to approach 15 to 20 percent of total data size (i.e., 30 to 40 gigabytes in Jane's example) and the demands for more sort space do not abate, start to question the validity of what the query developers are doing. Maybe they can make use of indexing rather than Parallel Query Option. Maybe they should create summary tables to *preaggregate* data, instead of aggregating "on the fly" all the time.

OTHER TABLESPACES

In addition to the SYSTEM, tools, rollback and temporary tablespaces, it is common to create another special tablespace generally called USERS. Create a USERS tablespace if any of the warehouse users will be allowed to create their own objects, perhaps to store temporary results between multiple analysis steps.

Also, if you will be using the Oracle auditing features (as described later in this chapter) you may wish to move the audit trail table (SYS.AUD$) to its own tablespace to avoid interfering with the other operations of the SYSTEM tablespace.

Redo Log Space Requirements

Last, but certainly not least, is the need to provide space for online redo logfiles. Think of these structures almost as representing a second copy of the database. The datafiles contain the *current* image of the database. The redo logfiles (on-line and archived) represent a *historical* image of the database, every action ever taken, in sequential order. While this image of the database is not useful for general use, it serves an extremely important function: in the event of some kind of failure, actions recorded in the redo logfiles can be replayed against the datafiles to bring them up to date. The sizing of redo logfiles is important mainly for controlling checkpoints and the archiving process.

Because we can control the frequency of *checkpointing* using initialization parameters such as LOG_CHECKPOINT_INTERVAL and LOG_CHECKPOINT_TIME-OUT, the size of redo logfiles should only provide an upper bound for checkpoint frequency; checkpoints must occur during the switch of online redo logfiles. If redo logfiles are sized too small, then database activity will cause *redo switches* every few seconds or minutes. As a rule of thumb, you don't like to see redo logfile switches more frequently than every thirty minutes on a consistent basis. Occasionally, "freak" high volumes of transactions may cause redo logfile switching to occur more often, but if this occurs frequently and regularly, then it is not a "freak" occurrence. In this event, you want to size your redo logfiles larger. As a starting point, you should not be uncomfortable to size the redo log-files at 50 to 100 MB.

Of course, there is an upper limit to the size of redo logfiles. When archiving (and there are very few reasons not to enable ARCHIVELOG mode in Oracle!), the destination for archived redo logfiles is typically a file system directory. In many versions of UNIX, the maximum file system size is 2 gigabytes (although several ports now allow much larger sizes). If you sized redo logfiles at close to or larger than 2 gigabytes, you run the risk of overwhelming the LOG_ARCHIVE _DEST directory and file system. This would cause your Oracle database to halt dead in its tracks. No data would be lost, but any activities causing updates to the database would freeze until space for redo logfile archiving is opened up.

Another consideration is tuning the ARCH background process. You want ARCH to promptly archive the online redo logfiles as quickly as possible, but you do not want the effect of the ARCH process while it is working to cause a system "brownout," or temporary performance degradation. Ideally, the ARCH process should be able to finish copying the redo logfile to the archive log desti-nation in less than one-third the time it takes the LGWR process to fill up a redo logfile, on average. If LGWR is filling up a redo logfile every thirty minutes, then it should be quite easy for the ARCH process to accomplish the simple task of copying the file off to the archive log destination in ten minutes or less.

Try to size the redo logfiles so that it takes the LGWR process at least thirty minutes *at a minimum* to fill one up. The "alert.log" file records the times of redo logfile switches, as does the V$LOG_HISTORY view.

If the ARCH process cannot finish archiving one of the logfiles in less than ten minutes, then add more redo log groups. By default, the Oracle Installer will create a database with the minimum of two redo groups; most DBA handbooks recommend at least three. If the ARCH process cannot finish its job quickly enough, adding more redo logfile groups will provide additional time for ARCH to finish its job before the circular redo logging once again needs to reuse the file being archived. Of course, be sure that some kind of I/O bottleneck is not slowing down either ARCH or LGWR; the I/O subsystem underneath the redo logfiles should be optimized for sequential writes (by LGWR) and sequential reads (by ARCH). Be aware also of the I/O characteristics of the file system to which the ARCH process is writing; if I/O performance is slow there due to con-tention then it would be more efficacious to remove the contention there in-stead of adding more redo groups.

As a starting point for Oracle data warehouses, try three groups redo logfiles of 100 MB apiece. Even if RAID 1 volume mirroring is available, it makes sense to use multiple redo logfile members (i.e., mirroring at the Oracle level) to pro-tect against some additional failure scenarios. These recommendations imply 600 MB of space optimized for sequential writes and reads. Start with these guide-lines, make sure that neither LGWR and ARCH are not being overwhelmed, and tune checkpoints separately using LOG_CHECKPOINT_INTERVAL and LOG _CHECKPOINT_TIMEOUT. Set the LOG_CHECKPOINTS_TO_ALERT initialization parameter to TRUE to have a message inserted into the "alert.log" file when each checkpoint occurs, so that you can tune the frequency of checkpoints.

Resource Capacity Planning

What kind of platform should you get for your data warehouse?

Hopefully the discussions in Chapter 2 have helped you decide which architecture might be best suited for your needs. Once you have chosen a platform architecture, once you have designed your data warehouse, and once you have sized your database, you will need to forecast how much CPU, memory, and network resources you will require. Typically, this answer is easy: as much as you can afford! Your hardware vendor will help you size the CPU and memory resources for your environment; with the variety of platforms and the pace of advances in hardware, this book can't delve into that subject.

As an administrator, the best thing you can do is try to anticipate what kinds of operations will be running on the data warehouse. This analysis is a direct offshoot of requirements analysis: What kinds of things are end users expecting to do in the warehouse? This is also a result of system requirements analysis: What kinds of batch processing are necessary to load and prepare the data warehouse for end-user access?

However, since the story always changes (for the worse) after the analysis and design phases of a software project, the next best thing an administrator can do is plan system management for the new system, at as early a stage as possible. For this reason, the best approach to planning resource capacity might be to ensure that, during full production usage, all utilization can be monitored, understood, and controlled.

Monitoring is not difficult: many system management tools (including Oracle Enterprise Manager's Performance Pack) provide the ability to find the "top 10" or "top NN" processes in terms of resource consumption, to monitor locks and "waits" in the database, and to monitor space utilization in the database easily and graphically.

The understanding may be trickier, depending on your level of expertise. If a process is the top consumer of CPU resources on your system for sixty seconds, is that necessarily a problem? What if it is one of the top consumers of CPU resources for an hour? If someone is running some SQL statements that are continuously running out of rollback segment space, what can be done about it? What *should* be done about it?

Control involves the ability not only to run and cancel execution but also to limit resource utilization and queue execution. So, once again, we begin a discussion of system management tools, especially job control packages and end-user tools that are integrated with some sort of queuing system.

QUEUING

What role does queuing play in controlling the utilization of resources? Consider the standard textbook depiction of queuing theory. The classic case is an airline ticket counter. There are only a few ticket agents ready to serve, but potentially hundreds of passengers desiring service. One approach is to set up a single queue, allowing each ticket agent to service the next passenger at the head of the line.

But consider the fact that not all passengers are equal. Some belong to the frequent-flier program and the airline wants to treat them well. First class passengers should also be given priority. Also, some passengers have long transactions (to purchase tickets) and others will require only a few minutes to check in and receive their boarding passes. Clearly the airline can accomplish a lot by setting up multiple queues and devoting different levels of resources (i.e., agents) to each queue. On the other hand, the airline may be guaranteeing customer unhappiness if it can't react quickly to changing volumes of passengers in the various queues.

The same situation confronts Oracle data warehouse administrators. Most data warehouses are opened with no consideration for limiting the access of end-users to system resources. As a consequence, many warehouses resemble a free-for-all melee with each transaction vying for resources as soon as it is submitted. Oracle8 does not provide a scheme for assigning different processing priorities to different users or jobs. The administrator must attempt to control demand by limiting the number of simultaneous users, the degree of parallelization, and the scheduling of batch operations. The best approach is to plan for a crushing volume of demand for system resources and to line up the appropriate end-user tools and system management facilities to deal with the demand during the earliest phases of planning.

Development, Test, and Training Environments

A data warehouse is a production environment, generally with availability requirements similar to a production OLTP system. As such, developers and end users should not be performing development activities inside the production environment, and there needs to be a separate "QA test" environment for new applications, software versions, and tools, just like in "real" system environments. Finally, new end users need to be trained in the data warehouse, so a training area separate from the development, test, and production areas should be available.

However, this begs the question: Since data warehouses are so often huge, how do we support not one but *four* copies of this huge database?

The best answer probably is: We don't. The best approach is to use sampling techniques to extract subsets of the production data to populate smaller versions of the database. This can be done in two ways: load sampling or data sampling.

Load sampling is when a filtering processing is performed against the original data to be loaded (see Figure 8.7). This filtering process is inserted ahead of the load process and feeds the load process a subset of the original records to be loaded.

Data sampling (see Figure 8.8) is similar in that instead of extracting the subset from original load data, the subset is extracted from the data warehouse database after the loads are completed. As such, the data sampling becomes yet another extract from the data warehouse.

Samples can be chosen at random (or near random) or chosen by some well-known non-random attribute, such as geography (see Figure 8.9).

Figure 8.7 Load sampling.

Figure 8.8 Data sampling.

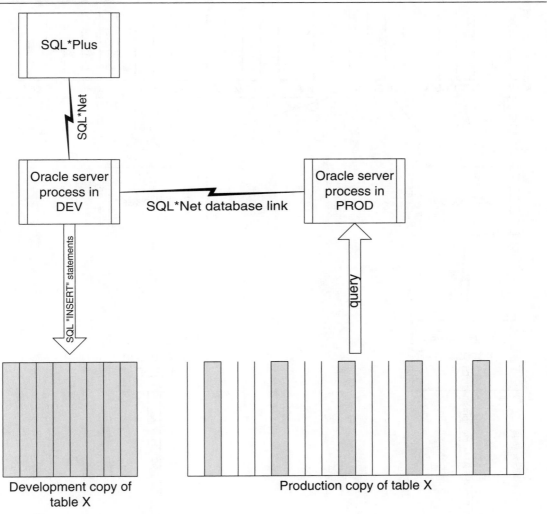

Take the example of a national retailer that does business in all fifty states in the United States and all the provinces and territories of Canada. They may decide that a valid sample would be to select from five geographically distributed states and one province, effectively selecting about 10 percent of the total production population.

Or, it may be equally valid to select from particular months, weeks, or days (see Figure 8.10). This may be easier to perform while you are data sampling as opposed to load sampling, as most load processes involve data from a certain recent period of time.

Figure 8.9 Sampling by geography.

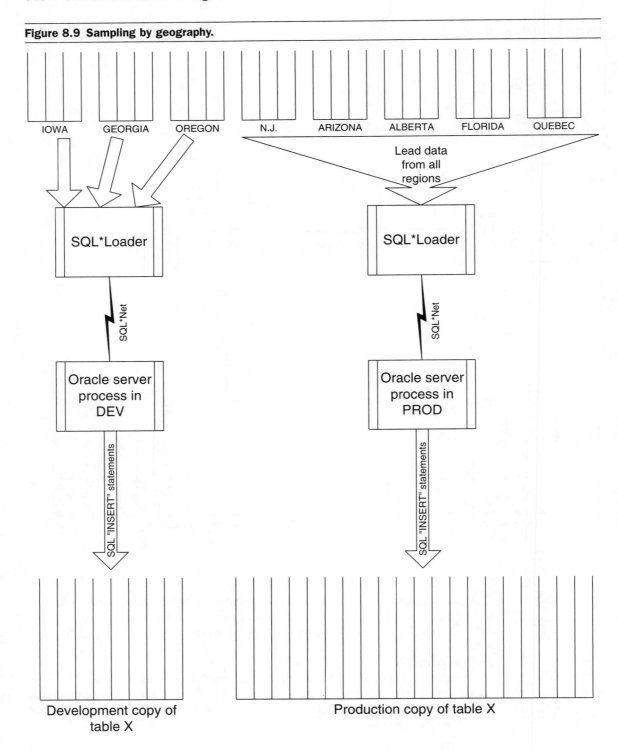

IOWA   GEORGIA   OREGON   N.J.   ARIZONA   ALBERTA   FLORIDA   QUEBEC

Lead data from all regions

SQL*Loader

SQL*Loader

SQL*Net

SQL*Net

Oracle server process in DEV

Oracle server process in PROD

SQL "INSERT" statements

SQL "INSERT" statements

Development copy of table X

Production copy of table X

Figure 8.10 Sampling certain months, weeks, or days.

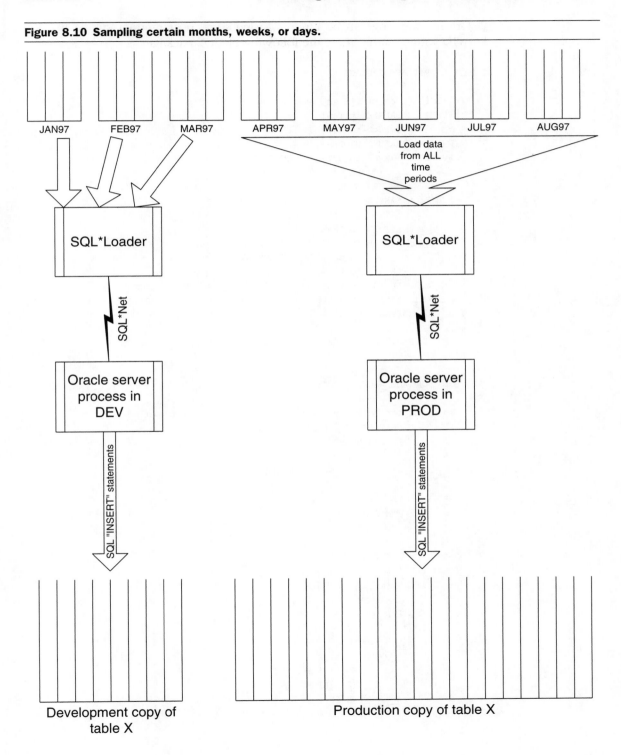

Or, the sampling can be random, using some near random criteria like the ROWID within a table. Take the following PL/SQL package:

```
CREATE OR REPLACE PACKAGE RANDOM
AS
     /* ~function SAMPLE is "overloaded" by datatype" */
     FUNCTION SAMPLE(in_rowid    IN ROWID,
                     in_pct      IN NUMBER)
            RETURN BOOLEAN;
     FUNCTION SAMPLE(in_date     IN DATE,
                     in_pct      IN NUMBER)
            RETURN BOOLEAN;
     FUNCTION SAMPLE(in_nbr      IN NUMBER,
                     in_pct      IN NUMBER)
            RETURN BOOLEAN;
     FUNCTION SAMPLE(in_str      IN VARCHAR,
                     in_pct      IN NUMBER)
            RETURN BOOLEAN;
     /* ~make PL/SQL "certify the purity" of the SAMPLE function at
  compile-time, to ensure that it can be used inside the WHERE clause
  of a SQL statement~
 */
     PRAGMA RESTRICT_REFERENCES (sample, RNDS, WNDS, RNPS, WNPS);
END RANDOM;
/
CREATE OR REPLACE PACKAGE BODY RANDOM
AS
     /* ~function to calculate the next higher prime number~ */
     FUNCTION NEXT_PRIME (in_nbr IN NUMBER)
              RETURN NUMBER
     IS
                          w      NUMBER;
                          i      NUMBER;
     BEGIN
          w := IN_NBR;
          IF w <= 2 THEN
               w := 3;
               RETURN w;
          END IF;
          IF MOD(w, 2) = 0 THEN
               w := w + 1;
          END IF;
          LOOP
               i := 3;
               LOOP
                    IF i * i > w THEN
                         RETURN w;
                    END IF;
                    IF MOD(w, i) = 0 THEN
                         EXIT;
                    END IF;
```

```
                    i := i + 2;
              END LOOP;
              w := w + 2;
      END LOOP;
END NEXT_PRIME;
--
/* ~sample using ROWIDs as criteria~ */
FUNCTION SAMPLE(in_rowid    IN ROWID,
               in_pct       IN NUMBER)
        RETURN BOOLEAN
IS
BEGIN
     RETURN sample(rowidtochar(in_rowid), in_pct);
END;
--
/* ~sample using DATE values as criteria~ */
FUNCTION SAMPLE(in_date     IN DATE,
               in_pct       IN NUMBER)
        RETURN BOOLEAN
IS
BEGIN
     RETURN sample(TO_CHAR(in_date, 'YYYYMMDDHH24MISS'), in_pct);
END;
--
/* ~sample using NUMBER values as criteria~ */
FUNCTION SAMPLE(in_nbr      IN NUMBER,
               in_pct       IN NUMBER)
        RETURN BOOLEAN
IS
BEGIN
     RETURN sample(TO_CHAR(in_nbr), in_pct);
END;
--
/* ~sample using character strings as criteria~ */
/* ~essentially, this function does a kind of "ckecksum" on the
   string, and decides whether the resulting value is a multiple
   of the IN_PCT value~
 */
FUNCTION SAMPLE(in_str      IN VARCHAR,
               in_pct       IN NUMBER)
        RETURN BOOLEAN
IS
               val          NUMBER := next_prime(in_pct);
BEGIN
     FOR i in 1..LENGTH(in_str) LOOP
         val := val + TO_NUMBER(CHR(SUBSTR(in_str, i, 1)));
     END LOOP;
     IF MOD(val, in_pct) = 0 THEN
         RETURN true;
     ELSE
         RETURN false;
```

```
                END IF;
          END;
          --
END RANDOM;
/
```

Now the packaged function RANDOM.SAMPLE can be used inside simple SQL statements to perform data sampling. For example,

```
SELECT *
  FROM table-X
 WHERE RANDOM.SAMPLE(rowid, 100) = TRUE;
```

Or:

```
SELECT *
  FROM table-Y
 WHERE RANDOM.SAMPLE(char-column, 75) = TRUE;
```

These SELECT statements can now be used as subqueries for pCTAS as described in Chapter 7. Be sure to test this first, to ensure the returned sample size is close to the requested size and that the returned sample is fairly random.

Backup and Recovery

There are already several terrific books on this subject:

- *Backup and Recovery Handbook* by Rama Velpuri, published by Oracle Press.
- Oracle7 *Server Administrator's Reference*, part of the standard Oracle documentation set, has several chapters devoted to backup and restore.
- Oracle8 *Server Backup and Recovery Guide*, part of the standard Oracle documentation set, is an entire book devoted to the subject in general and the new features of Oracle8 and Recovery Manager in particular.

Get your hands on at least one of these books and read it thoroughly. This book is not going to repeat what is covered so thoroughly in these standard references, especially the Oracle8 *Server Backup and Recovery Guide*.

While none of these three is explicitly devoted to data warehouses in particular, they still do an excellent job presenting the technical details related to backup and restore, and they also map to the business requirements behind each option.

THE DBA's RESPONSIBILITY FOR BACKUPS

Contrary to common opinion, a DBA does not have a responsibility to backup a database. The DBA's real responsibility is to be able to *recover* the database. In most cases that will require a program of regular backups and archive logging.

All in all, the *how* of backup and recovery is already very well covered, and this chapter will not delve far into the basic details of backup and recovery. We will skim briefly over the basics of backup and restore and then concentrate on the main issues: *what, when, how often,* and *why* to backup.

First, let's understand the basics of backup and restore in the Oracle environment. . . .

Backup and Restore Basics, or "What to Back Up?"

The most minimal backup strategy for Oracle databases involves the use of the Oracle EXP (export) utility. The use and capabilities of EXP are described in the Oracle *Server Utilities Guide,* part of the standard Oracle documentation set. Doing a *full database export* using EXP allows you to perform a complete restore of a database, but you may have to re-create the database from scratch, and you cannot recover to the point in time of the failure. A restore using the Oracle IMP (import) utility will only restore to the points in time while the export was running. It is quite possible that there will be referential integrity problems with the restored data unless either the EXP utility's CONSISTENT=Y option was used or access to the database is limited from users by RESTRICT mode. Last, the EXP and IMP utilities are each *single-threaded* processes writing to and reading from a single file. Because of this, they are both slow and constrained by file size limits. Relying on EXP and IMP as the sole components of a backup strategy is feasible only for smaller, unimportant databases. EXP and IMP should be considered only as a complementary part of backup strategy for a database with any kind of importance.

The next level in backup strategies involves "cold" backups with ARCHIVELOG mode disabled. Backup (both "hot" as well as "cold") are explained in more detail in the Oracle7 *Server Administrator's Reference* and the Oracle8 *Server Backup and Recovery Guide.* This means that the database instance is shut down successfully and all the files comprising the database are simply copied to backup media while it is down. The files that need to be copied are as follows:

- all datafiles (see V$DATAFILE), control files (see V$CONTROLFILE), and online redo logfiles (see V$LOGFILE)
- configuration files (i.e., all "*.ora" files, including those for SQL*Net) and password files (i.e., "orapwd.dat")

What does a "cold" backup in this manner buy you over full exports? First, there is no risk of referential integrity problems; since the database is shut down successfully while the backup is happening, the state of the database is completely consistent. Also, since a "cold" backup is done with operating system utilities, it is likely that many file copies can be done in parallel, making "cold" backups and restores quicker. Last, since each file in the database (just listed) is being copied separately, "cold" backups are not constrained by file size limits resulting from trying to pack the entire database into a single file.

However, beyond those substantial advantages, "cold" backups still require a complete restoration of the database, and recovery is only to the point in time of the backup, not to the point in time of the failure. Also, if there are any failures at all in the backup media (i.e., bad tape), the entire backup is useless and you will have to restore from a previous backup. This is true both for full database exports as well as "cold" backups. Last (but not least) a "cold" backup means that the database is unavailable, as does performing an export with the database in RESTRICT mode.

How do we get past these limitations?

Enabling ARCHIVELOG mode means that the Oracle database instance will now save all the information kept in the redo logs. To visualize why this is important, think of the redo logs as one of two databases kept by Oracle. The first database is, of course, the database itself. This database shows the current image of the data and is useful to humans. The second database is a different view of same data, and is the redo logs. The redo logs are also a database, but they do not have the same image of the data, the *current image* of all the data, that the regular database has. Rather, the database of the redo logs is a sequential record of every action against the database. If you are looking for a blow-by-blow account of what has changed in the database, the redo logs have that information readily available. If you are looking for the current state of all the data in the database at the current time, the database in the datafiles (and SGA database buffer pool) has that information.

Of course, nobody actually accesses that second database, the redo logs, directly. Rather, the Oracle instance uses that second database to provide recoverability for the datafiles.

The *online redo logfiles* provide the basic required level of recoverability, which is the ability to recover from *instance failure*. Should a running database instance fail for any reason, the online redo logfiles contain enough of the sequential history of changes to rebuild the database. This is known as *instance recovery*, and it happens automatically and transparently during the next startup after the database instance is shut down with SHUTDOWN ABORT or is terminated due to a system failure.

However, the online redo logfiles represent a circular buffer. There is a finite number of them, and when the last logfile is filled up the database *circles back* and overwrites the first logfile. When the database is not in ARCHIVELOG mode, this means that the historical data that was overwritten is now lost forever. When ARCHIVELOG mode is enabled, this overwrite will not be allowed to occur until the online redo logfile is *archived* or copied to an offline destination. In ARCHIVELOG mode, the combination of the archived redo logfiles and the online redo logfiles represents a solid, continuous history of all changes made to the database.

This means that if one or more datafiles are restored to points in time that are not consistent, the history of all changes in the redo logfiles can be used to bring all the datafiles to the same, consistent point in time. This mechanism is known as *roll-forward*.

Why doesn't everyone use ARCHIVELOG mode? There are some extra responsibilities that come with enabling ARCHIVELOG mode, namely, ensuring the safety of the archived redo logfiles. This is not a trivial task, as a busy Oracle database can generate several gigabytes of archived redo logfiles per day, requiring continuous backup to tape or other backup media. Additionally, tapes containing archived redo logfiles should be kept available for several weeks or months (depending on the frequency of backups), so the demands for proper tape handling and storage procedures can grow quite expensive for smaller IT departments.

However, adding ARCHIVELOG mode to a regimen of "cold" backups resolves most of the drawbacks associated with the other methods of backup. In addition to backing up all the files for a standard "cold" backup, you must now do the following:

- Provide a "staging" area for redo logfile archiving, specified with the initialization parameter ARCHIVE_LOG_DEST or archive logfile destination.
- Make sure that this staging area always has sufficient free space to archive newly filled redo logfiles.
- Ensure the safety of archived redo logfiles by copying them to backup media as soon as possible.

In return, you get the following advantages:

- Recovery to the point in time of failure or until a specified point in time between the time of backup and the failure
- The ability to perform a *partial restore* of an individual tablespace or datafile instead of having to restore the entire database
- Fault tolerance for backup media failures—if one tape from a backup set is bad, you only need to fall back to a previous backup set for just the bad tape rather than the entire backup set

For a production, mission-critical database application, these features address almost all availability concerns, except one: the downtime required to perform a "cold" backup. The remedy? Online or "hot" backups, which are performed while the database instance is "up," running, and fully available for all functions. The ability to perform "hot" backups is possible only when ARCHIVELOG mode is enabled, and it implies a little more administrative complexity for DBAs, as each tablespace must explicitly be placed into and out of BACKUP mode.

All in all, a complete backup/restore strategy for an Oracle database includes the use of ARCHIVELOG mode to enable "hot" (or "online") backups if desired, point-in-time recovery, incomplete recovery, and partial restores of specific datafiles and tablespaces as opposed to full restore of the complete database. Without ARCHIVELOG mode enabled, the only possible way to back up the database is "cold," or while the database instance is shutdown or "offline." The use of "cold" backups impacts uptime right away, as it implies regularly scheduled downtime or unavailability. Not enabling ARCHIVELOG mode also forces any database restore to be a complete restore of the entire database rather than restoring only those datafiles that were corrupted. Thus, for a database sized over one terabyte, corruption (due to media failure or some other reason) to a single datafile in a critical place—underneath the SYSTEM tablespace or underneath the primary *fact table* in the data warehouse—can be recovered by restoring the one lost file and then replaying the changes to that file from the archived and online log files.

A complete backup strategy for an Oracle database may also include the use of Oracle EXP (export utility) to save "snapshots" of specific tables or schemas for selective restore of those tables or schemas, if desired. The advantages of having exports to supplement backups include the following:

- Ability to restore individual tables or schemas within tablespaces; backups and restores have a minimum granularity of databases, tablespace, or datafiles
- Ability to restore indexes, constraints, and triggers related to individual tables or schemas
- Ability to restore PL/SQL packages and stored procedures related to individual schemas

While the ability to restore these objects is certainly included with a standard backup scenario, there are many advantages to being able to do it at the level of granularity made possible by the IMP utility. When an object is lost or damaged through a user (or administrator!) error, IMP can allow that single object to be restored to its condition at the time of the export.

When and How Often?

How frequently should backups occur?

The only correct answer is derived from the business's required mean–time–to–repair or MTTR. The basic formula is quite simple: the more frequent the backups, the quicker the recovery. This is due to the fact that the *roll-for-ward-then-rollback* phase of Oracle database recovery can be shortened by restoring from a more recent backup. If a month-old backup is used for restore, then the recovery process will have to roll forward through a month's worth of archived redo logfiles. Certainly, this takes longer to accomplish than restoring from a day-old backup and doing a roll-forward through only a day's worth of archive redo logfiles.

However, in a data warehouse environment, there are some additional considerations that impact this simple formula.

In a data warehouse, there might be a *load phase* during which data is refreshed completely or during which data is appended to existing data (see Figure 8.11). Quite often, this load phase is not continuous but rather happens at certain predefined times. Data changes to the data warehouse occur quite rapidly during a load phase, after which the data warehouse is used primarily in a *read-only* manner, during which queries are run, reports are generated, and analysis is performed. It makes sense to schedule backups to occur *after* such a load phase, upon completion of the loads, data cleansing, and aggregations.

Figure 8.11 Weekly load phases and backups.

This provides the additional benefit of immediately capturing data loaded or summarized with the UNRECOVERABLE or NOLOGGING options.

Since the numbers of changes and updates to the database are minimal following the backup, a restore followed by a media recovery roll-forward can proceed quite quickly for the simple reason that the number of archived redo logfiles is likely to be relatively small. If the backup were taken prior to the load phase, you might see that a roll-forward from that point would have to use over a hundred archived redo logfiles. On the other hand, imagine scheduling backups according to the timetable shown in Figure 8.12.

Although the simple formula of increasing frequency to reduce roll-forward still holds true, the cost-benefit ratio is not as clear. Having to roll forward through two archived redo logfiles as opposed to ten is not as dramatic a difference as rolling forward through ten archived redo logfiles instead of one hundred.

Figure 8.12 Daily backups with weekly load phases.

Backup Utilities

In general, there are five methods for performing backups:

- operating system
- third-party packages (i.e., Datatools' SQL*BackTrack)
- Enterprise Backup Utility (Oracle 7.3 only)
- Recovery Manager (Oracle 8.0 only)
- Export

Backups from the *operating system* are by far the most prevalent backup method in use. This involves using operating system utilities such as *cp*, *dd*, *tar*, or *cpio* on UNIX or *COPY* or *EXCHANGE* on VMS. For Windows NT, Oracle supplies *ocopy73.exe* or *ocopy80.exe*.

The basic method for such backups was to copy the datafiles, logfiles, and control files to tape using one or more of these operating system utilities. If database was in ARCHIVELOG mode, then *hot* backups would be possible if the file copy occurred while the tablespace involved was in BACKUP mode, using ALTER TABLESPACE . . . BEGIN/END BACKUP.

The third-party packages such as Datatools' SQL*BackTrack and Oracle7's own short-lived Enterprise Backup Utility (OEBU) essentially provide a more user-friendly layer to operating system backups. Additionally, they document backups and provide assistance during restores by recording backup details in a *recovery catalog*. EBU interfaces with underlying tape management software such as Hewlett-Packard's OmniBack.

All three methods described so far perform only *image backups*. Image backups are exact copies of the original physical datafiles, logfiles, and control files. Oracle8 Recovery Manager (RMAN) is capable of creating both image backups as well as incremental backups which copy only the blocks within the file that have been changed since the last backup. Although third-party utilities such as Datatools' SQL*BackTrack are also capable of performing incremental backups, Oracle Worldwide Support may not support a database that has been restored by a third-party product which has modified the contents or structure of the data files. RMAN is the only supported incremental backup/restore utility.

Recovery Manager can store the information from multiple datafiles (or archive logs, but not both) in a *backup set*. Backup sets are stored in a proprietary format that can't be processed directly. Backup sets are strictly for use by RMAN when database recovery is needed.

RMAN will perform either *cold* (offline) or *hot* (online) backups. It uses Oracle server processes known as backup I/O slaves instead of operating system utilities to perform the backups. If the backups will be written to tape, then RMAN will require that an approved *media manager*, such as Legato Systems' NetWorker product or IBM's ADSTAR Distributed Storage Management (ADSM), be linked to Oracle.

Incremental backups are extremely useful in data warehouse environments. This is due to the nature of load phases in data warehouses and the fact that the majority of data in the warehouse remains static between load phases. Thus, with incremental backups, it will be possible to take a full (incremental level 0)

Is Complete Recovery Even Necessary?

Even if the database is not in ARCHIVELOG mode, thus eliminating the possibility of recovering the database to the point in time of the failure, the use of incremental backups may facilitate more frequent backups, allowing complete restoration of the database to a point in time close to the failure. In a data warehouse environment, this might even be *good enough* under some circumstances. Data warehouses, because they are generally composed of data originating from other systems, may not jeopardize the organization's ability to run the business if they are not fully restored after a failure. This decision can only be made based upon the documented business requirements for the warehouse. Don't make this call unless all users are aware and in agreement.

backup immediately after the completion of a load phase and then take frequent higher-level incremental backups after that, to record only the changes since the level 0 backup. In a recovery situation, it is likely that any corrupted datafiles will be able to be restored to a point in time very close to the failure. As a result, the *roll-forward* recovery from the redo logfiles would complete very quickly, as relatively few transactions would need to be replayed.

Export (using the Oracle utility, EXP) provides a logical backup of the data. EXP has very little value in the backup strategy for the large objects typically found in a data warehouse. This utility was discussed in Chapter 6 and is fully documented in the Oracle7 and Oracle8 *Server Utilities* manuals.

Why? And Why Not? Rebuild versus Restore

Many people point out that a data warehouse is comprised of derived data and therefore does not need backup and restore to recover from failure. For databases sized in terabytes and mainly composed of data derived from other sources, performing regular backups to offset the seemingly remote possibility of media failure might seem unnecessary.

If you ask people how quickly a mission-critical order entry system should recover after a failure, the reply is likely to be instantaneous as well as nonnegotiable: "Recovery must be as brief as possible and it must be to the point in time of the failure." At least that would be the response from the technical people; the business unit being supported by the order entry system is likely to respond with: "What?! The system is down? Nobody told me the system is down! Find out when it's going to be back up! AND DON'T LOSE ANY ORDERS!"

When the same question is asked regarding a DSS, data mart, or data warehouse system, the response is much less predictable. All too often, a decision-support system is viewed as not being mission-critical, as in the statement, "Well, if the data warehouse goes down, the company doesn't grind to a halt." Or, "If my boss doesn't get those reports today, tomorrow will do." This perception, plus the scale of most data warehouses, leads project managers, system administrators, and DBAs to try to implement something less than a complete backup strategy.

The arguments against a complete backup strategy can be compelling:

- Availability requirements for decision-support systems are not as stringent as those for operational systems.
- Data can be reloaded and reaggregated as quickly as it can be restored.
- We invested in redundancy and fault-tolerance features (such as "mirroring" or RAID 5) to drastically reduce the probability of media failure.
- ARCHIVELOG mode is "overkill" for decision-support systems because they're read-only.
- Capacity and throughput of backup media is insufficient for regular backups.

In summary, this debate, which is generally discussed (at one point or another) during every large-scale data warehouse implementation, can be described as *Rebuild versus Restore*.

The arguments in favor of *rebuild* were just itemized. While they have some clear elements of truth, it is important to discuss the pros and cons of each thoroughly.

AVAILABILITY REQUIREMENTS FOR DECISION-SUPPORT SYSTEMS

Each of the following paragraphs is formatted as an individual reflection on this subject, intended to help stimulate points of view counter to the opinion that data warehouses are not mission-critical.

- Be sure to stay focused on the purpose of the decision-support systems. If they are perceived as not being mission-critical, then imagine what life would be like without them. Strategic reporting and analysis *are* mission-critical. Being able to accept orders does not guarantee business success if your products and services are not priced correctly.
- The stated mean-time-to-repair (MTTR) is sometimes based on a presumed favorable Mean-Time-Between-Failure (MTBF); should the MTBF worsen for any reason, the MTTR is likely to tighten significantly. For example, if the end-user community had agreed to an MTTR of 12 hours, it may not be bothered if the MTBF is six months. However, if the MTBF becomes three days, an MTTR of 12 hours will undergo reconsideration; count on it!
- Be sure to define precisely what constitutes downtime. Certain parties may consider downtime to mean that the machine is not powered on. Other parties may define downtime as the inability to log onto the machine due to operating system problems, database problems, or network problems. Yet other parties may define downtime as absolutely any condition that prevents *them* from getting *their* work done in a timely manner, such as any of the conditions listed earlier, and including performance degradation beyond 50 percent. In this last case, the line between performance and availability blurs, and who can argue with that?
- Generally, the end users of a data warehouse are senior management or their designees. Who else uses or needs strategic reporting? While it is true that the promptness of strategic reports will not cause a business to shut down, frequent unavailability of a data warehouse will erode confidence in

the data, cause reliance on alternative methods of obtaining the data, and essentially negate the purpose of the whole warehouse effort.

- Analyzing strategic data is difficult enough without performance problems making it more difficult. Unavailability is the ultimate performance problem; a downed system is racking up zero MIPS, and strategic analysis is not happening.

ASSERTION: RELOADING IS AS FAST AS RESTORING

Because the data loaded into a data warehouse generally originates on one or more other "sources of record," there is an accurate perception that the database in a data warehouse can sometimes be rebuilt and reloaded as quickly as it can be restored from a backup. *Rebuild-then-reload* may take the same amount of time or even more than *restore-from-backup*, but at least you did not expend time, resources, and effort performing the backups.

It is tough to argue against this approach, but it is important to remember the following points if you choose to go this route:

- Source data may not be available for reload after initial load. Make certain that the data used to load the data warehouse is not overwritten after use. Are those initial load files *really* still available?
- Rebuilding as a recovery strategy implies significant automation and testing of the rebuild procedures. This is not a trivial amount of development, and it is likely to require a lot of custom development as few (if any!) system management packages aid in automating the process of rebuilding tablespaces, tables, indexes, constraints, and triggers. This is not an activity to perform extemporaneously during a crisis!
- Only data that is completely refreshed is likely to be reloaded readily. Data that is accumulated over time may be difficult to restore in this manner, especially if it wasn't saved.
- Data that requires some form of postprocessing (i.e., cleansing and/or aggregation) may be postprocessed differently if the reference data or supporting data has been changed over time. For example, if data is aggregated using demographic or psychographic reference data that is refreshed on a monthly basis, chances are good that this reference data has changed over time. Aggregating 24 months' of data against the current month's demographic data will not produce the same data that had been aggregated over the past 24 months, each against its own current demographic data. In brief, be ready to accommodate data dependencies for time-series data. This is a data warehouse design issue, not something that the DBA should be dealing with at three o'clock in the morning during a recovery. The prospect of storing reference data over time to facilitate reloads is not something that would necessarily occur to a data warehouse designer who hasn't been faced with a recovery situation.

ASSERTION: INVESTMENT IN FAULT TOLERANCE ELIMINATES THE NEED FOR BACKUPS

Some people actually believe that an investment in fault-tolerant components (such as mirrored disk drives) actually eliminates the need for database recovery. In reality, corruption due to human mishap or some kind of software failure can occur just as easily as media failure. Fault-tolerant system components only mitigate one kind of risk—failure by one of the components that has been duplicated. And who is to say that simple disk mirroring cannot be defeated by bad luck? Who is going to guarantee that a raw partition won't be accidentally re-allocated and destroyed? Who is to say that both a volume as well as its mirror cannot fail at the same time? Yes, it's unlikely, but . . .

ASSERTION: ARCHIVELOG IS OVERKILL

This sentiment is closely related to "reloading is as fast as restoring"; if we don't want to back up derived data, we also do not want to save archived redo logfiles that are just full of this same data as it's being loaded into the data warehouse.

Once again, this is absolutely true. For reasons like this, Oracle has, since release 7.1, 7.2, and 7.3, successively implemented several UNRECOVERABLE (known as NOLOGGING in Oracle8) operations that minimize the generation of redo almost to the point of elimination. Loading using direct path SQL*Loader, CREATE TABLE . . . AS SELECT, and CREATE INDEX are all operations that can be run in UNRECOVERABLE mode, which generates virtually no redo and no rollback information. As a result, you can perform most of the data loads as well as much of the postprocessing without generating any redo logging to be archived and backed up.

Feature	Introduced in release
SQL*Loader direct path UNRECOVERABLE	7.1
CREATE TABLE . . . AS SELECT UNRECOVERABLE	7.2
CREATE INDEX UNRECOVERABLE	7.2
INSERT INTO . . . SELECT NOLOGGING	8.0

If this is the case, then what is the benefit of ARCHIVELOG mode?

It is this. There must be hundreds of other actions that take place in the data warehouse that have nothing to do with loading data. End users create "scratch" tables for holding their intermediate results from hours of work. Administrators create objects for testing. Our audit trail records user resource consumption, possibly for internal billing. Wouldn't it be inconvenient for them to be wiped out by re-creating the database? Wouldn't it just be easier to back them up and restore them if the need arises?

The problem with the rebuild-then-reload strategy is that it demands that every step of the recovery process be documented, understood, and performed during a recovery. Frankly, it may not be possible to do this. While it may be cost-effective to do this in a few areas, it can't possibly be cost-effective to do for everything. Why not let the database remember all these actions and perform them during a restore? Life is too short to custom develop a duplication of one of Oracle's major features.

ASSERTION: IT IS TOO BIG TO BACKUP!

It is not unusual to hear people say "That database is just too big to backup and restore." No matter how big a database gets, you really have to be able to move the whole thing to back up media and restore it in a reasonable amount of time. If you can't do that with your existing backup resources, invest in more hardware. If it is too big to be backed up, then the reload tasks are going to be even more overwhelming. Hot backups, incremental backups, and READ ONLY tablespaces can make the backup load more manageable.

If it seems too expensive to invest in more tape drives and in better backup media, then quite frankly you are out of your depth. You have no business creating a database that size. Hate to be so blunt, but there it is. . . .

Summary of the Rebuild versus Restore Debate

Both strategies have their place. Because of all the flexibility and availability benefits it provides, the basic strategy should be a complete backup strategy as described previously. If circumstances warrant it, use READ ONLY tablespaces to reduce the amount of data that must be backed up. Use ARCHIVELOG mode, but also use UNRECOVERABLE options to reduce the volume of redo logging if the data can be backed up immediately afterward.

In circumstances where data is refreshed completely and not postprocessed, consider using the rebuild-then-reload approach.

The two approaches are not mutually exclusive. But the rebuild approach should only selectively complement a backup strategy that protects key database structures using ARCHIVELOG mode.

Enabling and Optimizing Auditing

Auditing has a lot of benefits for a data warehouse environment. It can be used for its most obvious purpose: enhancing security by tracking what, when, and where people query or manipulate specific tables. But it also has usefulness in providing some other important functionality in a decision-support environment:

- information for usage chargeback
- information for determining proper RESOURCE PROFILES for various types of users
- failed connect or abnormal disconnect analysis
- usage analysis of all or certain tables

A data warehouse environment is actually well suited for an option like Oracle database auditing even though it carries a relatively high cost in terms of overhead. For each operation being audited, Oracle can either log an audit record to a database table (i.e., SYS.AUD$) or to an operating system file. If session connections and disconnections are being audited, this is usually a very light price to pay since connections and disconnections are relatively infrequent. However, if SELECT statements against all objects are being audited, then it is possible that the impact of auditing might be noticeable, as each SELECT statement would generate an INSERT into the audit trail.

Enabling AUDIT SESSION, which audits session connections and disconnections, is a relatively low-cost but high-value form of auditing in a data warehouse environment. Among other things, AUDIT SESSION records the following:

- operating system user name
- Oracle user name
- the machine or host the user had logged in from
- the terminal the user had logged in from
- the time of connection
- the time and manner of disconnection
- the number of logical reads, physical reads, and logical writes accumulated during the session

The duration of the connection or the I/O statistics could be useful in calculating accurate chargeback values. They could also be used for setting up valid and useful RESOURCE PROFILES for limiting resource consumption. The manner in which sessions were disconnected could be used to locate users who are having difficulties in a client-server environment, who think that CTRL-ALT-DEL is a valid way to log out of the data warehouse, for example.

Refer to the Oracle *Server Concepts* manual and the Oracle *Server SQL Language Reference* for more information on the breadth and depth of auditing.

If you choose to keep the audit trail in the database (a good choice, as it allows easy query of the audit information), there is one important thing to do. The audit trail in the database is a table named AUD$ owned by the Oracle account named SYS. By default, the table SYS.AUD$ is created in the SYSTEM tablespace. Depending on the amount of auditing activity, it is probably advisable to move this table out of the SYSTEM tablespace in case it grows large enough to "crowd" the data dictionary tables, indexes, and clusters in that tablespace. It is a common task, and simple enough, as Figure 8.13 illustrates.

```
CONNECT SYS/sys_password
CREATE TABLESPACE AUDIT_DATA DATAFILE 'file-specification';
CREATE TABLE new_aud$
       TABLESPACE AUD
       STORAGE (appropriate storage parameters)
    AS SELECT *
         FROM aud$;
RENAME aud$ TO old_aud$;
RENAME new_aud$ TO aud$;
<test by connecting to database and then verify the entry in the new table>
DROP TABLE old_aud$;
```

Sizing of the new audit trail table will be governed by how frequently you will report, summarize, and then delete from the table. If you are using audit extensively, such as monitoring each select against many tables, you should specify multiple freelists when constructing the NEW_AUD$ table.

As a starting point, plan to summarize usage each week or month into a series of permanent administrative tables. Depending on what you've elected to audit you may want to summarize activity by user, by day, by warehouse table, by time of day, and so on. After the summary is saved the detailed audit data may be deleted. You will want to support both the usage analysis and charge-

Figure 8.13 Moving SYS.AUD$ out of the SYSTEM tablespace.

back functions described earlier in this chapter. You will also want to use the historical record to monitor processing trends over time.

Two important reminders:

Be very careful while connected to the Oracle SYS account. This is the equivalent of UNIX root and accidents can cause irreparable harm to the database.

Also, be sure to monitor the growth of the AUD$ table and schedule regular purges. If you enable auditing and then forget about it, eventually AUD$ will consume all the available space (or number of extents) and all (audited) database activity will come to a halt.

Configuration Rules of Thumb

SYSTEM Tablespace

Data warehouse systems generally do not involve the creation of a great number of objects in the database. The data dictionary (i.e., objects belonging to SYS) of a basic installation of Oracle7.3 typically consumes about 20 to 30 MB initially; for Oracle8, this expands to 40 to 50 MB. The number of tables, columns, indexes, views, stored procedures, and packages created in the database will impact space consumption in the SYSTEM tablespace.

Large-scale packaged applications (such as Oracle Financial and Manufacturing applications) tend to create thousands of tables, indexes, synonyms, and stored procedures and packages. It is not uncommon for such databases to require 0.5 gigabytes or 1 gigabyte for the data dictionary alone. Data warehouses, by contrast, typically feature more simplistic, consolidated, denormalized data models. As a result, the number of tables, indexes, views, and stored procedures and packages tends to be relatively small.

A good starting point for a data warehouse is 100 MB for the SYSTEM tablespace. Even if the dictionary only ends up needing 60 MB, the "wasted" space is a very small percentage of the total warehouse usage. It is better to spend time on more profitable pursuits than trying to accurately estimate the SYSTEM tablespace needs in advance.

TEMP Tablespace

Set the tablespace status of this tablespace from PERMANENT (the default) to TEMPORARY. This will permit only TEMPORARY segments to be created there. It will also no longer deallocate segment extents when the segment is dropped, leaving them instead in the tablespace for reuse. This will lower contention for space management activities when there are many sorting operations going to disk, which is a common situation in data warehouse environments.

Since temporary space allocations are done implicitly by Oracle, there is no opportunity to explicitly set storage parameters. Storage parameters for temporary extents will be taken from the DEFAULT STORAGE clause specified in the CREATE TABLESPACE or ALTER TABLESPACE commands. PCTINCREASE should always be set to 0. Both INITIAL and NEXT should be set to the following:

```
1 database-block + (factor * SORT_AREA_SIZE)
```

where *factor* is a value between two and twenty (usually two, three, or four are used). Setting extents according to this formula minimizes the number of times a temporary segment used for sorting will have to allocate additional extents. This will also relieve contention on space management activities in the database.

Think about it. When Oracle starts a sorting operation, it uses private process memory, attempting first to complete the sort in memory. The amount of memory used is restricted to a maximum indicated by the "init.ora" parameter SORT_AREA_SIZE. When a sort has to move from memory onto disk, it will require a chunk of space at least the size of SORT_AREA_SIZE. Setting the factor value to two or more simply leaves room for more growth before further extent allocations become necessary. The one extra block in the formula above allows for the segment header.

The total size of the TEMP tablespace should depend on the number of concurrently executing operations. If a single nonparallel query can consume 100 MB of sort space, then fifty simultaneously executing queries could consume 5 gigabytes or more.

Be aware that the use of Parallel Query Option or Parallel DML can greatly exaggerate the number of users from a sort space standpoint. If the single non-parallel query consumes 100 MB, then it is conceivable that the same query using a parallel degree of eight could possibly consume 800 MB, although presumably for a shorter period of time. Multiple that value by fifty simultaneously executing queries, and you are now talking about needing 40 gigabytes for the TEMP tablespace. If you are using the parallel query feature extensively, you will probably want to use a smaller value for SORT_AREA_SIZE than if all queries are being run serially.

Of course, these sizes are very dependent on the sizes of the tables, the "raw" data to be sorted. It's unlikely that any query would require 100 MB of sort space if the largest table in the database is only 40 MB. However, since many data warehouses contain tables sized at hundreds of gigabytes, it is conceivable that some queries may require that much space for sorting. As a rule of thumb, use the following equation to set initial expectations for sizing the TEMP tablespace:

```
min((total-data-in-db * 0.5), (largest-table-size * 2))
```

If you have about 100 gigabytes of "raw" data in tables in your data warehouse and the largest table is 15 gigabytes, then sizing the TEMP tablespace at around 30 gigabytes is reasonable. If the largest table is 30 gigabytes, then sizing TEMP at 50 gigabytes would be reasonable. If the largest table is 55 gigabytes, then sizing TEMP to 50 gigabytes might still be reasonable because the best approach at this point would be to either partition this table or prevent most sorting operations during a full table scan. In other words, there is a limit to the amount of sorting you want to support. Beyond that, you should tune or limit the application.

Rollback Segments and the RBS Tablespace

Oracle gives some good rules of thumb for rollback segments. Use the following formula

```
4 <= #-of-rollback-segments <= 50
```

where the number of rollback segments is determined by dividing the number of concurrently active DML transactions by four. It would be surprising if a data warehouse application ever needed more than ten rollback segments using this formula. Don't forget to ignore UNRECOVERABLE or "direct path" operations as they do not generate rollback entries.

Since rollback entries for transactions occupy entire extents in the rollback segments, it is a good idea to preallocate plenty of extents for each rollback segment. For relatively "quiet" systems such as data warehouses, using MINEXTENTS 20 should be sufficient unless very large batch processes are going to be executed without the UNRECOVERABLE or NOLOGGING feature. For relatively busy OLTP-type systems, MINEXTENTS 40 should work.

The OPTIMAL parameter should be set to match MINEXTENTS. If MINEXTENTS implies 20 MB of space, then OPTIMAL should be set to 20 MB.

All that is left is to determine the extent sizes. Again, using basic rules of thumb, a starting value of 1 MB seems reasonable for data warehouse systems. For most OLTP-type systems, a starting value of 128 KB or 256 KB is reasonable.

When sizing the RBS tablespace, use the values determined earlier in the following formula:

```
((#-of-rollback-segments + 8) * MINEXTENTS * extent-size)
```

This would allow one of the rollback segments to grow to eight times its original size to handle long-running transactions. When possible, treat all the rollback segments the same. Define an appropriate value of OPTIMAL so that they can grow and shrink as needed. Then give them room to grow. If individual rollback segments are having to grow and shrink frequently and dramatically then consider creating one or more very large rollback segments. This will avoid the additional allocation and deallocation overhead and also prevent the occasional "unable to extend rollback segment" error if one needs to grow very large but another has not yet shrunk.

DB_BLOCK_SIZE

For data warehouses, use 8 KB database blocks as an absolute minimum; 16 KB is common for data warehouses and is now accepted as the standard recommendation. Larger block sizes are only supported by a few operating systems at this time (i.e., DEC UNIX), and the Oracle Very Large Memory (VLM) option is usually required to support database blocks this size in Oracle7.

If you believe block contention (see "Monitoring Latch Contention and Locking," later in this chapter) is occurring, then increase INITRANS and FREELISTS to reduce contention. INITRANS controls how many simultaneous transactions can be active in a fully loaded data or index block. Multiple freelists avoid contention when doing simultaneous INSERTs to a table. The FREELISTS parameter

Named Rollback Segments Are Not *Dedicated* to the Transaction

While it is possible to dedicate a transaction to a particular named rollback segment using SET TRANSACTION, there is no way to keep other transactions from using that "special" rollback segment. Oracle attempts to balance the number of transactions active in every rollback segment (other than the SYSTEM rollback segment) regardless of their relative sizes. Thus, having one or more "big" rollback segments for long-running transactions does not guarantee that the rollback segment in question won't already be in use when the long-running transaction is assigned to it. Multiple transactions can share a rollback segment, so it is possible that even the special large rollback segment may need to grow.

can only be set at the time of table creation. If you are using Parallel Server and you expect to insert to the table through multiple instances, also set FREELIST GROUPS to at least the number of instances.

As a last resort, you can selectively simulate a smaller DB_BLOCK_SIZE for certain tables or indexes by setting PCTFREE high on certain heavily contended segments and/or partitions. This will essentially lower the amount of data per database block, simulating a smaller DB_BLOCK_SIZE. For example, to simulate PCTFREE 10 on 4 KB database blocks when DB_BLOCK_SIZE is 8 KB, set PCT-FREE to 55. To simulate PCTFREE 0 on 2 KB database blocks when DB_BLOCK_SIZE is 16 KB, set PCTFREE to 80. It should be noted that this trick is very infrequently needed in a data warehouse because it is extremely rare to ever have multiple transactions simultaneously modifying a table.

Setting "init.ora" Initialization Parameters

Use the values for the LARGE profile supplied with the sample "init.ora" file provided as part of the Oracle install to start. Don't modify the values provided in this default file unless you have a good empirically proven reason to do so. See the section on monitoring rules of thumb later in this chapter for some empirically proven reasons.

When you change a parameter, comment out the old value and leave comments with your initials and the date next to the new values. A brief explanation on the reason for the change is helpful, too. This allows you a backout route should the change prove harmful. Also, when attempting to tune performance it is helpful to only change one parameter at a time so that its effects can be measured. Of course, there are some parameters that work together and need to be changed together, but don't attempt to change a dozen parameters and then determine why an unexpected effect materialized.

Redo Logfiles

Use at least three redo log groups per instance, with the files of each group of at least 100 MB for a start. Each redo group should be multiplexed, mirrored, or both. If you need to resize the logs later, you can add new log file groups with files of the proper size using ALTER DATABASE ADD LOGFILE. Then switch logging to one of the newly added groups using ALTER SYSTEM SWITCH LOGFILE. Finally, you can drop the old, smaller logs with ALTER DATABASE DROP LOGFILE.

Monitoring Rules of Thumb

In this section we cover guidelines for monitoring the following:

- the "worst" SQL statements
- the top consumers in the operating system
- AUDIT session statistics
- rollback segment contention
- latch contention and locking

- the number of extents
- free space
- tablespace fragmentation
- invalid compiled objects

Monitoring the "Worst" SQL Statements

Use the following query (borrowed from Oracle Consulting's System Performance Group APS toolkit) to determine the "worst" SQL statements being executed on your system:

```
SELECT hash_value "SQL Stmt ID",
       disk_reads "Physical Reads",
       buffer_gets "Logical Reads",
       sorts "Sorts"
       users_executing "Runs",
       loads "Cache Loads",
       (((disk_reads*100)+buffer_gets)/1000)/users_executing "Load"
  FROM v$sqlarea
 WHERE disk_reads > 100000
    OR buffer_gets > 1000000
 ORDER BY (((disk_reads*100)+buffer_gets)/1000)/users_executing DESC;
```

This will identify the worst SQL statements, in descending order of horror. The query will only consider those SQL statements that exceed a threshold. In this example, that threshold is either 1 million logical reads against the buffer cache or one hundred thousand physical reads on disk.

The sorting emphasizes the physical reads, multiplying by a weighting factor of 100. To this number is added the number of logical reads, after which the total is divided by one thousand to make it a more manageable number. Finally, to emphasize those statements that cost the most every time they are run, this total figure is divided by the number of executions. The result is a number that means little by itself but is useful for ranking the cost of various SQL statements.

Data in V$SQLAREA reflects the contents of the shared SQL area, cumulatively since database startup. Naturally, the shared pool is fixed in size, so seldom-used SQL statements do get cycled out, but they are of no concern to us. It is the statements that persist in the shared pool for long periods of time that are of interest.

Once the bad statements are identified, a DBA should strive to understand how it is being used. First, it is useful to know who is using it. The following query may help identify who is executing the statement, if it is currently in use:

```
SELECT username,
       osuser,
       machine,
       terminal,
       process,
       program,
```

```
      sid,
      serial#
 FROM v$session
WHERE sql_hash_value = <SQL-stmt-ID-from-previous-query>;
```

The column USERNAME is the Oracle account name, the column OSUSER should show the operating system account name of the client executing the statement. The column MACHINE should show the IP host name of the machine from which the client is executing the statement. In the event these first three columns do not positively identify the end user executing the SQL statement, the remaining column values might be helpful.

Once the end user executing the SQL statement is identified, then more can be learned about the reasons why the SQL statement is running, and why it is running as it is.

The tuning of SQL statements will be discussed in greater detail in Chapter 9, but for now simply identifying these resource hogs will have the greatest impact on system performance. You can buy the biggest computer in the world, you can tune all of its subsystems until they scream, but if the application is simply doing too much work, it will still appear sluggish.

There are many ways to tune a SQL statement, and optimizing its execution plan is only one. Sometimes, the SQL statement is simply unnecessary and should not be executing at all. This would be the case if a query was being executed against too low a level of detail, when the same information could be obtained faster from a higher level of summarization or aggregation. Perhaps the higher level of aggregation does not yet exist, but it should.

Perhaps the SQL statement is joining too many tables, indicating a problem with the data model or with the end user's understanding of the data model. Perhaps it would be useful to create a denormalized version of a certain set of tables by *prejoining* these tables as a final step in the data warehouse's load phase.

It should be the job of the DBA to identify these questions and help drive them through to resolution. It does not make sense to tune the database and tune an operating system to handle more load than is necessary. Saying this in a slightly different way, it doesn't make sense to tune unnecessary work—eliminate it! Identification is the first step.

Identifying the worst three or five SQL statements and fixing them will have absolutely the most impact on overall system performance. Doing this iteratively, every week or several times per month, will virtually ensure that any Oracle system performs to the utmost of its capabilities. If anybody complains that an Oracle database is sluggish or performing poorly, this is the first place to look for the culprits.

Monitoring the Top Consumers in the Operating System

Most operating systems have a "top ten" utility, which will display information about the top ten resource (usually CPU) consumers on the system. Such utilities are available for Sun Solaris, HP-UX, and Windows NT.

If you are on a UNIX system and such a utility is not available, you can use the following:

```
$ ps -eaf | sort -n +3 | tail
```

This uses the UNIX *ps* utility (i.e., *process status*) to display information about all processes on the system. This output is piped to the UNIX *sort* utility, which sorts numerically on the fourth column of the *ps* output. Finally, this output is piped to the UNIX *tail* utility, which displays only the last ten lines of output. Thus, the last line should be the most active CPU consumer on the system.

The operating system process ID or PID (i.e., the second column in the output of the command just shown) is represented in Oracle in the V$PROCESS dynamic performance view if the name of the process is *oracle<ORACLE_SID>*. For example, if the name of the process starts with the string "oraclePROD," where the ORACLE_SID is "PROD," then this is an Oracle server process. In the V$PROCESS view, the operating system PID is stored in the column SPID. On Windows NT, it is stored in hexadecimal format, which is a shame because the NT Task Manager utility displays the PID as decimal. On UNIX, the representation of the PID both in V$PROCESS as well as in UNIX is decimal.

Once an Oracle server process is identified as a resource "hog" in this fashion, it would be worthwhile to determine what the process is doing. This can be done by joining from V$PROCESS to the V$SESSION, V$SQLAREA, V$SESSTAT, and V$SESSION_WAIT views as follows:

```
SELECT username, osuser, machine, process, terminal, program,
       sql_hash_value, sql_address, sid, serial#
  FROM v$session
 WHERE paddr IN
       (SELECT addr
          FROM v$process
         WHERE spid = 'O/S PID');
```

This information may help identify who the user of the Oracle server process is, and (perhaps) what they are doing. For more definitive information on what they are doing, use the following:

```
SELECT sql_text, disk_reads, buffer_gets, sorts, loads, users_executing
  FROM v$sqlarea
 WHERE hash_value = <sql_hash_value-from-the-previous-query>
   AND address = <sql_address-from-the-previous-query>;
```

From this query, you will know exactly what SQL statement the user is executing at the moment. Additionally, you will see cumulative statistics (since database instance startup) on disk reads, logical reads, sorts, SQL cursor cache loads, and the number of times the SQL statement has been used.

But it would be interesting to know exactly what the SQL statement is waiting on. For this information, use the following query:

```
COLUMN p1 FORMAT A15
COLUMN p2 FORMAT A15
COLUMN p3 FORMAT A15
SELECT event,
       p1text || ' ' || p1 p1,
       p2text || ' ' || p2 p2,
       p3text || ' ' || p3 p3
  FROM v$session_wait
 WHERE sid = <SID-from-the-first-query>;
```

Each event indicates whether the session is waiting on network access, physical I/O, a latch or a lock, or some other kind of contention. See the table in Chapter 9 for a list of the most common events and a brief explanation of what they mean.

Last, it might be useful to know something about the kinds of run-time statistics that the session has been racking up. The following query can help:

```
SELECT n.name, s.value
  FROM v$sesstat s, v$statname n
 WHERE s.statistic# = n.statistic#
   AND s.value > 0
   AND s.sid = <SID-from-the-first-query>;
```

Monitoring the AUDIT Session Statistics

Another way to find users who are using an inordinate amount of system resources is to periodically query the audit records produced by AUDIT SESSION. To find the worst offenders, use the following query:

```
COLUMN os_username      FORMAT A10
COLUMN username         FORMAT A10
COLUMN userhost         FORMAT A10
COLUMN terminal         FORMAT A10
SELECT os_username, username, userhost, terminal,
       avg(logoff_lread + logoff_lwrite) l_io,
       avg(logoff_pread) p_io
  FROM dba_audit_session
 WHERE logoff_lread > 1000000 or logoff_pread > 100000
 GROUP BY os_username, username, userhost, terminal;
```

If this query identifies any particular person or group of people, it would be wise for the DBA to become familiar with what they are doing to offer assistance in tuning the SQL statements they are running. It may be that these are the power users who are legitimately exercising the warehouse. Or (more likely), they are submitting poorly tuned SQL statements. A third possibility is that they are doing legitimate work against detail tables that you, as the administrator, can make easier by creating additional indexes or summarizations.

Monitoring Rollback Segment Contention

The view V$ROLLSTAT contains run-time statistics on rollback segments since database startup. High values for the column WAITS indicate that transactions are being forced to wait for an available slot in that rollback segment. This is not an issue with end users' queries but with transactions that are updating the warehouse. If this is happening for all the segments, then consider adding more rollback segments or rescheduling some of the workload.

```
SELECT n.name,
       s.writes,
       s.waits
  FROM v$rollstat    s,
       v$rollname    n
 WHERE s.usn = n.usn;
```

What is a *high value?* There is no ready formula, but bear in mind the number of hours that the database instance has been running. Also keep in mind that your system probably has *off hours* as well as *peak hours*, so simply dividing these figures by the number of hours is bound to water down the rate during peak hours. Try to sample the table several times during peak periods of DML activity, and use the difference between the first sampling and the last sampling to calculate the current hourly rate.

Another good approach is to simply use the Oracle-provided SQL scripts *utlbstat.sql* and *utlestat.sql*, which reside in the directory *$ORACLE_HOME/rdbms /admin*. Commonly called BSTAT/ESTAT, these scripts sample the majority of the V$ performance tables for a particular time period. To use them, connect as SYS and run *utlbstat.sql* at the start of the sample period. Then, at the end of the sample period, connect again as SYS and run *utlestat.sql*. Each script takes a "snapshot" of many of the critical V$ performance views at the time they are run. The *utlestat.sql* script then takes an ending snapshot of the same views and calculates the differences between the beginning and ending snapshot values. It then produces a report and spools it to the current working directory as a file named *report.txt*. The rollback segment statistics are easy to find in *report.txt*.

If the hourly rate of WAITS is into double digits at peak hours, then certainly there is a need to add more rollback segments. If the hourly rate is nonzero but in the single digits, then the choice is less clear. Certainly, if there is room readily available, add more rollback segments. If space is tight, then consider the risk incurred by cramming more rollback segments into the RBS tablespace and possibly not leaving enough space for each of the rollback segments to extend, causing long-running transactions to fail for lack of space.

Another place to look for rollback contention is the V$SYSSTAT view, using the following query:

```
SELECT class, count, time
  FROM v$waitstat
 WHERE class LIKE 'undo%';
```

Again, bear in mind that the statistics in this table are cumulative since database instance startup. Raw numbers are meaningless; only differences are useful. Use that knowledge to come up with an hourly rate, especially during peak hours. Lots of waits on *undo header* (i.e., segment header for rollback segments) indicates the need for more rollback segments. Many *undo block* waits (i.e., blocks within rollback segments) can be solved by adding additional rollback segments or additional extents to the current rollback segments.

Monitoring Latch Contention and Locking

Yogi Berra once said, "You can observe a lot by watching." This is certainly true for Oracle databases, particularly if you know what you are looking for. The following query might be helpful for detecting various kinds of contention in your database:

```
COLUMN latch FORMAT A35
COLUMN p1 FORMAT A15
COLUMN p3 FORMAT A15
SELECT w.sid,
       n.name latch,
       w.p1text || ' ' || w.p1 p1,
       w.p3text || ' ' || w.p3 p3
  FROM v$session_wait w, v$latchname n
 WHERE w.event = 'latch free'
   AND n.latch# = w.p2;
```

An *enqueue* latch means that there is a lock on an object. The V$LOCK view would have more information for the session identified by the value of SID.

The *cache buffers chains* latch is used by server processes to serialize updates to a specific block in the buffer cache. Several blocks in the buffer can get hashed to the same latch. Many waits on this latch typically indicate block contention. Verify this finding by querying V$WAITSTAT where CLASS = 'data block.' If block contention appears to be occurring, use V$SESSION and V$SQLAREA to try to determine which table or index the contention is occurring on. If the SQL statement is an UPDATE or DELETE, increase INITRANS. If the SQL statement is an INSERT, increase FREELISTS (which requires rebuilding the table). In either case, if increasing INITRANS or FREELISTS doesn't help, consider lowering the number of rows in the database blocks for this segment by re-creating the segment with increased PCTFREE.

The *cache buffer lru chains* latch is used for moving buffers around in the SGA buffer cache. Excessive contention on this latch may indicate either a buffer cache that is much too small or a buffer cache that is much too large. In the former case, an extremely small buffer cache is being updated rapidly because blocks are aging out of the buffer cache too quickly. In the latter case, the buffer cache is so large that manipulations of the LRU (least recently used) chain takes an excessive amount of time. In either case, excessive waiting on this latch may indicate that DB_BLOCK_BUFFERS should be increased or decreased, respectively. As in all cases, DB_LRU_STATISTICS or DB_LRU_EXTENDED_STATISTICS should be used to determine the proper size for DB_BLOCK_BUFFERS; see the Oracle7 or Oracle8 *Server Tuning Guide* for more information. In an Oracle8 warehouse it is possible to manually tune the buffer cache for different types and sizes of tables by subdividing the buffer pool, as described in Chapter 3.

The *redo allocation* latch is used to allocate the redo buffers in the redo log buffer. It is also used during *checkpoints* to advance the System Commit Number (SCN). If anything, excessive waiting on this latch may indicate that database instance is checkpointing too frequently. This may be due to the redo logfiles being too small or LOG_CHECKPOINT_INTERVAL or LOG_CHECKPOINT _TIMEOUT is set too low.

The *redo copy* latch is used when the size of a redo entry is greater than the value of the configuration parameter LOG_SMALL_ENTRY_MAX_SIZE; the solution might be to raise this value. The number of *redo copy* latches is set by the configuration parameter LOG_SIMULTANEOUS_COPIES, and the LGWR process will grab all these latches before writing from the log buffers to the redo logfiles. Thus, excessive waiting on this latch might also mean that LGWR is writing too often, which might mean that the application is committing too often, or it might mean that the LOG_BUFFER value is too low.

The *row cache objects* latch guards the data dictionary cache in the shared pool. When loading, referencing, or freeing any data dictionary objects in the shared pool, this latch must be obtained by the Oracle server process. If this latch is being waited on and there is a lot of *recursive SQL* being generated by SQL statements, then the SHARED_POOL configuration parameter should be raised. If there is excessive waiting on this latch and there is not much recursive SQL being generated by SQL statements, then it simply means that the data dictionary is effectively cached in the shared pool already and is simply being referenced often. There is nothing to be done in this case.

There are at least seventy other latches used by Oracle. Contact Oracle Worldwide Support for help if you believe you are having problems with them.

Monitoring the Number of Extents

Although the MAXEXTENTS UNLIMITED clause became available in Oracle7.3, it is a mistake to use it. Always set a finite value for the number of extents, even if that value is 1000. To explain, imagine receiving this particular wish: a table or index with hundreds of thousands of extents. In such a situation, it is virtually guaranteed that each extent is tiny because hundreds of thousands of any sizable extent size would probably be obscenely large. Simply put, tens of thousands of extents, hundreds of thousands of extents, or millions of extents puts an unnecessary burden on Oracle space management. There is no need for the data dictionary tables to grow this large. MAXEXTENTS UNLIMITED combined with inappropriate values of INITIAL, NEXT, PCTFREE or PCTUSED can lead to this situation. Once the data dictionary tables (specifically SYS.UET$, the used extent table, and SYS.FET$, the free extent table) grow unnecessarily large, they will remain so for as long as the database exists.

Performance Impact of Many Extents

There has been unnecessary concern for years about the performance impact of working with tables with many extents. Random reads are not affected at all. Sequential reads (during full table scans) are only impacted when the extent size is very small. As long as Oracle can obtain DB_FILE_MULTIBLOCK_READ_COUNT contiguous blocks in a single I/O request the read will operate at full efficiency. Only when it receives a smaller number of blocks (at the end of an extent) will it be impacted. The worst case would be when each extent is one block larger than the value of DB_FILE_MULTIBLOCK_READ_COUNT. In this situation, every other sequential read would receive only a single block. If the extent size is any exact multiple of this parameter's value then there is no adverse effect at all. If it is anything greater than four or five times this value then the performance impact will be minimal.

Also, be aware that all space management transactions are single-threaded through the ST (space transaction) latch. Only one space management transaction can occur at any given moment in Oracle. Thus, if one or all space management operations begins to consume more time (by having to work with an unnecessarily large FET$ table, for instance), this means that the single-threading on the ST latch will become very noticeable.

Plan on setting MAXEXTENTS to a manageable value like 50, 100, 200, or 400. No value should be larger than 1000. Period. Finding any segments in DBA_SEGMENTS with MAX_EXTENTS > 1000 should be cause for concern, in any environment. Also, find out if any segments are approaching their MAXEXTENTS using the following:

```
SELECT s.owner,
       s.segment_name,
       s.partition_name,  /* only for Oracle8 */
       s.segment_type,
       s.max_extents,
       COUNT(distinct e.extent_id) nbr_extents
  FROM dba_segments   s,
       dba_extents    e
 WHERE s.segment_type <> 'CACHE'
   AND e.owner = s.owner
   AND e.segment_type = s.segment_type
   AND e.segment_name = s.segment_name
                        /* only for Oracle8 */
   AND NVL(e.partition_name, '~') = NVL(s.partition_name, '~')
 GROUP BY s.owner,
          s.segment_name,
          s.partition_name, /* only for Oracle8 */
```

```
          s.segment_type,
          s.max_extents
 HAVING COUNT(distinct e.extent_id) > (s.max_extents - 5);
```

It is really quite embarrassing for a DBA to be told that an application operation failed because a table or index exceeded its MAXEXTENTS. This query will warn of all segments within five extents of exceeding their current MAXEXTENTS.

Monitoring Free Space

One of the surest ways for upper management to get the impression that a DBA is not doing his or her job is to find unexpected failures occurring because of a lack of space. This is the classic *unnecessary error*, and if it can't always be avoided it certainly can be anticipated.

To find out if any tables, indexes, or clusters are about to run out of space, use the following query:

```
SELECT tablespace_name,
       segment_name,
       initial_extent,
       next_extent,
       max_extents
  FROM dba_segments x
 WHERE NOT EXISTS
          (SELECT NULL
             FROM dba_free_space
            WHERE tablespace_name = x.tablespace_name
              AND bytes > x.next_extent);
```

Be aware that this query may take a long time for databases with a lot of segments. It may be useful to copy the full contents of each of these views into tables first (using CREATE TABLE . . . AS SELECT), index the table by TABLESPACE _NAME and BYTES, and run this query off those tables instead.

Monitoring Tablespace Fragmentation

Tablespace fragmentation occurs when segments within a tablespace each have their own customized storage parameters, causing each segment to have differently sized extents or, through the use of a nonzero PCTINCREASE parameter, extents that are successively growing or shrinking in size.

Tablespace fragmentation becomes harmful when DROPs occur in such tablespaces. Dropping segments will leave the formerly occupied extents as differently sized *free extents*. Newly created segments can reuse these free extents, but over time, as segments are added and dropped, the free space in the tablespace will become "chopped up" into smaller and smaller widely scattered free extents. Eventually, what may happen is that a significant amount of free space is available, but only in hundreds or thousands of tiny free space extents, each too small to use. As a result, either more datafiles must be added to the tablespace, or all the segments in the tablespace will need to be dropped and re-created. This latter move is also known as a *tablespace reorganization*.

It is common to use the Oracle EXP and IMP utilities for this purpose, and there are several third-party utilities (such as Platinum's TSReorg product) to facilitate this activity. The sad fact is it is all completely unnecessary.

Craig Shallahamer of Oracle Consulting Services has written a paper entitled "Avoiding a Database Reorganization," which is available on the World Wide Web at www.europa.com/~orapub. This document explains how to understand, detect, and eliminate all kinds of fragmentation in an Oracle database. There is another fine paper at the same Web site by Cary Millsap, also of Oracle Consulting's System Performance Group, entitled "Oracle7 Server Space Management," which covers in fine detail all the issues and myths surrounding Oracle space management.

To supplement these documents, the following analogy can be used to picture what is happening when tablespace fragmentation occurs.

Think about tiling—specifically, tiling the floor of a kitchen. In this analogy, the floor of the room is the Oracle tablespace. The tiles themselves are extents. A tablespace is created out of one or more datafiles. Typically, determining the size of those datafiles did not take into consideration the size of the extents that would be contained within. The same is true for a kitchen. Chances are good that the kitchen was sized without any particular regard for the tiles that would be used on the floor.

In this analogy, laying tile down on the floor is similar to creating segments and their extents in a tablespace. There is one major departure from real life in this analogy: when segments and their extents are dropped or truncated, this would be similar to picking up and removing tile. Normally, that doesn't happen in real life unless a cracked tile has to be replaced.

Anyway, if kitchen floors were tiled the way most people create tables and indexes in Oracle tablespaces, then the floor would be composed of many differently sized tiles. Of course, our objective in both cases is to be able to cover as much floor as possible, but as you can visualize, this would start to become difficult when all the tiles are sized differently. Ultimately, there would be many situations where many of the tiles do not fit against one another neatly, leaving gaps. As the floor started to fill up, it would become progressively more difficult to find places to lay the remaining tiles.

The same is true of extents in Oracle tablespaces. In the beginning, there is no issue; finding space for all the extents is quite easy. But over time, as the tablespace fills up, it starts to become more difficult to find contiguous patches of open space in which to fit new extents.

Then, in Oracle we have the case of dropping extents, which in the analogy would be like removing some of the tiles previously laid down. That would potentially open new slots in which to place additional tiles, but the additional tiles would certainly have to be either the same size or smaller than the open slots.

Clearly, this analogy makes it easier to visualize how difficult this all becomes.

Now, using the same analogy, add one additional rule: all tiles will be either the same size or multiples of one another. Suddenly, the problem of covering every square centimeter of flooring becomes quite simple (except around the walls and cabinets, which we'll ignore for the sake of simplicity). Even when you throw in the additional scenario of removing tiles (to simulate dropping tables and indexes), what is left as gaps will be quite easy to refill. All the tiles are the same size, or are sized as multiples of one another.

Next time you have to tile a floor, consider whether you will use uniformly sized tiles or randomly sized ones. Unless you are an artist, you almost certainly must choose the former. After all, unless you feel quite strongly about it, who has time to make artwork out of the kitchen floor? The same is true with Oracle space management. Who has time to make artwork about segments, extents, and free space? Life is simply too short, and there are much more demanding issues on which to vent creative urges.

Coming up with sizes for INITIAL and NEXT for tables, clusters, and indexes should not be a matter of calculation at all. Rather, database objects should fit one of a very few profiles, such as SMALL, MEDIUM, LARGE, and HUGE. Tablespaces should be available for each profile, and each tablespace should use a small number of uniformly sized extents; only one extent size per tablespace is ideal.

Oracle8 has a new option to help enforce this:

```
ALTER TABLESPACE . . . MINIMUM EXTENT nn;
CREATE TABLESPACE . . . MINIMUM EXTENT nn;
```

If MINIMUM EXTENT is specified for the tablespace, then all extents in that tablespace must be at least the size specified, and if they are larger they must be multiples of the size specified. For example,

```
CREATE TABLESPACE dw01_huge
    MINIMUM EXTENT 32M
    DEFAULT STORAGE (INITIAL 32M NEXT 32M MAXEXTENTS 400 PCTINCREASE 0);
CREATE TABLESPACE dw01_large
    MINIMUM EXTENT 4M
    DEFAULT STORAGE (INITIAL 4M NEXT 4M MAXEXTENTS 400 PCTINCREASE 0);
CREATE TABLESPACE dw01_medium
    MINIMUM EXTENT 128K
    DEFAULT STORAGE (INITIAL 128K NEXT 128K MAXEXTENTS 400 PCTINCREASE 0);
CREATE TABLESPACE dw01_small
    MINIMUM EXTENT 16K
    DEFAULT STORAGE (INITIAL 16K NEXT 16K MAXEXTENTS 400 PCTINCREASE 0);
```

In the tablespace DW01_HUGE, you would be able to create tables, indexes, or clusters with extent sizes of 32 MB, 64 MB, and so on. By setting MAXEXTENTS to 400, you are implying that the largest object you can have in that tablespace is at least 12.5 gigabytes, assuming the smallest extent size of 32 MB.

Databases that have their space managed in this manner will never have problems with tablespace fragmentation, and they will make extremely efficient use of the space they have available.

There is a myth in Oracle performance tuning that many extents present a performance problem. Proponents theorize that skipping from extent to extent must cost *something* in terms of performance. The truth is that this is absolutely false. All extents are equally available for random as well as sequential access; there is no "chaining" from one extent to the next. The *extent map* residing in the segment header contains the address of all extents.

Only in the extreme case of extents being sized small enough to impair multi-block reads for full table scans is this supposition true. Again, the floor tile analogy covers this scenario quite graphically. When you want to tile a floor with the minimum amount of trimming, you want to use as small a tile as possible, so you can fit into tight corners and get close to rounded edges. On the other hand, there is a limit to how small you want to make the tile. What if you had to count the tiles every day for as long as you live in the house? In effect, that is similar to what Oracle has to do during space management operations. If the extent size is too small, you are building a mosaic, and once again you are indulging in artwork. If you care to indulge in art in such a mundane area, simply be aware of the costs involved.

Visualize a tiled floor next time you are trying to determine space management policy for your database.

Monitoring Invalid Compiled Objects

If your application is making heavy use of database VIEWs or PL/SQL stored procedures, stored functions, or packages, then there is the possibility that DROPs and reCREATEs on tables or views or PL/SQL stored objects could cause *invalidations* of those objects. While this situation would usually cause applications to fail with an error message from the Oracle server, sometimes the server attempts to recompile the object at run-time, and sometimes the application disregards the error message. As a result, multiple sessions are constantly running into the same error situation repeatedly, and processing the error and/or trying to recompile the object on the fly is burdensome to the Oracle server.

Periodically running the following query may help prevent this simple-to-fix but difficult-to-diagnose problem from occurring:

```
SELECT owner, object_name, object_type, status
  FROM dba_objects
 WHERE status <> 'VALID';
```

For Oracle8 databases, it might be useful to include the column SUBOBJECT _NAME as well.

Summary

There is much that has not been covered in this chapter. For example, we did not begin to cover system management or database monitoring tools, such as Oracle's Enterprise Manager or CA-Unicenter. Instead, this chapter covers most of the basic concepts outlining the administration and monitoring of an Oracle data warehouse; indeed, any Oracle database.

We also did not get heavily into security; there are numerous reference works that cover this subject adequately, and the issues are the same for any kind of Oracle database application, data warehouse or otherwise. Our primary recommendation is to use the roles facility to quickly provide a set of privileges to a group of users. Use session auditing and Oracle8 password management features to control unauthorized access.

What this chapter did attempt to cover was basic configuration, tuning, and troubleshooting issues. In the very large database (VLDB) environments occupied by many data warehouses, these are the issues that could make or break an implementation.

The basic message is that Oracle provides application developers, end users, and project managers with a huge array of tools, some of which may be more harmful than helpful. The DBA needs to steer people toward the proper usage of these tools and away from the harmful uses of other tools. The administrators have the responsibility to keep the systems available for all users.

DATA WAREHOUSE
PERFORMANCE TUNING

In the last scene of the movie *Indiana Jones: Raiders of the Lost Ark*, the Ark of the Covenant is crated by U.S. government drones and stored in a vast, anonymous warehouse, presumably never to be seen again. That chilling scene seems to mirror the impression that people have of warehouses in general. This misconception carries over into data warehouses as well. There seems to be a wide misconception among people new to this arena that a data warehouse is a place where all data goes to die.

In reality, if you have ever worked in a real warehouse, the image couldn't be further from the truth. Warehouses are highly organized. Everyone knows where everything is located and how much is there. Warehouses accept huge quantities of materials from one mode of transport and ship huge quantities of material on other modes of transport. While the materials are in the warehouse, they are frequently transformed from homogeneous product shipments from wholesale manufacturers into palletized mixes of products, suitable for delivery to retail destinations. There are not many warehouses like the one portrayed in the Indiana Jones movie, where things are just stored for all eternity.

So, just like a real warehouse, a data warehouse is not a place to which old data is archived. It is not a *data graveyard* or a *data attic*. Like a real warehouse, it is a dynamic place, and it only contains stuff that is going to be used.

Think of the system underlying a data warehouse as a *data pump*, as illustrated in Figure 9.1. More than any other kind of database, data warehouses have to move larger volumes of data faster. Think about the size of most data warehouses: several hundred gigabytes or even many terabytes. Where do they get their data from and how regularly? The answer is they get their data from other databases, and they get it quite often.

Going back to real warehouses, think of the view of a large warehouse from the air. Large warehouses are usually located near railroads, interstate highways, airports, and shipyards. Most of the outer walls of the warehouse building itself

Figure 9.1 The data warehouse as pumps and pipelines.

consist of loading docks to facilitate the fast simultaneous transfer of large amounts of material. On one side of the building may be a rail loading dock. On two or three other sides may be truck loading docks.

A data warehouse is not unlike its real-world counterpart. On one side of the data warehouse are the many data sources. Data enters the warehouse through tape drives, through network connectivity, through file transfers, and through direct connections to the operational data sources. On the other side of the data warehouse are the many outbound data destinations. Data leaves the warehouse using the same variety of media on which it arrived.

In the middle is the data warehouse system itself. Inbound source data is cleansed, transformed, and aggregated. Outbound data is sorted, subsetted, and aggregated—downloaded, spooled, and cubed. While all this is going on, certain enterprising souls may be performing ad hoc or tactical reporting or data mining.

Facilitating all this movement and activity requires a lot of attention to the foundation of the system, the I/O subsystem, the CPUs, the operating system, and the database itself.

Sizing Your System

A complete refresh from the legacy operational data sources could involve several hundred gigabytes being loaded from a tape drive or across the network. Many complete refreshes occur on a monthly or weekly basis, and some data warehouses even deal with daily refreshes. Additionally, incremental loads may account for hundreds of megabytes or several gigabytes, and generally these take place on a daily or weekly basis.

That's only the start of it. Once data has been loaded, cleansing and aggregation must take place, which generally involves making extra copies of the data to preserve your ability to restart the cycle in case something goes wrong. It is not unusual for each row of the *raw* detail data that is loaded into the warehouse to be copied two or three times, doubling or tripling the amount of space needed to store it. Redundancy of data in a data warehouse is sometimes necessary, if the redundancy occurs as part of a process. Redundancy, in this case, also provides the ability to checkpoint and restart a long involved process of transforming raw detail data into clean, strategic, summarized data.

Not only is the amount of storage mindboggling, but the realization that every byte of this storage will be picked up and put back—perhaps two or three times—on a regular basis in the shortest amount of time should disabuse one of the notion that data warehouses are like quiet, serene libraries, where the only activity is reading. If you share this popular perception of a data warehouse as a "reading room" or "library," imagine the data warehouse as a public library where every week the entire inventory of books is removed and reshelved, in six or eight hours!

Once the loading, cleansing, and aggregation is complete, the overall *load phase* is complete, and the data warehouse must shift from a *read/write* application to a *read-only* application. Ad hoc reporting, operational and strategic summary reporting, online analysis, data mining: these are all activities that typically involve massive queries against the extremely large volumes of data.

Again, to debunk the image of a data warehouse as a quiet, serene "reading room" or "library," think of it not as a place where people calmly stroll among the aisles and pick out a book here and there to sit down with and read at leisure. Instead, think of it as a place where readers madly rush through the aisles, sweeping entire shelves of books into carts from which they will be digested and read. It is a place where every single book must be read because, in a week or in a month, the whole place is turned upside down and reorganized again.

Setting Up the I/O Subsystem

When people think about sizing their system, especially the I/O subsystem, they generally think in terms of disk space, in terms of capacity. The I/O subsystem may be described as being 100 gigabytes, 400 gigabytes, or 6 terabytes in size.

But try to imagine 100 gigabytes of disk drive attached to a 1985-era IBM PC AT. Plainly, the CPU of such a computer would be overwhelmed by the amount

Figure 9.2 Subsystems as data pumps.

of data those modern-day disk drives would be able to pump at it. Such a configuration would be CPU-bound (i.e., bottlenecked at the CPU) right from the start. Conversely, imagine a Sun UltraSPARC E10000 with 100 gigabytes of disk in the form of 5.25-inch, 40-MB drives manufactured in 1985. In this case, obviously we would be I/O-bound (i.e., bottlenecked at the I/O subsystem).

Invoking these images is not intended as a form of sadism (well, not entirely!) but rather to illustrate the point by describing extremes. Each component of the system is a pump, and little good comes of mismatching the flow rates between the components. Another way of thinking of it is to remember the old adage that a chain is only as strong as its weakest link. In the same way, a pumping system will only provide as much throughput as its narrowest pipeline or its least capable pump.

In fact, it is very effective to think of the entire I/O subsystem (disk drives or DASD, tape drives, network) as pumps with which to drive data at the CPUs (see Figure 9.2). Thinking of the I/O subsystem as simply a repository in which to store data is terribly one-dimensional and it doesn't help design a system capable of performing the tasks asked of it nor does it aid in figuring out why a system is not performing up to expectations. Remembering that each component of the I/O subsystem has a *throughput rate* in addition to a *capacity* helps us construct a more useful picture of system components.

What do you see in Figure 9.2? Drives A, B, C, and D all have equivalent throughput. And the single CPU is able to handle eight drives with this through-

Figure 9.3 Subsystems as data pumps with *capacities*.

put. If all these components are used to their maximum effectiveness, how is this system likely to bottleneck?

Now, add back in the concept of capacity, and see how the picture in Figure 9.3 changes:

Where will the bottleneck occur in this scenario? As you can see, the majority of the capacity is on drives A and B, but they have equivalent transfer rates to drives C and D. This means that all the data stored on drives A and B can only be retrieved half as quickly as all the data stored on drives C and D. All four drives have the same transfer rate, but the larger drives have twice as much data. If all the data on these four drives had to be read or written, it would take as long as the times shown in Figure 9.4.

In contrast, consider the configuration shown in Figure 9.5. Obviously, this I/O subsystem would perform better than the previous one.

Just as obviously, you're not always going to be dumping or loading all the data on all your disk drives as illustrated in these figures, but the same basic principle holds true for smaller amounts of data. For example, let's say that you have a hundred megabytes of data to retrieve. Suppose that Figure 9.6 is the scenario.

The amount of time needed to retrieve the data is simply a function of the amount of data times the transfer rate. However, what if the data was organized on the disk as in Figure 9.7? It might then be possible to have all eight drives returning the data at once, making the read almost eight times faster. So far, so good. But *how* the data is spread across these eight drives is important, too.

Figure 9.4 Retrieval times.

Figure 9.5 RAID versus SLED.

RAID = Redundant Array of Inexpensive Devices

SLED = Single Large Expensive Devices

Figure 9.6 No striping of data.

Let's take a table of 1 gigabyte and eight disk drives. Spreading the data across these eight drives might mean dividing the table into eight distinct pieces and laying them down on the drives. This would fulfill the idea of spreading the data onto eight devices, but would a sequential scan of the data run any faster? The answer is no, for the reason shown in Figure 9.8.

As Figure 9.8 shows, each read operation scans 128 KB at a time, meaning that it should take about 8,192 read operations to read 1 gigabyte of data. Notice that each read operation is still being serviced by only one device at a time, as the scan will make 1,024 reads (of 128 KB apiece) across each disk drive before moving on to the next. Since the number of read operations is the same and

Figure 9.7 Data spread across eight drives.

Figure 9.8 *Stripe width* **equal to** *partition,* **or** *concatenation.*

1 Scan

each read operation takes the same amount of time, laying the data across many drives in this fashion will not cause a single scan to speed up.

However, imagine that ten such scans were going on at roughly the same time. Instead of a single disk drive device trying to service all ten scans, you might now have eight disk drive devices doing so. Depending on how the scans are distributed across the data, it may be possible for the ten scans to concurrently complete in roughly the same amount of time as if each were running alone. Thus, spreading data across multiple devices, even in as rudimentary a manner as concatenation, may cause *scaleup* for multiple concurrent operations, even if it doesn't cause *speedup* for individual operations—see Figure 9.9.

Obviously, with stripe widths of 128 MB apiece, we would have to get quite lucky to experience this kind of scaleup. Who can say that ten concurrent scans will each be called with enough time in between each so that all eight drives are in use at once? Who can say that all ten concurrent scans won't be seeking data on the same drive at the same time?

The solution is to reduce the size of the stripe widths, using RAID 0 striping. If the stripe width were reduced to 1 MB, then a new drive would be hit every eight read operations (of 128 KB apiece) during a scan of 1 gigabyte. Again, each read operation would not speed up, and one scan running on the system

Figure 9.9 Ten concurrent scans experiencing scaleup.

would not run any faster than if the entire 1 gigabyte were on one disk drive. But now throw ten or twenty concurrent scans at the system. Instead of one disk drive frantically trying to return 20 gigabytes (i.e., twenty scans of 1 gigabyte apiece), now eight drives would be involved, almost certainly improving performance.

So, to build a data warehouse system that will meet the needs of not one solitary user but dozens or hundreds of concurrent users, keep in mind that the foundation of the system is in the I/O subsystem. If you only buy your storage devices for their capacity, you will lay the foundation for a data warehouse that will probably fulfill all performance expectations when testing with one or two users, but it will quickly "hit the wall" when several dozen users start pounding on it.

Striping the data is important, not because the technique of striping necessarily provides any kind of speedup, but because it allows many concurrent operations to scaleup. Spreading the I/O load across many devices doesn't improve any single device's transfer rate, but it helps each device sustain its own transfer rates without degrading. Chapter 2 in this book provides a more detailed explanation of the issues surrounding RAID 0 striping.

Pretuning the Data Warehouse

In Chapter 8 we mentioned that the DBA must be aware of where and how all data is to be cleansed, transformed, and aggregated, as well as knowing when and how all data was going to be extracted to outbound destinations. The reason for this tall order is to make the most of proactive tuning opportunities. You can't be proactive unless you know exactly what is going on and when it is going on.

Once the Oracle database is optimally installed on a platform with an optimized I/O subsystem and an optimal CPU configuration with optimal RAM, there are some strategies available for proactively pretuning, namely:

- partitioned UNION-ALL views
- partitioned tables (RDBMS 8.0+ only)
- summary tables (preaggregating)
- "hinted" views (prejoining)

With the popularity of end-user query tools and browsers (such as Oracle Discoverer) and online analytical processing (OLAP) tools such as Cognos Impromptu, Business Objects, and Oracle Express, it seems that hardly anyone actually writes SQL statements anymore. The good news is the ease of use and the popularity of these tools. The bad news is that many of these tools only know how to generate SQL statements that do the job, but they frequently do not create SQL statements that do the job *well*.

With some knowledge of the kinds of activities and queries that end users will be performing, it could be helpful to optimize data structures toward those usages and forestall potential problems by creating preaggregated tables or prejoining tables inside "hinted" views.

Figure 9.10 Pre-7.3 UNION-ALL views.

VIEW ACCOUNT ACTIVITY

Query time = 8 scans in sequence even though
desired data in only two partitions.

Partitioning

UNION ALL view were available in Oracle7 prior to release 7.3, but only in an elementary way (see Figure 9.10). Each query in the UNION ALL statement had to be processed in turn, sequentially. Such views were created in the following manner, and there was no way to eliminate any of the queries from being evaluated:

```
CREATE OR REPLACE VIEW account_activity
AS
    SELECT * FROM account_activity_fy96_q1
UNION ALL
    SELECT * FROM account_activity_fy96_q2
UNION ALL
    SELECT * FROM account_activity_fy96_q3
UNION ALL
    SELECT * FROM account_activity_fy96_q4
UNION ALL
    SELECT * FROM account_activity_fy97_q1
UNION ALL
    SELECT * FROM account_activity_fy97_q2
UNION ALL
    SELECT * FROM account_activity_fy97_q3
UNION ALL
    SELECT * FROM account_activity_fy97_q4;
```

Figure 9.11 Oracle7.3 partitioned UNION-ALL view.

| FY96_Q1 | FY96_Q2 | FY96_Q3 | FY96_Q4 | FY97_Q1 | FY97_Q2 | FY97_Q3 | FY97_Q4 |

ALL PQ SCANS AGAINST 2 PARTITIONS SIMULTANOUSLY.

Using this view, a query such as the following

```
SELECT SUM(activity_amount)
  FROM account_activity
WHERE activity_date BETWEEN '13-DEC-96' AND '02-FEB-97';
```

will evaluate all eight queries in the UNION-ALL view one at a time, sequentially.

Even so, the big disadvantage is that only two of the tables in the view needed to be evaluated: ACCOUNT_ACTIVITY_FY96_Q4 and ACCOUNT_AC-TIVITY_FY97_Q1; any work performed against the other six tables is merely a waste of time.

Oracle7, release 7.3, has advanced abilities in using "partitioned UNION-ALL views," specifically in parallelizing access to all the "partitions" (i.e., individual queries in the UNION-ALL statement) and in eliminating irrelevant "partitions" (see Figure 9.11). In this situation, CHECK constraints, that are normally used only to enforce integrity rules when records are being inserted into, updated, or deleted, are now also used by the Oracle query optimizer to eliminate certain partitions from evaluation (see Figure 9.12). This can be done because the CHECK constraints, which are enabled when the table is created or with an AL-TER TABLE statement, guarantee that data not meeting the constraint will not be present in the table.

Partition Views in Oracle8

Even though Oracle8 supports the partition view facility for upward compatibility for databases migrated from release 7.3, the true partitioning available in Oracle8 is vastly superior in performance and administrative ease. This new capability is a key reason to move the data warehouse to Oracle8 technology.

Partition views have many limitations, including no DDL or DML support, no utilities support (no loader, import, export), no parallel index scans, and many other restrictions (see the Oracle 7.3.3 Tuning Guide). The ReadMe release for Oracle8, 8.0.4, states that partition views will be supported in a future release.

Figure 9.12 Check constraints to enable partition elimination.

VIEW ACCOUNT ACTIVITY

Oracle8 extends this functionality by creating true partitioned objects, which include the benefits of partitioned views from 7.3 (parallel evaluation and partition elimination) but have additional capabilities. Chief among these is *partition transparency*. Under Oracle7, only queries could be performed against the "logical table" presented by a UNION-ALL view. Inserts, updates, and deletes had to be performed against the "base tables" or actual physical tables that comprise the view. This results in significant administrative and programming *complexity*, perhaps making their use prohibitive. Oracle8 partitioned tables can be treated exactly like nonpartitioned tables by end-user SQL statements, eliminating any downside (see Figure 9.13). Following is code for creating a partitioned table, similar to the previous examples of UNION-ALL views:

Figure 9.13 Oracle8 partitioned table.

```
CREATE TABLE account_activity
(
     . . .(column-definitions). . .
)
PARTITION BY RANGE (activity_date)
PARTITION account_activity_fy96_q1 VALUES LESS THAN ('01-APR-96')
     TABLESPACE aa_ts9601
PARTITION account_activity_fy96_q2 VALUES LESS THAN ('01-JUL-96')
     TABLESPACE aa_ts9602
PARTITION account_activity_fy96_q3 VALUES LESS THAN ('01-OCT-96')
     TABLESPACE aa_ts9603
PARTITION account_activity_fy96_q4 VALUES LESS THAN ('01-JAN-97')
     TABLESPACE aa_ts9604
PARTITION account_activity_fy97_q1 VALUES LESS THAN ('01-APR-97')
     TABLESPACE aa_ts9701
PARTITION account_activity_fy97_q2 VALUES LESS THAN ('01-JUL-97')
     TABLESPACE aa_ts9702
PARTITION account_activity_fy97_q3 VALUES LESS THAN ('01-OCT-97')
     TABLESPACE aa_ts9703
PARTITION account_activity_fy97_q4 VALUES LESS THAN ('01-JAN-98')
     TABLESPACE aa_ts9704;
```

Note that each partition in Figure 9.13 is located in a different tablespace. This is possible to do with Oracle7 "partitioned views" as well, so there is no specific advantage here. However, unlike the Oracle7 views, you can run IN-SERT, UPDATE, and DELETE against ACCOUNT_ACTIVITY.

What are the advantages to partitioning? Whether you are using Oracle7 partitioned views or Oracle8 partitioned tables, the purpose is to break very large tables that can be unmanageable into a series of smaller tables that are much easier to manage.

Consider a ten-billion row table. A table this size is likely to consume 100 gigabytes or more. This means that you would have to create a tablespace of at least that size. Also, this table is likely to have a few indexes. Certainly, those indexes would be a fraction of the size of the table, but 10 percent of 100 gigabytes is still 10 gigabytes. Two or three indexes of that size would require several huge tablespaces as well, take hours or days to create, and possibly have ten or more B*Tree levels to boot. Therefore, each access of a single row using an index would require a single read of a block at each level of the index before it finally reads the row from a block on the table. This would be a very expensive table to access.

Inserts, updates, and deletes would present their own problems. It is a common practice to drop all indexes during a large-scale bulk load; can you imagine having to rebuild two or three 10-gigabyte indexes every night? Performing a backup of a 100-gigabyte tablespace would probably tax the capabilities of any backup media, and any errors occurring during a restore would probably wipe out the entire structure. Can you imagine losing a 100-gigabyte table and all its indexes due to a single bad sector on a magnetic tape?

Partitioning makes this problem much more manageable. Each partition can have its own index (or, more precisely, a separate partition of the table's index), which makes queries, inserts, updates, and deletes more manageable. Rebuilding the indexes becomes less scary.

Preaggregating

The idea here is quite simple and as old as data warehousing itself—even older, as this technique was originally used in operational environments to optimize reporting. The advent of data warehouses was in response to this kind of reporting in such operational environments.

To be sure, a feature like Parallel Query Option allows you to take a huge query that used to take hours and perform it in minutes. However, as we discuss in Chapter 10 on Parallel Query Option, using PQO does not reduce the overall amount of work that is performed to process the query. Rather, it does it faster by dividing the job into many smaller components and processing those pieces in parallel.

But what if that PQO-enabled query, or close variations of it, is being run dozens of times an hour? Isn't it a waste of resources to be continually performing the same massive amounts of work? Wouldn't it be better to save the basic results from one of those queries into a *summary table* and direct users to query from that table instead?

For example, given a query like the following:

```
SELECT activity_date, AVG(activity_amount)
  FROM account_activity
 WHERE  . . .(search-restrictions). . .
 GROUP BY activity_date;
```

and:

```
SELECT activity_date, SUM(activity_amount)
  FROM account_activity
 WHERE  . . .(search-restrictions). . .
 GROUP BY activity_date;
```

wouldn't it make sense to create a summary table with all manner of aggregations for each ACTIVITY_DATE? If the original ACCOUNT_ACTIVITY table contains 100 million rows and covers two years' worth of data, then a summary table of this sort would contain only about 720 rows. Repeated queries against a 700-row table have got to be better than repeated queries against a 100 million-row table! The following example shows the creation of a summary table. The simplified syntax in the subsequent query against the newly created summary table is illustrative of the benefits that both ad hoc query tools as well as OLAP tools will realize in terms of simpler, more fool-proof generated SQL statements:

```
CREATE TABLE ACCOUNT_SUMMARY
AS
    SELECT activity_date,
           AVG(activity_amount) avg_amount,
           SUM(activity_amount) tot_amount
      from account_activity
     GROUP BY activity_date,
           (. . .columns-used-in-search-restrictions. . .);


SELECT activity_date, avg_amount
  FROM account_summary
 WHERE  . . .search restrictions. . . ;
```

Some query and reporting tools, such as Oracle's Discoverer, store all the SQL statements they generate. This SQL is then analyzed for potential summary tables, just as a programmer/analyst might. Repeated aggregating queries are flagged as potential summary tables, and the data warehouse administrator is given the statistics on the number of times the aggregations are run. The administrator, in turn, can then make a judgment as to whether creating a summary table would make sense. If a decision is made to go ahead with the creation of the summary table, Discoverer creates an Oracle "snapshot" after prompting the administrator for a refresh frequency, and now the summary table is automatically refreshed by the database itself.

Prejoining

Here once again, the concept is very simple. Imagine that users are using an end-user access tool such as Business Objects, which is repeatedly going out into the data warehouse performing massive or complex joins. For one reason or another, the Oracle optimizer is just not getting it *right*. Whether the tables and indexes need to be analyzed more often or whether some initialization parameters have to be set to better values, the SQL being generated by the end-user utility is simply not performing well.

The DBA knows that the queries can perform better because SQL code proving this may have already been written using Oracle *optimizer hints*. These optimizer hints, to be discussed later in this chapter, tell the optimizer what to do instead of letting it decide what it wants to do by itself.

Database views can be created that incorporate these hints to *prejoin* complex SQL statements. This technique has several advantages: It ensures that joins happen exactly as you have determined to be optimal, and it can simplify the image or table structure that end users have of the data. Instead of having to worry about joining several different tables together, they see a single view.

In essence, a series of such views could be used to abstract the actual tables from end users, creating an *end-user layer* of simplified, prejoined views for end-user presentation.

Optimizing the Load Phase

There are only a few main issues concerning loading into the data warehouse:

- Use SQL*Loader direct path for large loads.
- Use SQL*Loader direct path parallel for very large loads.
- Drop and re-create indexes for large volume loads.
- FOREIGN KEY constraints are unnecessary in the data warehouse.
- On UNIX, use *named pipes* to load data directly from another system.

SQL*Loader Direct Path vs. "Conventional SQL"

Many people have a misconception that anything written in C or C++ has got to be faster than any other method. This may be sometimes be true, but it is distinctly untrue when loading data into Oracle.

The issue is *Application Programming Interfaces* or *APIs*. For programming languages, Oracle has two:

- Oracle Call Interface or OCI
- Precompilers (i.e., PRO*C/C++, PRO*Ada, PRO*COBOL, PRO*Fortran, PRO*Pascal, etc.)

In reality, the Precompiler APIs are a layer of software abstraction atop OCI; OCI is in fact the only API for programming languages into Oracle. When you use the Precompilers, you are using OCI. OCI supports only "conventional" SQL, such as INSERT, UPDATE, DELETE, and SELECT. It supports all the SQL commands listed in the Oracle *Server SQL Language Reference* manual, except those listed as *embedded SQL*. Embedded SQL commands are supported by the Precompilers. Any program written in the Precompilers or OCI can therefore only use INSERT statements to insert data into the database. This includes any utility programs written by Oracle except SQL*Loader direct path and also any programs written by vendors other than Oracle.

In brief, as we explained in Chapter 6, conventional-path SQL*Loader (see Figure 9.14) really operates against cached database blocks in the SGA buffer cache. At the time of the changes, the log writer process (LGWR) logs the changes. At a later time, the database writer (DBWR) process writes the changes in the buffer cache to the datafiles.

All in all, this buffering mechanism works very well for large numbers of processes simultaneously accessing and modifying the same database blocks. But this mechanism actually becomes a hindrance when one process simply wants to shovel data into a table. In this case, the need to manipulate buffers in a memory cache, about which all changes have to be logged and then flushed to disk by another process, can seriously stress the locks and latches designed to keep everything running smoothly. This buffered mechanism is designed for lots of different activities, not for a long-running, intensive activity like a bulk load. For a bulk load, all the locking, logging, and flushing becomes a bottleneck.

Figure 9.14 Conventional SQL.

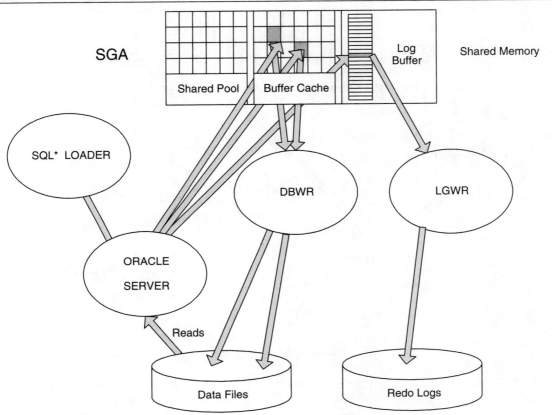

In response to this, Oracle introduced *direct path* loads. In short, using the direct path mechanism means that an SQL*Loader process bypasses the buffer cache and the rollback mechanisms, largely bypasses the redo log mechanism, and writes directly to the datafile (see Figure 9.15). In one sense, the direct path mechanism is very *sociopathic*, as it does not adhere to the general rules for co-operation and largely operates by itself.

The direct path mechanism reserves space outside the area currently utilized by the rest of the Oracle processes. In that area outside the bounds, the direct path does its work, populating database blocks and writing them directly to disk. When a direct path operation is complete, it notifies the rest of the Oracle instance and performs the necessary space management manipulation to add the formerly out-of-bounds area to the existing table data.

In fact, because it does almost pure I/O, SQL*Loader direct path is a very good testing mechanism for your I/O subsystem. It tends to read from the input data file very quickly, and when it's not reading it is writing Oracle database blocks directly onto the Oracle datafiles. Unless there is some kind of translation

Figure 9.15 Direct path mechanism.

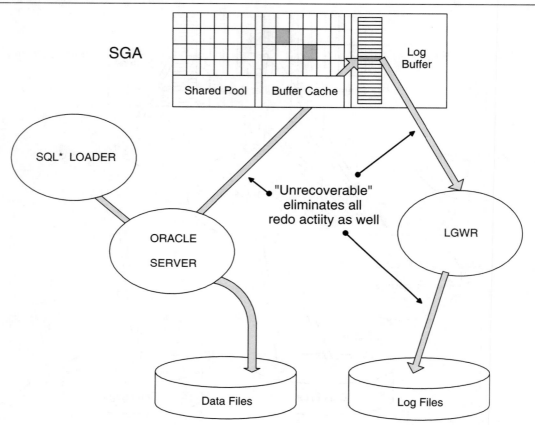

involved (like parsing variable-length, delimited input records or converting EBCDIC character sets to ASCII), SQL*Loader direct path spends all of its time reading or writing.

The direct path mechanism was first introduced in Oracle7, version 7.0, in SQL*Loader only. Later, in version 7.1, it was expanded to include an UNRE-COVERABLE option, whereby logging to the redo logs can largely be disabled. Disabling redo logging is not necessarily a performance boost in and of itself. Only if the system upon which the database is running is near capacity in terms of I/O throughput or CPU utilization will the lack of redo logging be immediately useful. But the other primary benefit of selectively disabling redo logging is to reduce the amount of redo being generated, archived, and backed up.

So using the UNRECOVERABLE option will certainly reduce demands on CPU utilization and I/O throughput; whether this translates into a performance benefit depends on whether these subsystems are near capacity.

Of course, disabling redo logging has ramifications on the recoverability of the table. A table loaded with SQL*Loader direct path UNRECOVERABLE can

Figure 9.16 Parallel CREATE INDEX.

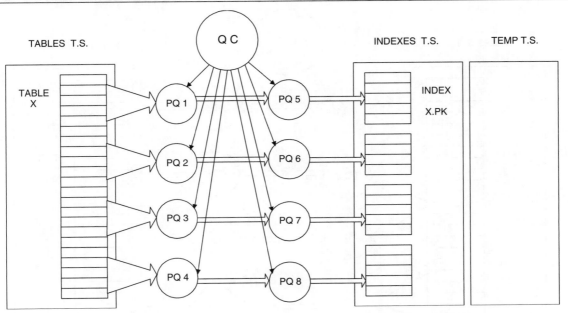

only be restored from a backup; it cannot be recovered by the roll-forward of redo logs. Therefore, unless you are prepared to reload a table all over again (which is actually a common strategy—see Chapter 8), you should perform a backup after loading a table UNRECOVERABLE.

Oracle7, version 7.1, also saw the introduction of the Parallel Query Option (PQO), which included another use of the direct path mechanism in the parallel CREATE INDEX (pCI) command (see Figure 9.16). Parallel CREATE INDEX also has an UNRECOVERABLE option.

Oracle7, version 7.2, saw the introduction of the parallel CREATE TABLE . . . AS SELECT (pCTAS), which also uses the direct path mechanism and has an UN-RECOVERABLE option as well (see Figure 9.17).

So, to load tables from a "flat file" fast, resist the temptation to write a "screamingly fast" program in C or C++. Use the direct path mechanism, available only in SQL*Loader.

Parallel Loads

After SQL*Loader direct path was introduced in version 7.0, it became clear that even the direct path mechanism was not fast enough. For one thing, on most multiprocessor platforms, a single SQL*Loader direct path process would probably only utilize one CPU at a time. This can be unsatisfactory if you have twelve CPUs and most of them are sitting idle. Since the direct path mechanism operated *outside the bounds* in terms of Oracle storage, the initial release of the di-

Figure 9.17 Parallel CREATE TABLE . . . AS SELECT.

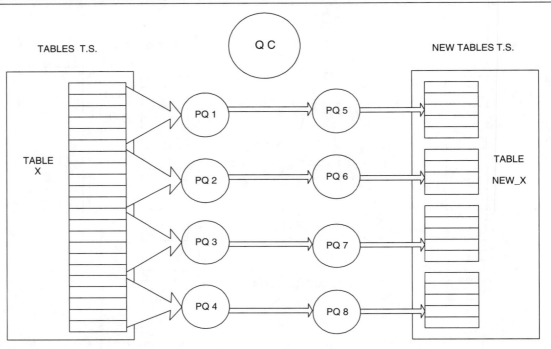

rect path mechanism did not allow more than one SQL*Loader process to operate on the same table at a time.

But, starting with the introduction of the Parallel Query Option (PQO) in version 7.1, it became possible to run more than one SQL*Loader direct path process against the same table (see Figure 9.18). To enable this, set both the DIRECT= and the PARALLEL= parameters to TRUE either on the SQL*Loader command line or in the SQL*Loader control file. Running more than one SQL*Loader process to load into the same table implies that each process has its own input data file.

It is possible to "partition" an input data file into segments for multiple loader processes, using the SKIP= and LOAD= parameters, either on the SQL*Loader command line or in the SQL*Loader control file (see Figure 9.19).

However, be aware that SQL*Loader direct path processes can be so efficient at loading that they can cause a bottleneck on the input data file, because the disk drive(s) on which they are located suddenly find not one but several processes intensively issuing read requests. The SKIP= parameter in SQL*Loader does not actually "skip over" or forego actually reading the records to be skipped; it just fails to load from them. So, when using the SKIP= parameter, SQL*Loader will actually read the skipped records, but not load them.

Figure 9.18 Multiple direct path loaders using multiple input files.

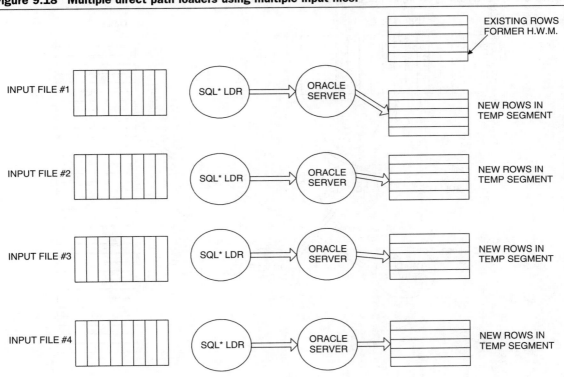

Drop and Re-create Indexes for Large-volume Loads

Whether using conventional path INSERT statements or direct path loads for large-volume loads, the load will go faster if there are no indexes on the table during the load.

Dropping the indexes and re-creating them after the load is complete can boost load performance many times. Using parallel CREATE INDEX, the index could be rebuilt much faster than if it were maintained during the load. Also, the resulting index would be more compact than an index that has been inserted into, as each database block comprising the index would be filled up to the point of PCTFREE—as opposed to being half full as would inevitably be the case from index block-splitting due to INSERTs.

The downside of dropping and re-creating indexes is, of course, that the table being loaded is unusable while it is being loaded. If this is not possible because of business requirements, consider using partitioned UNION-ALL views, partitioned tables (Oracle8), or leaving the indexes in place and taking the performance hit.

Figure 9.19 Partitioning an input file using SKIP= and LOAD=.

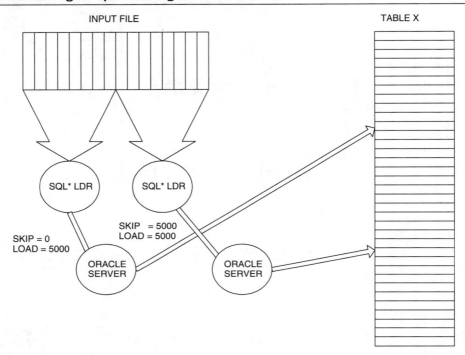

Constraints in the Data Warehouse

Many people new to data warehousing come from the world of "operational" systems. Inevitably, people who are used to creating data models for "operational" systems consider the use of integrity constraints such as PRIMARY KEY, UNIQUE KEY, and FOREIGN KEY to be mandatory for all relational databases.

But, this is not true for data warehouses.

Think about it. A data warehouse does not need referential integrity constraints. The operational system from which the data is loaded needs referential integrity. This is to ensure that declared relationships between PRIMARY KEYs and FOREIGN KEYs are valid, because a FOREIGN KEY in a "child" entity demands the existence of a PRIMARY KEY in a "parent" entity. Orphaned "child" records violate the relational model.

Data warehouses are not tasked with maintaining referential integrity. They exist to provide a reporting base for the data as it exists. If there is a referential integrity error on the source operational system, then this same error should be propagated to the data warehouse. This is because the operational system is *the source of record*, whether that data is *right* or *wrong*. If it is inappropriate for incorrect data to be in the data warehouse, then the correction should be made in the operational system, not in the data warehouse.

Of course, data cleansing routines and processes can be used to correct these errors in the data warehouse if desired, but referential integrity constraints are not a cost-effective mechanism to use in cleansing large amounts of data.

Data warehouses implemented in Oracle should use indexes to facilitate access. These indexes could be NONUNIQUE or UNIQUE, depending on which is more efficient at accessing the data. PRIMARY KEY and UNIQUE constraints should not arbitrarily be used to enforce entity integrity in a data warehouse because the terms are quite meaningless in this environment.

Pipelining Instead of "Staging" Flat Files

Frequently, the "flat files" used to load data into the data warehouse come from a remote system. Although it may be possible to run SQL*Loader from that remote system and use SQL*Net to connect into the data warehouse, this may not be optimal in terms of performance. Certainly, this is the most simple solution, if it is available. But SQL*Net's performance characteristics when performing a bulk operation over a network are quite well known; it's really not optimized for bulk operations. And it may not be possible to run SQL*Loader on the remote system.

Whatever the case is, it is quite common to use *ftp* or some other similar file-transfer utility to copy the "flat file" from the remote system to the local system, staging it locally, so that SQL*Loader can load the data into the Oracle database (see Figure 9.20). The problem here is *latency*. The file transfer has to finish before SQL*Loader starts to be sure that all the records to be transferred are actu-

Figure 9.20 Staging a file transfer.

Figure 9.21 SQL*Loader reading from pipes.

ally loaded. If SQL*Loader "catches up" to the file-transfer process and encounters a premature END-OF-FILE, then it will stop loading.

On UNIX systems, there is a mechanism available to eliminate this delay in starting SQL*Loader (see Figure 9.21). UNIX *named pipes* are actually one of the oldest interprocess communication (IPC) mechanisms still in use. Also called FIFOs (for *First In, First Out*), they appear in the UNIX file system much like a regular file. However, they do not occupy any actual space. They are essentially a memory buffer of fixed size. Although the details vary from one UNIX implementation to another, they essentially operate as a *circular memory buffer*. All writes to a pipe are blocked until a process opens the pipe for reading. Once a pipe is opened for reading, the pipe's memory buffer can be filled. However, once the memory buffer fills, any further writes are blocked until the reading process issues read requests. All data written into a FIFO is guaranteed to be read in the same order.

Conversely, a process that tries to read from a FIFO or pipe will block until another process writes data into it. Once enough data has been written to satisfy the pending read request, the read will complete. Using this mechanism, the delay while waiting for the file transfer to complete can be eliminated.

First, create the named pipe. Then start the SQL*Loader process, indicating the UNIX named pipe as the input data file. Once the SQL*Loader process is running, it will "hang" immediately as its read request from the pipe is blocked. Then, start the file transfer, directing the file-transfer program to write the remote data into the same UNIX named pipe that the SQL*Loader process is reading from.

Data will be loaded into Oracle as soon as it arrives on the local system. Also, it is not necessary to provide massive amounts of "staging" space for huge file transfers, as the data going through the UNIX named pipe never actually "lands" anywhere but inside Oracle. Therefore, this method might be the only alternative in the event the input data file is too large to fit into a UNIX file or is too big to fit anywhere given the existing disk capacity.

Tuning the SQL

The tuning of SQL statements is as much an art as a science; at least that is what people would have you believe. Frankly, people who give that impression are likely not sure enough of what they are doing to explain what they are doing. The author Arthur C. Clarke is credited with explaining that "any sufficiently advanced technology is indistinguishable from magic." That beautiful little aphorism can be slightly modified to fit the subject at hand: "Any sufficiently arcane technology can be confused with magic."

In reality, the key is to use the right tools; then tuning SQL statements becomes as easy as determining the lesser or greater of two numbers. Couple that with the spirit of experimentation and some background knowledge of access methods in Oracle, and anyone can become a guru overnight.

The right tool is SQL tracing and the TKPROF utility. SQL tracing gathers important statistics about an SQL statement while it is running, and TKPROF summarizes those statistics into a formatted report, supplementing the information with EXPLAIN PLAN information as well. These tools are among the oldest in the Oracle product set, having existed with little modification for over a decade. One would think that any tool so venerable would have been well documented. One would be wrong.

Historically, far too many Oracle developers and DBAs have been blissfully ignorant of the power of SQL tracing and TKPROF. Lack of documentation in earlier releases, combined with a lack of coverage in training classes, has stratified the community of would-be Oracle tuners. Those who have stumbled across SQL tracing and TKPROF and have actually learned to use it effectively are the "haves," the keepers of the keys. Those who have not yet discovered these tools remain the "have-nots," doomed to perpetually attend seminars and buy books on how to write SQL (not that buying books is a bad thing!) without ever becoming effective at Oracle tuning.

Documentation for using and interpreting these tools has been sparse and spare. Doubtless, there are those who will find this chapter wanting as well. At the moment, the Oracle *Server Tuning Guide* for both versions 7.3 and 8.0 are quite good on this subject, the best yet. Recent publications from Oracle Press and O'Reilly and Associates provide more information on using SQL tracing and TKPROF.

Understanding SQL Tracing

The idea behind SQL tracing is very simple. It started as a development debugging tool, much as any large-scale system would have a debugging tool. When

Figure 9.22 SQL tracing output stream on the server.

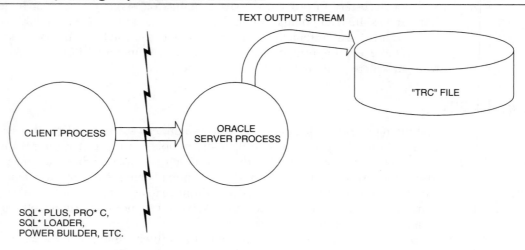

SQL tracing is enabled, the background Oracle server process opens an output file stream on the server (see Figure 9.22).

If you were writing a complex program using C or some other third-generation programming language, this is pretty much how you would handle debugging, both during the development phase and later on into production. By default, no such tracing output would be produced, but using one or more methods of signaling, the debugging output can be turned on or off.

In Oracle, there are five ways to enable or disable SQL tracing. But first, we will briefly discuss relevant initialization parameters that may need to be set or reviewed.

Relevant Initialization Parameters

- **USER_DUMP_DEST** This refers to a directory on the server where the instance is located that will hold all SQL trace files generated by that database instance. Valid values are dependent on the operating system; check your *Oracle Server Installation and Configuration Guide* for details.
- **TIMED_STATISTICS** This Boolean parameter defaults to FALSE. If set to TRUE, then the database instance will capture CPU and elapsed time statistics for every operation performed by the instance. Naturally, this adds some processing overhead to everything the database instance does, but it is certainly worthwhile in a development environment and even in some low-intensity production environments.
- **MAX_DUMP_FILE_SIZE** The maximum number of operating system blocks (check the *Oracle Server Installation and Configuration Guide* again) that an SQL trace file can grow to. The default is usually 500. Setting this parameter low helps keep SQL trace files from filling the file system

too quickly. However, leaving this value too low may cause valuable SQL tracing information to be lost due to file truncation.

Setting the Current Session Using ALTER SESSION

The first means of invoking SQL tracing is the most well known; the ALTER SESSION command. As this SQL command implies, it will change a characteristic of the current session for the duration of the session or until it is countermanded. Thus, once a connection to an Oracle instance has been established, any front-end utility such as SQL*Plus, PRO*Precompilers, Oracle Forms, PowerBuilder, Microsoft Access, or Business Objects can issue the following:

```
ALTER SESSION SET SQL_TRACE = TRUE
```

Or:

```
ALTER SESSION SET SQL_TRACE TRUE
```

Although this command can be issued any time during a session, it is best to make this the first SQL statement issued after establishing the connection to an Oracle instance. For example, in PRO*C it would be as follows:

```
/*
 * . . .set up error handling in case any EXEC SQL statements return an error. .
 .
 */
WHENEVER SQLERROR DO err_exit();

/*
 * . . .connect to the Oracle instance using the username, password, and
 * possibly the SQL*Net connect-string stored in the host "bind"
 * variable "username_password". . .
 */
EXEC SQL CONNECT USING :username_password;

/*
 * . . .if a UNIX environment variable named "SQL_TRACE" is set to TRUE,
 * then use ALTER SESSION to turn on SQL tracing. . .
 */
if ((p_env = getenv("SQL_TRACE")) != (char *) 0)
{
     if (strcmp(p_env, "TRUE") == 0)
     {
          EXEC SQL ALTER SESSION SET SQL_TRACE TRUE;
     }
}
```

Of course, you are going to need the ALTER SESSION system privilege granted to your Oracle account.

Setting the Current Session Using DBMS_SESSION

Another way to enable SQL tracing is by using the DBMS_SESSION package in PL/SQL. If you are programming in PL/SQL, you can still execute an ALTER SESSION command, but you would have to use the DBMS_SQL package for dynamic SQL, which requires many separate steps. A shorter, more intuitive method might be to use the SET_SQL_TRACE procedure as follows:

```
DBMS_SESSION.SET_SQL_TRACE(true);
```

This is exactly equivalent to the ALTER SESSION command. Of course, using FALSE instead of TRUE, just like in the ALTER SESSION command, will disable SQL trace if it is running. Make sure that your Oracle account (or PUBLIC) has been granted EXECUTE on the package DBMS_SESSION. Now you have two choices in enabling or disabling SQL tracing; either using the ALTER SESSION statement or using the PL/SQL packaged procedure DBMS_SESSION.SET_SQL_TRACE.

Setting Another Session Using DBMS_SESSION

In addition to setting SQL tracing in your own session, you may want to set it in another session running against Oracle. This is useful for tracing a session that is running from a program that cannot turn SQL trace on by itself. For example, most client-server applications that connect into Oracle databases were not written to enable SQL tracing using either the ALTER SESSION command or the DBMS_SESSION package. Therefore, there might be no way to tune SQL statements being generated from this tool unless the application is rewritten. This, of course, almost never happens!

However, never fear! You can log on to Oracle in another session and enable SQL trace from the first session. But first you must obtain some unique information about the session to be traced. To get this information, query the V$SESSION view:

```
SELECT username, osuser, machine, process, sid, serial#
  FROM v$session
 WHERE . . .
```

In the WHERE clause of this query, use whatever information available to you about the session to be traced. If you know the Oracle account to which they have connected, use WHERE USERNAME = '<username>'. If you know what machine or host name they are connecting into Oracle from, use WHERE MACHINE = '<hostname>'. Or, if worse comes to worst, dump the whole V$SESSION view and try to browse the results.

```
SQL> SELECT username, osuser, machine, process, sid, serial#
  2    FROM v$session
  3*  WHERE TYPE = 'USER'
SQL> /
```

```
USERNAME     OSUSER      MACHINE         PROCESS       SID   SERIAL#
----------   ----------- --------------- ---------  ---------  ---------
TED          ted         fester          9845              8       101
SYSTEM                                                     9        43
```

It helps to have a quiet system if you're going to browse the whole thing! Since I know that I'm logged in as SYSTEM, my only other possibility must be user TED.

What you need from V$SESSION are the primary key values of that view, namely SID (a.k.a. session ID) and SERIAL#. These values can then be used in the SET_SQL_TRACE_IN_SESSION procedure to enable (or disable) SQL tracing in the other session, as follows:

```
SQL> EXECUTE DBMS_SESSION.SET_SQL_TRACE_IN_SESSION(8, 101, TRUE);

PL/SQL procedure successfully completed.
```

Again, you will need to have EXECUTE permission for the DBMS_SESSION package granted to your Oracle account.

Setting Another Session Using Server Manager

Another method for setting SQL tracing in another session, which is functionally equivalent to using DBMS_SESSION, is by using the ORADEBUG facility in Server Manager. To do this, enter Server Manager; on UNIX, use the line-mode Server Manager:

```
$ svrmgrl
```

On Windows NT, use the Command prompt to run:

```
C:\> svrmgr30
```

Once you've logged on as SYSDBA, you can use the ORADEBUG commands:

```
SVRMGR> oradebug setospid <nnnnn>
Statement processed.
SVRMGR> oradebug event 10046 trace name context forever, level 0
Statement processed.
SVRMGR> oradebug unlimit
Statement processed
```

What these three commands have done is the following:

- "attached" the current Server Manager session to the process indicated by the operating system PID "nnnnn"; this is the same operating system PID (in decimal format) that we discussed earlier in the chapter
- enabled Oracle event 10046 (i.e., SQL tracing)
- disabled the MAX_DUMP_FILE_SIZE initialization parameter so the resulting SQL trace file can grow to an unlimited size if necessary

It is almost an application of Murphy's Law that the most interesting things that happen while you are tracing a session occur after you have exceeded the MAX_DUMP_FILE_SIZE limit imposed for all SQL trace files generated by the Oracle instance. To prevent this from happening on a very selective basis, enabling SQL tracing from Server Manager gives you the ability to override this limit just for the single session indicated.

WARNING: ORADEBUG Is Not for Experimenting

Please be aware that the Server Manager ORADEBUG facility is originally intended for debugging. Please do not experiment with it. The purpose of ORADEBUG is to provide Oracle Worldwide Support with the capability to debug the RDBMS in a wide variety of situations. While it will become obvious that ORADEBUG is capable of a great deal more than setting higher values of SQL Trace, it would be extremely foolish to play with it.

Setting SQL_TRACE for the Entire Instance

Last, but not least, you can set SQL tracing to TRUE for all the processes in the entire database instance. More often than not, this will generate too many trace files to be examined and therefore is generally overkill. Also, the extra processing overhead incurred by having every single Oracle background process (i.e., PMON, SMON, etc.) as well as every single Oracle server process producing SQL trace output can bring a system to its knees. Also, the number of files can easily run a file system out of space, if the system administrators are not prepared. Needless to say, you should be very careful whenever using this option.

But this technique has its uses. There can be times when a system is so busy that you may want to "snapshot" it. If you have the freedom to take the database up and down, you can set the initialization parameter SQL_TRACE=TRUE for a short time (i.e., 1 hour, 4 hours, 8 hours, etc.), then take the database down and set SQL_TRACE back to FALSE. What you will have gathered during the time when SQL_TRACE=TRUE is dozens or hundreds of SQL trace files, which you can examine at your leisure.

But, now that we have gathered SQL trace information into a file, what have we really got? What does that information look like? And how can we use it?

What Is Inside a SQL Trace File?

Upon completion of the ALTER SESSION command, the Oracle server process will have created or reopened a file somewhere on the machine where the Oracle instance resides. The directory in which this file resides is determined from the initialization parameter USER_DUMP_DEST, which is set by the Oracle DBA. By default, on UNIX this directory is "$ORACLE_HOME/rdbms/log" and on Windows NT it is "%RDBMSnn%\TRACE" where the "nn" in "RDBMSnn" is either "73" or "80" depending on your version of Oracle. However, best practices (codified by Oracle's Optimal Flexible Architecture [or OFA]) suggest that it be located somewhere else, not under the "ORACLE_HOME" directory structure. For more on OFA, see Chapter 8.

The name of the file can be constructed if you know a few things about your session. Query the V$SESSION and V$PROCESS views in the data dictionary, and you can find out what the operating system process ID (or PID) is. For example, on Windows NT run the following:

```
SQL> SELECT spid FROM v$process WHERE addr =
  2  (SELECT paddr FROM v$session WHERE audsid = USERENV('SESSIONID'));


SPID
---------
0010A
```

On Windows NT, the column SPID contains a hexadecimal number that must be converted to decimal; on UNIX, the value will already be in decimal representation. Given this value, the name of the SQL trace file can be pasted together as follows:

```
USER_DUMP_DEST || fixed-string || to_char(SPID,'00000') || '.trc'
```

where

- *USER_DUMP_DEST* is the directory name specified in the initialization parameter of the same name
- *fixed-string* is dependent on the operating system. On some UNIX platforms, this string is "ora_" or "$ORACLE_SID_ora_" or "ora_$ORACLE_SID_". On NT, it is simply "ora".
- *to_char(SPID, '00000')* is the operating system PID (in decimal format) zero-padded to five places
- *'.trc'* is just a file extension

After running the ALTER SESSION statement, go to the USER_DUMP_DEST directory and look for this file. It is simply a text file, so feel free to view it, but be aware that on some operating systems the file may be locked for use by the process writing to it, or output to it may be buffered and therefore not yet written.

ACCESSING TRACE FILES

The initialization parameter TRACE_FILES_PUBLIC will change the UNIX permissions of the generate trace files so that they may be read by users other than DBAs.

What you see when you view the file may not be very helpful for performance tuning, but it ought to give some insight into what is going on "behind the scenes." For example, the following SQL*Plus session was traced using ALTER SESSION:

```
SQL*Plus: Release 4.0.2.0.0 - Beta on Sun Jul 6 18:22:5 1997

Copyright (c) Oracle Corporation 1979, 1994, 1996.  All rights reserved.

Connected to:
Oracle8 Server Release 8.0.2.0.2 - Beta
With the distributed, heterogeneous, replication, objects
and parallel query options
PL/SQL Release 3.0.2.0.2 - Beta

SQL> select spid from v$process where addr =
  2  (select paddr from v$session where audsid = userenv('SESSIONID'));

SPID
---------
0010A

SQL> select value from v$parameter where name = 'user_dump_dest';

VALUE
------------------------------------------------------------------
%RDBMS80%\trace

SQL> alter session set sql_trace true;

Session altered.

SQL> select 'x' from dual;

'
-
x
```

At this point, the resulting trace file at "%RDBMS80%\trace\ora00266.trc" (i.e., hex '0010A' translates to decimal "00266") shows the following:

```
Dump file C:\ORANT\RDBMS80\trace\ORA00266.TRC
Sun Jul 06 18:38:58 1997
ORACLE V8.0.2.0.2 - Beta vsnsta=1
vsnsql=c vsnxtr=3
Windows NT V4.0, OS V5.101, CPU type 586
Oracle8 Server Release 8.0.2.0.2 - Beta
With the distributed, heterogeneous, replication, objects
and parallel query options
PL/SQL Release 3.0.2.0.2 - Beta
Windows NT V4.0, OS V5.101, CPU type 586
Instance name: orcl

Redo thread mounted by this instance: 1
```

```
Oracle process number: 10

pid: 10a

Sun Jul 06 18:38:58 1997

*** SESSION ID:(9.43) 1997.07.06.18.38.58.687
APPNAME mod='SQL*Plus' mh=3669949024 act='' ah=4029777240
=====================
PARSING IN CURSOR #2 len=33 dep=0 uid=5 oct=42 lid=5 tim=0 hv=1538466435
ad='30ce0c0'
alter session set sql_trace true
END OF STMT
EXEC #2:c=0,e=0,p=0,cr=0,cu=0,mis=1,r=0,dep=0,og=4,tim=0
=====================
PARSING IN CURSOR #2 len=21 dep=0 uid=5 oct=3 lid=5 tim=0 hv=2888538493
ad='30cb850'
select 'x' from dual
END OF STMT
PARSE #2:c=0,e=0,p=0,cr=0,cu=0,mis=1,r=0,dep=0,og=4,tim=0
EXEC #2:c=0,e=0,p=0,cr=0,cu=0,mis=0,r=0,dep=0,og=4,tim=0
FETCH #2:c=0,e=0,p=0,cr=1,cu=2,mis=0,r=1,dep=0,og=4,tim=0
FETCH #2:c=0,e=0,p=0,cr=0,cu=0,mis=0,r=0,dep=0,og=0,tim=0
STAT #0 id=1 cnt=1 pid=0 pos=0 obj=171 op='TABLE ACCESS FULL DUAL '
. . . more . . .
```

At the top of this file we see a banner announcing context: the name of the trace file, the current system date and time, the type and versions of the operating system and the machine it is running on, the Oracle product versions, the Oracle internal process ID and the operating system (Windows NT) process ID, and an acknowledgment that the application (i.e., SQL*Plus) had registered itself using the DBMS_APPLICATION_INFO package.

For each SQL statement, there will be an entry headed "PARSING IN CURSOR #nnn". The cursor number is a numbered entry in the Oracle program global area's (PGA) cursor cache, which is private to each session. The other data in this entry is as follows:

```
len=          the length in bytes (octets) of the SQL statement text
dep=          recursive call depth (0=user SQL, >0=recursive SQL)
uid=          the Oracle user ID (column USER_ID in DBA_USERS)
oct=          the Oracle command type
lid=          the privileged Oracle user ID
tim=          timestamp (hundredths of seconds)
hv=           hash value of SQL statement (column HASH_VALUE in V$SQLAREA)
ad=           address of SQL statement (column ADDRESS in V$SQLAREA)
SQL           the text of the SQL statement itself
```

The *Oracle command type* is documented in the *Oracle Call Interface User's Guide.*

Also, depending on what kind of SQL statement is being executed there will be entries for the different suboperations of an SQL statement, such as *parse, execute,* and *fetch.* Each of these entries will have the following format:

```
<oper> #nnn      "oper" is either PARSE, EXECUTE, or FETCH
                 "nnn" is the cursor number from the PARSING entry
c=               CPU time (hundredths of seconds)
e=               elapsed time (hundredths of seconds)
p=               number of physical reads
cr=              number of buffers gotten for consistent reads
cu=              number of buffers gotten for current reads
mis=             number of misses in the library cache
r=               number of rows retrieved
dep=             recursive call depth (0=user SQL, >0=recursive SQL)
og=              Optimizer goal (1=ALL_ROWS,2=FIRST_ROWS,3=RULE,4=CHOOSE)
tim=             timestamp (hundredths of seconds)
```

Additionally, there are entries called STAT with information about the amount of work performed at each level in the SQL access method, also known as the EXPLAIN PLAN:

```
id=              the ID of the step in the EXPLAIN PLAN of the SQL statement
cnt=             the number of rows visited during this step
pid=             parent ID of this step in the EXPLAIN PLAN
pos=             ordering of all steps with the same ID in EXPLAIN PLAN
obj=             value of column OBJECT_ID in the view DBA_OBJECTS
op=              the actual operation performed at this step
```

Altogether, this information provides a very detailed, if cryptic, look into the inner workings of Oracle.

Familiarity with the format of the SQL trace file is useful for debugging applications. How many times have you wished you could retrieve a log of all the SQL statements executed by a batch program, a form, or a report? As you can see, that is exactly what the "raw" SQL trace file is. It is a sequential record of everything that an Oracle server process does and is therefore a record or a log of everything that comes into the Oracle server process from the front-end program, whether it is a batch program, an OLAP tool, a PowerBuilder form, or an SQR report.

But nobody recommends that you examine a "raw" SQL trace file for SQL tuning purposes. Instead, there is a utility, called TKPROF, which can be used to reformat the "raw" SQL trace information into an actual report, and more.

Formatting a SQL Tuning Report with TKPROF

The TKPROF report format program takes "raw" SQL trace information from an SQL trace file and reformats it into an aggregated report. When used properly, it can sort the SQL statements in the "raw" trace file so the worst SQL statements show up first, making it very easy to identify the problem.

Figure 9.23 The TKPROF utility at work.

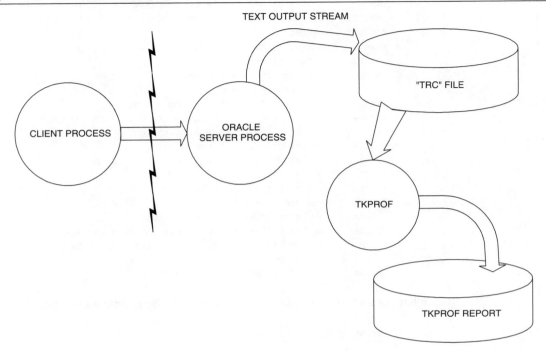

The tough part about using TKPROF is that it must be called from the operating system command line, making it rather archaic in terms of user interface! On UNIX, it must be called from the UNIX command line; on Windows NT, it must be called from the Command prompt.

Anyway, the TKPROF utility is quite basic; it takes the "raw" SQL trace file as input and produces a report (see Figure 9.23).

To find out the syntax of TKPROF, just enter the command itself with no parameters on the command line:

```
$ tkprof
Usage: tkprof tracefile outputfile [explain= ] [table= ]
               [print= ] [insert= ] [sys= ] [sort= ]
        table=schema.table    Use 'schema.table' with 'explain=' option.
        explain=user/pswd     Connect to ORACLE and issue EXPLAIN PLAN.
        print=integer         List only the first 'integer' SQL statements.
        aggregate=yes|no      Default: yes
        insert=filename       Create SQL script of SQL stmts and data.
        sys=no                Do not list SQL statements run as user SYS.
        record=filename       Record non-recursive SQL stmts in trace file.
        sort=option           Set of the following sort options:
            prscnt     number of times parse was called
            prscpu     cpu time parsing
```

```
prsela     elapsed time parsing
prsdsk     number of disk reads during parse
prsqry     number of buffers for consistent read during parse
prscu      number of buffers for current read during parse
prsmis     number of misses in library cache during parse
execnt     number of execute was called
execpu     cpu time spent executing
exeela     elapsed time executing
exedsk     number of disk reads during execute
exeqry     number of buffers for consistent read during execute
execu      number of buffers for current read during execute
exerow     number of rows processed during execute
exemis     number of library cache misses during execute
fchcnt     number of times fetch was called
fchcpu     cpu time spent fetching
fchela     elapsed time fetching
fchdsk     number of disk reads during fetch
fchqry     number of buffers for consistent read during fetch
fchcu      number of buffers for current read during fetch
fchrow     number of rows fetched
userid     userid of user that parsed the cursor
```

But what are all these options for? Let's start with the most basic syntax:

```
$ tkprof80 \orant\rdbms80\trace\ora00266.trc \temp\x.tkp
```

In this example here in a Windows NT environment, TKPROF is reading from the "raw" SQL trace file named *ora00266.trc* and will write output to another text file named *\temp\x.tkp*. In this and all examples, the name given for the output file is completely arbitrary.

This raw SQL trace file was generated by the preceding example, where we pretty much ran a single query, SELECT 'x' FROM DUAL, in SQL*Plus. What resulted in the output file was the following:

```
TKPROF: Release 8.0.2.0.2 - Beta on Sun Jul 6 21:59:29 1997
Copyright (c) Oracle Corporation 1979, 1994, 1996.  All rights reserved.
Trace file: ora00391.trc
Sort options: default


**************************************************************************
count    = number of times OCI procedure was executed
cpu      = cpu time in seconds executing
elapsed  = elapsed time in seconds executing
disk     = number of physical reads of buffers from disk
query    = number of buffers gotten for consistent read
current  = number of buffers gotten in current mode (usually for update)
rows     = number of rows processed by the fetch or execute call
**************************************************************************
```

```
alter session set sql_trace true

call     count    cpu    elapsed      disk      query    current       rows
-------  -----   -----  ----------  ----------  ----------  ----------  ----------
Parse        0   0.00       0.00           0           0           0           0
Execute      1   0.00       0.00           0           0           0           0
Fetch        0   0.00       0.00           0           0           0           0
-------  -----   -----  ----------  ----------  ----------  ----------  ----------
total        1   0.00       0.00           0           0           0           0

Misses in library cache during parse: 0
Optimizer goal: CHOOSE
Parsing user id: 5
*****************************************************************************

select 'x' from dual

call     count    cpu    elapsed      disk      query    current       rows
-------  -----   -----  ----------  ----------  ----------  ----------  ----------
Parse        1   0.00       0.00           0           0           0           0
Execute      1   0.00       0.00           0           0           0           0
Fetch        2   0.00       0.00           0           1           0           1
-------  -----   -----  ----------  ----------  ----------  ----------  ----------
total        4   0.00       0.00           0           1           0           1

Misses in library cache during parse: 0
Optimizer goal: CHOOSE
Parsing user id: 5
*****************************************************************************

select parameter, value
from v$nls_parameters     where (upper(parameter) in ('NLS_SORT','NLS_CURRENCY',
  'NLS_ISO_CURRENCY',                    'NLS_DATE_LANGUAGE',
  'NLS_NUMERIC_CHARACTERS',                      'NLS_LANGUAGE','NLS_TERRITORY'))

call     count    cpu    elapsed      disk      query    current       rows
-------  -----   -----  ----------  ----------  ----------  ----------  ----------
Parse        1   0.00       0.00           0           0           0           0
Execute      1   0.00       0.00           0           0           0           0
Fetch        1   0.00       0.00           0           0           0           7
-------  -----   -----  ----------  ----------  ----------  ----------  ----------
total        3   0.00       0.00           0           0           0           7

Misses in library cache during parse: 0
Optimizer goal: CHOOSE
Parsing user id: 5


*****************************************************************************
```

```
OVERALL TOTALS FOR ALL NON-RECURSIVE STATEMENTS

call      count    cpu    elapsed        disk       query     current        rows
-------   -----   -----  ----------  ----------  ----------  ----------  ----------
Parse         1    0.00        0.00           0           0           0           0
Execute       2    0.00        0.00           0           0           0           0
Fetch         2    0.00        0.00           0           1           0           8
-------   -----   -----  ----------  ----------  ----------  ----------  ----------
total         5    0.00        0.00           0           1           0           8

Misses in library cache during parse: 0

OVERALL TOTALS FOR ALL RECURSIVE STATEMENTS

call      count    cpu    elapsed        disk       query     current        rows
-------   -----   -----  ----------  ----------  ----------  ----------  ----------
Parse         0    0.00        0.00           0           0           0           0
Execute       0    0.00        0.00           0           0           0           0
Fetch         0    0.00        0.00           0           0           0           0
-------   -----   -----  ----------  ----------  ----------  ----------  ----------
total         0    0.00        0.00           0           0           0           0

Misses in library cache during parse: 0

    2  user  SQL statements in session.
    0  internal SQL statements in session.
    2  SQL statements in session.
*****************************************************************************
Trace file: ora00391.trc
Trace file compatibility: 7.03.02
Sort options: default

    1  session in tracefile.
    3  user  SQL statements in trace file.
    0  internal SQL statements in trace file.
    3  SQL statements in trace file.
    3  unique SQL statements in trace file.
   42  lines in trace file.
```

Although there isn't much going on in this example, its simplicity allows us to examine a few basics. First of all, the header of the report lists information such as the version of TKPROF and when it was run. It shows the name of the input file, the raw SQL trace file, and the sorting options provided. In this example, none were provided.

The bottom of this report header is a standard legend for the statistics displayed in the report:

```
count    = number of times OCI procedure was executed
cpu      = cpu time in seconds executing
```

```
elapsed = elapsed time in seconds executing
disk    = number of physical reads of buffers from disk
query   = number of buffers gotten for consistent read
current = number of buffers gotten in current mode (usually for update)
rows    = number of rows processed by the fetch or execute call
```

An OCI procedure refers to the Oracle Call Interface, which is the lowest-level application programming interface into Oracle. An OCI procedure could be a parse, an execute, or a fetch.

If TIMED_STATISTICS is FALSE, then TKPROF is always going to show 0.00 for both CPU and ELAPSED. As these statistics are so dependent on other factors, such as the current load on the machine and the type of machine, they are not all that useful by themselves anyway. At best, they provide supplementary information to augment more concrete information provided by some of the other statistics, so it is not necessary to have TIMED_STATISTICS enabled to get useful information from TKPROF.

The statistics for QUERY and CURRENT together make up the more commonly known statistic of *logical reads*. Logical reads are the number of buffers obtained from the Oracle buffer cache in the SGA. All SELECT, INSERT, UPDATE, and DELETE operations in Oracle operate out of the buffer cache first. If the necessary database blocks cannot be found in that buffer cache then a *physical read* occurs, which is the statistic DISK on this report. The ratio of physical reads to logical reads is typically referred to as the *hit ratio*. More precisely, the hit ratio is calculated as

```
(1 - (physical-reads / logical-reads)) * 100
```

which in terms of the statistics available in TKPROF would become

```
(1 - (DISK / (QUERY + CURRENT))) * 100
```

Following the header is an entry for each of the SQL statements. The first thing printed is the text of the SQL statement itself. Following this are the run-time statistics, which should be vaguely familiar from our examination of the contents of the raw SQL trace files:

call	count	cpu	elapsed	disk	query	current	rows
Parse	1	0.00	0.00	0	0	0	0
Execute	1	0.00	0.00	0	0	0	0
Fetch	2	0.00	0.00	0	1	0	1
total	4	0.00	0.00	0	1	0	1

Except for the *count*, the PARSE information is generally quite insignificant. If you are looking at SQL generated by a form, report, or a batch program, you generally like to see the PARSE operation happen only once for a SQL statement, even if the SQL statement is run several times. If the SQL was generated by an ad hoc tool like SQL*Plus, it is generally not so important that the PARSE operation be minimized.

The EXECUTE operation of a SQL statement can mean different things. For an INSERT, UPDATE, DELETE, or SELECT . . . FOR UPDATE command, all the work pertaining to the entire SQL statement occurs during the EXECUTE operation. In the case of a SELECT . . . FOR UPDATE statement, all the rows are fetched and locked during the EXECUTE operation.

The FETCH operation occurs only for SELECT statements other than SELECT . . . FOR UPDATE statements. During SELECT statements, the EXECUTE operation does not retrieve any data. It simply resolves the access methods and leaves "pointers" to the various data structures current inside the cursor. Then, the FETCH operation actually uses those "pointers" to visit the index entries or the rows in the tables, and the data is retrieved. Because a SELECT statement does not have any way of knowing how many rows are eventually going to be fetched, it is common to see an extra FETCH operation occur. This extra FETCH comes up empty, which tells the cursor that no more data can be retrieved.

Last, there is some extra information about the SQL statement:

```
Misses in library cache during parse: 0
Optimizer goal: CHOOSE
Parsing user id: 5
```

From Oracle7 on, there have been two components to a PARSE operation: parsing the SQL statement to obtain the execution plan and storing this information in the Oracle instance's global SQL *shared pool* and parsing the SQL statement for a particular session.

The PARSE statistic mentioned earlier pertains to the number of times this particular session tried to parse the SQL statement. If the application is using Oracle's shared pool correctly, only one of these PARSE operations will actually result in a true PARSE, where the execution plan is determined and an entry for the SQL statement is created in the shared pool. This is known as a *hard parse*. All subsequent PARSE attempts should reuse this entry, making for a very fast, lightweight PARSE operation, also known as a *soft parse*.

However, if the application is not using the shared pool properly, each PARSE operation issued by the application might result in a hard parse. In a data warehouse environment, this might not be as much of a cause for concern as in OLTP environments, but it can become a problem for frequently executed SQL statements. By far the most common cause of excessive hard parsing is the failure to use *bind variables*. This technique of using a *placeholder* in the text of the SQL statement and then substituting that placeholder with a value stored in a *variable*, is strongly encouraged for batch programs, forms, reports, and analysis tools. Oracle *caches* SQL statements in the shared pool based on the text of the SQL statement, and any variations in that text, no matter how slight, cause a new shared pool entry to be created for a SQL statement. If data values are embedded in the text of the SQL statement and these data values are constantly changing, then serious performance degradation could result.

Of course, in a data warehouse environment, there might be a significant amount of ad hoc querying. Also, the sheer number of SQL statements might be small enough to make this problem insignificant. Altogether, like many things, determining the statistic for "misses in library cache during parse" might indicate a problem requires some knowledge of how frequently the SQL statement is being executed. If the SQL is executed rather infrequently, then "misses in the library cache during parse" may not indicate a problem. If the SQL statement is executed every thirty seconds, twenty-four hours a day, then perhaps there is a problem that should be examined further.

The Optimizer Goal is also displayed, along with the USER_ID parsing the SQL statement. Both these factors can have a huge impact on how a SQL statement's execution plan is determined.

For example, remember that there are four Optimizer Goals: ALL_ROWS, FIRST_ROWS, CHOOSE, and RULE. The Optimizer Goal represents a "bias" on the part of the Oracle Optimizer when it tries to choose an execution method. ALL_ROWS emphasizes throughput, telling the Optimizer to choose a plan that retrieves all the rows the fastest. FIRST_ROWS emphasizes response time, telling the Optimizer to choose a plan that will retrieve the first rows the fastest, even at the expense of throughput. RULE is the old rule-based optimizer, which precedes the cost-based optimizer introduced in Oracle7. The rule-based optimizer is very familiar to most SQL programmers, but its rules haven't changed since Oracle version 6, and no new enhancements are being made to it. CHOOSE is the default goal, and it indicates that the Optimizer should choose between using the rule-based and cost-based optimizers, depending on whether there are any statistics on the tables involved in the SQL statement. If even one table has cost-based optimizer statistics, then CHOOSE will choose to use the cost-based optimizer. If none of the tables has ever had the ANALYZE command run to generate statistics, then CHOOSE will choose the rule-based optimizer.

The optimizer goal can be set for the whole database instance using the initialization parameter OPTIMIZER_MODE; valid values are ALL_ROWS, FIRST_ROWS, RULE, and CHOOSE (the default). Alternatively, the Optimizer Goal can be set for a single session using the following ALTER SESSION command:

```
ALTER SESSION SET OPTIMIZER_GOAL = ALL_ROWS | FIRST_ROWS | RULE | CHOOSE;
```

Last, the Optimizer Goal can be specified for a particular SQL statement using *hints*:

```
SELECT /*+ all_rows */ . . .
UPDATE /*+ first_rows */ . . .
DELETE /*+ rule */ . . .
SELECT /*+ choose */ . . .
```

Unfortunately, the Optimizer Goal cannot be set for a particular account, so that each time a user connects his or her own preferred Optimizer Goal would be used. On the other hand, perhaps this is a good thing, as absolute chaos might result if the Optimizer Goal is not kept as uniform as possible across all users.

Another factor affecting how a SQL statement execution plan is generated is the schema from which the parse information was derived. The schema for user Joe might present an entirely different set of tables by the same name than those seen by user Mary. User Joe might be looking at the tables belonging to the data warehouse, while user Mary may have made her own copies of those tables, and those much smaller tables are the ones she is querying. This fact should certainly be taken into consideration before trying to use SQL statements generated by Mary against the much larger tables Joe is seeing.

Now that we've had an initial look at some of the information provided by TKPROF, let's use some more of the TKPROF options. Let's use a slightly different example this time, querying the DBA_OBJECTS view in the Oracle data dictionary:

```
SQL> alter session set sql_trace true;

Session altered.

SQL> describe dba_objects
 Name                            Null?    Type
 ------------------------------- -------- ----
 OWNER                                    VARCHAR2(30)
 OBJECT_NAME                              VARCHAR2(128)
 SUBOBJECT_NAME                           VARCHAR2(30)
 OBJECT_ID                                NUMBER
 DATA_OBJECT_ID                           NUMBER
 OBJECT_TYPE                              VARCHAR2(15)
 CREATED                                  DATE
 LAST_DDL_TIME                            DATE
 TIMESTAMP                                VARCHAR2(75)
 STATUS                                   VARCHAR2(7)
 TEMPORARY                                VARCHAR2(1)
 GENERATED                                VARCHAR2(1)

SQL> select owner, object_type, count(*) from dba_objects
  2  group by owner, object_type;

OWNER                           OBJECT_TYPE        COUNT(*)
------------------------------- ---------------- ---------
DBSNMP                          SEQUENCE                 1
DBSNMP                          SYNONYM                  5
DBSNMP                          TABLE                    8
DEMO                            INDEX                   10
DEMO                            TABLE                   10
DEMO                            VIEW                     1
PUBLIC                          SYNONYM                659
SCOTT                           INDEX                    2
```

```
SCOTT                    TABLE                  4
SYS                      CLUSTER                9
SYS                      INDEX                116
SYS                      LIBRARY                4
SYS                      PACKAGE               95
SYS                      PACKAGE BODY          92
SYS                      PROCEDURE              4
SYS                      SEQUENCE              15

(. . .60 lines of output removed . . . )

76 rows selected.

SQL> exit
```

Look in the USER_DUMP_DEST directory for the most recently created file:

```
C:\> cd \orant\rdbms80\trace
C:\ORANT\RDBMS80\TRACE> dir *.trc
 Volume in drive C has no label.
 Volume Serial Number is 8899-58CB

 Directory of C:\ORANT\RDBMS80\TRACE

07/06/97  09:57p              110,852 ORA00266.TRC
07/06/97  09:58p                2,434 ORA00391.TRC
07/06/97  11:18p               12,181 ORA00435.TRC
07/06/97  03:45p               13,430 orclCKPT.TRC
07/06/97  03:45p               13,430 orclDBWR.TRC
07/06/97  03:45p               13,430 orclLGWR.TRC
05/26/97  02:28p                  170 orclPMON.TRC
07/06/97  03:45p               13,430 orclRECO.TRC
07/06/97  03:45p               13,430 orclSMON.TRC
07/06/97  03:45p               13,260 orclSNP0.TRC
07/06/97  03:45p               13,260 orclSNP1.TRC
              11 File(s)        219,307 bytes
```

This shows that the file *ora00435.trc* is the most recently created trace file. On most systems, unless lots of users are tracing their session, this is sufficient to locate a raw SQL trace file. So now execute TKPROF, but use the EXPLAIN= clause to run EXPLAIN PLAN in the report (see Figure 9.24). When EXPLAIN= is specified, TKPROF actually connects to the database instance as the specified user and runs EXPLAIN PLAN at that time for each SQL statement.

Syntactically, we are using the following:

```
C:\ORANT\RDBMS80\TRACE> tkprof80 ora00435.trc x.tkp explain=sys/manager

TKPROF: Release 8.0.2.0.2 - Beta on Sun Jul 6 23:27:56 1997

Copyright (c) Oracle Corporation 1979, 1994, 1996.  All rights reserved.
```

Figure 9.24 TKPROF connecting to perform EXPLAIN PLAN.

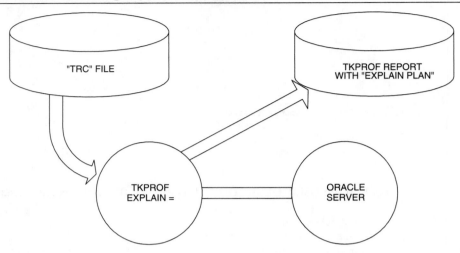

As you can see, it becomes necessary to write out the password to the SYS account in clear text; using the EXPLAIN= option for TKPROF is a clear security problem. For some reason, there is no way to have TKPROF prompt you for the password, allowing it to be hidden. The user SYS is being used only for this example, as SYS privileges are needed to perform EXPLAIN PLAN against data dictionary tables. Normally you may specify the username and password used in the original session.

Looking at the output file *x.tkp*, we see the following:

```
(. . . approximately 14 pages of output removed . . .)


**************************************************************************

select privilege#,nvl(col#,0),max(nvl(option$,0))
from
 objauth$ where obj#=:1 and grantee#=:2 group by privilege#,nvl(col#,0)

call     count   cpu    elapsed       disk      query    current      rows
------- ------  ----  ----------  ---------- ---------- ---------- ----------
Parse        1  0.00        0.00           0          0          0          0
Execute     10  0.00        0.00           0          0          0          0
Fetch       10  0.00        0.00           0         20          0          0
------- ------  ----  ----------  ---------- ---------- ---------- ----------
total       21  0.00        0.00           0         20          0          0

Misses in library cache during parse: 0
Optimizer goal: CHOOSE
Parsing user id: SYS    (recursive depth: 1)
```

```
Rows      Execution Plan
-------   ----------------------------------------------------
      0   SELECT STATEMENT    GOAL: CHOOSE
      0    SORT (GROUP BY)
      0     TABLE ACCESS (BY ROWID) OF 'OBJAUTH$'
      0      INDEX (RANGE SCAN) OF 'I_OBJAUTH2' (NON-UNIQUE)
```

****

```
select owner, object_type, count(*) from dba_objects
group by owner, object_type
```

call	count	cpu	elapsed	disk	query	current	rows
Parse	1	0.00	0.00	0	0	0	0
Execute	1	0.00	0.00	0	0	0	0
Fetch	6	0.00	0.00	137	11412	4	76
total	8	0.00	0.00	137	11412	4	76

```
Misses in library cache during parse: 1
Optimizer goal: CHOOSE
Parsing user id: 5  (SYSTEM)
```

```
Rows      Execution Plan
-------   ----------------------------------------------------
      0   SELECT STATEMENT    GOAL: CHOOSE
   5376    SORT (GROUP BY)
   5376     VIEW OF 'DBA_OBJECTS'
   5376      UNION-ALL
   5375       NESTED LOOPS
     98        TABLE ACCESS (FULL) OF 'USER$'
   5443        TABLE ACCESS (BY ROWID) OF 'OBJ$'
   5543         INDEX (RANGE SCAN) OF 'I_OBJ2' (UNIQUE)
      1       NESTED LOOPS
     98        TABLE ACCESS (FULL) OF 'USER$'
      1        TABLE ACCESS (BY ROWID) OF 'LINK$'
     99         INDEX (RANGE SCAN) OF 'I_LINK1' (NON-UNIQUE)
```

****

```
OVERALL TOTALS FOR ALL NON-RECURSIVE STATEMENTS
```

call	count	cpu	elapsed	disk	query	current	rows
Parse	8	0.00	0.00	0	0	0	0
Execute	8	0.00	0.00	0	0	0	0
Fetch	12	0.00	0.00	138	11457	4	86
total	28	0.00	0.00	138	11457	4	86

```
Misses in library cache during parse: 6
Misses in library cache during execute: 1

OVERALL TOTALS FOR ALL RECURSIVE STATEMENTS
```

call	count	cpu	elapsed	disk	query	current	rows
Parse	18	0.00	0.00	0	0	0	0
Execute	29	0.00	0.00	0	0	0	0
Fetch	57	0.00	0.00	0	132	0	40
total	104	0.00	0.00	0	132	0	40

```
Misses in library cache during parse: 0

     9  user  SQL statements in session.
    18  internal SQL statements in session.
    27  SQL statements in session.
    18  statements EXPLAINed in this session.
********************************************************************************
Trace file: ora00435.trc
Trace file compatibility: 7.03.02
Sort options: default

     0  session in tracefile.
     9  user  SQL statements in trace file.
    18  internal SQL statements in trace file.
    27  SQL statements in trace file.
    19  unique SQL statements in trace file.
    18  SQL statements EXPLAINed using schema:
          SYS.prof$plan_table
            Default table was used.
            Table was created.
            Table was dropped.
   392  lines in trace file.
```

Here we had to remove about fourteen pages of output to keep this chapter to reasonable size. As you can see, although the SQL*Plus session shows that we only executed three statements (an ALTER SESSION, a DESCRIBE, and the SELECT), the summary at the bottom of this report shows that nine "user SQL statements" were captured and no less than eighteen "internal" or recursive SQL statements were generated and captured.

The reason for this inflation is related to the fact that SQL*Plus itself runs a few SQL statements before the first results are returned. That is, as we ran the first SQL statement ALTER SESSION, SQL*Plus wanted to know what NLS language and conventions we were using, so it checked the view V$NLS_PARAMETERS after the ALTER SESSION was run but before it returned any response from the statement.

Also, the SQL*Plus DESCRIBE command can really best be described as a *macro*, in that SQL*Plus actually expands it into four or five SQL statements. Additionally, these four or five SQL statements generated by SQL*Plus recursively generated about ten or twelve additional "internal" SQL statements. All in all, twenty-six SQL statements, both "user" and "internal," result from the ALTER SESSION and the DESCRIBE commands. Finally, the twenty-seventh SQL statement is the query on the DBA_OBJECTS view.

In the output just displayed, note the EXPLAIN PLAN output that has now been added to the run-time statistics. This part of the report comes from two sources: the STAT lines, briefly discussed when we were examining the raw SQL trace output files, and the EXPLAIN PLAN command run during TKPROF. The "rows" information, representing the number of table or index rows visited during the step of the execution plan, comes from the STAT entries from the raw SQL trace file. The rest of the EXPLAIN PLAN output was generated by TKPROF, which created its own PLAN_TABLE, populated it, and dropped it.

TKPROF's EXPLAIN PLAN MAY NOT BE THE SAME PLAN THAT WAS EXECUTED

Note that the EXPLAIN PLAN is done at the time of TKPROF reporting and will be based on the available indexes and statistics at that time; this plan may not match the plan which was in effect when the trace file was created.

As illuminating as it is to see all the additional SQL statements resulting from "recursive" or "internal" SQL, there are times when we'd just prefer not to see it, especially in the interests of brevity. So, TKPROF comes with a SYS=NO clause, which filters out all "recursive" SQL statements from the body of the report. However, statistics from the recursive SQL is still summarized at the bottom of the report:

```
C:\TEMP> tkprof80 ora00435.trc x.tkp explain=sys/manager sys=no
```

Unfortunately, when we read the resulting report, we still have to read through the all the nonrecursive SQL statements generated by SQL*Plus "expanding" the DESCRIBE "macro" before we get to the query on DBA_OBJECTS. What would be most useful would be the ability to sort the SQL statements in the TKPROF report so that the most *interesting* ones "percolated" to the top of the report and the least interesting SQL statements filtered to the bottom of the report. To do this, we would want to use one or more of the twenty-three different sort options provided by TKPROF:

```
prscnt    number of times parse was called
prscpu    cpu time parsing
prsela    elapsed time parsing
prsdsk    number of disk reads during parse
prsqry    number of buffers for consistent read during parse
prscu     number of buffers for current read during parse
prsmis    number of misses in library cache during parse
```

```
execnt    number of execute was called
execpu    cpu time spent executing
exeela    elapsed time executing
exedsk    number of disk reads during execute
exeqry    number of buffers for consistent read during execute
execu     number of buffers for current read during execute
exerow    number of rows processed during execute
exemis    number of library cache misses during execute
fchcnt    number of times fetch was called
fchcpu    cpu time spent fetching
fchela    elapsed time fetching
fchdsk    number of disk reads during fetch
fchqry    number of buffers for consistent read during fetch
fchcu     number of buffers for current read during fetch
fchrow    number of rows fetched
userid    userid of user that parsed the cursor
```

Which ones should we use? Well, let's start eliminating, if we can.

Surprisingly, the statistics involving CPU and elapsed seconds are probably the least useful. This is because these values are extremely dependent on what kind of activity is happening elsewhere on the system. If there are forty other people running huge queries, then both the CPU and elapsed seconds are going to be affected through no fault of the SQL statement being examined. Naturally, differences in these values even over consecutive executions of the same query must be questioned; did the query actually run faster the second time or did the system load ease by the time the query ran again?

So, typically, any sort options ending in ". . . ela" and ". . . cpu" can be eliminated. That eliminates six options, leaving seventeen.

You may have already noticed "parse" times are usually quite small, and in fact they usually measure around 0.00. These small values with small differences between them make them bad sort criteria. Parsing is usually not much of a concern anyway, especially in a data warehouse environment, as we discussed earlier. Without ignoring parse statistics completely, let's eliminate them as a sort option. That eliminates another five options, leaving twelve.

The statistics pertaining to "misses on library cache" are related to parsing. Again, without ignoring this completely, let's eliminate them for the purposes of finding the most horrible SQL statements. Eliminating all options ending in ". . . mis" takes away one more option, leaving eleven.

Let's also eliminate USERID, as we're not likely to find much in the way of poor performance based on who parsed a cursor. While it may be useful for other investigations, it is not a good option for finding the worst performers. This leaves ten. Let's also eliminate the row counts, as we're not so much concerned with how much data is being returned as with how much work is performed to return it. After all, a SQL statement returning a single row may require 95 percent of the work performed, while another query returning a million rows may perform hardly any work to do so. This eliminates two more options, leaving eight. We're now down to the following:

```
execnt        number of execute was called
exedsk        number of disk reads during execute
exeqry        number of buffers for consistent read during execute
execu         number of buffers for current read during execute
fchcnt        number of times fetch was called
fchdsk        number of disk reads during fetch
fchqry        number of buffers for consistent read during fetch
fchcu         number of buffers for current read during fetch
```

For the same reasons as row counts, let's get rid of "number of XXX was called" because the number of executes does not have much bearing on performance. It does have some, as operations that are called more frequently certainly rack up higher statistics, but let's not sort on that criteria for now. This leaves six options.

We're down to the ". . . dsk" options, which are physical I/Os, and the ". . . qry" and ". . . cu" options, which are also known as *logical I/Os*. In a testing environment, *physical I/Os* may not be all that relevant, since the buffer cache may be sized smaller. Also, the pattern of usage of the buffer cache may vary widely, resulting in more physical I/Os for a particular SQL statement while testing than would normally result in the production database. The same can be true in reverse: In a development environment, the smaller volumes of data might be more easily cached in the buffer cache, resulting in an abnormally optimistic picture due to fewer physical reads than would result in production. Therefore, let's eliminate the ". . . dsk" parameters.

```
exeqry        number of buffers for consistent read during execute
execu         number of buffers for current read during execute
fchqry        number of buffers for consistent read during fetch
fchcu         number of buffers for current read during fetch
```

Finally, this leaves us with four sort options, which altogether happen to represent logical I/Os. If you think about it, it just so happens that logical I/Os are the perfect metric for determining the amount of work being performed by an Oracle server process. Logical I/Os are affected only by the execution plan; a less efficient execution plan results in more logical I/Os while a more efficient execution plan uses fewer. Logical I/Os are not affected by other processes or operations on the system. Logical I/Os are even portable from one platform to another; a query requiring one thousand logical I/Os on a UNIX system is likely to require the same number on Windows NT, on VAX VMS, or on MVS.

So, since sort options in TKPROF are additive, we can find the worst SQL statements by using the following SORT= clause:

```
SORT=EXEQRY,EXECU,FCHQRY,FCHCU
```

What TKPROF will do is add these four statistics for each SQL statement and sort the report by the sum. Now running TKPROF with the SORT= option as well will now give us a TKPROF report with the most expensive SQL statement at the top and the least expensive (and therefore the least important, for our purposes) at the bottom. Let's go further. Standard tuning methodology (whether the subject is Oracle, any other database system, or an operating system) dictates an iterative methodology. Attack the three worst, the five worst, or the ten worst problems only; ignore all the others. Fix those first three, or five, or ten. Then, after they are fixed, reevaluate again. Again, attack only the worst few problems. Fix them. And reevaluate . . .

Using this approach, all effort is directed at the worst problems. There is no expense of effort on small problems or nonproblems. Also, by reducing the scope, it becomes easier to focus on the worst problems. It is easier to focus on five issues than it is to focus on fifty or one hundred issues.

The TKPROF report can support this. The PRINT= clause will limit the TKPROF report output to only the number of SQL statements specified in the PRINT= clause. For example, if you specify PRINT=10, then TKPROF will print report details for only ten SQL statements, after all the other clauses and options have been processed. So, if you are sorting by EXEQRY, EXECU, FCHQRY, FCHCU, and you have specified SYS=NO to eliminate recursive SQL, then TKPROF will only print the ten least efficient (according to the sort criteria) nonrecursive SQL statements.

More options. Let's suppose you just wanted a quick report listing the SQL statements that were not recursive, in the order they were called. The RECORD= clause allows you to specify an output file for such a report.

Now, let's suppose that you did not want TKPROF to aggregate statistics for multiple executions of the exact same SQL statement. This might be the case if different executions of the same query are resulting in vastly different response times not explained by different users parsing the query. In this case, AGGREGATE=NO might be useful; the default, of course, is AGGREGATE=YES.

If a large number of people were using TKPROF at the same time, then having each of those TKPROF sessions create, populate, and then drop their own PLAN_TABLES to run EXPLAIN PLAN could get expensive. In this situation you may want to specify a fixed, permanent PLAN_TABLE for TKPROF to use when it does EXPLAIN PLAN; this involves the TABLE=*schema.tablename* clause.

The last option is by far the most intriguing. The INSERT= clause produces, instead of a formatted report, a SQL script that can be run through SQL*Plus or Server Manager to insert all the SQL trace information into a table called TKPROF_TABLE. From this, if you wish, you can generate your own reports, similar to TKPROF. What is so intriguing about this is the possibility of doing advanced analysis on performance statistics. Think about using this feature in conjunction with setting the initialization parameter SQL_TRACE = TRUE to enable SQL trace globally for an entire instance. Once all the raw SQL trace files have been gathered, TKPROF can generate SQL scripts for inserting all the SQL trace information into a table in the database.

Now imagine using an OLAP tool or some other advanced data warehouse analysis tool, not against marketing or campaign data, but against database performance data. The possibilities are quite exciting, especially with data mining techniques. You may be able to find something important that can't be gleaned from poring over traditional TKPROF reports.

But the most important thing that TKPROF provides is hard numbers, an empirical set of results against which different hypotheses can be either validated or invalidated. TKPROF allows a person doing tuning to unambiguously determine whether one technique works better than another. Is this index more efficient for this query than that one? Test it out. Enable SQL tracing against one version of the query and then against the other. TKPROF the results, and compare.

Would clustered tables be more efficient than regular tables? Test it out; create the necessary clusters and compare results in TKPROF. Would the optimizer goal of FIRST_ROWS provide better results than CHOOSE? Test it out, either using hints or the ALTER SESSION SET OPTIMIZER_GOAL command.

Looking for Problems

We've covered three major areas of tuning in Oracle data warehouses:

- adequately sizing the I/O subsystem
- pretuning the data warehouse
- optimizing the load phase
- tuning SQL statements

Are there more areas to cover? Absolutely! In particular, we need to discuss the techniques necessary to find processes that are taking an inordinate share of resources. Once we can *screen* for the worst resource hogs, we can then *drill down* on those intensive processes and fix them. In the previous section on SQL trace and TKPROF we showed how to do this drill down, this surgical focus on an already identified problem. When you are using SQL tracing and TKPROF, you are not scanning the system looking for problems. When you are using those tools, you have already identified the problem and you are now using very exact tools to fix the problem.

But what do we use to find the problem on a busy system? Finding out who is bringing a busy database to its knees is somewhat similar to trying to find out which cars are emitting the most pollution on a bumper-to-bumper freeway. It's probably not possible to hook up test equipment to every vehicle's tailpipe; personally, we would want to wear a bullet-proof vest to do that. You have to have some way of surveying all the vehicles from a distance to determine who is likely emitting the most exhaust first, and then put on the bullet-proof vests and try to convince just those drivers to submit to a more invasive, but more definitive, test.

It's the same with databases and data warehouses in particular. In a data warehouse, everyone is using tremendous amounts of resources; just as on the freeway everyone is emitting pollution. The trick is to detect who may be doing too much.

This exercise is usually reactive in nature. Pretuning techniques and SQL tuning can be proactive, in that potentially resource-intensive processes can be examined to determine whether they will consume too many resources. Scanning a system in use for performance problems, however, is strictly reactive.

Here are some tips and techniques for enabling and performing reactive performance tuning.

Keep a Baseline

Question: "Why is the system so slow?"
Answer: "Slow compared to what?"

Yes, it's easy to tell this conversation went downhill from that point, but the response is really quite valid. What specifically is happening (or not happening) that makes the person asking the question assert that the data warehouse is performing poorly?

There should be some facts available to lend credence to the assertion. For example, it should be possible to determine whether overall CPU utilization at present is different from an hour ago, or a day ago, or the average over the course of a week for this time of day. The same for "percent busy" statistics on the I/O subsystem and "waiting for I/O" statistics for the CPU. These are all statistics that come from the operating system and are therefore very dependent on the operating system. But it is crucial to be able to find this information and then save it for trend analysis.

On UNIX systems, a simple utility for this is "sar" (a.k.a. System Activity Reporter). This utility can be run in either a statistics-gathering mode, a reporting mode, or both at the same time. It's useful to run regularly in its statistics-gathering mode, perhaps once every five minutes. It can gather statistics on the following:

- CPU utilization (system or "kernel" usage, usage by "user" processes such as Oracle, "wait for I/O," and idle)
- swapping, paging, and memory utilization
- disk devices (percent busy, average queue length, average wait)

All of these statistics are valuable in determining how the *data pumps* (i.e., CPU, memory, I/O) supporting the data warehouse are working.

Finding Resource Hogs

When a system is running "slow," the reason is either

- a bottleneck or
- a *resource hog*

As mentioned earlier, many implementations of UNIX include some form of a "top" command, which displays the top ten processes in terms of CPU consumption. This is usually a volatile display in that the top ten processes probably keep shifting around, one sometimes ranking first, then at other times falling out of the top ten altogether.

If the UNIX platform you are using does not have a "top" command (or anything similar), you can do essentially the same thing using the following:

```
$ ps -eaf | sort -n +3 | tail
```

This command sequence will first run the UNIX *ps* command, which retrieves UNIX *process status*. The "-eaf" obtains a fairly complete display of information about each process, including the name of the process, the cumulative CPU time, the time when the process started, and the current CPU "clock ticks" consumed. It is this last statistic (CPU "clock ticks") that is most interesting. By passing the output from *ps -eaf* into the UNIX *sort* command, we are instructing *sort* to resort the output by the fourth field, which is the CPU "clock ticks" column. Then, to retrieve ten processes with the highest number of CPU "clock ticks," we are filtering the output from *sort* using the UNIX *tail* command. Using this homegrown top ten command, the heaviest consumer of CPU resources will be the last process displayed.

Whichever method you use, any process that stays consistently near the top of the list merits attention. Especially if it is an Oracle server process. If it is, it may be useful to find out exactly what it is doing. But that would be a *drill-down*; we would no longer be looking for a possible culprit, we would be looking more closely at a single suspect.

Drilling Down into Oracle Resource Hogs

Once you've identified a process as a possible problem, it might be useful to find out exactly what it's doing. To do that, we can go back to SQL tracing, but at a different level. The default level of SQL tracing, level 0, shows all the statistics necessary for generating a TKPROF report, for tuning SQL statements.

But there is additional information that SQL tracing can provide. Although TKPROF does not use this extra information, you can use it by viewing it in the raw SQL trace file.

Server Manager

As we mentioned earlier, one of the methods for enabling SQL tracing in another Oracle session uses the Server Manager's ORADEBUG utility. This is the only way to enable the two extra levels of SQL tracing, which are as follows:

- **Level 4:** provides all the information with SQL trace's default level (i.e., level 0), and it displays the values for any bind variables
- **Level 8:** provides all the information with SQL trace's default level (i.e., level 0), and it adds information on WAIT events
- **Level 12:** provides all the information of levels 0, 4, and 8 combined

Tracing WAIT EVENTS

From Server Manager, issue the following command:

```
SVRMGR> oradebug setospid NNNNN
Statement processed.
SVRMGR> oradebug event 10046 trace name context forever, level 8
Statement processed.
SVRMGR> oradebug unlimit
Statement processed.
```

This series of commands will first cause Server Manager to "attach" to the Oracle server process whose operating system process ID (i.e., O.S. PID) is the decimal number represented by *NNNNN*.

Remember: On Windows NT, you have to translate the hexadecimal value you get from the column SPID in the V$PROCESS view. If you acquired the PID from Windows NT Task Manager, then it is already in decimal format.

Once Server Manager is attached to the other Oracle server process, you can set the Oracle event number 10046 (i.e., SQL tracing) in that other process. This event will remain set "forever," which means until it is countermanded or until that process terminates. Since level 8 will probably mean more SQL trace output in the trace file, it might be a good idea to remove the size restriction on trace files imposed by the MAX_DUMP_FILE_SIZE parameter. This is not required, but it could keep you from missing something in case there is a lot going inside the process being traced, and the trace file becomes truncated.

Once SQL trace level 8 (or higher) is enabled, you will see lines starting with the phrase "WAIT #" in the SQL trace file. The format of these lines is as follows:

```
WAIT #<cursor>: nam="<event>" ela=N p1=N p2=N p3=N
```

where

```
cursor    The cursor whose execution is waiting
event     The name of the Oracle event we're waiting for
ela=N     Elapsed time in hundredths of seconds we've been waiting
p1=N      parameter #1 for the event
p2=N      parameter #2 for the event
p3=N      parameter #3 for the event
```

If you read backward in the trace file, you can find the PARSING IN CURSOR #<cursor> statement that identifies the SQL statement that is waiting. If you read backward from the WAIT event line, you can find the last operation (i.e., PARSE #<cursor>, EXEC #<cursor>, FETCH #<cursor>) that was executed, which would be the operation (or "step") of the SQL statement that the session is waiting on.

The ELA=*N* shows the amount of time this event was waited upon. This is in hundredths of seconds and should not be considered "gospel." Many operations complete far more quickly than 0.01 seconds, so many times this value will be

Wait Events

Events are basically information internal to Oracle, so documentation about them is not normally published publicly. But the following are some of the basic events most commonly seen:

SQL*Net message from client	The Oracle server process is waiting for a message to arrive from a client process.
SQL*Net message to client	The Oracle server process is sending a message to a client process.
SQL*Net more data from client	The previous operation was a message from a client process, and this is a continuation.
SQL*Net more data to client	The previous operation was a message to a client process, and this is a continuation.
buffer busy waits	A block is being read into the buffer cache by another session.
client message	The Oracle server process is idle and waiting for an SQL*Net packet.
db file scattered read	The Oracle server process is waiting on a full table scan (i.e., multiblock read).
db file sequential read	The Oracle server process is waiting on an indexed scan (i.e., single-block read).
enqueue	The Oracle server process is waiting on a lock (see V$LOCK).
free buffer waits	DBWR needs to free up some buffers by writing some "dirtied" blocks.
Null event	The Oracle server process is idle.
latch free	The Oracle server process is waiting on a latch (see V$LATCHNAME for P1).
log file sync	The Oracle server process has COMMITed or ROLLBACKed; LGWR has been posted to write the log buffer to the redo logfile.
parallel query dequeue wait	The Oracle server process is waiting on interprocess communication between PQ slaves, which takes place on internal queues.
pmon timer	PMON is idle, waiting to awaken.
rdbms ipc message	DBWR, LGWR, LCKn background processes are idle, waiting to awaken.
rdbms ipc reply	One of the background processes is waiting on a reply from another background process.
smon timer	SMON is idle, waiting to awaken.
write complete waits	The Oracle server process is waiting for DBWR to finish writing a "dirtied" block.

Of course, there are many more events. Contact Oracle Worldwide Support for additional explanations, if necessary. If the event contains information that Oracle feels is proprietary, they may not provide you with any details.

rounded, frequently to 0. The remaining information fields are all dependent on the value of NAM=, which is the name of the event.

These events are also seen in the dynamic data dictionary view V$SES-SION_WAIT. However, rows in that view exist only for the duration of the wait. Once the process is no longer waiting, the row is removed.

The V$SESSION_WAIT view provides a good snapshot of what all the sessions in the database instance are waiting on at a certain point in time, but it is rather difficult to track what a particular session is waiting on from moment to moment. This level of SQL tracing logs that same information to the trace file, so you can track what an individual session has been waiting on.

Tracing BIND VARIABLE Values

If an Oracle process is doing something unusual or returning unexpected results, it might be useful to see what data values are being passed to each SQL statement that uses bind variables. Of course, it is easy to see what data values are being passed when bind variables are not used, as these values are embedded right in the text of the SQL statement itself. Thus, these data values can be viewed using the default level of SQL tracing.

However, in order to effectively use the SGA Shared Pool and cache SQL statements, it is usually necessary to use bind variables. To dump the values of bind variables from an Oracle session currently running, use Server Manager to enable SQL tracing:

```
SVRMGR> oradebug setospid NNNNN
Statement processed.
SVRMGR> oradebug event 10046 trace name context forever, level 4
Statement processed.
SVRMGR> oradebug unlimit
Statement processed.
```

SQL trace level 4 provides all the information provided by level 0, plus the following entries to display bind variable values:

```
BINDS #<cursor>:
 bind <var>: dty=N mxl=N(N) mal=N scl=N pre=N oacflg=N
  bfp=0xNNNNNN bln=NN avl=NN flg=NN
  value=<value>
```

where

cursor	The cursor to which the bind variable belongs
var	positional number assigned to the variable within the SQL statement (i.e., first variable is "0," second variable is "1," etc.)
dty	data type in internal representation (see OCI Reference Manual)
mxl	maximum length of the bind variable

```
mal       array length
scl       scale (if numeric)
pre       precision (if numeric)
oacflg    bit-field indicating internal details about variable
bfp       hexadecimal bind address
bln       bind buffer length
avl       actual value length
flg       bit-field indicating internal details about variable
value     actual value of the bind variable
```

CAUTION: BE CAREFUL WITH THIS!

Be cautious when using the ORADEBUG facility. Be aware that it is intended primarily for use by Oracle Development and Oracle Support only and that the syntax of these commands is subject to change without prior notice.

Don't abuse this facility by exploring. You may give Oracle Worldwide Support a good reason to hang up on you.

Summary

This chapter is by no means a complete rundown on tuning Oracle databases or tuning Oracle-based data warehouses. Use the Oracle Server tuning guides; they are quite well written and contain useful advice that did not make sense to duplicate here. Consider this chapter something of a supplement to that standard piece of Oracle documentation.

Most questions about the behavior of an Oracle process can be answered by examining SQL trace files. If at all possible, ignore the "experts," ignore the pundits as they pontificate, even ignore most of the assertions in this book. Go out and find out for yourself. Trace it. Figure it out. Draw your own conclusions based on the empirical evidence.

PARALLEL OPERATIONS IN THE ORACLE DATA WAREHOUSE

Parallel operations in Oracle are a direct outgrowth from the trend toward data warehousing. From queries, inserts, updates, and deletes, to index and table creation, to loading, to media recovery, almost every facet of Oracle has gradually been retrofitted with a parallel option.

What Is Oracle Parallel Query Option?

In Oracle7, the Parallel Query Option (PQO) is sometimes confused with Parallel Server Option (PSO). Parallel Query Option allows certain individual SQL statements to be transparently divided into several, concurrently executing operations, providing a dramatic speedup in certain conditions. PQO can be used with single-instance exclusive-mode Oracle and it does not require PSO. It can also be used in conjunction with PSO to transparently divide certain operations not only among several processes on a single node but across several nodes as well. While PQO and its ability to scale operations within a system are available on just about all the one hundred-plus platforms Oracle runs on, the availability of the Parallel Server Option is more restricted. Fortunately, the most popular (at least in the United States) operating environments, such as IBM AIX, Sun, HP-UX, Sequent, Pyramid, DEC, and now even Windows NT, have specific configurations that will support Parallel Server. In many cases, however, this facility also requires purchase or licensing of particular hardware or operating system options. For example, to run the Parallel Server Option on Sun Solaris, the user must also acquire the PDB (Parallel Data Base) software from Sun Microsystems.

One additional point of possible confusion: With Oracle8, the Parallel Query Option becomes a standard feature of the Enterprise Edition of the Oracle8 Server. This has been a long-standing tradition of Oracle: What is originally offered as an unbundled additional option is later folded into the base product as standard functionality. This occurred previously when Oracle7 debuted and PL/SQL and row-level locking (together known as the Procedural Option under Oracle version 6) became standard functionality, for instance. The Parallel Server Option, covered in Chapter 11, remains a separately licensed option with Oracle8.

PQO first became available with Oracle7, version 7.1, and consisted of the following operations:

- parallel queries
- parallel direct-path SQL*Loader
- parallel CREATE INDEX (pCI)
- parallel instance recovery

Later, with Oracle7, version 7.2, the following were added:

- parallel CREATE TABLE . . . AS SELECT (pCTAS)
- parallel execution of partitioned UNION-ALL views

And with Oracle8, the following features appear:

- parallel queries on partitioned tables
- parallel DML on partitioned tables

Later on in this chapter we will be discussing each of these operations in detail. But first, we will discuss the appropriateness of parallelized operations in general terms.

When Are Parallel Operations Useful?

This issue is neatly summarized by considering the following question: "If it takes a woman nine months to produce a baby, could nine women take one month to do the same?" The answer is *probably not*; the reason the answer isn't *absolutely not* has to do with recent technological advances in cloning and the desire of certain people to appear on late-night talk shows. You just can't tell anymore . . .

Such speculation (and kidding) aside, it seems certain that parallelism is not the right strategy for speeding up all operations; it may be impossible (due to present technology) or not worth the effort. The same is true with database operations.

The main criterion in deciding whether to apply parallelism to a particular operation probably has to do with the duration of the operation. All other issues, such as the number of discretely identifiable steps in the operation, can be altered.

AVOID PARALLEL QUERY ON A BUSY SYSTEM

Parellelizing any operation adds work to the system. The same amount of actual processing effort is required plus the work of dividing the task up and then later recombining results. If the hardware (CPU or disk subsystem) is already running at capacity, then parallelizing will result in diminished throughput on the system.

Figure 10.1 Attempting to parallelize brief operations.

But if an operation already completes relatively swiftly, there may be little advantage to trying to speed it up. It is the operations that take a long time that are likely to benefit from the effort involved in parallelizing.

To arbitrarily name a figure, let's say that it generally takes about ten seconds to break a transaction into several smaller sub-transactions. Then, let's say that about 10 percent extra overhead is imposed on these sub-transactions during run-time for synchronization. Last, let's say that it takes an additional ten seconds to collate the results from all these sub-transactions to form a single unified result from a single transaction. (These timings aren't representative of real queries, but they make the following example easier to follow. In reality, PQO can frequently perform this task in less than a second, but longer times may be required for large queries spread over many instances.)

Now, let's apply these overheads to a small transaction that takes about two seconds to complete without parallelization (see Figure 10.1). Imagine that we are going to try to execute this query using ten separate distinct threads of execution. Each of the ten threads of execution might take one-tenth of two seconds, or 0.2 seconds. Tack on the additional 10 percent run-time overhead, and we get 0.22 seconds. Immediately, you can see that the original two-second transaction would probably take at least 20.22 seconds to complete after parallelization. Certainly, there is no advantage to parallelization here.

On the other hand, consider a query that takes two hours to complete (see Figure 10.2). Initiating the parallelized operation may take about ten seconds, but if the operation is farmed out equally to ten parallel threads of execution, it

Figure 10.2 Parallelizing long-running operations.

seems reasonable to assume that each thread of execution should take approximately one-tenth of two hours, or twelve minutes, to complete. Tacking on the extra 10 percent overhead (just because we're conservative) leaves us with an expected execution time of 13.33 minutes. Including another ten seconds to consolidate the results of the ten separate threads of execution and close them down, we could now reduce the two-hour query to under fourteen minutes. Now that's worthwhile.

The majority of "operational" systems can be characterized as online transaction processing, or OLTP. These kinds of systems are designed to process hundreds, thousands, or millions of transactions per hour, each transaction being a relatively short-lived operation. As a result, parallelized operations typically do not benefit OLTP systems except for a few limited exceptions, such as index creation.

In contrast, many of the operations performed in a data warehouse are huge, long-running affairs: a load from a huge "flat file"; a massive query against several huge tables loaded with detailed data; summarization of these same huge detailed queries into smaller "summary" tables. Therefore, parallelized operations generally benefit data warehouses and other decision-support systems (DSSs) immensely. Almost the entire feature set of the original PQO benefits data warehousing and should be exploited.

Parallel Queries

The ability to transparently execute a SELECT statement in parallel is one of the biggest technical triumphs of the Oracle7 product. It first became available with version 7.1 and is the "flagship" feature of the PQO.

Most of Oracle's parallelized operations share some common traits. The decision to run in parallel is either completely transparent or can be chosen with a simple clause like PARALLEL (DEGREE nn). Behind the scenes, the Oracle server process, which would normally be tasked with performing all the work of the query, is promoted to a management role known as the *query coordinator* (QC). The QC is responsible for the following:

- dynamically partitioning the work to be done
- recruiting a *crew* of *parallel query slave* processes to perform the actual work
- assigning partitions to each of the parallel query "slaves"
- receiving and collating the results returned by the parallel query slaves to the initiating process

After these tasks are done, the parallel query slave processes used during the operation return to a *pool* of such processes owned by the database instance, and the QC reverts to being just a normal everyday Oracle server process. If the next operation is not parallel, then it will do all the work, as normal. If the next operation is to be in parallel, then the whole process of becoming a QC starts all over again.

Consider the following example:

```
SQL> SELECT degree, instances FROM user_tables
  2 WHERE table_name = 'BILLING_DETAIL';

DEGREE      INSTANCES
---------- ----------
         1          1

SQL> SET TIMING ON
SQL> SELECT count(*) FROM billing_detail;

    COUNT(*)
------------
    12384004

Elapsed: 00:58:49.01
```

The first query merely confirms that the table BILLING_DETAIL is currently not set up for parallel queries. The default value of 1 is in effect for both DEGREE and INSTANCES. Please bear in mind that values greater than 1 for INSTANCES are useless unless this is a Parallel Server database with as many active database instances as specified.

The second statement turns on SQL*Plus timing, which will display elapsed time in hours, minutes, and seconds. The third statement is a query that merely counts the number of rows in the BILLING_DETAIL table, and it took just under one hour to complete.

Behind the scenes, the Oracle server process might look as it is shown in Figure 10.3.

Now, let's see what happens when we set a default DEGREE of parallelism on the table. The DEGREE of parallelism is the requested number of concurrent threads of execution to be used on one database instance in order to complete the query. The other parameter, INSTANCES, indicates the number of database instances to expand the DEGREE over and, as previously mentioned, is usable only in conjunction with Oracle Parallel Server. The resulting number of concurrent threads of execution requested, also known as the *scan factor*, is the product of these two numbers, or DEGREE times INSTANCES. So, if DEGREE = 4 and INSTANCES = 3, then a total of four threads of execution will be requested across each of three database instances, for a total scan factor of 12.

So, let's alter the PARALLEL characteristics of the table and reexecute the same query.

```
SQL> ALTER TABLE billing_detail PARALLEL (DEGREE 8);

Table altered.

SQL> SELECT degree, instances FROM user_tables
  2 WHERE TABLE_NAME = 'BILLING_DETAIL';

DEGREE      INSTANCES
---------- ----------
         8          1
```

```
SQL> SET TIMING ON
SQL> SELECT COUNT(*) FROM billing_detail;

    COUNT(*)
-------------
    12384004

Elapsed: 00:08:13.23
```

The row count returned by the query was the same, but the elapsed time dropped from 58 minutes to 8. This is not quite an eightfold improvement, and we'll explore the reasons why shortly. However, it's not a bad performance improvement, gained with little or no effort on the part of the end user.

Behind the scenes however, there was a lot happening.

Step 1: Dynamic Partitioning

PQO uses dynamic partitioning to divide the total work to be performed by a query. Each time a parallel query is executed, this process of partitioning the

Figure 10.3 Nonparallel query.

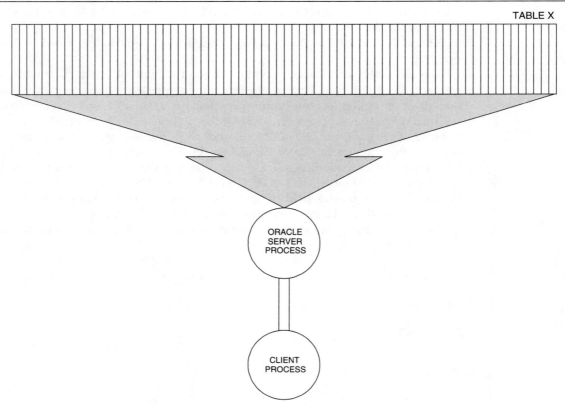

table to be queried must be done over again, even if the previous operation was the exact same query. It's not as if everything is thrown away, however; partitioned queries executed by each concurrent thread of execution are saved in the SGA's Shared SQL area, just like other queries. So there is some reuse.

The fact that PQO provides *internal parallelism* is important, because the end user issuing a SELECT statement need not change the SQL statement at all or use a different front-end tool to reap the advantages of parallelism. Many database systems provide functionality similar to PQO, but they do so *externally*, by forcing the end user to use a different front-end tool or connect to the database differently. PQO can be entirely transparent to the end users if they wish.

Dynamic partitioning allows Oracle to adjust, at run-time, to factors such as changing data volume and available CPU resources. *Static partitioning*, available with Oracle8 partitioned tables and solely employed by most other databases vendors, is based primarily upon a predetermined partitioning scheme formulated by the system administrator (see Figure 10.4 for a comparison of the two modes). As you might suppose, poor guesses by the system administrator or the DBA will result in queries that perpetually execute poorly. To react to changing

Figure 10.4 Comparison of dynamic and static partitioning.

data volumes and system resources, static partitioning schemes require at minimum that the rules of data partitioning be changed and at worst may require a reorganization of the tables involved.

Dynamic partitioning schemes such as Oracle's do incur *front-loaded overhead* because each query must draw on information in the data dictionary to determine how to create partitions. So systems that use dynamic partitioning schemes, like Oracle PQO, can experience initial delays while the task at hand is divided equally and each subtask is handed off to parallel query slaves.

In Oracle7, PQO implemented parallelism for full-table scans only. With Oracle8, parallel index scans also become possible on partitioned tables which have local indexing. A parallel query slave process can be assigned to each partition, and each PQ slave will scan the index for each partition concurrently. This is similar to parallel index scan functionality offered by other database vendors.

Non-partitioned tables in Oracle8 are subject to the same PQO limitations as Oracle7, but the addition of parallel index scans on partitioned tables is a powerful feature greatly augmenting Oracle's arsenal of tools for manipulating large bodies of data.

Let's look at how PQO dynamically partitions our example query, which is run against a non-partitioned table, thus requiring a full table scan. Parallelism is defined or determined for each individual table. It has two components, DEGREE and INSTANCES, as described earlier. The DEGREE and INSTANCES values can be specified three different ways:

- at the instance level, using initialization parameters
- at the individual table level, using CREATE/ALTER TABLE
- at the individual SQL statement level, using *hints*

Instance Level, Using Initialization Parameters

The initialization parameter PARALLEL_DEFAULT_INSTANCES can be used to set a standard value for the INSTANCES clause. Only tables with INSTANCES set to DEFAULT will use this value, and tables with values other than DEFAULT will not use the value defined by this parameter.

```
SQL> ALTER TABLE billing_detail PARALLEL (INSTANCES DEFAULT);

Table altered.

SQL> SELECT degree, instances FROM user_tables
  2 WHERE table_name = 'BILLING_DETAIL';

DEGREE      INSTANCES
---------- ----------
        8   DEFAULT
```

CALCULATING DEGREE IN ORACLE7

For the DEGREE clause, it gets a little more complicated for Oracle7 (and then simpler for Oracle8). For Oracle7, the initialization parameters PARALLEL_DE-

FAULT_SCANSIZE and PARALLEL_DEFAULT_MAX_SCANS are used together to calculate a value for DEGREE. Like the INSTANCES clause, to use these values a table must first have its DEGREE value set to DEFAULT.

```
SQL> ALTER TABLE billing_detail parallel (DEGREE DEFAULT);

Table altered.

SQL> SELECT degree, instances FROM user_tables
  2 WHERE table_name = 'BILLING_DETAIL';

DEGREE     INSTANCES
---------- ----------
   DEFAULT    DEFAULT
```

To calculate a value for DEGREE, the two parameter values are used in the following equation:

```
MIN((size-of-table/PARALLEL_DEFAULT_SCANSIZE), PARALLEL_DEFAULT_MAX_SCANS)
```

The size of the table in terms of database blocks (stored in and retrieved from the data dictionary) is first divided by this PARALLEL_DEFAULT_SCANSIZE value to get an initial value to use as DEGREE. As you can see, this value is proportional to the size of the table to be queried.

However, there has got to be a limit on this sort of thing. It doesn't take much imagination to see how this initial calculation could yield a number in the hundreds, thousands, or millions. Most computer systems will balk at supporting millions of parallel query slave processes.

To prevent this, the value specified for PARALLEL_DEFAULT_MAX_SCANS is used. If the value resulting from the previous division is smaller than the value of PARALLEL_DEFAULT_MAX_SCANS, then it gets used. Otherwise, the value of PARALLEL_DEFAULT_MAX_SCANS is used instead.

So, given the following initialization parameter values,

```
PARALLEL_DEFAULT_SCANSIZE = 500
PARALLEL_DEFAULT_MAX_SCANS = 3
PARALLEL_DEFAULT_INSTANCES = 4
```

if a full table scan on a table comprising 1,150 database blocks is to be scanned, then

```
MIN((1150/500), 3)
```

which results in a value of 2, since 1150/500 = 2 is less than 3. This will result in a value of DEGREE 2 and INSTANCES 4.

However, if the table is 11,000 database blocks in size, then

```
MIN((11000/500), 3)
```

will result in a value of 3, since 11000/500 is 22, and 3 is less than 22. As a result, a query against this table will result in parallelism of DEGREE 3 and INSTANCES 4.

CALCULATING DEGREE IN ORACLE8

For Oracle8, the situation becomes much simpler. The PARALLEL_DEFAULT _MAX_SCANS and the PARALLEL_DEFAULT_SCANSIZE parameter both disappear. They are replaced by Oracle RDBMS internal calculations that factor the number of CPUs on the node and the number of datafiles on which the table to be scanned is stored. The CPU information can be verified by examining the configuration parameter CPU_COUNT, and the datafile information can be retrieved from the DBA_EXTENTS view.

It is far better to base query parallelism on the resources of the machine (i.e., CPUs and disk drives) to be applied to the table scan rather than simply on the size of the table. Anyway, a move toward simplicity is a good thing, don't you think?

Individual Table Level, Using CREATE/ALTER TABLE

As we demonstrated earlier, you can also set the DEGREE and/or INSTANCES to hard-coded values for each table. Naturally, the values of DEFAULT and numeric hard-coded values can be mixed. Setting DEGREE and INSTANCES this way can be used to override the instance-level defaults. Or the instance-level defaults can be completely unused, and this method can be used exclusively. For example:

```
ALTER TABLE x PARALLEL (DEGREE DEFAULT INSTANCES DEFAULT);
ALTER TABLE y PARALLEL (DEGREE 10 INSTANCES 6);
ALTER TABLE z PARALLEL (DEGREE 4 INSTANCES DEFAULT);
```

Table X will use the instancewide specifications for both DEGREE and INSTANCES. Table Y will use only the hard-coded values specified. Table Z will use the hard-coded value for DEGREE and the instancewide default value for INSTANCES. In this way, you can set instancewide defaults but override those defaults for certain individual tables if you wish.

Individual SQL Statement Level, Using Hints

If you wish to override the instancewide specifications or the specifications for the particular table you are querying, you can specify SQL *hints*. Hints look very similar to standard SQL *comments* and are specified immediately after the first keyword of the SQL statement. Relevant hints are the following:

```
full(<tbl>)
parallel(<tbl>, <d>, <i>)
```

where

```
tbl   is the name of the table or an alias
d     is either a number or the word "default" to be used for DEGREE
i     is either a number of the word "default" to be used for INSTANCES
```

For example, let's use hints to override the instancewide defaults to be used for the BILLING_DETAIL table:

```
SQL> SELECT degree, instances FROM user_tables
  2 WHERE table_name = 'BILLING_DETAIL';

DEGREE      INSTANCES
---------- ----------
   DEFAULT    DEFAULT

SQL> SET TIMING ON
SQL> SELECT /*+ FULL(billing_detail) PARALLEL(billing_detail, 8, 4) */
  2        COUNT(*)
  3   FROM billing_detail;

   COUNT(*)
-------------
   12384004

Elapsed: 00:08:13.23
```

Alternatively, a SQL table *alias* can be used in the hint to make the SQL statement a little more concise:

```
SQL> SELECT /*+ FULL(x) PARALLEL(x, 8, 4) */
  2        COUNT(*)
  3   FROM billing_detail x;
```

TABLE ALIASES AND HINTS

If a table alias has been specified for a table in the SQL statement, then any hint that references the table MUST use the alias. Specifying the actual name of the aliased table will result in the hint being ignored.

Hints are probably too much of a pain to use in regular usage, but they are ideal for testing. Using hints, you can try out various values for parallelism in sequence without affecting anyone else.

Performing the Partitioning

The product of DEGREE and INSTANCES determines the *scan factor*. This number, in addition to being the number of parallel query slave processes that will be requested, is also the divisor used when performing dynamic partitioning (see Figure 10.5).

The Oracle data dictionary contains all necessary information about the number and distribution of database blocks comprising the table to be scanned; the views DBA_EXTENTS or USER_EXTENTS also display this information. The query coordinator (QC) will use the scan factor computed from the requested DEGREE and INSTANCES along with the table size information in the Oracle data dictionary to divide the table into N roughly equal-sized partitions, where N is the number of *scans*.

However, the QC does not stop with this initial partitioning. It then divides each of the initial partitions into one large, one medium, and one small subpartition (see Figure 10.6).

Regarding the Oracle Cost-Based Optimizer

Prior to Oracle7, the Oracle optimizer was rule-based, meaning that a list of prioritized rules that were used to determine the access path that each SQL statement would use. The rule-based optimizer (RBO) will be available through the Oracle8 releases, but it is no longer being enhanced. The cost-based optimizer (CBO), which debuted with Oracle7, has been the primary focus for new features.

It is well-known that the CBO was almost useless for version 7.0, and that there were significant problems in version 7.1. All in all, even Oracle Corporation did not heartily recommend the use of CBO in those releases. The CBO was much improved in version 7.2, but there were still a few well-documented glitches to erode customers' confidence.

In version 7.3, the CBO became "ready for prime-time," provided that cost statistics in the data dictionary are kept up to date using the ANALYZE command. Naturally, this caveat is to be expected for a cost-based optimizer, as valid cost data must be available at all times.

Hints, therefore, while remaining a valuable development and testing tool, are generally unnecessary once table default parallelism is defined and statistics are gathered.

The one remaining issue with the CBO in version 7.3 was the fact that the ANALYZE command itself was still not "parallelized," but reportedly that has been fixed in the production versions of version 8.0.

A warning: Do not neglect to regularly ANALYZE database objects when using the CBO, as the default values programmed into the optimizer rarely satisfy anybody. Conversely, do not allow cost statistics to exist in the data dictionary when using the RBO. Although it may seem counter-intuitive, the default OPTIMZER_MODE of CHOOSE does not ignore the cost data! Perplexing performance issues can result, which are only cleared up using ANALYZE . . . DELETE STATISTICS.

Use ANALYZE faithfully when utilizing CBO, and avoid ANALYZE like the plague when utilizing RBO (except ANALYZE . . . DELETE STATISTICS).

Figure 10.5 Partitioning the table by the scan factor.

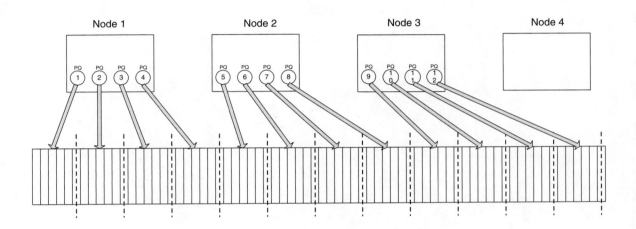

PARALLEL (DEGREE 4 and INSTANCES 3)

Let's take an example. Starting with DEGREE 4 and INSTANCES 2, we got a scan factor of 8. This resulted in eight initial partitions that were further subdivided into three subpartitions each. If the table we were querying was 20,000 database blocks in size, then the initial partitioning would have resulted in eight initial partitions of about 2,500 blocks apiece. Each of these partitions would then be subdivided into a large, medium, and small subpartition, for a total of twenty-four subpartitions.

Figure 10.6 Subpartitioning the initial partitions.

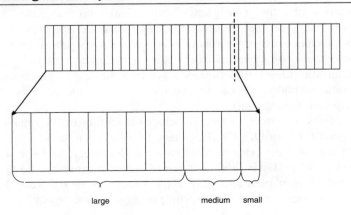

Figure 10.7 Parallel threads of execution consisting of 1 PQ slave.

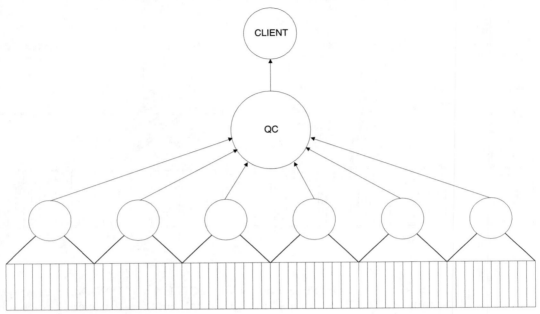

Step 2: Recruiting a Crew of Parallel Query Slaves

Finally, the partitioning is complete. Given DEGREE 4 and INSTANCES 2, we now have eight initial partitions (equal to the scan factor) and a total of twenty-four subpartitions. Now, to hire a crew to work on those subpartitions. In our example, we have a scan factor of 8, so the QC is going to try to recruit eight threads of execution.

The term *thread of execution* is used because each thread of execution can consist of either one parallel query slave process, used simply for scanning (reading) data (see Figure 10.7), or two parallel query slave processes that form a producer-consumer relationship. When two processes comprise a thread of execution, one parallel query slave process acts as the *producer* by scanning data; the other parallel query slave process acts as the *consumer* by performing some additional processing on the scanned data, such as sorting and aggregating (see Figure 10.8).

Thus, whenever a query includes a sorting or aggregation phase, such as a GROUP BY or ORDER BY clause, or a hash join or sort-merge join, each thread of execution is composed of two parallel query slaves in a producer-consumer relationship. Given a scan factor of 8, this means that the QC will attempt to recruit sixteen parallel query slave processes (see Figure 10.9). Whenever the query does not include a sorting or aggregation operation, then the QC will at-

Figure 10.8 Parallel threads of execution consisting of 2 PQ slaves.

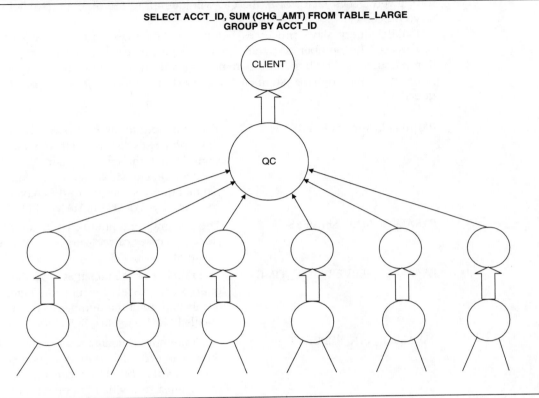

Figure 10.9 Parallel query slave processes.

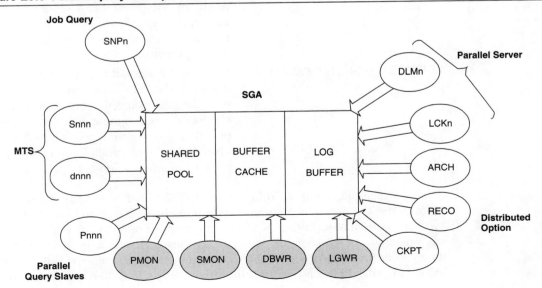

tempt to recruit one parallel query slave process per thread of execution. There-fore, given a scan factor of 8, the QC will attempt to recruit eight parallel query slave processes.

Parallel query slave processes belong to a database instance, as a pool of processes. The number of parallel query slave processes is set using initializa-tion parameters. The first three parameters given in the following list control this pool; the remaining two parameters are used in determining how a parallelized query will run.

PARALLEL_MIN_SERVERS	The minimum number of parallel query slave processes for an instance, which are started when the instance starts. As needed, Oracle will increase the number of parallel query slaves up to the maximum specified by PARALLEL_MAX _SERVERS.
PARALLEL_MAX_SERVERS	The maximum number of parallel query slave processes or recovery slave processes for an instance.
PARALLEL_SERVER_IDLE_TIME	The number of minutes that a parallel query slave process remains idle before it is terminated, until the number of processes equals PARALLEL_MIN_SERVERS.
PARALLEL_MIN_PERCENT	The minimum percentage of requested threads in order for a query to be exe-cuted. A value of 100 indicates that a query must run with 100 percent of re-quested DEGREE and INSTANCES or else return an error message. A value of 1 guarantees that a query will at least run nonparallel. A value of 0 disables the use of this parameter.
OPTIMIZER_PERCENT_PARALLEL	Specifies the amount of parallelism that the optimizer uses in its cost functions. A value of 0 (default) means that the optimizer chooses the best nonparallel plan. A value of 100 means that the optimizer uses each object's degree of parallelism in computing the cost of a full table scan operation.

In our example, using DEGREE 4 and INSTANCES 2 representing a scan fac-tor of 8, the QC now has to *recruit* eight threads of execution, four threads on each of two database instances. If the QC cannot find four (or eight, if neces-sary) parallel query slaves on two different instances, then it checks each in-stance's PARALLEL_MIN_PERCENT parameter value (set in "init.ora"). If PARALLEL_MIN_PERCENT is 100, then that means that 100 percent of all requested parallel query slave processes should be recruited in order for the query to proceed. If the query cannot proceed, an error message will be returned to the user indicating why the query failed.

If PARALLEL_MIN_PERCENT is 50, it means the DBA has determined that a query can proceed if the QC can only recruit 50 percent of the requested number of parallel query slaves. In our example, this means that at least four threads of execution are necessary for the query to be executed. If PARALLEL_MIN_PER-CENT is 1 (which is the default), it means the QC can be demoted back to plain old Oracle server process, the partitions will be discarded, and the query will be executed in *serial* instead of using PQO.

The DBA determines how many parallel query slaves can be run on each database instance using the initialization parameter PARALLEL_MAX_SERVERS. If PARALLEL_MAX_SERVERS is set to 50, it means that no more than fifty parallel query slave processes can be running at one time on that instance. If there is more than one database instance, Parallel Server is being used, then all the instances should have the same value for PARALLEL_MAX_SERVERS.

Once a parallel query slave process has been used and the query it was working on has ended, the DBA can determine how long the process will wait for another QC to recruit it. If the number of minutes specified by the instance's initialization parameter PARALLEL_SERVER_IDLE_TIME is exceeded, then the parallel query slave process will die off.

Many DBAs will recognize that constantly *spawning* parallel query slave processes, which each then *die* after a period of time, only to be *respawned*, can take a performance toll on a system. To make sure that a pool of inactive parallel query slave processes is available, the DBA can set the initialization parameter PARALLEL_MIN_SERVERS to a nonzero integer. When the instance is started, this number of parallel query slave processes will be started automatically. Depending on demand, additional parallel query slave processes can be started, up to the maximum number dictated by PARALLEL_MAX_SERVERS. If PARALLEL _MAX_SERVERS is greater than PARALLEL_MIN_SERVERS, then eventually unused parallel query slave processes will die off after PARALLEL_SERVER _IDLE_TIME minutes have passed, down to the minimum value specified by PARALLEL_MIN_SERVERS.

In this way, the costs of spawning these slave processes can be mitigated, if not eliminated. It is common practice to set PARALLEL_MIN_SERVERS and PAR-ALLEL_MAX_SERVERS to the same value. There is nothing inherently wrong in this, as idle processes consume almost no system resources. Also, the slave processes themselves are spared the task of having to constantly check if it is time to die off.

In this way, by setting up a pool of available parallel query slave processes and by setting a guideline on whether queries requesting PQO can proceed if an insufficient number of slave processes are available, the DBA can control the consumption of resources and also control the expected elapsed time of a PQO query.

Setting PARALLEL_MIN_PERCENT to 100 enforces a somewhat uniform elapsed time for each PQO query, depending on the requested DEGREE and IN-

STANCES. If a query should run with DEGREE 4 and INSTANCES 2, it will either do so or fail. Thus, fluctuations in query elapsed time will be due purely to overall system load on the cluster.

Setting PARALLEL_MIN_PERCENT to 1, while perhaps making the fullest possible use of PQO resources, can also cause severe fluctuations in query elapsed time. The elapsed time for the query to complete will not only be due to overall system resource consumption (i.e., the *busyness* of the system) but also to the number of parallel query slave processes that actually operate on a query at any one time. When a certain query is run at one point in time when the Parallel Server is relatively idle as a whole, elapsed time on the query can be blindingly fast, as the full number of requested (DEGREE and INSTANCES) parallel query slave processes is actually allocated to work on the query. Should the number of available parallel query slave processes dwindle, the query may actually be processed by fewer and fewer parallel query slave processes. This means that, in addition to query performance being affected by overall system load, it is also affected by a smaller than expected number of parallel query slave processes working on the query. If PARALLEL_MIN_PERCENT is set to 1, then the query may not even utilize PQO at all and will execute in serial.

It should be clear that PQO does not reduce the total amount of work the system must perform in order to perform a query; as a matter of fact, when you add in the overhead incurred by the PQO query coordinator's duties, the overall amount of work required to perform the query is actually greater. However, PQO can significantly shorten the elapsed time consumed while performing the query by breaking a large task into many smaller tasks and executing these smaller tasks in parallel.

It should be clear then that PQO will work only if there is overcapacity of CPU resources, memory resources, and disk throughput. If your system is nearing capacity on any of these resources, then running a job in parallel may not result in a speedup. But this is where Oracle Parallel Server provides the ability to scale performance. As we've described, if any excess processing capacity exists on any of the machines in your cluster, then PQO can utilize it dynamically. If the machine on which the data actually resides has no excess resource capacity, PQO can utilize another machine in the cluster that does.

Also, because the partitioning of work occurs dynamically, PQO can react to changing volumes of data in database objects at run-time. This avoids the need to continually monitor space consumption by large tables and possibly unload/reload these tables to reorganize the static partitioning structure.

If it becomes clear that there are great inefficiencies in accessing data from a node on which the data does not actually reside, then the DBA can set yet another "init.ora" parameter on all the instances in Parallel Server: _NODE_AFFINITY. If _NODE_AFFINITY is TRUE, then the QC will check the datafiles in which each of the dynamic partitions resides. If the operating system can provide information about what node the datafile resides on, then the QC process will use this information to attempt to acquire parallel query slave processes from the instance on that node. Thus, parallel query slave processes can be assigned to work only on data partitions that are local to the node they are running on.

Of course, effective use of _NODE_AFFINITY then puts extra responsibility on the DBA to make sure that data for each large table is distributed as evenly as possible across as many nodes as possible. This would prevent PQO from using _NODE_AFFINITY to overuse one node to the exclusion of others. But as we described earlier, striping of data (using RAID 0 or by concatenating datafiles in a tablespace) is a vital consideration when creating the Parallel Server database.

Moreover, the setting of OPTIMIZER_PERCENT_PARALLEL will determine from the start whether the Oracle optimizer chooses between a non-parallel access method, a parallelized full table scan, or parallelized index scan, should such a choice exist. For example, consider a query like this:

```
SQL> SELECT COUNT(*) FROM billing_detail WHERE acct_id > 500000;
```

The column ACCT_ID may have an index on it that can be used by this query. If OPTIMIZER_PERCENT_PARALLEL is left at the default of 0, then the Oracle optimizer will probably choose to use the index. If OPTIMIZER_PERCENT_PARALLEL is set to 100, then the optimizer may consider the size of the table along with the DEGREE and INSTANCES on the table and may choose to ignore the index and use a parallelized full table scan to perform the query. If the index on ACCT_ID were partitioned (for instance by transaction date) then the optimizer could additionally choose to scan each of the index partitions in parallel to find the requested data. (If this index had been partitioned on ACCT_ID ranges then the optimizer could use partition elimination to search only the index partition(s) in which these values could occur.)

Step 3: Assigning Partitions

Once the subpartitions have been designated, a crew of parallel query slave processes has been recruited, and the query is going to proceed in parallel, then the QC is in charge of keeping the crew busy. Communication between the QC and the various parallel query slave processes is conducted using "queues" in the SGA.

What is the reason for all this subpartitioning? Why wasn't one round of partitioning sufficient?

The key to optimizing a parallelized query is to keep all concurrently executing parallel query slave processes continuously working, each with an equal amount of work. If some kind of guarantee could be made that the initial partitioning would result in equal amounts of work for each parallel query slave process, then it would not be necessary to subpartition. Take the pie, cut it into eighths, and keep eight slaves busy.

However, there is no guarantee that each initial partition will contain the same amount of work. Perhaps some of the extents in the table contain lots of deleted rows. Perhaps an additional filter in the WHERE clause of the query causes most rows found in some of the extents to be skipped over.

Using our simple example, this does not cause much trouble. The rows have to be scanned anyway. But suppose this parallelized table scan is simply the

Figure 10.10 Uneven distribution of work in PQ partitions.

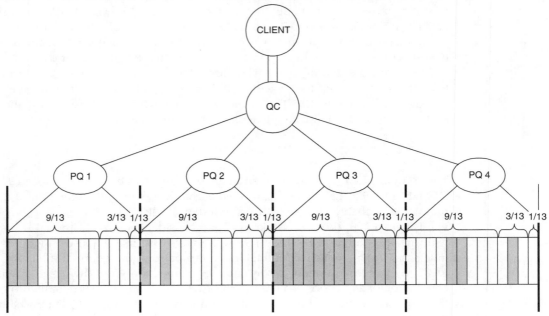

first stage of a complicated join? In this case, each row is not simply something to be scanned and counted, as in our example. Instead, each row could result in joins to other tables. Here, each row represents a discrete and significant *unit of work*. Each row in the driving table might require joins (via indexes, hash joins, or even further full table scans) to several other tables.

Now, with this in mind, the uneven distribution of rows across the initial partitions becomes quite important. Simply dividing the table by the scan factor would more often than not result in some partitions being full of work and others having hardly any work at all. As you can see in Figure 10.10, the overall response time of a parallelized query is determined by the longest-running parallel query slave.

When the parallel query starts executing, the first subpartitions to be assigned are the large ones. Once there are no more large subpartitions, then the next assigned are the medium subpartitions. Once those are all assigned, the last to be assigned for processing are the small subpartitions.

In this way, parallel query slave processes that finish faster will be assigned more work. Those processes that are given more work initially will probably not have to process as many partitions (see Figure 10.11).

Step 4: Receiving and Collating the Results

Communications between the QC and the parallel query slaves is accomplished via queue tables in the Oracle SGA. Messages from the QC are sent by putting requests on the queue. Replies from the parallel query slave processes are sent

Figure 10.11 Some processes process more partitions than others.

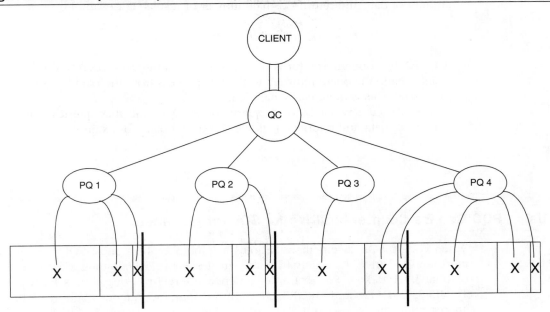

the same way. See Figure 10.12 for an illustration of interprocess communication in PQO.

The arrangement in Figure 10.12, with queue tables, should make something clear: Whenever the parallel query slave processes are returning large amounts of data, the QC can be overwhelmed. Just looking at the diagram should make that clear as well; the QC is a bottleneck.

Figure 10.12 Interprocess communication in PQO.

So, the absolute best kind of query for PQO is one that processes a massive amount of data and returns a small number of results. For example,

```
SQL> SELECT COUNT(*) FROM very-large-table;
```

A COUNT(*) operation returns only one row. During a COUNT(*), only one bit of information is being returned to the QC process from the parallel query slave processes. This is quite easily handled.

The absolute worst kind of query for PQO is one that queries a massive amount of data and returns a massive amount of data, for example:

```
SQL> SELECT * FROM very-large-table;
```

Using PQO Can Be Counter-Intuitive for SQL Programmers

When coding SQL statements with joins to multiple tables, most SQL programmers tend to "drive" the query from the smallest set of data, joining to larger sets of data by indexes. For example, given a query involving tables for CUSTOMERS, ORDERS, and ORDER_LINES, most non-PQO queries might have first attempted to query a set of CUSTOMERS rows. From each row in CUSTOMERS, the query would then be expected to join to related ORDERS rows. From there, once the proper ORDERS are identified, the idea is to join to related ORDER _LINES rows.

The use of parallel queries reverses this set of assumptions. Whether partitioned tables with parallel index scans are used, or whether non-partitioned tables with parallel full-table scan are used, the presence of PQO means that the "driving table" of the query should be the largest, not the smallest table. Then, the query can perform indexed joins to the next, smaller tables. In the example involving the CUSTOMERS, ORDERS, and ORDER_LINES tables, this would probably be the ORDER_LINES table. Drive the query from the ORDER_LINES table so that PQO can be utilized (parallel index scans if it's partitioned, parallel full-table scans if non-partitioned), and join to the smaller ORDERS table then to the yet smaller CUSTOMERS table. Note that in this example, we are reaping the additional benefit of utilizing the UNIQUE indexes which support the PRIMARY KEY constraints during the joins, as we are joining in the direction of FOREIGN KEY to PRIMARY KEY. Using the traditional set of assumptions, joining in the direction from PRIMARY KEY to FOREIGN KEY means utilizing the NONUNIQUE indexes which support the FOREIGN KEYs, which generally means less efficient range scans on the index.

This reversal of basic assumptions generally feels counter-intuitive to experienced SQL programmers, and frequently it is the most experienced programmers who have the greatest difficulty with PQO. Just remember that PQO is most effective in scans against large sets of data, not small sets. Give PQO room to run, and lose the assumptions based on prior experience once in a while!

Figure 10.13 SQL*Loader conventional path.

Essentially, this query will probably run slower in parallel than it would if run serially. The QC process would be overwhelmed by the volume of data returned by the parallel query slaves.

For data warehouses, the queries that work best are huge queries that summarize, aggregate, filter, or subset the data that is being queried. Huge queries that dump entire tables or otherwise return huge amounts of data will not make effective use of PQO.

Parallel Direct Path SQL*Loader

SQL*Loader has been available by that name since Oracle6; before that it was known as ODL (Oracle Data Loader). SQL*Loader was designed to read input data files and execute the INSERT commands necessary to load the data into the database. Today, this is still available and is known as SQL*Loader *conventional path*, since it uses conventional INSERT statements (see Figure 10.13). To speed up loads or to load huge amounts of data, you could concurrently run several copies of SQL*Loader against the same table (see Figure 10.14).

The direct path option was added to SQL*Loader with the initial release of Oracle7. (See Figure 10.15.) By specifying DIRECT=TRUE on the SQL*Loader command line or in the SQL*Loader control file, the performance of SQL*Loader was dramatically improved by bypassing normal SQL operations and having the SQL*Loader process itself format the data into database blocks and write those

Figure 10.14 Multiple concurrent SQL*Loaders.

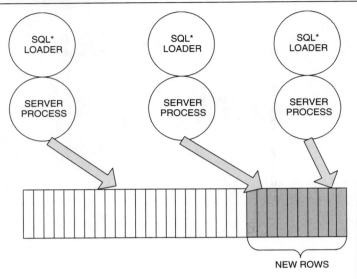

Figure 10.15 SQL*Loader direct path.

blocks into the datafiles. To accomplish this without interrupting queries against the table, the blocks were added above the *high-water mark* (HWM) of the table. This is done by allocating a new extent for the table but temporarily marking it as TEMPORARY, which means that it is not really associated with the table. When the load finishes, the *block type flags* are changed from TEMPORARY to DATA, and the extent is linked to the table itself.

Another advantage of the direct path option becomes apparent. During the load, database blocks belonging to the table are not being changed. Instead, the data is being placed into extents marked TEMPORARY. While the load is happening, the data is not available for query, and if the load should fail the TEMPORARY extents are simply removed. This means that it is not necessary to record *undo information* in order to perform ROLLBACKs, which means that direct path SQL*Loader does not impact rollback segments.

Starting with Oracle7, version 7.1, the UNRECOVERABLE option (specified only in the SQL*Loader control file) became available, which meant that redo logging could be disabled for the loaded data. However, the direct path option did not allow more than one SQL*Loader process at the same time to load the same table. Thus, for really huge loads, direct path was limited to the speed of a single process, albeit an efficient loading process.

To improve this situation, Oracle7, release 7.1, introduced *parallel* direct path SQL*Loader. By specifying PARALLEL=TRUE along with DIRECT=TRUE, multiple direct path SQL*Loader processes could load data into the same table (see Figure 10.16). Each concurrently executing SQL*Loader process allocates its own extent, located above the high-water mark of the table and temporarily marked as a TEMPORARY extent. There is no contention for this extent; each SQL*Loader process owns one absolutely, unlike the extent with concurrently executing con-

Figure 10.16 Multiple concurrent direct path SQL*Loaders.

ventional path SQL*Loaders. The end result is that each direct path SQL*Loader process can work as fast as it can run. Only table data is loaded, and neither *undo entries* (i.e., rollback segment entries) nor, if specified with the UNRECOVERABLE or NOLOGGING option, *redo entries* (i.e., redo logging) need to be created. No other utility, from Oracle or from other sources, can load data into Oracle as swiftly.

Parallel CREATE INDEX (pCI)

Also available since Oracle7, release 7.1, is the ability to create indexes in parallel. Normally, a single Oracle server process does the job, performing a full table scan on the table in question, sorting the data and then finally creating the index.

Consider the following example:

```
SQL> SET TIMING ON
SQL> CREATE UNIQUE INDEX billing_detail_pk
  2  ON billing_detail (acct_id, bill_date)
  3  TABLESPACE idx_01;

Elapsed: 03:23:56.33
```

This took over three hours to complete. See Figure 10.17 for an illustration of a normal CREATE INDEX.

Figure 10.17 Normal CREATE INDEX.

When the PARALLEL clause is added to the CREATE INDEX command, the Oracle server process becomes a query coordinator (QC). Its first job is to recruit enough parallel query slave processes from the database instance to perform the job. The actual number of parallel query slave processes acquired to create the index is dependent on the value of the initialization parameter PARALLEL_MIN_PERCENT, just as with parallel queries. If PARALLEL_MIN_PERCENT is 100, then the CREATE INDEX will proceed only if 100 percent of the requested number of query slaves can be recruited.

```
SQL> SET TIMING ON
SQL> CREATE UNIQUE INDEX billing_detail_pk
   2  ON billing_detail (acct_id, bill_date)
   3  TABLESPACE idx_01
   4  PARALLEL (DEGREE 12);

Elapsed: 00:20:12.05
```

In this case, performing the index creation with twelve concurrent threads of execution on the same instance dropped the elapsed time to create the index from over three hours to just about twenty minutes. See Figure 10.18 for an illustration of parallel CREATE INDEX (pCI) on one instance. If this were a Parallel

Figure 10.18 Parallel CREATE INDEX on one instance.

TEMP EXTENTS LATER SWITCHED TO "INDEX"
EXTENTS AS FINAL INDEX STRUCTURE

TEMP EXTENTS USED FOR
SORTING

Server database with four separate database instances accessing the same database, you might be able to run the following:

```
SQL> SET TIMING ON
SQL> CREATE UNIQUE INDEX billing_detail_pk
  2  ON billing_detail (acct_id, bill_date)
  3  TABLESPACE idx_01
  4  PARALLEL (DEGREE 12 INSTANCES 4);

Elapsed: 00:05:38.13
```

In this case, the index creation was performed with twelve concurrent threads of execution on each of four separate database instances, for a total of forty-eight concurrent threads of execution. In this case, the index creation that originally took over three hours now takes a little under six minutes! See Figure 10.19 for an illustration of parallel CREATE INDEX with Parallel Server.

Please note that the PARALLEL clause in CREATE INDEX is utilized only at runtime during the index creation itself. The values for the PARALLEL clause do not get stored in the data dictionary for later use by parallel queries, as is the case with the PARALLEL clause used in the CREATE TABLE or ALTER TABLE commands.

The pCI operation utilizes the direct path mechanism, which means that it generates no undo entries in the rollback segments. Additionally, pCI comes with an UNRECOVERABLE option (NOLOGGING in Oracle8) to eliminate the generation of redo entries for the redo logfiles. The pCI operation is equally useful in OLTP and data warehouse/DSS environments because no matter what

Figure 10.19 Parallel CREATE INDEX with Parallel Server.

Figure 10.20 Instance recovery.

types of transactions are typically executed, everyone needs to create indexes as rapidly as possible.

Parallel Recovery

Available since Oracle7, version 7.1, parallel recovery is completely transparent. During database startup, parallel recovery performs either instance recovery or media recovery in parallel, significantly hastening the *mean time to repair* (MTTR) after an abnormal shutdown of the database or the corruption of a datafile.

Instance recovery (see Figure 10.20) occurs after the database has been shut down in an abnormal manner, either due to system failure or a SHUTDOWN ABORT by the DBA. Behind the scenes, when the abnormal shutdown is detected during the STARTUP command, the SMON background process performs a *roll-forward* of all logged operations since the last checkpoint using the information stored in the online redo logfiles. All these operations are replayed (the roll-forward), and when the last operation is replayed then any uncommitted transactions are *rolled-back*.

Media recovery must be performed when one of the datafiles in the database has been corrupted or lost and therefore had to be restored from a backup. The restored datafile(s) is then brought *up to date* by replaying all changes made to it from the redo logfiles. Usually, the changes to be replayed will have to be recovered from *archived redo logfiles*, so the ability to perform media recovery means the database must be in ARCHIVELOG mode.

As you can imagine, the amount of roll-forward that has to occur during media recovery is dependent on the following:

- the number of datafiles corrupted and restored from a prior backup
- the amount of time since the backup was taken
- the number of operations recorded since the backup was taken

If 20 datafiles were somehow corrupted and had to be restored from a backup taken five days ago, that means five days' worth of operations have to be replayed for those 20 datafiles. Will this take five days to replay? Hopefully not! Generally, replaying operations recorded in the redo logfiles takes a fraction of the time required for the original operations because the database is usually not open for general use while instance recovery or media recovery is happening. Also, just the update actions themselves are being applied; in real life, there are frequently dozens or hundreds of queries supporting these INSERTs, UPDATEs, and DELETEs. Lastly, when these update actions are being reapplied, there is no need to generate undo entries for the rollback segments nor is there any need to generate redo logging, both of which are usually necessary in real life.

However, media recovery can take a long time, and applying parallelism to this process can help significantly. Just like normal recovery, the SMON process reads the redo logfiles. However, it is no longer tasked with actually replaying the operations; instead, it has a pool of parallel query slaves available to actually perform the updates to the datafiles. This is necessary because, obviously, roll-forward operations have to be replayed in exactly the same order they were originally played in real life. Single-threading the read phase of recovery is the best way to accomplish this. (SMON further ensures that two changes to the same block are properly serialized through its handoff algorithm.)

Implementing parallel recovery (illustrated in Figure 10.21) requires nothing more than the setting of an initialization parameter:

```
recovery_parallelism = NN
```

where "NN" is the desired number of *parallel recovery processes* available to the SMON process during recovery. The default value of 0 implies that SMON does

Figure 10.21 Parallel recovery.

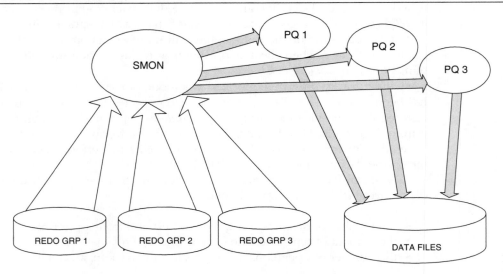

all the work. Since no other activity can occur in the database until instance recovery is completed, it makes sense to use the available system resources for this task.

Parallel recovery is a parallel feature that is equally useful both in OLTP and data warehouse or DSS databases. The types of transactions normally executed on the system are irrelevant; recovery is something that anybody wants to complete as swiftly as possible.

Parallel CREATE TABLE . . . AS SELECT (pCTAS)

Available starting with Oracle7, version 7.2, the parallel CREATE TABLE . . . AS SELECT operation (pCTAS) has turned into one of the most valuable features introduced to benefit data warehousing. Data in data warehouses does not sit still. There are constant reloads and refreshes, and with each load (complete or incremental) there usually comes the need to update summarized data. Whether these summarizations or aggregations take the form of a standalone summary table or whether they exist as part of a *star schema* as a *dimension table*, this operation must be performed frequently and completed swiftly.

Before the advent of the pCTAS operation, data warehouse implementers were faced with having to use a variety of more conventional methods not designed for bulk operations. In some cases, when the base tables in the warehouse were being loaded incrementally, with additional data being appended to existing data, it made sense to update summary tables or dimension tables incrementally as well (see Figure 10.22). This could involve significant programming in PL/SQL triggers or stored procedures or third-generation languages like C or COBOL.

Figure 10.22 Incremental updates to summary tables.

NEWLY ADDED ROWS

BATCH PROGRAM

UPDATE OR INSERT LOGIC

SUMMARY TABLE

DETAIL TABLE

Figure 10.23 INSERT INTO . . . SELECT.

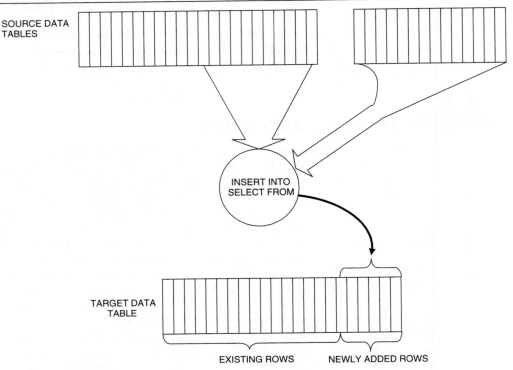

As the very simplest option, an INSERT INTO . . . SELECT statement could do the job (see Figure 10.23), but this operation might have its difficulties, for example, operating too slowly against massive amounts of data. Parallelizing the SELECT portion of this operation could help in certain circumstances (see Figure 10.24), but only if you remember one of the important limitations of parallelized queries: They work best on operations that scan massive amounts of data but only return small amounts of result data.

A number of questions inevitably arise about incremental updates to summary tables and dimension tables. The first involves the fact that *nothing grows forever*. Inevitably, it is necessary to purge. Although this might be easy to do on detail data, it may occasionally become necessary to subtract from related summary tables while the deletions from the detail data are occurring. This is neither an easy nor a swift operation.

The second question grows out of the first one. Because of all the possible complexity involved in custom programming—both the insertion of new data into the summary tables and the purging of old data—how accurate is the summary data after several iterations of both the load operations and the purge operations? And, if it's not accurate, how can it be fixed?

The major problem here is that the incremental approach can be painfully slow even if the programs are written to take advantage of parallelism or multi-

Figure 10.24 INSERT INTO . . . SELECT in parallel in Oracle7.

SOURCE DATA
TABLES

PQ 1

PQ 1

PQ 1

QC

EXISTING ROWS   NEWLY ADDED ROWS

ple concurrent streams of execution. Also, since they were forced to use conventional SQL—with its attendant requirements to generate rollback entries in the rollback segments and redo entries in the redo logs—bulk operations written this way put a great deal of stress on the system.

While the incremental approach may offset this inherent slowness by reducing the amount of work that has to be done (i.e., processing only the changes or *deltas*), the question of *how accurate the summary data is* raises the question of what can be done if it is found to be inaccurate. Reloading the summary tables using processes intended only to perform incremental changes may be unrealistic.

The eventual answer to all these concerns might be to always reload the summary tables. Don't bother with a complicated incremental approach, even if the detail data is substantially unchanged from load to load. Of course, if the detail data is completely reloaded or *refreshed* with each load phase, there is no choice: The summary tables have to be completely re-created. Unless a scheme for saving old copies of the detail data and detecting changes by comparing the old and new copies of detail data is implemented there is no way to detect incremental changes.

The pCTAS operation operates somewhat like an INSERT INTO . . . SELECT where the query is parallelized, but with two important differences:

Figure 10.25 CREATE TABLE . . . AS SELECT.

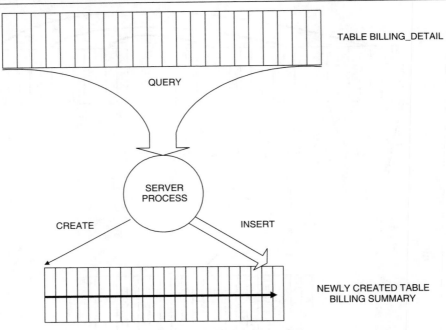

- The INSERT phase of the operation is parallelized in sync with the SELECT.
- The INSERT phase uses the direct path mechanism, similar to SQL*Loader.

A nonparallel CREATE TABLE . . . AS SELECT (see Figure 10.25) has existed since the early versions of Oracle:

```
SQL> CREATE TABLE billing_summary
  2  TABLESPACE summ_data01
  3  STORAGE (INITIAL 4M NEXT 4M PCTINCREASE 0)
  4  AS
  5  SELECT bill_dt, SUM(bill_amt) total_bill_amt
  6  FROM billing_detail
  7  GROUP BY bill_dt;

Table created.
```

In this situation, the new table is created according to the TABLESPACE and STORAGE specifications (which can default if they are not specified). The column names and data type definitions are derived from the elements in the SELECT list of the query (unless specified in the CREATE TABLE's column list). The new table is then populated with the results from the query.

After parallel queries were introduced, it was possible to enhance this command so that half of it was run in parallel, but the INSERT phase of the command was still single-threaded (see Figure 10.26).

Figure 10.26 CREATE TABLE . . . AS SELECT using parallel query.

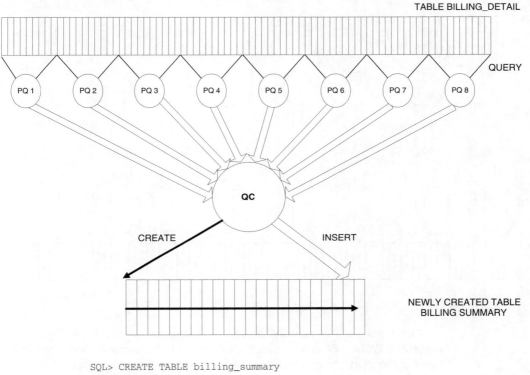

```
SQL> CREATE TABLE billing_summary
  2  TABLESPACE summ_data01
  3  STORAGE (INITIAL 4M NEXT 4M PCTINCREASE 0)
  4  AS
  5  SELECT /*+ PARALLEL(billing_detail, 8, 1) */
  6         bill_dt, SUM(bill_amt) total_bill_amt
  7    FROM billing_detail
  8    GROUP BY bill_dt;

Table created.
```

What the pCTAS operation brings to the situation is the full parallelization of both the INSERT and the SELECT phases, so that (with adequate I/O capacity) there are no bottlenecks to impede performance (see Figure 10.27).

```
SQL> CREATE TABLE billing_summary
  2  PARALLEL (DEGREE 8 INSTANCES 1)
  3  TABLESPACE summ_data01
  4  STORAGE (INITIAL 4M NEXT 4M PCTINCREASE 0)
  5  AS
  6     SELECT bill_dt, SUM(bill_amt) total_bill_amt
  7       FROM billing_detail
  8      GROUP BY bill_dt;

Table created.
```

Figure 10.27 Parallel CREATE TABLE . . . AS SELECT.

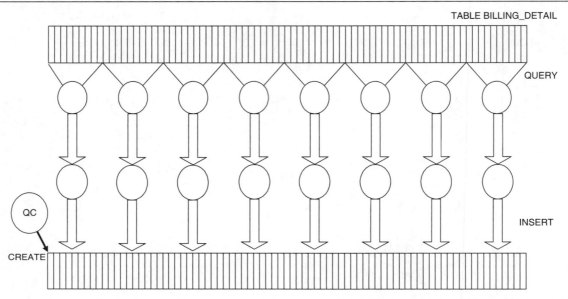

Please note that a *parallel hint* is no longer necessary in the SELECT statement; the PARALLEL clause in the CREATE TABLE statement functions both as a run-time specification for the degree of parallelization during creation and is stored as the table's DEGREE and INSTANCES values in the data dictionary for future parallelized queries against the new table. If the parallel hint is specified, it will be ignored. If the table being queried from (i.e., in this case, BILLING _DETAIL) has its own DEGREE and INSTANCES values in the data dictionary, they will also be ignored in favor of the CREATE TABLE's PARALLEL clause.

Unlike the INSERT INTO . . . SELECT statement and the older CREATE TABLE . . . AS SELECT operations—whether each used a parallelized SELECT or not—the new pCTAS operation uses the direct path mechanism originally introduced with SQL*Loader. Therefore, while the table is being created and populated, the pCTAS operation allocates TEMPORARY extents to load into (see Figure 10.28).

The parallel query slave processes themselves are not performing INSERT statements using the conventional SQL mechanism that operates through the SGA buffer cache and the LGWR and DBWR processes. Rather, they are bypassing the SGA buffer cache and log buffer, formatting the database blocks directly and writing directly to the datafiles (see Figure 10.29).

Therefore, not only has the pCTAS operation removed bottlenecks from its architecture, but it also uses a mechanism ideally suited for bulk data loading. This mechanism, by loading into TEMPORARY extents, eliminates the need for undo information to be generated in rollback segments. Additionally, like other Oracle operations that employ the direct path mechanism, an UNRECOVERABLE

Figure 10.28 pCTAS using TEMPORARY extents.

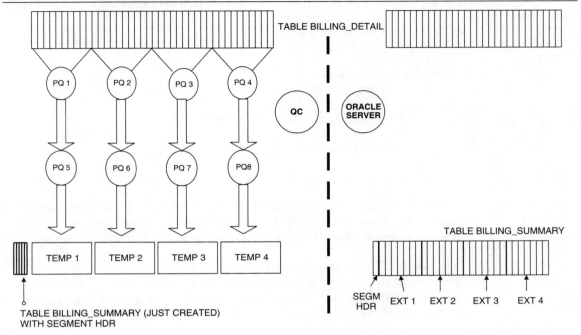

Figure 10.29 pCTAS using direct path mechanism.

or NOLOGGING clause is available to also eliminate much of the redo information logged to the redo logfiles by the LGWR process for future recoverability.

```
SQL> CREATE TABLE billing_summary
  2 PARALLEL (DEGREE 8)
  3 UNRECOVERABLE
  4 TABLESPACE summ_data01
  5 STORAGE (INITIAL 4M NEXT 4M PCTINCREASE 0)
  6 AS
  7    SELECT bill_dt, SUM(bill_amt) total_bill_amt
  8      FROM billing_detail
  9     GROUP BY bill_dt;

Table created.
```

So now we have an operation that allows summary tables and dimension tables to be re-created quickly and efficiently. In data warehouses, this opens all kinds of possibilities for data cleansing, data transformation, and data mart creation.

In any kind of database—OLTP, data warehouse, or otherwise—the pCTAS operation is also useful for performing mass UPDATEs or mass DELETEs. For example, if the following DELETE statement will be deleting a large portion of the following large table, it could literally take days to perform:

```
SQL> SET TIMING ON
SQL> DELETE
  2 FROM BILLING_DETAIL
  3 WHERE BILL_DT < '01-JAN-96';

1803773 rows deleted.

Elapsed: 22:44:55.03

SQL> COMMIT;

Commit complete.
```

Instead, the following pCTAS operation could perform this operation in a fraction of the time:

```
SQL> SET TIMING ON
SQL> CREATE TABLE new_billing_detail
  2 PARALLEL (DEGREE 8 INSTANCES 4)
  3 TABLESPACE bill_data01
  4 STORAGE (INITIAL 4M NEXT 4M PCTINCREASE 0)
  5 AS
  6    SELECT *
  7      FROM billing_detail
  8     WHERE bill_dt >= '01-JAN-96';
```

```
Table created.

Elapsed: 00:50:03.43

SQL> RENAME BILLING_DETAIL TO OLD_BILLING_DETAIL;

Table renamed.

Elapsed: 00:00:01.01

SQL> RENAME NEW_BILLING_DETAIL TO BILLING_DETAIL;

Table renamed.

Elapsed: 00:00:02.03
```

The exact same result is obtained in less than an hour as opposed to almost 23 hours. The downside is that the new table does not have any indexes (yet), table GRANTs have been lost, and any views or procedures referencing BILLING_DETAIL will have to be recompiled.

A similar operation can be performed for mass UPDATEs.

Extent Trimming in Oracle7

In Oracle7, the operations for parallel direct path SQL*Loader, parallel CREATE INDEX, and parallel CREATE TABLE . . . AS SELECT all have something in common: They all use a parallel implementation of the direct path mechanism. This is a good thing. The direct path mechanism is well optimized for writing massive amounts of data into the database, and that is—after all—the primary goal of each of these operations. See Figure 10.30 for an illustration of direct path operations.

But, in achieving the goal of throwing data into the Oracle database by the truckload, one of the basic assumptions of Oracle7 space management was in danger of being violated, and the remedy is one that will likely irritate many DBAs. When the direct path mechanism is in use, it does not share the space in which it is working with other processes. The space in which it is loading is "private," temporarily marked as a TEMPORARY segment, accessed and modified only by the single process doing the work.

All other "conventional" SQL operations (see Figure 10.31) work through the SGA buffer cache, performing all modifications on database blocks located in the shared memory buffer cache. Conventional SQL operations (i.e., INSERT, UPDATE, DELETE, and CREATE) do not write to the datafiles; rather, the memory-resident images of the database blocks in the buffer cache are modified, and those modifications are later written to the datafiles by the DBWR process.

So far, so good. However, direct path operations running in parallel have a special problem. In this case, there are multiple independently executing operations, none of which are sharing anything with each other. They are all (by defi-

Figure 10.30 Direct path operations.

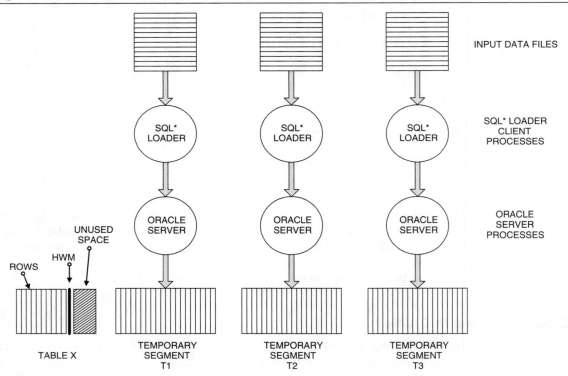

nition) operating on the same task on the same object, but they are working independently.

This in itself is not a problem, except for a basic rule about Oracle space management that was in effect until Oracle8: Each segment (table, cluster, or index) extent has all used space contiguously allocated, and all unused space is also contiguous. In other words, think of a table or index as being a sequential array of information, allocated by extents. Naturally, since the space for the segment is allocated in extents and space is used row by row, this means that unused space will exist at the "end" of the allocated space. The imaginary line drawn at the last row in a table (or entry in an index) is called the high-water mark (HWM), and space beyond that line is referred to as being *beyond (or above) the high-water mark* (see Figure 10.32).

So, up until Oracle8 and the advent of partitioned objects, one of the basic rules of Oracle space management indicated that, for each segment, one and only one extent could house a high-water mark, and only that extent could have unused space above that high-water mark.

Now, rewind to the discussion about direct path operations. What you have is umpteen processes, each operating independently of one another. Each of N processes is going to load a certain number of rows into however many extents are required, and when they each finish you can bet that each of those N

Figure 10.31 Conventional SQL operations.

processes is going to find that it has not completely filled the last extent it was working on. See Figure 10.33 for an illustration of parallel direct path operations each leaving a high-water mark.

Figure 10.32 The high-water mark and unused space.

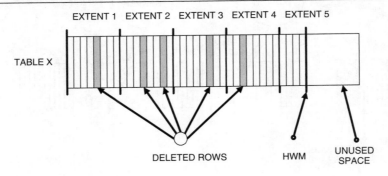

Figure 10.33 Parallel direct path operations each leaving a HWM.

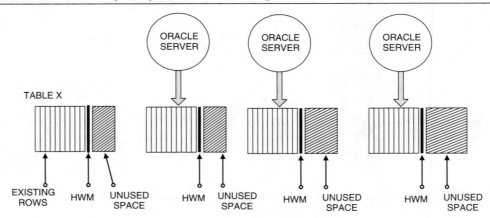

Although the direct path operations are ongoing, each process is working on its own TEMPORARY segments. But, when all the parallel operations are finished, the QC will change the BLOCK_TYPE flag in the headers of each of those segments, flipping them from TEMPORARY to DATA (for tables) or TEMPORARY to INDEX (for indexes). At this point, the QC is also supposed to merge these formerly TEMPORARY segments into the base table or index being loaded.

But, to do so while each of the TEMPORARY segments had unused space above the high-water mark would violate the rule stated earlier. So, the very last thing each parallel query slave process has to do after finishing direct path operations is "trim" its last extent to eliminate any unused space above the high-water mark from the TEMPORARY segment (see Figure 10.34).

Then, and only then, can all the TEMPORARY extents be merged into the base object. Why might this be a problem? A basic and well-known goal of experienced Oracle DBAs is to eliminate fragmentation by utilizing uniform-sized

Figure 10.34 Extent trimming.

Figure 10.35 Tablespace fragmentation.

extents in various tablespaces. Tablespace fragmentation (see Figure 10.35) is the often-discussed problem wherein the space inside a tablespace is "chopped up" into many differently sized extents. This in itself is not a problem, but eventually after tables and indexes get dropped and re-created, the resulting odd-sized extents of free space can make it impossible to create or extend anything in that tablespace. This topic was discussed in depth in the "Monitoring Tablespace Fragmentation" section of Chapter 8. Recall the analogy of laying floor tiles of different sizes.

In this way, there can be huge amounts of free space available in a tablespace, but it's all chopped up into small enough extents that it becomes practically unusable. In response to this, a number of products from a number of vendors have sprung up to *reorganize* tablespaces. What they do is export all the table and index definitions in a given tablespace, drop and re-create the tablespace, and then reimport all the tables and indexes. Typically, the INITIAL storage parameter of all these tables and indexes has been reset so that all data in the tables and indexes resides in a single extent. After this export/import is finished, all the free space in the tablespace formerly scattered in many unusably small chunks of space is now coalesced into one large usable chunk.

The problem with these reorganization utilities is that when they coalesce a table or index into a single large extent they only address the symptoms instead of fixing the problem. After all, these utilities would only get used once per tablespace if they actually solved the problem, wouldn't they?

There is a myth about Oracle space management that states "a segment should only have one extent" for optimal performance. It implies that multiple extents, especially hundreds of extents, are somehow bad for performance. This is almost always complete balderdash. There is no performance advantage to having data compressed into a single extent versus having it spread out over hundreds of extents, all other factors being equal. The habit of *compressing extents* for a segment into a single extent simply perpetuates the segment fragmentation problem, which suits the vendors of reorg tools just fine.

The permanent solution to tablespace fragmentation is to use uniformly sized extents, for all segments (table, clusters, and indexes) within a tablespace. If every extent in a tablespace is 1 MB (to pick a number) in size, then tablespace fragmentation cannot exist.

Some may argue that objects aren't always sized at 1 MB or whatever number is chosen. True, that's why Oracle allows multiple extents. Those steeped in the one-extent-only myth just mentioned may argue that multiple extents hurt performance. False, so there's nothing to worry about (unless the extents are very, very small in relation to DB_FILE_MULTIBLOCK_READ_COUNT). The only thing to worry about when letting segments extend is not to exceed MAXEXTENTS. Prior to release 7.3, the maximum value of MAXEXTENTS for a segment is tied to the database block size:

DB_BLOCK_SIZE	Maximum MAXEXTENTS
1 KB or 1,024 bytes	57
2 KB or 2,048 bytes	121
4 KB or 4,096 bytes	249
8 KB or 8,192 bytes	505
16 KB or 16,384 bytes	1017

The most common DB_BLOCK_SIZE for data warehouse databases is usually 4 or 8 KB. Realizing this, experienced Oracle DBAs try to keep the number of different extents to a minimum; ideally only one size, but possibly two, three, four, or five. As a result, these DBAs never have to worry about segment fragmentation, and they never need to buy one of those reorganization utilities.

Into the midst of this idyllic world come valuable operations like parallel direct path SQL*Loader, parallel CREATE INDEX, and parallel CREATE TABLE . . . AS SELECT, which make it almost impossible to keep *uniform-sized extents* in a tablespace. Very annoying! The problem does not get fixed until Oracle8, when extent trimming is no longer necessary and does not occur for these operations. For Oracle7, the problem is not addressed until version 7.3.3, when event 10901 can be set to disable extent trimming. Call Oracle Worldwide Support for information on setting this event if you are using version 7.3.3 or above.

Parallel Execution of Partitioned Views

Database views that include the UNION and UNION ALL operator have been available in Oracle for quite some time. But until Oracle7, version 7.3, each SELECT statement in the UNION or UNION ALL statement had to be executed sequentially, one after another (see Figure 10.36).

Consider the following example:

```
SQL> CREATE OR REPLACE VIEW accts
  2 AS
  3 SELECT * FROM accts_northeast
  4 UNION ALL
  5 SELECT * FROM accts_southeast
  6 UNION ALL
  7 SELECT * FROM accts_northcentral
  8 UNION ALL
```

Figure 10.36 UNION and UNION-ALL views prior to 7.3.

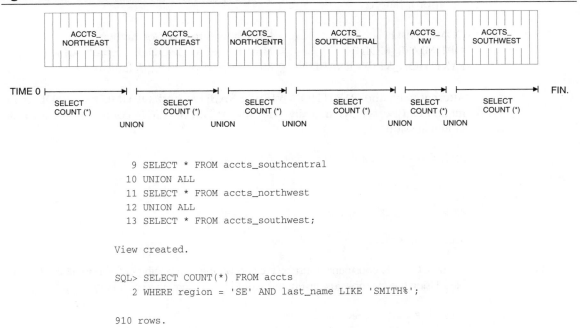

```
 9 SELECT * FROM accts_southcentral
10 UNION ALL
11 SELECT * FROM accts_northwest
12 UNION ALL
13 SELECT * FROM accts_southwest;

View created.

SQL> SELECT COUNT(*) FROM accts
  2 WHERE region = 'SE' AND last_name LIKE 'SMITH%';

910 rows.
```

After parallel queries became available in 7.1, the situation improved somewhat as each of the SELECT statements could be executed in parallel, if the optimizer deemed it appropriate. But the performance of such views was far from adequate for most uses. With version 7.3 of Oracle7 came two important features:

- partition elimination
- parallel execution of partitions

Partition Views in Oracle8

Even though Oracle8 supports the partition view facility for upward compatibility for databases migrated from release 7.3, the true partitioning available in Oracle8 is vastly superior in performance and administrative ease. This new capability is a key reason to move the data warehouse to Oracle8 technology.

Partition views have many limitations, including no DDL or DML support, no utilities support (no loader, import, export), no parallel index scans, and many other restrictions (see the Oracle 7.3.3 Tuning Guide). The ReadMe release for Oracle8, 8.0.4, states that partition views will be supported in a future release.

To enable these features in 7.3, the following initialization parameters must be set appropriately:

COMPATIBLE	Must be set to 7.3.2 or higher
OPTIMIZER_MODE	Must be set to CHOOSE (default value)
PARTITION_VIEW_ENABLED	Must be set to TRUE; default is FALSE

Alternatively, the PARTITION_VIEW_ENABLED and OPTIMIZER_MODE parameters can be set dynamically with the ALTER SESSION command for an individual session:

```
SQL> ALTER SESSION SET PARTITION_VIEW_ENABLED = TRUE;

Session altered.

SQL> ALTER SESSION SET OPTIMIZER_GOAL = CHOOSE;

Session altered.
```

Also, CHECK constraints must be created on the partitioning column in all the base tables. Using the example just given, this would be implemented as follows:

```
SQL> ALTER TABLE accts_northeast
  2       ADD CONSTRAINT ne_region CHECK (region = 'NE');

Table altered.

SQL> ALTER TABLE accts_southeast
  2       ADD CONSTRAINT se_region CHECK (region = 'SE');

Table altered.

SQL> ALTER TABLE accts_northcentral
  2       ADD CONSTRAINT nc_region CHECK (region = 'NC');

Table altered.

SQL> ALTER TABLE accts_southcentral
  2       ADD CONSTRAINT sc_region CHECK (region = 'SC');

Table altered.

SQL> ALTER TABLE accts_northwest
  2       ADD CONSTRAINT nw_region CHECK (region = 'NW');

Table altered.

SQL> ALTER TABLE accts_southwest
  2       ADD CONSTRAINT sw_region CHECK (region = 'SW');

Table altered.
```

Figure 10.37 UNION-ALL views after 7.3.

Last, all the base tables must be defined and indexed identically, each UNION ALL branch of the view must be a SELECT * FROM <table-name>, and all base tables and indexes must be ANALYZEd.

In essence, all the partitions can now be examined in parallel, and partitions that do not need to be examined are not examined. So now the example just given would be evaluated as shown in Figure 10.37.

An important point: The Oracle optimizer does not handle the use of either OR operators (including the IN operator) or SQL functions when specifying the CHECK constraint on the partitioning column or when evaluating a query on the view at run-time. So, none of the following CHECK constraint definitions would yield the desired result in terms of partition elimination:

```
SQL> ALTER TABLE accts_west
  2         ADD CONSTRAINT w_region CHECK (region IN ('NW','SW'));

Table altered.

SQL> ALTER TABLE accts_west
  2         ADD CONSTRAINT w_region CHECK (region = 'NW' OR region = 'SW'));

Table altered.

SQL> ALTER TABLE accts_west
  2         ADD CONSTRAINT w_region CHECK (region LIKE '%W'));

Table altered.

SQL> ALTER TABLE accts_west
  2         ADD CONSTRAINT w_region CHECK (SUBSTR(region,2,1) = 'W'));

Table altered.
```

Also, if a query against a correctly created partition view includes an OR or IN operator in the predicate containing the partitioning column, the Oracle optimizer will not eliminate partitions as expected:

```
SQL> SELECT COUNT(*) FROM accts
  2 WHERE (region = 'SE' OR region = 'NW') AND last_name LIKE 'SMITH%';

1730 rows.
```

Note that the CHECK constraint syntax is correct and that the query does return results; either of these conditions simply "turn off" the partition elimination feature, causing worse than expected performance.

Parallel Queries on Partitioned Tables

Queries against partitioned tables operate much the same way as queries against partitioned UNION-ALL views have since version 7.3. Like partitioned views, there is parallel execution of queries against the partitions and partition elimination. But there are fewer restrictions than with partitioned views:

- no restriction on performing DML on partitioned tables, as on partitioned views
- no requirement that each table partition be indexed exactly the same, as with partitioned views
- no restriction on the types of WHERE predicates to be used on the partition key columns, such as multiple OR operators and SQL functions

Partitioned tables are significantly easier to manage and are completely transparent as partitioned objects to end users. The only real reason to use partitioned views is because you are still on Oracle7, where partitioned tables are not available.

Parallel DML on Partitioned Tables

In Oracle7, only a query could be parallelized. Specifying the PARALLEL hint in an UPDATE or DELETE statement specified parallelism only for the query portion of the statement, not for the UPDATE or DELETE portion itself. If this hint was specified following the INSERT keyword of an INSERT INTO . . . SELECT statement, once again it would specify parallelism only for the SELECT portion of the statement.

Similarly, if the table being UPDATEd or DELETEd had its parallel characteristics, DEGREE and INSTANCES, set in the data dictionary, then the parallelization is applied only to the query portion of the statement. The same goes for the table specified in the FROM clause of the SELECT portion in an INSERT INTO . . . SELECT statement.

In Oracle8, this changes if you explicitly enable PARALLEL DML using the following:

```
SQL> ALTER SESSION ENABLE PARALLEL DML;
```

In this case, the use of hints or the presence of table settings for parallelism will enable the parallelism of the UPDATE or DELETE operation, as well as the query scan. This functionality, however, is limited to partitioned tables. A maxi-

Figure 10.38 Parallel UPDATE or DELETE on partitioned tables.

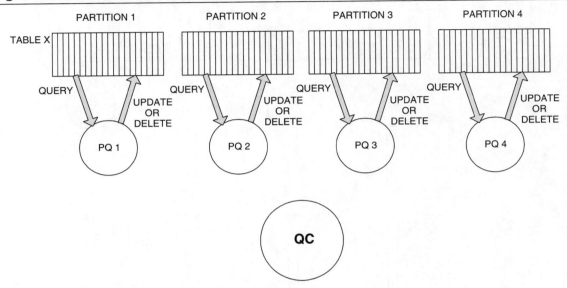

mum of one parallel query slave process per partition will be used to perform the UPDATE or DELETE; smaller numbers are possible, but each parallel query slave process will operate on only one partition at a time. There will also be another set of parallel query slaves performing the scan portion of the statement, so here we will employ a *consumer-producer* relationship between parallel query slave processes. One set of queries scans the table in parallel as *producers*, while the other set of processes performs the actual UPDATE or DELETE operations on their assigned partition (see Figure 10.38).

Parallel UPDATE and DELETE operations use the conventional SQL mechanisms and can only be performed on partitioned tables. If such an operation is attempted against a nonpartitioned table or a cluster, then the UPDATE or DELETE operation will be performed in serial. INSERT operations are different. Just as in Oracle7, serial INSERT operations are still available. For INSERT statements using the VALUES clause, this is still the only option. However, the options broaden from here, which (of course) means that things get more complicated.

Parallelized INSERT INTO . . . SELECT statements can now be performed on both partitioned as well as nonpartitioned tables. There is an APPEND option, which is a keyword that represents our old friend the direct path mechanism. APPEND means that the direct path mechanism is used; NOAPPEND means that the conventional SQL mechanism is used. There are limitations to how each is used.

For nonpartitioned tables, only the APPEND option is available. This means that a parallel INSERT INTO . . . SELECT operation works much like the pCTAS operation (see Figure 10.39).

Figure 10.39 Parallel INSERT APPEND on a nonpartitioned table.

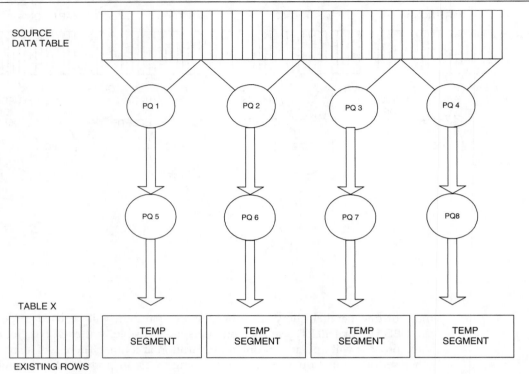

```
SQL> ALTER SESSION ENABLE PARALLEL DML;

Session altered.

SQL> INSERT /*+ append parallel(X, 8, 1) */ INTO non-partitioned-table X
  2 SELECT . . .
  3 FROM . . .
  4 WHERE . . . ;
```

For partitioned tables, both the APPEND and the NOAPPEND mechanisms are available but only if the there are no GLOBAL indexes on the partitioned table.

Using the APPEND option (also known as the direct path mechanism), a parallel INSERT statement requires that triggers and constraints be disabled for the duration of the operation (see Figure 10.40). Like other direct path operations, existing indexes are automatically disabled and rebuilt by the operation.

```
SQL> ALTER TABLE partitioned-table DISABLE CONSTRAINT . . . ;

Table altered.

SQL> ALTER TRIGGER trigger-name DISABLE;
```

Figure 10.40 Parallel INSERT using APPEND into partitioned tables.

```
Trigger altered.

SQL> ALTER SESSION ENABLE PARALLEL DML;

Session altered.

SQL> INSERT /*+ append parallel(X, 8, 1) */ INTO partitioned-table X
  2 SELECT . . .
  3 FROM . . .
  4 WHERE . . . ;
```

Immediately after each parallel DML statement, a COMMIT or ROLLBACK must be issued; any other SQL statement will fail until the transaction is ended.

Summary

Parallel operations in Oracle are a direct reaction to the rise of data warehousing. Bit by bit, since Oracle7, version 7.1, in 1994, more and more operations in Oracle can be transparently decomposed and run in parallel. With Oracle8 and its partitioned tables and indexes, this trend has leaped forward impressively.

Additionally, Oracle has "spun on a dime" and branched off into a completely unexpected direction with *direct-path* operations. Until Oracle7, version 7.1, the obvious primary focus of the Oracle RDBMS was toward supporting large numbers of concurrent OLTP operations. Since version 7.1, that evolution has continued, but there has been dramatic movement toward adding non-shared direct-path operations, optimized for speed and volume, that bypass the all-important buffer cache. This is a shift toward supporting a relatively small number of very large concurrent DSS operations.

With Oracle8, there is now a single RDBMS that can be optimized for both major kinds of databases: OLTP and data warehouse. This is no *one-trick pony*, like Red Brick or Sybase. This is a technological tour de force, and it's still improving.

WAREHOUSING WITH ORACLE PARALLEL SERVER

There are occasions when the demands of the application exceed the capacity of a single machine. There are also situations when the demands for nonstop availability exceed the probable reliability of a single machine and its subsystems. To address these situations, Oracle Parallel Server is available for clustered and Massively Parallel Processing (MPP) systems.

CLUSTERED AND MPP SYSTEMS

Refer to Chapter 2 in this book for a detailed discussion of clustered, MPP, NUMA, and other multi-node computer architectures.

What Is Oracle Parallel Server?

The Parallel Server option of the Oracle RDBMS allows a single database to be accessed and maintained by more than one instance. The usual arrangement for most Oracle installations involves a database with a single instance, whereas the files of an Oracle *database* are accessed and maintained by the processes of only one *instance* of Oracle. When the Parallel Server option is purchased and installed, more than one instance can be used to access and maintain a single database. See Figure 11.1 for an illustration of an exclusive database versus a parallel database.

In the vast majority of Parallel Server implementations, each instance resides on a separate node in a cluster. Each node, with its Oracle instance, has complete, equal, and full read/write access to all the files or volumes that comprise the Oracle database. This is the concept of *shared* disk (see Figure 11.2). Oracle

Figure 11.1 Exclusive database versus parallel database.

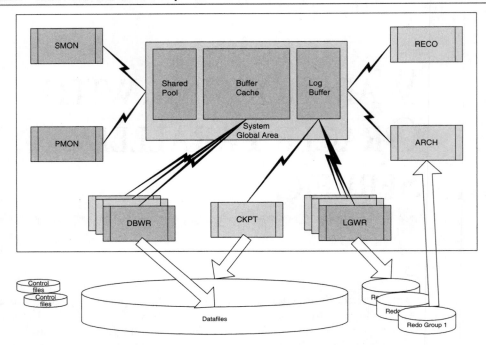

is the only major database vendor with this requirement on clustered systems; all other vendors implement what is known as a *shared nothing* parallel database architecture (see Figure 11.3). With shared nothing implementations, each database instance on each node of the cluster has exclusive access to the por-

Figure 11.2 Shared disk parallel database architecture.

Figure 11.3 Shared nothing parallel database architecture.

tion of the database residing on that node. Examples of shared nothing parallel database architectures include IBM DB2/PE, Informix XPS, and Teradata. As we just mentioned, Oracle has the only shared disk parallel database architecture.

There is another parallel database architecture that is possible for clustered or massively parallel processing (MPP) machine architectures: *shared everything* (see Figure 11.4). But so far, there has yet to be a commercial implementation of

Figure 11.4 Shared everything parallel database architecture.

Figure 11.5 Availability in Parallel Server.

a shared everything architecture. It could be argued that exclusive, non-Parallel Server Oracle on NUMA architectures presents this architecture, but NUMA platforms are only now becoming available, and there is nothing to indicate that the availability of NUMA systems can survive component failures.

In Oracle Parallel Server, each database instance is a *peer*; there is no concept of a *master* instance or of *subordinate* instances. Therefore, should one or more instances become unavailable for any reason (i.e., node "crash"), the remaining instance or instances can keep the database fully operational, provided that full access to all the files and volumes that comprise the physical database continues (see Figure 11.5).

Parallel Server vs. Distributed Databases

The concept of Parallel Server should also not be confused with the concept of a distributed database. A distributed database is a logical concept, consisting of two or more separate physical databases, each operating completely independently of one another. Each can be backed up and recovered separately; each can be started up or shut down independently. Distributed Oracle databases are linked together using Oracle "database links," which allow transparent server-to-server communication. Distributed Oracle databases are discussed in more depth in the next chapter. A distributed homogeneous database is illustrated in Figure 11.6.

In heterogeneous environments involving Oracle and other database vendors, *gateway* products may be used to represent the foreign data stores as part of the Oracle database, and vice versa (see Figure 11.7). Alternatively, access to each of the heterogeneous data stores can be presented to end users by middleware using X-Open's XA distributed transaction control protocol, which is used by

Figure 11.6 Distributed homogeneous databases.

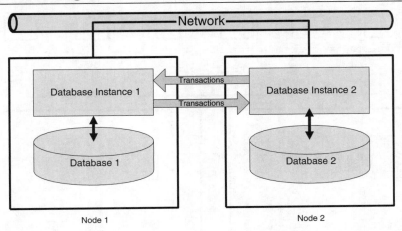

Figure 11.7 Distributed heterogeneous databases and gateways.

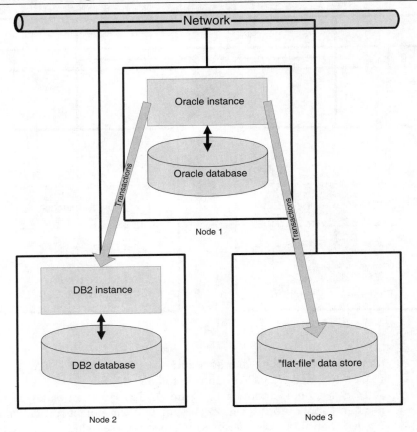

Figure 11.8 Distributed environment using XA.

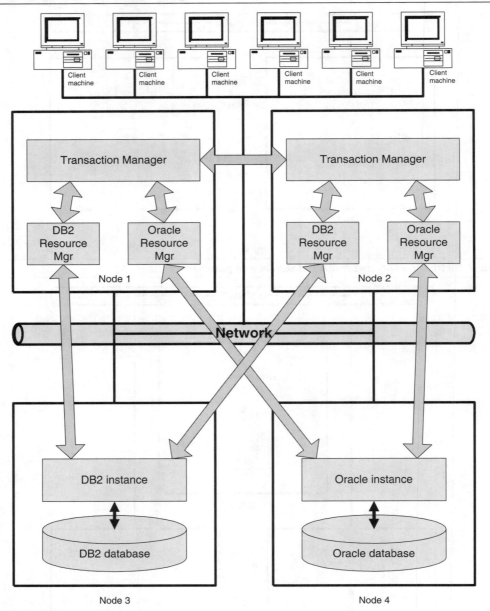

transaction processing monitors such as BEA's Tuxedo, IBM Transarc's Encina, IBM's CICS, and NCR's Top End (see Figure 11.8).

Last, distributed and/or heterogeneous databases can be linked together by the front-end applications; many development environments provide transparent connectivity to various data stores simultaneously (see Figure 11.9). Of course, a net-

Figure 11.9 Distributed environment joined by application.

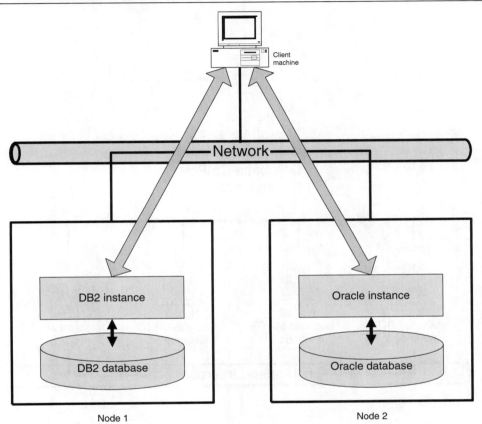

work of distributed databases could also include Parallel Server databases. In fact, it is not uncommon to see one or more so-called data marts, implemented as either single-instance exclusive Oracle databases or multiple-instance, multiple-node Parallel Server databases, extracting data from a centralized data warehouse, which also might be a single- or multiple-instance database (see Figure 11.10).

Again, What Is Parallel Server?

Bear with us while we employ a simple analogy to illustrate the following:

- the difference between an Oracle database and an instance
- how reads and writes are performed by an Oracle instance
- how Oracle with the Parallel Server option is different from single-instance Oracle
- how reads and writes are performed by many Oracle Parallel Server instances

Some of these issues were also covered in Chapter 3, but they bear revisiting.

Figure 11.10 Distributed environment including Parallel Server.

File Cabinets and File Clerks

The distinction between a database and an instance can be illustrated with a simple example involving file cabinets and file clerks. File cabinets, where paper files are stored, are just racks, drawers, and cabinets where information, in the form of file folders, is stored. However, someone or something has to organize these file cabinets and store data there in an orderly fashion, otherwise data would be stored there in a jumble, with no hope of being able to retrieve it again. That someone or something is the file clerk.

So, in this analogy, the role of the Oracle database itself is played by the file cabinets, which are just places to store data. On a computer, operating system files or disk volumes are used. The role of the Oracle database instance is played by the file clerks, who decide where and how data will be stored to facilitate retrieval. A database is inert storage, while an instance is active processes and data structures. In an office, the file cabinets are inert storage bins, while file clerks are the people who access those file cabinets.

Now to build on this analogy a little and make it more closely fit the reality of what an Oracle database is and how Oracle works. (Bear with us on this; if it gets too corny, then just go and skip ahead to the next section . . .)

Because they hold valuable data the file cabinets themselves reside in a room set apart from the rest of the office. Anybody accessing these file cabinets has to walk to this other room, which takes a little bit of time. Because of the amount of time it takes to walk from their office to the room where the file cabinets are kept, the file clerks keep the most frequently accessed files with them, on their desks in their office. This tends to save many trips back and forth to the file cabinets.

This part of the analogy illustrates the expense of accessing disk drives. The desks in the file clerks' office represent the Oracle SGA, which contains caches of information stored in shared memory. The file cabinets themselves, because they represent Oracle datafiles on disk drives, are depicted as being a certain distance away from the file clerks and their desks.

Now, there are some rigid rules defining how file clerks and their co-workers work together. It has been decided that, when anybody wants to access data, either to just read it or to update it, he or she should first check to see if the appropriate file or folder is already present on the file clerks' desks. If so, then the information should be read or updated right there. Once again, this scheme cuts down on the number of trips back and forth to the file cabinets.

However, if the information to be read or updated is not present on the file clerks' desks, then the co-workers themselves, not the file clerks, must trek out to the file cabinets and retrieve the information. They are not allowed to update the data (if that is their intention) at the file cabinets, but rather they must make photocopies of the files and then bring the copies with them back to the file clerks' desks. Then and only then are they allowed to read or update the data contained in the files.

This makes sense, because if the small group of file clerks were tasked with performing every single request to retrieve data from the file cabinets, the clerks would quickly become overloaded. Rather than keep people idle while a clerk retrieves information from the file cabinets, they go and do it themselves. This arrangement is much more *scalable*. The file clerks themselves, however, are responsible for making sure that *changed* file folders get back to the file cabinets.

So the basic rules in the fictitious office in this analogy are rather simple, as they are in real life in an Oracle database. Any Oracle server process (i.e., a co-worker) must first check in the buffer cache (the file clerks' desks) to see if the information to be accessed or manipulated is already there. If it is not, it makes the trek to the database (file cabinets) to bring a copy back to the buffer cache (file clerk's desks), where the data can then be used.

Once an Oracle server process (a co-worker) has used a file folder, it can just leave the folder in the buffer cache (file clerks' desks). If the data gets updated, the background processes of the database instance (file clerks) are responsible for putting the changed data back into the database (file cabinets).

There is an additional responsibility not previously mentioned: Because only so many file folders can fit on the file clerks' desks, the file clerks are also responsible for removing little used files to make room for more heavily used ones. This is, of course, analogous to the least recently used (LRU) buffer cache recycling scheme employed by Oracle, which allows a fixed-size buffer cache to efficiently accommodate a database of unlimited size, for all intents and purposes.

Extending the Analogy to Include Parallel Server

Okay, take a deep breath, because we're not quite through with this analogy yet . . .

Adding Parallel Server option to the picture simply extends this analogy. Now there are two or more separate sets of file clerks, all of whom are operating on the same file cabinets. Each set of file clerks, however, is located in a different building (i.e., different computers), but they all have equal access to the same set of file cabinets.

Each instance (set of file clerks) caches data locally in its buffer cache (on the file clerks' desks). Oracle server processes (co-workers) in each computer (building) work with their local database instance (set of file clerks). When a server process (a co-worker) wants to access or update data, it must first do so in the local instance's buffer cache (on the local set of file clerk's desks).

Now, perhaps you can see a problem. As long as the server processes (i.e., workers) are only reading the data, they can both do so at the same time and not cause a problem. But if both server processes (coworkers) wish to simultaneously update the same bit of information from the same file folder, then there could be a problem. Both instances could cache the information and make their updates in their respective caches. Subsequent reads and updates of this same information would then be different, as each instance has its own (now different) copy of what was read from the database. Eventually, each instance will write different information back to the same location in the disk drives, corrupting the database. If there are going to be multiple caches, they have to be kept *coherent.*

What has to happen to prevent this is a form of locking called *parallel cache management* (PCM). PCM is only necessary when two or more instances are trying to update the same parts of a database. If update activity (which includes INSERTs, UPDATEs, and DELETEs) is not occurring, if the environment is *read-only*, then there is no need for PCM. Oracle performs parallel cache management by assigning individual PCM locks to cover one or more database blocks in the database (see Figure 11.11).

The tables used to map from *database blocks* to *PCM locks* are in the Oracle SGA. Before any process can update the database block in the buffer cache, it must first acquire the related PCM lock in *exclusive* mode. By definition, before an exclusive lock can be acquired, any other instance holding an exclusive lock has to release it. Before it can do that, the other instance has to write all changes it has made to the database block back to the database. This is known as a *ping.*

Additionally, any instances that had acquired the PCM lock in *shared mode* must also release the lock, so the copies of the database blocks resident in the

Figure 11.11 PCM locks covering one or more database blocks.

cache cannot be used again. To read those database blocks again, a shared lock on the related PCM lock must once again be acquired. Figure 11.12 shows one instance trying to change a cached block.

When the process performing the change finally acquires the exclusive lock, it makes the change. It is not immediately required to write the changed buffer to the database unless someone else requests another shared or exclusive lock. So multiple changes to the same block can occur until another lock request comes across. At that time, the block can be written down to the database, and if the requested lock mode is shared, the exclusive lock will then be converted to shared as well.

In the terms of our analogy, these locks are *sign-up sheets* that each co-worker must sign before he or she takes a file folder back to his or her reading room. That way, if each bit of information is "signed out" when it is read up to the local buffer cache, then any later co-workers, perhaps from different buildings, know whether they can safely change the data or whether they must first inform all other departments about the change. If everyone is just going to read the file folder, then they simply indicate this on the sign-up sheet. Reading is no problem; many people are allowed to read at the same time, as long as you tell everyone else that you're reading.

But think about what happens when a change occurs. There are numerous copies of the file folder in different departments. If someone makes a change to his or her copy, then this change must be immediately propagated to the other copies in the different departments, so that everyone sees the same data.

Figure 11.12 One instance tries to change a cached block.

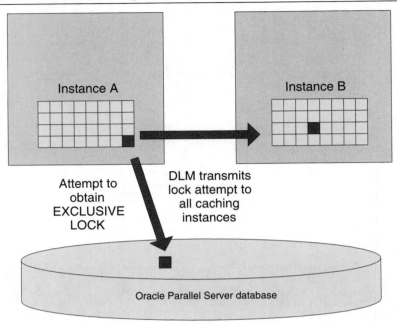

How can this propagation occur? Continuing with our analogy, it's possible that whoever is going to make the change gets on an intercom and announces the change to the whole company. A less obnoxious alternative might be to set up a telephone system from each of the clerk's desks; anybody about to make a change has to first notify all the other departments. This is *messaging*, and Oracle does this. A message, similar to a short telephone call, is sent to all instances holding locks, telling them someone is going to change that database block. Each instance must surrender its shared lock in order for the updating instance to obtain the necessary exclusive PCM lock covering the block to be changed.

The data changes themselves are not transmitted in the message. In Oracle, the data changes are made to the database block and are then written to the database. Any instances wishing to see those changes must read the block from the database back into their buffer caches. See Figure 11.13 for an illustration of messages and database writes.

Completing the analogy (finally!), the different departments (i.e., machines in a cluster), each with their own sets of file clerks (database instance) and their local supply of information on top of the clerks' desks (buffer cache) copy file folders (database blocks) from the file cabinets (database). To copy the file folders, the workers in the company (Oracle server processes) have to check out the file folders on a sign-up sheet, telling everyone that they've got the folder. Then they can carry a copy of it back to the file clerks' desks and read it.

If anyone in any of the departments wishes to change the contents of a file folder at their file clerk's desk, they first have to check the sign-up sheet and call

Figure 11.13 Messages and database writes.

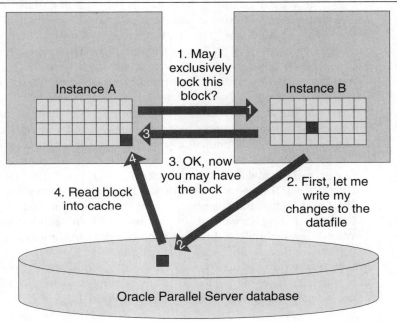

all the other departments on the list, telling them that the file folder is going to be changed. Once they've been notified, the copies of the file folders in the other departments are discarded, and their entry on the sign-up sheet is deleted. When the sign-up sheet for the file folder is finally clear, the change is made, right at the file clerk's desk.

Is there any need to put the changed file folder back in the file cabinet? Not until some other department wants to read it or write it. Once again, this write-down is known as a ping.

In real-life terms, Oracle Parallel Server uses what is called a *distributed lock manager* (DLM) to manage PCM locks. PCM locks have three basic states: *null*, *shared*, and *exclusive*. The DLM maintains a list of all the PCM locks and their current states. It is part of a class of program peculiar to networked environments known as a *distributed service*. It is available anytime, from any computer. If it is updated on one computer, it must be instantaneously updated across all computers. If one computer is shut down or crashes, the DLM must be able to continue running on all other nodes in spite of that (also known as *fault tolerance*).

For Oracle version 6.2 and Oracle7, the DLM is external to the Oracle instances. On some hardware platforms, the DLM is *kernelized* as an integral part of the operating system. On other platforms, the DLM is just another application running under the operating system, similar to the Oracle RDBMS itself. Check with your hardware vendor or Oracle Corporation to determine whether the DLM for your platform is provided by the hardware vendor (i.e., kernelized DLM) or by Oracle (i.e., nonkernel DLM).

With Oracle8, the DLM becomes an integrated part of the Oracle database instances. The advantage of this approach is that you don't have to rely on differing DLM implementations on different platforms. Now, on all platforms, the DLM works the same way. The DLM maintains a list of locks in shared memory on each computer node. Each instantiation of the DLM on each node communicates with each other over a network, preferably a very reliable and very high-speed network. In MPP environments, this network is known as the *interconnect*.

The DLM has a very simple job. The application (in this case, the local instance of the Oracle RDBMS) requests locks in different modes: null, shared, and exclusive. The DLM grants those requests according to a series of rules. The main trick is to tell everyone the same thing at the same time.

In our earlier analogy, these mysterious sign-up sheets seem to be everywhere at once. This is the magic of the DLM: to be everywhere at once, to be reliable, and to be fault tolerant. As you may have guessed, all this messaging and pinging is replacing what, in "normal" exclusive-mode Oracle, used to be simple accesses of buffered database blocks in shared memory. What was once a very fast, efficient, and scalable operation—caching—is now a liability. The operation of writing to a cached database block now involves an expensive operation that includes writes to the database known as pinging. This effect is referred to as the *paradox of pinging* (see Figure 11.14).

Figure 11.14 Paradox of pinging.

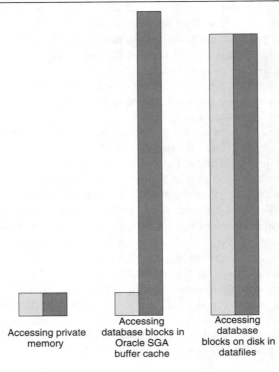

Accessing private memory

Accessing database blocks in Oracle SGA buffer cache

Accessing database blocks on disk in datafiles

Pinging is, therefore, to be avoided if possible. Is the way to avoid pinging to simply avoid using local buffer caches? Figure 11.14 would suggest so. But no, this would be an erroneous conclusion. Rather than avoiding buffer caching, one should try to avoid *cross-instance writes*, the situation that spawns the necessity for pinging. If the database itself can be *partitioned* effectively among the database instances, then cross-instance writes wouldn't happen, and therefore pinging could be eliminated or minimized. This too will be discussed later in the chapter.

We've now discussed the basics of how the Oracle RDBMS and the Oracle Parallel Server option work. This discussion outlines some of the complexities of using Parallel Server option and hopefully helps form a framework for understanding Parallel Server to help decide whether Parallel Server option is a suitable choice for your data warehouse.

Why Use Parallel Server?

In general, Parallel Server provides the following benefits:

- performance and capacity scaleup through additional instances operating against the same database
- higher availability through redundancy
- performance speedup when used in conjunction with Parallel Query option

In general, these advantages could be offset by the following costs:

- reliability problems caused by greater complexity
- much greater system management complexity
- some applications must be built (or rebuilt) specifically to be "parallel-aware"; if not, the expected performance benefits can readily turn into a performance degradation; query intensive applications typical in a data warehouse do not generally suffer from this potential disadvantage

So the decision whether or not to use the Parallel Server option should be made carefully. This chapter is intended to provide you with most of the knowledge necessary to make that decision. We will not, however, cover all details of all concepts related to Parallel Server. We highly recommended that you read the *Parallel Server Concepts and Administration Guide* for the version of Oracle you are using. If you are using a version of Oracle earlier than 7.3, this Guide was significantly less useful than the versions available with 7.3 and above; try to acquire this newer manual anyway, even if all the features do not apply to your particular version.

Benefit: Performance and Capacity Scaleup

It's simple. You've estimated how much disk storage and how many concurrent users the data warehouse is going to need, and the hardware vendor is skeptical that one machine could handle that load. Or worse, you've proved this empirically, finding out after the fact that your machine is not able to handle the load.

But perhaps two, ten, or a hundred machines can handle the load. Perhaps more machines can provide the necessary storage capacity. Parallel Server allows one database to be spread over two or more machines in a clustered environment.

There are several alternatives for dividing the load across several machines. In the case of two-tier (i.e., client-server) or multitier applications, the load can be distributed vertically by tier. For example, starting with the initial client-server application on one machine, the "client" tier can be moved onto one or more separate machines. Thus, the "horsepower" required to drive the client-side programs can be separated from the Oracle instance and the server processes. This is a common remedy for Oracle Applications, such as Oracle General Ledger or Oracle Inventory, which are primarily two-tier.

Another option is to distribute the load horizontally. If two thousand online users are too much for one machine, buy another machine and put one thousand online users on each. If you choose this route, there are again two choices. The existing database can be divided up into two (or more) separate databases. If each of the resulting databases need to access or manipulate data in the other database, then partitioning can be made syntactically transparent to the application by using database links and Oracle7's distributed database option (which becomes a standard part of Oracle8). See Figure 11.15 for an illustration of distributed databases.

Figure 11.15 Distributed databases.

Figure 11.16 Parallel server.

Data
Warehouse
end-users

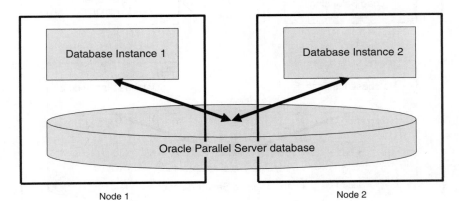

Database Instance 1

Database Instance 2

Oracle Parallel Server database

Node 1

Node 2

Creating two databases linked together is relatively easy if there is some natural partition (as in Figure 11.15). For example, perhaps application A is primarily financial data while application B is primarily marketing data. But if there is no clear separation point, it might work best to leave the database whole and distribute this single database across several machines as shown in Figure 11.16.

How can the load be distributed evenly between each instance? SQL*Net version 2.3 (which comes with Oracle7, version 7.3) had a feature called Connection Load Balancer (CLB) (see Figure 11.17). This feature was not, however, included in the first release of Net8, which was distributed with Oracle8, release 8.0.3. As the name implies, CLB distributes *connections*, not *transactions* (i.e., SQL statements). When you connect to Oracle, the *balancing listener* decides which database instance you should connect to. It currently makes this decision based on either a *sequential* (or simple round-robin) algorithm, or it can make this decision using a *random* algorithm. In the future, two load-based algorithms will be added, so you are connected to the database instance with the least load. These algorithms will be based on *operating-system load* and *Oracle instance load*.

Using CLB will ensure that each machine on the cluster has roughly the same number of Oracle sessions, thus helping ensure that each machine's resources

Figure 11.17 SQL*Net Connection Load Balancer (CLB).

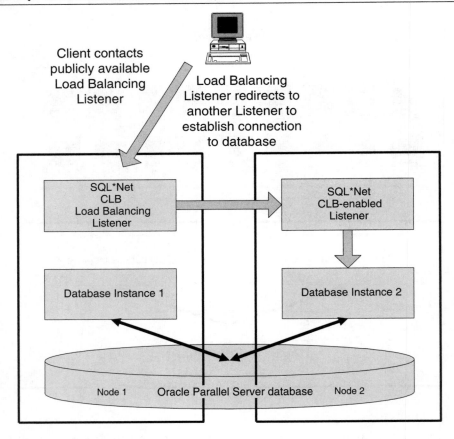

are utilized most efficiently. Vertical load partitioning does not have any special system hardware or software requirements, just the ability to network. Horizontal load partitioning using distributed databases also does not have any special system hardware or software requirements. However, horizontal load partitioning using Oracle Parallel Server requires the presence of clustered or MPP systems. See Chapter 2 for a more complete description of these kinds of systems.

Benefit: Higher Availability

Higher availability in traditional mainframe systems was usually the result of higher reliability of components. Mean Time Between Failures (MTBF) in mainframe components was generally quite high, meaning that component failure occurred infrequently enough to enable close to 100 percent system uptime. The problem here is that such component reliability is expensive.

Open systems such as UNIX rely on component redundancy, not component reliability, to enable close to 100 percent system uptime. Components produced on a commodity basis have lower MTBF individually, but their lower price allows

Figure 11.18 Machine failure in parallel server.

redundancy. Moving beyond component redundancy, Oracle Parallel Server enables the use of clustered systems to provide *system redundancy*. Each individual database instance in Parallel Server can continue to operate as long as all parts of the database are still available. So, if one machine should fail or be shut down, the remaining database instances can continue operating unimpaired (see Figure 11.18).

Additionally, SQL*Net CLB is tolerant of these kinds of failures and can also *failover* the *load balancing listener* if necessary.

How can disk drives survive machine failure? For the most part, disk drives used in clustered systems do not physically reside in the same cabinet as the CPU. Rather, storage arrays residing on their own power supplies can be connected to more than one CPU. Should one CPU or node in the cluster fail, the partner node detects this and orders the storage array to failover or transfer control of the array to itself (see Figure 11.19).

So, in addition to having all parts of the database available to each database instance on each node, each disk drive is usually connected to two or more nodes. Most of the technology to implement this redundancy has only been developed in the past decade. At the moment, most of this complexity is exposed to developers and administrators, making redundant open system environments exceedingly difficult to manage. However, the evolution continues. Within a few more years, administering redundant systems will be almost as simple to manage as individual systems. In fact, the redundancy may be quite transparent, blurring the lines of separation between mainframes and large open systems. The mainframe is not going away. Open systems are rapidly acquiring mainframe-quality features, and the expertise necessary to implement mainframe-quality applications will be necessary in greater numbers than ever.

It has taken UNIX about a decade to scale up to rival the mainframe in terms of performance, availability, and manageability. Many will argue successfully

Figure 11.19 Storage failover in clustered systems.

that it is not there yet in the last two categories. It will be interesting to watch how long it takes Windows NT-based systems to match this feat. UNIX still has a long way to go and NT even further, but both have a lot of momentum.

Benefit: Performance Speedup

As we mentioned in the previous chapter on parallel operations, on some UNIX platforms (IBM RS/6000 SP and Pyramid RM1000, for example) the Parallel Query Option (PQO), in conjunction with Parallel Server, can transparently scale a query across nodes. Instead of the query being executed by a single process, or multiple processes on the same machine, it can actually be scaled across multiple database instances (see Figure 11.20). This is actually quite an awe-inspiring feat. The IBM RS/6000 SP has a wonderful graphical 3-D performance statistic monitor named, appropriately, "3dmon." If a particular table is striped properly across all disk drives on all nodes, it is possible to execute a simple query, such as:

```
SQL> SELECT COUNT(*) FROM <really-big-table>;
```

and watch "3dmon" display all the little three-dimensional colored columns representing the disk drives on all the nodes in the cluster just stand right up and start pumping. Querying a 20-gigabyte table could take a single machine that is otherwise idle 20 minutes; spreading the table across 20 machines and having all 20 participate in the query can result in the query finishing in well under a minute.

Cost: Reliability Problems

As we mentioned earlier, the overall technology underpinning clustered and massively parallel systems is still relatively new. Mainframe-based systems of similar (and larger) scale have hardware and software components with twenty to thirty years of general availability behind them. The open systems market is maturing rapidly, and reliability is being addressed effectively. But while few of the "bleeding edge" aspects of this technology remain, it might be fair to label most of the organizations using clustered and massively-parallel UNIX systems as "early adopters." Those organizations using newly-introduced clustered Windows NT systems are still, as of this writing, very much "bleeding edge."

To put it simply, these systems have not been in existence long enough to clearly demonstrate the kind of reliability amply demonstrated by "legacy" mainframe-based systems. Whereas high-availability in the mainframe-based environment has been attained by the reliability of the components, high-availability in the open systems environment is accomplished in a slightly different fashion. Open systems components are generally produced as commodities; cheap and plentiful. High-availability is thus implemented by means of the *redundant* components, as opposed to *reliable* components. The reliability and manageability of open systems components is increasing, but the expectations for unscheduled downtime should be higher than for competing mainframes.

Why raise this discussion? Clustered and massively-parallel systems are commonly portrayed as suitable *mainframe replacement* platforms. While the performance and storage capacity of these systems are undoubtedly in the same class as the largest mainframes, availability and manageability are still evolving. As open systems vendors address these issues, hardware and software upgrades and maintenance patches become more frequent. These upgrades and patches imply additional, usually scheduled, downtime. Don't allow the impressive performance and storage characteristics of these architectures to overshadow the real risks posed by that which is new.

Can you run a "production" decision-support system (DSS) based on these availability figures? Can your strategic decision-makers live with this? Possibly, if they're made aware of it ahead of time.

Cost: Greater Management Complexity

Consider the maturing status of the components in clustered and massively parallel systems. Features and performance are clearly top priority, while manageability may be considered last, or not at all. Initial manageability weaknesses are shown in the tools supplied by the hardware vendor as well as in other systems management packages from third-party suppliers.

Figure 11.20 Parallel query scaling across instances.

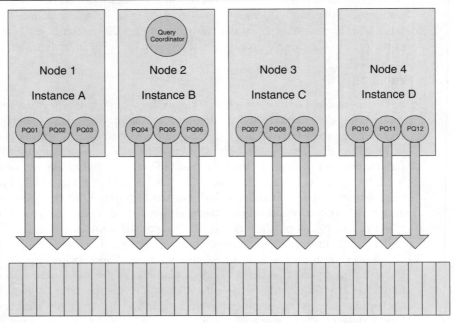

Table X

Illustrating this, Oracle Parallel Server did not have any database- or system-management utilities prior to Oracle7, version 7.2. Starting with version 7.2 (circa 1995), a short-lived utility named "dbtool" was introduced to facilitate startup and shutdown. With Oracle7, version 7.3 (circa 1996), "dbtool" disappeared and another utility named "opsctl" appeared, which also performed startup and shutdown only. Additionally, Oracle Enterprise Manager was introduced in 1996, and it was instrumented to manage many additional Parallel Server operations. Currently, startup and shutdown operations can be scripted for batch execution using the "opsctl" utility and most other operations can be performed using the GUI-based Oracle Enterprise Manager.

This illustration is not an indictment of Oracle's administration tools—the same points can be made about the evolving nature of all management tools for these new, somewhat exotic, clustered environments. The point is that you must not assume that the same level of monitoring and control that you have over your existing systems will be available on the "bleeding edge." Be prepared to develop additional shell scripts to bridge the gap until the system administration tools mature.

If your organization is seasoned, has good policies and procedures, and thrives on making new gizmos work, then clustered systems and Parallel Server should work out just fine. Mainframe-trained users invariably liken UNIX systems to tinker toy sets that are used to build Ferraris: All the pieces are there for you to use, but you have to fit them together yourself. If your organization likes doing this, then this is good news. If the organization is not technically confident, seems overwhelmed, has limited success adapting to change, or doesn't welcome a possible tinker toy Ferrari, then perhaps the project should scale back somewhat.

Cost: Not Transparent to Some Applications

To avoid pinging, some applications may require partitioning the database in such a way that each database instance does not frequently try to access database blocks outside of its partition. Obviously, most applications are not written this way. Therefore, most applications not originally designed for Parallel Server will not perform well if re-hosted without change to a Parallel Server environment. In fact, if no effort is made to tune for Parallel Server, it is quite likely that an application will run much slower in Parallel Server than when it was running on a single machine! So, applications must be written in such a way that they perform well on Parallel Server, and the cost of making those changes might very well be prohibitive.

Hey! We'll Just Use One Instance for Real Work and One Instance for Reporting!

As Oracle consultants, we frequently hear from customers who are aware of the fact that applications not built explicitly for Parallel Server will suffer serious performance problems. However, they want to make use of clustered or MPP systems for the availability benefits. So, they propose a two-node configuration with Parallel Server, each node with one instance accessing the same database. On one node, the "primary," they intend to place their existing application, unaltered. In the event of node failure, then the second instance on the second "backup" node can act as a "hot standby," continuing normal operations of all but transactions which had been "in-flight."

So far, so good. However, it is difficult to allow the second backup node to remain "unused" under normal circumstances. Thus, the proposal includes the scheme to use the second node with its second database instance as a "reporting" server. While all the "real work" is performed on the primary node, the backup node (while it is still a "backup") will be used for read only "reporting."

An attractive thought, but even read-only activities cause pinging when requesting blocks that have been updated in another instance. As a result, the performance of "real work" on the primary node will be severely impacted by contention with the read-only query activity on the backup node.

In brief, this scheme won't work; the backup instance must remain completely quiescent to avoid contention with the primary. To put it another way, for this primary/backup use of Parallel Server to work as intended, the backup node will have to be a "room warmer" until the primary fails.

One possibility: The backup node can be used to perform backups. Backup activities are generally image copies of the underlying datafiles to the Oracle database, and do not cause pinging (although Oracle8's Recovery Manager does have modes that do block reads and would induce pinging).

The other alternative: Retrofit the application to accommodate Parallel Server.

Luckily, data warehouse applications do not suffer from many of these issues. For the most part, data warehouses are read-only during most of their available hours, and read-only is not a problem. During the load phase, when inserts, updates, and deletes are occurring, it may be easier to partition load programs than it would be to partition, say, online forms. So, because of the need to enforce partitioning, it might be more properly said that the cost of making changes to accommodate partitioning may be prohibitive for OLTP applications. For DSS applications, the batched nature of the loads may make the task much easier.

There are a few ways to group database objects to make partitioning easier. There are two primary ways to group tables, clusters, and indexes for Parallel Server partitioning: read-only objects and read/write objects. Since pinging is only a problem when objects are being written to, a significant amount of work can be performed just by separating read-only objects into separate tablespaces from read/write objects. Isolating the objects that are being written to may make a large task a little smaller.

In a data warehouse, the vast majority of objects are *supposed to be* read-only. The catch is load cycles, when even read-only objects must occasionally be written to, so some objects may switch between read-only and read/write modes depending on whether or not they are in a load cycle. Since read-only segments cause no PCM difficulties, they should be grouped into tablespaces according to whether the following is true:

- They contain data (i.e., tables and clusters) or are indexes.
- They are on the same load or purge schedule (i.e., they are updated similarly at the same time).
- They have similar size and growth characteristics.

Data segments such as tables and clusters should be separated from indexes. Primarily, this is because tables and their associated indexes have different I/O characteristics: Indexes are always accessed with single-block, random I/Os, and tables could be accessed with either single-block random I/Os or with multiblock, sequential I/Os. These characteristics have direct impact on how PCM locks will be allocated. Also, tables and indexes typically have different size and growth characteristics; typically, indexes are smaller than the tables they are associated with and grow more slowly. Last, indexes don't necessarily have to be backed up, as they are *derived supporting* data structures and do not actually contain data. This brings up the whole debate over how to recover from a media failure: *restore from backup* or *rebuild*. With the size of data warehouses and the somewhat less stringent *mean-time-to-repair* recovery requirements associated with decision-support databases as a whole, it may be much more attractive to rebuild indexes and their tablespaces rather than back them up.

If tables are on different load schedules from each other, they should be placed into different tablespaces. This allows maximum flexibility in using the ALTER TABLESPACE . . . READ ONLY command in Oracle to reduce PCM contention by setting entire tablespaces into READ ONLY mode, thus absolutely preventing writes.

As far as size and growth characteristics are concerned, placing similar-sized segments in the same tablespace allows you to use a single extent size for that entire tablespace. This issue was discussed back in Chapter 8. If all extents for all segments in a tablespace are the same size, then there is no problem with *free space fragmentation*, which can cause "bubbles" of unusable space to form, which can subsequently lead to false "out of space" conditions or simply wasted space. Many software vendors make a pretty fair living for themselves by selling "database reorganization" products to facilitate unloading and reloading tablespaces. The typical reason for wanting to do this in Oracle is generally free space fragmentation. What the vendors of these reorg tools fail to mention is that free space fragmentation is *completely unnecessary* if segments are assigned to tablespaces so that uniform-sized extents can be used. For example, for a tablespace containing segments that range in size between 10 MB and 500 MB, setting the tablespace's DEFAULT STORAGE to INITIAL 4M NEXT 4M PCTINCREASE 0 MAXEXTENTS 400 and then removing STORAGE clauses for all segments created in that tablespace will result in nothing but 4 MB extents in that tablespace. Some segments will only use three or four such extents, and other segments may use one hundred or even up to four hundred such extents, but there would be absolutely no fragmentation issues. The Oracle8 parameter, MINIMUM EXTENT, may be applied to a tablespace to ensure that all extents are multiples of this size.

If tables are to be read/write at all times, then further break down the types of update that will occur: INSERTs or UPDATEs. DELETEs should be considered a given, as all data must eventually be purged, but the manner in which purges occur is not necessarily in online transaction. They can be done via periodic batch transactions, or they can be grouped under the category of UPDATEs for the purposes of further discussion. Also, in a data warehouse environment, deletions can frequently be performed using the TRUNCATE command or by simply DROPing the table altogether. For now, let's just consider DELETEs as being the same as UPDATEs.

If tables are primarily INSERTed into but rarely UPDATEd, then they can be partitioned in at least two ways: either data-routing or randomly using FREELIST GROUPS. If tables are INSERTed into and UPDATEd frequently, then the best method for partitioning involves data-routing only.

Partitioning Using Data-routing

Data-routing means that data will be manipulated according to the value of a key column or group of columns (see Figure 11.21). With Parallel Server, it means that each instance will be assigned to work on data according to the value of this key. This simplified example might involve customer information, keyed by CUST_NAME. Data is routed to Parallel Server instances according to the initial letter in the CUST_NAME. If there are four instances accessing the Parallel Server database, then each instance will be responsible for INSERTS, UPDATEs and DELETEs to any customer information where the CUST_NAME starts with a letter from the pre-assigned range.

Data-routing can be performed explicitly by the application software or it can be performed by a Transaction Processing Monitor (TPM), the middle tier in a three-tier application architecture.

The data routing (sometimes called application partitioning) and data partitioning schemes must be coordinated. This helps to ensure that the set of transactions routed to one Parallel Server instance will require a different subset of blocks than those transactions routed to each other instance. Data partitioning may be implemented in an Oracle8 database through the use of *partitioned tables* and *local partitioned indexes*. As long as the data routing is done by the same ranges as the data partitioning, then the Parallel Server will be able to efficiently distribute the work load without inducing excessive pinging.

Unfortunately, for the data warehouse designer, the most common data partitioning plan is based upon date ranges. This approach facilitates warehouse ad-

Multi-column Partitioning Keys

Partitioning keys based upon multiple columns can be tricky. The data values supplied are compared against the partition range bounds in the order in which the partition key has been defined. The first column (from the left) in the row's partition key which is not equal to a partition's corresponding boundary value will determine which partition will hold the data row.

This behavior can be confusing. As an example, if you specify REGION and TRANS_DATE as the partitioning key, rows with different values in the REGION column may end up in the same partition. In the following example, the COMMENTS column tells where the row will be inserted:

```
CREATE TABLE multikey
    (region            VARCHAR2(4),
     tx_date           DATE,
     comments          VARCHAR2(20))
  PARALLEL (DEGREE 4)
  PARTITION BY RANGE (region, tx_date)
    (PARTITION P1 VALUES LESS THAN
              ('EAST',to_date('19970101','YYYYMMDD'))),
     PARTITION P2 VALUES LESS THAN
              ('EAST',to_date('19980101','YYYYMMDD'))),
     PARTITION P3 VALUES LESS THAN
              ('EAST',to_date('19990101','YYYYMMDD'))),
     PARTITION P4 VALUES LESS THAN
              ('WEST',to_date('19970101','YYYYMMDD'))),
     PARTITION P5 VALUES LESS THAN
              ('WEST',to_date('19980101','YYYYMMDD'))),
     PARTITION P6 VALUES LESS THAN
              ('WEST',to_date('19990101','YYYYMMDD'))) );

insert into multikey values ('CENT','15-oct-98','partition 1');
```

ministration through simplified purges and read-only tablespaces. Partitioning by date does not, however, generally lend itself to data routing or application partitioning because most activity occurs only within the most recent time partition. On the other hand, application partitioning by, say, region would nicely balance workload across OPS instances, but would hinder the easy administration of the database. One compromise solution might be to build your table and local index partitions based upon a two-part partitioning key of region and transaction date. This leads to the creation of many more partitions. But, it does allow OPS to perform inserts into new partitions while preserving many of the advantages of managing partitions. Whether this approach will work well for your warehouse will depend upon the specific keys and the nature of the queries being submitted. If most queries are constrained by region, then this approach may work extremely well. If most queries cross all regions they may end up requir-

```
insert into multikey values ('EAST','15-oct-96','partition 1');
insert into multikey values ('EAST','15-oct-97','partition 2');
insert into multikey values ('EAST','15-oct-98','partition 3');
insert into multikey values ('EAST','15-oct-99','partition 4!');
insert into multikey values ('EAST', null,       'partition 4!');
insert into multikey values ('WEST','15-oct-96','partition 4');
insert into multikey values ('WEST','15-oct-97','partition 5');
insert into multikey values ('WEST','15-oct-98','partition 6');
insert into multikey values ('WEST','01-jan-99','rejected');
insert into multikey values ('WEST', null,       'rejected');
insert into multikey values (null,  '15-oct-98','rejected');
commit;
```

Several rows end up rejected or in partitions other than where you might intuitively expect them! A user who queried specifically from partition P_4 thinking that this partition includes just the 1996 transactions from the WEST region might be surprised to also receive two EAST region transactions!

A null value in the partition key column of an inserted row is sorted above all other values and will therefore sort into the highest partition which satisfies the boundary criteria of any columns defined earlier in the partition key. Therefore, there should be a partition bounded by MAXVALUE in any column which may contain nulls or the row containing the null value will be rejected or inserted into the next higher partition based on previous columns. (Inserts 6, 11, and 12 in the example demonstrate this behavior.) Better still, try to avoid partitioning on columns which allow null values.

Using a date column to define partition boundaries (single column or multicolumn) can also be confusing. Although it isn't well documented, you must specify the boundary value with a to_date function that includes century along with the year, month and day in the date format. The example just presented demonstrates this. Failing to specify the century (YYYY) as part of the date format will result in an error.

Figure 11.21 Data-routing.

ing multiple probes into the local index partitions and may not perform up to expectations.

Another compromise might be to partition detail data by date to facilitate administration of these large objects and to partition some summary data by region to facilitate the division of compute-intensive summarizations across OPS instances.

There are other schemes for implementing data-routing. End users can connect to different Oracle accounts, one for each instance. Each Oracle account has the same table names, but these table names actually resolve (via SYNONYMS) to table partitions dedicated to the instance.

Partitioning Randomly

Freelist groups are a mechanism used by Oracle during INSERTs. When a row is to be inserted into a table, a database block in which to place the row has to be identified. A freelist identifies database blocks that have sufficient room to allow a new row to be inserted. A segment can have multiple freelists; this can be specified during table creation only. Multiple freelists reduce contention when many different processes are rapidly inserting rows into the same table (see Figure 11.22). They do this by keeping separate lists of available database blocks.

Freelist groups are separate groupings of one or more freelists. When FREELISTS GROUPS is set to a value greater than 1, a separate database block is added to the segment header for each freelist group. Having each group in a separate

Figure 11.22 Multiple FREELISTs reducing contention.

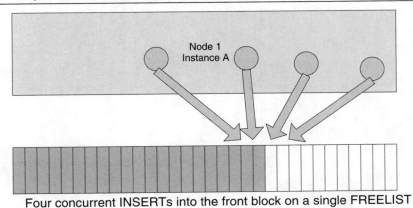

Four concurrent INSERTs into the front block on a single FREELIST

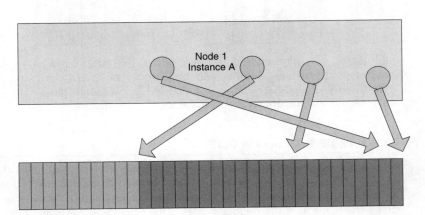

1st INSERT into first block of FREELIST 3, 2nd INSERT into front block
of FREELIST 1, 3rd INSERT into front block of FREELIST 2, 4th
INSERT into front block of FREELIST 3

database block allows Parallel Server to avoid pinging when accessing and manipulating freelists. Therefore, in a Parallel Server environment, the value of
FREELIST GROUPS is usually set to the number of instances, allocating different
groups of FREELISTs for each instance. When an insert into that table occurs, it
will attempt to find a block on a FREELIST belonging to a FREELIST GROUP belonging in turn to the instance performing the insert. If none of the FREELISTs
belonging to an instance has any space for additional rows to be inserted, then a
new extent will need to allocated, and either the entire new extent or just a portion of it will be allocated to this session's FREELIST in this instance's FREELIST
GROUP. See Figure 11.23 for an illustration of multiple FREELIST GROUPs reducing contention.

Figure 11.23 Multiple FREELIST GROUPs reducing contention.

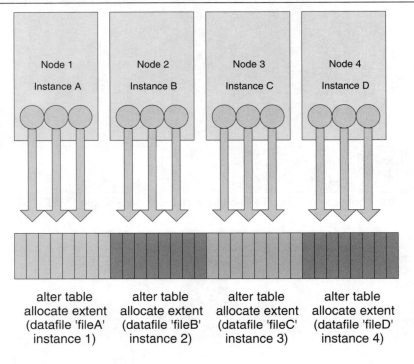

2-TIERS FOR DSS, 3-TIERS FOR OLTP

The cause of inter-instance contention is update activity, meaning INSERT, UPDATE, and DELETE activity. Most update activity in data warehouses is generated by batch programs such as loads; the vast majority of online activity is read-only. As a result, partitioning of data warehouses is easily controlled, as only the batch programs need to be partitioned.

OLTP systems are a different story. Update activity comes from online as well as batch modules, making it extremely difficult to partition effectively.

The best way of implementing partitioned applications is by the use of data routing. The most controllable way to implement data routing is by using a 3-tier architecture involving a transaction processing (TP) monitor such as BEA's Tuxedo. The front-end tier handles business and presentation logic, the middle tier handles the routing of transactions to various instances according to a key value embedded in the data, and the back-end tier is the Oracle Parallel Server database.

When considering Oracle Parallel Server, start off with the assumption that a data warehouse application can be 2-tier (client-server), while an OLTP application should be expected to be 3-tier (client-monitor-server).

More on PCM Locks

There are two kinds of PCM locks: *hash* locks, which are statically allocated and *DBA releasable* locks, which are allocated and deallocated dynamically on demand. Hash locks are assigned to database blocks within datafiles and tablespaces using the GC_FILES_TO_LOCKS "init.ora" parameter at instance startup. DBA releasable locks are assigned to specific database blocks that are about to be updated and are released when the updated transaction is ended.

The "init.ora" parameter GC_DB_LOCKS controls the total number of hash locks to be used by all database instances and the DLM; the parameter GC_RELEASABLE_LOCKS does the same for DBA releasable locks. How these pools of locks are assigned is specified by the parameter GC_FILES_TO_LOCKS.

PCM locks cover only database blocks occupied by tables, indexes, and clusters. Other non-PCM locks are used to cover data structures such as segment headers, rollback segments, and temporary tablespaces. Therefore, the parameters GC_DB_LOCKS, GC_RELEASABLE_LOCKS, and GC_FILES_TO_LOCKS should not cover tablespaces containing rollback segments and tablespaces designated for temporary segments only or explicitly marked as TEMPORARY tablespaces.

The GC_FILES_TO_LOCKS parameter is specified with a rather complicated syntax:

```
GC_FILES_TO_LOCKS="{file-list=#locks[!blocks][EACH]}[:] . . . "
```

where

file-list is the FILE_ID of each datafile to be covered. FILE_ID values can be translated from filenames using the following query:

```
SELECT FILE_ID, FILE_NAME FROM DBA_DATA_FILES;
```

The FILE_IDs should be specified as follows:

```
FILE_ID{-FILE_ID}[,FILE_ID{-FILE_ID}]
```

For example, "1" would indicate FILE_ID = 1 by itself; "1,2,3,4,5" indicates files with FILE_IDs 1 through 5. This last can also be specified using "1-5," indicating all FILE_IDs in the range from 1 through 5, inclusive. Individual FILE_IDs as well as ranges of FILE_IDs can be specified in comma-separated lists, such as "1-5,10-20,23,30-40."

#locks is the number of PCM locks to cover the datafiles specified by the *file-list*. For example, "1-5=100:10-20= 200:23=300:30-40=400" indicates that files 1 through 5 are to be covered by 100 PCM locks, files 10 through 20 are to be covered by 200 PCM locks, file 23 is to be covered by 300 PCM locks, and files 30 through 40 are to be covered by 400 PCM locks.

Unless the "R" qualifier is used, these locks will be *static* or *hashed* PCM locks. If the "R" qualifier (see below) is used, then these locks will be *fine-grain* or *releasable* PCM locks. These locks, also known as *dynamic* or *fine-grain* or *DBA* (Data Base Address) locks, are not permanently assigned to specific database blocks for the duration of the database instance, as static or hashed PCM locks are. Instead, these locks are assigned to individual database blocks as needed, drawn from the fixed-size pool of locks specified by the GC_RELEASABLE_LOCKS parameter.

The two locking schemes, *static* and *releasable*, can be used together at the same time in the same database. However, each data file can only use one or the other locking scheme; they cannot be mixed at that level. Therefore, some tablespaces or data files can use static PCM locks while other tablespaces or data files can use releasable PCM locks.

How are the two locking schemes intended to be used? What are the advantages and disadvantages of each?

Static locks inherently require less processing. As a database block is requested, its physical address on disk is converted using a hash algorithm into a lock number. This is a very simple and very fast operation. The database instance does not need to maintain a mapping of blocks to locks, as each block's address simply hashes to a lock number. Also, each of these locks can cover more than one database block, so this scheme is useful for covering large numbers of database blocks with small numbers of locks. Since each lock occupies several hundred bytes in the shared memory allocated by the distributed lock manager, this is an important consideration. If PCM locking required a lock for each database block, then databases would either quickly run out of shared memory as the numbers of locks increased or databases would have to limit their size. Naturally, this is an unacceptable requirement with most data warehouses.

Releasable locks reside in a fixed-size pool associated with the database instance, whose size is specified by the parameter GC_RELEASABLE_LOCKS. When a database block is about to be accessed by any Parallel Server database instance, a releasable PCM lock is allocated from the pool. This lock is associated with one and only one database block. This scheme requires more processing for maintenance of the pool of locks, but it also allows a relatively small pool of locks to cover a large number of database blocks, as long as the simultaneous number of database blocks being accessed does not exceed the size of the pool of locks.

Static locks are more efficient for covering large numbers of database blocks that are being read by more than one Parallel Server database instances. But since the setting of a single static PCM lock to *exclusive* mode can cause a large number of database blocks to be locked, this scheme can be very problematic when updating occurs. Contention between database instances for exclusive locks on the same database blocks is known as *true pinging*. When pinging results from database instances contending for exclusive locks on different database blocks that are covered by the same PCM lock, it is known as *false pinging*. True pinging cannot necessarily be avoided; if two or more instances need to update rows in the same database block, then contention cannot be avoided. But false pinging is unnecessary, and can be reduced by allocating larger numbers of static PCM locks to the data file. This will not eliminate false pinging, but make it less likely.

Since releasable PCM locks are each assigned to one and only one database block, false pinging is not a possibility at all. Thus, in tablespaces which will be updated heavily and often, releasable PCM locks are a favorable choice. In tablespaces which are predominately read-only or read-mostly, static PCM locks are suitable.

!blocks is the blocking factor for the database blocks to be covered. It is a nonzero positive integer value. If !blocks is not specified, it defaults to a value of 1. Syntactically, it is specified like this: ",1-5=100!20:10-20=200!20:23=300!30:30-40=400!20", which indicates that all the files specified (i.e., 1-5, 10-20, 23, and 30-40) will have a blocking factor of 20, except for file 23, which was specified with a blocking factor of 30. The significance of the blocking factor, as well as guidelines for setting it, will be discussed in more detail shortly.

R, if specified, indicates that this entry uses *releasable* or *fine-grain* or *dynamic* PCM locks, not the default *static* or *hashed* PCM locks. If you are using Oracle7, please be aware that releasable PCM locks were not generally available until version 7.3.3.

EACH, if specified, means the *#locks* and *!blocks* values will apply to each of the files in the *file-list*, instead of cumulatively to all.

To determine how each of these values are derived, let's approach them separately. The value of #locks is dependent on the amount of expected update activity in the datafile and the size of the datafile. Datafiles from tablespaces with high levels of update activity should get more PCM hash locks; datafiles from tablespaces that are marked READ ONLY only need 1 PCM hash lock.

The value of !BLOCKS is dependent on what kind of activity will be performed in the tablespace. If it will be primarily random index scans, smaller values of !BLOCKS are suggested. If it will be primarily full table scans with multiblock reads (as specified by DB_FILE_MULTIBLOCK_READ_COUNT), then the value of !BLOCKS should be two to four times the value of DB_FILE_MULTI-BLOCK_READ_COUNT.

Administering Parallel Server

There are a few requirements for implementing Parallel Server that are different from normal "exclusive"-mode Oracle:

- install and link Parallel Server option (PSO) into the Oracle RDBMS kernel (required)
- create separate threads of redo logfiles for each Parallel Server database instance (required)
- optimize each redo logfile thread for its associated Parallel Server database instance
- create separate rollback segments and tablespaces to hold them for each Parallel Server database instance

- optimize temporary tablespaces for the clustered environment
- optimize the loading of data

Installing and Linking in the Parallel Server Option (required)

The Parallel Server option is additional code that must be installed with and linked into the Oracle RDBMS. It is not a separate product, and only a few key sections in the Oracle RDBMS software are made different by linking the Parallel Server option.

All instances of Parallel Server must be running the same Oracle RDBMS software. This means that Oracle Parallel Server must run on a homogeneous cluster of nodes. A Parallel Server database cannot run partly on one platform and partly on another; for example, a four-node cluster cannot consist of a Sun server, an HP server, a Pyramid server, and a DEC Open VMS server. Generally, the hardware manufacturer stipulates that all nodes in a cluster must be running the same operating system (i.e., UNIX, Open VMS, MVS) and the same version of the operating system. This is a requirement just to get the clustered systems up and running.

The same is true for Oracle. Separate Parallel Server instances for the same database must be running the same platform (i.e., platform and platform version) as well as the same version of Oracle. Oracle RDBMS version numbers have five separate digits: *version, major release, minor release, port-specific release*, and *patch level.* For example, Oracle RDBMS 7.3.2.3.1 can be read as follows:

- version 7
- major release 3
- minor release 2
- port-specific release 3
- patch level 1

Oracle Parallel Server instances should be running the same platform of software—always. Instances are also required to be running the same version and major release of the software components. However, even though Oracle says it's OK if the minor release, port-specific release, and patch level are different among different instances on the same database, it is not recommended.

The reason? Oracle Development does not test all possible combinations of Parallel Server releases for all the platforms it supports. If a primary reason for choosing to use Parallel Server was availability, why would you jeopardize availability unnecessarily by simply not keeping versions of software synchronized?

Separate Threads of Redo Logfiles (required)

Each database instance in Parallel Server must have its own separate set of redo logfiles. These sets of redo logfiles are also known as *threads*.

Redo logs are essentially a sequential record of every action performed in the database. In one sense, they are a second copy of the Oracle database. The database itself is consistent in time; it presents a consistent image of all its composite data to a single point in time: right now. Archived redo logfiles, along with the online, active redo logfiles, present a different picture of the exact same database. The redo logfiles present a record, collected over time, of all the changes that have been made to the database by a database instance.

Since Parallel Server can consist of more than one instance, and since each instance has its own record of changes applied to the database, or *redo thread*, Parallel Server databases must consist of multiple, separate threads of redo. This is actually quite easy to implement. The creation of a Parallel Server database starts off exactly like the creation of a "normal," single-instance database: with the CREATE DATABASE command. The CREATE DATABASE command creates the following data structures:

Data structure:	Filenames specified in:	Size determined by:
control files	"init.ora" configuration file	the following clauses in the CREATE DATABASE command: MAXDATAFILES, MAXLOGFILES, MAXLOGMEMBERS, MAXLOGHISTORY, MAXINSTANCES, etc.
SYSTEM tablespace	DATAFILE clause in CREATE DATABASE command	SIZE qualifier to DATAFILE clause in CREATE DATABASE command
redo logfile thread #1	LOGFILE clause in CREATE DATABASE command	SIZE qualifier in LOGFILE clause in CREATE DATABASE command

Following a successful CREATE DATABASE command, additional redo logfile threads can be added using the ALTER DATABASE ADD LOGFILE THREAD command. The number of groups in the thread, the number of members in each group, the size of each member, and the filenames of the members are specified in this command insofar as they were specified for the redo logfile thread 1 in the CREATE DATABASE command. After a new logfile thread is created, it must be enabled using the ALTER DATABASE ENABLE LOGFILE THREAD command.

How are redo logfile threads assigned to the instances?

In the "init.ora" configuration file, there is a THREAD parameter that defaults to a value of "1" when not specified. This is useful when not using the Parallel Server option; since CREATE DATABASE implicitly creates redo logfile thread 1 and since the THREAD parameter defaults to "1," a DBA not using Parallel Server option can ignore the whole issue quite safely.

After the database has been created (with redo thread 1) and threads of redo have been added for the other instances, the additional instances can be started as long as the THREAD parameter is set appropriately in each instance's "init.ora" configuration file. For the instance using redo thread 2, the parameter THREAD should be set to "2." For the instance using redo log thread 3, the parameter THREAD should be set to "3."

Please note that it is not strictly necessary to have the redo threads numbered sequentially starting with 1; it's merely a convention. Although the CREATE DATABASE command does not allow you to change redo thread 1 to another number initially, there is nothing to stop you from dropping redo thread 1 and assigning the instance that formerly used it to a different thread.

How can a user detect which instance and redo logfile thread they are currently connected to from inside Oracle? Query the V$PARAMETER view for the row where the NAME column has the value "thread." The column VALUE on that row will contain the redo logfile thread number. Additionally, if you wish to know the value of ORACLE_SID for the instance to which you are connected, execute the following query:

```
SELECT instance
  FROM V$Thread
 WHERE thread# =
           (SELECT value
              FROM v$parameter
             WHERE name = 'thread');
```

Optimizing Parallel Server for Data Warehouses

Some of the characteristics of Parallel Server call for the consideration of additional issues when optimally configuring the database. These issues may not be present for non-Parallel Server environments.

Initialization Parameters

The following are some suggestions for setting Parallel Server-specific configuration parameter values. For more information, see the Oracle7 or Oracle8 *Parallel Server Concepts and Administration Guide*.

GC_SEGMENTS

GC_SEGMENTS covers segments headers for tables, indexes, and clusters. Maximum value can be determined using the following:

```
SELECT COUNT(*)
  FROM dba_segments
 WHERE segment_type in ('DATA','INDEX');
```

The actual value to be used should be the number of simultaneously active segments on the system (excluding rollback segments and temporary segments), globally.

This parameter is for Oracle7 only; the integrated DLM in Oracle8 makes it obsolete, as the DLM is now capable of querying the Oracle data dictionary for this information on its own.

GC_FREELIST_GROUPS

GC_FREELIST_GROUPS covers FREELIST GROUP blocks in the extended segment header for simultaneously accessed FREELIST GROUPS. Maximum value can be determined using the following:

```
SELECT SUM(freelist_groups)
  FROM dba_segments
 WHERE freelist_groups > 1;
```

As with GC_SEGMENTS, the value to be used should be gauged by the number of simultaneously active DATA and INDEX segments with multiple freelist groups on the system, globally.

This parameter is for Oracle7 only; the integrated DLM in Oracle8 makes it obsolete, as the DLM is now capable of querying the Oracle data dictionary for this information on its own.

GC_ROLLBACK_SEGMENTS

GC_ROLLBACK_SEGMENTS covers rollback segment header blocks. At least one lock per rollback segment, systemwide. Each rollback segment requires one distributed lock, specified by this parameter, in addition to the number specified by the GC_ROLLBACK_LOCKS parameter. The total number of distributed locks for rollback segments is as follows:

```
(GC_ROLLBACK_SEGMENTS * (GC_ROLLBACK_LOCKS + 1))
```

This parameter is for Oracle7 only; the integrated DLM in Oracle8 makes it obsolete, as the DLM is now capable of querying the Oracle data dictionary for this information on its own.

GC_ROLLBACK_LOCKS

In Oracle7, GC_ROLLBACK_LOCKS is the number of distributed locks available for simultaneously modified rollback segment blocks. The default is adequate for most applications. These distributed locks are acquired in exclusive mode by the instance that acquires the rollback segment. They are used to force the instance to write rollback segment blocks to disk when another instance needs a read-consistent version of a block.

In Oracle8, this parameter changes entirely. Whereas under Oracle7 it was a simple integer value, it now takes a lengthy, complicated string value with syntax very much like the GC_FILES_TO_LOCKS parameter, except that the items in the list are individual rollback segments, not data files.

The GC_ROLLBACK_LOCKS parameter string consists of one or more entries, separated by a colon (":") character. Each entry has the format of:

```
rbs-list = #locks [ EACH ]
```

The rbs-list is either a single integer, or a comma-separated list of integers, or an integer range, or a combination of all these. Each integer is a rollback segment number, as shown in the view DBA_ROLLBACK_SEGS by the column SEGMENT_ID.

The #locks value is an the number of PCM locks to devote to the list of rollback segments. If rbs-list has more than one item in the list, then the keyword EACH is required as PCM locks cannot be shared across rollback segments.

For example, in Oracle8 the GC_ROLLBACK_LOCKS string might look like:

```
gc_rollback_locks="1=100:2-10=50EACH:11-20,30,33-36=30EACH"
```

which means that rollback segment segment 1 (i.e. the SYSTEM rollback segment) has 100 PCM locks, while rollback segments 2 through 10 each have 50 PCM locks. For rollback segments 11 through 20, 30, and 33 through 36, each is allocated 30 PCM locks.

GC_SAVE_ROLLBACK_LOCKS

GC_SAVE_ROLLBACK_LOCKS covers "deferred" rollback segments, which are those rollback segments containing undo entries for (active or committed) transactions in tablespaces that were taken offline. The default should be adequate for one or two instances but should be increased in proportion to ten per instance for more instances if you need to take tablespaces offline while Oracle is running in parallel mode. This may be necessary if performing media recovery on individual tablespaces, for example.

This parameter is for Oracle7 only; the integrated DLM in Oracle8 makes it obsolete, as the DLM is now capable of querying the Oracle data dictionary for this information on its own.

GC_TABLESPACES

GC_TABLESPACES is the maximum number of tablespaces in a parallel server that can be brought offline/online simultaneously. The default should be adequate unless there is an increased risk of media failure or if offlining tablespaces is a frequent occurrence for any reason.

This parameter is for Oracle7 only; the integrated DLM in Oracle8 makes it obsolete, as the DLM is now capable of querying the Oracle data dictionary for this information on its own.

GC_DB_LOCKS

GC_DB_LOCKS sets the maximum total number of statically allocated "hash" locks specified in GC_FILES_TO_LOCKS. You should consider setting this value higher than the total specified in GC_FILES_TO_LOCKS to allow coverage for datafiles added in the future, unless GC_RELEASABLE_LOCKS is nonzero.

This parameter is for Oracle7 only; it was not carried forward into Oracle8.

GC_RELEASABLE_LOCKS

Not "production" or "generally available" until 7.3.3, this parameter should be set explicitly to zero in prior versions because it defaults to the value of DB_BLOCK_BUFFERS, wasting shared memory both in the SGA as well as in the DLM. It sets the maximum total number of "fine-grain" releasable locks for datafiles with zero PCM locks specified in GC_FILES_TO_LOCKS.

GC_FILES_TO_LOCKS

GC_FILES_TO_LOCKS maps "hash" or "releasable" PCM locks to datafiles and also sets "blocking factor." Essentially, datafiles that will use *releasable locks* will have zero locks assigned to them in GC_FILES_TO_LOCKS. Datafiles that have a nonzero number of locks assigned to them in GC_FILES_TO_LOCKS will be using static *hash locks*.

A good rule of thumb for determining how many hash locks to assign to a datafile is to start with the idea of a *density*, namely, the density of database blocks per PCM lock. For want of a better rule, it's probably a good idea to start with a density of 100:1. That is, 100 database blocks to 1 PCM hash lock. Once this is determined, it is not difficult to start calculating how many locks will be required for each datafile. The following query can help:

```
SELECT file_id, blocks, ROUND(blocks/<density>,0) LOCKS
  FROM dba_data_files
 WHERE tablespace_name <> 'TEMP'
   AND tablespace_name NOT LIKE 'RBS%'
 ORDER BY file_id;
```

Remember, the TEMP tablespace used for sorting is not covered by PCM locks (either hash or releasable), and the other GC_ parameters cover rollback segments, so tablespaces containing nothing but rollback segments should be excluded from the calculations as well. The output from this query may look something like the following:

FILE_ID	BLOCKS	LOCKS
1	25600	256
2	4096	41
4	1024	10
5	1024	10
6	2048	20
7	1024	10
8	1024	10
9	4096	41
10	4096	41

The GC_FILES_TO_LOCKS string that results from this output might look something like this:

```
GC_FILES_TO_LOCKS="1=256:2,9,10=41EACH:4-5,7-8=10EACH:6=0"
```

What this translates to is this: file 1 has 256 hash locks; files 2, 9, and 10 each have 41 hash locks; files 4, 5, 7, and 8 each have 10 hash locks; and file 6 has 0 hash locks, meaning that it will be covered by dynamic releasable locks.

Of course, if some tablespaces are likely to receive heavier amounts of write activity, then perhaps it would be a good idea to lower the ratio from 100:1. If the total number of locks resulting from this calculation using the 100:1 ratio is too high, or if some tablespace is going to receive very low write activity, then feel free to raise the ratio from 100:1 to 1000:1 or higher. Of course, if you are going to set the tablespace in question to READ ONLY, then a single PCM hash lock can be used to cover all the datafiles belonging to the tablespace.

What is not addressed in this example is the blocking factor, which would probably differ depending on whether the tablespace contains tables that are frequently full scanned or indexes that are randomly accessed. In the former case, you would want to use a higher blocking factor of about twice the value of the configuration parameter DB_FILE_MULTIBLOCK_READ_COUNT. For randomly accessed objects, you would want to use the default blocking factor of 1. See the section explaining PCM locks and GC_FILES_TO_LOCKS syntax earlier in this chapter.

GC_LCK_PROCS

The number of LCKn processes for the database instance (default: 1). Up to 10 processes can be allocated (i.e. LCK0 through LCK9), each of which handles communications between the database instance and the DLM.

This parameter is valid for both Oracle7 and Oracle8.

GC_LATCHES

The number of latches for each LCK process (default: 2 * CPU_COUNT).

This parameter is new for Oracle8 and did not exist under Oracle7.

ALLOW_PARTIAL_SN_RESULTS

This parameter allows partial results on queries to global dynamic performance views (GV$), in the event a process could not be allocated on the remote instance or in the event the instance is not running.

This parameter is new for Oracle8 and did not exist under Oracle7, due to the fact that the "GV$" views did not exist under Oracle7 either.

FREEZE_DB_FOR_FAST_RECOVERY

Setting this to TRUE speeds instance recovery by freezing I/O from all Oracle processes. If it is set to FALSE, then other database instances continue processing as normal, which can delay the completion of instance recovery due to contention.

This parameter defaults to FALSE if all datafiles are using static, hashed PCM locks. Else, if any datafiles are using dynamic, releasable PCM locks, it defaults to TRUE.

This parameter is new for Oracle8 and did not exist under Oracle7.

LM_RESS

This parameter specifies the total number of locking resources that the DLM can handle. It should be same on all instances of the database; it has a minimum value of 256, defaults to 6000, and should be set to a value less than (DML_LOCKS * 2) + 20.

This parameter is new for Oracle8 and did not exist under Oracle7, since the DLM was not integrated with the RDBMS in Oracle7.

LM_LOCKS

This parameter specifies the number of locks that the DLM can handle, and should be the same on all instances of the database. It has a minimum value of 512, defaults to 12000, and can be set according to the formula "LM_RESS + (LM_RESS * (nbr-nodes – 1)) / nbr-nodes."

This parameter is new for Oracle8 and did not exist under Oracle7, since the DLM was not integrated with the RDBMS in Oracle7.

LM_PROCS

This parameter specifies the number of processes that the DLM can handle, and should be the same on all instances of the database. It should be set using the formula "(PROCESSES * nbr-nodes)," where PROCESSES is the Oracle configuration parameter PROCESSES and "nbr-nodes" is the number of instances for the database.

This parameter is new for Oracle8 and did not exist under Oracle7, since the DLM was not integrated with the RDBMS in Oracle7.

DML_LOCKS

This parameter controls whether "table locks" will be acquired for processes that are performing row-locking. These "table locks" (i.e. "TM" locks from V$LOCK) ensure that DDL (i.e. CREATE, ALTER, DROP) commands are not performed while a process is changing data in the table. If the data warehouse application will not (foreseeably) be issuing DDL commands, then the acquisition of "table locks" during DML (i.e. INSERT, UPDATE, DELETE) can be disabled, thereby optimizing performance. Since these are data dictionary locks, this can help Parallel Server performance in particular, since the data dictionary (i.e. SYSTEM tablespace) is shared among all database instances, and is sometimes a source of unavoidable contention. Eliminating DDL during run-time, by setting DML_LOCKS = 0, can eliminate a major source of contention in Parallel Server. Of course, this comes at a cost to flexibility during run-time, as DDL commands will not be permitted, but this can be a win for controlled change-management anyway.

This parameter and its usage as described here is valid for both Oracle 7.3 and Oracle8.

DB_BLOCK_SIZE

Larger database block size can impact Parallel Server at least two ways. One negative impact is that larger database blocks can result in greater contention as each block contains more rows of data. But if steps have already been taken to partition the application for Parallel Server, this should not be an issue at all. A positive impact is that larger database blocks can reduce the number of PCM locks necessary to manage a database of a given size. If a database is about 100 GB, then it will contain about 13.1 million Oracle database blocks, if each is 8 KB in size. This means that any PCM locking scheme may have to cover up to around 10 million blocks. However, if the same 100 GB database was created with DB_BLOCK_SIZE = 16384 (16 KB), then of course the number of blocks would be roughly half. Halving the number of blocks to cover might halve the number PCM locks to cover them, in the event that system memory is short in supply.

Although 2048 bytes or 2 KB is the default Oracle database block size, current recommendations by Oracle Consulting's System Performance Group state that the standard configuration today should be at least 8192 bytes or 8 KB, with data warehouse databases using DB_BLOCK_SIZE = 16384 (16 KB) or higher to optimize read-intensive I/O. Database block size is changeable only at database creation.

Detecting Contention in Parallel Server

How can you determine whether Parallel Server is having problems with pinging or not?

Oracle provides a series of dynamic performance ("V$") views and dynamic database instance statistics to help determine whether additional contention is being introduced by parallel cache management.

The *Oracle8 Parallel Server Concepts and Administration Guide* contains a more complete source of information on all these topics. There is little purpose served in duplicating the excellent treatment of this topic by the standard documentation set, but we'll just discuss some information that may be supplemental.

Dynamic Performance (V$) Views

CATPARR.SQL SCRIPT

The dynamic performance views for Parallel Server are created by the *catparr.sql* script, which is run under Server Manager while you are connected as SYS or CONNECT INTERNAL. This script is run at installation time, as part of the install of the Parallel Server option, but in fact it will be necessary to run this script regularly whenever you attempt to use the Parallel Server dynamic performance views.

The reason is that, while some of these views only read internal memory structures in the Oracle SGA (i.e. fixed or "X$" tables), others use a derived internal table named EXT_TO_OBJ which is dropped and re-created during the *catparr.sql* script. All that EXT_TO_OBJ does is store the current contents of the internal space management tables in the data dictionary. These data dictionary tables are not optimized for query performance, which you are undoubtedly aware if you have ever tried to query them.

To prevent "V$" dynamic performance views that need to translate addresses in the database to object names from querying sluggish data dictionary structures, the *catparr.sql* script creates the EXT_TO_OBJ table, which provides far better access performance.

The defect in this plan is that the EXT_TO_OBJ table represents a *snapshot* or a point-in-time view of the data in the data dictionary space management tables, one which can rapidly become obsolete. To prevent this, run the *catparr.sql* script, which is generally located under the ORACLE_HOME directory in the *rdbms/admin* subdirectory, before attempting to use the Parallel Server "V$" dynamic performance views.

It might be advisable to run the job regularly, using a job scheduler or even the UNIX *cron* or Windows NT *at* utilities. On a busy system in which many extents are being added quickly, it might simply be best to just run *catparr.sql* immediately prior to using these views.

Be aware that these views may show inaccurate information if *catparr.sql* has not been run recently, and the data in EXT_TO_OBJ has been allowed to become obsolete.

The *catparr.sql* script itself provides some interesting documentation of the dynamic performance views, in addition to what can be found in the standard documentation. Take the time to read through this script.

V$PING

The V$PING view, as the name implies, displays information about pings, or I/O activity resulting purely from parallel cache management. The following table briefly describes the columns shown in the view and the meaning of their values:

Column Name	Description		
FILE#	the file number of datafile (see column FILE_ID in DBA_DATA_FILES)		
BLOCK#	the database block in the datafile (see column BLOCK_ID in DBA_EXTENTS)		
CLASS#	*Value*	*Description*	*GC parameter*
	0	SYSTEM rollback segment	N/A
	1	data block	gc_files_to_locks
	2	temporary segment block	N/A
	3	rollback segment block in off-lined TS	gc_save_rollback_locks
	4	segment header block	gc_segments
	5	rollback segment header in off-lined TS	gc_save_rollback_locks
	6	freelist group header block	gc_freelist_groups
	7 + (N*2)	rollback segment header block	gc_rollback_segments
	8 + (N*2)	rollback segment data block	gc_rollback_locks

(Note: "N" is the rollback segment number from V$ROLLNAME.USN)

(continues)

STATUS	Value	Description
	FREE	not in use
	XCUR	held exclusive by this instance
	SCUR	held shared by this instance
	CR	only valid for consistent read
	READ	is being read from disk
	MREC	in media recovery mode
	IREC	in instance (crash) recovery mode
XNC		number of times block has converted from *exclusive* (X) to *null* (N) for this database instance
FORCED_READS		number of times block had to be re-read from disk because another instance had forced it out of cache by requesting a PCM *exclusive* lock
FORCED_WRITES		number of times block was written by DBWR because another instance had requested a *shared* or *exclusive* PCM lock
NAME		name of the segment
PARTITION_NAME		name of the partition within the partitioned segmen
KIND		type of segment
OWNER#		owner of the segment (see column USER_ID in DBA_USERS)
LOCK_ELEMENT_ ADDR		foreign key to V$LOCK_ELEMENT view, which contains one row for each static (hashed) lock specified by GC_DB_LOCKS
LOCK_ELEMENT_ NAME		the name of the lock element

The columns FORCED_READS and FORCED_WRITES provide a good picture of the amount of wasteful I/O occurring due to parallel cache management only. The column XNC is provided for backward compatibility to previous versions of Oracle Parallel Server. It is not very useful, since it only tracks PCM lock conversions from *exclusive to null*, and will miss conversions from *exclusive to shared*.

By querying this view, you can detect exactly which objects (or their partitions) within which tablespaces or datafiles are suffering the most from *pinging*:

```
SELECT   F.TABLESPACE_NAME,
         F.FILE_NAME,
         U.USERNAME || '.' ||
             P.NAME || decode(P.PARTITION_NAME,
                              null, null,
                              ':' || P.PARTITION_NAME) NAME,
         DECODE(P.CLASS,
             0, 'SYSTEM RBS',
             1, 'DATA',
             2, 'TEMPORARY',
             3, 'RBS DATA OFFLINE',
             4, 'SEG HDR',
```

```
                              5, 'RBS SEG HDR OFFLINE',
                              6, 'FREELIST HDR',
                              DECODE(MOD(P.CLASS, 2),
                                      0, 'RBS DATA',
                                      'RBS HDR')) LOCK_CLASS,
                              P.STATUS LOCK_STATUS,
                              SUM(P.FORCED_READS) FORCED_READS,
                              SUM(P.FORCED_WRITES) FORCED_WRITES
            FROM     V$PING          P,
                     DBA_DATA_FILES  F,
                     DBA_USERS       U
            WHERE    F.FILE_ID = P.FILE#
            AND      U.USER_ID = P.OWNER#
            GROUP BY F.TABLESPACE_NAME,
                     F.FILE_NAME,
                     U.USERNAME || '.' ||
                           P.NAME || decode(P.PARTITION_NAME,
                                            null, null,
                                            ':' || P.PARTITION_NAME),
                     DECODE(P.CLASS,
                            0, 'SYSTEM RBS',
                            1, 'DATA',
                            2, 'TEMPORARY',
                            3, 'RBS DATA OFFLINE',
                            4, 'SEG HDR',
                            5, 'RBS SEG HDR OFFLINE',
                            6, 'FREELIST HDR',
                            DECODE(MOD(P.CLASS, 2),
                                    0, 'RBS DATA',
                                    'RBS HDR')),
                     P.STATUS;
```

One way to reduce pinging is to increase the value of the parameter associated with the block class (see CLASS# column in table above). If this value is already judged to be high enough, then it may be wise to consider other ways of reducing inter-instance contention, such as implementing FREELIST GROUPS (if the pinging is due to INSERT activity) or data-routing (if the pinging is due to UPDATE or DELETE activity).

V$FALSE_PING

If *static* or *hashed* PCM locks are being used in the datafile in question, then remember that there are two categories of pinging that can occur: *true* and *false*. *True pinging* results from contention between two (or more) database instances for the same exact database block. *False pinging* results from a database block buffer being pinged because it is covered by the same hashed PCM lock as a database block buffer which is actually being locked. To determine whether this is so, query the view V$FALSE_PING, which has all the same columns as V$PING. In V$FALSE_PING, the view is making an *educated guess* at whether blocks are being pinged due to the fact that they belong to the same hashed lock and the fact that they have been converted more than 10 times.

If V$FALSE_PING shows large numbers of rows, then consider either increasing the hashed PCM locks on the affected data files or changing the locking scheme from hashed PCM locks to *fine-grain* or *releasable* PCM locks, which never cause false pinging.

V$LOCK_ACTIVITY

Another useful view is V$LOCK_ACTIVITY which summarizes the types of PCM activities performed on the system. Columns for this view are:

Column Name	Description
FROM_VAL	PCM lock conversions from: NULL (unused), S (shared), X (exclusive), SSX (shared exclusive)
TO_VAL	PCM lock conversions to: NULL, S, X, SSX
ACTION_VAL	description of the FROM/TO action
COUNTER	total number of conversions

Healthy PCM lock activity includes any number of actions like "Lock buffers for read" and "Lock buffers for write". Contention between database instances is indicated when all the other actions achieve high numbers, relative to the "Lock buffers for ..." actions.

Global Dynamic Performance Views

All of the dynamic performance ("V$") views display information for an individual database instance. With Oracle8, *global* dynamic performance ("GV$") views are available, which display information on *all* running instances of the Parallel Server database. The GV$ views have all the columns of the V$ views, with the addition of a column INST_ID, which is an integer corresponding to the INSTANCE_NUMBER configuration parameter value. All of V$ views have corresponding GV$ views, except for V$ROLLNAME.

Parallel Server-specific Statistics

The following statistics can be queried from V$SYSSTAT for cumulative statistics since the database instance was started or from V$SESSTAT for cumulative statistics for a particular Oracle session.

GLOBAL LOCK GETS

The actual statistics are "global lock gets (non async)", "global lock gets (async)", and "global lock get time". These are the total requests made to upgrade PCM locks to either shared or exclusive mode, starting from null mode.

GLOBAL LOCK CONVERTS

The actual statistics are "global lock converts (non async)", "global lock converts (async)", and "global lock convert time". These are the total requests made to either upgrade PCM locks from shared to exclusive mode or downgrade PCM locks from exclusive mode to shared mode.

GLOBAL LOCK RELEASES

The actual statistics are "global lock releases (non async)", "global lock releases (async)", and "global lock release time". These are the total requests made to release PCM from shared or exclusive mode to null mode.

RELEASABLE FREELIST WAITS

The number of times the database instance exhausts the pool of releasable PCM locks specified by the configuration parameter GC_RELEASABLE_LOCKS. Naturally, this value should be kept as close to zero as possible. This may include increasing the GC_RELEASABLE_LOCKS value or reducing usage of releasable PCM locks.

REMOTE INSTANCE UNDO REQUESTS

The number of times this instance tried to read the "before image" stored in a rollback segment belonging to another database instance, for the purpose of satisfying a "consistent read".

REMOTE INSTANCE UNDO WRITES

The number of times this instance had to write down "dirtied" (or changed) rollback segment blocks so that another instance could read the "before image" information, for the purpose of satisfying a "consistent read".

DBWR CROSS INSTANCE WRITES

The number of "dirtied" (i.e. changed) database block buffers written to disk to allow another instance to acquire a shared or exclusive PCM lock on the block.

PHYSICAL WRITES

The total number of "dirtied" (i.e. changed) database block buffers written to disk by the DBWR process(es).

The ratio of "(DBWR cross instance writes/physical writes)" indicates how many of the writes performed by DBWR were due to pinging. When this ratio approaches 1.0, then use the V$PING and V$FALSE_PING views to locate the sources of cross-instance contention and to mitigate the pinging problem.

Once again, the standard Oracle8 documentation set has an excellent section on tuning Parallel Server in the *Oracle8 Parallel Server Concepts and Administration* guide; read it thoroughly and utilize it.

Optimizing Redo Logfiles in Parallel Server (optional, but highly recommended)

One important thing to remember about redo logfiles in general, Parallel Server option or not: The redo logfiles are likely among the busiest objects in the Oracle database in terms of I/O. They are always receiving large sequential writes from the Oracle LGWR background process, and if the database is in

ARCHIVELOG mode, they are frequently receiving large sequential reads from the Oracle ARCH background process.

As a result, the redo logfiles should be situated on the most optimal disk devices for large sequential writes and reads. What represents an "optimal disk device"? At the most basic level, it simply means a "fast" device. Redo logfiles are typically not accessed concurrently by more than one process at a time; LGWR is the only process that writes to redo logfiles when they are active; the ARCH process is typically the only process that reads from them. Of course, it is possible to start more than one ARCH process manually, but each ARCH will only read from one redo logfile apiece.

Because the level of concurrency of redo logfiles is very low, good performance gains can be achieved by utilizing RAID 0 nonredundant data striping with a fine-grain stripe width to parallelize the write- and read-requests across several devices at once. The fine-grain stripe width, which indicates that the stripe size is relatively small (i.e., 4,096, 8,192, or 16,384 bytes), implies that each LGWR write-request or ARCH read-request will make I/O requests of several different devices at once, achieving a degree of parallelism.

While RAID 0 data striping cannot improve upon the inherent data-transfer rates of the devices included in the RAID "parity group," the parallelism achieved by writing to and reading from multiple devices does improve overall data-transfer throughput.

Please note the phrase *nonredundant* in the name "RAID 0 nonredundant data striping." By itself, RAID 0 striping is a classic example of how a feature with clear *performance* advantages can have serious negative *availability* consequences. In this case, the fact that data is striped across multiple devices without any redundancy considerations means that the data is *more susceptible* to device failure than if data striping is not employed. Luckily, the solution is quite simple: RAID 1 mirroring (or *shadowing*) or RAID 5 block-interleaved distributed-parity mirroring can be employed to provide the necessary redundancy to guard against device failure. Check with your hardware vendor or system administrator for the most advantageous option.

Whatever option is chosen, be sure to optimize I/O to the redo logfiles. In general terms, the use of the combination of RAID 0 striping plus RAID 1 mirroring (also known as RAID 0+1 or RAID 01 or RAID 10) is the best option for the high I/O rates that Oracle redo logfiles generate.

On many clustered systems where Parallel Server option is used, there is another factor to be considered when creating the redo logfiles: locality of storage. Some clustered environments (i.e., Digital Equipment Corporation Clusters) use a *star-coupler* arrangement to provide each node with access to the cluster's disk drives. Other clustered environments (i.e., IBM RS/6000 HACMP) provide *direct connections* from each node to each disk drive. Therefore, each drive might have *multi-tailed* connections to two or more (up to eight) different nodes. With both of these arrangements, each storage device is equally accessible to all the nodes, and there is no disk drive that may be considered *local* to a particular node.

However, with some environments (i.e., IBM RS/6000 SP) disk drives are actually connected to particular nodes, and the ability to provide access to all disk drives from all nodes in the cluster is provided via *virtual shared devices*, which operate over a high-speed network interconnect. Therefore, while each node can access all disk drives, some disk drives (because they are local and do not have to be accessed over the interconnect) are more advantageous to use than others.

If the clustered environment you are using falls into the category of clustered systems with *local* and *nonlocal* disk drives, be sure to situate the redo logfiles for each instance on disk drives local to that node. With the combination of local disk resources and fine-grain RAID 0 striping, you can be certain that the Oracle background processes that write to (i.e., LGWR) and read from (i.e., ARCH) the redo logfiles will do so most optimally. When using RAID 1 mirroring/shadowing or RAID 5 interleaving in conjunction with the striping, you can be more comfortable that these all-important data structures are not subject to device failure.

One last note: Which is better? Mirroring provided by the hardware or operating system (i.e., RAID) or mirroring provided by the Oracle RDBMS (i.e., multiple members for each redo logfile group)? In general, there is nothing wrong with trying to use both methods at once. Naturally, this can be considered wasteful in terms of space utilization: twice the level of redundancy or essentially four copies of data! As with all redundancy schemes, the duplication is wasteful if the data structures being protected are unimportant. Oracle's redo logfiles, however, are crucial to the Oracle RDBMS's ability both to run and to recover from any kind of failure. Since redo logfiles generally consume a fairly small percentage of the total warehouse database size, extra redundancy may not be that costly to implement. But since Parallel Server needs a separate complete set (or thread) of redo logfiles for each instance, it stands to reason that the more instances you use, the more space the redo logfiles will consume in total. If you are mirroring logfiles at the hardware/operating-system level and again at the Oracle RDBMS level, using both methods of mirroring together may become prohibitively expensive.

If this is the situation, there is one extra failure scenario that mirroring at the Oracle RDBMS level (i.e., multiple members per redo logfile group) can cover and that mirroring at the hardware/operating-system level (i.e., RAID 1 or RAID 5) cannot handle: corruption of write requests issued by Oracle. Since the Oracle RDBMS method of mirroring can handle one more small scenario than the other option (even if the probability of this failure scenario is infinitesimally rare), we would tend to choose to create multiple members for redo logfile groups rather than use RAID 1 or RAID 5 for redo logfiles.

Optimizing Rollback Segments in Parallel Server (optional, but highly recommended)

There are two kinds of rollback segments in Oracle: public and private. The concept of public rollback segments was originally designed specifically for use in Oracle Parallel Server environments, but they are rarely (if ever) used even here, and it is advisable to avoid them. Rollback segments (both public and private) are claimed by a database instance and used exclusively by that instance until the instance is shut down. The difference between the two kinds of rollback segments lies in how they are claimed by an instance.

Private rollback segments are the default (and preferred) type. They can be claimed by an instance by specifying a list of rollback segment names in the ROLLBACK_SEGMENTS parameter in the instance's "init.ora" configuration file so they are claimed (and onlined) by the instance upon startup. Or they can be claimed by an instance after instance startup using the ALTER ROLLBACK SEGMENT . . . ONLINE command.

Public rollback segments were designed to be used as a pool of rollback segments, which are intended to be claimed by any instance that needs extra rollback space on demand. The idea sounds attractive but is actually faulty in practice. The reason public rollback segments are a bad idea is twofold. The first reason concerns the fact that, after the redo logfiles, the rollback segments can be considered the second-busiest data structures in the typical Oracle database in terms of I/O. Of course, this depends on the type and nature of the application being run on the database; some applications may access other data structures more heavily, of course. Also, I/O to and from the rollback segments can usually be reduced by increasing the size of the buffer cache in the SGA; this is not an option for redo logfiles. But regardless of the type of application, the rollback segments can usually be counted on to provide very high levels of I/O. This can be true even in primarily read-only environments like data warehouses.

Because of this, it is advantageous to separate rollback segments into their own tablespaces, separate from all tables, indexes, clusters, and especially temporary (sorting) segments. This prevents the expansion of these other types of segments from interfering with the growth of the rollback segments. Conversely, this also prevents the dynamic expansion of rollback segments from interfering with the growth of these other types of segments.

Temporary (sorting) segments and rollback segments are particularly incompatible, since they both have the same nasty habit of growing very rapidly in a short amount of time. Detecting a conflict between temporary segments and rollback segments can be made more difficult by the fact that temporary segments tend to disappear when they're no longer in use. If an operation requiring a sort fails because the associated temporary segment was unable to grow any further due to a clash with an active, growing rollback segment, the temporary segment disappears after the operation finishes. Additionally, via the use of the OPTIMAL storage clause, rollback segments themselves can shrink back to an optimal size. Because of the ability of both of these kinds of segments to "cover their tracks" (as it were) following a clash (one disappears completely, the other can shrink so it doesn't appear to be a problem), detecting the cause of a space shortage in a tablespace where temporary segments and rollback segments can coexist can be like chasing the will-o'-the-wisp.

It is also advantageous to try to situate the rollback segment tablespaces on the most optimal devices for I/O, if possible. The reasons here are the same as those cited for redo logfiles: You should situate data structures that you know are likely to generate the most I/O on devices capable of providing the fastest I/O. If the concept of local disk drives is relevant on your clustered system, then the devices capable of providing the fastest I/O differ from instance to instance.

By explicitly naming rollback segments for each instance, they can be isolated into different tablespaces and therefore made local.

The second reason public rollback segments are a bad idea involves the way Parallel Server handles contention between instances. Although it is possible for two or more instances to update data in the same tablespace or segment or extent, it is easiest to guarantee that there will be no interinstance contention if the contents of tablespaces can be *dedicated* to a specific instance. Since rollback segments are effectively dedicated to the instance that brings them online, this makes it possible to guarantee that an entire tablespace, if it contains only private rollback segments for a particular instance, handles reads and writes only from that particular instance. The same guaranteed dedication to an instance cannot be made for tables, indexes, or clusters.

For all these reasons, the best practice is to create separate tablespaces for rollback segments only, one tablespace per instance, in a Parallel Server database. Each tablespace should be created on disk devices optimized for the node on which each particular instance resides. Each tablespace should contain private rollback segments for that one—and only one—instance. Upon startup, each instance should bring its own private rollback segments online using the ROLLBACK_SEGMENTS parameter in the instance's "init.ora" configuration file.

Optimizing Sorting in Parallel Server

With Oracle RDBMS version 7.3, the TEMPORARY clause became available with the CREATE TABLESPACE and ALTER TABLESPACE commands. By default, tablespaces can contain both "permanent" segments (i.e., tables/clusters, indexes, rollback segments) and temporary segments. When an entire tablespace is created as TEMPORARY, or if it already exists and contains nothing and is altered to TEMPORARY, then it is optimized for use only by the temporary segments used during sorting.

Before version 7.3, and in PERMANENT tablespaces from 7.3 on, temporary segments are allocated upon demand and are removed as the final task of the SQL statement that created them. All this allocation and deallocation can strain the Oracle RDBMS and its data dictionary. When a tablespace is marked TEMPORARY, then the extents belonging to temporary segments are not deallocated once they are created. The extents remain allocated but available for use by subsequent SQL statements. The fact that extent deallocation and reallocation no longer occurs can remove quite a bit of contention from each Oracle instance, as well as the database's data dictionary, which is global to all the instances. If multiple instances no longer have to update the global data dictionary when a lot of sorting is happening, then the performance of each instance as well as the overall performance of all instances is improved.

Also, marking a tablespace TEMPORARY further emphasizes the nature of I/O performed on that tablespace. Since tables, clusters, indexes, and rollback segments can no longer be created in the tablespace, the datafiles that comprise the tablespace can be optimized for the kind of I/O generated by sorting operations. If a lot of sorting is performed by the SQL statements used by the data warehouse application, then you may want to consider placing these tablespaces on optimal I/O devices as well. However . . .

Temporary tablespaces can safely be shared by all the instances of a Parallel Server database, so you may only need one such tablespace. But that one tablespace may have to be huge, and here's why: Data warehouse applications on Oracle typically require *very large* amounts of sorting space. The kinds of SQL statements issued against data warehouses are generally large queries that perform summarizations, aggregations, or filtering against massive amounts of data. Sometimes these massive queries might also involve joining several tables, which may require additional sorting.

Add to this the probable involvement of the Parallel Query Option (PQO), which transparently takes a single SQL query running on one Oracle server process and divides the work to be performed so that many concurrently executing parallel query slave processes can perform the work, in parallel. If the original query was large enough, then instead of a single long-running query process generating huge temporary segments for sorting, you may have dozens of parallel query slaves each generating large temporary segments for sorting. Where only one process was consuming space at a relatively slow pace, you may now have dozens of processes each clamoring for more sorting space at the same time. If you have a handful of such queries running at the same time, each using PQO, then Oracle can gulp down sort space at a dizzying rate and just as quickly release it when the queries finish.

Quite frequently, the temporary tablespace in an Oracle data warehouse is the single largest tablespace in the database. In fact, in a data warehouse that makes heavy use of both Parallel Query Option and Parallel Server option, the temporary tablespace can represent anywhere from 10 to 25 percent of the total size of the Oracle database. To illustrate this, in a Oracle data warehouse database that measures 750 gigabytes in total, it is not unreasonable to have a temporary tablespace sized at 100 to125 gigabytes. The size of the temporary tablespace is dependent partially on the amount of "raw" data in the database (i.e., tables and clusters, not including indexes) and partially on the number of concurrently executing query processes requiring sort space.

Another issue that arises when optimizing temporary tablespaces and sorting in general is to set the SORT_DIRECT_WRITES parameter in each instance's "init.ora" configuration file to TRUE (default is FALSE). Enabling this parameter causes each query process to write directly to the temporary segments, bypassing the buffer cache in the SGA. As a result, there is less contention in each instance's SGA, each query server process performs the I/O to the temporary tablespace's datafiles (instead of the DBWR background process), and the overall code path in performing sorting is made significantly shorter.

All in all, the redo logfiles, the rollback segments, and the temporary tablespace may put huge demands on the I/O subsystem underneath an Oracle data warehouse, whether Parallel Server is in use or not. If Parallel Server is in use, then the redo logfiles and rollback segments should be partitioned and optimized for the instances and nodes they are associated with. Since it can be shared by all the instances in the Parallel Server database, the temporary tablespace should probably be striped or concatenated across all the nodes in the cluster to ensure that no single node (or group of nodes) bears the brunt of the I/O associated with sorting.

Concatenating, as the word is used here, is similar to data striping, but at a less sophisticated level. RAID 0 striping causes the data to be striped in small discrete chunks (i.e., 4 KB, 16 KB, 64 KB, etc.). Concatenation merely means dividing the tablespace evenly into a certain number of separate files and then placing each one of those files on a separate node or device.

An example of tablespace concatenation is shown in the following CREATE TABLESPACE command:

```
CREATE TABLESPACE TEMP DATAFILE    '/dev/dsk/node1/temp01.dbf' SIZE 1024M,
     '/dev/dsk/node2/temp02.dbf' SIZE 1024M,
     '/dev/dsk/node3/temp03.dbf' SIZE 1024M,
     '/dev/dsk/node4/temp04.dbf' SIZE 1024M,
          TEMPORARY;
```

In this example, a temporary tablespace named TEMP is created with an initial size of 4 gigabyte (i.e., 4,096 MB). The datafile named *temp01.dbf* is created on *node1*, the datafile named *temp02.dbf* is created on *node2*, and so on. This tablespace is concatenated across four nodes, each chunk (or stripe width) being 1 gigabyte in size.

Of course, each datafile itself might be RAID 0 striped across several disk devices. For example, the datafile named *temp01.dbf* may actually reside on sixteen disk drives on *node1*. The size of each chunk (or stripe width) on each disk drive might be 16 KB. Whether or not each datafile is itself striped at the hardware or operating system level is, of course, completely transparent to Oracle.

Some clustered systems, such as the IBM RS/6000 SP, provide the ability to perform RAID 0 striping not only across disk drives within a node but also across nodes. On the SP platform, these are referred to as *hashed shared devices* or HSDs. In this case, the four datafiles in the example just shown may themselves be RAID 0 striped in relatively small widths (i.e., 16 KB) across all four nodes, as well as being RAID 0 striped across all sixteen disk drives on each node. In this situation, the only reason for using four datafiles to create the tablespace is due to a possible 2 gigabyte file size limitation on AIX, not because of a desire to spread I/O across all four nodes. If the AIX operating system (as well as Oracle for AIX) fully supported file sizes larger than 2 gigabytes (which will be true with AIX 4.2 and above), then the tablespace TEMP in the preceding example could have been created with a single HSD and still provided all the benefits of RAID 0 striping across all nodes and all disk drives.

Optimizing Data Loading in Parallel Server

Strategies for populating the data warehouse were discussed in detail in Chapter 6, but there are two basic methods for loading data into Oracle:

- using "conventional" SQL
- using direct path

The first approach includes any mechanism involving SQL: "conventional path" SQL*Loader, custom-written programs using Precompilers or OCI, or third-party vendor solutions using Precompilers or OCI. The other approach has only one alternative: direct path SQL*Loader. Oracle does not provide an API for using the direct path mechanism, so SQL*Loader is the only utility available for loading data that uses it.

The best approach to loading with Parallel Server is the same regardless which mechanism is being used: The fastest approach is to use as many instances as possible. However, partitioning the loads so that there is no contention between instances varies based on the mechanism.

Direct Path Loading

The SQL*Loader utility can be used with the direct path mechanism in parallel, that is, with several concurrent such programs running at the same time. SQL*Loader does not transparently "parallelize" the way parallel queries do. Rather, parallel direct path SQL*Loader just means that you can have two or more SQL*Loader processes running in this fashion at the same time. For example:

```
$ sqlldr control=x.ctl data=x1.dat direct=true parallel=true . . .
$ sqlldr control=x.ctl data=x2.dat direct=true parallel=true . . .
$ sqlldr control=x.ctl data=x3.dat direct=true parallel=true . . .
```

What will happen here is that the SQL*Loader processes will each create their own "private" TEMPORARY segments to load into, each essentially *appending* data onto the table in question.

The problem here is that we have provided Oracle no guidance about where to physically locate these extents, so in Oracle7 it guesses. It may guess well and locate the extents in datafiles that are "local" to the node on which the SQL*Loader processes are running, or it may guess poorly and locate these extents in datafiles that are not "local." This is illustrated in Figures 11.24 and 11.25. Naturally, you can see that locality can be important for performance; having to send data across a network, even a high-speed network, is certainly much slower than sending the data to locally connected disk drives. You can also see that, all other things being equal, it would be even more advantageous to locate each of these three SQL*Loader processes on separate database instances. But which of the scenarios illustrated in Figures 11.26, 11.27, and 11.28 is more efficient?

Obviously, it's Figure 11.28. Little or no networking is involved; each process is simply shoveling data from the input flat files and loading the local datafiles in the tablespace. Oracle7 chooses where the extents will go if you don't. Frankly, you shouldn't allow it to do so if you are concerned about optimizing performance. So, using the FILE= clause you can explicitly specify where the extents will be located, ensuring locality of work.

```
$ sqlldr control=x.ctl data=x1.dat direct=true parallel=true file='x1.dbf'
$ sqlldr control=x.ctl data=x2.dat direct=true parallel=true file='x2.dbf'
$ sqlldr control=x.ctl data=x3.dat direct=true parallel=true file='x3.dbf'
```

Figure 11.24 Loading into extents located on local datafiles.

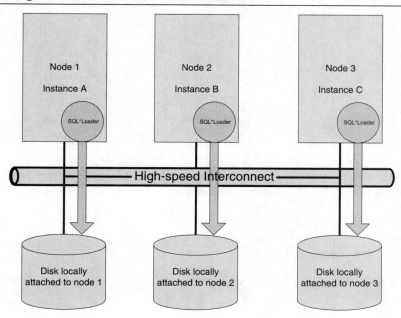

Figure 11.25 Loading into extents located on nonlocal datafiles.

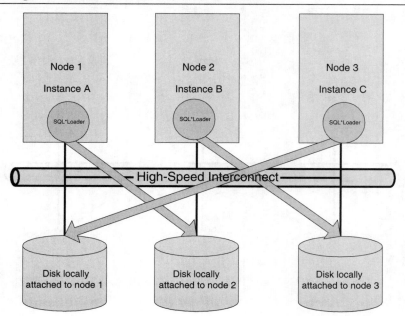

Figure 11.26 From separate instances onto a single datafile.

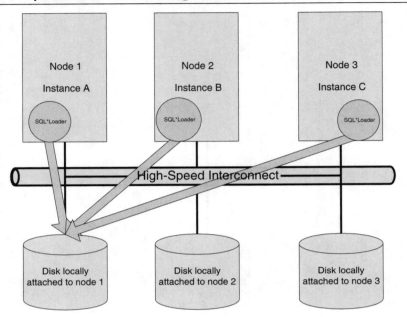

Figure 11.27 From separate instances onto different datafiles.

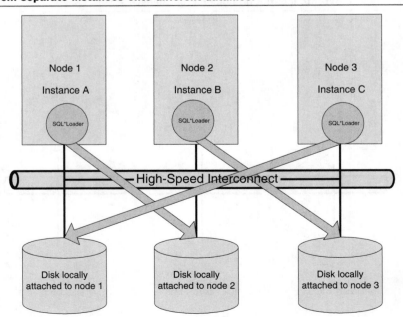

Figure 11.28 From separate instances onto local datafiles.

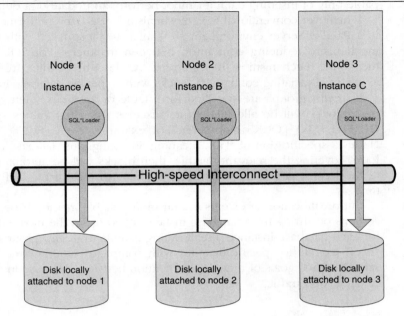

The FILE= clause can also be specified inside the SQL*Loader control file; in some cases, this is the only option: for example, when data from the input file is being loaded into two or more different tables or when data from the input file is being loaded into two or more different partitions in a partitioned table. Check with the *Oracle Server Utilities Guide* or Chapter 6 in this book.

Conventional SQL Loading

For some reason, many people are under the impression that any program written in C, COBOL, or Fortran simply must be faster than SQL*Loader. Even if the task at hand is simple insertion, they still feel that writing a program in a third-generation language (3GL) such as C simply must be faster than SQL*Loader conventional path.

Not true. To help explain this, just think of SQL*Loader as a C program that has already been written. All you have to do is write a control file that describes what the input data looks like. Right away, this is a performance increase; creating a 3GL program takes a lot of time to write and test, and writing a control file is a heck of a lot faster and easier.

SQL*Loader can handle a surprising number of complex file formats and situations, such as loading from one input file into several tables or partitioned tables or merging multiple input records into a single input record. But there are a few basic ones that it cannot handle: For example, if data from each input record must go to more than one table or if data from two or more input files must be merged, to be loaded into one or more tables. Also, SQL*Loader is capable only of inserting data; it cannot perform an update of a duplicate record.

Whichever conventional SQL mechanism is used, the performance challenges in a Parallel Server environment are similar to those faced with the direct path mechanism: reducing contention between instances. For SQL INSERT statements, the mechanism is *freelist groups*. As described earlier, freelist groups are a way of associating contiguous blocks with a specific database instance.

If freelist groups are specified for a table or an index, then groups of database blocks will be allocated to an instance using the values specified in the GC_FILES_TO_LOCKS parameter. For example, if GC_FILES_TO_LOCKS includes a specification of "!50", meaning 50 contiguous database blocks for PCM locks covering the relevant datafile, then blocks will be automatically allocated to the freelist group for the current instance in increments of fifty blocks at a time.

But preallocation of extents is a far more reliable method for ensuring that insertions occurring from database instances end up in the most efficient location for each database instance. Preallocating extents to freelist groups allows you to "map" extents to specific datafiles with complete certainty, and they therefore serve the dual goals of reducing contention between database instances and "localizing" disk traffic.

```
SQL> CREATE TABLE X
  2 (. . .)
  3 STORAGE (INITIAL 1 NEXT 8M PCTINCREASE 0
  4 FREELISTS 4
  5 FREELIST GROUPS 3);

Table created.

SQL> ALTER TABLE X ALLOCATE EXTENT
  2       (DATAFILE '/dev/rv_node1_02_X.dbf' INSTANCE 1);

Table altered.

SQL> ALTER TABLE X ALLOCATE EXTENT
  2       (DATAFILE '/dev/rv_node2_03_X.dbf' INSTANCE 2);

Table altered.

SQL> ALTER TABLE X ALLOCATE EXTENT
  2       (DATAFILE '/dev/rv_node3_04_X.dbf' INSTANCE 3);

Table altered.
```

Here, table X is initially created with a minimally sized initial extent; note that only one byte was requested. This initial extent will not belong to any particular freelist group, so the best way to mitigate this fact is to make the extent as small as possible. On most platforms, this should result in an initial extent of only one database block, as a part of the following:

- one database block for segment header
- three database blocks for freelist groups
- one database block for initial extent

The result should total five database blocks upon table creation. Then the subsequent ALTER TABLE commands will add three additional extents, each sized at 8 MB, and each assigned to one of the freelist groups, which are associated with INSTANCES 1, 2, and 3, respectively.

Summary

Data warehouse applications are better suited to Oracle Parallel Server than any other kind of database application. The risks are much lower due to the nature of data warehouses. Troublesome data manipulation is largely programmatic and performed in "batch," and if this can be partitioned to prevent interinstance contention, Parallel Server can be demonstrate impressive scalability during the load phase. But the real strength of Parallel Server data warehouses comes during queries. This is when the full power of Oracle's parallelized operations, described in Chapter 10, can fully exploit the hardware architecture.

DISTRIBUTING THE ORACLE DATA WAREHOUSE

CHAPTER 12

Data warehouses are without any doubt the largest relational databases being developed today. Data warehouses tend to push the limits of database storage capabilities and performance. Oracle8 has greatly increased the physical limits on the size of a database and has provided new capabilities for managing the larger databases. Physically storing and administering data warehouses with multiple terabytes of data is now feasible. At the same time developments in both hardware and Oracle Parallel Server have greatly increased the capability of data warehouses to handle hundreds or even thousands of simultaneously connected users.

With such capabilities available to the warehouse development team, one has to wonder why any organization would ever need to consider any architecture more complex than a single large database. There are several reasons for considering a distributed database architecture. Chief among these is cost. While modern (exotic) MPP hardware combined with Oracle Parallel Server makes it *possible* to develop and administer a multi-terabyte warehouse, the economics of this architecture may make it unfeasible.

It may be far less expensive to maintain the large central data warehouse using conventional SMP or newer NUMA computer technology. The storage cost of disk and controllers is not reduced in this configuration, but processor costs can be reduced by literally millions of dollars. What is given up by making this hardware change, of course, is the ability to support hundreds of simultaneous parallel queries. Many of the queries that need to be processed in the warehouse, however, are using relatively small summary tables for which parallel operation across dozens of CPUs is not required. It is possible, in some cases, to move some of the data and some of the users to separate servers and databases and thereby reduce total costs.

Another reason to consider a distributed database is to provide "local" access to a data mart that contains a subset of the data stored within the total warehouse. By keeping a copy of the data most likely to be needed by a particular department or workgroup on a server nearby, we can reduce the need for our entire user base to access the centralized warehouse, which reduces our need for massive computing resources. Because the department's data mart is physically close to its users we can reduce telecommunications cost and network delays for widely dispersed global corporations. Using data marts in this way will generally increase the total warehousing costs for an organization but will provide increased availability and performance in return.

Reasons to Consider a Distributed Data Warehouse

Cost provides one criterion by which distributed data warehouses are justified. Let's consider a hypothetical MPP hardware architecture that costs $10 million for sixteen interconnected SMP nodes and 1.2 terabytes of shared disk storage. We anticipate that we will need the processing capability of those sixteen nodes to handle the query load of several hundred users. To support the loading, indexing, summarizing, and other administrative tasks of our terabyte warehouse, we determine that we will need the processing power of four of those nodes. The cost of those four MPP nodes (and the same amount of disk) might be $3 million. We might be able to satisfy the query processing needs of our large user community by purchasing four large SMP machines at $1 million each. Figures 12.1 and 12.2 provide an idea of these two configurations and the potential savings.

The databases on each of these four query databases can be much smaller since they will not store the very large volumes of detail data. If each of these machines is assigned to a different group of users, we may well find that we can further limit the local storage on each to even a subset of the various summaries that we produce. Thus, with a distributed configuration we might provide the same or better level of query performance at a cost savings of $2 million dollars.

Further, the four machines serve as backups to each other so that, in case of one machine's failure, users can reach another of the servers to have their query processed. So, in addition to saving money, we may actually be able to increase net system availability.

For global corporations, another advantage to this distributed architecture is that the four secondary servers in our example may be placed in different parts of the world. This can improve query performance by keeping the database closer to a selected group of users. It can greatly decrease the total telecommunications costs of the warehouse since most queries can be performed "locally." This leaves periodic data load file transfers and occasional drill-down queries (which need to access detailed data) as the only warehouse demand on the global network connections. This advantage also extends to simplified administration. Since each machine is potentially supporting a group of users spanning only a few time zones instead of the entire world, it is easier to schedule loads and cold backups in times when the users aren't needing access. A database supporting only query users in the United States and Canada may be easily taken offline every Sunday evening; if the database supports worldwide users,

Figure 12.1 Potential hardware cost of an MPP data warehouse.

1.2 Terabytes of
Disk Storage

16 Node MPP
Cost: $10M

Figure 12.2 Potential hardware cost of a distributed data warehouse.

300 Gigabytes of
Disk Storage

300 Gigabytes of
Disk Storage

1.2 Terabytes of
Disk Storage

300 Gigabytes of
Disk Storage

300 Gigabytes of
Disk Storage

4 Node MPP
Cost: $3M

4 SMP Servers
Cost: @$1M = $4M

Total
Hardware
Cost $7M

there never is a "Sunday evening" window since for users in Europe it is now Monday morning and for those in Asia it is already Monday evening!

This alternative architecture with a smaller central complex augmented with four large SMP servers does, however, come at some additional operational costs. After the data has been loaded onto our central server and then summarized and indexed we have another generation of data loading to perform. We must create several extracts of the summarized (and perhaps some of the detailed) data and then transport, load, and index our four additional databases. This process is greatly simplified, however, because the hard work of organizing and integrating the data was performed during the load of the central server. Extracting data from an architected warehouse to build these smaller warehouses (often called "data marts") requires minimal additional analysis to decide which subset of the total warehouse should be copied closer to each user group.

Also, because of the redundant nature of this distributed architecture, we may well be able to forego making backups of the four secondary warehouse databases. Should one of these machines suffer a disk failure, we may find that reloading the data into the affected tablespaces from either the MPP central database or one of the other secondary servers is faster than performing database recovery.

If we decide that we should do backups on the distributed servers' databases we will find our task simplified by the fact that we are doing very simplified processing on each of these servers. We can take full advantage of read-only tablespaces so that much of our recovery only requires file restoral from backup.

Our backup and recovery of the distributed data marts is made simpler by another feature of this design. Most of our loads and index builds can be done with the UNRECOVERABLE (Oracle7) or NOLOGGING (Oracle8) options and therefore will generate minimal redo. Not having to perform large summarizations or other processing will minimize the redo generation on these satellite systems. This means we may avoid the usual complexities while still running the database in ARCHIVELOG mode—we are likely to have fewer archived log files to manage and may be able to retain them on disk until the next system backup.

NOARCHIVELOG Mode

Whenever you are operating an Oracle database in NOARCHIVELOG mode you can easily recover any read-only tablespaces in the event of media failure. The SYSTEM tablespace and the tablespace holding rollback segments cannot be made read-only. These tablespaces must be given additional protection from failure through some form of disk mirroring. When running NOARCHIVELOG, you cannot perform hot backups so warehouse downtime for cold backups after each load must be scheduled. When loads are performed weekly or monthly and the warehouse is not being accessed globally, this backup window is usually easy to schedule. If a disk failure does occur to a database operated in NOARCHIVELOG mode, the administrator must either restore the entire database from the last cold backup or re-create the database and reload all of its data.

Given these potential advantages of a distributed data warehouse, let's consider Oracle's distributed database features and then examine several alternative distributed architectures.

Distributed Database Terminology

Before examining the specific Oracle features that support distributed data warehousing, it is appropriate to introduce some terminology used to describe database operations in both local and distributed configurations.

We use the term *query* to describe a retrieval of data that does not attempt to modify any database data. In the Oracle SQL language, queries are performed using the SELECT command. A *transaction*, on the other hand, may involve multiple SQL statements and makes some modifications to data through some combination of data manipulation language (DML) verbs, namely INSERT, UPDATE, and DELETE. Each of these commands locks the specific rows being modified so that no other transaction is able to make additional changes until the first transaction completes. (There are other SQL statements that can lock data for the purpose of making changes—SELECT . . . FOR UPDATE and LOCK TABLE request locks without actually changing any data. This type of intention locking allows the transaction to ensure that the data it needs will be available and not locked by another transaction.)

A transaction is terminated by the SQL COMMIT statement. COMMIT (or COMMIT WORK to meet ANSI SQL standard syntax) makes all the modifications permanent and releases all the locks held by the transaction. Alternatively, the transaction can be ended with the ROLLBACK (or ROLLBACK WORK for ANSI compliance), which restores all the data modifications to the state they existed in before the start of the transaction. ROLLBACK reverses the effects of the transaction and releases all its locks. A new transaction is started by the first DML statement after the initial user connection to the database or the last COMMIT or ROLLBACK that ended a previous transaction.

A local query is a SELECT statement that is executed entirely within the database where the user is connected. In Oracle's two-task implementation this type of query follows the client-server model. The user process passes the query to an Oracle server process that will perform the work and then return results to the user process. The user process may reside on the same server as the database instance or it may submit the query over SQL*Net from another computer, typically a PC. Only a single database is required to satisfy the local query.

A local transaction is a transaction that locks and/or modifies data only within the single database to which the user is connected. Again, only a single database is required to complete the entire transaction. There are several query and transaction processing models, however, in which more than the single connected database is required. These include remote and distributed queries and transactions. A special case of prepackaging distributed transactions, known as replication, is also available.

Remote Query

The most basic distributed database operation is the remote query. A remote query requires data from only one database, but not the database to which the user is connected. The database to which the user is connected determines that the entire query can be shipped to a remote database for processing.

Figure 12.3 A remote query.

Figure 12.3 illustrates a query submitted by the client while connected to the database instance LOCL on Database Server number 1. However, LOCL recognizes that the query only requires data that is located in the database instance RMOT on Database Server number 2. LOCL reissues the query directly to RMOT using its own client-server connection. The query is executed entirely on RMOT, and then the final results are passed back to LOCL, which merely passes them along to the client user.

Distributed Query

A distributed query is a SELECT statement that requires data from more than one database. The data from one database must be combined (either through a join or a set operation such as UNION ALL) with data residing on another database. Figure 12.4 demonstrates a distributed query being submitted to LOCL. The query requires data from both LOCL and RMOT, so the LOCL instance examines the statistics about both tables (and their indexes) to determine the optimal plan for combining the data. In some cases, the amount of data from LOCL is much smaller than the amount of data needed from RMOT. In such a case, LOCL will reformulate the query and ship it, along with the LOCL data, to RMOT for processing. In other situations, RMOT data will be much smaller than LOCL data, and LOCL will generate a query to RMOT to bring back the needed data for processing in LOCL. Wherever the data is combined, it will be passed back through LOCL to the requesting user.

Figure 12.4 A distributed query.

Remote Transaction

A remote transaction involves locking or changing one or more rows in a single database other than the one to which the user is connected. As long as each subsequent DML statement continues to refer to the same remote database, the local instance continues to simply pass the DML statements along to that remote instance for processing. When the transaction-ending COMMIT is issued by the client, the local instance verifies that all INSERT, UPDATE, and DELETE and other locking statements were directed to the same instance. If so, the COMMIT statement is passed along to the remote database instance for normal single-phase completion.

An example of a remote transaction is provided in Figure 12.5. One row is updated in the RMOT database instance. The UPDATE statement is passed along to that database. When this single statement is committed, only the RMOT instance will have any changes to make permanent. No special two-phased commit protocol will be required.

Distributed Transaction

A distributed transaction involves data manipulation in more than one database that must be treated as a single unit of work. The changes in the two (or more) databases have to be coordinated and either made permanent (committed) or reversed (rolled back) identically at each site.

Ensuring that all the sites either commit or roll back together requires special processing at the end of the distributed transaction. This special processing is known as a two-phased commit. The local database instance where the client is connected will coordinate the two-phased commit processing. In the first phase all sites but the coordinator are put into a *prepared* state. From this state each site is guaranteed to be able to either roll back or commit the transaction. In Oracle terms this means that all the transaction's changes, including the prepare request, are written out to the online redo log. Once all sites have responded to the coordinator that they are prepared, then the second phase, *commit,* is initiated.

LOCKING DURING TWO-PHASED COMMIT

All but one site in the distributed transaction will require special locks to be taken on the blocks which have been modified in the transaction. These locks are called in-doubt transaction locks and are generally held only for a short period between the two phases of the commit process. These locks are, however, very expensive because they prevent any user from updating or even reading any data in the in-doubt blocks. This is necessary during the normally brief period of committing since the local Oracle instance cannot accurately rebuild a consistent view of the block until it receives the commit or rollback message in the second phase.

This can cause concurrency problems when distributed transactions need to modify data in the same blocks as other transactions or queries. Another concurrency problem is introduced when, in rare circumstances, a failure of the network, a server, or a database instance prevents completion of the second phase of the commit after a site has entered the prepared state. In such a situation the expensive, in-doubt transaction locks will be maintained until the failure is corrected and the commit processing can be completed.

To minimize the impact (and perhaps the probability) of such situations, Oracle7 and Oracle8 allow the administrator to set the initialization parameter COMMIT_POINT_STRENGTH in each instance. Whichever participating database instance has the highest value of COMMIT_POINT_STRENGTH, it will become the commit point site of the transaction and will not have to enter the prepared state. The commit point should be directed to the database in which in-doubt transactions would have the greatest impact. In many cases, this will be the busiest database; in others it might be the one supporting the most critical application. A database instance on an unreliable server, however, would not be a good choice because failures of the commit point site can leave in-doubt blocks of other databases unavailable.

Oracle also provides a means for the administrators of the distributed database to manually force the local portion of a distributed transaction to complete the commit (or rollback) when an outage causes a severe contention problem. Care must be taken, though, to ensure that any manually forced transaction is handled consistently with the action taken by the commit point site. Commiting part of a distributed transaction at one site and rolling back at another will cause an inconsistency (also known as corruption!) in the distributed database.

A simple distributed transaction, with one data change in LOCL and another single row modified in RMOT is illustrated in Figure 12.6. The LOCL instance that receives each request from the connected client determines which statements it can process and which must be passed along to another instance. As

Figure 12.5 A remote transaction.

Figure 12.6 A distributed transaction.

Figure 12.7 A replicated transaction.

soon as a DML statement is encountered that must be handled by a second in-stance, the transaction is marked as distributed and two-phased commit process-ing will be required when the transaction ends.

Replication

Replication is a facility for propagating changes made in one database to an-other. When a row is inserted, updated, or deleted in one database, a corre-sponding insert, update, or delete is automatically performed in the other. Replication may be either synchronous or asynchronous. Synchronous replica-tion occurs as part of the initial transaction—if the change can't be propagated immediately then the transaction fails. The advantage in performing synchro-nous replication is that both databases are kept perfectly synchronized. The drawback, however, is that a failure of either server or network component pre-vents the transaction from completing.

In asynchronous replication, changes are propagated after the initial transac-tion by a separate independent transaction. Asynchronous replication is more resilient to outages of either the network or the remote database and server. Per-formance of the original transaction is also less impacted by asynchronous repli-cation than by immediately performing the remote work with synchronous replication. Figure 12.7 shows a simple transaction inserting a single row into the database associated with instance LOCL. Replication has been defined on the particular LOCL table that received the insert. Oracle's replication facility will automatically copy the row as part of a separate transaction into the database opened by the RMOT instance. The second, asynchronous replication transaction (shown in the darkest shading) operates independently of the first under a schedule defined during the setup of replication. Should the network connection to RMOT be unavailable for some reason, the row will be replicated when the connection is restored.

Oracle Distributed Database Technology

The Oracle RDBMS has included distributed database features since version 5. The same basic "SQL*Star" architecture that provided distributed query capability ten years ago has been preserved with several major enhancements. Chief among these has been the introduction of distributed transactions in Oracle7. Building upon this capability, Oracle's replication facilities allow changes made in one database to be automatically propagated to a corresponding table within another database. Finally, constant improvements in the Oracle optimizer have greatly improved the performance characteristics of distributed queries. The Oracle8 cost-based optimizer is able to use statistics on both local and remote database objects to determine an efficient plan for moving data between the databases in order to complete a distributed query. Although such queries are never as quick as the equivalent query performed entirely within a single database, they are far more efficient than in earlier releases, which were not able to determine the relative volumes of data and available indexes in each database.

Beyond changes in the optimizer several Oracle features provide location transparency—the ability for the administrator to hide distributed complexities from the end user.

Database Links

A *database link* is Oracle's means of establishing a connection from one database to another. Just as user connections are made over SQL*Net to allow client application code to communicate with an Oracle database using SQL and PL/SQL, one database can become a client requesting services from another database. The connection between databases is defined through an underlying network protocol, such as TCP/IP, and a layer of SQL*Net, Oracle's communication software. SQL*Net does not replace the network communication protocol but rides on top of it.

To avoid having to specify physical connection information as part of SQL queries, Oracle provides a means for predefining connection data. This predefined connection is called a database link. The syntax to create a database link is as follows:

```
CREATE PUBLIC DATABASE LINK rmot
       CONNECT TO username IDENTIFIED BY password
       USING 'connect_string';
```

In this example "*rmot*" is the name given to the database link. This name will be used as part of each remote query or DML statement. This avoids having to specify the other details again in the query or transaction. To query data from the PROJECTS table in the database pointed to by this link, the user would add the database link name to the table name in his or her SELECT statement:

```
SELECT *
  FROM projects@rmot;
```

The keyword "PUBLIC" can be used by the DBA to define a link that can then be used by any user of the database. General users may be allowed to create their own private database links without the "PUBLIC" keyword.

The "CONNECT TO . . . IDENTIFIED BY . . . " clause allows a remote operation to be conducted through a connection to a specific schema and password within that remote database. The administrator might use this feature to direct all remote queries to a particular schema that has read-only access to all the warehouse tables in a database. If this clause is not included in the definition of the database link then connections will be made using the same username and password that were used to make the initial local connection. This is common practice when each user has been provided with an account in each database that they are allowed to access. This would allow the administrators of each database to control what data is visible to each individual user or group of users. It does, however, require the user to change his or her password in every database each time one is changed.

The final clause, "USING '*connect_string*'" is where the detailed database connection is defined. Usually the connect string is the name of a service already defined to SQL*Net (or Net8). This definition is made by an administrator, not a general user, as an entry in either a TNSNAMES.ORA file or within an Oracle Name Server.

When an Oracle Name Server has been configured, a third type of database link can be used—a *global* database link. This is the simplest type of link for the administrator to create and maintain since only a single, centralized definition needs to be made. There is no need for the administrator of each database (or any user) to issue a CREATE DATABASE LINK command. For a large distributed database environment this can be a great time-saver. However, using global database links still requires each database administrator to carefully control the privileges provided to users who can now reach any database in the network. Whether they should have access to the data in every database is not as straightforward as providing the connection path!

RESOLVING CONNECT STRINGS IN NET8

Net8 (the upgraded and renamed SQL*Net product shipped with Oracle8) also allows for resolving connection strings through host naming (such as Domain Name Services, or DNS) or through external naming (such as the NetWare Directory Service). These features are defined in the *Net8 Administrator's Guide*.

Synonyms

Synonyms provide another level of location transparency to the distributed Oracle environment. A synonym may be created to define an alternative name for some database object, either local or remote. The SQL SELECT statement used in the database link example earlier had to include the "@RMOT" designation appended to the PROJECTS table name. The user would be required to remember that the PROJECTS table was physically stored in the database pointed to by the RMOT link.

To avoid this burden on the user, the administrator might predefine a public synonym that would incorporate both the table name and the location definition:

```
CREATE PUBLIC SYNONYM projects
   FOR projects@rmot;
```

(Note that the synonym name does not have to be the same as the name of the object it refers to.) Now any user who needs to reference this remote PROJECTS table can simply use the synonym in the SQL statements:

```
SELECT *
  FROM projects;
```

Without the "PUBLIC" keyword, an individual user may create a private synonym that can be used to simplify his or her own personal accesses but will be unknown to other users.

Views

Views are created by the administrator (or by a user) for a variety of reasons. In some cases, the view will be used to predefine complex join or selection logic. In other situations the view might be used to provide a level of security or convenience by limiting the amount of data visible to user.

Views can also serve the same purpose as a synonym when the goal is to make a remote object appear to the user as if it were a local object:

```
CREATE VIEW projects
   AS SELECT *
 FROM PROJECTS@RMOT;
```

This view would provide the same function as the synonym definition in the previous example. However, the view processing requires some additional overhead not needed by the synonym. Therefore, the view approach would be used only if some requirement other than transparency were to be met. An example would be when an optimizer hint or WHERE clause restrictions were needed to control the access to the remote data. Another example would be where the local administrator wishes to impose a level of security on the access. An explicit grant of privileges is required before a user can access the view; no privileges are associated with public synonyms, so the only security would be enforced at the remote site where the object physically resides.

UNION ALL Views

UNION ALL views are a special case of using a view to simplify the accessing of multiple remote objects as if they were one. We may wish to allow our users to easily select from identically defined tables containing different data rows located in multiple databases. By defining a UNION ALL view that includes the data rows from each of these tables, the user query can appear to select from just a single local object:

```
CREATE VIEW all_projects AS
    SELECT *
      FROM projects
  UNION ALL
    SELECT *
      FROM projects@canada
  UNION ALL
    SELECT *
      FROM projects@europe
  UNION ALL
    SELECT *
      FROM projects@asia;
```

This view will present all PROJECTS data from these four databases to the user who enters a simple query such as the following:

```
SELECT project_name, start_date
  FROM projects;
```

Of course, there are performance considerations with retrieving data from multiple remote databases. As we'll discuss later in this chapter there are trade-offs in deciding to distribute the data.

Gateways

Oracle provides a series of gateway products that provide a different type of transparency. These gateways allow data maintained by another RDBMS or file management system to be made to appear like another Oracle database. The Oracle Open Gateway serves as a black box that translates the Oracle dialect of SQL into the appropriate dialect for the RDBMS.

Some of the Oracle Open Gateway products allow read-only queries while others allow for additional DML commands. Additionally, Oracle provides procedural gateway capabilities that allow a programmer to write procedures in the language of a non-Oracle application and then invoke those procedures via an Oracle PL/SQL procedure.

Figure 12.8 illustrates an Oracle Open Gateway that transparently allows Oracle queries to be directed to a DB2 database. The Gateway modifies the SQL as necessary to meet the requirements of the DB2 RDBMS. Although this example shows a remote query, the Gateway may also be incorporated into a distributed query or transaction.

Location transparency of the homogeneous RDBMS connection through a gateway is provided through the same synonym or view facilities as remote or distributed Oracle. Overview documentation of the Oracle8 Open Gateways is provided in the Oracle8 *Server Distributed Database Systems* manual, with more

Figure 12.8 An Oracle Open Gateway.

detailed documentation provided in separate manuals for each of the specific gateway products.

Oracle Replication Facilities

Basic replication facilities were first introduced in Oracle7, release 7.0, which allowed the creation of read-only snapshots. Additional capabilities for advanced (symmetric) replication were incorporated with release 7.1. Releases since then have incorporated many small enhancements to these facilities, especially related to increased performance and throughput in Oracle8.

Basic Replication

Basic replication consists of the ability to create read-only snapshots. A snapshot is an automatically maintained copy of remote data. In the simplest form, the snapshot is a complete copy of a remote table. Whenever a row in the base table is added, modified, or deleted, Oracle performs a corresponding INSERT, UPDATE, or DELETE statement in the snapshot. These secondary changes are not made as part of the original transaction but are propagated as part of an asynchronous refresh process controlled by Oracle. The snapshot definition includes a declaration of how and when the refresh should take place.

Oracle can refresh a snapshot (or a group of snapshots) automatically under a regular schedule such as every fifteen minutes or at 1:00 A.M. each day. The snapshot owner or DBA may also choose to manually refresh a snapshot group.

The refresh can be a COMPLETE refresh in which the copy is truncated and then all rows are retrieved to repopulate the snapshot. Any snapshot can be refreshed in this manner.

An alternative for doing FAST refreshes, in which only changed rows need to be copied, is available only for so-called simple snapshots. A simple snapshot is one whose defining query is based on a single table without joins, set operations, or GROUP BY functions such as SUM() or COUNT(). It may include some or all of the columns in the base table and may include all the rows or restrict the copy to a subset of the base table rows. Snapshots that do include joins of data from multiple tables or are defined using summary functions are considered complex snapshots and cannot be FAST refreshed.

The query that defines the simple snapshot could not, prior to Oracle8, include a sub-query. This new feature greatly extends the capability of Oracle8 replication to precisely define the appropriate rows to be included in a simple snapshot. Consider, for instance, a snapshot site which is designed to keep only information about West area consultants and their timecards. No column in the CONSULTANT table or the ACTIVITY table provides the area. This information is maintained in the ORGANIZATIONS table, based upon the consultant's ORG_ID. In Oracle7 it would be necessary to either denormalize both the CONSULTANT and ACTIVITY tables at the master site, to include this additional data or to use a complex snapshot based on a view which joins these tables to ORGANIZATIONS.

In Oracle8, it is possible to code the query using a sub-query to help filter the necessary rows using filters defined in a parent table. In the following example, three snapshot logs are created on the tables in the master database. Two snapshots with sub-queries are then defined in a remote west area data mart.

```
CREATE SNAPSHOT LOG ON organizations WITH PRIMARY KEY (area);
CREATE SNAPSHOT LOG ON consultants WITH PRIMARY KEY;
CREATE SNAPSHOT LOG ON activity WITH PRIMARY KEY;

CREATE SNAPSHOT west_area_consultants
      REFRESH FAST WITH PRIMARY KEY
      AS
      SELECT * FROM consultants@dw_master c
       WHERE EXISTS
             (SELECT o.org_id
                FROM organizations@dw_master o
               WHERE c.org_id = o.org_id
                 AND o.area = 'West');

CREATE SNAPSHOT west_area_activity
      REFRESH FAST WITH PRIMARY KEY
      AS
      SELECT * FROM activity@dw_master a
       WHERE EXISTS
             (SELECT c.employee_id
                FROM consultants@dw_master c
```

```
WHERE EXISTS
      (SELECT o.org_id
         FROM organizations@dw_master o
        WHERE c.org_id = o.org_id
          AND o.area = 'West')
    AND a.employee_id = c.employee_id);
```

There are many restrictions on the use of sub-queries in defining simple snapshots. These are documented in the Oracle8 Server Replication manual.

Basic snapshots allow for only query access at the remote site. All changes to the data must be made at the base site upon which the snapshots are defined. This limitation is not generally a problem with data warehouse replication but sometimes is inappropriate for certain OLTP requirements. Allowing for data modifications in multiple distributed databases requires more advanced replication facilities.

Advanced Replication

Oracle7, release 7.1, provided new replication facilities that have been carried forward into each subsequent release. *Advanced Replication,* or symmetric replication as it was originally titled, allows for updatable simple snapshots so that DML activity at any of the snapshot sites can be replicated back to the master database site. Multiple master sites can also be defined in which each site serves an equal partner in owning the replicated objects.

Oracle Advanced Replication further allows the combination of these facilities so that snapshots, both read-only and updatable, can be defined based on any of the masters in a multimaster configuration. Since data changes can occur to the same data at multiple sites, Advanced Replication introduces the possibility of conflicts. A conflict might occur when two users, at different sites, each make a change to copies of the same data row. One might delete the row while the other updates a column. Advanced Replication provides conflict detection features to identify such a conflict. The person implementing replication then has to define an appropriate conflict resolution strategy.

ORACLE8 SNAPSHOT REPLICATION BY PRIMARY KEY

Snapshot replication in Oracle7 is maintained based on the ROWID of each row in the master site. This capability is maintained in Oracle8, but an improved method based on the primary key values of the table data has been added. Primary key snapshots require the master table to have a primary key constraint. To facilitate migration, an Oracle8 master can support both primary key and ROWID snapshots. Unless data needs to be replicated between an Oracle7 and an Oracle8 database, it is recommended that the newer primary key method be used in pure Oracle8 replication environments.

Such configurations with multiple masters and many snapshots can become very complex to administer. The Oracle8 Replication Manager is used to help the administrator control the distributed environment and maintain the replication catalogs maintained at each participating site.

One final capability of replication that may have merit within a distributed data warehouse environment is to automatically maintain two identical copies of the warehouse for performance and throughput by supporting twice as many users. Using replication in this way has another advantage in that it also provides a backup site for continued availability in case of a server crash or other outage that would prevent access to a single warehouse database. This should not be considered a complete disaster recovery solution, but it can increase warehouse availability. It is probably not possible to replicate all detail data in this manner, but keeping copies of all summary tables may be feasible.

STANDBY DATABASE

Using replication to maintain a backup site contrasts to the Oracle standby database feature (introduced in release 7.3) that maintains a complete remote copy of a database by constantly applying redo log files from the primary database to the backup database, which is kept in recovery mode. The replicated site can be accessed and queried by users whereas the standby database (in recovery mode) cannot be opened unless the primary database is lost.

Because of the nature of data warehouse processing, there are limited opportunities or requirements to utilize Advanced Replication to propagate changes within the warehouse environment. Since most activity is read-only, basic replication of some tables between databases is generally sufficient.

The other problem with both basic and advanced replication features in the data warehouse environment is based on data volume limitations. The commonly accepted rule of thumb for Oracle7 replication has been to expect propagation of no more than 20 or so rows per second in any single replication group. Major rewriting of replication code in Oracle8 provides for significantly higher throughput, but extremely high propagation rates of many hundreds of rows per second should not be depended upon without adequate testing.

Another facility, however, exists within the Oracle Advanced Replication facility, which is designed to handle certain large volume operations within the distributed warehouse. Procedural replication allows for a remote procedure call (RPC) to a PL/SQL stored procedure on a different database. If your warehouse has a monthly purge procedure that is expected to delete a very large number of rows, row-based replication would require a very large number of individual rows to be deleted in each data mart. Network performance of this operation would likely be unsatisfactory. By disabling the normal replication of row deletes and then defining a packaged procedure to issue the same delete statement at each site, the warehouse can propagate a single call to each data mart. Procedural replication will ensure that the procedure is completed at each site. Consider using procedural replication whenever a single large set operation can be defined which will perform the needed maintenance at each site based on a general WHERE clause condition rather than individual primary key (or rowid) values. Note, however, that Advanced Replication's normal row-level conflict detection is disabled for these RPCs so care must be taken to ensure correct handling of any possible conflicts.

One final replication feature which is new to Oracle8 is the ability to propagate changes from one database to another in parallel. Parallel propagation uses the same query slaves mechanism as Oracle Parallel Query (as described in Chapter 10). Unfortunately, this feature is incorporated into the Advanced Replication facility and does not support refreshes of individual simple snapshots.

"Roll Your Own" Replication with Triggers

Before symmetric (or advanced) replication was introduced in release 7.1 we had occasional application requirements to keep two updatable copies of data in different databases. Database triggers can be used to perform synchronous replication as part of the transaction that changes data. The row-level trigger is written to immediately propagate the equivalent row modification to the remote database. Synchronous replication has the disadvantages of decreased availability and performance. Availability is reduced since a failure of either server, either database, or their network connection prevents the transaction from completing. Performance is diminished because of the additional work required to perform distributed transactions and the requisite two-phased commit.

Database triggers can also be used to develop your own primary key–style asynchronous replication. The database trigger is written to insert a row into a separately defined "to do list" table every time a row is inserted, updated, or deleted in the base table. This "to do list" tracks the primary key and type of action performed. A user-written process is scheduled to periodically read from the "to do list," perform the required action in the remote database, and then delete the row from the "to do list." The entire transaction is then committed using the two-phased commit protocol. This approach is very similar to the Oracle8 design. The only reasons to consider building your own asynchronous replication facility in this manner would be to implement primary key replication in Oracle7. Since this is all custom code that has to be developed, tested, and maintained, there would have to be an extremely strong reason for going this route!

These distributed database features of Oracle7 and Oracle8 can be used in a variety of ways within an Oracle data warehouse environment. The remainder of this chapter will look at these distributed warehouse design alternatives.

Alternative Distributed Architectures

Both Oracle7 and Oracle8 provide multiple alternatives for developing a data warehouse in configurations other than a single database. Some of these alternatives are, however, more reasonable than others. We discuss each of them in the following sections.

Data Marts

It is a tempting euphemism for warehouse developers (and warehouse product vendors) to justify laziness or sloppiness by invoking the mantra of "distributed"

Figure 12.9 Improper data mart design.

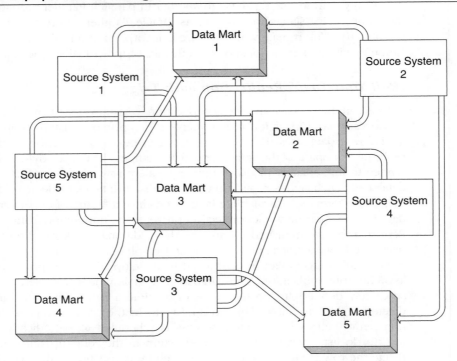

and "data mart." The term *data mart* is, unfortunately, misused in many cases where what is actually being created is a series of disjointed data warehouses. Figure 12.9 portrays this dangerous situation.

Each of what might (incorrectly) be called data marts in Figure 12.9 is really an independent data warehouse. As such, there is no coordination in the identification of source systems or in the extract, reformatting, and summarization processing. Each of the warehouses has some data that overlaps the data in the others, but none of them is consistent with the others. Developing independent data warehouses in this uncoordinated manner should be avoided. The end result will frustrate users who obtain conflicting answers and will undermine any possible success of the data warehousing effort.

A data mart is not just a small, independent data warehouse—avoid the temptation to build small data warehouses without an overall integrated design! Remember the analogy of a warehouse that distributes products to various retail outlets. This is the model to follow in creating your data mart strategy.

A proper data mart design, as illustrated in Figure 12.10, shows data from various sources being integrated into a centralized warehouse. The integrated data then flows from the data warehouse to the various data marts. This approach provides the true benefits of local data marts without forfeiting control. The proper data mart approach takes as much work as building the single centralized data warehouse (even a bit more). Any attempt to circumvent that neces-

Figure 12.10 Proper data mart design.

sary work by throwing together a handful of quick and dirty mini-warehouses will inevitably lead to the chaos of Figure 12.9.

The data marts shown in Figure 12.10 can be maintained using the Oracle RDBMS or alternatively by using an Express Server. Using the Oracle Express Server as the manager of a data mart is covered in the next chapter.

Distributed Data Warehouse

A single data warehouse need not be housed entirely within a single Oracle database. A single logical database design may be physically distributed. This physical distribution of a single logical model requires careful analysis in order to avoid a chaotic mess like that shown in Figure 12.9. It is not acceptable to simply create separate data warehouses for different departments as a means of avoiding the tough analysis and design necessary to create the unified data model. The data warehouse can, theoretically, be distributed in three ways: we can separate objects from subject areas or we can partition specific objects either horizontally or vertically. Only the first two of these three options are likely to be used in data warehousing with current technology.

Distributing Warehouse Subject Areas

When there is a clear line of demarcation between certain subject areas and we can be sure that very few (or no) queries will want to access tables from more

Figure 12.11 A data warehouse distributed by subject area.

Data Warehouse Logical Design
Data Model

FINANCIAL RESULTS Subject Area

EMPLOYEES
Subject Area

Data
Warehouse
Physical
Distribution
Model

than one subject area, then the two subject area's tables can be placed in separate databases. Figure 12.11 illustrates the separation of two subject areas in the data model that have no anticipated intersection.

Extreme care must be exercised to ensure that data that is likely to be needed together is stored in the same physical database. Although Oracle is able to distribute a query to more than one database, there is a performance penalty incurred whenever joins (or subqueries) are forced to operate over the network. This performance penalty has been greatly reduced with the improvements in the Oracle cost-based optimizer introduced in each successive release of Oracle7 and Oracle8.

Distributing the warehouse as a first deployment strategy leads to a risk of slipping into the easy (read: "lazy") approach of "wishing" that two areas be completely separable when more careful analysis or experience would indicate they are not. While the warehouse is small there are probably no hardware limitations that force the issue of distribution. This type of distribution may be a better direction after the organization has gone through several iterations of data warehouse rollout. Consider migrating to this approach as the warehouse grows and requires either a major hardware upgrade or a second server. Delaying the distribution action while doing the initial analysis and logical design will help enforce the necessary discipline for a successful design.

This approach of distributing the data warehouse later in its life is facilitated by the recommendation made in Chapter 4 to place each subject area into its own schema during physical design. If you have initially separated the subject areas in this way, you will have an easier time physically separating them to multiple databases later.

By using roles to control user access to the various subject areas (as recommended in Chapter 8) it will be easy to verify whether users accessing one subject area are or are not also accessing the other. In the example of Figure 12.11 we expect that financial analysts should have roles that permit them to query various subject areas of a financial nature. The analysts in the human relations group are probably only working with roles that allow them to see data relating to the EMPLOYEES subject area. If we discover a group of users who have requested both roles, then they need to be questioned to determine how they see the data—are they using the tables of the different subject areas completely separately or have they found some unexpected connection in the data?

Horizontal Partitioning of Data Warehouse Objects

Partitioning refers to the dividing of a single object into multiple objects. Horizontally partitioned tables have the same logical design of columns, but rows are placed into one of the partitions based on some specific criteria. The new partitioned tables (and indexes) in Oracle8 are horizontally partitioned. Each partition has an identical table layout but contains a different subset of the total table's rows. Oracle8 allows the different partitions of a partitioned object to be placed in different tablespaces of a database. In some future release of Oracle there may be an enhancement of the distributed capabilities to include distributed support for partitions, but in the current release the partitions must remain in the same physical database.

True horizontal partitioning, such as the partitioning of Oracle8, ensures that the rows entered into a partitioned table are unique and no duplicates can "sneak" into different partitions. (In the case of vertical partitions, the DBMS would ensure that a matching row piece would occur in every partition. A single INSERT or DELETE statement would operate on all vertical partitions at the same time.) Of course, in the data warehouse we frequently relax the normal OLTP constraint requirements, and we may also choose to distribute parts of a logical table without insisting that the database enforce all the strict rules of a distributed database.

If the warehouse designer has a valid reason to do so he or she may manually "partition" by creating separate tables (with the same column layout) in separate databases. Oracle7 and Oracle8 will treat these as completely separate objects, and any rules for which rows are placed into which table will be entirely the responsibility of the programmers building the extract and load processes. Duplicated rows in different partitions will not be automatically prevented by an Oracle primary key constraint. An example of partitioning by division in our case study warehouse is illustrated in Figure 12.12. In this case there is a "clone" of each table in each database. Some dimension tables, such as FISCAL_PERIOD and FUNCTION_CODE are likely to contain the same data in each database. Others, such as ORGANIZATION, PROJECT, and CONSULTANT, along with the ACTIVITY facts table, can be expected to only contain the rows that pertain to the specific division being stored.

Figure 12.12 A horizontally partitioned data warehouse table.

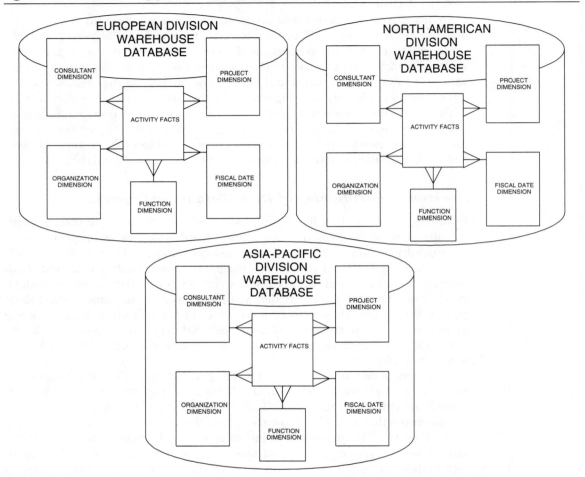

A decision to separate our European Division warehouse data from our Asia-Pacific Division and North American Division data is not one to be entered into lightly. The ability of each division to work with its own data may be enhanced by having the data physically closer to its divisional headquarters and by having a smaller collection of data to process. For a company with totally autonomous operations this might be an overwhelming advantage. However, by taking this approach we have surrendered an easy way to do comparisons of operations across the divisions. This might be an important type of query for an operations analyst in worldwide headquarters to perform.

Oracle can allow a single query to access the data in the three physical databases, but there will be a severe performance penalty if large amounts of data from one database need to be retrieved to another database to complete the query. A SELECT . . . GROUP BY, for instance, on any dimension other than organization will have to retrieve data from two remote databases and then sort it in the database instance where the user is connected.

Vertical Partitioning of Data Warehouse Objects

Less common than separating entire subject areas or horizontal partitioning of logical tables is the possibility of partitioning a table vertically. Vertical partitioning refers to the division of a logical table based on one subset of columns being stored in one physical table and other columns being stored in a separate table.

ORACLE SUPPORT FOR DISTRIBUTED PARTITIONING

Vertical partitioning is not directly supported by Oracle7 or Oracle8 although a foreign key constraint and two identically defined primary keys can provide most of the required support for vertical partitioning within a single database. Database triggers are needed to automatically support any partitioning across distributed databases. The performance impacts of this approach make it infeasible for most warehouse tables.

VERTICAL PARTITIONING IN OLTP SYSTEMS

Vertical partitioning is sometimes used to improve the performance and storage efficiency within an OLTP application when a large amount of data potentially needs to be stored for a particular entity but only a small portion of the total attributes are commonly needed for online update.

Figure 12.13 shows a table that has been partitioned vertically in order to separate a LONG column from the rest of the table's data. By separating the infrequently used LONG data from the other columns that are used regularly, the designer provides for more rows of data to be stored in each block of the primary table and thus reduce the possibility of chaining rows across multiple blocks. The LONG data is stored in a table that has different storage parameters defined and in which possible chaining may be isolated and better controlled.

While each consultant's resume might well be "normalized" into the same logical table as the rest of the data about consultants, it isn't required in the operational time card system. The resume data is used infrequently to aid in staffing projects but is not used by the various online TEAM system's screens or by the billing system. The designer chose to vertically partition the CONSULTANTS table so the resume data wouldn't slow down OLTP access to the other data.

The designer might have chosen to further separate the resume data by storing it in a completely separate database. If the two tables are not stored in the same database then it would be impossible to define the foreign key constraint as shown in Figure 12.13. Maintaining this referential integrity rule across multiple databases would require creating database triggers. Most OLTP systems designers would attempt to avoid enforcing referential integrity across multiple databases for both performance and availability issues.

Figure 12.13 A vertically partitioned OLTP table.

VERTICAL PARTITIONING IN THE DATA WAREHOUSE

Vertical partitioning data in the data warehouse environment is even less common than in OLTP systems. The primary objective in the warehouse is not to perform online access and updates. Making data accessible in a useful and convenient format is more critical. Because vertical partitioning is not widely used in data warehousing, we will have to stretch a somewhat artificial example to demonstrate the concept. We will close this section with an example of partitioning across data marts that has more practical value.

Warehouse design sometimes leads to a denormalized structure in which a time series of data is stored within a single row. An example might be a summarization of consultants' monthly utilization that includes a separate column for each month. Certain types of analysis may be enhanced by storing the data in this manner. Figure 12.14 illustrates such a denormalization, which includes

Figure 12.14 A denormalized warehouse table.

three years' utilization data for each consultant. In this example, we would create a monthly summarization job that would update each row to populate the utilization column for the most recent month and calculate the appropriate quarterly and annual utilization columns.

The simple denormalization adopted in Figure 12.14 leads us to make another design decision, however. Once we decide to store multiple months' values in the utilization table, we have to determine how many months of data should be included. If we are expected to retain summarization data for 5 years we would require 60 monthly columns, 20 quarterly columns, and 5 annual columns. Ten years would therefore require a total of 165 columns.

Figure 12.15 Vertically partitioning the denormalized warehouse table.

Partitioned Denormalized Table #1	Partitioned Denormalized Table #2	Partitioned Denormalized Table #3

CREATE TABLE CONS_UTILIZATION_95_SUM
  (EMPLOYEE_ID   NUMBER(10),
   EMPLOYEE_NAME   VARCHAR2(40),
   JAN_UTIL_PCT   NUMBER(4,3),
   FEB_UTIL_PCT   NUMBER(4,3),
   MAR_UTIL_PCT   NUMBER(4,3),
   Q1_UTIL_PCT   NUMBER(4,3),
   APR_UTIL_PCT   NUMBER(4,3),
   MAY_UTIL_PCT   NUMBER(4,3),
   JUN_UTIL_PCT   NUMBER(4,3),
   Q2_UTIL_PCT   NUMBER(4,3),
   JUL_UTIL_PCT   NUMBER(4,3),
   AUG_UTIL_PCT   NUMBER(4,3),
   SEP_UTIL_PCT   NUMBER(4,3),
   Q3_UTIL_PCT   NUMBER(4,3),
   OCT_UTIL_PCT   NUMBER(4,3),
   NOV_UTIL_PCT   NUMBER(4,3),
   DEC_UTIL_PCT   NUMBER(4,3),
   Q4_UTIL_PCT   NUMBER(4,3),
   FY_UTIL_PCT   NUMBER(4,3))
TABLESPACE SUMMARY_DATA;
	CREATE TABLE CONS_UTILIZATION_96_SUM
	  (EMPLOYEE_ID NUMBER(10),
	   EMPLOYEE_NAME VARCHAR2(40),
	   JAN_UTIL_PCT NUMBER(4,3),
	   FEB_UTIL_PCT NUMBER(4,3),
	   MAR_UTIL_PCT NUMBER(4,3),
	   Q1_UTIL_PCT NUMBER(4,3),
	   APR_UTIL_PCT NUMBER(4,3),
	   MAY_UTIL_PCT NUMBER(4,3),
	   JUN_UTIL_PCT NUMBER(4,3),
	   Q2_UTIL_PCT NUMBER(4,3),
	   JUL_UTIL_PCT NUMBER(4,3),
	   AUG_UTIL_PCT NUMBER(4,3),
	   SEP_UTIL_PCT NUMBER(4,3),
	   Q3_UTIL_PCT NUMBER(4,3),
	   OCT_UTIL_PCT NUMBER(4,3),
	   NOV_UTIL_PCT NUMBER(4,3),
	   DEC_UTIL_PCT NUMBER(4,3),
	   Q4_UTIL_PCT NUMBER(4,3),
	   FY_UTIL_PCT NUMBER(4,3))
	TABLESPACE SUMMARY_DATA;
		CREATE TABLE CONS_UTILIZATION_97_SUM
		  (EMPLOYEE_ID NUMBER(10),
		   EMPLOYEE_NAME VARCHAR2(40),
		   JAN_UTIL_PCT NUMBER(4,3),
		   FEB_UTIL_PCT NUMBER(4,3),
		   MAR_UTIL_PCT NUMBER(4,3),
		   Q1_UTIL_PCT NUMBER(4,3),
		   APR_UTIL_PCT NUMBER(4,3),
		   MAY_UTIL_PCT NUMBER(4,3),
		   JUN_UTIL_PCT NUMBER(4,3),
		   Q2_UTIL_PCT NUMBER(4,3),
		   JUL_UTIL_PCT NUMBER(4,3),
		   AUG_UTIL_PCT NUMBER(4,3),
		   SEP_UTIL_PCT NUMBER(4,3),
		   Q3_UTIL_PCT NUMBER(4,3),
		   OCT_UTIL_PCT NUMBER(4,3),
		   NOV_UTIL_PCT NUMBER(4,3),
		   DEC_UTIL_PCT NUMBER(4,3),
		   Q4_UTIL_PCT NUMBER(4,3),
		   FY_UTIL_PCT NUMBER(4,3))
		TABLESPACE SUMMARY_DATA;

We have to consider how, with this design, we'll handle the rolling window of the data to be kept. We can't easily drop the initial 17 columns (12 months, 4 quarters, 1 annual). Reusing the same columns within the long list of columns for the new year could easily lead to confusion. A further complication arises when we consider that we have consultants joining and leaving our practice each month. Storing 60 months' history for a consultant who started last month (or who left 3 years ago) is a bit wasteful.

Figure 12.15 takes the denormalized table of Figure 12.14 and partitions the data into separate tables to hold the monthly data from each year. (Note that because of the chosen denormalization to store time-series data, this vertical partitioning scheme actually looks a lot like horizontal partitioning based on year.) With this approach, retention or deletion of particular years' data is simplified, and we waste at most 11 months' storage for a consultant who doesn't remain with us for a full 5 years.

If these partitioned tables were used in different ways or by different users, they could be moved to different warehouse databases. An entire database could be created to house data older than 1996. Assuming that this old data was not needed often, we might choose to house this data on a low-powered server, saving our high-powered server resources for more critical queries on more current data.

This example illustrates the concept of vertical partitioning without demonstrating much practical benefit. As a slightly more practical example, consider a warehouse table that maintains data about customers. Some of the columns store data about our customers' sales history. Perhaps other columns are used to contain information about the history of warranty claims and technical support calls made by each customer account.

Figure 12.16 Vertical partitioning in extracting for data marts.

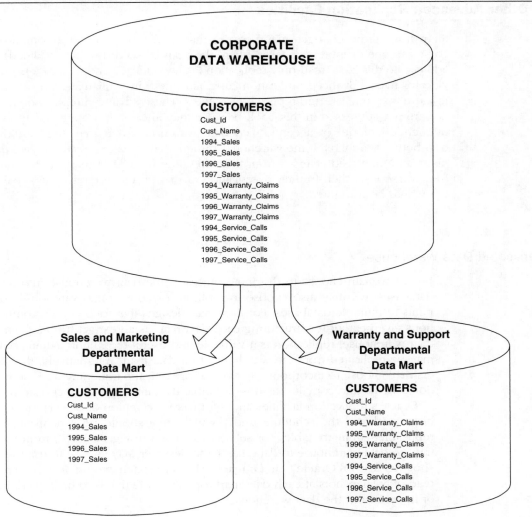

If we have decided to create multiple departmental data marts with subsets of the warehouse data, we may find it helpful to vertically subset the table when extracting it to the data marts. Figure 12.16 shows this situation. The data mart in the sales department may include a different subset of data than the data mart created for our warranty and support department. Each user community has quick, local access to the customer information that is of primary interest to them. Because the data marts are all fed from an integrated warehouse the risk of inconsistent data is greatly reduced. Note that this flavor of vertical partitioning as part of an extract can be implemented using Oracle replication. A different snapshot query would be used to perform each extract.

Other Advanced Replication Facilities

Snapshots allow changes made to the master database to be automatically copied to one or more databases where they can be seen (but not modified). In addition to this basic read-only replication facility, Oracle7 and Oracle8 also provide for more advanced replication capabilities in which changes can be made in more than one site and replicated to others. These advanced replication facilities are not addressed in this book because they are not appropriate in the recommended model of a centralized data warehouse that may feed multiple distributed data marts. If the warehouse designer chooses to directly update data marts and then feed changes from them to either other data marts or a centralized warehouse, then further investigation of the advanced replication capabilities would be warranted.

Replicated Data Warehouse

Just as we can choose to distribute pieces of the data warehouse into multiple databases, we may also choose to replicate or copy some warehouse components to multiple databases. For data mart designs that follow the recommendations given earlier for structuring each data mart as an extract from a centralized data warehouse, replication is a valuable and useful tool. Entire summary tables may be replicated from the warehouse to a data mart. Alternatively, the designers may choose to incorporate horizontal or vertical partitioning into the replication scheme and copy just a subset of table data into each distinct data mart.

Oracle's replication facilities allow for easy declaration of objects that need to be copied and the schedule under which they should be synchronized. For replicating summary tables (or subsets as shown in Figure 12.17) from the centralized warehouse to data marts, the designer may choose to use the snapshot feature of Oracle7 or Oracle8. This approach would involve creating read-only snapshots at each data mart for each table that is to be copied, in total or in part, from the data warehouse.

REFERENCE

The snapshot facility is part of Oracle8's replication features and is documented in the Oracle8 *Server Replication* manual. (For Oracle7, release 7.3, this information is provided in volume 2 of the Oracle7 *Server Distributed Systems* manual.) The Replication Manager tool is provided to aid the administrator in managing the replication environment. Unfortunately this tool is not described in these manuals. Review the text files which are supplied with Replication Manager for documentation.

The snapshot creation process involves defining a query that will be used to refresh the snapshot. The refresh may be performed automatically by the replication facility based on a time schedule defined at the time the snapshot is cre-

Figure 12.17 Replicating data warehouse objects.

ated. Alternatively, the refresh process may be executed manually by the administrator. In the data mart and data warehouse environment there may be good reasons to choose to ignore the automatic refresh capability. The administrator will want to ensure that the data mart snapshots are not performed until after the warehouse summary tables have been completely updated or rebuilt and then validated. Since the automatic refresh capability is based on a time sched-

Snapshot Groups

It is possible to maintain and refresh snapshots as individual objects. It is recommended, however, that they be included in snapshot groups and refreshed as a group. For the data mart this is particularly important in order to ensure that all related data in various summary tables get updated simultaneously. If individual snapshots are individually refreshed, it is possible for one query to get a different answer than a second query issued against a different level of summarization. Refreshing snapshot groups with a large number of tables containing large volumes of changed rows will require the entire snapshot refresh process to be handled as a single large transaction. The administrator should be prepared for this and assign an appropriately large rollback segment to this transaction.

ule and our regular warehouse loads and summarization processes may have varying execution times (or may occasionally not even complete), we will want to prevent the data mart refresh from starting before the warehouse processing is done. We would also like to avoid scheduling our data mart refresh based on a "worst case" schedule—we probably don't want to regularly waste hours or even days updating our data marts only to allow for occasional processing delays in the warehouse.

A better alternative to using Oracle replication's normal automatic time-based refresh of data mart snapshots may be to trigger the refreshes based on completion of the final step in the warehouse processing. A manual refresh is invoked by calling the DBMS_REFRESH.REFRESH procedure. This causes all the snapshots in a refresh group to be refreshed together, maintaining consistency across the various snapshots. Where possible, all snapshots related to a particular subject area should be included in a single refresh group.

Snapshot refreshes are based on a pull model—the snapshot site must initiate the query against the master, so this command has to be issued from the data mart where the snapshot is created. Remember, normal Oracle snapshot replication will initiate this pull based on the passage of time. To trigger it based on an event in the warehouse we have two choices. We can have the data mart poll the warehouse—issue regular queries against the warehouse metadata store to determine whether a particular job has ended. These queries might be issued every fifteen minutes starting at the time we expect to be ready and continuing until we find the successful completion record in our job status metadata table. This approach requires somewhat sophisticated scripting, either with shell script and cron (assuming the data mart is running on a UNIX platform) or with PL/SQL and the DBMS_JOB utilities inside the Oracle database.

There's a disadvantage, however, to placing all of these scripts at each remote data mart server. In general, we want to maintain as simple an environment as possible at each data mart. We'd like to perform the majority of our administration from the centralized warehouse. This is partly because of an assumption that the data marts may be located in sites without a regular Oracle administra-

DBMS_JOB

DBMS_JOB is one of several utilities built into the Oracle database kernel. It provides a job scheduler function similar to the UNIX cron utility. Oracle snapshots use this facility to automatically invoke refresh jobs at scheduled times. When snapshots were initially introduced in Oracle7, the job queue was created to manage the refresh processes but not documented for other customer use. Because of its usefulness in various situations other than just refreshing snapshots, the facility was documented and made available for customer use in Oracle7, version 7.2. This utility is documented in Chapter 7 of the *Server Administrator's Guide* for both Oracle8 and Oracle7, version 7.3.

tor. The simpler each site's programming and administration can be made, the more likely it is that the mart will remain functional and available. Another motivation for centralizing our control of the data mart refresh cycles is to provide a simple capability for adding additional data marts. If our administrator can monitor, administer, and tune all refreshes from one site, then the additional burden of adding an additional site is minimal. If, on the other hand, he or she needs to specifically connect to each remote data mart database to verify its status and possibly perform some administration tasks then each new site will add significant additional workload for each routine task.

In keeping with this desire for distributed data with centralized control we have a second way to approach triggering the remote "pulls" of data from the warehouse. Oracle's distributed capabilities provide for execution of remote procedure calls. These RPCs are developed in PL/SQL and allow for execution of a stored procedure on a remote database. In this case, when the centralized warehouse completes the load, summarization, and validation cycle, a remote procedure call is issued to each satellite data mart to invoke the refresh. The centralized job would call the DBMS_REFRESH.REFRESH procedure on each remote database. In this model all of the scheduling and triggering scripts can be maintained on the centralized warehouse server. (If a customized replication facility were used instead of the standard snapshot facility, then the centralized job would call DBMS_JOB.SUBMIT to request execution of a custom procedure.)

Unfortunately, neither of these two approaches is as simple as using the default snapshot timing mechanism. If, as expected, the central warehouse has occasional processing delays which delay the time when data is ready to be replicated, then it is important to assume manual control of the replication timing.

Summary

There are several potential motivations for creating a distributed database architecture for an organization's data warehouse. Among these are decreased cost, increased availability, and increased performance. Oracle provides several distributed database facilities that allow the warehouse designer to implement a distributed warehouse solution. Among these are database links, synonyms, and views that enable remote and distributed queries. Oracle gateway products allow non-Oracle data to be queried and in some cases updated as if it were managed by Oracle. Oracle's snapshot facility allows for automatic copying of selected data from one database to another. This greatly simplifies the development of data marts as satellites of the central warehouse.

These Oracle features allow the designer to adopt any of several styles of distributed warehouse architecture. One of these options is the data mart, in which a subset of the centralized warehouse is copied to a smaller, local database for user access. Another option is a truly distributed data warehouse in which certain subject areas are physically housed in one database while others are maintained in a separate database. Variations allow for the partitioning of certain objects or for replication of objects (or even subsets of the data in those objects) to be replicated to more than one database in the distributed warehouse.

OLAP PROCESSING IN THE ORACLE DATA WAREHOUSE

What is OLAP and why is it so different from relational technology? This chapter will shed some light on these questions and give some idea how to go about implementing an OLAP system. Online Analytical Processing (OLAP) utilizes software that adds value to the huge volume of data most organizations collect through their transaction processing. Most of this data remains unused in large data stores until it is purged or archived and forgotten.

What Is OLAP?

The term *OLAP* was coined by Dr. E. F. Codd to describe a technology that could bridge the gap between personal computing and enterprise data management. The relational model falls short of providing the analytical capabilities required by management, analysts, and executives. Dr. Codd recognized the need for an additional multidimensional model that would allow faster and more capable analysis of the growing relational databases. A multidimensional model would allow the data to be represented in ways that more closely fit the way managers and analysts understand their businesses. Marketing and salespeople tend to think of their sales in terms of products, markets, and time, and financial managers tend to view their data by line, organization, and time.

The multidimensional model allows users to change their "reports" by simply reorienting their dimensions. Frequently, the multitude of reports requested within an organization are merely different orientations of the same data, perhaps only viewed at different levels of summarization across various keys. It should be possible to change the selection of data and the view interactively,

Figure 13.1 Multiple views of the data.

without rerunning complex queries or creating many separate reports. It should not require large amounts of time to rewrite the report just for simple changes in layout. With an OLAP engine, the calculations and design work are done once, resulting in a multidimensional database that, by its very nature, can deliver reports and analysis with flexibility and power that standard relational technology cannot match. Figure 13.1 illustrates multiple views of the same data as required by various managers.

The multidimensional model is inherently better at representing different views of the business by comparing different facets of the business environment at different levels of detail. Some of the terms used in OLAP are *slicing*, *dicing*, *rotating*, and *drill-down*. The true power of a multidimensional structure is in its ability to quickly and easily manipulate or rotate the view to do a comparison along different criteria. The other "abilities" are more technology-specific. Express is particularly good at slicing and dicing and has powerful analytical functionality built into the engine.

What does "slicing and dicing" mean? To easily visualize an example it is best to limit ourselves to a three-dimensional cube. For example, you may have a cube of hours worked. The cube may be dimensioned by project, organization, and time. Let's assume the organization dimension has several summary levels, like region, cost center, and consultant at the lowest level of detail. *Slicing* means limiting the view of the data to a selection of consultant, region, or cost center. It would take a "slice" of data from the cube as shown for the three managers' views in Figure 13.1. You could have a slice for a particular cost center or a slice for a particular quarter or one for a particular project.

Dicing, just like in cooking, is slicing in multiple directions—making the selection along more than one dimension. Using persistent selections, you essentially keep the slice of data already selected and refine the selection by adding or removing more of the data cube. This could be the number of hours or revenue for a particular cost center during a specific time period. It could represent region and quarter for specific projects. When you add the other features of an analytical engine to the picture it gets interesting since you can select via interrelationships of the data, perform exception analysis, and calculate rankings by a wide variety of criteria.

Rotating data is changing the axes along which you orient your data. If we review cost centers by placing organization down the page, we might analyze our data across time or across projects. In a case where we have multiple hierarchies in a project, like industry or service line, we can compare cost centers across those too. Another rotation would be to set cost centers as page values, with each page displaying time for one cost center across the page and projects on the vertical axis.

Drilling is being able to open up a subset of data that corresponds with a particular value of a dimension. A good example in our sample data schema would be drilling down within an organization. By starting at region, perhaps "EAST," "CENTRAL," and "WEST," the analyst might click on WEST to examine the next lower level of detail, the cost centers in Seattle, San Francisco, and Los Angeles.

Other typical operations in the analysis of the data would involve top/bottom or exception analysis. *Top/bottom* analysis selects the top and/or bottom ranges based on certain other criteria. For example, we could look at the top five cost centers based on margin. Within a cost center, we could select the top ten *and* bottom ten projects based on the ratio of expenses to revenue. Exception reporting involves selecting data based on exceptions—all the data that does not meet some specification. For instance, one could request the cost centers where margin is less than 10 percent.

So why bother with an OLAP component to a data warehouse? Keep in mind that different types of systems (OLTP, warehouse, and OLAP) all serve specific purposes and are optimized accordingly. The complex analytical queries of an OLAP engine might bring a relational system to its knees. The Express engine, on the other hand, is not capable of handling many simultaneous online transactions.

The following table is a popular way of comparing the different types of systems and their typical characteristics. There are other characteristics not mentioned, but this gives a pretty good comparison. Obviously, there are many similarities between the relational warehouse and OLAP characteristics. If some users have a need for strong analytical capabilities then an OLAP component to the warehouse may be desirable.

	Operational	*Relational Warehouse*	*OLAP*
Activity	Updating	Reporting	Analysis
Queries	Periodic	Ad hoc and Periodic	Ad hoc
Transaction size	Small	Small to Large	Large/Complex
Transaction volume	Large	Medium	Small
Age of data	Current	Current and Historical	Current, Historical, and Future
Data sources	Internal/Keyed	Internal and External	Internal and External
Predictability of usage	Predictable	Unpredictable	Unpredictable
User interaction	Low	Medium to High	High

Two striking differences between relational and OLAP processing are the OLAP capabilities for performing different types of time-series analyses and complex calculations such us multiple linear regressions, forecasting, or other built-in financial or statistical functions. Anyone who has written SQL for time-series reporting should appreciate multidimensional OLAP on first sight. The general user can change the selections and selected periods with ease, interactively. This interactive use is a keystone of decision-support systems (DSS), since the investigative nature of analysis requires the reformulation of queries to further narrow down areas of interest. There is no need to reexecute queries just to see the new selections or format.

The Express Data Model

In discussing the Express data model, it is important to understand the different components and how they fit together. On the client side we often speak of *cubes* that represent the data elements, even when they represent data with five, six, or more dimensions as opposed to only three. Data with more than three dimensions is still represented as an essentially three-dimensional view, with the extra dimensions grouped on either the x-, y-, or z-axis. A dimension may also be hierarchical, allowing us to drill down, but this is not required. In the engine itself a dimension is a specific type of database object. What is called a dimension in the application is really a composite structure of dimensions and other database objects, such as relations, variables, and value sets that support the functionality of the application's front-end.

Dimensions

Dimensions are the keys to the data. It is through the dimension values that you select the data that is to be analyzed. They are also the means of indexing into the data. For example, in the time dimension we may have the months JAN97, FEB97, and MAR97 as values, while a geography dimension may have specific cities or sales offices. Dimensions correspond to the key values in a relational table. Just as the key values define the data, the dimensions define the measures in a multidimensional database, so that if our variable is dimensioned by time, there exists a "bucket" for each and every value of time. Unlike a relational database, when analyzing or reporting Express data you do not generate a result set of data. Instead, you manipulate the data available to the Express analytical engine by setting the *status* of the dimensions. The dimension status is a selected subset of the dimension's values. One way to describe this is that all values not included in the current status are invisible. You cannot see other data and Express calculations, reports, and other commands won't have to deal with it. From a relational perspective, think of status as a dynamically created view that limits the underlying table's view which is visible.

Hierarchies

Dimensions are usually used in the form of *embedded total hierarchies*. These special hierarchies are made up of a dimension whose values include all the different levels within a hierarchy. This means that the summary levels are in the same database object (dimension) as their children. It is through this structure that the most effective drill-down is made possible. The embedded total dimension is actually a complex object made up of several components. It usually will have the dimension itself, a relation to itself that represents the parent-child relationship, and also related dimensions for hierarchies and levels. In its simplest form, the embedded total hierarchy in Express is similar to a self-join in a relational database.

Hierarchies are made up of different levels of detail, each value having a parent relation and a level relation, indicating the parent value and level for at least one of the hierarchies. Because Express is multidimensional relations can also be multidimensional. This allows for multiple hierarchies. For example, if the project dimension has two hierarchies, one for industry and one for service line, the relation would contain a parent value for each of the two hierarchies. The hierarchy dimension is one that allows the main dimension to have alternative or multiple hierarchies. In the following Express example, P1.HIERDIM is the hierarchy dimension, while P1.LEVELDIM is the level dimension, and the P1.PARENT and P1.LEVELREL are the parent and level relations, respectively:

```
DEFINE PROJECT DIMENSION TEXT

DEFINE P1.PARENT RELATION PROJECT <PROJECT P1.HIERDIM>
LD Parent-child relation for PROJECT

DEFINE P1.LEVELDIM DIMENSION TEXT
LD List of hierarchy levels for PROJECT

DEFINE P1.LEVELREL VALUESET P1.LEVELDIM <P1.HIERDIM>
LD Levels used by each PROJECT hierarchy

DEFINE P1.LEVELREL RELATION P1.LEVELDIM <PROJECT P1.HIERDIM>
LD Level of each PROJECT in each PROJECT hierarchy
```

Within the Express environment, we refer to the relationships between the dimension members using the family tree metaphor. Terms like parents, siblings, children, ancestors, and descendants are all used here. Dimensions are grouped together by level. Month, quarter, and year would be typical levels for the time dimension.

- **Parent:** The dimension value that represents the next higher level of aggregation within each hierarchy.
- **Sibling:** Other dimension values at the same level of detail.
- **Children:** Those dimension values that have the dimension value as parent.
- **Ancestors:** The dimension values above each value (the parents, the parents' parents, etc.).
- **Descendants:** The corresponding lower level values (the children, the children's children, etc.).

Attributes

Sometimes we would like to select, sort, or categorize data without calculating all the totals for each category. In such cases, it is wise to use attributes. *Attributes* are really just relations to the dimensions. Attributes are similar to lookups or joined tables in relational databases. For instance, if we may want to select projects by type, but are not interested in totals by type, we would use type as an attribute. We accomplish this by defining another dimension called type and then defining a relation between the two. Indeed, you could also create an aggregate or other calculation using this relationship.

Measures

Express includes two basic types of measures: variables and formulas. *Variables* are predefined "buckets" in which calculated or loaded data is stored, either permanently or temporarily during a session. *Formulas* calculate or retrieve their values as they are accessed.

THE IMPORTANCE OF MULTIPLE CUBES

Some other OLAP tools only support single cubes and are limited by requiring all data to have the same dimensionality. This is a serious limitation when trying to model the complexity of the real world.

Express allows multiple cubes, which may or may not share common dimensions. Having multiple cubes is an important feature because it allows different data to have different dimensions. Calculations can be performed even where all dimensions are not shared. Take our example where we have measures of HOURS, EXPENSES, and REVENUE. Measures share dimension values where the dimensions are common. If HOURS and EXPENSES are both dimensioned by PROJECT, then they are both dimensioned by the *same* PROJECT dimension. If the variables do not share dimensionality then the natural dimension set of the result is the union of the input variables' dimensions. The following example demonstrates a result that has the full set of the variables' dimensions:

```
DEFINE HOUR_RATE VARIABLE  DECIMAL <TIME ORGANIZATION CONSULTANT MONTH>
DEFINE HOURS_BILLED VARIABLE DECIMAL <TIME ORGANIZATION PROJECT
LIMIT TIME TO AUG97 TO DEC97
LIMIT PROJECT TO FIRST 2


REPORT HOURS_BILLED*HOUR_RATE


PROJECT: 334535
                 ---------------HOURS_BILLED*HOUR_RATE----------------
                 ------------------------TIME------------------------
ORGANIZATION     AUG97      SEP97      OCT97      NOV97      DEC97
-------------    ---------- ---------- ---------- ---------- ----------
BOB              2,061.93   2,044.37   1,560.21   3,102.57   3,928.67
JIM              2,496.12   5,447.33   5,462.96   3,168.02   2,451.28
MARY             6,393.59   4,952.59   5,527.89   5,349.60   4,026.10
CINTHIA          2,263.69   1,752.84   1,900.22   1,683.16   1,874.65
JOANNE           1,665.23   1,453.19   2,980.58   1,574.94   2,585.95
ELROY            1,734.90   2,912.60   3,616.01   2,063.45   2,649.98


PROJECT: 124858
                 ---------------HOURS_BILLED*HOUR_RATE----------------
                 ------------------------TIME------------------------
ORGANIZATION     AUG97      SEP97      OCT97      NOV97      DEC97
-------------    ---------- ---------- ---------- ---------- ----------
BOB              2,324.71   4,087.13   3,906.41   4,314.90   2,148.17
JIM              2,025.50   3,055.48   4,149.35   4,445.50   2,363.84
MARY             5,762.75   6,763.80   6,481.53   7,761.13   8,158.61
CINTHIA          2,230.26   2,325.09   3,729.94   1,794.86   1,992.37
JOANNE           1,195.04   1,533.00   3,320.61   2,215.31   1,532.00
ELROY            2,982.99   2,832.65   2,010.95   1,339.40   2,101.53
```

Variables

Variables are the Express structure used to represent stored data. They are usually quantitative; however, other types are supported. Most of the labeling for the data is indeed just text variables, defined by the dimension they describe. Sometimes there might also be a language dimension to provide for multiple-language versions. For the purposes of the application, variables are collected under a dimension that allows the user to rotate and use the selector tool to add and remove different measures to and from the view.

Formulas

Formulas are measures that are evaluated on the fly when accessed. Essentially, each is a stored procedure, like an Express program, which has dimensions (similar to a variable) and can be accessed precisely like a variable. When a formula is accessed, Express loops over its dimensions to perform the specified calculations. The Express engine is extremely efficient at calculating formulas. In many cases formulas may be used quite efficiently instead of storing derived variables.

In its most simple form, a formula is just a calculation based on existing values in the Express database. For example, if we have the variables HOURS and REVENUE, dimensioned by PROJECT, ORGANIZATION, and TIME, we could divide REVENUE by HOURS to obtain REVENUE_RATE. To perform this calculation, Express would have to open two separate data areas and then perform the calculation. Depending on how it would be used, this could be a pretty large transaction. We could make a smaller, simpler calculation by predefining a RATE variable that was just dimensioned by CONSULTANT and TIME. Figure 13.2 shows another simple example of calculating SALES as the product of UNITS multiplied by PRICE.

More complex formulas can use Express functions or logical operators or call stored procedures. For instance, the data may reside in a relational database and be queried and summarized for display. Oracle Sales Analyzer, Analyzer, and Express Objects allow users to create what are called *custom aggregates*. The user creates these by selecting a set of dimension values for which a total is then calculated. This custom aggregate gives the flexibility of reporting or analyzing totals on an ad hoc basis, even where the values haven't been precalculated.

Figure 13.2 Formula arithmetic.

Programs and Models

Express includes a powerful language for developing stored procedures. These procedures are the basis for applications developed in Express. Various front-end options exist, but the Express 4GL does the data manipulation work. Programs and models are compiled objects within the Express environment. Programs are independent and free-standing while models are defined to perform calculations over dimensions. Models are heavily used in financial applications such as Oracle Financial Analyzer.

History of Express

Express was originally written in the early 1970s by MIT graduate students Jay Wurths and Rick Karrash while they were doing marketing analysis programming for three MIT professors, John Little (ex-dean of MIT's Sloan School of Business, now professor emeritus), Glen Urban (current dean of Sloan), and Len Lodish (currently at the University of Philadelphia's Wharton School). The software was first used to model market data for several large consumer products companies, to which John Little was consulting. This early work resulted in the founding of a company, Management Decision Systems (MDS), which did consulting in consumer market research.

Express started out as a mainframe system available only under the IBM VM/CMS operating system. It was later ported to Prime. In the beginning, Express was made available via time-sharing service. It was made available for customer installation in the early 1980s.

Information Resources, Inc. (IRI) purchased MDS in 1985, primarily to acquire the Express technology. They wanted to use Express for analysis of scanner data and therefore had a strict marketing focus. Shortly thereafter, Express was converted to the C language, resulting in a two-tier product architecture comprised of PcExpress as PC-based client and MDB as a back-end server component. Some features for advanced statistical analysis (factor, cluster, or discriminant analysis) that were present in the early product are no longer included. IRI later expanded from its strict marketing focus and developed FMS, the Financial Management System.

Oracle acquired the Express software from IRI in July 1995. This acquisition included the set of products based on Express technology. About two-thirds of the IRI field staff and the development teams in Waltham, Massachusetts, also joined Oracle in the acquisition. PcExpress and MDB were renamed Oracle Personal Express and Oracle Express Server, respectively. The other IRI application products then evolved into Oracle Sales Analyzer, Oracle Financial Analyzer, Or-

ONGOING ENHANCEMENTS

Since the acquisition, Oracle has greatly improved the integration of Express to relational (SQL) databases using RAA/RAM (Relational Access Administrator/Relational Access Manager) and added new composite dimensions to transparently handle sparse data. Continued product development is underway under Oracle Corporation's ownership.

acle Analyzer, and Oracle Express Objects. (Note that the Financial Analyzer database names are still prefixed with "FMS.")

The fundamental data model is still very similar to that of the original product. It has undergone very few changes over the years. Express has always been both multidimensional and relational. Yes, relational. When Dr. Codd composed the twelve rules for relational database management, Express met more rules than many accepted "relational" databases at the time. However, just because Express meets many of the rules documented for relational databases does not mean it has been designed to be used as a transactional database. The arena where Express performs best is where it should be—in analytical processing. Incidentally, Dr. Codd documented the rules for OLAP tools in 1992, twenty years after Express was first made available!

The Express Technology

The following section introduces a few elements of the Express technology. Express is a robust product, and this book does not allow a complete discussion of the technology. We will explore a few areas that can have an impact on the performance of an Express database implementation. Perhaps this discussion can help you understand enough about how Express works to avoid problems. Other issues can also be read about in the Express product documentation.

Data Storage and Access

Express manipulates the data as multidimensional arrays with indexes on each dimension object. It does this by storing each variable, both on disk and in memory, in pages whose layout is mapped to the dimensional array. This means that each and every cell in the database is indexed, allowing very rapid retrieval of data from the database. As long as the dimension values are already defined, the keys are not stored with the variables so as not to require more segments, which makes data storage very compact on pages. This is important for performance considerations.

This is quite different from typical relational storage where the key values are stored along with the data values, and related rows might be spread across multiple pages. (The nearest Oracle RDBMS structure is an index cluster.) Figure 13.3 illustrates the storage of all values for HOURS together and all values of EXPENSES together, organized by their dimensions. Retrieving a large number of data values across time, for instance, will be much faster than scanning through a correspondingly large table to collect key values for every data item retrieved. This reduces I/O significantly and also allows matrix arithmetic and complex functions to be performed very efficiently.

Offset Addressing

Offset addressing is another facet of the way Express organizes measure data on whole pages. Offset addressing helps retrieve data that has a high degree of lo-

Figure 13.3 Data access.

cality. For instance, when you are viewing January data and next want to look at February's, it is not necessary for the engine to seek the next "chunk" of data; it knows to look "4 bytes to the right" to find the value corresponding to that dimension's next value. This is especially important to time-series analysis, where you may be performing calculations involving many data "buckets" that are literally stored next to each other.

Persistent Selections

Much analysis is performed on specific slices or views of data. For example, a particular cost center may show a higher result on some measure than other cost centers. It is normal to make comparisons during analysis, frequently across some other dimension. It may be interesting to take the results from the current month and expand the time dimension to the past half year. This second selection doesn't affect the status of the first selection. It is persistent. In this way, the user can add or take away dimension values very quickly, not by generating new results tables, but just by reshaping the current view.

Inversions

An inversion is an internal structure that holds information about relationships between dimensions. It is essentially the set of related values that correspond to a particular dimension value. Here is an example based on the demo database:

Relation		
1	ATLANTA	EAST
2	BOSTON	EAST
3	CHICAGO	CENTRAL
4	DALLAS	CENTRAL
5	DENVER	WEST
6	LOS ANGELES	WEST
7	NEW YORK	EAST
8	PHILADELPHIA	EAST
9	SAN FRANCISCO	WEST

Inversion	
EAST	1, 2, 7, 8
CENTRAL	3, 4
WEST	5, 6, 9

The inversions allow very fast lookups and limit operations on related dimensions. The level relations in the hierarchies we discussed earlier are an excellent example.

XCA Communications

The Express Communications Architecture (XCA) is a high-performance, peer-to-peer architecture that allows databases to communicate with each other across different platforms in a way that is transparent to the user. This topological independence can be important in maximizing performance when working in distributed architectures. It is important to evaluate the communications requirements and methods for transferring/loading data when designing the Express architecture. The various architectures supported by Express will be discussed in the next section.

The retrieve command is useful for exchanging data between host and client sessions where the information is for a specific purpose and expected to be used infrequently. It provides seamless integration of the remote and local data. It allows the user to get any data so long as the dimension of the data exists in both sessions. The formula would check against the local memory cache to see if the value had been retrieved and, if not, would call a program to query the details and return them.

The *EIF* (Express Interchange Format) *pipeline* is best for transferring larger amounts of data between Express sessions. It uses data compression to make the transfer more efficient. This transfers data via an EXPORT directly from one session into the objects of another. Arguments can be used to transfer only data, only definitions, or both. Dimension values can be appended or replaced. This technique is also useful in updating slices of data.

An *EIF file* is especially effective for cases where communications may be undependable or where the client must be able to work with the data while disconnected from the primary database. A manager may wish to perform analysis using a laptop while flying to a meeting. An EIF file is created using the XCA compression algorithm to compress and store the data in a platform-independent binary file. The platform independence of this file also makes it an excellent method for distributing data in cases where no network connection is available. (An EIF file is conceptually similar to the dump file used by Oracle EXP and IMP utilities.) As with the EIF pipeline, the import command can be used to transfer just definitions, only data where dimension values are present, or even to replace all objects.

Application Architectures

When implementing an Express OLAP solution, there are several different options for the overall application architecture that can be implemented. There are many factors that play a role in determining how the application should be structured. These factors can be grouped as follows:

- **Data distribution architecture:** How the data is distributed to or accessed by users. The architecture options include thin client, thick client, web access, or a combination of several different approaches depending on the needs of the user community.
- **Load and storage strategy:** The overall style of solution, whether purely multidimensional, relational access (ROLAP), or a hybrid, with summary-level data stored in the OLAP tool but detail maintained by a relational database.
- **Physical database design:** The structure of the database objects themselves and how the data will be organized.

We will explore the first two groupings next. The third, database design, will be covered throughout the rest of this chapter.

Data Distribution Architectures

Express applications can be set up to allow access or distribution of data following three basic configurations. The primary drivers for determining how information will be distributed are going to be whether the user needs a local copy of data for disconnected use, the maintenance costs of installed software, and the performance issues surrounding both loads of distributed "slices" and system response. The three alternatives are as follows:

- Client-server with either thick client, thin client, or via a browser using Web Agent
- LAN installation with shared databases on a LAN
- PC installation

Figure 13.4 presents a graphical view of these three architectures.

The three variations on the client-server model are discussed in the following three sections. They are shown in Figure 13.5.

Thick Client-Server

Thick client typically consists of the client application (running under Microsoft Windows), a local version of the database engine (Personal Express), and the

Figure 13.4 Application architecture alternatives.

Figure 13.5 Client-server variations.

Express server located on a host system. The local database on the PC client communicates with the host using XCA to retrieve and load data from Express Server. This means that when the server has new data, the client can refresh the local database with the new version of server data. This is particularly useful when Personal Express is used on a laptop and usually presents a slice of data. The data can be refreshed, then used as needed, while you are disconnected from the server. The thick client is limited by disk space and network performance, so care must be taken in determining the slices of data that will be distributed to the clients. A complete copy of a large database may not be appropriate. The PC is the most common client component in a typical Express implementation. This will probably change as more web applications are made available and network computers appear on more desktops.

Thin Client-Server

A somewhat "thinner" alternative to the thick client on which data is permanently stored involves the use of a local cache database. The GUI application communicates with the local cache database via SNAPI (Structured N-dimensional Application Program Interface), and the cache uses XCA to retrieve data from the host as needed. The data is stored in the cache (memory) for the duration of the session, minimizing the repetitive retrieval of data.

One advantage the cache has over a true thin client without cache is that the cache database eliminates the need to retrieve data from the server more than once per session. Once the data has been retrieved, it resides in the cache, so that further analysis using that data can use the Express engine to manipulate it. There is, however, a negative impact on performance because the IF clauses check to see if the buffer is filled. This can be significant in cases where the cache database has a large number of dimension combinations to check.

Starting with Express Server version 5.03, a true thin client is available. In this scenario, the client application uses SNAPI to communicate directly with the Express Server component. Only the Windows application itself is installed on the client machine, with no local copy of data maintained.

Web Browser Client-Server

Web-enabling the Express Server allows the thinnest client of all—any standard web browser. This development is also in line with Oracle's Network Computing Architecture and may represent a significantly lower cost for maintaining all implementations where remote sessions are necessary. The Express Web products are constructed as four-tier CGI and four-tier Java applications.

Web access to Express can currently be provided in three ways. In all cases, Express Web Agent provides the environment to produce dynamically generated Web pages through Express's stored procedure language. Provided with the Web Agent is the Express Developer's Toolkit, with which you can create Express programs that generate dynamic HTML pages that, in turn, contain views of Express data. These programs also support special formatting such as tables, frames, and other capabilities defined by the HTML 2.0 standard.

The Express Web Publisher is used in conjunction with either Express Objects or Express Analyzer. With it, Web "sites" can be created and managed and tables and graphs published. Within Web Publisher you can create and publish *Web-Sites* that are units of storage for *WebBriefings*. WebBriefings are, in turn, groups or subsets of *WebPages* that contain tables, graphs and other HTML content. The published Web pages are supplied within briefings and include the controls for selecting pages, rotating, and exporting data.

Sales Analyzer version 1.6 is also Web-enabled, and through its administrative features it allows users to publish their own reports to libraries. The public libraries are then accessed from the Web via the Sales Analyzer Web Server. The Web pages generated by Sales Analyzer are like the Web Publisher pages and provide the same toolset for later rotating and selecting from a Web browser.

LAN Installation

In a LAN installation the application code, shared databases, and even the user's databases would exist on the shared disk of a server on the local area network. The tempoary data files used for paging should always be on the client side. It is important to note that the software is run completely in the memory space of the client PC using the client CPU. This can cause a significant amount of network traffic as data is transferred between the database and the client. The chief advantage of this architecture is that it provides the analytical independence of a PC installation, but simplifies the software and database maintenance through centralization. The release of Express Server on Windows NT has made the more efficient client/server model available to smaller systems. Increasing acceptance of NT Server has virtually eliminated new LAN installations of Express.

PC Installation

A single user installation of Personal Express can be performed on a personal computer. With the processing power of modern PCs, this is a viable solution for many analysts. A local installation on a notebook computer allows Express capabilities to become completely portable for small- to moderate-size databases.

Load and Storage Strategy

While there are many ways to strategize storing data, the first alternative stores data within an Express multidimensional database. This approach will most surely deliver the best performance in data retrieval and presentation.

Multidimensional OLAP

Such activities as drilling down, rotation, and analytical calculations have the best response in a purely multidimensional setup. Frequently, though, there is a great deal of corresponding relational data that needs to be processed to load the multidimensional database. Achieving "speed-of-thought" multidimensional database performance requires that staging, loading, and aggregating of data be

Figure 13.6 Multidimensional OLAP.

performed in batch. This process can take quite a bit of time depending, of course, on the structures being updated. Figure 13.6 illustrates Express retrieving data from its own database.

This approach is especially suited for systems where the data is updated on a periodic basis, typically monthly or even quarterly. The time required for the loading and aggregating makes this less suitable for situations requiring frequent updates. There is also some inflexibility in making changes to the multidimensional front-end, as it is heavily dependent on the database structure. Making significant structural changes involving large amounts of data will require correspondingly long times associated with reloading and aggregating along the new structures. Even changes in hierarchies involving no "structural" changes can have a significant impact on the build process.

Relational OLAP

The ROLAP alternative uses the relational database to store the data, which is then mapped into a multidimensional cache where the structures are more tuned for display and analytical purposes. On the relational side, the data would be stored in either a star (or snowflake) schema. Ideally, the Express metadata layer would then be maintained as relational tables so that a variety of end-user applications could be used, depending on the individual needs of the user or group. The data is queried into the Express database as needed and kept there

Figure 13.7 Relational OLAP.

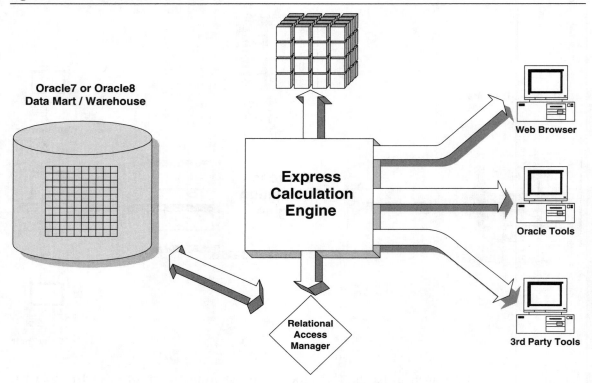

for the session. This marriage of the Express engine to a relational warehouse database is shown in Figure 13.7.

The drawback with any pure ROLAP solution is that every time the system is started it must start from scratch and reload the cache. Heavily indexed databases with summary tables can mitigate degradation in response time. This, however, comes at the cost of introducing more overhead during updates of the relational database. Performance of this architecture depends greatly on the relational server platform. If this is the desired solution, be sure to invest in adequate hardware. Each loading of the Express cache can represent a significant query load on the warehouse server.

Hybrid

The hybrid approach uses the power of the multidimensional structures and storage for performance in analytical processing while allowing "reach-through" to the relational system for more detailed data supporting the summary data the user is analyzing (see Figure 13.8). In this model, some of the data is preloaded and aggregated in the Express database, while the rest of the data is left in a relational database. This is accomplished by defining a local cache with a reach-through to a

Figure 13.8 Hybrid OLAP.

ROLAP database. Then, with the Express database attached with write access, the upper levels of summary data are loaded into the Express database.

Relational Access Administrator (RAA) and Relational Access Manager (RAM) are special tools to assist in the development of ROLAP and hybrid configurations. These tools are discussed in the section on Oracle Express Applications at the end of this chapter. For a database generated with RAA/RAM, the status of all the dimensions is limited to those values for which data should be loaded and stored. At this point the "normal" fetch program is run, just as it would have been in a reach-through situation, except that the database is attached read/write. This process loads the data into the buffer usually used to hold data during the session. Once loaded, we can update Express, saving the loaded values in the cache database. Now when the data is accessed, the formula that evaluates whether the buffer is already populated will determine that it is and avoid the additional cost of reaching through.

Using the hybrid approach also allows an extra degree of "tuning" for performance by adjusting how much data is stored in the multidimensional side and how much remains in the relational. Use of the two environments can also be optimized by splitting the different reporting needs by the applicability of the different technologies—some reports are better provided in the purely relational world. Don't assume that Express must be used to satisfy all needs. This awareness may save loading a lot of detail into Express for very little additional benefit.

Implementing an OLAP Solution

This section deals with some of the issues related to implementing an OLAP application. Most conventions for application development and implementation can be adapted to apply to OLAP. It is not within the scope of this chapter to discuss project methodology or coding, naming, documentation, and project administration issues, except where those issues are specific to OLAP or to Oracle Express. That said, this section delves into basic project phases in order to group certain issues together. Be aware, however, that many activities are intertwined, and the related issues are not unique to a particular project phase.

Requirements Definition

If the OLAP implementation is part of a larger data warehouse project much of the requirements definition has more than likely been done. Even so, at minimum a review of the business requirements, data sources, and extraction and loading plans as well as the resultant entity relationship models is necessary from the point of view of the OLAP implementation process. In OLAP implementations it is good to keep in mind that it will be the analysts and business managers who will determine the success of the project. While the reporting and analysis needs for a given group of users will change to keep pace with evolving the business environment, the underlying data needed to support the information requirements will generally remain fairly stable. To support a wide array of decision support needs, the data model must be very flexible.

Business Requirements

To fully understand what the objectives and informational needs of the business users are, it is useful to review current and proposed report layouts as well as any proposed organizational changes and any external factors expected to alter how the business will be run. It is critical that the business issues are fully understood and represented in the business model and that all calculations and models currently in use are fully documented. An organization chart of the users should be created as well as documentation of the business entities and how they relate to each other. At this point, a high-level data model should be created containing the main entities and data elements needed to support the business views.

Data Sources

The analysis of the data sources should compare the data requirements coming out of the business requirements analysis with the existing data sources. If the data sources do not exist within the existing schema other sources may need to be found or else the business views need to be adjusted to balance the availability of data with the users' expectations. If an Express OLAP solution is being added to an existing relational data warehouse, much of this work will already be complete.

Data quality should also be addressed because data of poor quality can have a severe impact on the success of an OLAP project. The source data's granularity needs to be documented and correlated between the different source systems since comparison of data will require a set of common keys. This may mean that for some external sources you will only be able to load data at a very high summary level. Often, information from associations or governmental agencies is based either on some geographic code like country or by some industry-unique identifier.

This can pose a difficult problem. You may wish to combine your internal sales figures with data from the OECD, the United Nations Statistical Office, or the Direct Marketing Association. Users may demand state-level summaries but want to look at their data by DMA code. This, of course, would seem simple for many DMA codes, since in areas like the northeastern United States the codes may be like supercounties. This is not true in other areas where population density may be much lower. Here we find DMA codes that overlap state boundaries! It should also be noted that DMA codes don't exist internationally. This is just one example. Reports should be evaluated carefully to identify data that is "grouped" by some of these codes. As often as not, even if it makes sense to the users, careful investigation will reveal that it is in error because of mismatches in groupings. Some of these reports can easily be produced via SQL, where a subtotal will be generated by each of these groups. If you add up the subtotals, you may find either double counting, missing data, or some of both.

STAR AND SNOWFLAKE SCHEMAS

The star schema is the simplest relational schema that supports the multidimensional model effectively. To what extent summary tables are created (and how extensively they are indexed) is determined by factors such as the available Express load window, the frequency and volume of updates, and the type(s) of access to the relational warehouse. The star (or snowflake) simplifies loading in that all the dimension maintenance can be done on smaller lookup tables instead of the fact tables, which usually represent the largest component of the relational data.

Extraction and Loading

There is a good chance that source data for a standalone OLAP database will be coming from several places. Ideally, however, data reconciliation and integration is all done through the relational data warehouse. If the data is coming directly from source transaction systems, it should first be extracted to either intermediate tables in a relational database or flat files. This can either be accomplished using extraction tools or just as reports/extracts from the systems in question.

The most efficient method for reading data into an Express database is by using the FILEREAD command. This advantage may be outweighed by other factors, such as maintenance of the source data in a warehouse or data cleansing issues.

CLEANSING THE DATA

If the data is not coming from a verified data warehouse and an extraction tool with data scrubbing capabilities is not being used then the data will need to be verified and corrected. Care must be taken to assure that all the necessary parent values exist so that rollups can be successful. Express (starting with version 6) has a utility called HIERCHECK for checking hierarchies for circularity. To deal with circular references prior to version 6, refer to the ROLLUP command in the *Language Reference Manual* for sample code to write your own verification programs.

Distribution and Access Control

Requirements for access and distribution of data should be determined based on the need of the various users or user groups. Generally, it makes the most sense to allow export of slices to those who either need a local copy of data to update during the analytical cycle or to those who need to view the data while disconnected from the network. This is especially true with Financial Analyzer because of its budgeting capability.

Distributing data may make sense if the user base is skilled with regard to computers or if the users' workstations are powerful. This can be a way of distributing the processing load. Generally, this is not an issue since the server is likely to have enough capacity to outperform even the fastest PCs. Creating and distributing EIF files or exporting via the pipeline would also require host CPU and disk resources, so the distribution of data may not greatly reduce the total load on the server.

Another consideration regarding access and distribution is, naturally, security. Allowing users to take slices of data may complicate the management of data security. This is a general issue related to how people use laptops and personal workstations. As such it is beyond the scope of this chapter.

Analysis

With the requirements fully understood and with clearly identified sources, it is possible to put together some size estimates and some predictive metrics regarding performance. During the analysis phase, we will want to take those requirements and determine the best of the many alternative methods for structuring the database. This will be done by assessing the characteristics of the data, determining the appropriate dimensions and granularity of the data, and determining how dense or sparse the data may be. Finally, we need to establish the impact of the available time window, the frequency of loads, and any processor and disk constraints.

Dimensionality

An important issue is the dimensionality. When should an entity be considered in a separate dimension? When is it just a level within a hierarchy? In typical hierarchies, the relationships are always one to many. Should you try make separate dimensions out of them they are likely to be extremely sparse. If, for example, you would make state and city separate dimensions and then view the data in table form, it would normally be fairly sparse. Denver would probably only have data for Colorado, leaving the remaining rows and columns empty. This obvious example illustrates the potential use of a hierarchy. It might not be so obvious, however, if the data is billing information for a telephone company and CITY is the origination city and STATE the destination state. In this revised example, the CITY and STATE fields are not hierarchically related. Making separate dimensions of them would result in a cube that would probably be very dense. So the entity relationship diagram can't be simply mapped directly to a physical model in OLAP. Care needs to be taken to understand how the elements relate to each other.

Likely candidates for dimensions are naturally TIME, since a particular month is always in a specific quarter, year, and so on. Others are PRODUCT, ORGANIZATION, and GEOGRAPHY hierarchies. For example, Denver is always in Colorado, which in turn is always in the United States.

Another common question is how many dimensions a cube can have. Theoretically, Express can support objects with up to thirty-two dimensions. This is really not necessary. Try to imagine a table on your screen with the columns across the screen representing TIME, and with GEOGRAPHY as the vertical axis, and then the unique combination of thirty keys defining each page definition. Now think about drilling down or making a specific selection. This would mean that to truly use the tool, you would need to drill and select through all thirty-two dimensions as keys. The relational equivalent would be equally complex. Imagine having to specify thirty-two key columns in each SELECT statement. That wouldn't be user-friendly by anyone's definition. A far better solution is to utilize the Express multiple cube facility. Then smaller cubes could be defined to support different types of analysis. In our case study database project time accounting, we probably wouldn't want to include the Strategic Service Line, Industry, or Project dimensions in a simple report of consultant utilization. A smaller cube of the data which had dimensions of Consultant, Organization, and Time would be sufficient for this analysis.

Granularity

The level of detail stored in the Express database will have an impact on loading and maintenance performance as well as responsiveness. Less detail will allow enhanced performance but will limit the users' ability to drill down. Balancing these objectives is an important function of analysis.

Sparsity of Data

Generally, we refer to data as being 80 percent sparse when only 20 percent of the variable's cells—unique combinations of the dimensions—for that variable contain data. Where data is sparse, dimensions should be set up as either *composite* or *conjoint*. If the database is large or if the data is sparse for certain subsets of dimensions, there may be other methods for managing the sparse data and improve performance. Some other techniques (which are discussed later in this chapter) are subsetted dimensionality, record relational structures, indirect references and capstone databases. Most of these techniques partition the data into smaller pieces and then join them together through the use of formulas. This corresponds to the definition of a relational view which predefines a join of multiple tables.

Precision of Data

The required precision of data should be evaluated carefully. Both variables and dimensions should be defined with the least precise definition possible. Is rounding error going to be a problem for the type of analysis to be performed? Whether to maintain SALES data with whole dollar values or with dollars and cents will be determined by whether you're selling cars for thousands of dollars or canned foods for less than a dollar.

Reducing precision will make the dimensions smaller, so they'll take less storage and be more efficiently accessed. Specifying a decimal variable instead of a short integer will double the amount of storage for that variable. Need we say more? It is, however, important to provide sufficient precision to meet the analytical needs of the business.

Order of Dimensionality

In determining the order of dimensions for the variables, certain things must be taken into consideration. Data loading and typical view layouts are factors that influence the order. In the example data, we assume that time should be used as an "across" dimension in many views—this is fairly typical. Time is expected to be one of the "most variable" variables. If we take a look at our case study data, we see that we have thousands of consultants and projects and even hundreds of organizations. It is typical that a consultant will work on one project and perform one function for several months. Therefore, time is the dimension that

Defining Sparse Dimentions

In Express version 6 the definition for hours would include the sparse keyword to designate which dimensions are sparse:

```
DEFINE HOURS VARIABLE INTEGER <TIME SPARSE <CONSULTANT PROJECT FUNCTION>>
```

In releases prior to version 6 you would more than likely use a conjoint dimension to manage the sparsity:

```
DEFINE MAIN.CJT DIMENSION <CONSULTANT PROJECT FUNCTION>
DEFINE HOURS.CJT VARIABLE INTEGER <TIME MAIN.CJT>
```

varies fastest—it changes every period even when other aspects of a consulting assignment remain the same.

To optimize our application for performance we want to represent time as the fastest-varying dimension. This would make it the "across" dimension in the default layout of a table. The second fastest is the down dimension, and third, fourth, and so on become pages. Since the order of dimensions will also dictate how the data is physically stored, this decision will make this setup the fastest for retrieval as well.

Some systems will have frequent loads or updates and will need to have the dimensions ordered accordingly. If you are loading data daily, you may want time to be the slowest-varying dimension. This would allow the data for a single data to be loaded together onto a single page (or small set of pages).

Design and Build

The design of a multidimensional database is conceptually quite different than that of an OLTP relational database. Of course, there are some characteristics that are common to both types of systems. The largest difference is in the approach to design. It is important to remember that the primary reason for the development OLAP databases is for decision support. For a decision-support system (DSS) to be successful it must accurately represent the business model, not an effective transaction processing model.

Many of these multidimensional relationships will be similar to joins that could be done at run-time in an RDBMS. Within the multidimensional database, they must be defined carefully to fit within the business model. Although this requires more work at design time, a properly designed multidimensional database can offer a great deal of versatility and flexibility at run-time because of its very nature.

One of the more difficult transitions for experienced relational database designers to make is working in more than two dimensions simultaneously. One typical mistake is to develop the design of the multidimensional database based on reports from either a legacy or current relational system. While this input is an important part of the information needed for analysis and design, it is not an end. The physical schema should be optimized for interactive performance and for maximum flexibility in regard to reporting layouts.

Do the planning up front—it will save countless headaches later on.

Constructing a small prototype of the multidimensional database is always a very good idea. Don't forget that multidimensional databases are new to many people. The users may do a thorough job of describing their current reporting and analysis needs, but if they haven't worked in a multidimensional database before, they won't be able to conceptualize what they want in the appropriate terms. After working in a prototype for a short while, they will be much more prepared to give appropriate feedback.

One of the first steps in the actual design of the multidimensional database is to determine which data elements should be included. Next it will be necessary to determine the source of the data or how it will be entered. The atomic level "facts" need to be identified first. Then the corresponding hierarchies are determined for each dimension. Finally, the key values for each dimension must be verified. These elements and the necessary dimensional objects will form the basis for the database design.

Design Trade-offs

Just as in relational database design, the primary activity during the design of an OLAP environment is evaluating the trade-offs between multiple objectives and alternative solutions. Most trade-offs revolve around how much work to do ahead of time during and directly after the load process and how much to do on the fly. Some of the trade-offs to consider are the following:

- load time versus retrieval time
- load time versus required granularity
- precalculation of aggregates versus calculated-on-demand
- loaded aggregates versus rolling up in Express
- loading of detail versus reach-through-on-demand
- loading all desired data versus disk limitations
- object definition versus cell limitations

CALCULATED VARIABLES

Whether or not to precalculate and store variables often depends on how the calculation affects performance and the load window. Calculating on the fly saves storage space but may adversely affect the performance. Some calculations are simple or require a small subset of data, perhaps by utilizing offset addressing.

When presenting cumulative sums, one could use the *cumsum() function.* This would require calculating over the entire time series—and would probably take much too long for on-the-fly calculations. However, if the cumulative sum is precalculated and stored, you could use a formula to present the monthly values by calculating the difference between the current and previous month. This calculation would be very fast since Express just needs to look a few bytes to the left and return the difference.

If your database size is not an issue and your load window is adequate, precalculating and storing both of these variables may be the best alternative. Where processing speed is the primary concern, lean toward calculating and storing a variable. When database size or load processing are critical consider calculating on the fly.

Entity Relationship Diagram

An entity relationship diagram (ERD) of the data and various entities is a typical method for determining what needs to be in the database and what objects will be defined. Using standard modeling techniques will help the database designer to better communicate the data feeds and source requirements necessary to support the multidimensional database. The ERD is ideal for understanding the various elements and their interrelationships and dependencies. The data model will be somewhat different than an OLTP database design, but the ERD can be the link between different technologies. This will be particularly important if Express is being used to reach through to an underlying relational database.

Mapping to Multidimensional Structures

Entities and relationships map to dimensions, levels, and attributes, while facts generally map to variables and formulas. One of the core concepts in OLAP terminology is the *datacube*. A datacube is the multidimensional object, referred to as a *financial data item* in Financial Analyzer or as a *measure* in other Express front-end tools. These structures are indeed multidimensional arrays; a three-dimensional object would be conceptually similar to a Rubik's cube. These normally dimensioned structures are fine for densely populated datasets, but in many cases the data is not at all dense. To compare the different alternatives for the physical structure of our database, we will start with our example database consisting of ORGANIZATIONS, PROJECTS, and TIME. This example is simple and easy to follow.

To create our sample database, suppose our dimensions are defined as follows:

```
DEFINE PROJECT DIMENSION TEXT
DEFINE ORGANIZATION DIMENSION TEXT
DEFINE TIME DIMENSION TEXT
```

and we define our data in a simple cube by placing it within the three dimensions:

```
DEFINE HOURS VARIABLE INTEGER <TIME, ORGANIZATION, PROJECT>
```

Furthermore, suppose our dimensions had ten values each, 10 PROJECTS, 10 ORGANIZATIONS, and 10 MONTHS Our cube could then store up to 1,000 values of HOURS. If only 250 of these distinct combinations contained values, the cube would be 1,000/250 or 25 percent dense. (This is the same as 75 percent sparse.) The cube may not, however, be uniformly dense. For instance, it is possible that each actual PROJECT and ORGANIZATION combination might have corresponding values for every value of TIME. This would mean that TIME is dense relative to PROJECT and ORGANIZATION. PROJECT and ORGANIZATION, however, would be sparse relative to each other.

Normal Multidimensional Structures

Where data is dense across its defining keys, normal dimensional structures can be used. For instance, as we demonstrated earlier:

```
DEFINE HOURS VARIABLE INTEGER <TIME, ORGANIZATION, PROJECT>
```

Using standard dimensional and hierarchy structures simplifies both the build process and aggregation and facilitates using various tools and functions. The standard structures keep all of the hierarchical information in a simple set of relations that are then used for both aggregating the data as well as drilling down from a front-end tool. Alternative structures, in which the applications can become more complicated, are discussed in the following sections. The direct, simple structures allow all the analytical power to rotate, slice, dice, and drill down via the dimensions. If it is possible to keep the application simple, do it!

Conjoint Dimensions

In Express versions prior to 6.0, the *conjoint dimension* was one of the primary methods for controlling sparse data. A conjoint dimension is a dimension whose values point to values of its base dimensions and represent an intersection. This allowed the variables to be stored very densely. The downside to conjoint dimensions was the extra work required to set up hierarchies. Additionally, conjoint dimensions can get very large. The indexing algorithm for conjoint dimensions should be hashed. (If it is initially defined as *nohash* the indexing algorithm can be reset to either *hash* or *btree*.) Were our example to have sparse data, we would first need to define the conjoint dimension:

```
DEFINE ORGPROJ DIMENSION <ORGANIZATION, PROJECT>
```

The data would then be stored using the conjoint dimension rather than the original two dimensions:

```
DEFINE HOURS_CJT VARIABLE INTEGER <TIME, ORGPROJ>
```

Reporting on this structure wouldn't be very convenient or flexible. Because HOURS_CJT is dimensioned by ORGPROG means that the combination of ORGANIZATION and PROJECT must always be on the same axis. This limits the ability to rotate the output. In the following example we limit the time to only four months:

```
LIMIT TIME TO LAST 4
REPORT DOWN ORGPROJ HOURS_CJT
```

| | | -----------------HOURS_CJT----------------- | | | |
| ---------ORGPROJ--------- | | --------------------TIME-------------------- | | | |
ORGANIZATION	PROJECT	SEP97	OCT97	NOV97	DEC97
BOB	334535	60	57	55	80
BOB	124858	63	63	73	69
JIM	334535	55	61	52	63
JIM	124858	75	59	79	79
MARY	334535	67	63	68	72
MARY	124858	58	64	56	69
BOB	394893	73	64	78	75
BOB	342382	56	65	70	79
MARY	394893	75	76	67	74
MARY	342382	73	78	70	61

```
JOANNE      124858                    59          62          62          53
JOANNE      394893                    79          77          69          53
JOANNE      342382                    65          59          51          53
```

The hours variable could be represented via a formula instead, so that the full dimensional power could be used to allow pivoting, rotating, and the like:

```
DEFINE HOURS_F FORMULA INTEGER <TIME, ORGANIZATION, PROJECT>
EQ HOURS_CJT

REPORT HOURS_F

PROJECT: 334535
                  -----------------HOURS_F-----------------
                  -----------------TIME-------------------
ORGANIZATION    SEP97       OCT97       NOV97       DEC97
-------------   ----------  ----------  ----------  ----------
BOB                 60          57          55          80
JIM                 55          61          52          63
MARY                67          63          68          72
JOANNE              NA          NA          NA          NA

PROJECT: 124858
                  -----------------HOURS_F-----------------
                  -----------------TIME-------------------
ORGANIZATION    SEP97       OCT97       NOV97       DEC97
-------------   ----------  ----------  ----------  ----------
BOB                 63          63          73          69
JIM                 75          59          79          79
MARY                58          64          56          69
JOANNE              59          62          62          53

PROJECT: 394893
                  -----------------HOURS_F-----------------
                  -----------------TIME-------------------
ORGANIZATION    SEP97       OCT97       NOV97       DEC97
-------------   ----------  ----------  ----------  ----------
BOB                 73          64          78          75
JIM                 NA          NA          NA          NA
MARY                75          76          67          74
JOANNE              79          77          69          53

PROJECT: 342382
                  -----------------HOURS_F-----------------
                  -----------------TIME-------------------
ORGANIZATION    SEP97       OCT97       NOV97       DEC97
-------------   ----------  ----------  ----------  ----------
BOB                 56          65          70          79
JIM                 NA          NA          NA          NA
MARY                73          78          70          61
JOANNE              65          59          51          53
```

As you can see, having the dimensions separated provides multidimensional functionality to the data. Even though creating a viewable structure is easy, it is more complex to build the structures for performing rollups of data, and to maintain the multiple levels and hierarchical information.

In order to perform a rollup of the data, store the aggregates, and provide drill down, you need to make parent structures for the conjoint. (Now comes the fun part!) For each of the base dimensions of the conjoint, a parent conjoint value must be added. First, we will need to define a parent relation for each of the base dimensions:

```
DEFINE ORGPROJ_ORG RELATION ORGPROJ <ORGPROJ O1.HIERDIM>
```

Notice that this relation is also dimensioned by the hierarchy dimension (its name shows that we assume the administrator tool is being used), so that the conjoint rollup can support multiple hierarchies. Otherwise a separate relation is needed for each hierarchy.

The following is a simple method for using the parent relation to build the parent structures; Sales Analyzer does this in a much more sophisticated way.

```
vrb lvlcount int
lvlcount=0
lvlcount=obj(dimmax 'O1.leveldim')
while lvlcount gt 0
do
  maintain ORGPROJ merge   -
  < O1.PARENT(ORGANIZATION -
  key(ORGPROJ PROJECT))>   -
  relate ORGPROJ_ORG

lvlcount=lvlcount-1
doend
```

After building the parent structures, the ROLLUP command can be issued as it normally would:

```
ROLLUP HOURS_CJT OVER ORGPROJ USING ORGPROJ_ORG
```

A later section of this chapter, "Aggregation/Rollup," will provide general rules on performing rollups.

Composite Dimensions

Starting with Express version 6.0, another means of dealing with sparsity is provided. As measures/variables are defined, combinations of their dimensions can be designated as being sparse. This allows Express to manage their storage more efficiently. Express version 6.0 handles this transparently. No extra structures need to be created or maintained as required with conjoint dimensions. Express maintains the *composite dimension* automatically.

The conjoint example above, if re-created using a composite dimension, would be:

```
DEFINE HOURS VARIABLE DECIMAL <TIME SPARSE <ORGANIZATION PROJECT>>
```

At this point the data is as usable as in the normal dimensional model. There is no need to create any extra structures just for viewing the data or aggregation.

```
PROJECT: 334535
                  ------------------HOURS------------------
                  ------------------TIME-------------------
ORGANIZATION    SEP97       OCT97       NOV97       DEC97
--------------  ---------   ---------   ---------   ---------
BOB               58.29       55.52       54.22       74.81
JIM               60.55       61.03       69.36       65.64
MARY              53.95       58.83       51.38       60.75
CINTHIA           70.66       57.45       74.29       73.96
JOANNE            64.19       61.03       64.80       68.72
ELROY             56.86       61.52       55.04       65.85

(Note: Full report output not shown.)
```

Subsetted Dimensionality

Creating subsets of large objects is one of the more common ways to improve performance when sparse data is not equally distributed but occurs in large "chunks." This places the data into separate cubes in which the data is dense. In some cases, it may even make sense to separate the data into separate databases. Using indirect references you can join them seamlessly. This can make the complexity invisible to the user.

Record Relational

Record relational structures can be useful as an alternative to building very large conjoint structures. A record relational structure makes use of the Express capability for storing data in a relational manner based on a record ID. This feature would only be used when you have a very large number of transaction details which need to be loaded into an Express database. One situation where this might be handy is where data must be counted using a dimension at the detail level. Calculating this type of measure requires the detailed base elements to be available.

Consider the need to maintain a count of the number of different projects that a consultant worked on during a specified period of time. The data could be calculated at the detail level but you will have to recalculate higher levels based on the lowest level. Simple aggregation would be wrong. As an example, Bob worked on three projects during January and his work on two of those projects extended into February along with work on a new project. If the two months' data were simply aggregated it would appear that Bob worked on six projects even though he actually worked on only four. To calculate the proper count for higher levels in the TIME hierarchy, the details must be preserved and used. To allow such a large number of records we could use the record relational structure.

In this scenario, a dimension would be created to act as a record identifier, and then the "columns" would be relations to the base dimensions. Accessing data dimensioned by the "record dimension" requires using qualified data references within formulas.

The primary drawback to this method is one of data integrity. It is conceivable that duplicate rows of data could quite easily be loaded into such a structure unless custom integrity checking code is written. One alternative is to use meaningful *record ID* codes. If the record ID were to be a concatenation of the "base dimension" values, then it would be relatively simple to check for duplications. The fact remains that it would be a customization.

As an example, we can take our example data and define a record ID dimension, some relations, and an hours variable that will act as "columns":

```
DEFINE RECDIM DIMENSION INTEGER
DEFINE REC_PROJ RELATION PROJECT <RECDIM>
DEFINE REC_ORG RELATION ORGANIZATION <RECDIM>
DEFINE REC_TIME RELATION TIME <RECDIM>
DEFINE REC_HOURS VARIABLE DECIMAL <RECDIM>
```

We can then define a formula to retrieve some data from the record relational structure:

```
DEFINE REC_HOURS.F FORMULA DECIMAL <TIME PROJECT ORGANIZATION>
EQ TOTAL(REC_HOURS REC_TIME REC_PROJ REC_ORG)
```

We may also use the REPORT command to view the record relational data:

```
REPORT REC_TIME REC_PROJ REC_ORG REC_HOURS

RECDIM          REC_TIME    REC_PROJ    REC_ORG     REC_HOURS
--------------- ----------  ----------  ----------  ----------
              1 JAN95       334535      BOSTON          321.50
              2 FEB95       334535      BOSTON          325.50
              3 MAR95       334535      BOSTON          430.50
              4 APR95       334535      BOSTON          576.00
              5 MAY95       334535      BOSTON          811.50
              6 JUN95       334535      BOSTON          890.00
```

A REPORT (or the graphical user interface, or GUI) can use the formula to provide us with a multidimensional view of the data. We could test this using our example data, rotating it a few different ways:

```
REPORT REC_HOURS.F

ORGANIZATION: BOSTON
```

```
                         --------------------REC_HOURS.F--------------------
                         ----------------------TIME----------------------
    PROJECT        JAN95        FEB95        MAR95        APR95        MAY95
    -----------  ---------    ---------    ---------    ---------    ---------
    334535          321.50       325.50       430.50       576.00       811.50
    124858          660.00       761.00       917.50     1,256.00     1,267.00
    133555          524.00       568.50       588.50       693.50       902.50
    394893          532.00       589.00       628.00       678.50       688.50
    342382          914.00       868.50     1,002.00     1,075.50     1,201.50
```

Or we might set ORGANIZATION across and set TIME down the y-axis. PRO-JECT then becomes the page dimension.

```
REPORT DOWN TIME ACROSS ORGANIZATION: REC_HOURS.F


PROJECT: 334535
--------------------------REC_HOURS.F---------------------- ------------------
----ORGANIZATION--------------------------
TIME        BOSTON     ATLANTA    CHICAGO     DALLAS     DENVER     SEATTLE
--------  ---------  ---------  ---------  ---------  ---------  ---------
JAN95        321.50     406.50     291.00     477.50     365.00     435.50
FEB95        325.50     442.50     290.00     501.50     336.50     412.00
MAR95        430.50     512.50     395.50     671.00     453.00     515.50
APR95        576.00     784.50     488.00     873.00     574.50     770.50
MAY95        811.50     936.50     666.00   1,154.00     795.50   1,043.50
```

Or, with ORGANIZATION defaulting as the page, we might report TIME down (and PROJECT across):

```
REPORT DOWN TIME REC_HOURS.F


ORGANIZATION: BOSTON
                    --------------------REC_HOURS.F--------------------
                    ----------------------PROJECT----------------------
TIME          334535      124858      133555      394893      342382
--------    ---------   ---------   ---------   ---------   ---------
JAN95          321.50      660.00      524.00      532.00      914.00
FEB95          325.50      761.00      568.50      589.00      868.50
MAR95          430.50      917.50      588.50      628.00    1,002.00
APR95          576.00    1,256.00      693.50      678.50    1,075.50
MAY95          811.50    1,267.00      902.50      688.50    1,201.50
```

Indirect References and Capstone Databases

One of the most common approaches to insulating the users from complex structures is the use of indirect references. Data can be partitioned into smaller components either in the same database or in separate databases. Indirect references can also be used to view and manipulate data stored in the record relational structures described in the last section. The downside of this approach is in the additional complexity of the application for administration and modification. The users are insulated from this complexity, however, since they are only able to see the formulas that then reference the otherwise awkward schema. These formulas are normally dimensioned and look like other multidimensional data.

Reconciling the physical and logical data models is achieved by creating a dimension that is a superset of the dimension values. This superset dimension serves like a view in an Oracle relational database that combines data joined from multiple tables. This approach insulates the users from the additional variables and dimensions (and possibly different databases) chosen by the designers.

In our example, this might allow the data to be physically separated regionally (e.g., Americas and Europe). This should be a pretty clean breakdown since most projects will be staffed by consultants from the same region as the organization owning the project. For each summary value at the top levels of the superset dimension, the formula would check whether there was a value and, if so, retrieve it from the subdatabase/cube. This is similar to the way a cache database is set up or to the use of the SQL reach-through feature.

A *capstone* is a shell database that is the only database the users directly access. Just like indirect references within a single database, they contain the supersets of dimension values and access the subordinate data slices residing in separate databases via formulas. One way of conceptualizing a Capstone implementation is to see it as a partitioned database. The databases can be partitioned vertically or horizontally. Figure 13.9 demonstrates a capstone database that retrieves its actual data from three other databases.

There are performance trade-offs in the use of capstone databases. There may be some loading advantages from spreading the load process over several file systems. There will be some extra overhead, however, from evaluating the formula to determine the proper location from which to retrieve data.

Using our PROJECT example, we could have a vertical partition by separating the different levels of the ORGANIZATION hierarchy into different databases. Given the following hierarchy within the ORGANIZATION dimension:

 ↵ Totorg

  ↵ Division

   ↵ Region

    ↵ Cost Center

     ↵ Consultant

then our formula for accessing the different "cubes" would be as follows:

```
DEFINE HOURS_F DECIMAL FORMULA <PROJECT ORGANIZATION TIME>
eq if  O1.LEVELREL eq 'TOTORG then
if isvalue(T.PROJECT PROJECT) and
               isvalue(T.ORGANIZATION ORGANIZATION) and
               isvalue(T.TIME TIME)
     then T.HOURS_F
else if O1.LEVELREL eq 'DIVISION' then
```

```
if isvalue(D.PROJECT PROJECT) and
   isvalue(D.ORGANIZATION ORGANIZATION) and
   isvalue(D.TIME TIME)
             then D.HOURS_F
else if O1.LEVELREL eq 'REGION' then
if isvalue(R.PROJECT PROJECT) and
   isvalue(R.ORGANIZATION ORGANIZATION) and
   isvalue(R.TIME TIME)
             then R._HOURS_F
else . . .
```

In this example, each of the objects within each "partition" database will need a prefix where the objects would otherwise have identical names. This is similar to the owner qualification required in the Oracle relational database when referencing objects from multiple schemas.

Figure 13.9 Capstone database.

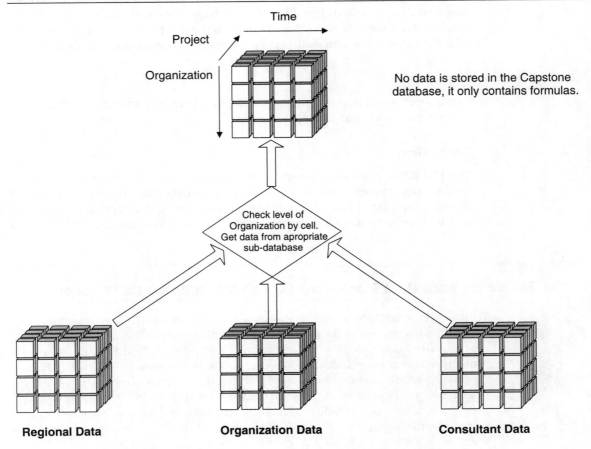

Data is retrieved from sub-databases where the actual values are stored.

You will also need an AUTOGO program to attach all the subdatabases when starting the system. An AUTOGO program would be run automatically upon attaching the Capstone.

```
DEFINE AUTOGO PROGRAM
PROGRAM

DTB ATTACH TOTORG.DB
DTB ATTACH REGION.DG
DTB ATTACH COSTCNTR.DB
DTB ATTACH CONSULT.DB

END
```

Data Loading and Integration with External Systems

Source data typically comes from many different places. It would not be at all strange to get financial data from the corporate general ledger system, production statistics/costs from text files, and perhaps sales and marketing data from another relational system such as a data warehouse, perhaps organized in a star schema. Express can efficiently load from diverse sources into one database.

Loading Data

Express provides alternative methods for loading data from extracted files or directly from a relational database.

Text Files

The FILEREAD command represents the most efficient (fastest) way for Express to load data. Express processes records very quickly using this method and still allows quite a bit of processing during the load. Using the Express administrator tool to map text files will generate code that simplifies the use of FILEREAD.

The Source for Each Data Mart Should Be an Integrated Data Warehouse

To maintain a consistent data snapshot across the enterprise it is important to control the integration of data from these multiple sources. The majority of readers of this book are likely to be incorporating Express and OLAP into an environment with a relational data warehouse. As we recommended in Chapter 12, a centralized warehouse should be used to bring data together from many sources before it is distributed to various data marts (whether Oracle relational or Express multidimensional). Individually sourcing multiple data warehouses or data marts is virtually guaranteed to eventually result in multiple users receiving different answers to what looks like the same question.

This generated code can then be further modified as needed to maintain conjoint dimensions.

FILEVIEW is used to individually read each record from the data file and process it. The FILENEXT command is then used to explicitly read and process the next input record. This is effective where more extensive processing would be necessary during the build/load of data. FILEVIEW and FILENEXT are used infrequently since FILEREAD usually has enough flexibility to deal with most load situations.

SQL/ODBC

The SQL capabilities in Express enable it to communicate with an ODBC-compliant (Open Data Base Connectivity–compliant) relational database. Express Server can also access Oracle7 or Oracle8 directly via OCI. This connection allows for both data retrieval and modification; however, it is less common to update the relational database from Express. Express uses embedded SQL for accessing the relational database. There are four primary uses for SQL connectivity in Express, as described in the following sections.

LOADING EXPRESS USING SQL

Express can use SQL to capture data from a relational database for storage in its multidimensional database. This is similar to loading from text files in that is is usually a batch loading process which happens to pull data from a relational source. Loading using SQL involves the creation of a data loading procedure which connects to the SQL database, declares and opens a cursor, and then fetches data from the cursor into Express dimensions and variables. Here are the significant parts of a load programs:

```
SQL.DBMS='ORACLE'
SQL CONNECT 'scott/tiger@projectdb'
SQL DECLARE c1 CURSOR FOR -
SELECT -
     month, -
     project_number, -
     delivery_org_id, -
     SUM(hours) -
   FROM PA_olap.activity -
   GROUP BY -
     month, -
     project_number, -
     delivery_org_id

SQL OPEN c1
_i = 0
WHILE SQLCODE EQ 0
  DO
_i = _i + 1
    SQL FETCH c1 INTO -
```

```
              :APPEND period     -
              :APPEND project      -
              :APPEND organization    -
              :hours_SQL_LOAD
DOEND
SQL CLOSE c1
SQL ROLLBACK
```

Drilling Through to Relational Data (Details)

In the ROLAP and HYBRID architectures, Express retrieves data from a relational database for temporary use. Express checks a local data cache location to see if it is populated. If it isn't then Express will fill the cache location by generating a SQL SELECT statement to retrieve the specific data requested. Here is a formula, as generated by the Administrator tool, for retrieving HOURS data when the local cache value is NULL:

```
DEFINE HOURS_SQL FORMULA DECIMAL <TIME ORGANIZATION PROJECT>
EQ IF bookdemo_CACHE0 EQ XP_NULL THEN NA -
ELSE NAFILL(bookdemo_CACHE0, XP_SQLGen('hours_SQL',-
          CONVERT(time, TEXT) -
          CONVERT(organization, TEXT) -
          CONVERT(project, TEXT) ))
```

Updating SQL Databases

SQL DML statements can be used within the Express embedded SQL model. Because most OLAP applications are limited to reporting and analysis, this type of direct updating or inserting data via SQL is very unusual. This feature might conceivably be used to store the results of some ROLAP analysis back into a relational table. Here is a somewhat contrived example:

```
SQL PREPARE h1 FROM PA_OLAP.activity, -
   SET hours=:hours -
   WHERE :organization = TO_CHAR(delivery_org_id)-
   AND :project = TO_CHAR(project_number) -
   AND :time = TO_CHAR(month)


FOR organization
   DO
    _i = _i + 1
      SQL EXECUTE h1
      IF SQLCODE NE 0
      THEN BREAK
   DOEND
```

Dynamic Generation of SQL Code/Selections

This is really a variation of the first three categories for using SQL. The Express stored procedure language can generate SQL queries based on currently selected dimension values. These dynamically generated queries could, in turn, be passed to another tool or could direct SQL output to another window rather than filling a datacube. This technique can be used, for instance, to provide detailed reports to substantiate on-screen views.

Aggregation/Rollup

There are a several steps that should be taken to ensure good rollup performance. As long as the database design is sound, most steps are related to data storage or paging behavior. The most significant performance effects are related to how much data is to be aggregated.

When Express performs a rollup of data it loops implicitly though the dimensions of the data variable being aggregated. The status of the variable's dimensions determine how much of the data is used as input for the calculations. The rollup will populate the higher levels based on the current status of dimension values.

Storage

Before rolling up a variable, it should be changed to *INPLACE* storage. This can significantly cut down on paging since Express doesn't need to copy data back and forth into memory just to change the values and save it back to disk. Changing the storage to INPLACE just before rolling up the data means that the rolled-up data is written directly to the address on disk. To do this safely, you must assure that no one else will have access to the database while the rollup is in progress, since the database will be in a state of change.

If other users must be attached (with read-only access), set the storage to PERMANENT—users will then see the last saved version of data when they load from disk. This will, of course, have an impact on the ROLLUP performance. Setting the storage of a variable to either INPLACE or PERMANENT is done with the CHGDFN command:

```
CHGDFN HOURS_CJT INPLACE
CHGDFN HOURS_CJT PERMANENT
```

Always use the UPDATE command to ensure that all data is written to the database. If you exit before updating the database, the data may be inconsistent because some of it may have been written to the database. To resolve the inconsistencies, just execute the ROLLUP again to ensure that it is complete then UPDATE.

Segment Size

Express stores data in segments of disk space allocated for each variable. The segments are divided into pages of 4 KB each. You shouldn't have to change the size of the segment in Express Server 6.01 since the default segment size is probably adequate.

In earlier versions of Express, however, it may be useful to calculate and then set the appropriate segment width needed for the variables. If all the dimension values are loaded first, Express will allocate enough segment space to keep the data for each respective variable all in one segment. If the dimension values will be loaded intermixed with the data, there may be a significant growth in the number of segments. Express will always add segments as each new dimension values is added, except for the last (slowest-varying) dimension. If a composite dimension is defined anywhere but in the last position, segment growth could be extreme—instead of a single segment, this can result in hundreds of thousands of segments.

To avoid creating a multitude of new segments each time a new dimension value is added, use the CHGDFN SEGWIDTH command to allocate enough space for all the values. Calculate the product of a variable's dimension lengths, and set the segment width to that value. In the case of conjoint or composite dimensions, calculate or estimate the total number of unique combinations of the conjoint/composite dimension and set the segment width equal to that. While use of this command will ensure the best performance of all variables, it is most critical to use the command on any variable where conjoint or composite dimensions are not in the slowest-varying (last) position.

Limit Status

Limit the status of the dimensions to those children without descendants by using the COMPLEMENT keyword. Note that this example does not show a rollup over a conjoint dimension. It also does not detach the database to free up memory between ROLLUPs—normally this would be done.

First, set the status for all dimensions of HOURS to the lowest level of detail. Then increase the status of each dimension before rolling up over its values. In this fashion, the rollup only loops over the dimension values for which values have been calculated. The values in status are the "input" for the rollup so each level becomes the input for the next level. The ROLLUP command will still process all the levels in the hierarchy, but based on the parents of the "input" that is in status. Rolling up over data that will be replaced either because it is null or just old data is only a waste of CPU and developer time. Once the first level of rollup is complete, then that level can be used to populate the next level.

Figure 13.10 illustrates the rollup of the HOURS variable as performed in the following example code:

```
LIMIT ORGANIZATION COMPLEMENT O1.PARENT
LIMIT PROJECT COMPLEMENT P1.PARENT
LIMIT TIME COMPLEMENT T1.PARENT

LIMIT TIME TO ALL
ROLLUP HOURS OVER TIME USING T1.PARENT
UPDATE
LIMIT PROJECT TO ALL
ROLLUP HOURS OVER PROJECT USING P1.PARENT
UPDATE
```

Figure 13.10 The rollup of the HOURS variable.

Limit all dimensions to
the lowest level of detail.

Limit TIME to all,
then rollup over time.

Limit PROJECT to all,
then rollup over project.

Limit ORGANIZATION to all,
then rollup over organization.

```
LIMIT ORGANIZATION TO ALL
ROLLUP HOURS OVER ORGNIZATION USING O1.PARENT
UPDATE
```

Rolling Up Selectively

Normally, data will be added incrementally. Corrections and regular monthly updates are two examples of this. If only a smaller subset of data is changing, why roll up all the data? To selectively roll up the data correctly, you must limit the dimensions in the hierarchy to the following:

1. The initial value(s) that changed
2. The changed value's siblings
3. All ancestors of the changed value
4. All siblings of the ancestors

If we take a look at our ORGANIZATION hierarchy once again, we see that at the lowest level we might have "Cost Center." Just imagine that cost center "DENVER" has just been updated. Figure 13.11 shows this situation.

Figure 13.11 Rolling up because one variable value has changed.

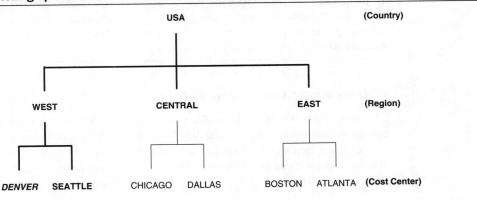

Here is the code that is needed to selectively rollup the changed HOURS for DENVER:

```
LIMIT organization TO 'DENVER'
LIMIT organization ADD ANCESTORS USING O1.PARENT
LIMIT organization ADD CHILDREN USING O1.PARENT
ROLLUP HOURS OVER organization USING O1.PARENT
```

Check for Circularities

It is critical that hierarchies not include circular references that would suggest a value was its own ancestor. To check for such anomalies in Express version 6.0 and above, you can run HIERCHECK either as a function or a program. As a function it returns a YES if the hierarchy is OK. When run as a program, it generates an error if the hierarchy contains loops.

The syntax for the HIERCHECK program is as follows:

```
Call HIERCHECK(relation)
```

where relation is the name of the parent relation being checked. NOSTATUS can also be supplied as a second argument to tell the program to ignore the present status of the dimension.

You can also access several system variables to check the results of the program. The variable HIERCHK.LOOPFND will contain a YES if a loop was found and NA if HIERCHECK terminated abnormally. If no loop is found, the HIERCHECK.LOOPEND will contain a NO. HIERCHK.LOOPVALS shows the dimension values where problems were found. This helps to identify where to begin correcting the data. HIERCHK.XTRADIMS provides the names of the hierarchy in which a loop was found in situations where the dimension has multiple hierarchies.

For versions of Express before 6.0, refer to the ROLLUP command in the *Express Language Reference Guide* for some example code to check for circularity.

USE SUBSETS OF DATA

If the amount of data being rolled up is larger than available memory, you can control the amount of thrashing and significantly decrease the amount of time the rollup takes by rolling up subsets of data. Set the status of the variable's dimensions then loop through the subsets explicitly in the rollup program.

Clustering of Dimension Values

The best performance will result if the physical order of the dimension values are clustered according to their level, as opposed to interspersed with the child values. At a minimum, cluster at least the lowest-level values since they account for the largest number of values. Also try to keep the children of the same parents adjacent to each other. This is best done by sorting the input files prior to

Figure 13.12 Clustering of the organizational hierarchy dimensions.

Bad for Rollups	Good for Rollups
USA	USA
EAST	**EAST**
BOSTON	**WEST**
ATLANTA	**CENTRAL**
WEST	BOSTON
DENVER	ATLANTA
SEATTLE	DENVER
CENTRAL	SEATTLE
CHICAGO	CHICAGO
DALLAS	DALLAS

loading the database. Otherwise, the values can be moved via the MAINTAIN MOVE command, then exporting and importing the EIF file into a new database. Figure 13.12 shows the effect of clustering dimension values.

Performance Issues and Tuning

In general, Express is self-tuning, and you are limited to adjusting memory allocation, job priority, disk allocation, and I/O settings. More critical to performance are changes in applications and data structures. There are several Express utilities for gathering information relating to performance. There are also operating system–specific utilities (commands) that can be useful. In many cases, upgrading hardware is the quickest and most cost-effective way to boost performance.

Always be sure that all objects related to or dimensioned by the dimensions you are maintaining are loaded into memory before the maintenance is performed. This will help prevent deferred maintenance, which is costly. For instance, if we are loading values or updating the ORGANIZATION dimension, we would do the following:

```
LIMIT NAME TO OBJ(ISBY 'ORGANIZATION')
LOAD &CHARLIST(NAME)
```

Then perform the required maintenance:

```
MAINTAIN ORGANIZATION ADD 'PHILADELPHIA'
UPDATE
```

Gathering Information to Help Tune

There are utilities and commands both within Express and at the operating system level that can give valuable information to help identify slow performing programs, I/O problems, and the like.

Express

The following list is a sample of the most common utilities and commands used to help tune an Express application and database. More detail on each of these is provided in the Express reference manuals. Not all these commands or their options are available on every operating system.

SYSINFO(CPUSECS) shows the number of CPU seconds accumulated since the start of the current session. The use of SYSINFO is platform-dependent. The CPUSECS option is available on most Express Server platforms (NT is different). Check the reference manuals for other choices, depending on your operating system.

DATABASE command can reveal information about the attached databases. Observing paging activity in a database can help you check the impact of stored procedures.

- **DATABASE(PAGEREADS 'databasename')** shows the number of pages read from this database during the current session.
- **DATABASE(PAGEWRITES 'databasename')** shows the number of pages written to this database during the current session.
- **DATABASE(PAGES 'databasename')** displays the total number of pages in this database.
- **DATABASE(FREEPAGES 'databasename')** provides the total number of pages available for reuse.
- **DATABASE(PAGESIZE 'databasename')** shows the number of bytes in the per page used by Express. (**DBPAGESIZE** provides the same information in versions prior to 6.0.)

OBJ (object) command provides information specific to a particular database object.

- **OBJ(NUMSEGS ['object-name'])** displays the number of storage segments associated with the object.
- **OBJ(DISKSIZE ['object-name'])** shows the number of disk pages used to store the object.
- **OBJ(INORDER ['object-name'])** indicates whether the object's logical order matches the physical order.
- **OBJ(NAPAGES ['object-name'])** provides the number of logical pages that are not physically stored because they are entirely filled with null values.
- **OBJ(NUMDELS ['object-name'])** displays the number of deleted cells for a dimensioned object.
- **OBJ(NUMCELLS ['object-name'])** shows the number of logical cells, both active and deleted, for a dimensioned object.

- **OBJ(NUMVALS ['object-name'])** shows the number of active cells for a dimensioned object.
- **OBJ(VALSIZE ['object-name'])** indicates the number of pages used to store the object's values.
- **OBJ(DISKSIZE ['object-name'])** displays the total number of pages used to store an object.

The following OBJ commands are related to RANSPACE (Random Access Pagespace). Even if you have been careful in capacity planning and sized the variables and dimensions, there can still be memory shortages. This is due to the shared memory pool that many objects use. The objects usually sized and planned for have their own pagespace allocated and therefore have that memory space independently managed. Objects that share the common pagespace are text variables, program object definitions, key value tables, and inversions.

- **OBJ(RSSIZE ['object-name'])** returns the amount of text in RANSPACE.
- **OBJ(IRSSIZE ['object-name'])** displays information about the size of inversions.
- **OBJ(KVSIZE ['object-name'])** shows the space used by key values.

In addition to the DATABASE and OBJ commands, there are several other Express utilities that provide important information for monitoring and tuning performance.

- **PRGTRACE = YES|NO** sets an option to force the redirection of all non-stripped code to the current output device. (*Stripped* code includes just the runtime application without source code.)
- **TRACE prgname** modifies the control list of programs and models that will be traced by the Express debugger.
- **TRACKPRG** command tracks the performance cost of all programs executed while it is turned on.
- **MONITOR** displays the amount of time spent on each line of executed code to help isolate poorly performing code.
- **DBREPORT** is included in the DBREPORT.DB database that comes with Express. When run, it produces three reports: the "Dimension Space Report," the "Detailed Space Report," and the "Summary Space Report."
- **REORGANIZE** is used to remove deleted values from dimensions and variables, remove segments from variables, and change the physical order of dimensions. The main results of this are usually that Express can access data faster. It also puts freed space into contiguous areas so that data can be written without expanding the database file size. Note: This will not make the database file smaller. On the contrary, it may actually make it larger. However, the file may not grow as fast after a reorganization. *Always make a backup before reorganizing!*
- **RANSHOW** is a monitoring tool to show the total RANSPACE used in the database. It is mostly used by Express developers but can give you a quick view of the RANSPACE utilization.

- **DBCACHE** can help performance when the application reads and writes to consecutive database pages. This option is not available in version 6. Instead, see the Windows NT section later in this chapter.

UNIX

The following tools can be useful in isolating issues with regard to CPU usage, disk utilization, memory usage and I/O requests:

```
iostat
vmstat
sar
ps
top
```

Space limitations prevent us from giving a detailed explanation of each of these UNIX utilities. If the reader is not already familiar with them, then the tuning effort should be coordinated with the UNIX systems administrator, who will be experienced in using these commands. Check the system vendor's command reference or use the UNIX *man* (manual) command for description and usage information. For example, to obtain the reference manual page on the vmstat command, enter the following:

```
man vmstat
```

Windows NT

On Microsoft Windows NT the Express Server is integrated with the Performance Manager. To enable this functionality, the Performance Manager module must be installed. In the Performance Monitor, Express Server provides the following counters:

- %Processing Time
- %CommittedBytesInUse
- PageFaults/Second
- FileReadOperations/Second
- FileWriteOperations/Second

Of these, the most commonly used are probably *%Processing Time* and *PageFaults/Second*.

Express NT Server Configuration Manager Settings

Express for Windows NT changes the way we work with configuration settings. The Express Configuration Manager, along with closer integration with the NT Performance Monitor, allows us to tune the way Express interacts with the operating system more easily than before. The three main areas we can affect are the Express cache, paging activity, and the I/O thread.

Express Cache

Adjusting the size of the Express cache can help the performance if there is operating system paging, Express paging, or both. Increase the Express cache to decrease Express paging when the operating system is not paging. Decrease the cache if there is operating system paging. The size of the Express cache is determined by the value of the *PageBufferCount* parameter in the Express Configuration Manager. By default Express uses 75 percent of the total number of pages available. To calculate the actual value divide the total system memory by 4,096 to determine the total number of pages. Express will use 75 percent of that total.

Paging

Two parameters that control how Express recycles pages are *FreePageLowCount* and *FreePageHighCount*. *FreePageLowCount* determines at what page count Express starts to discard pages, and *FreePageHighCount* defines the number of pages which need to be available before Express stops discarding them. If, while executing a rollup, there are spikes in the process time counter in the NT Performance Monitor, increasing both of these may be the solution. If the system provides more than 128 MB of physical memory then both of these should be set higher. The defaults are 100 and 250 respectively.

I/O Thread

You can adjust the parameters *ModifiedPageWriterSleep* and *ModifiedPageCount* to improve the performance of updating the database and of data loading procedures on multiprocessor computers. These determine how long the I/O thread waits to check for modified pages to write and how many modified pages to keep in modified state. The default for *ModifiedPageWriterSleep* is 30 seconds on a multiprocessor machine and 0 (zero, disabled) on a uniprocessor. The default setting for *ModifiedPageCount* is 200. Some performance improvements may be gained by experimenting with different values here if there are multiple processors.

Front-End Alternatives

There are several alternative interfaces by which a user may interact with an Express database. In selecting a front-end alternative, care must be taken to evaluate the administrative needs as well as the interface. The Express applications offer substantial functionality in maintenance, distribution, and standardization. When developing and defining the requirements, review the available Express applications to see how closely they fit the business's needs. It may even be worthwhile to revisit some of the requirements for cost justification of custom development as opposed to a more standard approach through the prepackaged applications.

Should a custom-developed solution be necessary, review the different tools available and choose wisely. Much can be said for Express Objects's tight integration with the Express engine. Consider building multidimensional data-aware objects using other programming environments.

The Oracle Express Applications

Sales Analyzer and Financial Analyzer are *packaged* applications that meet most of the needs of a large number of users. Both include many robust administrative and loading functions that would otherwise need to be custom developed. Sales Analyzer, as well as custom solutions developed with Express Objects, can make use of the Relational Access Manager. Financial Analyzer is tightly integrated with the Oracle General Ledger application through the G/L (General Ledger) Link. Cleansing and loading data can comprise a sizable portion of the project time line and budget—it may make sense to evaluate these products as components in an overall solution, even if they don't provide the complete solution for your data warehouse project.

Oracle Sales Analyzer

Originally used as a consumer goods marketing and sales analysis tool, Sales Analyzer has grown to be a versatile tool that can be used in a wide variety of ways. Sales Analyzer is expected to be a component in Oracle's Data Mart Suite for Sales and Marketing. It is the OLAP component of Oracle's Applications Data Warehouse. Sales Analyzer is also designed to work with Oracle's Relational Access Manager (which evolved from Sales Analyzer's SQL Bridge component). See the section on Relational Access Manager later in this chapter to gain a better idea of how this alternative works.

There is a utility to allow the Sales Analyzer to obtain its data from text files instead of RAA/RAM. Preparing for the Data Loader requires building sets of files for establishing dimensions, levels, hierarchies, variables, and measures. See the Data Loader Guide for details on the file structures and exact instructions for running the loads.

Oracle Financial Analyzer

Oracle Financial Analyzer was developed to support the specific needs of financial analysts. It can support multiple levels of administration and distribution.

There are essentially four types of workstations in a Financial Analyzer implementation: Super DBA, Sub-DBAs, Analyst, and Budgeting workstations. The users of Budgeting workstations can enter data via worksheets, submitting the budget data to their administrator. The subadministrators then review, combine, and submit the data from their users and so on.

The Super DBA sits at the top of the pyramid and controls the distributions of data, structures, and reports. The Super DBA also sets up the access privileges, user definitions, and other administrative functionality. The Super DBA is also responsible for launching the load processes to pull data from Oracle General Ledger, from other systems, or from text files. Through use of the G/L Link, the Super DBA can also submit budget data back to the Oracle General Ledger.

ORACLE FINANCIAL ANALYZER/GENERAL LEDGER INTEGRATION

The General Ledger (G/L) Integration has made the Financial Analyzer application extremely popular for performing financial functions. The G/L Link has two basic components:

On the General Ledger side there is an interface for mapping the G/L segments to dimensions and providing the administrator with functionality to set up and run the extracts. These screens are accessed through the Application Manager.

Generally, the Express Server side of Oracle Financial Analyzer needs to use the concurrent manager to find the extracts. So if Express Server cannot be installed on the same machine as the concurrent manager, you will need to ftp the files to a location accessible to Express Server. You must then update the *rg_dss_requests* table in General Ledger so it will be able to find the extracts. This must be done each time the extracts are run. The Super DBA can then load the data into the shared database and run Solves, distributions, and so on.

The budgeting capability has been extended to include uploads to the Oracle General Ledger by the OFA Super DBA. There are also hooks to enable drilling down into more detailed data. However, this is not standard functionality in the current release.

Relational Access Manager/Administrator

The Relational Access Administrator (RAA) and Relational Access Manager (RAM) are the client and server components (respectively), which allow the management of metadata conforming to standard as Discoverer and the Oracle Applications Data Warehouse. The metadata is stored as *projects*. Each project contains the necessary data for establishing connections and building the necessary Express structures for performing SQL reach through via mapped dimensions and facts.

The Relational Access Administrator is a graphical user interface tool for creating and managing projects that control the mapping of data in a relational star (or snowflake) schema to the dimensions and variables within an Express database. RAA uses ODBC to connect to the relational data warehouse. RAA provides two choices for building a project: The user may utilize the Project Wizard or manually define the multidimensional data model and then map the relational structures to it.

The Relational Access Manager then performs a build. This creates an Express database that is defined by the metadata layer of the relational warehouse. RAM uses a direct connection to the Oracle database (through OCI) to load data whenever it is requested through either Sales Analyzer, Express Objects, Express Analyzer, or an Express Web Agent access tool.

The Express engine handles the multidimensional representation and generates the necessary SQL code to fetch the data.

It is also possible to use a RAA/RAM database in a hybrid configuration. As discussed in the "Data Distribution Architectures" section earlier in this chapter, a hybrid configuration stores summary data within the Express multidimensional database while allowing reach-through through the relational database to obtain detail data for drill-down processing. To implement a hybrid architecture, the Express database needs to be attached read/write while the procedures for fetching data from the star schema are executed. Which data is fetched and stored depends on the status of the dimensions when the data is retrieved. During normal access Express checks the buffer to see whether or not the data has been retrieved. By preloading and updating the database the buffer can already be populated for certain values, improving performance. Upon drilling down to nonstored data, an empty cache is encountered, and the data is automatically retrieved from the relational database.

Oracle Express Objects and Express Analyzer

Express Objects is an object-oriented application development environment. It can be used to create Briefing Books or to create applications for Express Analyzer. A *Briefing Book* is an application that allows the user to create page objects and populate them with data-aware tables and graphs. Users can also modify Briefing Books created by Express Objects. Express Objects is the most effective way to build custom applications for Express multidimensional databases.

The Express Analyzer tool provides a subset of the tools available in Express Objects. Express Analyzer users can only run the application built in Express Objects but cannot alter it. The standard applications (such as Financial Analyzer) are more complete packages which can be executed by the Express Analyzer software but not modified.

Other Development Tools

The Express Structured N-dimensional Application Program Interface (SNAPI) allows custom development of applications using a variety of tools including C++, PowerBuilder, and Visual Basic. It is not within the scope of this chapter to provide details on the use of these tools.

Express and the Web

Beginning with version 6, Express is Web-enabled, that is, it is capable of generating dynamic Web pages. This is done through the Express Web Agent, which is a Web listener interface. It allows Express Server to respond to requests from the Web Request Broker in one of two ways. It can be configured either as a Common Gateway Interface (CGI) or as an Oracle Web Request Broker Cartridge. The Cartridge configuration is more efficient and can support many more users. Other components of the Web Agent include Web modules and the Web Agent Developers Toolkit.

Express Web Agent Developers Toolkit

The Express Web Agent includes the tools necessary to build custom web applications developed in the Express stored procedure language. This is a module of the Express Server (version 6.0+) that allows Express to produce HTML output in response to requests received from the Web Request Broker.

The Express Web Publisher

The Express Web Publisher is a component of the Oracle Express Objects development tool set that allows you to publish Web sites. Web sites are the containers for Briefing Books. With the Web Publisher, a user with no knowledge of HTML can publish tables and graphs on a Web site. The resulting pages are complete, with a rotation tool, an export tool, and a saved selection tool. Web Publisher utilizes either the Express Analyzer or Express Objects environments to develop the tables and graphs. The tool can also be started on its own and has features to create and manage Web sites and to create new Briefing Books.

Sales Analyzer Web Server

Publishing reports and graphs to the Web is as simple as copying the reports to a common library. The created Web pages are extremely similar to Web Publisher pages. They have folders like Briefing Books in Web Publisher, the rotation tools, a graph/table, an export-to-Excel button, and a saved selection button. One advantage of Sales Analyzer's Web capabilities is that the user doesn't need to do anything different from normal distribution policy. The objects are simply copied from the personal library into a public library just as they would be for other users of the client tool. Once made public, they can be viewed using a standard Web browser.

Summary

The Oracle Express products provide an OLAP component for the Oracle data warehouse. The features of Express extend the usefulness of the data warehouse by providing additional analysis capability not available in standard relational query tools. Express includes its own multidimensional database facilities. It has also been integrated with the Oracle7 and Oracle8 relational databases to allow the Express user to transparently access data stored relationally.

In this chapter we introduced several concepts of multidimensional databases and OLAP. We described elements of the Express technology as well as several alternative architectures for implementing Express. The chapter discussed topics related to analyzing, designing, building, loading, and tuning an Express database as well as several Express tools and alternative interfaces.

INDEX